SCEPTICAL PERSPECTIVES ON THE CHANGING CONSTITUTION OF THE UNITED KINGDOM

This book examines the far-reaching changes made to the constitution of the United Kingdom in recent decades. It considers the way these reforms have fragmented power, once held centrally through the Crown-in-Parliament, by means of devolution, referendums and judicial reform. It examines the reshaping of the balance of power between the executive and the legislature, and the way that prerogative powers have been curtailed by statute and judicial ruling. It focuses on the Human Rights Act and the creation of the UK Supreme Court, which emboldened the judiciary to limit executive action and even to challenge Parliament, and argues that many of these symbolised an attempt to shift the 'political' constitution to a 'legal' one.

Many virtues have been ascribed to these reforms. To the extent that criticism exists, it is often to argue that these reforms do not go far enough. An elected upper chamber, regional English parliaments, further electoral reform and a codified constitution are common tonics prescribed by commentators from this point of view. This volume adopts a different approach. It provides a critical evaluation of these far-reaching reforms, drawing from the expertise of highly respected academics and experienced political figures from both the left and right. The book is an invaluable source of academic expertise and practical insights for the interested public, students, policymakers and journalists, who too often are only exposed to the 'further reform' position.

Sceptical Perspectives on the Changing Constitution of the United Kingdom

Edited by
Richard Johnson
and
Yuan Yi Zhu

·HART·
OXFORD · LONDON · NEW YORK · NEW DELHI · SYDNEY

HART PUBLISHING

Bloomsbury Publishing Plc

Kemp House, Chawley Park, Cumnor Hill, Oxford, OX2 9PH, UK

1385 Broadway, New York, NY 10018, USA

29 Earlsfort Terrace, Dublin 2, Ireland

HART PUBLISHING, the Hart/Stag logo, BLOOMSBURY and the Diana logo are trademarks of Bloomsbury Publishing Plc

First published in Great Britain 2023

A catalogue record for this book is available from the British Library.

A catalogue record for this book is available from the Library of Congress.

ISBN: HB: 978-1-50996-370-6
        ePDF: 978-1-50996-372-0
        ePub: 978-1-50996-371-3

Typeset by Compuscript Ltd, Shannon

In Memory of Christine Morrissey – RMJ

To Alison Zhu – YYZ

ACKNOWLEDGEMENTS

The editors of this volume first met at Nuffield College, Oxford shortly after the UK had voted to leave the European Union. Richard Johnson was finishing his DPhil in Comparative Politics, and Yuan Yi Zhu was beginning his in International Relations. Neither officially specialised in the study of British politics. Yet, we both had a long-standing, deep-seated interest in the question of how the UK is governed. In spite of our different partisan attachments, we soon discovered a good deal of common ground on basic points about the importance of democratic self-governance, agenda control and political accountability, as well as a suspicion of legalistic remedies for problems that are inherently political.

This volume originated as a two-day conference in March 2021 called 'UK Constitutional Reform: What Has Worked and What Hasn't?', organised by Richard and at which Yuan presented. The conference was funded by a Quality-related Strategic Priorities Fund grant from Research England and was hosted by the Mile End Institute and the School of Politics and International Relations (SPIR) at Queen Mary, University of London (QMUL). The conference would not have been possible without the support of Bilen Barzaghi, Julie Becker, Tahmeda Khanam and Manisha Patel. Alex Wild and Rajiv Shah offered key support at the conference's early stages.

Held online during the coronavirus lockdown, the conference attracted 284 attendees. Although online conferences have their drawbacks, the format did mean that the attendees and the 35 speakers from six countries (UK, USA, Canada, Australia, New Zealand and Botswana) left a very low carbon footprint. One panel spanned 16 time zones and included speakers on four continents!

Many of the speakers became contributors to this volume, and they are named in the contributor list. The other speakers were Erin Delaney, Natascha Engel, Caroline Flint, Andrew Geddis, Paul Goldsmith, Tom Harris, Henry Hill, Martin Howe, Ruth Kelly, Philippe Lagassé, Andrea Leadsom, Jamila Michener, Sela Motshwane, Jo Murkens, Patrick O'Brien, Carina O'Reilly, Neil Pye, Peter Ramsay, Peter Roberts, Claire Sugdon, Mark Tushnet and Anne Twomey. We thank them for generously giving up their time (sometimes at unsociable hours) and for their excellent contributions. The panels were chaired by Patrick Diamond, Daniel Gover, Katharine Hall, Sophie Harman, Kim Hutchings, Tom Kelsey and James Strong.

In January 2022, the contributors to this volume were finally able to meet in person to discuss each of the chapters and strengthen the coherence of the work. We are grateful to the external readers who joined us at the workshop, namely Howard Anglin, Lee Evans, James Hallwood, Martin Loughlin and Rajiv Shah. We also thank Nikki da Costa for her interest and input.

Finally, we would like to thank the team at Hart, especially Kate Whetter, who has been an enthusiast for this project from the beginning, and Rosemarie Mearns. We are also grateful for the detailed, constructive and helpful feedback provided by the four anonymous reviewers. They are credited with some important changes, including to the title, which have improved the volume.

Richard Johnson (London)
Yuan Yi Zhu (Oxford)
August 2022

CONTENTS

CONTRIBUTORS

Professor Sir Vernon Bogdanor CBE FBA is Professor of Government at King's College, London. He has written widely on British constitutional matters, including *The People and the Party System*, *Monarchy and the Constitution*, *Power and the People: A Guide to Constitutional Reform*, *Devolution in the United Kingdom*, *The New British Constitution*, *Beyond Brexit: Towards a British Constitution* and *The Strange Survival of Liberal Britain: Politics and Power Before the First World War*. He was a Visiting Professor at Yale University in 2019.

John Bowers KC is Principal of Brasenose College, Oxford and Vice Chair of the Oxford University Conference of Colleges. He is a barrister and expert in employment law, having acted in high-profile cases such as the 1984 Miners' Strike, the 1989 Docks Dispute, the Wapping Dispute and the largest ever employment tribunal application. He sits as a Deputy High Court Judge and a Recorder on the South Eastern Circuit.

Rt Hon Sir Robert Buckland KBE KC MP has been the Conservative Member of Parliament for South Swindon since 2010. He has served in the Cameron, May, Johnson and Truss governments, including as Solicitor General for England and Wales (2014–19), Secretary of State for Justice and Lord High Chancellor of Great Britain (2019–21) and Secretary of State for Wales (2022).

Dr Conor Casey is Lecturer in Law at the University of Liverpool. He has published widely on constitutional and administrative law, as well as on the classical legal tradition. He was called to the Irish Bar in 2020.

Dr Robert Craig is Lecturer in Law at Bristol University. His evidence about the repeal of the Fixed-term Parliaments Act was cited multiple times in the report prepared by the House of Commons Public Administration and Constitutional Affairs Committee. His forthcoming book is entitled *Royal Law: Prerogative Foundations*.

Professor Richard Ekins KC (Hon) is Professor of Law and Constitutional Government at the University of Oxford and Fellow of St John's College. He is the author of *The Nature of Legislative Intent* and co-author of *Legislated Rights: Securing Human Rights through Legislation*. He leads Policy Exchange's Judicial Power Project and the Programme for the Foundations of Law and Constitutional Government.

Dr Michael Foran is Lecturer in Law at the University of Glasgow. His research focuses on constitutional theory and jurisprudence, with a particular focus on common law theory and natural law. His forthcoming book is entitled *Equality Before the Law: Equal Dignity, Wrongful Discrimination, and the Rule of Law*.

Joanna George is a Research Associate at the Faculty of Law at the University of Cambridge. She is a Research Fellow at The Constitution Society and a Steering Committee member of the Constitution Reform Group, which proposes a new Act of Union for the UK. Her research focuses on UK, EU and comparative constitutional law.

Professor Carol Harlow FBA KC (Hon) is Emeritus Professor of Law at the LSE. Her main research interests lie in the field of national and comparative administrative law, on which she has published widely. She was recently a Panel Member of the Independent Review of Administrative Law. She is a Fellow of the British Academy and Bencher of the Middle Temple.

Kate Hoey, Baroness Hoey of Lylehill and Rathlin was a Labour Member of Parliament for Vauxhall from 1989 until 2019. She now sits as a non-aligned peer in the House of Lords. Baroness Hoey was a minister in the Blair government and later served as Chair of the Northern Ireland Affairs Select Committee.

Dr Hayley Hooper is Associate Professor of Law at the University of Oxford and a Fellow of Harris Manchester College. She is an expert in constitutional and administrative law. She is the author of *Parliament's Secret War* and an academic affiliate at the Bonavero Institute for Human Rights.

Dr Richard Johnson is Senior Lecturer in Politics at Queen Mary, University of London. He writes on US and UK politics, with a focus on democracy, inequality and political institutions. He is the author of *The End of the Second Reconstruction*.

Dr Brian Christopher Jones is Lecturer in Law at the University of Sheffield. He is a member of the Executive Committee of the Society of Legal Scholars (SLS), and formerly co-convened the Public Law Section. He is the author of *Constitutional Idolatry and Democracy: Challenging the Infatuation with Writtenness*.

Dr Tony McNulty is a Teaching Fellow at Queen Mary, University of London. He was the Labour Member of Parliament for Harrow East from 1997 to 2010. He served in various ministerial roles in the Blair and Brown governments, including as Minister of State for Immigration, Citizenship and Nationality.

Dr Jasper Miles is Lecturer in Politics at the University of Lincoln. He has published on Labour Party history, including as co-author of *Peter Shore: Labour's Forgotten Patriot* and co-editor of *James Callaghan: An Underrated Prime Minister?*.

Professor Philip Norton, Lord Norton of Louth is Professor of Government at the University of Hull. He is the Director of the Centre for Legislative Studies. He is the author or editor of 35 books on British politics, including *The British Polity*. He is Chair of the History of Parliament Trust and President of the Study of Parliament Group. He is a Conservative member of the House of Lords.

Professor Gillian Peele is an Emeritus Fellow of Lady Margaret Hall, Oxford and an Emeritus Associate Professor of Politics at the University of Oxford. She is the author of many works on British and US politics, including *Governing the UK*. She served as an independent member of the House of Lords Appointment Commission. She now is now an independent member of the Committee on Standards in Public Life.

Peter Reid is a postgraduate researcher at the Edinburgh Law School, where he is a comparative legal scholar. He is writing a PhD thesis that explores constitutional change and hybrid systems in The Gambia, Guyana and Sri Lanka since independence. Peter has also worked on research projects in Sri Lanka and is Centre Secretary at the Edinburgh Centre for Constitutional Law.

Rt Hon Gisela Stuart, Baroness Stuart of Edgbaston was Labour Member of Parliament for Birmingham Edgbaston from 1997 to 2017. She was UK Parliamentary Representative to the European Convention, which drafted a new constitution of the European Union, and served as member of its Presidium. She served as Chair of the Vote Leave campaign in the 2016 referendum of EU membership. She was appointed First Civil Service Commissioner in 2022. She is a member of the House of Lords, where she sits as a crossbencher.

Dr Asanga Welikala is a Senior Lecturer in Public Law at the University of Edinburgh. He is the Head of the Public Law subject area at Edinburgh Law School, the Director of the Edinburgh Centre for Constitutional Law, and a Research Fellow of the Institute of Commonwealth Studies at the University of London. His teaching and research interests are in comparative constitutional law, applied constitutional theory, and Commonwealth constitutional history.

Professor Richard Tuck FBA is the Frank Thomson Professor of Government at Harvard University. He has published widely on political theory and the history of political thought. Among his many publications include *The Sleeping Sovereign: The Invention of Modern Democracy*. He is a Fellow of the British Academy.

Yuan Yi Zhu is Assistant Professor of International Relations and International Law at the University of Leiden, a Research Fellow at Harris Manchester College, Oxford, and a Senior Fellow at the Policy Exchange's Judicial Power Project.

Introduction: The Case for
the Political Constitution

RICHARD JOHNSON AND YUAN YI ZHU

I. Introduction

To its detractors, a group which includes many academic experts and public commentators, the British constitution is too old, too vague, too unwritten. In their view, it is, at best, something of an embarrassment and, at worst, a danger to democracy itself.[1] Unwritten constitutions such as the British one, so the argument goes, are more susceptible to either tyranny or 'populism'. Will Hutton warns that 'the weakness of Britain's constitution [is] to drive through toxic, divisive change [following] the manipulated will of the people'.[2] Anthony Barnett argues that Britain's unwritten constitution 'is the raw meat of dictatorship'.[3] Andrew Blick writes, 'a written constitution could protect politicians from making hasty, populist, media-driven promises in advance of general elections'.[4]

Yet it is not obvious that a written constitution delivers the magic fix that these reformers seek. As Brian Christopher Jones argues in the opening chapter of this book, most dictatorships around the world have constitutions, often containing very bold promises to protect individual rights and liberties. Equally, citizens of countries with written constitutions, such as the USA, France or the Philippines, may be surprised to learn that they have avoided either populism or a media-driven political environment thanks to their hallowed documents. As Montesquieu argued, the spirit of the law matters more than textual guarantees.[5]

The British constitution is unusual, but the importance of its unwrittenness is often overstated. To even say that it is unwritten is not entirely accurate for it contains many written parts. There are dozens of written statutes which pertain to constitutional matters. The numerous Representation of the People Acts clearly set out the rules of the parliamentary franchise. The Parliament Acts 1911 and 1949

---

[1] B Ackerman, 'Why Britain Needs a Written Constitution' (2018) 89 *The Political Quarterly*.
[2] W Hutton, 'The Sheer Scale of the Problem Facing Britain's Decrepit Constitution Has Been Laid Bare' *The Guardian* (1 September 2019).
[3] A Barnett, 'Why Britain Needs a Written Constitution' *The Guardian* (30 November 2016).
[4] A Blick, 'The Merits of a Written Constitution' (2016) 21 *Judicial Review* 52.
[5] Montesquieu, *The Spirit of Law* (1748).

establish the primacy of the House of Commons over the House of Lords. The Registration of Political Parties Act 1998 sets out the rules by which political parties may be established and operated. There is plenty of constitutional text in the UK.

A more moderate position can be found in Iain McLean's book, *What's Wrong with the British Constitution?*, in which he accepts that the British constitution is not fully unwritten, but argues that the problem lies in the fact that constitutional statutes are not afforded some higher status or embodied in a single codified text. In answer to his titular question, McLean replies, 'For a start, nobody knows what it is.'[6]

It is true that there are many aspects of the British constitution that are embodied in convention, tradition and practice. Not every single aspect of the constitution is written in statute or even in any official document at all. This is not, however, a distinguishing feature of the British constitution. It does contain written and unwritten elements, but so do all constitutions. No constitution in the world would be fully workable without convention, interpretation or precedent. As Akhil Amar has written, even the US Constitution, the inspiration for countless written constitutions since its enactment, is only intelligible and workable by numerous unwritten conventions and understandings.[7] The US Constitution is short – far shorter than any of the 50 American state constitutions.[8] There is simply no way that the 7,591 words in its articles and amendments could precisely spell out how all aspects of government should function.[9] The Constitution is silent on much, and this means that Americans, too, have an unwritten constitution in addition to their written one.

What distinguishes the British constitution, then, is not that it is unwritten, or even that it is uncodified. Codification is in large part a secretarial exercise. It would be easy enough to gather together a collection of statutes of 'constitutional importance' into the same volume, as is indeed done sometimes by legal publishers for the benefit of law students. No one but an election lawyer might wish to read a constitution that contains all 13 Representation of the People Acts passed between 1918 and 2000, but it is not impossible to find and collect them together. Some constitutions adopt this 'kitchen sink' approach to codification. The Constitution of India is 140,000 words long and contains hundreds of articles.[10] The Constitution of Alabama is even longer.[11]

---

[6] I McLean, *What's Wrong with the British Constitution?* (Oxford, Oxford University Press, 2009) vii.

[7] A Amar, *America's Unwritten Constitution: The Precedents and Principles We Live By* (New York, Basic Books, 2012).

[8] S Levinson, *Framed: America's 51 Constitutions and the Crisis of Governance* (Oxford, Oxford University Press, 2012).

[9] E Zackin, *Looking for Rights in All the Wrong Places* (Princeton, Princeton University Press, 2013).

[10] Z Elkins, T Ginsburg and J Melton, *The Endurance of National Constitutions* (Cambridge, Cambridge University Press, 2009) 106.

[11] B Thomson (ed), *A Century of Controversy: Constitutional Reform in Alabama* (Tuscaloosa, University of Alabama Press, 2002).

The difference between the British constitutional system and most other constitutional systems pertains to the hierarchy of law. In most other systems, constitutional provisions are treated as more sacrosanct than 'normal' legislation. If the legislature decides to pass some legislation which falls afoul of the constitution, then the statute can be declared 'unconstitutional' and struck down. Even if the democratic legislature supports a measure overwhelmingly, some things are 'beyond politics' under such an arrangement. Some countries go even further by forbidding amendments to certain constitutional provisions, entrenching them for all of eternity.

Let us take an example from the USA, where the US Constitution is supreme and courts have the power to strike down legislation which is deemed to be incompatible with it. In 1918, Congress passed a minimum wage for women and children in federal territory. Five years later, the Supreme Court struck down this legislation, invalidating the minimum wage. Justice George Sutherland, writing the court's majority opinion, explained that a minimum wage law was

> an unconstitutional interference with the freedom of contract included within the guaranties of the due process clause of the Fifth Amendment. That the right to contract about one's affairs is a part of the liberty of the individual protected by this clause is settled by the decisions of this court and is no longer open to question.[12]

Such a declaration would not be permissible from a British court. Once Parliament legislates for something, it is deemed *ipso facto* constitutional. Thus, as Richard Ekins sets out in chapter three, what makes the British constitution exceptional is that the absence of a hierarchy of law gives the UK Parliament total freedom to legislate without any legal limitations. Parliament, therefore, is at once a legislature and a constitutional assembly. To continue the American analogy, it would be as if the constitutional framers in Philadelphia never left.

The British constitution, therefore, maximises usable political power. This might concern some observers. What if a government uses its mandate to go 'too far'? Who will step in to save the public from their elected masters? For proponents of constitutional codification, the remedy is judges applying the rules of the constitution. Yes, they would admit, perhaps constitutional supremacy enables judges to stop elected governments from passing laws, including protections for workers or racial minorities, but at least such an arrangement guarantees a 'check' against the possibility of a 'tyrannical' elected government.[13]

The implication of this line of argument is that the British constitution lacks 'checks' against such dangerous excess. This is not correct. As Carol Harlow describes in chapter two, the British constitution is famously a 'political constitution', whose safeguards come from within democratic politics. In a system without a hierarchy of law, it is true that one statute cannot be used to

---

[12] *Adkins v Children's Hospital* 261 US 525 (1923).
[13] For examples, see R Johnson, *The End of the Second Reconstruction* (Cambridge, Polity, 2020) ch 2.

block the implementation of a new statute. There is nothing, legally speaking, stopping Parliament from repealing the Freedom of Information Act 2000 or the Minimum Wage Act 1998. Equally, a British government can use its prerogative powers to go to war, to sign treaties or to prorogue Parliament for a week longer than is usual.

Yet, the absence of legal 'checks' does not exclude the possibility of other ways of restraining government behaviour. While Parliament can technically legislate how it likes and while governments have sweeping prerogative powers, both are held back by what they believe the public is likely to accept. One check is the necessity of the government at all times to carry the confidence of the House of Commons. At any moment, if MPs feel that the government has gone too far, in one simple act – a vote of no confidence – they can bring down a government. Elections, then, become another way in which a check is exercised against MPs. If the MPs were wrong to bring down the government, then the British public can render their verdict in the pursuant general election.

Likewise, if the government feels unduly frustrated by MPs from implementing its agenda, it can dissolve Parliament and call an early election. If the election had been called unnecessarily, for the sake of the Prime Minister's advantage, the public could sanction the governing party at the ballot box. Edward Heath and Theresa May learned this lesson in 1974 and 2017. Robert Craig in chapter six demonstrates the importance of this delicate balance of confidence – one which helps governments to push their programme forward but also ensures that governments do not stray too far from popular sentiments.

This is a profoundly democratic system. The public's verdict hangs like a sword of Damocles over politicians. Misbehaviour, incompetence or failure to implement manifesto commitments do not go unpunished for long. Nick Clegg and his Liberal Democrats learned this in 2015 after having traded their manifesto pledges to support a Conservative government for five years. Boris Johnson, as Gillian Peele notes in chapter thirteen, was eventually ejected from office in 2022 not by a standards committee, but because the public showed that they were fed up with him. The government experienced repeated by-election defeats in a diverse array of constituencies, placing enormous pressure on Conservative MPs to remove their leader, lest the public render a similar verdict on the complicit MPs in their own seats at the next general election.

The contention that the British constitution is fundamentally democratic often raises heckles from commentators.[14] They often point to the unelected upper chamber and head of state as proof positive that the constitution is archaic and undemocratic. The Scottish Labour leader Anas Sawar proclaimed that Labour must 'renew democracy. The House of Lords, in its current form, as an institution

---

[14] J Dennison, 'A Proposal for Simultaneous Reform of the House of Commons and House of Lords' (2020) 91 *The Political Quarterly*.

has no place in twenty-first century politics.'[15] More furtively, similar points can be found against the monarchy.[16] Yet, such commentators need to go back and read their Bagehot.[17] They have confused the 'dignified' and the 'efficient' constitution. The former refers to the grand pomp and ceremony of British constitutional arrangements – epitomised in the Crown and the Lords. The 'efficient' constitution refers to where power actually lies – the House of Commons and the Cabinet. In the British system, there is almost an inverse relationship between how grand and splendid an institution is and the amount of power afforded to it. The King lives in grand palaces; the Prime Minister lives in a townhouse. Yet, it is the latter who wields real executive power. The chamber of the House of Lords is much more ostentatious than the rather plain House of Commons, despite power overwhelmingly resting with the Commons.

If you want to change Britain, do not waste time on the 'dignified' constitution; grab control of the 'efficient' constitution and use it to implement your political agenda. It is precisely because the House of Lords and the monarchy are out-of-place with modern democratic values that they pose no serious threat to the popular will expressed through the House of Commons. As Philip Norton sets out in chapter eight, these unelected actors have no legitimate claim to block the democratic will of voters expressed in the election of their MPs. This is not true in systems with elected upper chambers and elected presidents, who often feel empowered to block legislation that commands a majority in the lower chamber. Paradoxically, it is the lack of democratic legitimacy of the Lords and monarchy that acts as a democratic safeguard. Those who wish to change this will introduce greater possibilities to dilute the expression of the popular will. They have succumbed to a 'liberal' reading of constitutional reform, which fetishises process and form over outcomes.

II. The British Constitution and Policymaking

This is not a partisan book. The editors support different political parties, as do our contributors. The volume contains chapters from ministers who have served in both Conservative and Labour governments. However, all those involved are united by a willingness to take seriously the value of the political constitution and to treat efforts to depart from this model, if not with unified opposition, with a healthy scepticism.

It is curious, however, that opposition to the political constitution so often comes from the left of the British political spectrum. This was not always the case.

---

[15] H Stewart, 'Labour Would Scrap House of Lords, Says Scottish Party Leader' *The Guardian* (4 July 2022).

[16] R Ridyard, 'Abolishing the monarchy would remove an obstacle to genuine democracy in Britain' (*Democratic Audit*, 3 December 2014), available at https://www.democraticaudit.com/2014/12/03/abolishing-the-monarchy-would-remove-an-obstacle-to-genuine-democracy-in-britain/.

[17] W Bagehot, *The English Constitution* (London, Chapman & Hill, 1867).

Labour politicians like Clement Attlee and Aneurin Bevan understood the transformative potential of the 'old' British constitution.[18] The National Health Service, for example, is a unique creation of the British constitution. To socialise the entire healthcare system in the UK, which involved the appropriation of private hospitals into public hands with little or no compensation, the Attlee government simply needed a majority in the House of Commons.

In many other systems in the world, appeals might be made to an upper chamber, an elected head of state, a judge, or a state or provincial legislature to act as a block on such radical, transformative action. In a system of constitutional supremacy, there might indeed be some higher law which would protect private property rights from such appropriation. Yet, in the British system, if Parliament (and, in practice, a simple majority in the House of Commons) wishes to achieve something so radical, there is no one to stop it.

Raymond Seitz, who was US Ambassador to the UK in the early 1990s, marvelled at the British constitution compared to his own. He reflected:

> Coming from this kind of fractured, fractious federal background, an American arrives on British shores astonished to find how unfettered a modern British government is … It took me a long time to understand that a British government, with a simple majority in the House of Commons, can do pretty much what it wants to … I kept looking for the constitutional checks and institutional balances that could stay the will of the British government. But I could find none.[19]

His astonishment is understandable, for the USA has an exceptionally high number of 'veto players' in its Constitution.[20] A veto player refers to a political institution whose consent is required for the enactment of legislation.[21] In the US Constitution at the federal level, there as many as five veto players. In order to be enacted fully, legislation could need to receive assent from three institutional actors: a majority in the House of Representatives, a majority or (more commonly) super-majority in the malapportioned Senate and the president's approval. Sanford Levinson has called the US a *tricameral* system because the president wins approximately 95 per cent of all veto contests with Congress.[22] In addition, legislation must also sometimes withstand dissent from the Supreme Court and state governments, who, often working together, can scupper legislation that has, nonetheless, won approval from the House, Senate and president.

In the British constitution there is one effective veto player – a majority in the House of Commons. In practice, the House of Lords, Crown and courts must fall into line should the Commons wish something to become law. This absence of veto players has real implications for policymaking. Contrast the ease of establishing

---

[18] F Field (ed), *Attlee's Great Contemporaries: The Politics of Character* (London, Continuum, 2009).

[19] R Seitz, *Over Here* (London, Weidenfeld & Nicolson, 1998).

[20] A Stepan and J Linz, 'Comparative Perspectives on Inequality and the Quality of Democracy in the United States (2011) 9 *Perspectives on Politics* 841.

[21] G Tsebelis, 'Veto Players and Institutional Analysis' (2000) 13 *Governance* 441.

[22] S Levinson, 'Popular Sovereignty and the United States Constitution: Tensions in the Ackermanian Program' (2014) 123 *Yale Law Journal* 2661.

the National Health Service to the challenges which Barack Obama faced when he tried to implement a modest public health insurance reform: the expansion of the Medicaid public health insurance programme to all American families whose income fell below 138 per cent of the federal poverty line.

Medicaid expansion was a policy designed to provide public health insurance to millions of working-class people.[23] In 2010, this proposal passed the House (veto player 1), it passed the Senate (veto player 2) by a single vote and Obama signed it into law (veto player 3). Then, before it came into effect, the Supreme Court stepped in (veto player 4). The court ruled that it was unconstitutional for the government to force states to expand the Medicaid programme to millions of working-class people.[24] The expansion of healthcare became contingent on the acceptance of state governments (veto player 5).[25] As Pablo Beramendi once said, federalism is a 'breeding ground for political and economic opportunism'.[26] This was no exception. Federalism threw up racialised structural barriers to the expansion of Medicaid. Nearly half of African Americans lived in states where the governors refused to expand public health care.[27]

Far from being 'radical', the kinds of constitutional reforms often supported by Labour MPs of a recent vintage are the very devices that would constrain the power of a majority Labour government from implementing a socialist programme. Indeed, some mooted reforms, like proportional representation, would make a majority Labour government a virtual impossibility altogether.[28] The dearth of veto players in the British constitution provides enormous potential for a democratic socialist party. A socialist party which can secure a bare majority in the lower chamber of Parliament can rule the country with virtually no limitations whatsoever: no senate to block its legislation, no president to veto it, no judge to overrule it as 'unconstitutional', no devolved government to refuse to cooperate and no non-socialist coalition partners with whom to compromise. The Labour MP Peter Shore, who opposed all of these veto players, put it succinctly: 'I did not come into socialist politics in order to connive in the dismantling of the power of the British people.'[29]

Many on the left, however, are willing to sign away all this power if it means that Conservative governments cannot get their way, either. This, in effect, in the trade-off between the 'old' and 'new' British constitutions. The further Britain

[23] L Jacobs and T Skocpol, *Health Care Reform and American Politics* (Oxford, Oxford University Press, 2010).

[24] *National Federation of Independent Business v Sebelius* 567 US 519 (2012).

[25] B Merriman, *Conservative Innovators: How States are Challenging Federal Power* (Chicago, University of Chicago Press, 2019).

[26] P Beramendi, *The Political Geography of Inequality: Regions and Redistribution* (Cambridge, Cambridge University Press, 2012).

[27] J Michener, *Fragmented Democracy: Medicaid, Federalism, and Unequal Politics* (Cambridge, Cambridge University Press, 2018).

[28] R Johnson, 'Proportional Representation Would Spell Disaster for the Labour Party' *The Guardian* (27 September 2021).

[29] K Hickson, J Miles and H Taylor, *Peter Shore: Labour's Forgotten Patriot* (London, Biteback, 2020).

moves away from the 'old' constitution, the less likely it is for parties of either the right or the left to implement their programme untrammelled. What has been lost is faith in the power of the British people to act as a constitutional safeguard or true architects of their own future. When Labour gives up hope of defeating the Conservatives through the ballot box, it turns instead to trying to place constitutional restrictions on Conservative governments, even if it means reducing power for itself.

Labour's proposals to empower judges to quash government policies, empower an elected upper chamber to block a Commons majority or to devolve more power away from Westminster never really consider what they could mean: judges ruling against democratically enacted social legislation, a Senate that blocks transformative social policy and devolved governments cutting the social safety net to the bone. But the evidence is there in the comparative politics research should anyone care to look.[30]

To end the legislative freedom of Parliament is to end the political constitution as we know it and to turn judges into our ultimate political masters. It is, in effect, changing the title deeds of the guardianship over the British constitution from the British public to the judiciary. As the Labour leader Hugh Gaitskell said in similar, if not identical, circumstances, 'You may say "Let it end" but, my goodness, it is a decision that needs a little care and thought'. This volume is an opportunity to give a bit of care and thought as to whether these changes have delivered the benefits that they were purported to bring. Its contributors ponder whether further reform is in fact needed, or whether there was in fact something to be said for the old British constitution.

III. The New British Constitution: A Note of Scepticism

Since the late 1990s, the UK constitution has undergone a profound transformation. The New Labour (1997–2010) and Conservative–Liberal Democrat coalition governments (2010–15) implemented highly consequential structural changes to the British system of governance. The gist of these reforms was to weaken the power of the UK government and Parliament by creating devolved governments, increasing veto players in Westminster, elevating the role of unelected technocratic experts and strengthening judicial power. The role of national democratic 'politics' as the linchpin in the system was brought into question. Instead, policymakers sought to constrain politics through additional veto points, a greater role for 'neutral' experts, curtailed prerogative power and active judicial monitoring.

---

[30] A Lijphart, 'Democratic Political Systems: Types, Causes, and Consequences' (1989) 1 *Journal of Theoretical Politics* 33; G Rosenberg, *The Hollow Hope: Can Courts Bring About Social Change?*, 2nd edn (Chicago, University of Chicago Press, 2008); J Behrend and L Whitehead (eds), *Illiberal Practices: Territorial Variance within Large Federal Democracies* (Baltimore, Johns Hopkins University Press, 2016).

Sir Vernon Bogdanor wrote in his 2009 book *The New British Constitution* that

the constitutional reforms since 1997, together with Britain's membership of the European Union, have served to provide us with a new British constitution ... [T]he radicalism of the reforms should not be under-estimated, nor the challenge they offer to traditional assumptions about the constitution.[31]

We agree with this assessment. Bogdanor himself explores in chapter fourteen one such reform of profound constitutional consequence: devolution. He concludes that the devolution settlement has failed to live up to the promise of its 1990s devotees.

Regardless of their actual record of performance, many virtues are ascribed to these reforms. They are accepted as 'settled', rather than contingent, features of the political system. Few venture to question their value, even if, like devolution, they were controversial at the time of their introduction. To the extent that criticism exists, it has often been to argue that these reforms do not go far enough. An elected upper chamber, regional English parliaments, further devolution, electoral reform, citizens' assemblies and a codified constitution are common tonics prescribed by commentators from this point of view.

This volume adopts a different outlook. The editors of the volume are sceptical that it is necessary or even desirable to reduce the British constitution to a canonical text that can then be enforced by judges. We tend to regard Westminster parliamentarism as one which links both maximum government power with maximum accountability to the electorate. We are sceptical of attempts to redirect the safeguards of this model away from the British public and into the hands of a mandarin class of legal elites. While not dogmatic on questions of reform, we believe that arguments that depart from this model need very good justification and are not self-justified on their face. Ultimately, this book is an effort to restore faith in the possibility of democratic self-governance where the public are the ultimate masters of what can be achieved through politics.

IV. Outline of the Volume

The contributors to this book are a diverse array of voices, and they do not purport to be in full agreement on all matters of constitutional reform. Some are comfortable with, and see the case for, some reforms. Some might even call themselves 'reformers' of a certain kind. Other contributors are much more sceptical and argue strongly for a return to the 'old' constitution. These differences, we argue, are a strength of the volume. What unites them is a willingness to take the political constitution seriously and to acknowledge the virtues in the unique British constitutional system. The authors in this volume have reviewed the constitutional

---

[31] V Bogdanor, *The New British Constitution* (London, Bloomsbury, 2009).

reforms of the last quarter century and come to the conclusion that many of them have not delivered the cures which their proponents claimed they would. Along with their purported benefits, each change carried corresponding costs. In many, if not all, of these cases, the costs have outweighed the benefits.

A. Part I – The Political Constitution and the Law

Part I analyses the relationship between politics and law. Brian Christopher Jones (chapter one – 'A (Brief) Case against Constitutional Supremacy') begins by outlining a case against what he calls 'constitutional supremacy', the idea that laws produced by a democratically elected government can be overturned if deemed to be incompatible with a set of supreme or higher laws, embodied in a codified constitution. The British constitution has no hierarchy of law and, while this can carry some risks (eg to stability), Jones regards this system as fundamentally more democratic. Jones also points out that a codified constitution is no safeguard of democracy, with many of the most oppressive regimes in the world operating according to written constitutions.

Carol Harlow explores two key, interrelated questions in chapter two ('Judicial Encroachment on the Political Constitution?'): 'What exactly is the political constitution?' and 'what do we expect of our judges?'. To answer these questions, she turns to the work of JAG Griffith, one of the leading exponents of the idea of the political constitution. Griffith warned against moves to convert essentially political questions from contestable claims to enforceable rights, which he believed would involve a 'substantial transfer of power from Parliament and politicians to the judiciary'. One might wonder whether New Labour's creation of the Supreme Court of the United Kingdom represented such a move. Harlow sets out to assess how much the British judiciary has encroached on politics in recent years, especially during the heated controversies over implementing the 2016 vote to the leave the EU. She believes that 'a judiciary, emboldened by the passage of the Human Rights Act, extended its ambition and power'. However, she observes that the departure of Lady Hale in 2020 as President of the Supreme Court and her replacement by Lord Reed has seen 'a reversion to restraint'. In her assessment, 'The Supreme Court over which Lord Reed presides operates in a markedly different manner and has adopted a very different style to the court that decided *Miller and Cherry*, *Privacy International*, and *Evans*'.

In an important contribution, Richard Ekins (chapter three – 'Legislative Freedom and Its Consequences') defends the idea that the central rule of the UK constitution is the doctrine of parliamentary sovereignty. For Ekins, this means that the King-in-Parliament may enact any law except one that binds its successors. Even though this proposition was once entirely 'unremarkable', Ekins observes that some contemporary constitutional scholars have brought this idea into doubt, suggesting that the constitution has undergone 'a series of legislative qualifications of parliamentary sovereignty' in recent years. Usually, EU membership (until 2020), the Human Rights Act 1998 (HRA) and devolution are cited as implicitly limiting the legislative freedom of the UK Parliament. Ekins rejects this thinking. All of these, he writes, are contingent. Legislative freedom remains 'fundamental' to the UK's governing arrangements. Should Parliament wish to change these strictures, it is entitled to do so. Ekins emphasises that the political constitution relies on 'politics to direct and discipline the exercise of Parliament's vast legal authority'.

The New Labour government passed two major legal reforms that appeared to reshape the relationship between the law and politics. One of these was the HRA, which attempted to incorporate the European Convention of Human Rights into domestic law. Michael Foran (chapter four – 'A Great Forgetting: Common Law, Natural Law and the Human Rights Act') offers staunch criticism. The HRA, in his view, was neither a necessary nor a positive contribution to rights enforcement in Britain. He argues, 'In its most basic sense, the Human Rights Act represents an abdication of legislative responsibility'. The HRA enjoys a high status in much of the legal community, and any effort to repeal a law called the 'Human Rights Act' would likely be met with scepticism and even alarm. Yet, Foran discourages alarmism. 'We should be wary of adopting an uncritical view that the arc of the moral universe is long but it bends toward the Human Rights Act', he advises.

A second major legal reform was the Constitutional Reform Act 2005, which established the 'Supreme Court of the United Kingdom' and made major changes to the ancient position of Lord High Chancellor of Great Britain. The legislation removed the Lord Chancellor's roles as presiding officer of the House of Lords, head of the Law Lords, Chancellor of the High Court and President of the Supreme Court of Judicature. Simultaneously a member of the legislature, executive and judiciary, the Lord Chancellor was once the 'linchpin' of the constitution. Sir Robert Buckland, who held the role from 2019 to 2021, reflects in chapter five ('Law and Politics: The Nightmare and the Noble Dream') about what these changes meant for the relationship between politics and the law. Buckland makes no apologies for his view that government should be 'as effective as possible' in delivering on the agenda on which it was elected. However, Buckland, a King's Counsel, values the judiciary and its reputation, too. He believes the interests of both the government and the judiciary are best served when there is a 'clear delineation about where the power lies'. Judges must not be drawn into the political realm. Both MPs and government must play their part to ensure that they are not. Finally, he defends the constitutional vision of the post-coalition Conservative governments and argues that they were 'attempting to return to the political constitutional model that was the orthodoxy for much of the 20th century'.

B. Part II – Westminster and Whitehall

Part II analyses various attempts to reform the UK Parliament and UK government since 1997. At the heart of the British constitution is the idea of the political accountability of the executive. Sometimes pilloried as 'elected dictatorship', the British constitution enables majoritarian governments to win elections and deliver on their manifesto promises with few legal constraints. Increasingly, there have been efforts to limit executive power and prerogative, through statute (such as the Fixed-term Parliaments Act) and judicial intervention (the two *Miller* cases).[32]

Robert Craig (chapter six – 'The Fixed-term Parliaments Act 2011: Out, Out Brief Candle') offers a robust critique of these efforts to constrain executive power. In the crosshairs of Craig's chapter is the Fixed-term Parliaments Act 2011 (FtPA), which, until its repeal in 2022, abolished the prerogative power, held by the monarch and exercised on the advice of the Prime Minister, to dissolve Parliament and call a new general election. Craig shows not only why the FtPA was poor law, but also why it introduced an undesirable constitutional imbalance. It upset the 'mutually assured destruction' that both the government and the House of Commons hitherto enjoyed: at any moment, MPs could bring down a government through a vote of no confidence and, at any moment, a Prime Minister could dissolve Parliament and call for a new election. Both MPs and the Prime Minister had the power to remove the other from office, providing the public agreed with them, a balance which has now happily been restored since the FtPA's repeal. Craig's chapter also includes a valuable discussion about royal power and the prerogative more generally.

The role of the UK legislature has traditionally been seen as much less 'proactive' than other legislative assemblies. In the 1960s, Bernard Crick wrote that the UK legislature can offer 'influence, not direct power; advice, not command; criticism, not obstruction; scrutiny, not initiation'. The growth of the committee system and a variety of internal reforms have strengthened the legislature's ability to scrutinise. Yet, recently, some scholars have called for an even more proactive legislature, for example one which can wrest control of the parliamentary timetable from government.

Tony McNulty, in chapter seven ('Reform of the House of Commons: A Sceptical View on Progress'), regards the House of Commons as 'the fulcrum of the UK's constitutional settlement'. Therefore, 'the first point of reference of any constitutional reform should be an assessment of how it impacts on the Commons'. McNulty takes a dim view of recent efforts to reform the House of Commons, emanating from both parties. He argues that the Wright Committee's report of 2010, commissioned by Gordon Brown, was 'not rooted in a deep analysis'. Additionally, while the 2010–15 Conservative–Liberal Democrat government pursued 'constitutional change with all the piety and sanctimony of a religious cult', the reforms proposed by Deputy Prime Minister Nick Clegg made 'no attempt' to explain how the changes would improve the core functions of the Commons. McNulty, who served as a Labour MP for 13 years, views the

---

[32] *R (Miller and another) v Secretary of State for Exiting the European Union* [2016] EWHC 2768 (Admin), [2017] UKSC 5; *R (Miller) v The Prime Minister, R(Cherry) v Advocate General for Scotland* [2019] UKSC 41.

Commons as serving three key functions: as a forum for national debate, a place of scrutiny over the government and the body that sustains the government in power. Of these, McNulty argues, 'primacy needs to be given to the facilitation of the government's ability to govern'. Fundamentally, the Commons is 'a legislative factory', and McNulty strongly disagrees with present-day reformers who advocate further reforms 'from a fundamentally flawed premise of control of the order paper'. Parliament *should not* have control over parliamentary time because, as McNulty argues, 'the government needs to control business in the Commons to govern effectively'.

Another frequently floated reform is an elected upper chamber, which likely would reintroduce a veto player into the UK system that had been, effectively, abolished by the Parliament Acts 1911 and 1949. Unlike the resistance faced by David Lloyd George when he presented his reforming People's Budget, it is now understood that the House of Lords must ultimately defer to the will of the House of Commons (although some delay is possible). By being unelected, it is clear why this deference must take place, whereas an elected chamber would surely become more assertive and, over time, seek to weaken the primacy of the House of Commons. Philip Norton, who sits in the House of Lords as Lord Norton of Louth, argues in chapter eight ('The House of Lords: A Sceptical View of "Big Bang" Reform') that the unelected feature of the Lords, paradoxically, acts as a democratic safeguard. Lord Norton argues that while some reforms in the Lords are desirable, he favours a more incremental approach which focuses on improving the Lords' function rather than obsessing over its form.

Proponents of an elected House of Lords almost always advocate that such a chamber should be elected by some form of proportional representation (PR). More broadly, it seems that many academics would like to extend PR to the House of Commons, too. Electoral reform would lessen the likelihood of majority governments, making post-election coalition deal-making a new fact of life in British politics. Electoral reform would, therefore, not simply change the legislature of the UK, but would also have profound implications for the composition of the executive. It would weaken the clarity of political accountability, warns Jasper Miles (chapter nine – 'Accountability and Electoral Reform'). The case for first-past-the-post is a point of view that does not get much of a hearing in academia; although it certainly seemed to be the overwhelming choice of the British electorate in the 2011 electoral reform referendum. Implausibly, supporters of electoral reform argue that voters overwhelmingly voted to keep First Past the Post because the proposed Alternative Vote system was not proportional enough.

Hayley Hooper's chapter (chapter ten – 'Delegated Legislation in an Unprincipled Constitution') explores the use of delegated, or secondary, legislation. Parliament delegates powers to ministers under provisions sometimes called 'Henry VIII clauses', enabling them to make law without the usual parliamentary processes. For decades, legal academics have complained about the use of secondary legislation, warning that it evades essential parliamentary scrutiny. At the same time, there has been a begrudging acceptance that delegated legislation is a 'necessary evil' in order to help governments overcome the limits of parliamentary time and to accommodate the need for flexibility and detail that primary legislation struggles to provide. Delegated legislation gained renewed prominence during both the Brexit process and the COVID-19 pandemic. In this timely contribution, Hooper analyses how delegated legislation was deployed in the context of these two major episodes. She concludes that it is vital for Parliament to play its part, but the strength of the British constitution is that neither Parliament nor the government (neither 'Westminster' nor 'Whitehall') should completely dominate. A creative tension between the two is a strength of the system.

In an innovative contribution to this volume, Conor Casey (chapter eleven – 'A Defence of the Dual Legal-Political Nature of the Attorney General for England & Wales') disagrees with those who argue that the Attorney General should be carved out from partisan politics and reserved for a 'neutral' legal expert. Casey sees merit in the fact that the Attorney General emerges from the legislature, like other members of the Cabinet. As a politician, the Attorney General is better able to 'translate' law and politics for the Prime Minister and other members of the executive. Casey also argues that a politician Attorney General is less likely to be 'cautious' in the way that some technocratic advisers might be. Casey writes, a 'very cautious and highly risk averse approach to the provision of legal advice has the capacity to seriously hamstring the state's capacity to project public power to robustly respond to socio-economic challenges for the common good'. While Casey was referring specifically to the (un)desirability of relying on legal technocrats to dispense legal advice to the government, this point can be made more broadly. Relying on 'legal', 'neutral' or 'apolitical' devices to constrain government action carries costs. They shrink politics and, therefore, the range of possible policy interventions open to a government.

The final two chapters of Part II analyse public appointments and standards in public life, the subject of lively political contestation during the premiership of Boris Johnson (2019–22). John Bowers (chapter twelve – 'The Public Appointments System') argues that the system for public appointments has been quite haphazard and shaky. Public confidence has been undermined at times by a lack of perception of a fair process. He suggests some reforms to strengthen public confidence in the system.

Gillian Peele (chapter thirteen – 'Standards and the British Constitution') is both an Oxford University academic and a member of the Committee for Standards in Public Life, although she writes here in a personal capacity. Peele explains the origins of the committee, its function and its legal footing. She offers some suggestions for strengthening the role and work of the committee, while acknowledging concerns MPs frequently raise about their autonomy. She also acknowledges that, alongside parliamentary investigators, MPs themselves serve as an important vehicle in holding governments to account. Ultimately, it was a rebellion from his own MPs and Cabinet ministers that forced Boris Johnson to resign as Prime Minister in July 2022, rather than the long-awaited report from the Privileges Committee.

C. Part III – Beyond Westminster and Whitehall

Part III of the book examines the constitutional changes that are, to some extent, external to the operation of Parliament or the UK government but which, nonetheless, have serious ramifications for the doctrine of parliamentary sovereignty and political accountability. They also raise important existential questions about the continuation of the UK itself.

Devolution, once thought to be a device to protect the union, has seemingly weakened the UK's internal bonds dramatically. From a social policy perspective, devolution fragments the welfare state and makes universal, transformative social policy more difficult to implement. Paul Peterson said 'Federalism means inequality', yet some of the staunchest advocates for federalism in Britain seem to be from the British left. Sir Vernon Bogdanor (chapter fourteen – 'Devolving and Not Forgetting') argues that UK policymakers made a serious mistake when devolution was thought to transfer all responsibility for domestic social problems to the devolved parliaments and executives. He argues that it remains the responsibility of the UK government to ensure a high standard of living, a well-trained and educated workforce, and equality of opportunity, irrespective of where a person lives within the UK. Therefore, UK governments should feel more empowered to intervene to address social problems with respect to British citizens living in Scotland, Wales or Northern Ireland.

Scotland has witnessed the greatest loosening from the rest of the UK, with the Scottish Parliament being given more powers than the other devolved parliaments and being politically governed by a party whose primary purpose is to dissolve the UK. Far from 'killing nationalism stone dead', devolution has provided the institutional blueprint for a separate Scottish state.[33] Peter Reid and Asanga Welikala, both based at the University of Edinburgh, consider in their chapter (chapter fifteen – 'Scottish Secession and the Political Constitution of the UK') the remarkably relaxed approach the UK government has taken to Scottish separatism. Few other countries in the world would have simply consented, as David Cameron's coalition government did in 2014, to the breakup of their country on the basis of a simple legislative majority in a devolved region and with the threshold being a simple majority (on any turnout) in a referendum.

Across the Irish Sea, Kate Hoey, who sits in the House of Lords as Baroness Hoey, writes about the UK government's insouciance to British identity in Northern Ireland in chapter sixteen ('Northern Ireland's Constitutional Position in the UK'). Writing from her British Unionist perspective, Lady Hoey argues that the Northern Ireland Protocol, which was negotiated as part of the British withdrawal from the European Union, is an unacceptable disjuncture in trade across the UK. Just as people would not accept a customs barrier between the East and West Midlands, Hoey argues, such a barrier between Northern Ireland and the rest of the UK should be viewed as equally intolerable. At the same time, she argues that the Belfast (Good Friday) Agreement has been misused to argue that there

[33] HC Deb 6 May 1998, vol 311, col 735.

should be *no* border (in any form) between the Republic of Ireland and Northern Ireland, even though, she argues, this was never the intent of the Agreement. She recalls in the chapter her time as a London Labour MP, when she travelled to Northern Ireland in 1998 to campaign in favour of the Agreement, alongside the Ulster Unionist leader David Trimble. At the heart of the Belfast Agreement is cross-community consent, which ironically is now being violated by those who wish to impose the Protocol on the Unionist community.

The ructions caused by British membership (and exit) from the European Union are examined by Joanna George and Gisela Stuart, Baroness Stuart of Edgbaston in chapter 17 ('The European Union and the British Constitution'). Stuart, as a Birmingham Labour MP, served as Chair of Vote Leave during the 2016 referendum on European Union membership. George and Stuart regard joining and leaving the EU as fundamentally constitutional acts, with important implications for the operation of the UK constitution more broadly. They contend that British governments tended not to take seriously how constitutional reform *within the EU* would have knock-on consequences for the operation of the constitution *within the UK*. Stuart draws from her experience as the Parliamentary Representative to the European Convention, which drafted a new constitution of the European Union, and where she served as a member of its Presidium.

The volume concludes with a wide-ranging and fascinating discussion about representation and the British constitution by Richard Tuck (chapter eighteen – 'Against (Many Kinds of) Representation'). Tuck rejects schemes like citizens' assemblies and legislatures chosen by sortition because they remove any sense of a positive mandate for action or retrospective accountability for performance. A citizen who is not lucky enough (or unlucky, depending on one's perspective) to be chosen for a citizens' assembly has no power to instruct its members or sanction them, unlike in an elected system. All that ordinary citizens can do is present petitions and try to appeal to the beneficence of the members of the citizens' assemblies, who are under no obligation to listen to or follow their instructions. Tuck likens this situation to the petitions made by subjects to their king under the absolute monarchies of the *ancien régime*. Relatedly, Tuck rejects Edmund Burke's theory of representation articulated in his Address to the Electors of Bristol in 1774. In this speech, Burke, unlike his fellow Bristol MP Henry Cruger, rejected the common practice of mandation, whereby electors would vote on certain policy instructions that their MPs would need to follow. Burke wished to function effectively as an independent, which raises many of the same concerns as sortition and citizens' assemblies. In the old practice of mandation, Tuck sees the seeds of the party manifesto, 'a special document' that 'has played a powerful role in modern British politics'. Manifestos act as a form of mandation on MPs today, which Tuck regards as highly democratic and desirable. In addition, Tuck views referendums as a kind of national mandation of MPs, which they are duty-bound to accept, even if technically they could act otherwise. The attempt to revive a Burkean theory of representation during the hung parliament of 2017–19 was 'farcical' and 'a full-blooded Burkean position is no more persuasive now than it was in 1774'.

PART I

The Political Constitution
and the Law

1

A (Brief) Case against Constitutional Supremacy

BRIAN CHRISTOPHER JONES*

I. Introduction: We've Been Here Before

Written constitutions may capture the imagination, but whether they lead to better forms of government is certainly up for debate.[1] Not every country possesses a single written constitution, and some countries possess them in quirky forms. The UK famously does not have such a document. New Zealand possesses only a decorative one: an ordinary statute that has been labelled a constitution, and that can be amended the same as any other law. And Australia's 1901 constitution lacks what many consider the crown jewel of such documents: a bill of rights. Nonetheless, these countries remain some of the most free and democratic in the world. But these countries are swimming against the tide. There is little doubt the worldwide trajectory is towards more writing, more constitutions and less deference to elected representatives, legislatures and majoritarian rule. Many states have gone down the path of implementing 'constitutional supremacy': the idea that the written constitution sits above everything else within the state, containing the state's fundamental law. The idea sounds enticing, at least until one digs into what it actually entails. This chapter provides a brief case against constitutional supremacy, arguing that the UK doctrine of parliamentary sovereignty is a better option for upholding democracy.

This book is predominantly concerned with the past three decades of constitutional reform, and especially those reforms under New Labour. Much of these

---

*This chapter builds upon BC Jones, 'A Single Written UK Constitution May Only Make Things Worse' (*UKCLA Blog*, 25 May 2020) https://ukconstitutionallaw.org/2020/05/25/brian-christopher-jones-a-single-written-uk-constitution-may-only-make-things-worse/; BC Jones, 'What's So Great About a Written Constitution?' *The Atlantic* (9 October 2020).

[1] See, eg L Colley, *The Gun, the Ship, and the Pen: Warfare, Constitutions, and the Making of the Modern World* (London, Profile, 2021) 9: 'By their very nature, written constitutions are protean and volatile pieces of political technology. They hold out the enticing promise that the words and clauses contained within them will bring into being a new, improved reality. New constitutions offer, or can appear to offer, the prospect of benign and exciting transformations.'

reforms were focused on an increased 'writtenness' of the UK constitution: human rights, devolution, institutional reform, etc. Even publication of things like the Cabinet Manual was said to be aiming towards an idea of a written constitution.[2] Indeed, Gordon Brown had no qualms admitting that he preferred a written constitution for the UK, both when he was PM and afterwards.[3] Throughout the twenty-first century a plethora of individuals, from high-profile politicians to bestselling authors, have advocated for a written UK constitution.[4] But these suggestions for codification largely overlook the fact that semi-codification under EU membership proved difficult, and that the flexibility of the unwritten constitution has proved advantageous for both sides. Ultimately, far from demonstrating the need for more rigid structures and boundaries, the UK story demonstrates why a commitment to unwritten constitutionalism works.

Figure 1.1 References to a written constitution in *Hansard*, 1800–2022

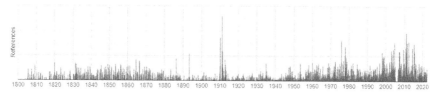

In the UK, the debate over written constitutionalism comes to a head every now and then, but there is strong evidence that it is always bubbling away in the background. As Figure 1.1 demonstrates, parliamentary discussion over written constitutions comes in peaks and troughs.[5] Talk of a written constitution is surprisingly consistent throughout the nineteenth century. Then, it drops off markedly until 1910, when talk skyrockets around the controversy over the People's Budget. After this, discussion trails off until just before 1950, when it seems to pick back up again. The period from 1975 to 2020, however, displays the most consistently intense period of discussion around written constitutionalism. Correspondingly, it should be noted that until the turn of the twenty-first century, there is virtually no talk of a 'codified constitution'.[6] From the 1970s onwards, there are some single mentions, but it does not go over five mentions per year until 2007. Thus, for all

---

[2] *The Cabinet Manual: A Guide to Laws, Conventions, and Rules on the Operation of Government*, 1st edn (October 2011).

[3] G Brown, 'How to Save the United Kingdom' *The New Statesman* (18 November 2020).

[4] Even high-profile authors feel the need to discuss the matter. See, eg R Jones, 'Author Hilary Mantel Says UK Needs Written Constitution' (*BBC News*, 21 May 2021) www.bbc.co.uk/news/entertainment-arts-57157878.

[5] Hansard search for 'written constitution' from 1 January 1800 to 7 July 2022, https://hansard.parliament.uk/search.

[6] Hansard search for 'codified constitution' from 1 January 1800 to 7 July 2022, https://hansard.parliament.uk/search.

the pedantic debate over the topic, in Parliament there seems to be little appetite for the use of 'codified' over 'written'.

A. Historical Attempts (or Recognitions) of Codified Constitutions within the UK or its Constituent Parts

The idea that the UK should draft a written constitution has been floated over the centuries, and there are certainly some documents that have attained – or at least been recognised at various points as – potential written constitutions. Below I attempt to navigate some of the significant developments throughout the years, but with an emphasis on the past four decades.[7]

In 1653, Cromwell's Protectorate penned what many consider the world's first written constitution: the Instrument of Government. For all intents and purposes, the document was a resounding failure, not least because of its unamendability and its concentration of power in the executive.[8] The same fate fell upon its successor, the Humble Petition and Advice.[9] Given the difficulties these initial attempts at codification presented, the decision not to draft another written constitution after the Glorious Revolution 1688 seems perfectly understandable. After the monarchy was restored, the Bill of Rights 1689 was passed,[10] but this was not akin to a written constitution. In fact, the document laid the basis for the operation of parliamentary sovereignty, as it guaranteed the rights of Parliament against the monarch.[11] This foundation ultimately commenced the UK's commitment to unwritten constitutionalism.

Perhaps the next major attempt at recognising a codified UK constitution came in the 1707 Act of Union with Scotland. Indeed, this has many features that a written constitution would have, such as the merging of the kingdoms and the establishment of the Parliament of Great Britain, including the representation Scotland would have at Westminster. The document has even been acknowledged as a constitutional text in the judicial sphere at times.[12] Himsworth and O'Neill state three reasons for according higher status to the treaty: its constitutive character, the language used in the treaty, and judicial recognition of the treaty.[13]

---

[7] During the last century, the UK Parliament did enact constitutions for many Commonwealth countries, including those for Canada, India, Australia and other states.

[8] GD Heath III, 'Making the Instrument of Government' (1967) 6(2) *Journal of British Studies* 15; P Gaunt, 'Drafting the Instrument of Government, 1653–54: A Reappraisal' (1989) 8(1) *Parliamentary History* 28.

[9] RCH Catterall, 'The Failure of the Humble Petition and Advice' (1903) 9(1) *American Historical Review* 36.

[10] The Claim of Right 1689 was passed in Scotland.

[11] G Lock, 'The 1689 Bill of Rights' (1989) 37 *Political Studies* 540.

[12] *MacCormick v Lord Advocate* 1953 SC 396, 1953 SLT 255.

[13] CMG Himsworth and CM O'Neill, *Scotland's Constitution: Law and Practice*, 3rd edn (London, Bloomsbury, 2015) 135–38.

However, the authors conceded that although it was fundamental in its time, the treaty has not been regarded as a codified constitution throughout the years.

The discussion around the People's Budget and subsequent developments brought forward much acknowledgement of a written constitution in Parliament. In fact, from 1800 to the present day, this period of parliamentary discussion has the highest number of references to a written constitution than at any other period. However, I have been unable to locate any formal proposals for a written constitution during this period.

The Government of Ireland Act 1920 provided Northern Ireland with a sort of mini-constitution from 1922 to 1972, and could also be considered recognition of a codified document for one of the UK's constituent parts.[14] This was replaced with the Northern Ireland Constitution Act 1973, which essentially provided for direct control of Northern Ireland to revert to Westminster.

The late 1980s and early 1990s witnessed an intense period of written constitutional desire. The Charter 88 Movement was one of three prominent efforts during this period to bring forward such a document. The Charter began in the pages of the *New Statesman*, receiving support from notable intellectuals in the Liberal and Social Democratic parties. The Charter commits to a bill of rights, proportional representation and a written constitution 'anchored in the idea of universal citizenship'.[15] In the early 1990s, the issue of codification came up again. In 1991, there were two major proposals for a written constitution: Tony Benn's Commonwealth of Britain Bill[16] and the Institute of Public Policy Research's (IPPR) Written Constitution for the United Kingdom.[17] Both of these were fairly radical proposals that would have significantly altered the current UK constitution. Benn's proposal would have turned the UK into a presidential system, eliminated the House of Lords in favour of a 'House of the People' and lowered the voting age to 16. The IPPR proposal would have replaced the Lords with an elected second chamber, changed the time periods that Parliament sat and moved to proportional representation.

Whilst New Labour did not have a commitment to codification, they did have a commitment to increased constitutional writtenness. As this book documents, many of the elements located in the constitutional documents above made their way into New Labour's legislative programme: a de facto bill of rights, devolution, House of Lords reform and the creation of a Supreme Court. These developments undoubtedly 'constitutionalised' the UK's unwritten constitution in many ways.[18]

---

[14] ibid 15, citing AS Quekett, *The Constitution of Northern Ireland* (Belfast, HMSO, 1928, 1933, 1946).

[15] D Erdos, 'Charter 88 and the Constitutional Reform Movement: A Retrospective' (2009) 62 *Parliamentary Affairs* 537.

[16] The Bill was presented by Tony Benn on 20 May 1991.

[17] J Cornford et al, 'The Constitution of the United Kingdom' (Institute of Public Policy Research, 1 September 1991) www.ippr.org/publications/the-constitution-of-the-uk.

[18] Some even characterised it as a 'new' constitution. See V Bogdanor, *The New British Constitution* (Oxford, Hart Publishing, 2009).

The implementation of the Human Rights Act 1998 accomplished the establishment of a statutory bill of rights, resulting in (arguably) strong form judicial review.[19] The devolution statutes have also been characterised as potential constitutions for the respective countries. Under these, the Westminster Parliament remains sovereign, but there is scope for the Supreme Court to review legislation emanating from the devolved legislatures.[20] Throughout this period of constitutional development, Tony Blair was non-committal in relation to a written constitution, but the post-Blair Labour governments steered the UK towards such a document.[21]

The 800th anniversary of Magna Carta brought forward numerous attempts to codify the UK constitution. Indeed, a major parliamentary report into such prospects was entitled 'A New Magna Carta?'.[22] But the report did not recommend a view either way. Three other notable attempts at codification were: Conor Gearty's Crowdsourcing the UK Constitution,[23] Robert Blackburn's article 'Enacting a Written Constitution for the United Kingdom',[24] and Andrew Blick's book, *Beyond Magna Carta: A Constitution for the United Kingdom*.[25]

Finally, as will be seen in section III, Brexit, the coronavirus response and the premiership of Boris Johnson have all brought forward more calls for a written constitution. However, in the section that follows, I outline an admittedly brief case against constitutional supremacy, followed by another brief analysis of the UK constitution during times of recent crisis.

II. A (Brief) Case against Constitutional Supremacy

Arguments for and against a single written (or 'codified') UK constitution often revolve around flexibility versus rigidity or transparency versus opacity.[26] Another, recent common objection is that it would just be inconvenient, or impossible, given the current levels of polarisation.[27] These objections are reasonable and

---

[19] A Kavanaugh, 'What's So Weak about "Weak-Form Review"? The Case of the UK Human Rights Act 1998' (2015) 13 *International Journal of Constitutional Law* 1008.

[20] Indeed, this has happened relatively frequently throughout the years.

[21] N Barber, 'Against a Written Constitution' [2008] *PL* 11; V Bogdanor, T Khaitan and S Vogenauer, 'Should Britain Have a Written Constitution?' (2007) 78 *The Political Quarterly* 499, 500.

[22] House of Commons Political and Constitutional Reform Committee, 'A New Magna Carta?' (HC 463, 10 July 2014).

[23] C Gearty, 'Crowdsourcing the UK Constitution' (*LSE Blog*, 16 January 2015) https://blogs.lse. ac.uk/lti/2015/01/16/crowdsourcing-the-uk-constitution/.

[24] R Blackburn, 'Enacting a Written Constitution for the United Kingdom' (2015) 36(1) *Statute Law Review* 1.

[25] A Blick, *Beyond Magna Carta: A New Constitution for the United Kingdom* (Oxford, Hart Publishing, 2015).

[26] See, eg J King, 'The Democratic Case for a Written Constitution' (2019) 72(1) *Current Legal Problems* 1.

[27] House of Commons Political and Constitutional Reform Committee (n 22). In discussing arguments against codification, the Committee notes that, 'The preparation of a written constitution would involve a huge and disproportionate amount of time and effort – in preparing the proposal and its various options, in carrying out consultation exercises, in holding debates in Parliament, and in arranging

legitimate, but they are hardly the full extent of the story. In fact, much room exists for a more principled stance: that implementing a single written constitution may just be unwise, will not result in better government and could ultimately lead to a number of democracy-hindering downsides. I believe that single written constitutions have been drastically and persistently oversold throughout the years and will not produce better democratic outcomes compared to unwritten constitutions or help solve increasingly sophisticated societal problems.[28]

A. Constitutional Supremacy ≠ We the People

Most contemporary constitutions begin with 'We the People' or place the idea of strong constituent power prominently within the written document. The idea is constitutional supremacy's most potent fiction; it certainly does not provide 'the People' with any enhanced powers or place them at the centre of the constitution. James Madison often boasted about the fact that the US Constitution did not allow 'the People' – in their collective capacity – to possess any share of government, and he considered this exclusion as one of the document's 'great virtues'.[29] Constitutional supremacy also lowers the significance and outputs of those most readily connected to the people: elected representatives. Parliamentary supremacy, on the other hand, preserves elected representative's status as the most important voice of citizens and the most direct connection to the people. Nevertheless, the UK's governmental system is regularly mocked – even by its own citizens and leading constitutional experts – for not possessing a constitution that identifies the people as the underlying authority.[30] But the notion that constituent authority goes unresolved in the UK constitution is a misrepresentation at best and a complete distortion of the truth at worst.

It is not clear that the presence of 'We the People' in a constitutional text actually matters. Advocates maintain that the phrase ultimately grounds the constitution in 'the People', producing better outcomes for ordinary citizens. But as a practical matter, the rhetorical invocation of 'the People' does not confer any

---

(most likely) a referendum. To attempt to foist a written constitution on the UK would be a diversion of scarce time and resources away from the most relevant social and economic problems facing this country' (17). Additionally, another reason against codification was: 'In the absence of any national crisis or catalyst making a written constitution necessary, it is idle to pretend that the main political parties could ever agree on the precise contents of a written constitution, even if all were to support the principle and desirability of codifying the constitution' (21).

[28] BC Jones, *Constitutional Idolatry and Democracy: Challenging the Infatuation with Writtenness* (Cheltenham, Edward Elgar Publishing, 2020).

[29] G Thomas, 'The Madisonian Constitution, Political Dysfunction, and Polarized Politics' in Z Courser, E Helland and KP Miller, *Parchment Barriers: Political Polarization and the Limits of Constitutional Order* (Lawrence, University of Kansas Press, 2018) 18.

[30] DJ Galligan, 'The Constitutional Future of the UK' in DJ Galligan (ed), *Constitution in Crisis: The New Putney Debates* (London, IB Tauris, 2017) 165. Galligan notes that even the Turkish Constitution is 'clear and accurate' on the matters of constituent power.

enhanced powers or special treatment on the citizenry. Nevertheless, ideas around popular sovereignty were present in England and Scotland well before the era of written constitutions came about. The Scottish Declaration of Arbroath, in 1320, contained language advocating popular sovereignty over the monarch, and in two seventeenth-century events in England – the Civil War and the Glorious Revolution – numerous accounts of such language have been documented.[31] Although the idea that citizens possess ultimate constitutional authority may have been a central focus of these events, the UK never felt the need to write this commitment down.

Yet if the UK decided to draft a constitution incorporating the words *We the People*, MPs would undoubtedly lose power and influence within the UK constitutional system. As Jutta Limbach, a former president of the German Federal Constitutional Court, identifies, constitutional supremacy 'means the *lower ranking* of statute' and also a '*lower ranking* of the legislator'.[32] This presents clear problems for the UK's unwritten constitution, which relies on parliamentary sovereignty and highly values both statutes and legislators. Without such a written document in place in the UK, no intentional lower ranking of statute and legislator takes place. This means that the governmental institution most accountable and responsive to the people, the legislature, retains the most power within the UK system. Judges remain in a powerful constitutional position but are unable to strike down legislation, and if laws need to be amended or repealed, the legislature must take action.

Equating constitutional supremacy with a deeper focus on 'We the People' is a misrepresentation. If anything, constitutional supremacy has brought forward strong examples of judicial supremacy around the world,[33] which has increasingly sidelined elected representatives and citizens.

B. Discouraging Popular Participation?

It is impossible to ignore the fact that since written constitutions, bills of rights and enhanced judicial review became increasingly prevalent throughout the twentieth and twenty-first centuries, levels of political participation have plummeted.[34] But the picture is certainly a complicated one, and it is not possible to draw a direct line between increasing constitutionalisation and decreasing political participation. There are some elements that may play a role, however.

Although a number of writers have noted that written constitutions can be 'inspiring', strengthen citizenship and bring government and citizens closer

---

[31] ES Morgan, *Inventing the People: The Rise of Popular Sovereignty in England and America* (New York, WW Norton, 1988).

[32] J Limbach, 'The Concept of the Supremacy of the Constitution' (2003) 64(1) *MLR* 1.

[33] CN Tate and T Vallinder (eds), *The Global Expansion of Judicial Power* (New York, NYU Press, 1997).

[34] See, eg BC Jones, 'The Legal Contribution to Democratic Disaffection' (2023) 75(4) *Arkansas Law Review* forthcoming.

together,[35] whether implementation may lead to any type of invigoration of the citizenry is highly questionable. In particular, there are questions about whether the implementation of single written constitutions have translated into higher citizen participation at the ballot box. A preliminary study on this topic reveals that after the implementation of new written constitutions, for whatever reason, voter turnout in a wide variety of jurisdictions noticeably dropped.[36] Surprisingly, a number of states also experienced their lowest recorded post-World War II voter turnout after implementation. In some cases, noticeable decreases were also found after the introduction of bills of rights and major constitutional amendments. Of course, voter turnout is a complex and multifaceted phenomenon that can change considerably from one election to the next. Nevertheless, if single written constitutions are designed to inspire citizens and strengthen citizenship, they do not appear to be encouraging people to exercise their most significant democratic power: the public vote.

Additionally, while protecting and upholding constitutional norms is a collective function within states that all citizens can participate in, constitutional supremacy has decreased this collective focus, coalescing guardianship around one branch in particular: the judiciary. Justification for this enhanced role is often premised around constitutions being displayed in written form as a legal document. Suffice it to say that judiciaries have embraced this enhanced role. Rather than acknowledging that other branches or institutions are better placed to resolve constitutional disputes or uphold constitutional norms, many judiciaries nowadays are becoming more adamant that *they alone* are the ultimate constitutional guardians.[37] Legal scholars and journalists have also perpetuated this misguided idea. Whilst judiciaries do play a significant role within any democracy, this overly paternalistic development is unhealthy for democracy and downplays the critical roles of citizens, journalists, and other constitutional actors. After all, if states are going to succeed and thrive, then they require active citizens willing to participate in and uphold the wider constitutional project; judiciaries alone cannot do this.

There is also a substantial risk that implementing constitutional supremacy will lead to a strong form of adjudicated constitutionalism, which contains its own pathologies. The new relationship brought about by constitutional supremacy is not one of equality between law and politics, but rather law asserting itself as *superior* to politics. For example, rather than attempting to ennoble the political realm to further the public good, adjudicated constitutionalism frequently attempts to belittle and infantilise politics, so that law and courts can assert its dominance over

---

[35] See, eg W Voermans, M Stremler and P Cliteur, *Constitutional Preambles: A Comparative Analysis* (Cheltenham, Edward Elgar Publishing, 2017) 93.

[36] BC Jones, 'Constitutions and Bills of Rights: Invigorating or Placating Democracy?' (2018) 38 *Legal Studies* 339.

[37] BC Jones, 'Constitutional Paternalism: The Rise and Problematic Use of Constitutional Guardian Rhetoric' (2019) 51 *NYU Journal of International Law & Politics* 773.

constitutional claims.[38] For a constitution that relies heavily on politics to solve sophisticated societal problems, such as the UK's, such a transition could come at substantial cost. After all, there are other downsides to adjudicated constitutionalism. Given the vast powers that many constitutional courts end up with under constitutional supremacy, there seems to be an undermining or breakdown of the separation of powers.[39] And not only that, but adjudicated constitutionalism only perpetuates juristocracy, which often sees constitutional law as primarily case law, or judge-made law.[40]

Democracy requires at least some level of citizen engagement and participation. Constitutional supremacy may not eliminate this, but it likely makes traditional methods of political participation (voting, party membership, campaigning, and generally attempting to win hearts and minds) less attractive.

C. Educating and Informing the Citizenry

One commonly cited benefit to states possessing written constitutions is that such devices perform an educative function, because citizens can easily consult and reference the documents. But in practice, constitutional knowledge does not work this way.[41] Indeed, the US Constitution is widely available on countless apps and websites, and its physical form consistently lands on bestseller lists. There is probably no written constitution that is more politically and culturally relevant than the US Constitution. Yet, US citizens undoubtedly struggle with knowledge of their revered text,[42] suggesting the answer does not lie in merely having the document available or taking a 'closer look' at it, let alone getting to grips with the vast layers of legal doctrines and precents that animate it.[43] Moreover, single written constitutions do not inform citizens on civic knowledge or constitutional operation any better than unwritten or partially written ones. A number of large comparative studies have found that those living in the UK, New Zealand and Australia are just as knowledgeable, if not more so, about politics, political structures and

---

[38] R West, 'Ennobling Politics' in HJ Powell and JB White (eds), *Law and Democracy in the Empire of Force* (Ann Arbor, University of Michigan Press, 2009) 78–79; Jones, *Constitutional Idolatry and Democracy* (n 28) 81–86.

[39] A Stone Sweet, *Governing with Judges: Constitutional Politics in Europe* (Oxford, Oxford University Press, 2000); M Tushnet, *Advanced Introduction to Comparative Constitutional Law*, 2nd edn (Cheltenham, Edward Elgar Publishing, 2018) 64.

[40] Stone Sweet (n 39) 146; West (n 38) 66.

[41] G Frankenberg, *Comparative Constitutional Studies: Between Magic and Deceit* (Cambridge, Cambridge University Press, 2018) 14–15. Frankenberg notes that constitutions 'hardly render an accurate description of social reality' and cannot be read as state instruction manuals. He notes that at best they 'indicate how societies … envision coping with or camouflaging the business of establishing and exercising authority and bringing about social cohesion'.

[42] Annenburg Public Policy Center, 'Americans' Civics Knowledge Increases During a Stress-Filled Year' (14 September 2021) www.asc.upenn.edu/news-events/news/americans-civics-knowledge-increases-during-stress-filled-year.

[43] AR Amar, *America's Unwritten Constitution: The Precedents and Principles We Live By* (New York, Basic Books, 2012).

constitutional operation as citizens in countries governed by easily accessed written constitutions.[44]

In fact, a large portion of citizens in countries with written constitutions do not even know these documents exist. In 2015, in celebration of the eight-hundredth anniversary of the Magna Carta, Ipsos MORI and the Magna Carta Trust sampled a number of jurisdictions around the world on how familiar citizens were with various constitutional documents.[45] The poll found that at least one-third of citizens in Australia, Belgium, Brazil, India and South Korea had *never even heard of* the constitution governing their country. In Romania, only 38 per cent of citizens were familiar with their present constitution. These results call into question the significance and effectiveness of merely having a single written document available.

The idea that a country's constitutional operation can be captured in a single document remains a powerful yet ill-considered fantasy. All constitutions rely on a combination of written texts, unwritten principles, conventions, judicial decisions, parliamentary rules and procedure, the quality of the relationship between central and local governments, the attitudes and rhetoric of the political class, and several other elements. Frankenberg questions whether we can even consider these 'road maps' when it comes to state operation.[46] No doubt he has a point. Many constitutions may contain provisions that have fallen into desuetude or do not accurately describe the current operation of the constitution in question.[47] And for a competent understanding of constitutional operation, many documents may need reference to supplementary texts and further explanation.

Ultimately, a single written UK constitution may not educate or inform the citizenry any better than the current arrangements do. These highly legalised documents are unable to capture the full range of constitutional activities within any given state, and in some cases may conceal or overemphasise certain aspects of constitutional operation.

D. Questionable Drafting Practices

Some constitutions engage in questionable drafting practices, such as actively encouraging praise of the written document or downplaying some highly contentious issues.

---

[44] J Torney-Purta, R Lehmann, H Oswald and W Schulzrk, *Citizenship and Education in Twenty-eight Countries: Civic Knowledge and Engagement at Age Fourteen* (Amsterdam, IEA, 2001) 45–56; W Schulz, J Ainley, J Fraillon, D Kerr and B Losito, 'ICCS 2009 International Report: Civic Knowledge, Attitudes, and Engagement among Lower Secondary School Students in 38 Countries' (International Association for the Evaluation of Educational Achievement, 2010) 75; K Grönlund and H Milner, 'The Determinants of Political Knowledge in Comparative Perspective' (2006) 29 *Scandinavian Political Studies* 386, 396.

[45] Magna Carta Trust, 'International Poll', https://magnacarta800th.com/projects/international-poll/.

[46] Frankenberg (n 41).

[47] R Albert, 'Constitutional Amendment by Constitutional Desuetude' (2014) 62 *American Journal of Comparative Law* 641; Chien-Chih Lin, 'Believe in the Ideal, not the Idol: Is Constitutional Idolatry Happening in Taiwan?' (*IACL Blog*, 12 January 2021) https://blog-iacl-aidc.org/cili/2021/1/12/believe-in-the-ideal-not-the-idol-is-constitutional-idolatry-happening-in-taiwan.

One of the major underexplored downsides of single written constitutions is the drafting of preambles. These constitutional preludes often contain language that advocates not adherence to any particular constitutional principles, but idolatry of the written document itself. For countries that adhere to questionable forms of democracy (or even openly flout democracy), preambles are often used to provide a veneer of legitimacy, employing 'We the People' rhetoric to hood-wink citizens into believing that the foundation of the constitution is built around them. Additionally, preamble language may also foment nationalism or enhance dangerous forms of patriotism. For example, Syria's preamble notes that the country is 'the beating heart of Arabism, the forefront of confrontation with the Zionist enemy and the bedrock of resistance against colonial hegemony on the Arab world and its capabilities and wealth'.[48] Some preambles even contain material that suggests that the hand of God helped write particular constitutions,[49] or that God's wisdom contributed to its drafting (eg the Philippines Constitution 1987).[50] Thus, it is unsurprising that constitutional idolatry remains so rampant, given that many preambles actively encourage it.

Another issue with the drafting of single written constitutions is the somewhat bizarre method of articulating judicial power. Given the wide growth of judicial authority since WWII, one would expect these awesome powers to be front and centre in any document. But they are actually quite tricky to find.[51] Although some may point to preliminary clauses declaring that 'statutes contrary to the constitution will be void', these clauses are highly problematic, as they usually do not explain how statutes can be voided or which branch does the voiding. In fact, some constitutions do not mention the fact that courts can strike down statutes, or that they often possess ultimate power to determine what the constitution means, until well over half-way into the document. Thus, it is no surprise that a portion of American citizens believe that 5–4 Supreme Court judgments are sent back to Congress,[52] or that over half of those recently polled in South Africa did not know that the top court could strike down statutes.[53] Whilst articulating the powers of the judiciary may not align with the 'We the People' rhetoric of such documents, constitutions must do a better job of making these tremendous powers explicit, especially if they are to serve an educative function.

---

[48] Syria Constitution 2012, preamble.

[49] Tunisia Constitution 2014, preamble.

[50] Philippines Constitution 1987, preamble.

[51] The German Basic Law does not articulate the power of the judiciary until Art 92, and the Japanese Constitution does not do so until Art 76.

[52] Annenberg Public Policy Center, 'Is There a Constitutional Right to Own a Home or a Pet? Many Americans Don't Know' (16 September 2015) https://cdn.annenbergpublicpolicycenter.org/wp-content/uploads/Civic-knowledge-survey-Sept.-2015.pdf.

[53] D Bilchitz et al, 'Assessing the Performance of the South African Constitution' [2016] *International IDEA* 19.

E. Is a 'Good' Constitution Essential for State Success?

There are major questions regarding what a 'good' constitution is: does it matter if it is long or short; does it contain certain 'essentials' (such as a bill of rights, an inspirational preamble or an element of 'cleverness'); has it sufficiently articulated the separation of powers; does it allow for judicial review by a supreme or constitutional court; and has its drafting and ratification had appropriate participation from relevant sections of society?[54] Constitutions that do not include these items or follow these paths may be less likely to succeed than those that do. Perusing the constitutional landscape, however, the development of many states seems to push back against the notion that a 'good' constitution can be found, let alone its particular elements readily identified.

Numerous 'unorthodox' constitutions do not fit the ideal of what a 'good' constitution should include in this day and age. Indeed, some states with what could be thought of as shaky constitutional foundations have undoubtedly succeeded. For example, some prominent imposed constitutions (ie constitutions heavily drafted by outsiders and forced on particular states),[55] have been successful in some instances. Germany's 1949 Basic Law was heavily written by outsiders, and yet it has survived post-war reconstruction and the unification of East and West Germany, and has allowed Germany to thrive well into the twenty-first century. Japan's 1947 Constitution was also heavily written by outsiders (in particular, two American army officers) and yet, to date, this Constitution has never been formally amended. Japan also scores very high on democracy and human rights indicators,[56] and has been a beacon of freedom in Asia for decades. There are even constitutions that have been written for completely different states, such as Taiwan's 1947 Constitution – which was written for a democratic China but has proven successful even under these strange conditions. Similar to Japan, Taiwan also performs well on international indicators,[57] and its impressive transition to democracy over the past few decades is a model for other states.

The Nordic states also contain an interesting counter-narrative when it comes to contemporary constitutionalism and whether there is a need for constitutional supremacy.[58] In particular, most of these countries' constitutional traditions

---

[54] H Landemore, 'What Is a "Good" Constitution' in T Ginsburg and A Huq (eds), *Assessing Constitutional Performance* (Cambridge, Cambridge University Press, 2016); JM Carey, 'Does It Matter How a Constitution Is Created?' in Z Barany and R Moser (eds), *Is Democracy Exportable?* (Cambridge, Cambridge University Press, 2009).

[55] David Law has pushed back in classifying some of these as 'imposed' constitutions: D Law, 'The Myth of the Imposed Constitution' in D Galligan and M Versteeg (eds), *Social and Political Foundations of Constitutions* (Cambridge, Cambridge University Press, 2013) 264–65.

[56] Freedom House, 'Freedom in the World Report 2022', https://freedomhouse.org/countries/freedom-world/scores; Economist Intelligence Unit, 'Democracy Index 2021: The China Challenge' (2022).

[57] ibid.

[58] R Hirschl, 'The Nordic Counternarrative: Democracy, Human Development and Judicial Review' (2011) 9 *International Journal of Constitutional Law* 449.

revolve around 'local and national democracy, popular sovereignty, parliamentary supremacy, and majority rule',[59] some of which have fallen out of favour in recent years (parliamentary supremacy and majority rule in particular). Yet, these countries are some of the highest performers on democracy and human rights indicators. Norway, Sweden and Finland score 100/100 on Freedom House's indicators, with perfect marks in civil rights and political liberties. Iceland and Denmark are not far behind, scoring 94 and 97, respectively.[60] All these countries are also in the top 10 of *The Economist*'s most recent Democracy Index.[61] The more restrained methods of rights protection used in these states demonstrate that 'rights and judicial review alone certainly do not do the trick when it comes to human development. They may not even be an across-the-board necessary … supplement to democracy'.[62] As noted at the beginning of this chapter, the same can be said about the UK, Australian and New Zealand constitutions, as they all possess quirks that in some ways are antithetical to constitutional supremacy. Yet, these countries also perform very well on democracy and human rights indicators.

The idea of a 'good' constitution remains elusive, with natural constitutional experiments demonstrating that certain 'core' elements of a contemporary democracy, such as the articulation of constitutional rights and strong judicial review by powerful constitutional courts, are far less important to state success than many seem willing to admit.

F. Frustrating Essential Constitutional Maintenance

Vibrant societies require structures that can change and evolve over time, but written constitutions often stifle much-needed constitutional maintenance, rely on tidal-wave constitutional moments, or place pressure on societal change to happen via the courts. None of these outcomes are ideal. About the only thing that scholars can agree on is that constitutional change needs to happen,[63] but there is less agreement about how that should happen, what the threshold for constitutional change should be and whether there are certain things that should remain off the table in terms of constitutional amendment.

In the UK's unwritten system, virtually nothing is too sacred to be amended: the prescribed length of time between general elections has fluctuated;[64] the balance of power between the Houses of Parliament has altered over time;[65] reform of

---

[59] ibid 450.
[60] Freedom House (n 56).
[61] Economist Democracy Index (n 56).
[62] Hirschl (n 57) 455.
[63] S Barber, *Constitutional Failure* (Lawrence, University of Kansas Press, 2014) 8; S Levinson, *Constitutional Faith* (Princeton, Princeton University Press, 1988) 9.
[64] It has gone from three (Triennial Act 1694) to seven (Septennial Act 1716) then to five years (Parliament Act 1911), where it currently sits.
[65] See the Parliament Acts 1911 and 1949.

the UK's top court has taken place;[66] historical government positions have been reformed or eliminated;[67] the role of the monarchy has changed significantly;[68] and even major constitutional principles, such as parliamentary sovereignty, have shifted throughout the years as political and economic developments arose.[69] Most of these have been responses to societal change, and did not require tidal-wave constitutional moments. Additionally, the prospects of ongoing constitutional change leads to a dynamic not seen in other jurisdictions: the debate is wider and more fluid, given that virtually anything is on the table.

The UK constitution has also been identified as one of the easiest – or, indeed, *the* easiest – constitutions to change.[70] Yet, there remain certain features that suggest such a classification could be quite far off the mark. The presence of the monarchy and an unelected House of Lords, in addition to the inability of the courts to nullify Acts of Parliament, suggests that some major aspects of the UK constitution are rather entrenched in the wider constitutional culture, even if not entrenched by a formal constitution or an amendment procedure. Nevertheless, the ease with which constitutional change can happen should not be downplayed. The scrapping of the Fixed-term Parliaments Act 2011 is a good example of how a significant constitutional change can quickly be done away with when it becomes problematic.[71]

Other countries seem to be stuck when it comes to constitutional change. The lack of formal constitutional change in the US over the past few decades has produced a strong form of disillusionment, both with the written Constitution and with the Supreme Court.[72] The main problem is that formal amendment procedures are so exceedingly difficult, but a 5–4 Supreme Court decision can produce significant constitutional change. Further, a focus on elusive constitutional moments – in which there must be intense and widespread constitutional discussion and debate among the citizenry – as opposed to constitutional maintenance has obscured the need for regular constitutional change to take place. Although the longevity of America's written Constitution remains impressive, many of its structures and operations have always been highly questionable.[73] But recent events

---

[66] Constitutional Reform Act 2005, Part 3.

[67] Constitutional Reform Act 2005, Part 2.

[68] R Hazell and B Morris, 'The Queen at 90: The Changing Role of the Monarchy, and Future Challenges' (UCL Constitution Unit, June 2016) www.ucl.ac.uk/constitution-unit/sites/constitution-unit/files/170.pdf.

[69] This was driven by the UK's membership in the European Union, which definitely affected the principle of parliamentary sovereignty.

[70] A Lorenz, 'How to Measure Constitutional Rigidity: Four Concepts and Two Alternatives' (2005) 17 *Journal of Theoretical Politics* 339, 359.

[71] Dissolution and Calling of Parliament Act 2022.

[72] S Barber (n 62); LM Seidman, *On Constitutional Disobedience* (Oxford, Oxford University Press, 2013); EM Chemerinsky, *The Case Against the Supreme Court* (New York, Penguin, 2015); A Cohen, *Supreme Inequality: The Supreme Court's Fifty-Year Battle for a More Unjust America* (New York, Penguin, 2021); LM Seidman, *From Parchment to Dust: The Case for Constitutional Skepticism* (New York, The New Press, 2021).

[73] RA Dahl, *How Democratic Is the American Constitution?* (New Haven, Yale University Press, 2002).

seem to have only exposed and exacerbated its flaws: a popularly elected leader should not be able to receive three million votes fewer than the challenger but still win the electoral contest; a system of checks and balances should ensure effective and responsible government, not sow political dysfunction; and generations of Americans should not have to live their life without a practical and reasonable opportunity to amend their Constitution. None of those outcomes advances 'We the People'.

Constitutional maintenance plays an important part in keeping the UK constitution dynamic, and able to respond to pressing societal issues and challenges. Implementing constitutional supremacy could significantly change that.

III. The Unwritten Constitution During Times of 'Crisis'

Nowadays, almost any problem or hiccup that occurs with the UK constitution brings talk of a potential written document as a solution. Some of these do not even have to be constitutional problems per se, but problems over high policy or more general questions about how best to hold people in power to account. Thus, in many respects, they are problems that every state – especially those with written constitutional documents – also face. Below, I focus on three particular incidents – Brexit, coronavirus, and the premiership of Boris Johnson – to examine how the UK's unwritten constitution fared during these so-called 'crises'.

A. Brexit

During the height of Brexit, and even now post-Brexit, commentators frequently complained that the UK constitution was 'in turmoil', 'in crisis', or simply 'broken'.[74] But it is difficult to see how a more rigid written constitution would have better navigated through the treacherous political gridlock surrounding Brexit.

There were signs during Brexit that the UK constitution was under strain: the referendum exposed stark differences between MPs' preferences and those of the electorate (something that parliamentary sovereignty is supposed to reconcile), and also differences between the UK's constituent parts; governments lost significant policy votes and continued in office (Theresa May's Brexit deal loss was historic); the opposition took over the Common's order paper from government; and the Supreme Court intervened on matters traditionally left to the executive. There is no doubt that these controversial situations raised questions and concerns about how the UK constitution was coping with Brexit. But whether a written constitution would have handled any of this better or provided clearer solutions is

---

[74] See, eg 'Next to Blow: Britain's Constitution' *The Economist* (1 June 2019).

certainly up for debate. As a former Supreme Court justice noted, 'the constitution showed itself to be remarkably resilient' and its 'famous flexibility enabled it to fight back' when under pressure.[75]

The idea of 'bend but don't break' seems to encapsulate the UK constitution during this period. Constitutional tensions were present and events occurred that potentially stretched traditional constitutional understandings. Whilst Brexit may not be a moment to pat the UK constitution on the back, as Lord Sumption has done – especially given the ongoing devolution tensions – neither is it worthy of sounding the alarm bells on its demise.

B. The Coronavirus Pandemic

If the recent pandemic has taught us anything, it is that having a written constitution during times of crisis means very little. Many written constitutions have emergency provisions, which allow the suspension of key parts of the constitution that affect basic rights, such as those of speech, association, and movement. The vast majority of countries triggered these emergency provisions when the coronavirus came to their particular region or passed special legislation in order to respond to the pandemic that allowed the restriction of basic rights.[76]

The UK constitution throughout the pandemic fared appropriately, if not relatively commendably. The government passed the Coronavirus Act 2020 in late March, and used this in conjunction with the Public Health (Control of Disease) Act 1984 when responding to the pandemic. As in many states, citizen activities were severely constrained. But the restrictions were eventually challenged, and both the High Court and the Court of Appeal upheld them as lawful.[77] Also, bad practice during the lockdown was exposed. Infamously, the 'Partygate' scandal dominated headlines for a long while in the winter of 2021 and spring of 2022, culminating in fines for the PM and other leading government members, in addition to the Sue Gray report.[78] But other government actions were found to be unlawful as well,[79] demonstrating that errors were not ignored simply because of convenience.

---

[75] J Sumption, 'Brexit and the British Constitution' (2020) 91 *The Political Quarterly* 107, 110.

[76] A Vedashi, 'COVID-19 and Emergency Powers in Western European Democracies: Trends and Issues' (*Verfassungsblog*, 5 May 2021) https://verfassungsblog.de/covid-19-and-emergency-powers-in-western-european-democracies-trends-and-issues/.

[77] *R (Dolan) v Secretary of State for Health and Social Care* [2020] EWCA Civ 1605.

[78] Cabinet Office, 'Investigation into alleged gatherings during Covid Restrictions: Final Report' (25 May 2022), www.gov.uk/government/publications/findings-of-the-second-permanent-secretarys-investigation-into-alleged-gatherings-on-government-premises-during-covid-restrictions.

[79] 'Covid: Matt Hancock Acted Unlawfully over Pandemic Contracts' (*BBC News*, 19 February 2021) www.bbc.co.uk/news/uk-56125462; 'Covid: Government's PPE "VIP Lane" Unlawful, Court Rules' (*BBC News*, 12 January 2022) www.bbc.co.uk/news/uk-59968037.

Coronavirus provided an altogether different test for the UK constitution, which was less obvious – but no less significant – than Brexit. No doubt there remain significant questions and criticisms about how the response occurred, and what could have been improved upon.[80] Ultimately, the ability to respond collectively to some matters, whilst also letting the UK's constituent parts control their own coronavirus responses, seemed to demonstrate a flexibility that Brexit did not offer. And that flexibility is worth holding onto.

C. The Leadership of Boris Johnson

Many people thought that the entire premiership of Boris Johnson was itself a sustained constitutional crisis.[81] But Johnson's downfall as PM displayed the UK constitution working almost perfectly. Just weeks before Johnson was ousted, he survived a confidence vote amongst Tory MPs on his premiership, meaning that he should have been safe for another year from challenge.[82] That the confidence vote happened was evidence enough that Conservative MPs were increasingly frustrated with Johnson's premiership. Although he may have won an 80-seat majority, the PM was unable to escape his many mistakes in office and soon felt the full weight of politics. The confidence vote win did not stop the PM from being ousted a few weeks later, after revelations came forward that he installed someone in a ministerial post knowing that person had sexual misconduct issues. That was the final straw. Johnson succumbed to a record number of resignations and intense pressure within his party to resign. It may not have been the exit many wanted, with Johnson staying on until a new leader was elected, but it demonstrated two insights in particular: (i) the UK constitution provides more exit points for troublesome leaders than most constitutions; and (ii) that even in a position of relative constitutional strength, the UK's wider political culture can exert immense pressure on leaders.

For those calling for a codified constitution because of Boris Johnson's leadership, it is almost as if they seem to have forgotten the fact that every 'strongman' leader around the world (Putin, Xi, Duterte, Erdogan, Trump, etc) has acted with a written constitution in place. I seriously doubt whether Johnson belongs in such a group. However, if he does, then the UK's unwritten constitution is the only system to have successfully deposed such a leader. And it did so efficiently and effectively.[83]

---

[80] PG Hildago, F de Londras and D Lock, 'Parliament, the Pandemic, and Constitutional Principle in the United Kingdom: A Study of the Coronavirus Act 2020' [2022] *MLR* 1463.

[81] DA Green, 'The UK's Constitution Is Not Working' *Financial Times* (19 September 2020) www.ft.com/content/27e55f9b-018e-4f52-80c7-97844629f351.

[82] J Nevett, 'Boris Johnson Wins Vote but Suffers Large Tory Rebellion' (*BBC News*, 6 June 2022) www.bbc.co.uk/news/uk-politics-61709441.

[83] Indeed, it even prevented a potential comeback by Mr Johnson as Conservative Party leader only a few months after being deposed (see BBC News, 'Boris Johnson pulls out of leadership race: Statement in full' (23 October 2022), www.bbc.co.uk/news/uk-politics-63368973).

IV. Conclusion: Accepting the Human Foundations of Laws and Constitutions

As the demise of Boris Johnson demonstrates, the human aspects of politics can remain definitive in the operation of constitutional government. Perhaps nobody has expressed the human component of law as eloquently as Clarence Darrow, a prominent criminal lawyer in Chicago in the early twentieth century. In making closing arguments during a case on 19 May 1926, Darrow said the following:

> [F]inally they were given their liberty, so far as the law goes – and that is only a little way, because, after all, every human being's life in this world is inevitably mixed with every other life and, no matter what laws we pass, no matter what precautions we take, unless the people we meet are kindly and decent and human and liberty-loving then there is no liberty. Freedom comes from human beings, rather than from laws and institutions.

A similar insight is true for constitutional government: constitutional success comes from human beings, rather than from constitutional provisions. And whilst constitutional replacement may change laws and institutions, it is highly unlikely to bring forward better leaders, ensure more trust in government, or radically change a state's political culture. All of these are human elements that rely on a wide range of social and cultural factors.

The current operation of the UK constitution possesses qualities that demonstrate its commitment to the human foundations of constitutions. A focus on parliamentary sovereignty is meaningful and beneficial because, first and foremost, it reflects the society at large. This means that the focus is on human nature, including the contemporary views of people that have been elected into office. And the doctrine that Parliament cannot bind its successors means that good policies stay for as long as they are working, and that if mistakes are made – which they will – then they have the opportunity to be corrected. Indeed, this ensures that constitutional mistakes cannot become too firmly entrenched, as at any moment they are subject to removal and replacement. It is this commitment to human principles, such as parliamentary sovereignty, that makes the UK constitution work.

The UK's unwritten constitution remains far from perfect; mistakes happen, much-needed reforms often stall, and reliance on politics can prove extremely frustrating. But when it comes to sustaining vibrant and healthy democracies, unwritten constitutions can go head-to-head with written constitutions any day.

2

Judicial Encroachment on the Political Constitution?

CAROL HARLOW

I. Politics and the Judges

What exactly is a political constitution? And what do we expect of our judges? These are difficult questions which have over the years provoked much controversy and occasionally spiralled into conflict. After the divisive Brexit election, two contentious cases were referred to the courts. *Miller (No 1)* involved a difference of opinion between Parliament and the government concerning the power to serve notice of UK departure on the European Union.[1] The three senior High Court judges who determined that parliamentary authorisation was necessary were clearly alert to the political implications. They took care in delivering their unanimous judgment to emphasise that the court was dealing with 'a pure question of law' and that their judgment was purely legal. But tempers were running high, and the judicial apologia was insufficient to assuage them. Claiming the decision purposefully blocked the Brexit process, the *Daily Mail* ran a front page article under the headline 'Enemies of the People', attacking 'out-of-touch' judges who had by their ruling 'defied 17.4m Brexit voters in a popular referendum' and 'declared war on democracy'.[2] Lawyers turned on Liz Truss, then Minister of Justice and Lord Chancellor, condemning her for her failure to defend the judiciary more openly,[3] while the President of the Supreme Court, agreeing that politicians could have been 'quicker and clearer' in defending the judiciary, warned that unjustified attacks on the judiciary undermined the rule of law.[4]

Again, in *Miller and Cherry*, where the Supreme Court was asked to pronounce on the legality of advice given by the Prime Minister to the Monarch that she should prorogue Parliament, the Court took care to emphasise that its unanimous

---

[1] *R (Miller and another) v Secretary of State for Exiting the European Union* [2016] EWHC 2768 (Admin), reported in the Supreme Court [2017] UKSC 5 (*Miller (No 1)*).

[2] *Daily Mail*, 4 November 2016. The headline provoked over 1000 complaints to the Independent Press Standards Organization.

[3] *BBC News*, 5 November 2016.

[4] *Today Programme*, BBC Radio 4, 16 February 2017.

ruling was not political.[5] The issue was not when and on what terms the UK was to leave the European Union, but only whether the prorogation of Parliament was lawful. As Lady Hale, President of the Court, explained:

> [A]lthough the courts cannot decide political questions, the fact that a legal dispute concerns the conduct of politicians, or arises from a matter of political controversy, has never been sufficient reason for the courts to refuse to consider it ... [A]lmost all important decisions made by the executive have a political hue to them. Nevertheless, the courts have exercised a supervisory jurisdiction over the decisions of the executive for centuries. Many if not most of the constitutional cases in our legal history have been concerned with politics in that sense.[6]

This was not enough to deter Professor John Finnis, in a note on the 'unconstitutionality' of *Miller and Cherry*, from calling the judgment 'a historic mistake'; it was 'wholly unjustified by law' and 'through and through political'. The Supreme Court had defied or rescinded settled rules which preserved the distinction between conventions and law and 'clearly forbade judicial involvement in questions of high politics'; moreover, its 'selection of irrelevant facts to record and of relevant facts *not* to record' illustrated the ineptitude of judicial forays into high politics.[7]

Debate over the place of the judiciary in the UK constitution is usually less heated, but it is by no means new. In this chapter, I want to pick the debate up at a point before the Human Rights Act came into force in 2000, and to use an exchange between Lord Justice Stephen Sedley, a moderate constitutionalist, and Professor John Griffith, with whose writing the term 'political constitution' is most closely associated, as exemplars of the two main sides in the debate: for or against a constitution that imposes no legal limitations on Parliament, for or against limitations, for or against a stronger role for the judiciary.

II. The Political Constitution

When Professor John Griffith used the term 'The Political Constitution' as the title for a 1978 lecture, it was notably without defining it.[8] Academic definition was

---

[5] *R (Miller) v The Prime Minister, R (Cherry) v Advocate General for Scotland* [2019] UKSC 41 (*Miller and Cherry*).

[6] ibid [1], [31].

[7] J Finnis, *The Unconstitutionality of the Supreme Court's Prorogation Judgment* (Policy Exchange, 2019) [6], [7]. Equally impassioned was the dispute between Professors Martin Loughlin and Paul Craig: see M Loughlin, 'The Case of Prorogation' (Policy Exchange, 15 October, 2019); P Craig, 'The Supreme Court, Prorogation and Constitutional Principle' [2020] *PL* 248; M Loughlin, 'A Note on Craig on Miller; Cherry' [2020] *PL* 278; P Craig, 'Response to Loughlin's Note on Miller/Cherry' [2020] *PL* 282.

[8] This may have been because it was not his first choice of title: see M Loughlin, 'The Political Constitution Revisited', LSE Working Paper 18/2017 (2017). For an academic definition, see G Webber and G Gee, 'What Is a Political Constitution?' (2010) 30 *OJLS* 273.

not Griffith's priority. He had in his sights a number of proposals for constitutional change circulating at the time, all of which involved a substantial transfer of power from Parliament and politicians to the judiciary.[9] These changes, Griffith believed, would take political decisions out of the hands of politicians and pass them into the hands of judges. This would change not only the locus of power, but also the character of the dialogue, and would inevitably involve a change of status from contestable political 'claims' to a reformulation as enforceable 'rights'. Griffith was no authoritarian; he thought laws expressed the ways in which 'the hegemon' seeks to manage society.[10] He recognised the need for accountability, but thought it should be through the political side of constitution, through Parliament and the media.[11] He called for 'more open government, less restriction on debate, weaker Official Secrets Acts, more access to information and stronger pressure from backbenchers' as a basis for democracy.[12] That, for Griffith, was the essence of a political constitution.

However, the debate between Sedley and Griffith, which grew acrimonious, did not start from 'The Political Constitution', but with a lecture series and mildly constitutionalist article in which Sedley lamented the absence of a governing principle in our constitution and argued for a measure of constitutional reform and a stronger role for the judges.[13] There were two main areas of disagreement. First, in 'The Sound of Silence', Sedley argued that the British constitution lacked a 'principled constitutional order' and stood in need of an 'understood, coherent and legally underpinned frame'. Sedley believed that the common law had both the capacity and the obligation to supply this.

Griffith, on the other hand, looked with suspicion at the word 'principle' and with disfavour at efforts to 'reintroduce natural law concepts' into law or to conceptualise law as 'undeniably good' and to be upheld at all times. He charged legal theorist Ronald Dworkin with setting up 'principles' that govern law 'because it is a requirement of justice or fairness or some other dimension of morality'.[14] Although he may not have realised this, Griffith was looking at an era in which a growing constitutionalist movement would work to build a 'common law constitution', implanting the ideas and values supposedly embedded in the common law,

---

[9] Notably proposals made by Lord Hailsham in *The Dilemma of Democracy: Diagnosis and Prescription* (New York, Collins, 1978) and a variety of proposals for a Bill of Rights: eg M Zander, *A Bill of Rights?* (Rose for British Institute of Human Rights, 1975).

[10] JAG Griffith, 'The Common Law and the Political Constitution' (2001) 117 *LQR* 42, 59. For Sedley's reply, see S Sedley, 'The Common Law and the Political Constitution: A Reply' (2001) 117 *LQR* 68.

[11] Griffith was interested in parliamentary reform and was an inaugural member of the Study of Parliament Group, set up by Bernard Crick, his friend and LSE colleague. See B Crick, *The Reform of Parliament* (London, Weidenfeld & Nicolson, 1964).

[12] JAG Griffith, 'The Political Constitution' (1979) 42 *MLR* 1, 18.

[13] S Sedley, *Freedom, Law and Justice* (London, Sweet & Maxwell, 2001); S Sedley, 'The Sound of Silence: Constitutional Law without a Constitution' (1994) 110 *LQR* 270.

[14] Griffith, 'The Political Constitution' (n 12) 10, citing R Dworkin, *Taking Rights Seriously* (Cambridge, MA, Harvard University Press, 1967), 22.

and empowering the judiciary as guardians of the rule of law.[15] Sedley, who stood on the edge of this movement, gave it moderate support in his article.[16]

The second and more profound area of disagreement concerned institutional balance. The UK constitution is commonly understood to rest, as Lord Reed, the current President of the Supreme Court, recently explained, on two 'long-established constitutional principles of fundamental importance': first, that government power must be exercised in accordance with the law – a narrow meaning for the rule of law with which it is hard to quarrel – and secondly, that 'ultimate sovereign power rests with the Queen in Parliament'.[17] This is a generally accepted formulation that incidentally deals the trump card decisively to Parliament.[18] Sedley made space for executive government, but portrayed it not as 'one of three sovereign and equal elements of the state [but as] subordinate both to Parliament and to the courts'.[19] Something similar was said in *Miller and Cherry* (discussed below), where the Supreme Court asserted that 'The Government exists because it has the confidence of the House of Commons. It has no democratic legitimacy other than that'.[20]

This analysis, which might surprise political scientists and bears little relation to how party leaders are chosen and how we vote in modern elections, infuriated Griffith. Griffith was one of a group of academics who recognised the need for a strong executive government capable of pushing through a reformist agenda, realised in the post-war Labour government of Clement Attlee.[21] For Griffith, the executive possessed its own independent legitimacy based on elected, democratic government. He had no wish to see brakes applied to government powers, especially if it was left to the judiciary to apply them. At no time did he accept the need for a new constitutional settlement or an accretion of power to the judiciary. Judges had to be judged by their policies, meaning their political attitudes. Griffith held very clear views on the political attitudes of the judiciary: they were for the most part conservative, perhaps even Conservative, and in many areas, such as property rights, trade unionism and race, judges' view of the public interest gave cause for concern.[22] Politicians were preferable to judges simply because they were more easily dismissed.

---

[15] See, notably, J Laws, 'The Constitution: Morals and Rights' [1996] *PL* 622; J Laws, 'Law and Democracy' [1995] *PL* 72; J Laws, 'Is the High Court the Guardian of Fundamental Constitutional Rights?' [1993] *PL* 59. See also TRS Allan, *Law, Liberty and Justice* (Oxford, Oxford University Press, 1993) 4.

[16] For an account of constitutionalist theory, see T Poole, 'Back to the Future? Unearthing the Theory of Common Law Constitutionalism' (2003) 23 *OJLS* 435.

[17] Lord Reed of Allermuir in evidence to IRAL: Ministry of Justice, *IRAL Review Report*, CP 407 (2021) [24].

[18] The antithesis is based on AV Dicey, *The Law of the Constitution* (JWF Allison ed, Oxford, Oxford University Press, 2013).

[19] Sedley, 'The Sound of Silence' (n 13) 273.

[20] *Miller and Cherry* (n 5) [55].

[21] C Harlow, 'Judicial Power, the Left and the LSE Tradition' in R Ekins and G Gee (eds), *Judicial Power and the Left* (Policy Exchange, 2017).

[22] Expounded at length in JAG Griffith, *The Politics of the Judiciary*, 5th edn (London, Fontana, 1997).

III. The Judicial Function

A well-known dictum of Lord Bridge cited by Sedley as 'a vital constitutional truth' lays out the bare bones of the judicial function in the constitution and reflects a general understanding of the role of the judge as restrained. He said, the rule of law rests on twin foundations, the sovereignty of the Queen [as she was then]-in-Parliament in making the law and the sovereignty of the Queen's courts in interpreting and applying the law.[23] This dictum downplays the judicial role by passing over the many ambiguities concealed in the notion of interpretation. Statutory language is seldom straightforward; as Australian justice Robert French acknowledges, it brims with possible meanings that judges, with the aid of a raft of common law assumptions, presumptions, rules and principles, can construct. It follows that statutory interpretation does not discover either the 'one true result' or the true 'legislative intention'. Statutory interpretation by courts is, in other words, a form of decision-making.[24] Griffith, however, did not make this point, but accepted Lord Bridge's dictum, albeit with caution: so long as 'law' is understood to mean statutes and subordinate or secondary laws made by the executive under statutory authority. Yes, 'under the constitution' judges interpret and apply these laws, but – and it is a big but – Griffith points to a separate body of rules, which is called the common law and is 'made' by the judges,[25] a crucial qualification on which he did not at this point expand.

At the time Sedley and Griffith were writing, however, both recognised that the judicial role was changing; this was, as both writers recognised, largely the handiwork of the judges, who were in any event happy to claim full credit for the change.[26] Sedley, who welcomed the development, credited the judges with occupying, unnoticed, 'areas of constitutional high ground which government had come to believe, and the public had come to fear, were beyond the reach of the law', from where they were now 'directing fire on entrenchments of the local and central state'.[27] He thought it too late to draw back, in which, at least until very recently, he was proved right.

How was this achieved? By the end of the 1970s, a series of breakthrough cases had established the outlines of our modern system of judicial review.[28] In *Ridge v Baldwin*,[29] the House of Lords had breathed new life into the centuries-old doctrine of natural justice, which had fallen into disuse in the course of two world wars. They reinforced the common law right for a person affected by an

---

[23] Lord Bridge of Harwich in *X v Morgan-Grampian Ltd* [1991] AC 1, 48.

[24] R French, 'The Principle of Legality and Legislative Intention' (2019) 40 *Statute Law Review* 40, 45.

[25] Griffith, 'The Common Law and the Political Constitution' (n 10) 46.

[26] See notably Lord Diplock, 'Administrative Law: Judicial Review Reviewed' (1974) 33 *CLJ* 233, 244.

[27] Sedley, 'The Sound of Silence' (n 13) 285.

[28] J Jowell, 'Administrative Law' in V Bogdanor (ed), *The British Constitution in the Twentieth Century* (Oxford, Oxford University Press, 2004); C Harlow and R Rawlings, *Law and Administration*, 4th edn (Cambridge University Press, 2021) ch 4.

[29] *Ridge v Baldwin* [1964] AC 40; Harlow and Rawlings, *Law and Administration* (n 28) ch 16.

administrative decision to make representations to the decision-maker and paved the way for the modern emphasis on procedural due process in public administration. In *Padfield*,[30] a landmark political ruling, the House of Lords required a minister of the Crown to give reasons for his refusal to follow a statutory procedure, indicating that a failure to give reasons must be accounted a bad reason. Thus, in *Miller and Cherry*, the government was criticised for declining to provide the Supreme Court with 'any reason – let alone a good reason' for its advice to the Queen on prorogation. 'We cannot speculate, in the absence of further evidence, upon what such reasons might have been. It follows that the decision was unlawful.'[31] Arguably an encroachment on executive discretion, *Padfield* marked the start of several decades of concerted assault by judges and academics on discretionary executive power.[32] It paved the way for the principles of reason-giving and rationality in decision-making that are the hallmark of both contemporary public administration and contemporary judicial review.[33]

A further important step in the direction of judicial control was taken in the celebrated *GCHQ* case, where the Prime Minister, as Minister for the Civil Service, had taken a decision to impose a ban on trade union membership for those working at GCHQ.[34] The Prime Minister, as she was perfectly entitled to do, had acted under the prerogative powers of the Crown, whose use was at the time considered virtually exempt from judicial review. Although the House of Lords declared prerogative power to be justiciable, the government was held to be exercising a security function, which the House refrained from reviewing. The courts nonetheless nibbled away at the prerogative powers in subsequent cases, declaring them one by one subject to judicial review.[35]

Perhaps the boldest of these four seminal decisions was *Anisminic*,[36] where a statutory provision specifying that the decision of a tribunal was to be 'final and binding' was found by judicial sleight of hand not to be binding at all. As we shall see, this decision had the effect of making it almost impossible for Parliament, though sovereign, to exclude the jurisdiction of the High Court of Justice.

---

[30] *Padfield v Minister of Agriculture, Fisheries and Food* [1968] AC 997.

[31] *Miller and Cherry* (n 5) [61].

[32] See R Austin, 'Judicial Review of Subjective Discretion; At the Rubicon – Whither Now?' (1975) 28 *Current Legal Problems* 150.

[33] Harlow and Rawlings, *Law and Administration* (n 28) ch 17. There is no general duty in UK administrative law for the administration to give reasons, but it is unwise not to do so: see Government Legal Department, *The Judge over Your Shoulder – a Guide to Good Decision Making* (updated October 2018) https://assets.publishing.service.gov.uk/government/uploads/system/uploads/attachment_data/file/1105680/The_Judge_Over_Your_Shoulder_JOYS_6th_edition_2022.pdf.

[34] *Council of Civil Service Unions v Minister for the Civil Service* [1985] AC 374.

[35] See T Poole, 'The Strange Death of the Prerogative in England' (2018) 43 *University of Western Australia Law Review* 42.

[36] *Anisminic v Foreign Compensation Commission* [1968] UKHL 6. See D Feldman, 'Anisminic v Foreign Compensation Commission (1968): In Perspective' in S Juss and M Sunkin (eds), *Landmark Cases in Public Law* (Oxford, Hart Publishing, 2017).

IV. Crossing the Boundary Line

The orthodox view after *GCHQ* was, as Lord Roskill had insisted, that the remedy for abuse of prerogative powers 'lay in the political and not in the judicial field'. He was quick to warn the judges off clearly political territory:

> Prerogative powers such as those relating to the making of treaties, the defence of the realm, the prerogative of mercy, the grant of honours, the dissolution of Parliament and the appointment of ministers as well as others are not, I think susceptible to judicial review because their nature and subject matter are such as not to be amenable to the judicial process. The courts are not the place wherein to determine whether a treaty should be concluded or the armed forces disposed in a particular manner or Parliament dissolved on one date rather than another.[37]

In *Miller (No 1)*, the Supreme Court did not go so far as to rule that exercise of the treaty-making power was reviewable; indeed, the majority judgment calls that 'rather a bold suggestion, given that it has always been considered that, because they only operate on the international plane, prerogative treaty-making powers are not subject to judicial review'.[38] The issue was sidestepped by taking the European Communities Act 1972 as the 'fixed domestic starting point', thus converting the issue from one of justiciability to whether the executive could draw on prerogative powers in such a way as effectively to set aside a statute. The majority felt that such a major change to UK constitutional arrangements could not be achieved by ministers alone; it 'must be effected in the only way that the UK constitution recognises, namely by Parliamentary legislation'. The Court also thought the political remedy of accountability to Parliament an insufficient safeguard against misuse; it would justify all sorts of powers being accorded to the executive, on the basis that 'ministers could always be called to account for their exercise of any power'.[39]

Whether or not the case was rightly decided,[40] it took the Supreme Court onto dangerous, disputed ground, provoking, as already explained, a political storm. *Miller and Cherry* bit more deeply into the prerogative; indeed, it is clearly arguable that the Supreme Court trespassed on political ground in declaring the prerogative power reviewable.[41] Essentially, this was done by drawing two bright lines: first, prorogation was treated separately from dissolution, a constitutional convention responsibility which was recognised to be political. Secondly, parliamentary 'accountability' was detached from parliamentary sovereignty, a doctrine said to be applicable in the realm of legislation, and stated to be 'a second constitutional principle ... no less fundamental to our constitution than Parliamentary sovereignty'.

---

[37] *Council of Civil Service Unions v Minister for the Civil Service* (Lord Roskill).

[38] *R (Miller and another) v Secretary of State for Exiting the European Union* [2017] UKSC 5, [92] (Lord Neuberger).

[39] ibid [82].

[40] For a selection of views, see the special section devoted to the case at (2017) 80 *MLR* 685.

[41] Prorogation marks the ending of a parliamentary session. Finnis (n 7) argues that prorogation is a 'proceeding in Parliament', exempt from review by virtue of Art 9 of the Bill of Rights 1689.

And the mere fact that a minister is politically accountable to Parliament does not mean that he is therefore 'immune from legal accountability to the courts'.[42]

V. Empowering the Judges

If, as Griffith suggested, the judiciary had declined in power during the Conservative governments of the 1980s, resurgence was largely the work of government and Parliament. Two legislative initiatives taken by Tony Blair's New Labour government were crucial to underpinning the judges' constitutional position: the Human Rights Act 1998 (HRA) and the Constitutional Reform Act 2005 (CRA), which replaced the Judicial Committee of the House of Lords as the final court of appeal with a new, and more obviously autonomous, Supreme Court. At first sight, the changes made by the CRA are only minimal. The Act did not create a constitutional court; the Supreme Court remains the final 'court of appeal' for the UK, though some of its functions are clearly constitutional: the Court hears cases involving devolution issues, Human Rights Act cases and cases involving the European Convention on Human Rights.[43]

In typical English drafting style, the Bill, which was rushed before Parliament without the customary consultations and deliberations, merely lists the appeals that the Supreme Court can hear. After some debate, a clause was inserted committing the Lord Chancellor – a post combined by the Act with that of Minister of Justice – to uphold the 'continued' independence of the judiciary and confirming the 'existing' constitutional principle of the rule of law, left undefined.[44] Nothing further is said about constitutional principle, justiciability or the role the Supreme Court is intended to fulfil. Deliberately, it seems, the government has left the Supreme Court to fill these important gaps. There could be no clearer illustration of Sedley's complaint about the 'sound of silence' in constitutional matters.

In the words of a former President of the Supreme Court, the CRA and its break with the House of Lords, marked physically by a new, separate building, helped the Court to gain 'a visibility and with it a strength that it did not have when it was hidden from view in the House of Lords'.[45] Under the CRA, the Supreme Court took over one clearly constitutional function from the House of Lords: the handling of appeals in devolution matters. This jurisdiction, I have argued elsewhere, helped the new Court to inch its way towards the status of a constitutional court.[46]

---

[42] *Miller and Cherry* (n 5) [33] and [46].

[43] The Supreme Court was the final court of appeal for purposes of preliminary references to the Court of Justice of the European Union, which is beyond the scope of this chapter.

[44] For the parliamentary story of the Bill, see *First Report of the Committee on the Constitutional Reform Bill* (HL 2004–05, 129–1).

[45] Lady Hale, 'What Is the United Kingdom Supreme Court For?' (Macfadyen Lecture 2019) 13, www.supremecourt.uk/docs/speech-190328.pdf; Lord Reed, 'The Supreme Court Ten Years On' (Bentham Association Lecture 2019) www.supremecourt.uk/docs/speech-190306.pdf.

[46] Harlow and Rawlings, *Law and Administration* (n 28) 55–80.

The HRA, which had come into force in 2000, had a more direct impact. Ostensibly passed in fulfilment of a promise by the Blair government to 'bring rights home', the HRA purported to maintain the balance of the traditional constitution.[47] Thus, Parliament was specifically excluded from the statutory obligation for all public authorities to act in a way compatible with Convention rights, while courts and tribunals were not. Legislation was so far as possible to be 'read and given effect' in a way compatible with Convention rights and where interpretative alignment was not possible, the courts gained a new judicial remedy, the 'declaration of incompatibility'. But the validity, continuing operation or enforcement of primary legislation was not affected, and it remained for the government of the day, under the watchful eye of the Parliamentary Joint Committee on Human Rights, to decide whether there should be remedial legislation.

The HRA nonetheless marked a significant empowerment of the judiciary. It underpinned their traditional interpretative function by enhancing their autonomous status. In arriving at their decisions, courts must 'take account of' the jurisprudence of the European Court of Human Rights (ECtHR), a formula that reserves a substantial discretion for the national court if it cares to use it – as Lord Irvine, who had piloted the Bill through the House of Lords, believed that Parliament intended.[48] New interpretative principles were soon formulated. The principle of legality now requires, for example, that before a court will interpret legislation so as to override human rights, the statutory provision must point unequivocally to the conclusion that this was the intention of Parliament.[49] Again, judicial review traditionally focused on the process by which decisions are taken or policies implemented and – as the courts in the two Brexit cases insisted – not with the rightness or wrongness of the policies concerned. Yet it is the function of the judge when deciding a Human Rights Act case to decide whether a given act or decision amounts to a violation of the ECHR and, in holding that parliamentary legislation does not comply with Convention law, it goes very near to allowing a court to decide whether a law is a 'good' law or not.

Review for unreasonableness was historically restrained; it covered only action that is capricious or absurd, bringing only an extreme degree of unreasonableness within the scope of judicial review.[50] It was, as Lord Sumption pointed out, 'a very undemanding test for administrative decision-makers', although it necessarily

---

[47] J Hiebert, 'Parliamentary Bills of Rights: An Alternative Model?' (2006) 69 *MLR* 7.

[48] Lord Irvine of Lairg, 'A British Interpretation of Convention Rights' [2012] *PL* 237. At first, courts had allowed themselves to be bound by the ECtHR: see *R (Ullah) v Special Adjudicator* [2004] UKHL 26. The current position is set out by the Supreme Court in *R (AB) v Justice Secretary* [2021] UKSC 28 as being that the domestic courts should follow a clear and consistent line of relevant ECtHR case law unless there are exceptional circumstances which justify a different approach, but they should not substantially develop the case law.

[49] See the debate between Australian justice Robert French and Supreme Court justice Lord Sales in R French 'The Principle of Legality and Legislative Intention' (2019) 40 *Statute Law Review* 40; P Sales 'Legislative Intention, Interpretation and the Principle of Legality' (2019) 40 *Statute Law Review* 53.

[50] Commonly known as 'Wednesbury unreasonableness' after *Associated Provincial Picture Houses Ltd v Wednesbury Corporation* [1948] 1 KB 223. See also Lord Irvine of Lairg, 'Judges and Decision-makers: The Theory and Practice of *Wednesbury* Review' [1996] *PL* 59.

involved some assessment of the merits of the decision. The proportionality test borrowed from European law is 'a much more exacting test, and even more obviously involves an examination of the merits'.[51] It requires the court to consider: (i) whether the decision answers a pressing social need; (ii) whether the decision-maker's objective is important enough to justify interfering with a human or fundamental right; (iii) whether a less intrusive measure could have been used without unacceptably compromising the objective; and (iv) whether, looking at matters in the round, a fair balance has been struck between the interests of the individual and the community.[52] These are clearly policy issues that can take a court deep into political territory, hence changing the nature of judicial review proceedings. Lord Sumption has more than once drawn attention to 'the propensity of judicial review of human rights to elide the boundaries of politics and law', and it is perhaps not surprising that the Johnson government should have the Human Rights Act, with its European origins and independent Human Rights Court with a transnational jurisdiction, in its sights.[53]

VI. Widened Boundaries, Deeper Scrutiny

We have been discussing high-level relationships between those at the apex of the judicial hierarchy and the political elite. We should bear in mind that applications for judicial review are heard in the Administrative Court or Upper Tribunal and seldom progress beyond the Court of Appeal. It is thus the practice of the less senior courts and tribunals that is likely to have a greater impact on officialdom. As Joanna Bell argues, the majority of these decisions are mundane and relate only to individuals; they have no wider implications and no clear-cut political dimension.[54] But the judicial system in the UK is hierarchical and the style and tone of the judicial process is inevitably dictated by the highest courts. Three Supreme Court decisions in particular helped to set the tone of judicial review from the 1990s, moving markedly away from the restrained approach of earlier days. Like *Miller and Cherry*, these cases opened the courts to accusations of political decision-making and government retaliation. After the Supreme Court invalidated the Fees Order in the *UNISON* case (below), an administrative compensation scheme had to be set up to assess claims for refunds of fees imposed unlawfully.

---

[51] Lord Sumption, 'Anxious Scrutiny' (ALBA Annual Lecture 4 November 2014) 7–8, www.supreme-court.uk/docs/speech-141104.pdf.

[52] For a helpful discussion, see J Jowell, 'Proportionality and Unreasonableness: Neither Merger nor Takeover' in H Willberg and M Elliott (eds), *The Scope and Intensity of Substantive Review: Traversing Taggart's Rainbow* (Oxford, Hart Publishing, 2015).

[53] The Bill of Rights Bill currently before the House of Commons sets out to repeal the Human Rights Act and 'clarify and re-balance' the relationship between the ECtHR and our courts: see Explanatory Notes, paras 3–4.

[54] J Bell, *The Anatomy of Administrative Law* (Oxford, Hart Publishing, 2020).

A. The Right to Know

Rob Evans was a *Guardian* reporter who applied under the Freedom of Information Act (FOIA) to see letters written by the Prince of Wales promoting causes of particular interest to him. The Cabinet Office refused disclosure, but access was ordered by the Information Commissioner and again, on appeal, by the Upper Tribunal. At this point, the Attorney General intervened to veto disclosure, relying on section 53(2) of the FOIA, which permits an 'accountable person' to override a decision notice if he certifies that he has 'on reasonable grounds formed the opinion' that disclosure should not be granted. The Attorney General gave reasons: he had acted in line with a partial statutory exemption for the Sovereign and other members of the royal family (section 37 FOIA) and with a convention that the heir to the throne should be 'instructed in the business of government'. He was also protecting the Sovereign's 'right to consult, to encourage and to warn her Government' and shielding the political neutrality of the Royal Family. On appeal, however, the Court of Appeal overrode these reasons, holding that disclosure was in the public interest. By a majority of 5–2, the Supreme Court agreed.[55] To permit the Attorney General, who had heard no argument and seen no new evidence, to override a decision of a judicial tribunal or court merely because he took a different view from that taken by the tribunal or court, would be 'unique in the laws of the United Kingdom' and would cut across fundamental components of the rule of law.

Arguably, the same can be said of judges, however eminent, who set aside the decision of 'an accountable person' because they disagree with his reasons, provided these are not manifestly unlawful or absurd. This was certainly the view of Lord Wilson dissenting in the Supreme Court. He thought the courts should have resisted the temptation to review. The Court of Appeal had not so much *interpreted* the FOIA as *rewritten* it and, invoking 'precious constitutional principles', had overlooked that 'among the most precious is that of parliamentary sovereignty, *emblematic of our democracy*' (emphasis added).[56] The Cameron government agreed; preserving the ministerial veto, they made the statutory exemption absolute.[57]

B. Covert Investigation

Privacy International is a campaign group, set up to protect democracy, defend people's dignity and demand accountability from institutions who breach public trust. Its special concern is government use of technology and it was fighting the

---

[55] *R (Evans) v Attorney General* [2015] UKSC 21.

[56] ibid [168]. See also R Ekins and C Forsyth, 'Who Judges the Public Interest? The Future of the Rule of Law' (Policy Exchange, 3 December 2015).

[57] See s 46 and sch 7 of the Constitutional Reform and Governance Act 2010.

practice of 'bulk hacking' to gain automated access to peoples' computers and mobile phones. The Investigatory Powers Tribunal (IPT), which handles appeals, is a specialist tribunal with the status of the High Court that was set up by the Regulation of Investigatory Powers Act 2000 (RIPA) to hear cases involving covert investigative techniques. It has 10 legally qualified members and is chaired by a Lord Justice of Appeal.

With a view to making the IPT the final court of appeal in such matters, RIPA contained what might be called an anti-*Anisminic* ouster clause, which provided:

> Except to such extent as the Secretary of State may by order otherwise provide, determinations, awards and other decisions of the Tribunal (including decisions as to whether they have jurisdiction) shall not be subject to appeal or be liable to be questioned in any court.

This seems clear, yet a majority of the Supreme Court, reading the word 'determination' to mean only a *legally valid* determination, felt able to conclude that the statutory words were insufficient to deprive the High Court of its jurisdiction in judicial review.[58] It was 'a necessary corollary of the sovereignty of Parliament that there should exist an authoritative and independent body which can interpret and mediate legislation made by Parliament'. Judicial review could consequently be excluded only by the most clear and explicit words, and this apparently unambiguous text was insufficiently clear. Without in any way questioning the doctrine of parliamentary sovereignty, the Court had tilted the constitutional balance towards the rule of law. The sting was perhaps taken out of a judgment that makes it virtually impossible to draft a judge-proof ouster clause by the fact that Parliament had already changed the law by creating a limited right of appeal from the IPT.[59]

But this should not blind us to the significance of the decision for the political constitution. Premised on an interpretative *presumption* against interpreting legislation so as to permit the exclusion of judicial review, *Privacy International* builds on *Anisminic* to turn presumption into implicit prohibition. By so doing, it 'heralds the limitation of Parliament through the rule of law'.[60] Lord Carnwath would have liked to go further, questioning in a non-binding section of his majority judgment whether a clause that ousted the supervisory jurisdiction of the High Court should *ever* be binding. Yet parliamentary sovereignty is emblematic, as Lord Wilson underlined in *Evans*, its function being, as Griffith firmly believed, 'to establish the constitutional primacy of political decision-making in the pre-eminent democratic institution of UK central government'.[61]

---

[58] *R (Privacy International) v Investigatory Powers Tribunal and others* [2019] UKSC 22.

[59] s 242(1) of the Investigatory Powers Act 2016 adds s 67A to the Regulation of Investigatory Powers Act 2000, allowing appeal where the appeal would raise an important point of principle or practice or where there is another compelling reason for granting leave to appeal to the Court of Appeal.

[60] M Gordon, 'Privacy International, Parliamentary Sovereignty and the Synthetic Constitution' (*UK Constitutional Law Blog*, 26 June 2019).

[61] ibid.

C. Executive as Legislator

In *UNISON*, a powerful trade union attacked the Fees Order, delegated legislation made by the Lord Chancellor, which for the first time imposed a substantial fee to make a claim in an employment tribunal. UNISON argued that the fees interfered unjustifiably with a constitutional right of access to justice, frustrated the operation of parliamentary legislation granting employment rights and discriminated unlawfully against women and other groups protected by the Equality Act. The argument was dismissed by the High Court and Court of Appeal, but persuaded the Supreme Court. Buttressing its reasoning with reference to statistical evidence that showed a dramatic and persistent fall in the number of employment tribunal claims post-Fees Order, the Court found that the Order created a 'real risk' that access to justice would be inhibited. Access to justice was 'not an idea recently imported from the continent of Europe but has long been deeply embedded in our constitutional law'. It was a common law right inherent in the rule of law, which is 'needed to ensure that the laws created by Parliament and the courts are applied and enforced'.[62] The Fees Order was ruled unlawful and quashed.

The impact of *UNISON* was undoubtedly wide-ranging. The government had to decide on a new fees regime and replace the Fees Order. A costly exercise was put in place for the refunding of fees. Moreover, the case set an important precedent, encouraging courts to probe government policy more deeply and signalling a move towards 'system checking' or 'structural review', which allows a court to evaluate the rules and structure of an administrative system rather than focusing on a single individual's rights. Public interest groups are encouraged to fight their political campaigns in court, turning the courtroom into a quasi-political process with an impact on the style of the judicial proceedings.[63] In the *UNISON* case itself, the evidence produced to the Supreme Court was akin to that available to a parliamentary committee, and the Court considered a government impact assessment, compared tribunal fees with court fees and evaluated the potential impact of the Fees Order in a range of hypothetical cases. For these reasons, Harlow and Rawlings called *UNISON* 'one of the most significant judicial review cases in the last decade'.[64] But does it stand, as some would like to think, as 'a testament to the vitality of the common law constitution'[65] or did it perhaps imperil that construct?

---

[62] ibid [64] and [66].
[63] C Harlow, 'Public Law and Popular Justice' (2002) 65 *MLR* 1; C Harlow and R Rawlings, *Pressure through Law* (London, Routledge, 1992).
[64] Harlow and Rawlings, *Law and Administration* (n 28) 741–47.
[65] A Bogg, 'The Common Law Constitution at Work' (2018) 81 *MLR* 509, 510.

VII. Back to Basics?

Judicial review has never gone unchallenged, and governments of all persuasions have engaged in 'striking back'.[66] Censured regulations have been redrafted and annulled legislation reinstated, sometimes even retrospectively – a dubious constitutional move.[67] Effective though less direct are financial disincentives to litigate: cuts in legal aid, 'cost capping' or, as in *UNISON*, high fees. Changes in judicial review procedure, such as tighter standing or intervention rules, can make it harder for public interest groups to go to court. Tony Blair, whose first government was responsible for the HRA, allegedly planned to overhaul it to give government power to override judicial decisions.[68] David Blunkett, Blair's Home Secretary, infuriated by lost immigration cases, tried to insert a stringent 'ouster clause' into an Asylum and Immigration Bill to restrict the powers of tribunals.[69] Michael Howard, while Conservative leader, threatened during the 2005 election campaign to 'overhaul or scrap' the HRA. David Cameron went somewhat further, threatening in the 2015 Conservative manifesto to replace it with a 'British Bill of Rights'.

On these and many other occasions, the judicial system weathered the political storm, emerging unscathed. The two Brexit cases were different. They took place in a changing political climate, as right-wing ideology was edging its way into the middle-of-the road politics of the previous decades. In the election that followed *Miller and Cherry*, the Conservative Party pledged a Constitution, Democracy and Rights Commission 'to examine the broader aspects of the constitution in depth' and come up with proposals 'to restore trust in our institutions', and to 'update the Human Rights Act and administrative law to ensure that there is a proper balance between the rights of individuals, our vital national security and effective government'. More threatening was the promise to 'ensure that judicial review is available to protect the rights of the individuals against an overbearing state, while ensuring that it is not abused to conduct politics by another means or to create needless delays'.[70]

It began to look possible that 'a political leader might do more than simply pressurise the judiciary. Moves might be made to circumscribe its ability to review the actions of the executive at all'.[71]

Remarks made by Lord Reed, newly made President of the Supreme Court, to the House of Lords Constitution Committee suggested that he was alive to the

---

[66] See C Harlow and R Rawlings, '"Striking Back" and "Clamping Down": An Alternative Perspective on Judicial Review' in J Bell et al (eds), *Public Law Adjudication in Common Law Systems* (Oxford, Hart Publishing, 2016).

[67] For the reasons why, see House of Lords Constitution Committee, Jobseekers (Back to Work Schemes) Bill, HL 155 (2013) [11]–[15].

[68] *The Guardian*, 14 May 2006.

[69] R Rawlings, 'Review, Revenge and Retreat' (2005) 68 *MLR* 378. The Bill became the Asylum and Immigration (Treatment of Claimants, etc) Act 2004.

[70] Conservative Party Manifesto (2019) 48. The threats have not so far materialised; instead, the Lord Chancellor set up an informal review by the IRAL small panel of advisers, which recommended minor changes to judicial review procedure, to be implemented in a Judicial Review and Courts Bill currently before the House of Commons.

[71] A Blick, 'Populism and the UK Constitution' (*Constitution Society Blog*, 3 June 2019).

dangers. Asked what role the Supreme Court had in protecting the constitution, he replied that it was 'limited but crucial'. The role of the courts was merely 'to ensure that the Executive behave according to the law, so that they exercise the powers that Parliament has given them within the confines of the statute'; crucially, he added: 'and we thus protect the principle of parliamentary supremacy'. Silent on *Miller and Cherry*, Lord Reed told the Committee that 'our constitution is one which is not fundamentally based on law but more based on political practices and conventions'; many aspects of the relationship between executive and legislature are 'not protected by the courts at all but by parliamentary and other conventions'. Defending *UNISON*, he explained that the level of fees had been so unaffordable that it would prevent rights which Parliament had conferred on individuals from being enforced, which would be 'the Executive frustrating Parliament's intention in passing the legislation'.[72]

Lord Howell, a Conservative peer, was not entirely convinced. He took a side swipe at the Supreme Court with a Griffith-like question about the view of the Court, and more particularly its previous President (Lady Hale), about the functions and role of Parliament. 'Some people' questioned this view as being 'rather narrow' and 'not taking account of the historic role of Parliament in supporting the Executive or enabling the Executive to exist and the Queen's government to carry on, which is rather important'. This had surprised 'a number of people', including Lord Howell himself.[73] Lord Reed, remarking that he shared the surprise, fell back on the 'one off' argument: we had just been through 'a rather extraordinary period in our constitutional history', which Lady Hale might have had in mind.[74]

The Supreme Court over which Lord Reed presides operates in a markedly different manner and has adopted a very different style to the court that decided *Miller and Cherry*, *Privacy International* and *Evans*. The years of progressive liberalism are seemingly at an end; there has been a reversion to restraint and the formalist style of earlier years. The Court takes a textbook approach to lines of precedent. *UNISON* survives, but only just;[75] no longer could it serve, as Harlow and Rawlings once suggested, as 'a benchmark for the growth of judicial power in general, and for the constitutional role of the UK Supreme Court in particular'.[76] New standards are in place for the evaluation of government policy, revived from the past in two unanimous Supreme Court decisions.[77] The 'real risk' test of *UNISON* is applicable *only* where access to justice is endangered; otherwise, an 'unacceptable risk' test for the lawfulness of policy would be 'a new departure

---

[72] Select Committee on the Constitution, 'Corrected Oral Evidence: Annual Evidence Session with the President and Deputy President of the Supreme Court' (4 March 2020) 4, 5.

[73] See questions at ibid 3–5.

[74] ibid 5.

[75] See *R (O (a minor)), R (Project for the Registration of Children as British v Secretary of State for the Home Department* [2022] UKSC 3, where a compulsory fee of £1012 for a child to register British citizenship was upheld by the Supreme Court.

[76] Harlow and Rawlings, *Law and Administration* (n 28) 742.

[77] *R (A) v Secretary of State for the Home Department* [2021] UKSC 37; *R (BF (Eritrea)) v Secretary of State for the Home Department* [2021] UKSC 38.

in public law' and would 'subvert existing principle'. Executive policy will only be ruled unlawful if it 'sanctions, positively approves or encourages unlawful conduct by those to whom it is directed'.[78]

In the first of these cases, the Court added two striking comments to its judgment, perhaps as policy guidance to lower courts, possibly as assurances to government of judicial good behaviour. The Court warned that, without a reasonably clear criterion of unlawfulness with a sound foundation in principle:

> the assertion of such a power of review by the courts in relation to functions (the operation of administrative systems and the statement of applicable policy) which are properly the province of the executive government would represent an unwarranted intrusion by the courts into that province ... [I]f one moves away from that principled foundation, there is a risk that a court will be asked to conduct some sort of statistical exercise to see whether there is an unacceptable risk of unfairness ... But a court is not well equipped to undertake such an analysis based upon experience ... The test for the lawfulness of a policy is not a statistical test but should depend ... on a comparison of the law and of what is stated to be the behaviour required if the policy is followed. Both aspects of this test are matters on which the court is competent and has the authority to pronounce.[79]

In his 2021 appearance before the Constitution Committee, Lord Reed underlined the desirability of harmony between the institutions of government:

> Domestically, in a time of change and uncertainty, confidence in the rule of law is especially important. At the moment, we need to challenge the idea that this involves a struggle for power between the courts and the Government or between the courts and Parliament. As I see it, our function of interpreting and applying the law does not set us in opposition to government. Our decisions support effective government within the limits of the powers conferred by Parliament. Nor do I see our function as trespassing on the domain of Parliament. On the contrary, it is an essential component of our democracy that the courts ensure that public bodies comply with the legislation that Parliament enacts.[80]

Griffith, who, as a mere academic, did not have responsibility for keeping the ship of state afloat, could afford to view contention and dispute as normal. A constitution is shaped, he declared, by the working relationships between its principal institutions and reflects the political conditions that prevail in practice at any given time:

> At different times in our history, Government, the Houses of Parliament, and the Judiciary have enjoyed more and less influence over each other. Most recently, the Government was dominant in the immediate postwar period and during the 1980s,

---

[78] [2021] UKSC 37, [65], applying the principle in *Gillick v West Norfolk and Wisbech Area Health Authority* [1986] AC 112.

[79] *R (A) v Secretary of State for the Home Department* (n 77) [65].

[80] Select Committee on the Constitution, 'Annual Evidence Meeting with the President and Deputy President of the Supreme Court' (17 March 2021) 2.

Parliament at its most influential during the early 1960s and the late 1970s, the Judiciary growing in strength during the 1960s, until its decline in the 1980s. The 1990s saw weak and strong Governments with correlative strong and weak Parliaments, with the Judiciary recovering some of its influence.[81]

Two decades after this was written, we could add that the late twentieth and early twenty-first centuries were years when a judiciary emboldened by the passage of the Human Rights Act extended its ambit and power. If, now and again, they encroached on the political constitution, they were arguably doing so with the implied assent of Parliament, more especially when human rights were directly involved. *Privacy International* and *UNISON*, with the two Brexit cases, went some way towards creating the idea of 'a struggle for power between the courts and the Government or between the courts and Parliament'. But times change. If the courts respond by redrawing political/legal boundaries, they are only affirming the political nature of the constitution.

[81] Griffith, 'The Common Law and the Political Constitution' (n 10) 42.

3

Legislative Freedom
and its Consequences

RICHARD EKINS KC (HON)

I. Introduction

The central legal rule of the UK constitution is the doctrine of parliamentary sovereignty, which provides that the King-in-Parliament may enact any law, save that it may not bind its successors. This legal rule grounds the UK's political constitution, making political support within Parliament imperative if the Crown is to govern effectively, or in the end at all, and relying on politics to direct and discipline the exercise of Parliament's vast legal authority. Legislative freedom is fundamental to our governing arrangements. It is open to Parliament, as a matter of constitutional law, to repeal any Act of Parliament, including constitutional statutes, and to enact new Acts, provided that they do not bind its successors. In this way, legislative freedom persists over time. This freedom is not exercised in the abstract. On the contrary, the political constitution frames its exercise, which means not only that the dynamics of parliamentary government and electoral democracy limit how Parliament legislates, but also that Parliament is itself subject to constitutional conventions, which entail that certain legislative choices would be unconstitutional.

Any plausible theory of British constitutional change or reform will grapple with Parliament's continuing legislative freedom. The significance of this freedom is that the UK's constitutional arrangements are contingent – they may be set aside or displaced by legislative action. This point requires careful handling, for Parliament cannot change convention by legislation. The constitution is more than law and legislative authority pertains to the latter. But Parliament may change the law to require action that is inconsistent with what convention would otherwise require. This contingency is extremely important. It is always open to parliamentarians or the people to agitate for far-reaching constitutional change, and an argument for such cannot be dismissed on the grounds that Parliament lacks legal authority to act. However, contingency is not instability. Many features of the UK's constitution are unlikely to be unsettled, precisely because there is widespread support for them or at least an absence of support for their change.

These are unremarkable propositions about constitutional change. They follow directly from the doctrine of parliamentary sovereignty and the idea of the political constitution. Still, some scholars and jurists question them,[1] arguing either that Parliament no longer enjoys the legal authority to change the constitution or that key constitutional changes introduced in the last quarter century cannot now be undone (reversed, qualified) by legislative action. The argument may aim simply to describe the constitution we now have or it may also commend, or agitate for, Parliament's incapacity to undertake far-reaching constitutional change.[2] This chapter defends the idea that legislative freedom remains fundamental. Parliament retains legislative capacity to change how we are governed, a capacity that means that political argument for change is not futile. On the contrary, our constitution makes institutional provision for change, including radical change, to our governing arrangements. The provision is self-tempering insofar as each Parliament enjoys this capacity, which is to say that changes introduced by one Parliament may be undone by the Parliament that follows, or even the same Parliament. The paper defends these claims by reflecting on Parliament's legislative authority in relation to the territorial constitution, EU membership, human rights law and judicial review. Each remains liable to legislative change, which is fundamental to the nature of – and the case for – the UK's political constitution.

II. Stability and Contingency in Historical Perspective

Parliament's freedom to make law is constitutional bedrock. It long predates the Glorious Revolution or the English Civil War.[3] Parliamentarians and royalists alike agreed that the King-in-Parliament brooked no rivals. Their dispute concerned the political balance of power between the King and Parliament (that is, *within* the King-in-Parliament), which spilled over into controversy about the scope of royal

---

[1] See, eg S Douglas-Scott, 'The Case against Parliamentary Sovereignty' *Prospect Magazine* (30 December 2021); Lord Hope of Craighead, 'Is the Rule of Law Now the Sovereign Principle?' in R Rawlings, P Leyland and A Young (eds), *Sovereignty and the Law* (Oxford, Oxford University Press, 2013) 89. More equivocal is M Elliott, 'Parliamentary Sovereignty in a Changing Constitutional Landscape' in J Jowell and C O'Cinneide (eds), *The Changing Constitution*, 9th edn (Oxford, Oxford University Press, 2019) 29.

[2] See, eg Lord Falconer of Thoroton, 'Labour's Constitutional Changes 1997–2010: Time for More' in M Gordon and A Tucker (eds), *The New Labour Constitution: Twenty Years On* (Oxford, Hart Publishing, 2022) 11–25, arguing for adoption of a written constitution in order to protect the Blair-era constitutional reforms.

[3] J Goldsworthy, *The Sovereignty of Parliament* (Oxford, Oxford University Press, 1999) 229–32; R Ekins and G Gee, 'Ten Myths about Parliamentary Sovereignty' in A Horne, L Thompson and B Yong (eds), *Parliament and the Law* (Oxford, Hart Publishing, 2022) 299–321.

authority to act without parliamentary assent in levying taxes, making law by fiat, or suspending or dispensing from statutes. The UK constitution is the successor to the English constitution. It changes over time, of course, including by way of legislative action. Many of the most significant changes, however, have been political, with the King over time yielding political initiative to parliamentarians, with responsible government democratising the Crown.

Key relationships in our constitution – between the King, ministers, government and opposition, and Houses of Parliament – are formed and framed by constitutional convention and political dynamics rather than positive law. Those relationships are often supported by positive law, and inform and justify acts of lawmaking, including the Bill of Rights 1688/1689, which deploys Parliament's legislative authority to disarm the Crown in various ways, making government more clearly reliant on continuing parliamentary support. It is not open to Parliament to change constitutional convention by legislating, but it can displace (override) convention with a legal rule or replace (supplement) a convention with a legal rule. The Parliament Act 1911, for example, was enacted in a response to the House of Lords' breach of convention.

The openness of the UK constitution to legal change does not entail that the constitution is unstable, for the political constitution frames how Parliament exercises its authority. It would be unconstitutional for Parliament to undermine responsible government, to change electoral rules for partisan advantage or to immunise government from the ordinary law. It would be politically difficult for a government to propose such changes, or for the Houses of Parliament to support them, partly because of how the electorate would respond, but also because parliamentarians (including ministers) would struggle to defend them to one another and to the country. If such changes were enacted, political contest about their merits would not come to an end but, on the contrary, might result in Parliament, before or after an election, undoing the change.

Parliament's freedom to change the law is thus self-tempering. The law Parliament makes now may be amended or repealed in the future, perhaps the near future, whether by a chastened Parliament that can see the law has misfired or is unpopular, or by a Parliament that is committed in principle and/or for political imperative to its reversal. The constitution provides a frame within which decisions can be made about how we are governed, including when and whether to change the law. This includes decisions about the constitution itself. When there is widespread consensus in support of some constitutional arrangement, legislative change will be politically difficult and may be unlikely even to be attempted. But parliamentarians are entitled to attempt to exercise leadership, to bring the people with them, and may succeed in enacting constitutional change. Whether their handiwork endures depends on whether their successors have good reason not to undo the changes they have made, which may turn not only on how the changes come to be perceived by the political classes and the electorate, but also on the scarcity of legislative time and the relative priority that reform has in any future programme for government.

Constitutional reform may of course concern the franchise,[4] the shape of Parliament[5] or the bounds of the realm,[6] in which case it directly changes the conditions under which Parliament's continuing authority is exercised. Parliamentary reform in the nineteenth century was immensely controversial. The Reform Acts of 1832 and 1867 could each have been undone by later Parliaments, but not without reopening the controversy in question, risking widespread political unrest and paying a heavy electoral price. The legislation in question changed the political constitution, which in turn helped protect the legislation from being unwound. That is, legislation to limit the franchise would have required the support of a House of Commons elected under the reformed franchise. When parliamentary government proved compatible with parliamentary reform, *pace* the arguments of its opponents, the political argument for its reversal withered away.

The Parliament Act 1911 changes the relationship between the Houses of Parliament, not only in relation to finance and general legislation, but also future reform of the House of Lords, as the preface to the 1911 Act itself records. That is, disputes between the House of Commons and the House of Lords are now mediated by the capacity of the Commons to act despite the Lords, and even to reform the Lords without its assent. The use of the 1911 Act to enact the Parliament Act 1949 proves the point. One could repeal the Parliament Acts, weakening the primacy of the Commons, but the political argument for such change would be very difficult to make, unless it were bundled with radical reform of the Lords and perhaps a new federal compact for the UK as a whole.

The expansion and contraction of the English, then British, state has been achieved in part by way of legislation.[7] The union of England (including Wales) and Scotland formed Great Britain, the Parliament of which, as the successor to the English Parliament, was free to change the law, including to dissolve the union.[8] For a time, the political strength of the union meant that no Parliament was likely to contemplate such a change, but the rise of Scottish secessionism has changed this. The union of Great Britain and Ireland was less happy, and the Parliament of the whole was forced to consider, and eventually to adopt, proposals for dissolving the union. In making legislative provision for the independence of former British colonies,[9] Parliament made possible the orderly dissolution (separation) of the political community over which it otherwise exercised legislative authority. When the community was changed in this way, when the British empire came apart,

---

[4] Reform Act 1832, Reform Act 1867, Representation of the People Act 1918.

[5] Life Peerages Act 1958, House of Lords Act 1999.

[6] See, eg the rather different Statute of Westminster 1931, the Indian Independence Act 1947, the Canada Act 1982 and the Australia Act 1986; see further P Oliver, *The Constitution of Independence* (Oxford, Oxford University Press, 2015).

[7] M Loughlin, *The British Constitution: A Very Short Introduction* (Oxford, Oxford University Press, 2013).

[8] The realm is, of course, now the United Kingdom of Great Britain and Northern Ireland.

[9] J Finnis, *Philosophy of Law. Collected Essays: Volume IV* (Oxford, Oxford University Press) ch 21; J Finnis, '*Brexit* and the Balance of Our Constitution' in R Ekins (ed), *Judicial Power and the Balance of Our Constitution* (London, Policy Exchange, 2018) 134.

Parliament's authority was not abrogated, but the set of persons who continued to recognise it contracted.

The relative stability of constitutional changes made by way of legislation thus depends on the politics that follows in their wake, which may include both the way in which that legislation changes the political dynamics in question and the perception of its political merits over time. Effective constitutional change will be adopted (secured) by a widespread political consensus, which makes it difficult for opponents even to move proposals to undo the change. The consensus may turn on the relative success of the legislation in practice or on wider social and political changes that bear on how it is remembered or evaluated, or the legislation may change the world in such a way that it is ever more difficult, politically or practically, to reverse, to unscramble the omelette.

I will turn in the sections that follow to analysis of some of the main features of the modern constitution, focusing in particular on the Blair-era changes. However, a more recent example helps confirm the contingency of constitutional change. The Fixed-term Parliaments Act 2011 was introduced by the Conservative–Liberal Democrat coalition government. It had support in principle from some academic lawyers and jurists who view it as a justified limitation on executive power insofar as it terminates the royal prerogative of dissolution.[10] However, the political consensus is now that the 2011 Act was a mistaken experiment, which undid an ancient constitutional arrangement to address an immediate political imperative (stabilising the coalition) without considering its wider consequences. The 2011 Act seemed ineffective in 2017, when an early election was held, and disastrous in 2019, when it made much more difficult any resolution of the long political crisis. In the December 2019 general election, the government campaigned on a commitment to repeal the Act, with the main opposition party also proposing repeal, and the Dissolution and Calling of Parliament Act 2022 has now swept it away and restored the law as it stood until 2011. This is an exercise of legislative freedom – and a justified one at that – setting the constitution to rights.[11] It confirms the contingency of constitutional innovation, especially when the innovation's failure is widely recognised.

III. The Territorial Constitution

Now that the UK has left the EU, the context in which legislative freedom is perhaps most often questioned is in relation to the devolutionary settlements in Northern Ireland, Scotland and Wales. The settlements were introduced by legislation in 1998. Each had a different origin, as well as a different trajectory in the years that

---

[10] See, eg evidence given to the Joint Committee on the Fixed-term Parliaments Act 2011 from Professors Phillipson and Young and Lord Sumption. The Committee published its report on 24 March 2021.

[11] See Robert Craig's chapter in this volume.

have followed, but they are related in important ways. The three settlements – the territorial constitution – constitute a major change in the UK's governing arrangements, empowering parliamentary government below the Westminster level, viz below the level representing the British people as a whole. My question is how this change intersects with (bears on) Parliament's legislative freedom.

The devolution legislation does not transfer Parliament's legislative authority to the Scottish Parliament, the National Assembly for Wales (now the Welsh Parliament) or the Northern Ireland Assembly. It delegates authority, empowering those institutions to make law. The statutes at first granted legislative competence in different ways, but now the model is a general grant of legislative competence subject to a limit on legislating in relation to reserved matters. The legislation expressly preserves Parliament's continuing authority to legislate.[12] That is, the Acts do not purport in any way, and indeed expressly disavow any intention, to limit Parliament's legislative authority. Nonetheless, some jurists have deployed the devolutionary settlements as part of an argument that parliamentary sovereignty is no more, that it is an outdated, English idea about the constitution, which cannot account for the new constitutional reality that sovereignty is shared.[13]

Nothing in the devolution legislation supports a legal argument that Parliament's authority is subject to limits. Section 1 of the Scotland Act 2016 introduces section 63A into the Scotland Act 1998, which says that the Scottish Parliament is a permanent part of the UK's constitutional arrangements, that the purpose of the provision is to signify Westminster's commitment to the Scottish Parliament, and declares that it will not be abolished save on the basis of a decision of the Scottish people in a referendum. The Wales Act 2017 makes equivalent provision. These provisions are framed to be politically significant without in any way asserting a legal limit on Parliament's legislative authority,[14] a limit that on the orthodox view of the constitution would be impossible. There is no good legal argument that Parliament is unable either to repeal section 63A or to abolish the Scottish Parliament without the support of the Scottish people voting in a referendum. This is not to say that the provisions are unimportant. They form part of the political compact between the Scottish people, and their institutions, and the British people, which includes the Scots, and their institutions. Breach of the compact would have political consequences, including perhaps provoking unlawful secession. However, much would depend on when and how Parliament were to abolish the Scottish Parliament, for example, without the support of the Scottish people in a referendum. It is possible to imagine social and political circumstances in which this would be politically defensible.

Parliament's continuing authority in relation to devolution may be misunderstood. The Petitions Committee of the House of Commons has taken the view

---

[12] Scotland Act 1998, s 28(7); Government of Wales Act 2006, s 93(5); Northern Ireland Act 1998, s 5(6).

[13] See Douglas-Scott (n 1); Lord Hope (n 1); see also M Loughlin and S Tierney, 'The Shibboleth of Sovereignty' (2018) 81 *MLR* 989; cf Ekins and Gee, 'Ten Myths' (n 3).

[14] R Ekins, 'Legislative Freedom in the United Kingdom' (2017) 133 *LQR* 582, 584.

that it should not publish petitions that call for the abolition of devolved institutions without consent because any legislation to this effect would breach Part 2A of the Scotland Act or Part 1A of the Government of Wales Act and the political principle of self-determination for the people of the devolved nations.[15] It may be open, as a matter of procedure, to the Committee to take this view, but it betrays a confusion about Parliament's responsibilities. The relevant provisions of the devolution legislation are contingent enactments, fully open to repeal or amendment. In abolishing the devolved assemblies, Parliament would not be *breaching* the legislation in question (which does not purport to forbid future legislation). The political principle the Committee invokes is controversial and is open to Parliament to question and reject in the course of its deliberations about future legislation. The people of the UK are entitled to petition their Parliament about the legislative provision that has been made in relation to devolution, provision for which Parliament was and remains responsible.

I have argued in more detail elsewhere that it is a mistake to imagine that devolution supports a legal argument against parliamentary sovereignty.[16] Much more plausible is the argument that, quite apart from the law, devolution limits Parliament's legislative freedom. The Sewel Convention, first articulated in the House of Lords in the course of the Scotland Act's passage through Parliament, provides that Parliament will not normally legislate in relation to matters that are within the competence of the devolved legislatures. The Convention has expanded over time to provide further that Parliament will not normally change the scope of that competence without consent, which is clearly a rather more demanding limitation on Parliament. The Sewel Convention bears more than a passing resemblance to the conventions that governed the relationship between the Imperial Parliament and the self-governing Dominions within the British Empire.[17] The former includes the caveat that it concerns what Parliament will 'normally' do, thus working into the substance of the Convention an important, routinely overlooked, opportunity for argument for an exception.

The Scotland Act 2016 recognises the Sewel Convention. The Supreme Court in 2017 rightly understood this statutory recognition to be intended *not* to establish a legal rule,[18] which entailed that the Court had no jurisdiction to consider whether triggering Article 50, or more precisely legislation authorising the Prime Minister to trigger Article 50, would engage the Sewel Convention. It remained open to Scottish nationalists, and to opportunistic opponents of Brexit, to argue

---

[15] On 24 March 2021, a petition to end devolution in Scotland – inviting Parliament to debate devolution – was rejected on the grounds that it was not a matter for which the UK government or Parliament was directly responsible. The editors to this volume subsequently corresponded with Catherine McKinnell MP, chair of the Petitions Committee, who outlined the position paraphrased in the main text.

[16] Ekins, 'Legislative Freedom (n 13).

[17] *Madzimbamuto v Lardner-Burke* [1969] 1 AC 645 (PC).

[18] *R (Miller) v Secretary of State for Exiting the European Union* [2017] UKSC 5, [146]–[148] (*Miller (No 1)*).

that the European Union (Notice of Withdrawal) Act 2017, enacted in response to *Miller (No 1)*, breached the Sewel Convention because the devolved legislatures had not consented to its enactment. Likewise, it remained open to Parliament to enact the 2017 Act, as it did with an overwhelming majority in the House of Commons, whether because parliamentarians doubted that the convention was properly engaged or because they reasoned that the decision to leave the EU was made by the British people as a whole and was not properly subject to veto by the devolved institutions.

It is striking how often the devolution statutes have been amended by Parliament in the past 25 years. The amendments have largely been with the consent of the devolved institutions, but the settlements have scarcely been etched in stone. On the contrary, one main criticism that may be made of devolution is that it has been developed (extended) thoughtlessly, with scant concern for the integrity of the UK as a whole. Constitutional tinkering in this way is a use of legislative freedom; it is reasonable to argue that it has also been a misuse of that freedom.

The Northern Ireland arrangements were suspended from 2002 to 2007, in accordance with the terms of the Northern Ireland Act 2000, and the arrangements broke down again from 2017 to 2020. In the latter period, the UK government did not restore direct rule but instead invited Parliament periodically to legislate to maintain a constitutionally anomalous state of affairs, in which there was no responsible government in Northern Ireland.[19] Legislation put forward to this effect in 2019 was hijacked by parliamentarians in order to gain advantage in the parliamentary manoeuvres about Brexit and in order to impose same-sex marriage and legalised abortion on Northern Ireland without the consent of the devolved authorities.[20] This was an unhappy legislative episode,[21] even if few commentators objected to its unconstitutional character, but it confirms the continuing vitality of Parliament's legislative freedom even in the devolved context.

The devolutionary settlements were introduced while the UK was a member of the EU and the relevant statutes rely on EU law to provide part of the framework for devolution, disabling the devolved institutions from legislating in breach of EU law. In anticipation of the EU Treaties coming to an end, Parliament enacted legislation making provision for the exercise of repatriated powers.[22] The devolved institutions argued that the legislation was a power grab, in breach of the Sewel Convention, insofar as it failed simply to devolve repatriated powers. The argument for the legislation was that wholesale devolution would be imprudent and that the functions otherwise undertaken by EU institutions or the rules operating by virtue of EU law had to replaced by domestic law in such a way as would work best for the country as a whole. The political argument was had, within

---

[19] Northern Ireland (Executive Formation and Exercise of Functions) Act 2018.
[20] Northern Ireland (Executive Formation etc) Act 2019.
[21] R Ekins, 'The Constitutional Dynamics of Brexit' (2022) 12 *Notre Dame Journal of International and Comparative Law* 46, 67.
[22] European Union (Withdrawal) Act 2018.

Parliament and beyond, and the legislation enacted. Parliament exercised its freedom to decide how best to make legal provision for the end of EU membership, taking into account, but not simply accepting, arguments made by the devolved institutions.

In the wake of the UK's departure from the EU but before the interim period came to an end, Parliament enacted the United Kingdom Internal Market Act 2020. This legislation was again controversial, with the devolved institutions protesting that it was enacted in breach of the Sewel Convention. The argument to the contrary was that the legislation was required in order to establish a workable internal market within the UK once the EU Treaties no longer applied. The enactment of the legislation confirms that Parliament's freedom to legislate remains, notwithstanding the importance of the Sewel Convention and the extent to which the devolved institutions have become part of the constitutional landscape. Whether to exercise this freedom, when doing so generates controversy, requires prudent judgement. It was clearly open to Parliament to conclude that legislation triggering Article 50, making provision for consequent legal change and regulating the internal market should be enacted, despite opposition from the devolved institutions, in the interests of the whole country, taking into account the risk of secession, but perhaps reasoning that the reforms in question would minimise this.

The law of the territorial constitution was made by Parliament, and related constitutional conventions have been accepted by Parliament. The law in question is an exercise of legislative freedom. It is liable to be changed over time by further exercise of that freedom, freedom which is framed by convention and by the practical (political) difficulties of making changes without consent. Nonetheless, Parliament's continuing legislative capacity clearly enables it to act for what it perceives to be the common good of the entire country, including by revising the territorial constitution, even when consent is not forthcoming. Parliament does not yet, and may well never, stand in relation to Scotland, Wales and Northern Ireland as it stood, in the early 1980s, to politically independent but legally related Australia and Canada. That is, Parliament's legislative freedom within the UK is not a relic of a previous constitutional regime, even if it should no doubt be exercised with much respect for devolved institutions. It remains indispensable in order to explain how the country is governed and how it may be governed in the future.

IV. European Integration and International Law

For an earlier generation of sceptics about parliamentary sovereignty, the main line of argument was that membership of the EU limited Parliament's authority to change the law. While the UK has now left the EU, reflecting on the constitutional significance of EU membership continues to be useful, helping reveal important truths about Parliament's legislative freedom and its relationship to the UK's international obligations more generally, quite apart from the EU Treaties.

In its 2017 White Paper on withdrawal from the EU, the government said that 'Whilst Parliament has remained sovereign throughout our membership of the EU, it has not always felt like that'.[23] This line was much mocked, but was good constitutional theory. Neither the UK's subjection to the EU Treaties nor the European Communities Act 1972 limited in any way the scope of Parliament's legislative authority. Parliament retained its capacity, as a matter of constitutional law, to enact any legislation it chose, including legislation that would place the UK in breach of the EU Treaties.

The 1972 Act operated not by limiting the scope of Parliament's authority, such that legislation that was incompatible with European law was invalid, but by forming the context in which later Parliaments exercised that authority, with each Parliament, in each successive Act, choosing to maintain the rule of priority (not a rule about validity!) that the 1972 Act introduced.[24] The latter Act made provision for the rights under the EU Treaties, including decisions made by European institutions, to have effect in domestic law without further enactment and to take effect notwithstanding other enactments, a priority maintained by successive Parliaments choosing to legislate consistently with (that is, taking up and maintaining) this rule of priority. It remained open to Parliament at any time to displace this default rule, including by implication, by making clear that it intended to legislate in a way that was incompatible with priority for European law. It is arguable that Parliament did this in legislating in the European Union Act 2011 and the European Union Referendum Act 2015,[25] but even if it did not do so then, it was clearly able so to do.

The contingency of European integration – its dependence on Parliament's exercise of legislative freedom – is confirmed by two judgments in 2014 and 2015,[26] where the Supreme Court entertained arguments to the effect that the 1972 Act did not give domestic effect either to European law that was inconsistent with fundamentals of the UK constitution or to decisions of European institutions that were clearly ultra vires the terms of the EU Treaties. The arguments in question were raised, rather than resolved, but they confirm that the domestic legal implications of European integration turned on the provision Parliament made, which might not extend to giving full effect to the EU Treaties or decisions purportedly made under the Treaties. The UK's dualist legal order reserves to Parliament responsibility for deciding whether the UK's treaty obligations, or the actions of international institutions over which the UK has very little control, are to have

---

[23] Department for Exiting the European Union, *The United Kingdom's Exit from, and New Partnership with, the European Union* (White Paper, Cm 9417, 2017) s 2.1.

[24] Ekins, 'Legislative Freedom (n 13) 585–91.

[25] Ekins, 'Legislative Freedom (n 13) 590–91; in relation to the 2015 Act, see *Shindler v Chancellor of the Duchy of Lancaster* [2016] EWCA Civ 469 (Elias LJ), suggesting that s 2(4) of the 1972 Act may not apply.

[26] *R (HS2 Action Alliance Ltd) v Secretary of State for Transport* [2014] UKSC 3; *Pham v Secretary of State for the Home Department* [2015] UKSC 19.

effect in domestic law.[27] The point of the reservation is to protect the fundamentals of the constitution from being changed by a side wind, which includes Parliament's freedom to legislate for the common good, and to protect the UK from imposition of obligations to which it did not in fact agree.[28]

In exercising its legislative authority, Parliament had to take into account practical and political limits on what legislation could responsibly be enacted. The EU is a complex treaty-based legal order, which imposes far-reaching legal obligations on its members and creates a sophisticated scheme for enforcing those obligations, both at the European level, per adjudication by the Court of Justice of the EU, and within the domestic legal orders of the Member States. Enforcement of European law within domestic law was entirely a function of Parliament's decision to enact the 1972 Act and was always subject to Parliament enacting legislation that was not intended to be subject to contrary European law. But it is no surprise that Parliament, led by successive governments (who have had to take responsibility for UK foreign policy), never enacted such legislation, for the consequences would have been difficult at best.[29] The consequences would have included the UK's liability to daily fines and, more importantly, the scandal of being held (and being perceived by other countries) to be in breach of common European treaty obligations.

European integration thus did not qualify the doctrine of parliamentary sovereignty but did limit the principle of legislative freedom. Parliament chose to exercise its responsibility for lawmaking consistently with the UK's international obligations, viz within the strictures of European law. For many students of our constitution, withdrawal from the EU was unthinkable and parliamentary sovereignty was a relic of an old constitution – it was said to be possible in theory for the 1972 Act to be repealed but impossible in practice, and thus not a point of constitutional significance. This line of thought mistook the contingent stability of EU membership, always much more contested than its enthusiasts realised, for a fixture of the constitution. It was always open to Parliament to repeal the 1972 Act (and for the government to terminate the EU Treaties), which meant that the constitution made provision for political support for withdrawal from the EU to culminate in action. As the EU changed, and the balance of domestic politics changed too, it was readily apparent that Parliament could legislate in relation to withdrawal.

Membership of the EU would have abrogated parliamentary sovereignty if the 1972 Act had been understood, by judges and parliamentarians alike, to establish that Parliament had no legal authority to legislate incompatibly with European law, unless or until either the 1972 Act was repealed or the UK had

---

[27] A point powerfully confirmed by a unanimous Supreme Court in *R (SC, CB and 8 children) v Secretary of State for Work and Pensions* [2021] UKSC 26; for comment, see R Ekins, 'Convention Rights, Child Tax Credits and the Constitution' (2022) 138 *LQR* 551–557.

[28] D Feldman, 'The Internationalization of Public Law and Its Impact on the UK' in Jowell and O'Cinneide (n 1) 121.

[29] See B Castle, 'Let Them Throw Us Out' *New Statesman* (17 September 1982).

withdrawn from the Treaties. An argument to this effect was made by Eleanor Sharpston QC[30] in the landmark *Thoburn* case,[31] but was roundly and rightly rejected by the court.[32]

One can see the significance of legislative freedom in the decade leading up to the UK's withdrawal from the EU on 31 January 2020. The changing character of the EU had become a cause of domestic political concern. The Labour government had promised a referendum before ratifying the proposed European Constitution, but when that treaty collapsed, the government committed the UK to the very similar Lisbon Treaty without a referendum. In 2010, the Conservative–Liberal Democrat coalition government proposed, and Parliament enacted, the European Union Act 2011, which imposed a so-called referendum lock on further European integration. In 2015, the Conservative government secured a parliamentary majority, having been elected on a manifesto commitment to hold a referendum on EU membership. Parliament enacted the European Union Referendum Act 2015 with support from an overwhelming cross-party majority. Forcing the question of continuing membership on to the parliamentary agenda was a remarkable victory for parliamentary democracy.[33] The decision to hold the referendum was an exercise, rather than an abdication, of parliamentary democracy. In making provision for the referendum, and in standing ready to act on its outcome, Parliament exercised its legislative freedom responsibly. The same cannot be said for the response of some parliamentarians (and many commentators) after the referendum, when Parliament was encouraged to break faith with the electorate and to refuse to support withdrawal from the EU or to make legislative provision for its reversal.[34] It was open to opponents of withdrawal to make this argument, of course, but the argument wrongly sought to leverage Parliament's freedom to legislate into an absolute freedom from constraint, immunising parliamentarians from the political consequences of defying the electorate.

In late 2020, the relationship between legislative freedom and international law arose again, this time in the context of clauses of the Internal Market Bill that made clear provision for ministers to make secondary legislation that would be inconsistent with the UK–EU Withdrawal Agreement and in particular with the Northern Ireland Protocol. Legislative provision was needed because the Agreement had otherwise been given legal force in domestic law, including priority over other legislation, by virtue of the European Union (Withdrawal Agreement) Act 2020. It was obvious that Parliament had legal authority to enact the legislation in question.

---

[30] She went on to serve as an Advocate General at the Court of Justice of the EU from 2006 to 2020.

[31] *Thoburn v Sunderland City Council* [2002] EWHC 195 (Admin).

[32] For similar argument, see P Craig, 'Britain in the European Union' in J Jowell and D Oliver (eds), *The Changing Constitution*, 8th edn (Oxford, Oxford University Press, 2015) 104 and 122. For criticism, see Ekins, 'Legislative Freedom (n 13) 587.

[33] R Ekins, 'Restoring Parliamentary Democracy' (2018) 39 *Cardozo Law Review* 997.

[34] See ibid; Ekins, 'The Constitutional Dynamics of Brexit' (n 20); see also R Ekins and G Gee, '*Miller*, Constitutional Realism and the Politics of Brexit' in M Elliott, J Williams and A Young (eds), *The UK Constitution after Miller: Brexit and Beyond* (Oxford, Hart Publishing, 2018) 249.

Some parliamentarians and other commentators argued that it was inconsistent with the rule of law, and thus unconstitutional, for ministers to propose such legislation. This argument went too far. International order is important and the UK would often act wrongly if it acted inconsistently with its treaty obligations. But the constitution does not proscribe, by way of the constitutional principle of the rule of law or otherwise, ministers proposing legislation that would place the UK in breach or Parliament enacting such legislation. Whether to do so turns on the merits, which means whether the legislation is a justified means to secure the common good, taking into account the importance of international order and the UK's reputation for good faith in foreign affairs.

The best argument for the controversial provisions of the Internal Market Bill would have been that they were necessary to protect the internal integrity of the UK if a further agreement with the EU could not be reached and that their enactment would help make such an agreement more likely, at which point the risk of substantive breach of international law would fall away.[35] Like other sovereign states, the UK is free to act incompatibly with its treaty obligations, although this comes with a cost in terms of its reputation, may expose the UK to retaliation or litigation, and in justice may require compensation of injured states and other parties. In relation to the Internal Market Bill, the government had a case to make in relation to the risk of Northern Ireland being divorced from the rest of the UK, but the problem for its argument was that the Agreement in question had been reached only a year ago and the government had campaigned for election promising to implement it. In refusing to approve the clauses in question, the House of Lords was well positioned to present itself as forcing the government to honour its manifesto commitment and to keep faith with the UK's international obligations. These were compelling arguments, highly relevant to how legislative freedom should have been exercised in this context. But they do not detract from the wider truth that legislative freedom extends to legislating in ways that place the UK in breach of treaty obligations, or in breach of decisions taken by international institutions about those obligations. In a world in which international law reaches far into domestic affairs, this freedom is an important safeguard, yet one that is often difficult to exercise.[36]

V. Human Rights Law Reform

The UK's withdrawal from the EU confirms the contingency of our constitutional arrangements. The political constitution, with a sovereign Parliament at its centre, made provision for constitutional change, even in relation to membership of a complex treaty-based organisation, which had been designed to make

---

[35] See the Northern Ireland Protocol Bill HL Bill 52 (21 July 2022).
[36] Feldman (n 27); see also P Sales and J Clement, 'International Law in Domestic Courts: The Developing Framework' (2008) 124 *LQR* 388.

exit very costly and thus in practice impossible. While the UK has left the EU, it remains a signatory to the European Convention on Human Rights (ECHR, the Convention), subject to the jurisdiction of the European Court of Human Rights (ECtHR, the Strasbourg Court). The question that arises is how European human rights law, and its domestic reception, bears on legislative freedom.

The ECHR was signed in 1950 and the UK agreed the right of individual petition to the ECtHR in 1966. It was not until 1998 that the UK enacted legislation to incorporate the ECHR into domestic law, legislation that did not come into force until two years later. Until October 2000, the UK handled its obligations under the ECHR, including its Article 46 obligation ('The High Contracting Parties undertake to abide by the final judgment of the Court in any case to which they are parties'), in the same way that it addressed other unincorporated treaty obligations. That is, it was for the government to decide whether, and if so how, to propose legislation that might change domestic law in ways that would avoid the risk of the ECtHR continuing to hold the UK in breach of its obligations. It was also for the government to deal with the Committee of Ministers (the Council of Europe's statutory decision-making body). For almost three decades, membership of the ECHR did not have much impact on British law, because the UK had not regressed from standards agreed in 1950. However, in the late 1970s, the ECtHR began to conceive of the ECHR as a 'living instrument',[37] thus setting in motion a decades long expansion of case law beyond the terms agreed in 1950. In the hands of the Strasbourg Court, the ECHR has thus been transformed into a dynamic treaty,[38] which raises an ongoing risk that the UK will be held to be in breach of the ECHR, even if the breach in question turns only on newly asserted (invented) law.

It is in this setting that the Human Rights Act 1998 (HRA) was enacted. Its aim was to 'bring rights home', incorporating the Convention rights, which would make it unnecessary to proceed to Strasbourg. If domestic law was likely to be compatible with the ECHR, the ECtHR would be unlikely to find the UK to be in breach of its international obligations. The HRA was framed in order to attain this end without limiting parliamentary sovereignty. That is, Parliament would remain free to enact whatever legislation it chose and no court would have authority to quash an Act of Parliament on the grounds that it was incompatible with Convention rights. The HRA carefully preserves Parliament's continuing legislative capacity in this way. It aims to maximise compatibility with Convention rights not by qualifying parliamentary sovereignty, but by framing how statutes should be interpreted, encouraging parliamentarians to address the question of rights-compatibility and equipping courts to denounce incompatible legislation.

While the HRA preserves parliamentary sovereignty, it is in tension with the principle of legislative freedom, for it distorts deliberation about what should

---

[37] J Finnis, 'Judicial Lawmaking and the "Living" Instrumentalization of the ECHR' in N Barber, R Ekins and P Yowell (eds), *Lord Sumption and the Limits of the Law* (Oxford, Hart Publishing, 2016) 73.
[38] Lord Sumption, *Trials of the State* (Cambridge, Polity, 2019) ch III.

be enacted, discouraging parliamentarians from taking full responsibility for legislating for the common good.[39] The whole structure of the HRA encourages a focus on compliance with ECtHR case law, or its domestic analogue, rather than direct engagement with the merits of legislation or policy. In introducing legislative proposals to Parliament, ministers must make a statement about their compatibility with Convention rights. Strictly, it is open to ministers to assert that legislation is compatible even if there is a strong risk that a court, domestic or European, will find it incompatible. But the practice that has developed is one in which the minister anticipates the court's reaction and, save in unusual cases, attempts to avoid such. For supporters of the Act, this is a feature and not a bug. For my part, this is litigation risk prematurely foreclosing parliamentary deliberation. Much the same can be said about declarations of incompatibility. Political litigation often aims to secure such a declaration, which would either arm the minister to amend the legislation by executive fiat, circumventing the full rigours of the legislative process, or would impose political pressure on the government and Parliament to act, lest they be charged with taking the risk that the Strasbourg Court will rule that the UK is in breach of its obligations. Whether the pressure is effective turns on the issue in question and the wider political context. But the dynamic in question is clear, with the Act designed to cajole the political authorities into action.

It was open to Parliament in 1998 to legislate in this way. The HRA does not strictly foreclose legislation that is incompatible with Convention rights, and Parliament has legislated in order to limit the risks that Convention rights will be wrongly deployed in litigation.[40] The risk is that the HRA fails to square a circle, with the Act's incorporation of European human rights law distorting the political constitution. The HRA is sometimes said to have introduced weak-form constitutional review, in contrast to the strong-form review one sees in North American and some continental European states. The contrast is sound insofar as UK courts cannot quash incompatible legislation, which is a vital point. However, the contrast is blurred in two other ways. The first and most important is the way in which some parliamentarians and officials take for granted that the principle of the rule of law and the UK's international obligations require Parliament to amend or repeal legislation if the ECtHR concludes that such legislation is incompatible with the ECHR. The second is the assertion made by some scholars that there is an emerging convention that Parliament must change the law in order to comply with a section 4 HRA declaration of incompatibility.[41]

---

[39] Ekins, 'Legislative Freedom (n 13) 595 and 605; R Ekins, 'Human Rights and the Separation of Powers' (2015) *University of Queensland Law Journal* 217.

[40] Overseas Operations (Service Personnel and Veterans) Act 2021, s 11; I take no view here as to whether the legislation will prove effective in practice.

[41] A Kavanagh, *Constitutional Review under the UK Human Rights Act* (Cambridge, Cambridge University Press, 2009) 320–22; J King, 'Rights and the Rule of Law in Third Way Constitutionalism' (2014) 30 *Constitutional Commentary* 101.

I deny that there is any such convention, which would in any case be an *unconstitutional* convention precisely because it is incompatible with the point of the HRA and would arbitrarily foreclose legislative freedom.[42] It is reasonable for Parliament to stay its hand in order to enable the devolved authorities to take responsibility for governing part of the UK in some respect. It would not be reasonable for Parliament to abandon its own responsibility for the statute book if or when litigants persuaded a domestic court to denounce legislation. The argument that Parliament must comply with ECtHR judgments, because the UK has an international obligation to this effect, is more challenging. No doubt Parliament should be slow to legislate in ways that would risk placing the UK in breach of its obligations, especially if this would undermine UK foreign policy. However, recall that the ECtHR treats the ECHR as a living instrument. What this means is, first, that the Strasbourg Court may well change its mind in future, especially if the political response from one or more Member States is robust. Parliament may reasonably enact legislation that is incompatible with current ECtHR case law in the hope, which may well be realised, that the case law in question will be qualified or corrected in due course. The living instrument cuts both ways. Further, the judicial transformation of the ECHR into a dynamic treaty qualifies the UK's obligation to comply with the ECtHR's judgments. The analogy with ultra vires action on the part of the Court of Justice of the EU, against which the Supreme Court railed in 2015,[43] is clear.[44] There is a strong case for principled defiance of select ECtHR judgments, where the UK maintains that the ECHR has been flatly misinterpreted, beyond the range of plausible error, and refuses to accept that it has an obligation to change its domestic law to comply with a newly invented standard. It would be open to Parliament to legislate on this basis, enacting legislation that is incompatible with recent ECtHR case law but which is compatible with the terms of the ECHR itself.

The prisoner voting saga is instructive. The ECtHR ruled that the UK was in breach of its obligation under Protocol 1, Article 3 of the HRA 'to hold free elections at reasonable intervals by secret ballot, under conditions which will ensure the free expression of the opinion of the people in the choice of the legislature' because the Representation of the People Act 1983 disenfranchised prisoners. But Protocol 1, Article 3 was deliberately framed not to confer a right to universal suffrage.[45] The ECtHR transmuted the Article into an individual right to vote, admitting at first of no exceptions, but in later cases of such limited exceptions as the Court was willing to tolerate. The House of Commons decried the judgment. The government came under considerable pressure to introduce legislation amending the 1983 Act but refused. For more than a decade, the government met

---

[42] Ekins, 'Legislative Freedom (n 13) 595.

[43] See n 25 above.

[44] R Ekins, 'Constitutional Conversations in Britain (in Europe)' in R Dixon, G Sigalet and G Webber (eds), *Constitutional Dialogue: Rights, Democracy, Institutions* (Cambridge, Cambridge University Press, 2019) 436.

[45] J Finnis, 'Prisoners' Voting and Judges' Powers' in Dixon et al (n 43) 337.

regularly with the Committee of Ministers, for talks in relation to compliance with the ECtHR's rulings, finally agreeing in 2017 to make 'administrative changes',[46] but not, crucially, changing the law. The Committee declared itself satisfied.[47] The saga makes clear that there is no convention that Parliament must amend or repeal legislation that is declared rights-incompatible. It makes clear also that the UK may maintain for many years legislation that the Strasbourg Court thinks incompatible, and may in the end negotiate a settlement with the Committee. This is in fact how states often deal with discordance between domestic law and international obligations – not by slavishly legislating as an international body dictates, but by careful diplomacy.

Principled defiance of select judgments, on the prisoner voting model or otherwise, is an option. But it is a costly option, which invites constant challenge from parliamentarians and jurists who equate the UK's non-compliance with an ECtHR judgment with a minister's non-compliance with a High Court judgment. The two are radically different. The UK is a sovereign state within which the King-in-Parliament is free to legislate as it thinks the common good requires. Neither the constitutional principle of the rule of law nor the value of international order at large justifies the conclusion that Parliament's freedom to legislate evaporates in such cases. Still, it may be that the practical and political difficulties of legislating in the shadow of ECtHR litigation warrant withdrawal from the ECHR, which would help restore more robust legislative freedom. The UK's membership of the ECHR is not a settled fixture of our constitution. Withdrawal could be realised by prerogative action, but might be held (wrongly I think) to require legislation.[48] The present government is committed to remaining in the ECHR, but has now proposed repealing the HRA and replacing it with a British Bill of Rights. This was government policy in 2015, but was displaced by withdrawal from the EU. The Conservative Party in 2019 undertook to 'update' the HRA and later launched an Independent Human Rights Act Review to this end. The Review, predictably, recommended only minor changes, but the government has determined to go further and has seemingly revived its 2015 proposals, which were never published, and inviting Parliament to enact a new Bill of Rights.[49]

If the new Bill of Rights is enacted, it will likely be a major change to the UK's statutory Bill of Rights. The Bill may be an improvement on the HRA if it limits rights-compatible interpretation and upholds the lawfulness of public action, including secondary legislation, in the face of political litigation. However, the Bill may be a step backwards if it invites UK courts freely to determine the meaning

---

[46] In particular, allowing prisoners on Temporary Licence to vote. The lawful basis for this action is obscure.

[47] For a helpful review of the chronology, see N Johnston, *Prisoners' Voting Rights: Developments since May 2015*, Briefing Paper 07461 (House of Commons Library, 19 November 2020).

[48] By analogy with *Miller (No 1)* (n 17); see further H Mountfield, 'Beyond Brexit: What Does *Miller* Mean for the UK's Power to Make and Break International Obligations?' (2017) 22 *Judicial Review* 143; for criticism, see Ekins and Gee, '*Miller*, Constitutional Realism and the Politics of Brexit' (n 33).

[49] R Ekins, *Thoughts on a Modern Bill of Rights* (London, Policy Exchange, 2022).

of Convention rights other than by giving effect to Parliament's specific choices. The point of the Bill may be in part to leverage the UK courts against the ECtHR, developing an autonomous, home-grown understanding of Convention rights that the UK may maintain in litigation in Strasbourg. This strategy risks improperly empowering domestic courts.[50] The proposed Bill also contemplates ministers making time for the Houses of Parliament to debate ECtHR judgments, the point of which may be to replicate the prisoner voting dynamic in other contexts. Whether the HRA is replaced by a new Bill of Rights remains to be seen. What bears noting is that the HRA has never been secure from the risk of repeal or amendment. The case for the HRA is that it preserves legislative freedom or that something like the HRA is inevitable if the UK remains party to the ECHR. The new Bill of Rights questions both propositions and would seem to be intended, in part, to restore legislative freedom that the HRA (and its model of ECHR incorporation) has curbed.

VI. Legislating about Judicial Review

In addition to human rights law reform, the present government has proposed legislation to reform the law of judicial review. Successive governments have had concerns about the expansion of judicial review, often in relation to immigration and asylum, but also in relation to powers and questions that were once not thought amenable to judicial review. There has been a decades-long expansion of judicial review, although of course its extent, and especially its merits, have been much contested.[51] The Supreme Court's judgment in September 2019 quashing the prorogation of Parliament was a striking departure from settled law, and a number of other high-profile judgments in the preceding years also exemplify the assertion of judicial power. In a handful of judgments, two in particular,[52] some senior judges have even questioned whether Parliament may truly enact any legislation it chooses and have asserted that there may be a (new) judicial power to quash legislation that flouts fundamental constitutional principle. The particular concern of these judges has been the prospect of legislation that might limit, or oust, the High Court's jurisdiction to entertain proceedings for judicial review.

In *Jackson*, Lord Hope and Lord Steyn, and to a lesser extent Lady Hale, reasoned that parliamentary sovereignty has been overtaken by events. They relied on the European Communities Act 1972, the Scotland Act 1998 and the HRA to establish that Parliament has chosen to impose limits on itself, which means, somehow, that (i) the rule of law has displaced parliamentary sovereignty as

---

[50] R Ekins and J Larkin, *Human Rights Act Law Reform: How and Why to Amend the Human Rights Act 1998* (London, Policy Exchange, 2021).

[51] R Ekins, *The Case for Reforming Judicial Review* (London, Policy Exchange, 2020).

[52] *Jackson v Attorney General* [2005] UKHL 56, [2006] 1 AC 262; *R (Privacy International) v Investigatory Powers Tribunal* [2019] UKSC 22.

constitutional bedrock and (ii) the courts may assert further limits on Parliament's legislative capacity and quash statutes that fall afoul of those limits. I have detailed the weakness of this argument elsewhere. It is a striking argument, not only because it publicly asserts a willingness to violate fundamental constitutional law, but also because it misunderstands the way in which the relevant statutes work and their contingency. The judges in question attempted to leverage significant exercises of Parliament's legislative freedom to justify rejecting the constitutional law that underpins this freedom. As I say, the arguments fail, but they reveal an undercurrent in legal thought, in which parliamentary sovereignty is taken to endanger constitutional principle, which judges should secure *against* Parliament.

This line of thought was restated in sharp form in *Privacy International*, with Lord Carnwath, with whom Lord Kerr and Lady Hale agreed, openly asserting that in a future case courts might not give effect to a statutory provision ousting judicial review. The case concerned judicial review proceedings that had been brought in relation to a decision of the Investigatory Powers Tribunal despite an ouster clause that seemed to proscribe such litigation. The majority held that, properly interpreted, the clause did not in fact prevent judicial review in this case. Lord Carnwath, speaking for three of the four judges in the majority (another three dissented), went on to say that there was a strong argument that, regardless of the words used, it would be for courts to decide whether to uphold a clause excluding judicial review. Likewise, he speculated that a future court might reject legislation that limited a right of appeal to the Court of Appeal or Supreme Court in relation to a decision of the High Court in judicial review proceedings. There is no good legal argument for Lord Carnwath's assertions, although it is notable that he sought to rely on section 1 of the Constitutional Reform Act 2005. His assertions are flatly inconsistent with constitutional law and any court that refused to uphold an ouster clause would be acting unconstitutionally.[53]

In the wake of the 2019 election, the government launched an Independent Review of Administrative Law, which recommended minor changes to the law of judicial review but also defended parliamentary sovereignty in strong terms. The Review affirmed the legitimacy of Parliament reversing particular judgments by legislation or even ousting judicial review altogether in some contexts, including, for example, in restoring traditional limits on judicial review. Thereafter, the government brought forward the Judicial Review and Courts Act, as it now is, which makes limited changes to the law of judicial review, overturning two Supreme Court judgments and in particular ousting judicial review in relation to certain decisions of the Upper Tribunal. In addition, section 3 of the Dissolution and Calling of Parliament Act categorically excludes judicial review in relation to the newly restored prerogative of dissolution, an exclusion required in order to address the risk of litigation in the wake of the Supreme Court's prorogation judgment. There may be further legislation in relation to other judgments or propositions.

---

[53] Ekins and Gee, 'Ten Myths' (n 3).

Legislating about judicial review is not straightforward. While it is open to Parliament to reverse particular judgments, or to limit or exclude judicial review in particular contexts, changing the premises of judicial reasoning in other cases is difficult. The willingness of Parliament to respond to what it perceives to be mistaken judgments may well chasten the courts, but reform of judicial review does partly require a change in judicial attitudes.[54] None of this is to deny that Parliament is free to legislate about judicial review – it clearly has such freedom and is set to exercise it – but there are limits to legislative technique that are relevant in this context. Parliament could overhaul the law of judicial review at large, codifying it in some detail, but prudence may dictate more limited legislative intervention, aiming to correct particular problems and spurring judges to return to a more disciplined understanding of their constitutional role.

VII. Conclusion

Much of the law of the constitution has been made by exercise of legislative freedom. Political support within Parliament makes reform of constitutional law possible. No Parliament may change constitutional *convention* by legislation and some statutes that Parliament might enact should be decried as unconstitutional, while still being upheld as legally valid until their repeal. Parliament's freedom to legislate is disciplined by the political constitution, including the prospect that its successors may undo its handiwork. Stable change to constitutional law requires legislation that is taken up by successive Parliaments, who may choose not to repeal or amend it, either because it would be imprudent so to do or because the political dynamics do not permit such.

Constitutional change in recent years confirms the continuing significance of legislative freedom. The introduction of the territorial constitution was a major development, sharply changing the political context in which Westminster has had to act. Yet Parliament clearly continues to exercise authority in relation to the devolution settlements, authority framed by the twin political imperatives of respecting other elected authorities (and the peoples they represent) and maintaining the integrity of the UK. Entry into and withdrawal from the European legal order was made possible by exercise of legislative freedom. The supposed constitutional fixture of EU membership was revealed to be only a fitting, with Parliament making legislative provision first to hold the referendum and then to implement withdrawal. Parliament's freedom to legislate during the course of EU membership was heavily circumscribed, not by domestic constitutional law, but by the practical and political (economic and diplomatic) strictures that the European legal order imposed. Withdrawal from the EU Treaties and repeal of the 1972 Act was thus a very significant undoing of a practical constraint on legislative freedom.

---

[54] There is some evidence that this is now underway.

International law frames the context in which Parliament acts. Parliament should often avoid legislating in a way that would place the UK in breach of its obligations, but our constitution carefully preserves its freedom to do so, if it thinks this is necessary. In the context of European human rights law, Parliament's freedom to legislate incompatibly with ECtHR case law is an important protection in view of that Court's approach to interpreting the ECHR. The HRA was enacted to minimise discordance with the ECtHR. While the Act aims to maintain legislative freedom, the HRA and the ECtHR's jurisdiction are important, if not insurmountable, practical limits on how Parliament chooses to legislate. Still, it is open to Parliament to legislate incompatibly with ECtHR case law, and repeal of the HRA is once again a live prospect.

It is a mistake to think that modern constitutional change in the UK has involved a series of legislative qualifications of parliamentary sovereignty. Constitutional statutes are important, contingent exercises of legislative freedom, the constitutional significance of which turns in large part on the way in which they frame the context in which later Parliaments act. Note that the 1972 Act has been repealed, the Scotland Act 1998 has been amended, the Internal Market Act 2020 has been enacted and repeal of the Human Rights Act has now been proposed; the Constitutional Reform Act 2005 may well be amended. The contingency of constitutional law, and the primacy of the political constitution, is thus a consequence of legislative freedom, for successive Parliaments, and thus the British people over time, are free to choose how to change the law.

4

A Great Forgetting: Common Law, Natural Law and the Human Rights Act

MICHAEL FORAN

I. Introduction

The enactment of the Human Rights Act 1998 is often heralded as a watershed moment within UK public law. It 'brought rights home', returning to British soil an international convention that was largely crafted by UK lawyers and politicians, informed by the common law tradition.[1] Yet the fact that there was a perceived need for domestic incorporation signals a tension between such rights as they were envisaged within their common law home and what they became once they had flown the coop and fell in with a different crowd. These are not the same children we sent out into the world. They have grown and changed and, in doing so, some things were gained. And some lost.

A lot has been said in praise of the Human Rights Act, much of it deserved. There is, however, a strand of argument in favour of domestic incorporation of the European Convention of Human Rights (ECHR, the Convention) which is premised on the inherent inadequacy of common law rights. The fact that ECHR rights are, in large part, based on common law rights is either forgotten or else used as further evidence of the benefits brought by incorporation, given the differences between them. Convention rights are presented as simply better versions of common law rights, where common law protection of fundamental rights is recognised at all. Often, we hear of a sharp divide between the 'old' constitution, characterised by liberties, and this 'new' one, which *finally* protects rights after centuries of barren, rights-deficient common law.[2]

One response to these claims is to reassert the similarity between common law rights and Convention rights.[3] This is important. Any attempt to contrast common

[1] Secretary of State for the Home Department, *Rights Brought Home: The Human Rights Bill* (Cm 3782, 1997).
[2] On the distinction between the 'old' and the 'new' constitution, see V Bogdanor, *The New British Constitution* (Oxford, Hart Publishing, 2009); NW Barber, *The United Kingdom Constitution: An Introduction* (Oxford, Oxford University Press, 2021).
[3] TRS Allan, 'Human Rights and Judicial Review: A Critique of "Due Deference"' (2006) 65 *CLJ* 671.

law rights and Convention rights must recognise how similar they are in many respects. Yet, for all that can be said for the claim that, in the end, courts will engage in a very similar process of interpretation and application of rights, be they derived from the common law or the Convention, it cannot be denied that something dramatic has occurred within UK public law over the last three decades. While the judiciary will always strive to provide justice to individual cases, upholding the fundamental principles of the common law which themselves informed the Convention, what judges must do in order to achieve this has altered significantly. The Human Rights Act has profoundly changed the way rights claims are brought within common law adjudication. It has also contributed to the gradual shift in how we conceptualise rights altogether.

Despite Convention rights being presented as sufficiently distinct from common law rights for them to be superior, our understanding of the nature and scope of common law rights has been diluted. Indeed, Tony Blair's government stressed that, while it was once understood that the rights and freedoms guaranteed by the Convention 'were already, in substance, fully protected in British law',[4] now 'it is not sufficient to rely on the common law and … incorporation is necessary'.[5] Common law rights are perceived to be unable to meet the requirements of a Convention inspired by common law principles and this failure is now the primary descriptor afforded to them. They are seen only in relief; understood in contrast to the radiant light cast by Convention rights, as pale imitations, unfit for the purposes we now expect rights to fulfil. The distinctiveness of common law rights is being lost, while their supposed inferiority is emphasised. They are now expected to look and operate as Convention rights, and their failure to do so is just one more reason to evidence their inadequacy. But this is a mistake. We should be wary of adopting an uncritical view that the arc of the moral universe is long, but it bends toward the Human Rights Act.

There are good reasons to think that common law rights are uniquely tailored to meet the constitutional structures and principles of the UK and that Convention rights are perfectly suited for international law, where domestic determination can be done according to a country's own constitutional arrangements, subject to their remaining within the margin of appreciation. But difficulties arise when an international standard which envisages tailoring of general, purposively vague norms to meet a domestic context is replicated whole cloth at the legislative level. This is particularly striking, given the Labour government's stated aim was to enable British judges to 'make a distinctively British contribution to the development of the jurisprudence of human rights in Europe'.[6]

Rights under the Human Rights Act are essentially values which ground a selection of entitlements which themselves ground duties that bind public officials.

---

[4] Secretary of State for the Home Department, *Rights Brought Home: The Human Rights Bill* (Cm 3782, 1997) [1.11].
[5] ibid [1.4].
[6] ibid [1.14].

Common law constitutional rights operate in reverse: common law values inform duties that bind public officials, which then ground entitlements that legal subjects may seek to have enforced should the duty be breached. The shift from common law rights to those protected under the Human Rights Act can therefore be characterised by the centring of value claims, moving them from the periphery to the core of adjudication. What were once background principles and values, developed gradually over centuries into doctrines and rules, are now foreground claims that require far more in the way of interpretation from judges. The advent of proportionality analysis has ensured that the very concept of a right under law has transformed, expanding to include extremely broad interest claims, unmoored from the idea of duty or obligation in any strict sense.[7]

This has had two important implications for rights adjudication: firstly, it has required the court to grapple far more explicitly with contested value claims and review the substance of policy decisions in a manner which they may be unsuited for, to say nothing of legitimacy. Secondly, it has collapsed much of the distinction within public law between such value claims and those derived duties and principles which courts are best suited to interpret and enforce. This has resulted in an increased expectation that common law rights take the form of Convention rights, with very little understanding of important differences between general, purposively vague standards set at the international level and concrete determinations of those standards within domestic law.

An older way of thinking about rights and duties is being lost, and the delicate interplay between various actors within a domestic constitutional setting is being replaced by a statutory framework which places great emphasis on this balance at the level of enforcement, but very little when determining the content of the rights themselves, notwithstanding attempts by courts to rectify this through doctrines of deference.[8] International obligations, because they apply to states as a whole, cannot account for the separation of powers within a given constitutional context. Common law principle has always included such considerations when determining the nature and scope of rights. Where there is a range of reasonable options open for the state to respect fundamental constitutional values, the traditional common law approach has been to police that boundary but leaving the final choice from within the range of reasonable options to other organs of state.

With the exception of declarations of incompatibility, the Human Rights Act has not necessarily empowered the courts to do much different with convention rights than they have historically done with common law rights. What has changed is the material that courts have been given to work with and the questions they are forced to ask in order to determine what a given right entails in a particular context. For all its genuine success, particularly with regard to the separation

---

[7] See J Tasioulas, 'Saving Human Rights from Human Rights Law' (2021) 52 *Vanderbilt Law Review* 1167, 1185–92; NE Simmonds, 'Constitutional Rights, Civility and Artifice' (2019) 78 *CLJ* 175.
[8] See A Young, 'In Defence of Due Deference' (2009) 72 *MLR* 554.

of powers at the remedial stage, the Human Rights Act fails at its primary aim: it did not actually legislate to provide domestic incorporation and articulation of Convention rights that was tailored to our constitutional tradition. Rather, it replicated international obligations in the domestic setting, making no effort to provide determination as to what these rights mean within the margin of appreciation granted to Member States. It enshrined a collection of values and passed the difficult task of concretising these values to the courts. Courts can and have developed doctrine around important constitutional principles and values in the past. But a key difference exists in this context; the nature of the Human Rights Act and the proportionality test developed from it means that, no matter how much doctrine develops around a value such as privacy or family life, the value is always at the centre of adjudication in these cases.

Usually when entitlements are enshrined within legislation, the judiciary is given more to work with than what the Human Rights Act provides. This raises issues of legitimacy, with the classic common law method being obscured. If the Human Rights Act is under threat, it is partially because of failures of its own making. But it is not exclusively at fault. Some of these failures are the result of a legal culture which has arisen around international human rights that seeks to simultaneously allow for diverse political input to determine the content of contested rights claims while also maintaining a strict absolutism concerning judicial determination of these very same contested claims. The common law, having woven a delicate path through these difficult questions, has now been supplanted by a legislative framework which has been equally as delicate in its approach to remedies but has given very little thought to the actual determination of the content of these rights.

II. Classic Common Law Rights

Barber, drawing upon Bogdanor's now classic distinction between the old and the new constitution, characterises the historic UK constitution by reference to the protection of liberty.[9] On this view, the old constitution placed a high premium on liberties, the residual space left over once legal duties and constraints have been fully articulated and understood. This is presented in sharp contrast to the modern protection of rights embraced by the new constitution via, among other statutes, the Human Rights Act. But nobody seriously contends that the UK only began to protect legal rights in the 2000s. Indeed, Barber himself stresses that rights must be distinguished from mere interests or valuable goods: they are the co-relative entitlements which derive from duties.[10] This being the case, however, it is unclear why rights are characteristic of the New constitution. There is nothing new about legal entitlements that one has co-relatively entailed by legal duties

[9] Bogdanor (n 2).
[10] Barber (n 2) 297.

that others have. They are a central feature of any legal system and so are necessarily present anywhere where there is a directed legal duty owed by one party to another. Where organs of state are subject to such duties, owed to legal subjects, we can call these constitutional rights. They have been an aspect of the common law (and the constitution) for centuries.[11] Indeed, Barber himself recognises that 'much of the legal order is an attempt to work through and, where appropriate, provide legal protection for, peoples moral rights'.[12]

The common law has all of the resources needed to protect and defend fundamental rights – breach of which would be beyond any reasonable conception of the common good and so would fall foul of the ordinary administrative law. Non-fundamental but still valuable rights can and should be protected through legislative enactment by a democratic authority capable of making determinative choices from among a range of reasonable options. Yet even here we should be wary of framing every positive social development as a right, fundamental or not. The important distinction between goods and rights should be maintained.[13] This is not to say that many of the goods now included within our modern notion of rights are not valuable aspects of, indeed necessary for, a just society. But their inclusion within the concept of rights manifests a distinct departure from the classic common law conception and eclipses the role of legislatures and the executive in pursuing the common good.[14] Something important has been lost in our understanding of rights. The requirements of justice may demand greater nuance in our thinking and more active effort on the part of Parliament than has currently been given. Judicial protection of genuinely fundamental rights has long been an aspect of the common law, with courts interpreting statute and common law rule to conform to the rule of law and its related fundamental principles. But this has always needed to be supplemented by legislative choice from within the realm of reasonable disagreement.

Fundamental rights are the floor below which no rule-of-law-compliant system can fall, but a society directed towards the flourishing of its members will obviously go beyond that. The court's role vis-à-vis Parliament and the executive, from Coke to Dicey, has been understood to police the outermost limits of reason so that statute and the related limits on executive action are interpreted in 'the spirit of legality'.[15] What has changed with the enactment of the Human Rights Act is the way in which we identify the scope and content of rights, moving from the particular under classic common law to the exceptionally general, purposively vague, under modern human rights law.

---

[11] Magna Carta is the emblematic statement of this commitment.
[12] Barber (n 2) 340.
[13] See Simmonds (n 7).
[14] See G Webber and P Yowell, 'Securing Human Rights through Legislation' in G Webber et al (eds), *Legislated Rights: Securing Human Rights through Legislation* (Cambridge, Cambridge University Press, 2018); Simmonds (n 7).
[15] AV Dicey, *An Introduction to the Study of the Law of the Constitution* (Oxford, Oxford University Press, 2013) 273.

Classic common law rights were first identified by reference to common law duties. While it is correct to say, as a matter of analytical philosophy, that rights and duties are correlatively entailed,[16] in practice, it matters doctrinally which grounds the other for the purposes of identification. Common law courts, within constitutional and administrative law, have historically identified the limits on the authority of public officials and only derivatively concerned themselves with the entailed rights of claimants, where they require such rights at all. For example, the ancient writ of habeas corpus is a remedy through which the lawfulness of a detention could be tested; it is not a general right to liberty. As a 'great and efficacious writ in all manner of illegal confinement',[17] it is a summons, addressed to a duty-bearer (for example, a custodian or prison official) to produce the body so that an inquiry can be undertaken to determine whether they have lawful authority to detain the prisoner. It is only through analysis of the authority of the duty-bearer that any conclusion can be reached regarding the liberty interest of the prisoner. As such, the entitlement is to test the lawfulness of a confinement with a presumption of non-authority. The duty-bearer must prove the lawful basis of their action, lest the court find for the petitioner, who may be any person. There is no requirement that the petitioner bring an individual right of theirs to court and demand enforcement. Habeas corpus is a remedy designed to test a breach of duty on the part of the respondent, not to vindicate the rights of the petitioner.

Obviously, we can derive certain entailed rights from this duty not to be unlawfully detained, but they are exactly as described: derived from conclusions pertaining to the presence or lack of lawful authority. The analytic and doctrinal work is done primarily in working out the limitations on a given agent's authority, even if important common law values – liberty and legality – operate as background considerations, giving rise to the presumption of non-authority and the lack of standing requirements. There is no directly justiciable general right to liberty, even if there are more concrete, defined rights deriving from duties which flow from the rule of law. It is for this reason that Dicey concluded that

> though this merely formal distinction is in itself of no moment, provided always that the rights of individuals are really secure, the question whether the right to personal freedom or the right to freedom of worship is likely to be secure does depend a good deal upon the answer to the inquiry whether the persons who consciously or unconsciously build up the constitution of their country begin with definitions or declarations of rights, or with the contrivance of remedies by which rights may be enforced or secured ... there runs through the English constitution that inseparable connection between the means of enforcing a right and the right to be enforced which is the strength of judicial legislation. The saw, *ubi jus ibi remedium*, becomes from this point of view something much more important than a mere tautologous proposition. In its bearing upon constitutional law, it means that Englishmen whose labours gradually framed the complicated set of laws and institutions which we call the Constitution, fixed their minds far more intently

---

[16] W Hohfeld, *Fundamental Legal Conceptions* (New Haven, Yale University Press, 1919).
[17] W Blackstone, *Commentaries on the Laws of England*, vol 3 (first published 1768, Oxford, Oxford University Press, 2016) 129–37.

on providing remedies for the enforcement of *particular* rights or (what is merely the same thing looked at from the other side) for averting *definite* wrongs, than upon any declaration of the Rights of Man or of Englishmen. The *Habeas Corpus* Acts declare no principle and defined no rights, but they are for practical purposes worth a hundred constitutional articles guaranteeing individual liberty. (emphasis added)[18]

The basic principle that where there is a common law right, there is a remedy speaks, as Dicey says, not just to the conceptual entailment of rights and remedies, but also to how the content of rights is identified under common law. Identifying remedies for breach of concrete duties enables us to identify the content of the right in question. It is thus important to have a focus both on remedies and on the identification of the duties which give rise to such remedies upon their breach. As will be explored below, the Human Rights Act has done an excellent job at one of these, but is lacking in the other.

There is no general right to individual liberty under classic common law. Rather, liberty is a central animating value of common law reason, and so it informs a number of defined duties, including duties not to unlawfully detain and the crucially important remedy of habeas corpus which renders this duty, and its entailed right, judicially enforceable and thus legally effective. On this view of rights, the identification of their content flows directly from analysis of the entailed enforceable duties and their remedies, not vice versa. This is reflective of modern administrative law doctrine, which focuses on the limits of executive decision-making – the duties that such actors are under – not necessarily the rights that claimants must prove breach of before remedy can be provided. Duties to act reasonably or fairly will, of course, entail derivative common law rights not to be treated unfairly or unreasonably, but adjudication focuses on the identification and enforcement of the duties and upholding the rule of law at a general level. As such, we will see within administrative law duties which are not directed towards identified others but are instead general, undirected duties which pertain to the duty-bearer and their own conduct in isolation from any specified rights-bearer. For example, requirements to direct oneself properly in law or to act only where there is lawful authority to do so are not directed duties and so do not give rise to specified entailed rights. Rights can, of course, arise even in these contexts – for example, where the duty to direct oneself properly in law entails respect for statutory entitlements, such as it does under section 6 of the Human Rights Act.

The classic approach of the common law to these questions of right can be compared to the natural law tradition, which focuses on identifying what our duties of justice demand. As Finnis, drawing upon Aquinas, notes,

the object of the virtue of justice, and thus the source of the justness of just acts and arrangements, is that people all get what is theirs by right. Which is to say: that (to the

---

[18] Dicey (n 15) 199–200. See also W Blackstone, *Commentaries on the Law of England* (first published 1768, Oxford, Oxford University Press, 2016) Book I, ch I, 119.

extent measured by one's duties of justice) each person's *rights* are respected and promoted.[19]

What one is owed as a matter of right has traditionally been understood to derive from conclusions about justice and one's duties under it. The object of justice – *ius* – can be translated to mean 'right', 'the just thing' or 'what is due'.[20] To act according to the demands of justice is therefore to do the right thing or to render to another what they are due.[21] The connection between rights and principles of justice has important implications for the identification of the content of these rights. Crucially, being parasitic upon duties under justice, rights are always connected to a wider corpus of principles of justice, themselves inseparable from the common good. In the classic sense, the identification and scope of individual rights are always dependent upon a proper understanding of our duties both to fellow members of our community and to the community as a whole. The consequence of this is that rights are usually very narrowly tailored to meet the actual duties owed, rather than the more general form they take now, reflecting an abstract value commitment to family life or privacy, for example.

III. Natural Law Roots

The natural law was heavily influential in the development of the common law and the doctrine of common law rights, at least as they were traditionally understood.[22] Far from being something to contrast the common law with, natural law was integral to its development, both as a source of common law and as a model for the systematic interconnectedness of legal concepts.[23] It was widely accepted at the seminal points of common law exegesis and by the seminal institutional writers, from Coke to Hale to Blackstone, that 'Natural Law was a body of self-evidently valid ideas antecedent to the Common Law and in some way superior to it'.[24] Coke and his contemporaries, in their description of common law, constantly referenced the law of nature as a source of common law doctrine.[25] Indeed, in cataloguing his library, Coke listed divinity books first, followed by 'the book of the laws of

---

[19] J Finnis, *Human Rights and Common Good: Collected Essays: Volume III* (Oxford, Oxford University Press, 2011) 2. See also Aquinas *ST* II-II, q 58, Art 1; J Finnis, *Natural Law and Natural Rights* (Oxford, Oxford University Press, 1980) 220–21.

[20] It can also mean soup, but we should confine our analysis to the non-culinary translations. See J Brown, 'Jus Quaesitum Tertio – a Res, Not a Right?' [2019] *Juridical Review* 53, 59 fn 72.

[21] Aquinas, *Summa Teologica* (London, T Baker, 1911–25) II-II, q 58.

[22] See the many examples provided in DJ Ibbetson, 'Natural Law and Common Law' 5 *Edinburgh Law Review* 4.

[23] ibid 6–7.

[24] ibid 8.

[25] AD Boyer, '"Understanding, Authority, and Will": Sir Edward Coke and the Elizabethan Origins of Judicial Review' (1997) 43 *Boston College Law Review* 43.

England because they are derived from the laws of God'.[26] The understanding that the natural law was integral to the common law was so widespread as to be banal.[27]

It should be no surprise, then, that the natural law conception of rights, principles of right action which entail duties, is reflected in common law doctrine. Indeed, common law in its medieval guise was regularly called common right or common justice, and was understood to draw upon general principles of natural law, concretise them through the development of custom and doctrine and, in so doing, provide a greater determination of justice:

> The common law of England sometimes is called right, sometimes common right, and sometimes *communis justitia*. In the grand charter the common law is called right … And all the commissions and charters for execution of justice are, *facturi quad ad justitiam pertinet secundum legem et consuetudinem Angliae*. So as in truth justice is the daughter of the law, for the law bringeth her forth. And in this sense being largely taken, as well the statutes and customs of the realm, as that which is properly [called] the common law, is included within common right.[28]

Common law rights are heavily influenced by the natural law tradition, understood first and foremost as the reasoned articulation of duties under justice, with entitlements flowing from such conclusions. Thus, the natural law requirement that husbands provide for their wives was well accepted as morally binding in the context of the seventeenth century, but it was precisely on the basis of this natural law duty that the common law courts developed the right of a wife to pledge her husband's credit in order to provide herself and her children with necessities.[29] The value which underpins this right, the natural law commitment to family life, was explicitly relied upon to ground a concrete entitlement under common law. Similarly, many of the core common law rights are informed by general commitments to values such as life, security and liberty, which then take more concrete purchase in doctrinal rules and duties under the criminal law, the law of trespass, habeas corpus and so on.[30] Similarly, the common law commitment to the values of liberty and legality, informed by natural law, is the foundation of procedural safeguards of a fair trial – the rules of natural justice – so that, for example, 'it is certain that natural justice requires that no man shall be condemned without notice'.[31] Essential to the substantive enforcement of common law rights, entailed and identified by reference to common law duties, was a strong commitment to the rule of law and the principles of natural justice and procedural fairness. There is

---

[26] E Coke, *A Catalogue of the Library of Sir Edward Coke* (Oxford, Oxford University Press, 1950); Boyer (n 25) 47.

[27] See RH Helmholz, *Natural Law in Court: A History of Legal Theory in Practice* (Cambridge, MA, Harvard University Press, 2015) 96–100; Ibbetson (n 22) 7–9.

[28] *Coke on Littleton* (London, Saunders and Benning, 1830) 142a–142b.

[29] *Manby v Scott* (1661–62) 1 Keb 80, 82, 1 Keb 361, 366.

[30] See Blackstone, *Commentaries on the Law of England*, Book I, ch I.

[31] *Rex v Cleg* (1721) 1 Str 475, 93 ER 643. See also W Fulbecke, *Parallel or Conference of the Civill Law, the Canon Law, and the Common Law of This Realme of England* (London, Thomas Wight and Anno Domini, 1601) Dial X, 58.

remarkable similarity between the ECHR and Blackstone's Commentaries, at least as regards many of the interests protected.

Natural law principles of right action, understood as duties under justice, helped to inform common law doctrine and could be invoked in hard cases to help further or correct the common law. When Lord Mansfield held that the common law 'works itself pure by rules drawn from the fountain of justice',[32] he meant the laws of nature.[33] As such, natural law could be relied upon as a source of common law where no positive law could be found. This was the foundation of the historic common law rejection of slavery. In the famous case of *Somerset v Stuart*, Lord Mansfield was tasked with defining slavery's status in English law.[34] Somerset was a slave who was brought into England from Virginia, with the ultimate destination intended to be Jamaica. A writ of habeas corpus was brought on his behalf and the Court of King's Bench held that he could not be held as a slave in England, nor could he be forced to leave the realm and be returned to slavery. In so holding, Lord Mansfield relied heavily upon the natural law because by its dictates, discovered through reason, all men were free. It could only be introduced via the positive law or the *ius gentium*. As such, Lord Mansfield held that slavery was 'so odious that nothing can be suffered to support it but positive law'.[35] Because England had no such law, Somerset could not lawfully be treated as a slave within its jurisdiction.

The concept of odious law is quite important here and would have been familiar to anyone knowledgeable of the continental jurists at this time.[36] Odious law referred to posited law which was incompatible with natural law principles. A statute authorising slavery is an obvious example. Continental jurists would treat such posited law in a very similar manner to how the Human Rights Act demands UK judges treat domestic legislation which is incompatible with the ECHR: by interpreting it, as far as possible, to be compatible with natural law principles of justice and, where they could not, confining its application as much as possible. Statutes which were in harmony with the natural law were given an expansive interpretation, whereas odious law was not. This is so, even though an odious statute may not necessarily have been struck down or voided. Under some institutional arrangements, they may be. But this is a peripheral issue.[37] It is true that many back of the napkin summaries of the natural law tradition begin and end with the maxim *lex inusta non est lex*, crudely and incompletely translated as the idea that an unjust law is no law. But this is incomplete even taken in abstraction from the rest of the natural law tradition. *Lex* is posited law, understood to be a good faith attempt

---

[32] *Omychund v Barker* (1744) 1 Atk 22, 33; 26 ER 15, 23. See also *James v Price* (1773) Lofft 219, 220; 98 ER 619, 621; *Jones v Randall* (1774) 1 Cowp 37; 98 ER 954, 955.

[33] See N Poser, *Lord Mansfield: Justice in the Age of Reason* (Montreal, McGill-Queen's University Press, 2013) 214–16.

[34] (1772) 98 ER 499. See also E Fiddes, 'Lord Mansfield and the Sommersett Case' (1934) 50 *LQR* 499.

[35] ibid 510.

[36] See Helmholz (n 27) 108–09.

[37] ibid 69–75.

to more concretely determine the requirements of the natural law – *ius*. It is not generally taken to be something which exists in abstraction from this connection to justice. *Lex* is an interpretation of *ius*, as applied to specific contexts. Thus, as early as the *Institutes of Gaius*, it was understood that 'considerations of civil law can destroy civil but not natural rights'.[38] But this was first and foremost a maxim about the interpretation of law, not the capacity of judges to strike down statute. Where the option existed to interpret positive law compatibly with natural law, it was taken over an odious interpretation.

This is exactly what happened in *Somerset*. Positive law which permitted slavery did exist, but it was foreign to England. When faced with an interpretation of common law that would be as odious as slavery, the common law courts favoured an interpretation which was compatible with natural law requirements of justice. In fact, for all its fame, *Somerset* did not establish much in the way of new precedent. Previous case law had accepted that it was 'against the law of nature for one man to be a slave to another' and so 'if the plaintiff had any right to the servitude of this negro, that right is now divested by his coming into England' because 'by Magna Charta, and the laws of England, no man can have such a property over another'.[39]

In this sense, natural law maxims and long-standing custom informed by natural reason were sources of common law; they could be drawn upon to answer more concrete questions.[40] They were not themselves independently justiciable when freed from common law principle or doctrine. Even in some of the more blatant examples of natural law directly informing common law principle, such as the neighbourhood principle grounding the law of negligence, one needed to concretise such arguments into more discrete doctrine. The central issue in such cases turns on the precise duties owed to claimants.

Values are in the foreground here obviously, but they are mediated through our existing practice, distilled by reference to common law principles and the interconnected duties under justice. The rule that an agreement between two persons could not prejudice the rights of a third party was cited as determinative in the classic common law, precisely because it was based on principles of 'the law of nature and reason'.[41] Value is always present, especially in instances where the natural law was explicitly dispositive, but value alone was insufficient without something more concrete to ground a legal claim. Under the classic common law, adjudication centred on the identification of duties and mechanisms for their enforcement. Rights, where they arose, did so derivatively. This is why the remedy of habeas corpus arose, not to vindicate a right to liberty, but to enforce a duty. Similarly, the entitlement of a wife to pledge her husband's credit did not derive

---

[38] *G Inst* 1.158 (F de Zulueta trans, 1946).

[39] *Chamberline v Harvey* (1696) 5 Mod 182, 190, 87 ER 596, 600.

[40] See, eg *Manby v Scot* (1661–62) 1 Keb 69, 363; 83 ER 826, 996: 'There being no presidents we must resort to the law of Nature.'

[41] *Sir William Elvis v Archbishop of York et al* (1619) Hob 315, 316; 80 ER 458, 458.

primarily from her right to necessities, but from his duty to provide. Her entitlement arose as a mechanism for enforcing his duty.

IV. The Hobbesian Turn

Common law principles can develop doctrine which concretises general or abstract values into more concrete duties and rights. The generative and evolving nature of the common law is such that the enumeration of new common law rights can be seen as little more than the application of existing common law principle to developing contexts, including the context of an emerging international human rights framework.[42] This was the understanding at the time the Convention was drafted and remained so until the late 1980s. So, what changed? There are many obvious parallels between the international human rights movement and the classic common law, informed by the natural law tradition. But there are also important distinctions. Two key differences between the modern human rights movement and the classic common law find their roots in the work of Thomas Hobbes. Firstly, our understanding of natural rights has changed dramatically, departing from the view that they were derived from interconnected duties under justice to embrace atomistic, individualistic entitlements which, in their Lockean guise, act as trump cards against the community. Secondly, the scope and character of rights has expanded to encompass interests cast in the broadest sense of the term. This results in a need to develop a method of adjudication which can account for this expanded notion of rights without rendering them determinative of legal duties or obligations, precisely because to do so would be to prohibit practically every exercise of public or private power.[43] Under this new adjudicative method, the fact of having a right, and even of it being infringed, means very little.[44] Because rights are now seen as an individual's protection against the majority, expanded to include any valuable interest which might be placed in conflict with it, the mere fact of conflict constitutes an infringement. But that alone tells us nothing, given how often individual and majoritarian interests conflict. What matters is how to mediate that conflict so that some infringements are justified, and others are not. This way of thinking about rights is very different from the classic common law conception, informed by the natural law tradition.

The Enlightenment heralded dramatic change in how common law judges understood natural law. In particular, the influence of Hobbes is hard

---

[42] See T Fairclough, 'The Reach of Common Law Rights' in M Elliott and K Hughes (eds), *Common Law Constitutional Rights* (Oxford, Hart Publishing, 2020).

[43] Tasioulas, 'Saving Human Rights from Human Rights Law' (n 7) 1186; *cf* R Alexy, 'Constitutional Rights, Balancing, and Rationality' (2003) 16 *Ratio Juris* 131, 132, 135.

[44] See M Kumm, 'Political Liberalism and the Structure of Rights: On the Place and Limits of the Proportionality Requirement' in G Pavlakos (ed), *Law, Rights and Disclosure: The Legal Philosophy of Robert Alexy* (Oxford, Hart Publishing, 2007) 139.

to understate.[45] His description of the 'state of nature', absent governmental authority and characterised by violence, suffering and death, is foundational to how modern rights are conceived. This is not to say that his own conception of rights was particularly influential. Indeed, Hobbes is usually dismissed as a theorist of rights because on his view they are simple freedoms or liberties, unconnected from any correlative duties or obligations on the part of others.[46] In the state of nature, one has a natural right to do whatever one pleases. Hobbes should not be taken to endorse this state, however. Recognising the brutality of this hypothetical situation, he concluded that people would value security above these rights and so would freely sacrifice them to a sovereign who could exercise absolute power to govern. It was John Locke who introduced a conception of rights that existed even in the Hobbesian state of nature and could never be voluntarily given up by individuals.[47] They were inalienable and served to limit governmental authority, which existed in conceptual tension with the individual. While Locke is presented as the progenitor of the modern natural (and later human) rights movement, it is important to see how he built upon the foundation Hobbes set down in his break from the classic tradition.

The key distinction between classic rights and Hobbesian rights (including their later Lockean variant) is their grounding. For the classic natural law and, I argue, the common law, rights were grounded in one's duties under justice. They were the output of an interpretative or deliberative process concerned with interconnected principles of right action, applied to specific contexts. Hobbes rejected this understanding. On his view, and the view later advanced by Locke and others, rights are individual entitlements which take their character entirely separated from society or community. Their grounding is not in duties but in one's personal interests.[48] In embracing the idea of the pre-political person and affording this fiction natural rights, whether given up to enter into society or maintained as against that society, these thinkers ushered in a radical departure from the classic understanding.

The Hobbesian conception of rights is premised upon a view of man that it has helped to foster: an atomistic, individualistic self, disconnected from the community except when they conflict. The interconnectedness of rights and duties, understood on the classic account as the product of determinations about what we owe to fellow members of our community, has been lost and replaced with the Hobbesian state of nature, where rights become an individual's bulwark against

---

[45] T Hobbes, *Leviathan* (Oxford, Oxford University Press, 2008).

[46] J Hampton, *Hobbes and the Social Contract Tradition* (Cambridge, Cambridge University Press, 1986); DP Gauthier, *The Logic of Leviathan* (Oxford, Clarendon Press, 1969); *cf* E Curran, 'Hobbes's Theory of Rights – A Modern Interest Theory' (2002) 6 *Journal of Ethics* 63. Curran argues that Hobbes can instead be seen as a genuine rights theorist, but one who broke with natural law.

[47] J Locke, *Two Treatises of Government* (Cambridge, Cambridge University Press, 1988) 265.

[48] See Curran (n 46). Note that modern theories of rights may also be grounded in one's will. See M Kramer, NE Simmonds and H Steiner, *A Debate over Rights* (Oxford, Oxford University Press, 2000). However, even a will-based theory of rights constitutes a break with the classic natural law tradition in that it sees rights as the product of individual powers and choice.

a society she is conceptually set up in conflict with. This notion of the human person, before the coming of civilisation and law, is presented as our natural state: nasty and brutish, lacking any collaborative impulse except when the majority gang up on the minority. The natural corollary of this is an understanding of the public interest, which is rarely, if ever, genuinely common. The public interest is taken to manifest in a utilitarian or consequentialist calculus wherein the minority are required to sacrifice for the good of the rest, except when an individual right can be adduced to protect against this incursion. On this account, rights find their scope and character free from any social or community concern, which may be present within legal or moral analysis but only as grounds for legitimate or justified infringements in the name of the majority – but rarely common – interest. Rights act as inputs into legal and political deliberations, pitched as wide in scope as possible in order to allow analysis of justification, where the right of the individual is 'balanced' against the needs of the majority. The output of this justification analysis is a conclusion pertaining to the legitimacy of a rights infringement rather than a final determination about the scope of one's rights. This may seem like a distinction without much difference, but it has wide implications for legal adjudication, as will be discussed below.

The advent of Hobbesian and then more explicitly liberal accounts of natural rights was heavily influential on how common law judges understood natural law during the Enlightenment. This does not, however, as I will argue below, mean that a similar reconceptualisation occurred for common law rights, at least not until very recently, if it can be said to have happened at all. Thus, Blackstone distinguishes absolute rights, 'such as would belong to their persons merely in a state of nature', from relative rights, 'which are incident to them as members of society, and standing in various relations to each other'.[49] This is not to say that the posited law is only concerned with relative rights, on this view. Rather, human law plays an important role in defining and enforcing both natural and posited rights.[50] Indeed, to Blackstone,

> the principle aim of society is to protect individuals in the enjoyment of those absolute rights, which are vested in them by the immutable laws of nature; but which could not be preserved in peace without that mutual assistance and intercourse, which is gained by the institution of friendly and social communities. Hence it follows, that the first and primary end of human law is to maintain and regulate these *absolute* rights of individuals.[51]

In one sense, this is a clear reference to the Hobbesian and later Lockean idea that there are fundamental rights which exist outside of society. But in another sense, it is entirely in conformity with the classic natural law tradition because these natural entitlements must be mediated through our social practices so that their final character and scope is determined through a process of regulation and

---

[49] Blackstone, *Commentaries on the Law of England*, Book I, ch I, 119.
[50] ibid 120.
[51] ibid.

definition; what the classic natural law tradition called *determinatio*. Yet there is an important difference here nonetheless. It is one thing to say that the natural law does not depend upon society for its existence, so that the rights which derive from it are not essentially contingent upon posited law, even if posited law is needed to provide greater determination under conditions of uncertainty. It is another thing entirely to say that natural rights sit outside society so that their scope and character can be determined in abstraction from one's relationship to others. On one view, we have our rights in a state of nature (including a natural liberty, 'absolute and uncontrolled' to do as we wish),[52] but we give these natural entitlements up to live in society. On another, our natural duties and rights do not exist in a vacuum and so depend upon comparative considerations of justice for their full articulation in exactly the same way that Blackstone ascribes exclusively to posited rights.

A prime example of the disconnect between the classic understanding and this new conception of natural rights concerns property. On Blackstone's view, there is an 'absolute right, inherent in every Englishman', to his property, including 'the free use, enjoyment and disposal of all his acquisitions, without any control or diminution, save only by the laws of the land'.[53] Of course, the laws of the land arise from within society and so the qualification here speaks nothing of the scope of the natural right and only of the means by which the right can be legitimately infringed in the name of the common good. We see here, as we see elsewhere, a description of an absolute natural or moral right which the posited law is not expected to uphold in its entirety. Our legal rights (at least those derived from natural rights) are the product of determination, regulation and concretisation of these natural entitlements. There is much to be said elsewhere about whether the natural law genuinely does provide absolute claims such as these. For our purposes, however, it is important only to focus on the fact that such general and wide-ranging entitlements are necessarily filtered through the existing practice of the common law.

For example, the classic case of *Entick v Carrington* illustrates the common law approach to the connection between rights and duties, and also the common law understanding of the connection between rights and natural law concepts such as the common good.[54] Carrington and others had broken into Entick's home and searched it for seditious material, causing considerable damage. They had been ordered to do this by Lord Halifax, the then Secretary of State for the Northern Department. Entick sued for trespass. In determining whether the warrant of Lord Halifax was valid, thus providing lawful authority to search the home and removing liability for trespass, Lord Camden concluded that

> [t]he great end, for which men entered into society, was to secure their property. That right is preserved sacred and incommunicable in all instances, where it has not been

---

[52] ibid 121.
[53] ibid 134.
[54] [1765] EWHC J98; 95 ER 807.

taken away or abridged by some public law for the good of the whole. The cases where this right of property is set aside by positive law, are various. Distresses, executions, forfeitures, taxes, &c. are all of this description; wherein every man by common consent gives up that right, for the sake of justice and the general good.[55]

When reading comments such as this, we should be very careful to recognise the distinction being drawn between natural right and common law right in this context. Lord Camden was referring to natural property rights being given up or taken away by the public law for the good of the whole. Common law property rights are those entitlements one retains, preserved sacred and incommunicable in all instances where they have not been abridged by the demands of the common good.[56] To determine what the content of one's common law property rights actually entails, one must determine what has been preserved and retained upon conclusion of a process of adjudication and interpretation. Common law property rights, being the output of this process, never extend to include that which is precluded by the common law or statute acting in furtherance of the common good. In this case, since the warrant lacked legal authority, no such common law or statutory rule could be found and so the conduct amounted to trespass.

Lord Camden (and many others writing about the relationship between common law and natural law at this time) mischaracterised the nature of natural law property rights, presuming them to be absolute claims to ownership and possession.[57] He was nevertheless correct that common law protects property interests in all instances where their enjoyment has not been legitimately abridged by public law for the sake of the common good. The failure here is not in how courts understood common law rights, but in how they conceptualised the natural rights that they distinguished the common law from. This is not to say that common law theorists departed from the classic understanding of the relationship between the natural law and the common law. A central point of agreement among classic common law theorists, even those who embraced a Lockean conception of natural rights, was the understanding that common law rules, duties and entitlements were derived from, and were thus greater specifications of, the natural law. The abstract moral standards contained within the natural law needed to be concretised and tailored to meet the circumstances of particular jurisdictions in a particular time and place. Common law was the working out of one's entitlements under justice. It was further down the chain of

---

[55] ibid.

[56] Note that protection of one's natural rights is an essential aspect of the common good and one key reason why a system to protect such rights – law – is essential for the common good. See Blackstone, Comm Bk I, Ch, 134–6. However, it will be shown below that Blackstone's understanding of natural law, informed by the Lockean tradition, is mistaken.

[57] On the fallacy of this understanding, see R Walsh, *Property Rights and Social Justice: Progressive Property in Action* (Cambridge, Cambridge University Press, 2021); R Walsh, 'Property and the Common Good: Reviving Old Debates' (*Ius & Iustitium*, 14 September 2021) https://iusetiustitium. com/property-and-the-common-good-reviving-old-debates/.

understanding from the more general principles and values of the natural law. As such, Blackstone notes:

> This law of nature ... is of course superior in obligation to any other. It is binding over all the globe in all countries, and at all times: no human laws are of any validity, if contrary to this, and such of them as are valid derive all their force, and all their authority, mediately or immediately, from this original ... But in order to apply this to the particular exigencies of each individual, it is still necessary to have recourse to reason: whose office it is to discover, as was before observed, what the law of nature directs in every circumstance of life.[58]

The natural law helped to set the outermost limits of what posited human law could be, but it also relied upon the actions of legitimate authorities to provide greater determination to its precepts as applied to specific contexts and circumstances. As such, Blackstone concluded that 'human laws are only declaratory of, and act in subordination to, [the natural law]'.[59] Where natural law or divine revelation was silent, on Blackstone's view, human law enacted for the common good could restrain even that liberty which is untouched by the superior moral law.[60] Common law rights were thus complementary to and derived from principles of justice drawn from the natural law. Under common law, the values which protect property interests operate in the background, as considerations which help to inform doctrines such as the law of trespass, forfeitures and so on. These doctrines and the enforceable entitlements which flow from them are the output of a process of determination which is heavily reliant on both existing common law principle and the constitutional entitlement of Parliament to make reasonable adjustments to these entitlements through legislation.

V. Custom and Deference

For all the discussion of Hobbesian natural rights as self-contained individual entitlements, manifest in the Lockean sense of trumps against the community, the common law did not historically approach rights in this manner. When dealing with posited law, courts incorporated principles of deference to help delineate the scope of one's entitlements under law, always drawing upon the wider corpus of political principles than Hobbes or Locke would have associated with natural rights. To understand how common law rights differed from the Hobbesian understanding of natural rights but remained consistent with the older natural law tradition, we need to examine this principle of deference and its roots within the natural law concept of *determinatio*.

---

[58] Blk Comm Bk I, Introduction, 41.
[59] ibid 42–43.
[60] ibid.

Under classic theory, the rules and principles of the common law were derived from the moral and social customs of the land. It is sometimes assumed that custom is simply a collection of practices, social facts which can be determined without recourse to moral deliberation.[61] But, just as is the case with constitutional conventions, mere practices must be distinguished from custom and tradition precisely because there is an important normative – moral – dimension to them.[62] In every community in the world, you will find a long-standing practice of murder. This is not a custom. To constitute a custom, social practices must be underpinned by moral reasons, which create social obligations that bind members of the social community. These customs form an important source of common law rules and doctrines, which are taken to be determinative and authoritative expressions of the principles which underpin our customary practices. Positivists may look at this and say that judges can and do provide this expression by reference to social fact alone: the fact that these practices are taken to be morally binding by members of the community. Legal realists may look at this and say that judges are making this all up, or are at best tactically choosing which customs and principles to derive doctrine from in pursuit of their own private aims. But common law theorists recognise that judges must exercise moral judgement and they often do that in good faith, attempting to provide determinative interpretation of our existing legal rules and doctrines, drawn from custom and shared moral practices and principles.

Under the common law, custom is a valid source of law, not because it is the *mere* practice of the community, but because it is the *moral* practice of the community, informed by considerations of justice. Often these practices are an attempt to provide determination to the more general moral commitments demanded by the natural law – the font of justice described by Mansfield. Our common law rights are therefore those entitlements which derive from the common law duties owed to us by identifiable others. In a private law case, the court is the only authoritative voice on the requirements of custom and, later, statute. Where there are two private parties in a case pertaining to one's duties under contract law or tort, these rules are derived from collective judicial deliberation and interpretation, carried out over hundreds of years, of what we owe to fellow members of our community.[63] Custom is their source; the judge is the interpreter of that custom and the entailed legal rules and duties which stem from it. The role of the judge is

---

[61] See F Jiménez, 'Legal Principles, Law, and Tradition' (2022) 33 *Yale Journal of Law and the Humanities* 59. Jiménez does recognise moral judgement as a part of custom but sees it was a historical social fact about the views held by members of a community rather than something that demands the engagement of our own moral judgement for its full understanding.

[62] TRS Allan, *The Sovereignty of Law: Freedom, Constitution, and Common Law* (Oxford, Oxford University Press, 2013) ch 2; *cf* G Postema, *Bentham and the Common Law Tradition* (Oxford, Oxford University Press, 1986) ch 1.

[63] Indeed, it is important to stress that the rule of law is as important for private law as it is for public law. See TRS Allan, 'The Rule of Law as the Rule of Private Law' in L Austin and D Klimchuk (eds), *Private Law and the Rule of Law* (Oxford, Oxford University Press, 2014).

not to create law but to apply it, acting as 'the personification of justice'.[64] In this manner, the judge becomes the mouthpiece of a law which transcends any organ of state, speaking for shared principles of justice held by the community, simply articulated or interpreted by the judiciary – *judex est lex loquens*.[65]

With this in mind, it is important to recognise the constitutional aspects of the common law tradition. In constitutional and administrative law, common law courts recognise that they are no longer dealing with two private parties, each subordinate to the courts' authority to speak on behalf of the community. In public law cases, one party has been granted specific authority to speak and act on behalf of the community, either through the election process or through delegated authority. In our modern administrative law, this translates into the maxim that courts will review the outmost limits of discretion but will not act as an appellate body tasked with retaking the decision themselves. In these cases, courts recognise an alternative, perhaps superior, voice speaking on behalf of the community – even if they must interpret that voice when adjudicating cases, drawing upon principles of justice in so doing. It is this authority which explains the courts deference to the more political organs of state. It is for this reason that Laws suggests that 'deference marks the courts' recognition that as regards the merits of the use of discretionary power in any given instance, the public body to which the power has been delegated by Parliament is the primary decision-maker'.[66]

The approach of the common law to questions of deference echoes the natural law concept of *determinatio*. In the classical legal tradition, posited laws, including the decisions of executive authorities, were attempts to provide greater determination to the very general requirements of justice and the natural law. With that in mind, there exists a realm of reasonably plausible concretisations or determinations of these requirements in any given context. As Aquinas notes, general ideas must be made particular as to details, 'for example the craftsman needs to turn the general idea of a house into the shape of this or that house'.[67] Within the bounds of reason, such determinations as to these particulars must be contextualised to varying circumstances across time and place: 'The general principles of the natural law cannot be applied to all men in the same way because of the great variety of human circumstances; and hence arises the diversity of positive laws among various people'.[68] Here we see the classical roots of the modern ECHR principle of the margin of appreciation, as well as the more historic principle of deference that is owed by courts to legitimate political authority, where it acts within the realm of its lawful authority. Determination will inevitably be in some way discretionary, so that, once within the bounds of reasonable disagreement, it may even

---

[64] T Aquinas, *Summa Theologica*, pt II-II, q 58, Art 1 in Aquinas, *Political Writing* (RW Dyson ed, trans, Cambridge, Cambridge University Press, 2002) 130.

[65] *Calvin's Case* (1608) 77 ER 377, 381.

[66] J Laws, *The Constitutional Balance* (Oxford, Hart Publishing, 2021) 90.

[67] T Aquinas, *Summa Theologica*, pt I-II, q 95, Art 2 in Aquinas, *Political Writing* (n 64) 130.

[68] ibid 131.

be 'rationally arbitrary'.[69] As such, 'The basis of deference, then, is that deference is how law respects the discretionary space of the public authority to engage in determination'.[70]

Common law courts recognise their own constitutional limits when adjudicating public law cases precisely because they are not the only ones who have a constitutional voice here. The upshot is that the scope and content of common law rights track the important distinction between a public authority acting within or outwith this realm of reasonable political determination. Where there is room for reasoned disagreement within the scope of discretion, the court will (or at least should) not intervene to impose its own determination of how best to pursue a given political aim. While the same is claimed of rights under the ECHR, the advent of proportionality calls this into question.

While common law rights can generally be contrasted with Convention rights, it is at least arguable that courts began to embrace a Lockean understanding of constitutional rights in the years following the drafting of the ECHR. One important shift, beginning in the early 1990s, was the gradual development of a doctrine wherein courts grounded common law constitutional duties in rights, explaining the content of constitutional and administrative law duties by reference to historic (and in some cases, developing) rights rather than the other way around. Thus, in *Leech*, the Court of Appeal relied on the right of access to court to determine the scope of discretion afforded under the Prison Act 1952.[71] The Secretary of State had been granted discretionary power to make rules for the management of prisons, and under rule 33(3) of the Prison Rules 1964, governors could read any correspondence to or from a prisoner. Leech sought to have this rule declared ultra vires insofar as it purported to authorise the interference with correspondence between prisoners and their lawyers. The Court agreed, drawing upon the previous dictum that a convicted prisoner retains all common law rights which are not taken away expressly or by necessary implication.[72] One such right was the 'principle in our law that every citizen has a right of unimpeded access to court … [which] even in our unwritten constitution … must rank as a constitutional right'.[73] Even here, though, the common law derived this right from long-standing doctrines pertaining to the rule of law. Thus, while it is certainly true that administrative law duties are here characterised by reference to a right, the scope and character of this entitlement are derived from well-established constitutional principles and the entailed duty of legal officials to uphold the rule of law.

A more blatant shift in our understanding of common law rights comes from the first instance decision of Laws J in *R v Cambridge Health Authority, ex parte B*,

---

[69] See A Vermeule, 'Rationally Arbitrary Decisions in Administrative Law' (2015) 44 *Journal of Legal Studies* S475. See also J Finnis, 'Natural Law Theories' (*Stanford Encyclopedia of Philosophy*, 3 June 2020) https://plato.stanford.edu/entries/natural-law-theories/.

[70] A Vermeule, *Common Good Constitutionalism* (Cambridge, Polity, 2022) 46.

[71] *R v Secretary of State for the Home Department, ex parte Leech* [1994] QB 198. See also *R v Lord Chancellor, ex parte Witham* [1998] QB 575; *R (UNISON) v Lord Chancellor* [2017] UKSC 51.

[72] See *Raymond v Honey* [1983] 1 AC 1, 10.

[73] *Leech* (n 71) 210 (Steyn LJ).

which challenged the decision of a health authority not to sanction an expensive experimental course of treatment with a slim chance of success. Laws J held that the authority had acted unreasonably, concluding that 'where a public body enjoyed a discretion whose exercise might infringe a fundamental human right, such as the right to life, it should not be permitted to perpetrate any such infringement unless it could show substantial objective justification for doing so on public interest grounds'.[74] Here, we see the right to life take on a much more expansive character compared to its historic common law counterpart. To Blackstone, the right to life included entitlements not to be unlawfully killed and to the enjoyment of bodily integrity, and the related defence of duress and self-defence when acting in preservation of one's own life or the life of others.[75] Casting this as a general common law protection of anything which could plausibly be covered by the interest of life vastly alters the concept of rights, potentially so much so that what remains is not properly understood as a right at all. This will be discussed in greater detail below. For now, it is important to note that the Court of Appeal in this case unanimously upheld the health authority's appeal, making no mention to a general common law right to life as described by Laws J.[76] Indeed, even under the ECHR, because the right to life is an absolute right, it generally takes on the character of classic common law rights, where scope is of much greater relevance, precisely because, unlike qualified rights, infringement is automatically unjustified.[77] This means that there is no room for an expansive protection of an interest in life where little attention need be paid to scope, all of the work being done at the justification stage.

Common law constitutional rights, being derived from fundamental constitutional and administrative law duties, police the outermost boundaries of legitimate political authority and discretion but leave this important sphere of determination open. Fundamental constitutional law principles demanding judicial respect for legitimate political determination are essential to the common law. The same is true for the Human Rights Act at the level of enforcement and remedy, but something different is occurring with regards to the scope, content and interpretation of the rights themselves, at least with regard to qualified rights.

VI. The Centring of Value

Returning to the distinction set out at the beginning of this chapter, we can conclude that it was the old constitution which was in fact characterised by duties and rights. In this final section, I will argue that the new constitution is characterised

---

[74] See R James and D Longley, 'Judicial Review and Tragic Choices: Ex Parte B' [1995] *PL* 367, 368.

[75] Blackstone, *Commentaries on the Law of England*, Book I, ch 1, 129–34.

[76] [1995] 1 WLR 898.

[77] See *R (Wa) v Secretary of State for the Home Department* [2021] EWCA Civ 12, where the court engaged in careful analysis of the scope of the right to life, concluding that it simply did not extend to include a right to have false documentation that would diminish the risk of suicide.

not by rights, but by values. Moral rights now inform legal doctrine not through the gradual working out of legal rules and duties in the form of distinct heads of action, but by directly invoking values which had previously been latent within the common law. The Second World War was an example of a complete degradation of the moral conditions necessary for a legal system to operate.[78] This led to a shift within Western legal thinking which manifested in the conscious commitment of states to uphold and defend the values which had so callously been abandoned. That is not a bad thing, but it has had a profound effect on legal reasoning when it comes to rights adjudication.

It is important to trace the underlying assumption motivating the advent of international human rights law. The narrative that legal systems need now to explicitly and actively commit to these values in order for them to avoid repeating the atrocities of the past presumes either that there was previously no recognition of the moral rights of subjects within law or that somehow being explicit about what was once taken for granted will prevent an evil tyrant from ignoring such statements and commitments. It is clearly incorrect to say that the historic common law, or the *ius civil* on the continent, had no commitment to the values contained within the Universal Declaration of Human Rights or the European Convention on Human Rights. Nor is it fair to say that domestic protection of human rights occurred only at common law. There has been a collective amnesia, prompting repeated inaccurate descriptions of our legal history as devoid of rights protection prior to the ratification of the European Convention.[79] Yet, as the above has shown, this is simply not true at common law. Equally, as Webber and Yowell point out, this description fails to account for the vast swathe of legislation which protects fundamental rights, from the Representation Acts to the Education Acts, the National Health Service Act 1947 and the vast swathe of labour law legislation.[80] Even after ratification and incorporation, much of the most effective means of protecting rights in the UK has come through legislation such as the Equality Act 2010, which provides detailed concretisation and determination to the more general values contained within the Convention.

International human rights treaties are necessarily pitched at such a broad level of abstraction that the ascription of rights to the commitments contained within is at worst purely rhetorical. At best, this signals a change in how we conceive

---

[78] L Fuller, 'Positivism and Fidelity to Law: A Reply to Professor Hart' (1958) 71 *Harvard Law Review* 630; G Radbruch, 'Statutory Lawlessness and Supra-statutory Law' (2006) 26 *OJLS* 1; R Alexy, 'A Defence of Radbruch's Formula' in D Dyzenhaus (ed), *Recrafting the Rule of Law: The Limits of Legal Order* (Oxford, Hart Publishing, 1999); TRS Allan, 'In Defence of Radbruch's Formula: Injustice, Interpretation, and Invalidity' in M Borowski, SL Paulson and J-R Sieckmann (eds), *Rechtspjilosophie und Grundrechtstheorie* (Tübingen, Mohr Siebeck, 2017).

[79] For example, Lord Neuberger has said that, prior to ratification, 'the UK simply did not recognise human rights other than through the common law': Lord Neuberger, 'The Role of Judges in Human Rights Jurisprudence: A Comparison of the Australian and UK Experience' (address at the Supreme Court of Victoria, Melbourne, Australia, 8 August 2014) para 1, www.supremecourt.uk/docs/speech-14080.pdf.

[80] Webber and Yowell (n 14) 2.

rights: no longer as the narrowly tailored correlatives of duties under justice, but as interests centred around a unifying value, with the value being the thing that is codified. On one view, what are protected by these treaties are not rights, but valued interests.[81] A commitment to respecting life, family life or even property, when pitched at so general a level, tells us very little about the actual duties that signatory states are under, nor the entitlements that legal subjects have as a result. This was purposeful, of course, because anything more detailed than what was eventually proposed would not have achieved the needed consensus. A commitment to privacy is all well and good, who could disagree with that? But a commitment to the legalisation of euthanasia on the grounds of privacy? That is much less likely to achieve the consensus. Thankfully, the ECtHR has recognised this and for the most part has been content to leave such contentious decisions to Member States.[82]

There is often an assumption amongst human rights lawyers that the historic legislative mechanisms for working through people's moral rights failed and will continue to fail, but that the new international order will succeed.[83] This framing is fundamentally mistaken because it neglects the essential role that legislatures can and should play within this process.[84] International conventions and declarations of human rights set out essential aspects of human well-being which demand respect, promotion and protection. But they cannot perfectly express the content of these rights, precisely because they are pitched at such a general level. The act of determination must still be done. We need to concretise these general value commitments. The shift within modern rights adjudication occurs where legislatures fail or refuse to do their part in this process, enshrining Bills of Rights which leave domestic courts in an uncomfortable position where they must balance the need to provide justice to individual claimants against their institutional limitations and the consequent desire not to usurp the democratic authority of the legislature.

It is here that the Human Rights Act fails most: it incorporated – without concretising – international standards which envisaged legislative work to be done to flesh out their general commitments. In doing so, it 'brought rights home', placing these general values above any domestic legislation which attempts to provide authoritative determination. Courts were given interpretative obligations and powers to declare a statute to be incompatible with the Convention. Such powers and duties were essential for full domestic incorporation and clearly represent the product of extensive and nuanced thinking about the separation of powers. This was not applied to the most important aspect of any domestic incorporation of international human rights: the content of the rights themselves.

---

[81] Simmonds (n 7).

[82] See *Pretty v United Kingdom* (2346/02); *Nichlinson and Lamb v United Kingdom* (2478/25; 1787/15).

[83] For example, some scholars argue that legislatures simply cannot be trusted to legislate for rights. See R Dworkin, *Taking Rights Seriously* (Cambridge, MA, Harvard University Press, 1977) 22, 90; *cf* P Yowell, 'A Critical Examination of Dworkin's Theory of Rights' (2007) 52 *American Journal of Jurisprudence* 93; Webber and Yowell (n 14).

[84] See Webber and Yowell (n 14).

In its most basic sense, the Human Rights Act represents an abdication of legislative responsibility.

The result is that domestic courts are placed in an extremely difficult position. They have been handed a purposively vague international treaty and obligations to interpret domestic law to be as compatible as possible with general values without much assistance in determining what these values actually require in concrete situations. For all the criticism of domestic courts, they have generally been quite reluctant to wade into contentious social or moral debates on the back of these general value commitments. But that reluctance does not do much to wave away their own obligations under the Human Rights Act. One solution has been for domestic courts to avoid exercising their own judgement on the content of these rights, either by abdicating responsibility to the ECtHR or to other – more democratic – domestic institutions via the doctrine of deference. Each of these solutions has proved controversial.[85]

For all that the courts have done to manage this issue, they cannot avoid the fact that the material they are working with requires them to provide their own determination at a level of abstraction that they are generally ill-equipped to do. This is especially salient for cases which fall within the margin of appreciation where no further guidance can be drawn from the ECtHR. The historic common law approach to these kinds of cases, where there are a range of reasonable measures open to democratic authorities, has been to confine their focus to reviewing reasonableness. This has never been so light-touch as to amount to a review for sanity,[86] but it clearly differed from the kind of proportionality analysis used within human rights adjudication. One should not be too quick to declare sharp distinctions here, however. Values are an unavoidable part of adjudication in hard cases. The difference here is one of degree, with adjudication under the Human Rights Act requiring far more direct engagement with abstract value commitments than the common law has previously required of courts.

The central difference here lies in an understanding of moral and legal rights as fundamentally tied to obligations or duties, and an understanding of them as being fundamentally tied to interests. When framed in this way, some have concluded that international human rights law does not actually focus on rights at all. As Tasioulas notes, moral rights are associated with obligations, which are their normative content:

> In speaking about human rights, one is not simply appealing to a universal human interest, such as freedom from pain, or the interests in autonomy, knowledge, or friendship. Nor is one appealing to some other kind of deontic value, such as human dignity. Both universal human interests and human dignity are values that lie at the foundations

---

[85] See R Masterman, 'Deconstructing the Mirror Principle' in R Masterman and I Leigh (eds), *The United Kingdom's Statutory Bill of Rights: Constitutional and Comparative Perspectives* (Oxford, Oxford University Press, 2013) ch 5; Young (n 8); *cf* Allan, 'Human Rights and Judicial Review' (n 3).

[86] See M Foran, 'The Constitutional Foundations of Reasonableness Review: Artificial Reason and Wrongful Discrimination' (2022) 26 *ELR* 295.

of human rights; they are the underlying values that ground human rights claims. But they are not to be identified with human rights.[87]

Classic common law rights are a far better articulation of the moral rights of persons, at least in terms of their structure and normative content. When rights are understood by reference to the concrete obligations or duties that derive from general value commitments rather than the values themselves, important implications obtain for rights adjudication. Tasioulas identifies three key considerations that arise when moving from the underlying values to duty-imposing rights:

> (a) the putative obligation must be possible to comply with; (b) the obligation must not impose excessive burdens on duty bearers and others; and (c) the obligations associated with a given rights must satisfy a holistic constraint of being generally consistent with other rights.[88]

International human rights law has generally failed to respect these considerations.[89]

The European Convention on Human Rights and the jurisprudence of the ECtHR tend to fair better on these metrics, partially because there is a court which is tasked with interpreting and enforcing these rights in such a way that they are generally capable of being complied with, not overly burdensome on states and broadly compatible with the democratic authority of Member States. Still, there is one area where the ECtHR exemplifies many of the concerns raised by Tasioulas: proportionality.[90] The doctrine necessitates an exceptionally broad interpretation of rights which equates them with 'virtually any legally cognisable interest an individual may possess'.[91] With this expanded scope and content of rights, proportionality then has a tendency to attribute any plausible interference with these broad interests as an infringement standing in need of justification.

This is generally not the case at common law, where the scope of rights is of central importance, precisely because common law rights are concerned with obligations and duties which are conceptually resistant (if not immune) to being overridden by countervailing considerations.[92] If sufficient attention is paid to the scope of rights, many ostensible infringements which might prompt proportionality analysis simply do not arise. One reason for this is that there is no actual conflict between the right in question and the countervailing public interest. For example, in *R (WA) v Secretary of State for the Home Department*, the court was faced with a claimant who demanded the production of an official Biometric

---

[87] Tasioulas, 'Saving Human Rights from Human Rights Law' (n 7) 1179. See also J Tasioulas, 'On the Foundations of Human Rights' in R Cruft, SM Liao and M Renzo (eds), *Philosophical Foundations of Human Rights* (Oxford, Oxford University Press, 2015).

[88] Tasioulas, 'Saving Human Rights from Human Rights Law' (n 7) 1167. See also Tasioulas, 'On the Foundations of Human Rights' (n 87) 56–63.

[89] Tasioulas, 'Saving Human Rights from Human Rights Law' (n 7) 1183–1185. Tasioulas, 'Saving Human Rights from Human Rights Law' (n 7) 1183–85.

[90] See Alexy, 'Constitutional Rights' (n 43).

[91] Tasioulas, 'Saving Human Rights from Human Rights Law' (n 7) 1167. See also Alexy, 'Constitutional Rights' (n 43) 135.

[92] Kumm (n 44).

Residence Permit with a date of birth that he was extremely emotionally attached to, but which fell outwith the plausible range of birth dates as determined by the Home Department.[93] WA was an asylum seeker who had sustained torture as a child in Gaza and then physical and sexual abuse in Italy whilst on his way to the UK. His birth date was unknown, but local authorities determined that it fell within a range of plausible dates and that his preferred date was far beyond that range. In response to the refusal of the Home Secretary to reissue documentation with his preferred date, he began to starve himself and claimed that continued refusal would violate his right to life.

This case was brought under the Human Rights Act, Article 2 of which, the right to life, is unqualified. As such, proportionality analysis was not open to the court, so it had to take very seriously the nature of the obligations which actually arise from this right. It was not open to the court to do what Laws J did in *ex parte B*, where he attempted to expand the scope of the common law right to life to include the underlying interest in its entirety, leaving the real work to be done at the justification stage. Instead, the Court of Appeal engaged in careful analysis of the scope of the right to life and concluded that, although WA's situation was tragic, no obligation to review or change administrative decisions which might cause distress, even severe distress, will usually arise under the right to life.[94] Because the analysis of this case required attention to be paid to the actual duties which arise under the right in question, it was not possible to cast the right to include such broad duties as a requirement to publish false documents which could then be justifiably infringed in the interests of accuracy. When framed in this way, it seems very obvious why the right to life will not ordinarily give rise to duties of this kind.

This different framing helps make sense of the different conceptions of rights at play here: on one view, the scope of rights is tied to the duties they give rise to; on the other, the scope of rights is tied to the underlying interest they seek to protect. In *WA*, it was not the case that his right to life was infringed; on balance, it was not breached because there were important countervailing considerations relating to the accuracy of government records. Instead, no infringement occurred at all because the scope of WA's right simply did not extend so far as to demand the publication of inaccurate documentation. Rather than engage in proportionality analysis, the court did what is demanded by the classic common law approach: it determined the scope and content of the duties themselves and came to a conclusion as to the nature of the claimant's rights as a result of that. This is the kind of reasoning that courts are generally adept at. It will inevitably involve recourse to moral judgement, but value operates in the background; the court's central focus in on duty and obligation.

When cast in these more defined terms, courts are also better equipped to assess infringement, where the duty associated with a given right is engaged but its

---

[93] [2021] EWCA Civ 12.
[94] ibid [61]–[62].

normative force is overridden or outweighed by other important considerations.[95] Some rights are not subject to this kind of override, but many common law rights are, although they will arise in rare circumstances and demand compensation for their breach, even if it is justified. An example of this is the interest of liberty and the derived right not to be falsely imprisoned. A custodial sentence is not a justified infringement on this right precisely because the right does not extend to create a duty not to imprison criminals. Where someone is imprisoned in a manner which does engage the right, say a requirement to quarantine or isolate to prevent the spread of a dangerous pathogen, the confinement may infringe this right justifiably. In this instance, the right is genuinely engaged and has been infringed, but for justified and exceptional reasons. In such cases, the residual normative force of the right will mitigate in favour of some form of compensation or, at a minimum, an apology from legal officials in recognition of the infringement. Unjustified imprisonment would simply violate this right and would be covered under the duties captured and remedied by habeas corpus.

Proportionality analysis demands something quite different from courts by way of adjudication. By conflating rights with interests, it fails to adequately address the important role that duties or obligations play in identifying the scope of rights. The result is that proportionality analysis is 'too ready to find conflicts where there are none and, as a result, massively inflate[s] the category of infringements'.[96] This has the important consequence of centring values without tying them to duties or obligations. There are two key concerns here. The first is that, as Tasioulas notes, 'this is inconsistent with the fact that the normative content of rights is given by their associated obligations and that it belongs to the very idea of such an obligation that it is robustly (if not absolutely) resistant to being overridden'.[97] The decoupling of rights from defined duties transforms them into interests which do not have the salient features of rights. As Simmonds puts it,

> when all moral concerns are expressed as involving 'rights', we lose any sense of the precise way in which rights possess a special moral force. Rights come to be thought of as simply important interests that are to be balanced against other interests.[98]

This balancing means that rights are no longer considered to be robustly resistant to being overridden. The result is that 'a rights-holder does not have very much in virtue of having a right' precisely because they no longer carry any special moral weight beyond mere interests.[99] As Simmonds notes, 'when every important interest comes to be spoken of as a right, the distinct logic of rights is obscured'.[100]

Secondly, in severing rights from duties, proportionality analysis demands that courts focus not on the identification of what obligations plausibly arise

---

[95] See J Tasioulas, 'Taking Rights out of Human Rights' (2010) 120 *Ethics* 647.
[96] Tasioulas, 'Saving Human Rights from Human Rights Law' (n 7) 1189.
[97] ibid.
[98] Simmonds (n 7) 186.
[99] Kumm (n 44) 139.
[100] Simmonds (n 7) 187.

from a given right, but on whether a given policy pursues a legitimate governmental aim, interferes no more than is necessary with the protected interest in its
pursuit of that aim, and strikes a fair balance between the needs of the community and the interests of the claimant all things considered. This kind of reasoning
is quite alien to the traditional common law approach, which, while never
severed from value or underlying principles, manifests in a distinct method of
adjudication focused on the identification and enforcement of concrete duties
and entails entitlements which have peremptory force. Once rights are identified with the underlying interests, they lose this peremptory force and 'what is
left is a supposed "right" that is to a large extent unfeasible; and it is readily and
systematically overridden by competing considerations'.[101] When placed into the
hands of a judge, these considerations are expected to be balanced against one
another, with very little in the way of guidance. Value and interest occupy the
core of adjudication here.

There clearly has been a dramatic shift in constitutional understanding over
the last few decades, but it was not a move from liberties to rights protection.
Instead, we have seen a marked shift in how we understand and come to identify
the content of rights, coupled with the expansion of the concept to include general
values and interests. The doctrine of proportionality, as it arises in this context
and because it begins by casting the scope of rights so broadly, has a tendency
to describe as disproportionate policies and statutes which, on any metric, fall
within the range of reasonable options open to a legitimate democratic authority.
The common law embracement of a proportionality test similar to that which is
employed at the ECHR level does not necessarily represent a radical departure
from reasonableness review.[102] A grossly disproportionate policy is an unreasonable one, but assessment of proportionality, at least under the current tests, must
only arise where a genuine right infringement has occurred. Were the court to
confine itself to genuinely disproportionate decision-making, concerning genuine
right infringement that would breach the outermost limits of common law reason,
the outcome would be similar to reasonableness review, understood correctly to
account for important common law rights and principles.[103]

The Human Rights Act is part of a wider trend within Western legal thinking,
one which has expanded our understanding of rights. Contemporary rights theory
and doctrine recognises that there is some connection between the rights of the
individual and the common good, but they have perverted it. Rather than the classic understanding that rights and the common good are co-constitutive, with the
scope and content of one being dependent upon proper understanding of the other,
they are not presented as oppositional.[104] Rights can now be understood wholly

---

[101] Tasioulas, 'Saving Human Rights from Human Rights Law' (n 7) 1185.
[102] See *R v Secretary of State for the Home Department, Ex parte Daly* [2001] UKHL 26.
[103] See Foran (n 86).
[104] See Vermeule, *Common Good Constitutionalism* (n 70) 164–67.

separately from the good of the community, their scope and content informed by widely cast interests. Where the common good enters the picture, it is either to set down justifications for the infringement of rights or it is itself trumped by the rights in question. This approach is mistaken. An older way of thinking about rights, one which ties them to our obligations under justice and the common good, is being lost and that should be resisted.

5

Law and Politics: The Nightmare and the Noble Dream

SIR ROBERT BUCKLAND*

I. Introduction

Those who are privileged to serve as Lord Chancellor, as I did, have a unique responsibility with regard to our constitutional arrangements. As part of the executive, the Lord Chancellor naturally wants the government to be as effective as possible in delivering on its agenda. We should not apologise or be defensive about that in any way; it is what voters expect from their government. But at the same time, the Lord Chancellor has an important – a vital – duty to protect the judiciary, not just in the single jurisdiction of England and Wales, but throughout the UK.

As our system continues to evolve to serve the needs of our citizens, as it has over many centuries, the delicate balance between our institutions and the ways in which they interact between the nations of the UK inevitably requires fine tuning. The Lord Chancellor has a vital role to play in carrying out that work and, when I was holder of the office, I took forward a series of reviews to examine the balance in different contexts.

The first of these, established in 2019, set up the Independent Review of Administrative Law. I am pleased to say that the panel produced a fine report, which analysed the trends seen in judicial review over the previous decades, as well as evaluating the diverse views that are held about them. The following year, I launched a consultation outlining my proposals for reform which emanate from the panel's recommendations. The second review was the Independent Review of the Human Rights Act, chaired by Sir Peter Gross and established in 2020. That review was concerned with the operation of the various aspects of the Human Rights Act.

* This chapter is based on two speeches: one delivered at the conference 'UK Constitutional Reform: What Has Worked and What Hasn't', Queen Mary, University of London (25 March 2021) www.gov.uk/government/speeches/lord-chancellors-speech-law-and-politics-the-nightmare-and-the-noble-dream and one at the conference 'Johnson's Constitutional Reform Agenda', University College London (17 June 2021) www.gov.uk/government/speeches/lord-chancellor-speaks-at-ucl-conference-on-the-constitution.

Finally, I wanted to examine the role of the Lord Chancellor itself, in the context of the Constitutional Reform Act 2005. The Act brought in some sensible reforms, such as a greater degree of transparency in judicial appointments, but there are strands that are worth examining – to ensure that they have kept pace with the developments and continue to provide the appropriate framework for the Lord Chancellor to exercise their duties in respect of our constitutional arrangements.

In the days when the Lord Chancellor was not only a parliamentarian and a Cabinet minister, but also sat on the bench and appointed all their judicial colleagues, the role was often described as a 'linchpin' that linked all three branches of the state and managed the relationships between them. Walter Bagehot was somewhat unimpressed with this arrangement, describing the role as 'a heap of anomalies'.[1] My predecessor, Ken, now Lord, Clarke, said the role was difficult to explain to people in other political systems as it 'sounded like something ... made up'.[2] The only other Lord Chancellor to have hailed from my home town of Llanelli, Lord Elwyn-Jones, described it perhaps as only he could in a more kindly way as 'an object of wonderment and perplexity'.[3]

This chapter sets out some of my thinking about the office I held, as well as outlines the key aspects of the British constitution which I undertook to be reviewed while Lord Chancellor. I explain my purpose in clarifying key concepts, such as judicial review and the rule of law, and where I think the role of the Lord Chancellor could be used to address problematical areas of ambiguity which have arisen in recent years.

II. The Lord Chancellor Today

The office of the Lord Chancellor has evolved and changed over many, many centuries. While it is something of a personal relief that the title 'Keeper of the King's Conscience' is no longer in the job description, the office continues to have a hugely important constitutional role – in maintaining that incredibly fine balance that exists between our institutions and the ways in which they make, shape and enforce the law.

The Constitutional Reform Act 2005 made sweeping reforms to the office of Lord Chancellor, the extent of which was brought home to me when, on assuming office in 2019, I was obliged to resign my position as a Recorder of the Crown Court, a part-time judge. The Act aimed to answer questions about separation of powers, but the reality is that we do not have a perfectly neat and defined

---

[1] W Bagehot, *The English Constitution* (London, Chapman & Hall, 1867) 117.
[2] K Clarke, The Office of the Lord Chancellor, 'Oral Evidence to the Select Committee on the Constitution' (QQ 76–85), 22 October 2014, 51.
[3] N Underhill, *The Lord Chancellor* (Sudbury, Terence Dalton, 1978) Foreword.

separation of state powers – and I say amen to that. As a Tory, I accept and embrace the imperfections of the human condition and, indeed, of government. Instead, we have a system which is based on checks and balances. By changing the role of the Lord Chancellor in the ways that the Blair government did – remaining as part of the legislature and the executive but no longer the judiciary – we have lost the sense of the office being the linchpin between all three.

It is worth reminding ourselves that, contrary to regular commentary, Parliament today is not in my view the supine body it has been at times. It is better informed by the way outside bodies interact with it; it is a stronger scrutinising body certainly since the Tony Wright reforms; and more recently, since 2016 it has demonstrated an ability to flex its muscles on issues of huge national importance. It is no longer the Victorian child, someone who is seen and not heard. The fact that Parliament matters a lot more today and is more assertive than it once was is to be celebrated in a healthy democracy such as ours. While it does not necessarily make the day-to-day work of politics any more straightforward, I very much valued the effect that it has on our ability to make better law – for instance, the kind of cross-party working we saw on the Domestic Abuse Act 2021.

Since 2007, Lord Chancellors have been drawn from the House of Commons, which means that they are much more in the hurly burly of politics, with responsibilities, amongst others, for piloting legislation through the House, as I did with the Police, Crime, Sentencing, and Courts Bill. At the same time as taking on all of these responsibilities on behalf of the executive within the legislature, the role of Lord Chancellor continues to demand that those who hold the office remain detached from partisan politics in their duty to defend the judiciary. The one benefit to no longer themselves being a member of the judiciary is that the Lord Chancellor is able to offer, shall we say, much more detached commentary in upholding their oath to defend it. This is particularly helpful in discussing the question of where power lies in our country.

III. The Executive

Let us look then at each of these institutions. Firstly, the executive. The role of a modern Lord Chancellor can only be understood in the light of a modern government, and it seems to me that modern government is caught between two positions: firstly, that of constant suspicion about executive power; and secondly, one of constant expectation about the need for the government to assume that very power to 'take swift action'. And nowhere is this more obvious than in the adoption of secondary legislative powers as a basis of lawful activity, and in the ability via secondary powers to amend primary legislation, the so-called Henry VIII power.

The COVID-19 pandemic threw this issue into stark relief. The government imposed legislative restrictions on the clear understanding that they were to be temporary only, with reviews and sunset clauses to assure every one of their intentions. Suspicion remained, however. There is a historical hangover, perhaps, from the Civil War struggle between Parliament and the Crown, or rather, between Parliament and a particular interpretation of prerogative power, namely the divine right of kings – and we still live with tensions between different arms of the state today. I will not deny that there have been instances in ancient and, indeed, more modern political times where governments have overreached and have had to be checked. Governments are not perfect, but neither, generally speaking, do they have that insatiable appetite to ever expand their power and reach.

This argument has been described to me by its opponents as somewhat redolent of the way in which Frederick the Great described the attitude of Empress Maria Theresa of Austria on the partition of Poland in the 1770s: 'She cried, when she took; the more she cried, the more she took.' I see the point, but it misunderstands motive. The idea that governments of all hues are on a ceaseless mission to expand their power is, frankly, for the birds.

The government is very often all too glad to share or cede responsibility. It is constantly faced with cries of 'there ought to be a law against it', and when it acts to address those calls, often it accrues a little more authority and a little more power. This has consequences. The government has to constantly balance the need for action with its actual capacity to deliver. This is the real struggle and is the true explanation for the reluctance of government in many instances to seek more power. Because with more power comes more responsibility, and with more responsibility comes more financial cost. This, in itself, is, in my view, a key check against unrestrained government and 'elective dictatorship', so well written about by my predecessor, Lord Hailsham. And there are many other restraints, both formal and practical. Modern government is more Prometheus bound than unbound.

IV. The Judiciary

When it comes to the judiciary, its role and its approach, nowhere do these issues become more pertinent than in the area of judicial review. I think it is helpful from my vantage point, uniquely connected to the judiciary but no longer of it, to consider issues raised by none other than Professor HLA Hart, one of the foremost legal philosophers of the last century, in his 1977 Sibley lecture at the University of Georgia, entitled 'American Jurisprudence through English Eyes: The Nightmare and the Noble Dream'.[4]

In addressing the question of adjudication, especially higher court judges, Hart explained that there were two views on how the courts approach such a task, which he termed the Nightmare and the Noble Dream. Setting aside the purist view that,

---

[4] HLA Hart, 'American Jurisprudence through English Eyes: The Nightmare and the Noble Dream' (1977) 11 *Georgia Law Review* 969.

when faced with a dispute, judges simply apply existing law and do not create new law, Hart saw two extremes: firstly, the Nightmare of judges deciding dockets of moral and political questions, and then the Dream of judges threading fundamental principles through every case.

The Nightmare in Hart's scenario 'is that this image of the judge, distinguishing him from the legislator, is an illusion, and the expectations which it excites are doomed to disappointment – on an extreme view, always, and on a moderate view, very frequently'.[5] If adjudication were a true form of law-making rather than the application of existing laws, this would lead to worrying questions about how far judges' personally held views could form the basis of their legal decision-making.

An easy defence is that here in the UK not only, when selecting our judges, do we disregard their personal political views, but our constitution does not allow for primary legislation to be struck down by the courts. The very existence of the sovereignty of Parliament is at odds with the idea that judges could ever act as legislators and 'create' law, but, as I shall return to, the core idea of the Nightmare – that judges are placed into the position of legislators or political decision-makers – is not unimaginable.

Hart's Noble Dream is the belief that even when the law appears unclear or there exists no precedent, judges can still apply existing law and underlying principles 'which if consistently applied, would yield a determinate result' to their cases – and do so without creating new law.[6] Whether this dream can be said to apply in the UK is questionable, given, as I shall return to, our legal systems can contain conflicting principles, and there may be a number of legal sources which could be examined in seeking clarification. Judges are then left in the unenviable position of having to make law-making choices.

Hart concludes ultimately that the truth, as with so many things in life, is somewhere in the middle. In many cases, judges simply apply the law, but in others they have a discretionary field of judgement and actually have a choice to make about what the law should be. As Hart put it, 'It is not of course a matter of indifference but of very great importance which they do and when and how they do it'.[7]

Whilst Hart was speaking of the USA, quite a separate and distinct jurisdiction to ours, it is useful nearly 50 years on to consider where Britain stands on Hart's oneiric spectrum – and how the modern Lord Chancellor should react. Before the Supreme Court heard the appeal in the first *Miller* case, a newspaper carried a feature analysing how supposedly 'Europhile' the 11 judges were.[8] The rating of each was based upon their formal links to European institutions, any views they

---

[5] ibid 972.

[6] ibid 979.

[7] ibid 989.

[8] *R (on the application of Miller and another) v Secretary of State for Exiting the European Union* [2017] UKSC 5; 'Enemies of the People: Fury Over Out of Touch Judges Who Have Declared War on Democracy by Defying 17.4m Brexit Voters and Who Could Trigger Constitutional Crisis' *Daily Mail* (3 November 2016).

publicly expressed that seemed to be sympathetic to the EU and their close links to individuals who themselves might be pro-EU.[9]

In the end, there was no correlation whatsoever between the rating given and the way in which the judges ruled. Lord Sumption, imagined to be the only Eurosceptic, ruled with the majority; whilst Lords Carnwath and Reed, each imagined to be a Europhile, dissented. In this case, the Nightmare proved to be just that – a nightmare; a rather ridiculous one, but not at all easy for the judges, whose integrity was impugned and who could not defend themselves.

At the same time, the Noble Dream – the view that judges do nothing more than interpret and apply the law – is frequently aired in our country. For example, a former President of the Law Society said, 'A judge's ruling is an expression of the law – not of their personal opinion. It would be disingenuous to conflate the two'.[10] However, I am not the first to consider that this is not always true in every case. In an interesting lecture in 2020, Lord Sales described *R (Nicklinson) v Secretary of State for Justice* as

> a case literally involving questions of life and death, which called for a decision which balanced competing fundamental moral values. It also called for a decision which balanced competing fundamental institutional values in terms of whether the court should or should not strike the balance of moral values itself or accept the balance as struck by Parliament.[11]

The judges of the Supreme Court, holding the highest legal offices in the land, were not of one mind on what was the first-order question here or how it should be answered. If the courts had to answer moral and not legal questions themselves, wholly different from the sorts of questions which even the apex courts are accustomed to considering, this raises questions of what the proper description of the judicial role should be, how the government and Parliament should relate to them and how the Lord Chancellor should defend them.

I do not think it is controversial to say that there are questions on which a court should not be required to adjudicate. On one famous occasion, a former Chief Justice, Sir Edward Coke, told James I that no level of natural reasoning abilities made the king qualified to decide a case personally. Coke distinguished between natural reason 'accessible to individual rational minds' and by which 'law is measured', and artificial reason – technical, legal reasoning which requires long study of the law.[12] On this analysis, legislators use natural reason but judges

---

[9] G Adams, 'The judges and the people: Next week, 11 unaccountable individuals will consider a case that could thwart the will of the majority on Brexit. The Mail makes no apology for revealing their views – and many have links to Europe', *Daily Mail*, 2 December 2016, available at www.dailymail.co.uk/news/article-3995754/The-judges-people-week-11-unaccountable-individuals-consider-case-help-thwart-majority-Brexit-Mail-makes-no-apology-revealing-views-links-Europe.html.

[10] See 'Response to Supreme Court ruling', Law Society press release, 24 September 2019, available at https://web.archive.org/web/20200918164433/https://www.lawsociety.org.uk/contact-or-visit-us/press-office/press-releases/response-to-supreme-court-ruling.

[11] Lord Sales, 'Proportionality Review in Appellate Courts: A Wrong Turning?' (November 2020) 3, www.supremecourt.uk/docs/speech-181120.pdf.

[12] GJ Postema, 'Classical Common Law Jurisprudence (Part I)' (2002) 2 *Oxford University Commonwealth Law Journal* 178.

use artificial reason, and this distinction is an important one in determining what is being asked of our judiciary and so, in turn, how the Lord Chancellor should act.

Without wanting to get into a debate about whether everyone is equally good at natural reason, there is no objective metric by which it can be measured. Even if there were, judges in the UK are not appointed on that basis. And, as the late US Supreme Court Justice Antonin Scalia pointed out of his own bench, they would have no more, and, indeed, would likely have less, legitimacy to decide a moral question than nine randomly selected citizens – an inference which must be true even of our great judiciary.[13]

In a jurisdiction where a body of law lay out the settled moral and philosophical view of the nation and catered for all possible scenarios, no judge would ever be asked to exercise their own discretion. Despite the work of codifiers from Hammurabi through to Justinian and Napoleon, such a jurisdiction has never existed and, indeed, in the increasing complexity of the modern world seems further away than ever.

The USA has pursued a solution of considering the moral, political and philosophical dispositions of would-be judges in the appointment process. And we have all seen the results of that. As Lord Chancellor, I felt that this would indeed be a nightmare for the UK, which we should seek to avoid. Imagine if the newspaper story I mentioned earlier had been about the judges' views on assisted suicide – here we are back to the nightmare once again. But how best can the modern Lord Chancellor use their roles in the executive and legislature, and as advocate and defender of the judiciary, to avoid that very nightmare?

V. The Intention of Parliament

In her response to the Independent Review of Administrative Law call for evidence, Baroness Hale wrote that 'in the vast majority of cases, Judicial Review is the servant of Parliament'. In this kingdom, we in the government – the executive and the judiciary – are all servants of Parliament, which derives its authority from the people. But how do we know what it wants – particularly how it wants the executive and the judiciary to treat each other?

When Parliament grants a power to the executive, it also sets limits to how it can be used. These are the familiar grounds of judicial review. How those limits apply in a particular case essentially comes down to a question of statutory interpretation: did Parliament intend for the decision-maker to have the power to do it? The courts should not imply any limitations on a power which Parliament did not actually intend; and if Parliament intended not to put in some limitations, this must be respected.

---

[13] *Cruzan v Director, Missouri Department of Health* (1990) 110 S Ct 2841, 2859 (Scalia J); cited approvingly by Ward LJ in *Re A (Conjoined Twins)* [2000] EWCA Civ 254.

There is a cautionary tale to be found in the case of *Roberts v Hopwood*, where the Appellate Committee of the House of Lords held that the powers Parliament granted to local authorities had the implied condition that they should be exercised in accordance with a so-called fiduciary duty towards ratepayers.[14] Using this limitation of power that they had just discovered, the courts decided that a council could not set a minimum wage for its employees. So much so that this rule was nicknamed by some mischievous souls as 'the rule against socialism'![15] The powers of local government have changed since then, but the legal problem of a constitutional problem raised is not simply theoretical.

On the other hand, the continued failure of the courts to give full effect to ouster clauses is a cause for concern. As Lord Chancellor, I sought to ensure that Parliament's instructions were clearer to both the executive and the judiciary. Although I am no longer personally a law officer of the Crown, I had a duty to uphold the rule of law. The Independent Review of Administrative Law panel said that ouster clauses, when they are used in relation to specific decisions and powers, do not contravene the rule of law, and so should be upheld.

Nonetheless, we are yet to see an ouster clause where Parliament was held to have been clear enough in its language to be given full effect by the courts. Indeed, even the previous Labour government, with a majority north of 150 at one stage, ran into problems in attempting to get an ouster clause through Parliament, which sought to clarify the law in the broadest terms possible. So, I believe it is for Parliament to clarify its instructions to the courts in this situation to ensure Parliament's intentions are observed.

More generally, the risk of the Nightmare arises most commonly from legislation which lacks the kind of clarity that the rule of law demands in a modern and mature democracy like ours. A legal system as complex and advanced as ours will always fills gaps in legislation – and that is in the interests of litigants. We must be honest about the fact that rushed and poorly drafted legislation leaves those gaps and judges have an unenviable task in filling them. At best, it is a Parliament shirking its duty which leaves jurists uncertain of whether it did or did not intend a certain outcome; at worst, it is contracting out its own decision-making function. That tendency only creates more problems for those who must interpret the law.

Governments of all complexions have a clear responsibility to draft better, clearer laws that protect the judiciary from having the responsibility to do our jobs for us. It must surely be an important part of the role of the modern Lord Chancellor to be the keenest advocate in government of precise and clear legislation. As a Cabinet minister, I had the tools to challenge my colleagues to produce only the best legislation, but as in all things, I could not guarantee perfection.

Like any minister of the Crown, I have a general responsibility to ensure that statutes passed through Parliament continue to be consistent with the rule of law. It was also my responsibility, along with the Leader of the House of Commons,

---

[14] *Roberts v Hopwood* (1925) AC 578.
[15] P Fennel, '*Roberts v Hopwood*: The Rule Against Socialism' (1986) 13 *Journal of Law and Society* 401.

as chair of the Parliamentary Business and Legislation Committee of Cabinet, to cajole and to encourage each and every government department to consider whether the legislation they put before Parliament was properly thought through, well drafted, unlikely to export policy questions to the courts and consistent with the rule of law.

For example, with the mental health provisions of the Coronavirus Act 2020, it was decided ultimately that, as the measures were not used, it made abundant sense not to renew them. Now, that review enshrined in the legislation was a useful process and proportional to the need at the time. It meant that renewal of the Act as a whole was not simply a rubber stamp exercise, which should never happen without proper regard to the rule of law.

Indeed, one of the core functions of the Law Officers of the Crown, and having been Solicitor General I am well familiar with its practice, is to make sure that the government acts lawfully and that it respects the rule of law. For example, if the government wants to propose retrospective legislation, this requires the consent of the Law Officers. This ensures respect for the principle of no excessive use of retrospective legislation, which is a core component of the rule of law, as well as certainty, which is an inherent element. But as the minister leading the Ministry of Justice, I believed it was incumbent upon me to ensure that the rule of law itself could not be misused to in effect weaponise the courts against political decision-making.

This is particularly acute when our domestic law interacts with that of another jurisdiction. In the EU, the supremacy of the European Court of Justice (CJEU) was the extreme answer to this tension between the Union and its Member States. New case law of the CJEU is, of course, no longer a matter for our courts, but how to maintain clarity for the courts was amongst the most technically and politically fraught parts of legislating for our exit. In the European Court of Human Rights, the evolution of the European Convention on Human Rights and our domestic law has increased the complexity and decreased the clarity of the law in cases like *Nicklinson*.

Achieving that clarity is a responsibility placed upon the Lord Chancellor and on the government, but each institution of the state has a responsibility to maintain and respect balance in our system. Writing about the recent decision of the Supreme Court in the *Shamima Begum* case – where the Court made the determination that ministers are better equipped than judges to make decisions relating to national security and that resolving such matters through litigation lacked democratic legitimacy – one of its former members, Lord Sumption, noted that it marked 'a return to a more cautious approach to the judicial control of ministerial decisions'.[16] His assessment – that it goes some way to restoring a balance between Parliament and the courts which understands the realities and the proper role of each institution within a democracy – has much more to say about the ongoing

---

[16] *R (on the application of Begum) v Secretary of State for the Home Department* [2021] UKSC 7.

relationship between the executive and the judiciary than it does about the decisions of the current government.[17]

VI. Judicial Review and the Rule of Law

Judicial review is a vital check on unbridled power, and it is precisely for this reason that we should review how it operates – to ensure that there remains that essential balance between Parliament and the courts.

While there are those who would say that there are too few occasions when the process of judicial review goes wrong and that this exercise is somehow a waste of energy, I would say that we have a clear responsibility as custodians of our constitution to make it work as well as possible for as much of the time as possible. And when I say 'we', I am talking about all of us – Parliament, the executive and the judiciary – it is a collective responsibility, and the way we arrive at solutions is through dialogue, whether that plays out in Parliament, the courts or, indeed, in government.

In the final analysis, however, we should be crystal clear that the executive and judiciary are servants of Parliament, which derives its authority from the people – and ultimately this is the place where all the debates culminate. I think it is unhelpful to be drawn into arguments about where power is derived from, and anyone who would make out that I have relegated the judiciary to 'mere servants' has frankly missed the point.

In any event, our preoccupation should be with intent, not function – so, for example, it should be with what Parliament intended for the powers it gives to others. I believe there are two important parts to this. In a democracy as mature and complex as ours – where any gaps in legislation will naturally be filled – parliamentarians have a responsibility to ensure that laws are carefully drafted and therefore to avoid situations where judges are called upon to adjudicate on avoidable ambiguity. Now, at the same time, it is incumbent upon judges to be cautious in their decision-making and to ensure that their judgments properly reflect the intent of our elected Parliament. In this regard, all of us have a responsibility to maintain the balance.

It is worthwhile, therefore, to examine precisely what is meant by the term 'rule of law'. In the modern context, there is, I believe, some confusion about what the rule of law really means. Now, it is true that there are a number of interpretations and potential component parts, but my worry is that it has been the victim of conceptual creep, which leaves it open to hijack from politically motivated interests. The effect this is having is to set up a false dichotomy between the rule of law and parliamentary supremacy itself.

---

[17] J Sumption, 'Supreme Court rules that home secretary is the best judge of national security risk', *The Times*, 4 March 2021, available at www.thetimes.co.uk/article/supreme-court-rules-that-home-secretary-is-the-best-judge-of-national-security-risk-rfs067gw9.

The task of the courts in interpreting legislation is to give effect to the intention of Parliament. This is done by looking at the words of the statute in context. As part of this exercise, courts will use certain general presumptions. Some of those presumptions can be said to reflect the value of the rule of law. For example, it can be seen by the presumption against retrospective legislation. As Bennion puts it, the rule is as follows:

- Unless the contrary intention appears, an enactment is presumed not to be intended to have a retrospective operation.
- The strength of the presumption varies from case to case, depending on the degree of unfairness that would result from giving the enactment retrospective effect.
- The greater the unfairness the clearer the language required to rebut the presumption.[18]

There are a couple of points to make about this. First of all, the presumption helps to ensure compliance with the rule of law; secondly, the presumption can be said to reflect Parliament's general intentions; and thirdly, the presumption is rebuttable – and, indeed, where the legislation is expressly retrospective, the courts will give effect to it even if they think it might be unfair. The Law Officers play an important role here through the consent process, and they give impartial and invaluable legal advice as independent guardians of the rule of law within the government.

A number of other presumptions and rules of interpretation can be said to give effect to the rule of law. There is also the principle of legality, according to which legislation, and in particular vague and general words, will be presumed not to be contrary to certain fundamental rights and principles. On a high level of generality, that is perfectly proper, but, as the late Sir John Laws put it: 'The rule of law is a Protean conception. Different meanings have been variously ascribed to it. It possesses many different facets, and has generated an enormous literature.'[19]

The rule of law itself is not a legal concept; rather, it is a concept of political morality about the way in which we are and should be governed. Although it is a political principle, it is one which is above, and must always be above, party politics – a commitment to the rule of law is something which we all share. This makes it an extremely powerful concept, and a failure to abide by it gives rise to criticisms which are not grounded in mere party politics.

This has given rise to the possibility of abuse in political debates. Those of both the left and the right have tried to read controversial political values into it. Hayek railed against the notion that policies such as the welfare state could be defended on the grounds that 'social justice' was a requirement of the rule of law.[20] Dicey thought that administrative discretion was incompatible with it, which for him

---

[18] D Feldman, D Bailey and A Norbury, *Bennion, Bailey, and Norbury on Statutory Interpretation*, 8th edn (London, LexisNexis Butterworths, 2020) 7.14.

[19] *Cart* [2009] EWHC 3052 (Admin), [35].

[20] F Hayek, *The Constitution of Liberty* (Chicago, University of Chicago Press, 1960).

meant that government involvement in the running of the economy, for example by issuing licences, was improper.[21]

This sort of argument suggests that one group's policies can be characterised as incompatible with the basic principles of our legal system and, thus, as illegitimate, without the need to engage with them on their merits. Now, does this not amount to moving the goalposts so that, no matter the will of the people and no matter the will of Parliament, a political result that is deemed undesirable by one side or the other can be deemed illegitimate in the name of the rule of law, no matter how loosely connected to that concept it really is?

That is not to say that the courts must never play a role in ensuring that the rule of law is respected – of course they should do so where it is right and proper. There will always exist a natural tension in that possibility – the question is how we respond to it. Part 5 of the UK Internal Markets Bill, regarding the Northern Ireland Protocol, is a classic example where that tension became abundantly clear. Some of the arguments around it were political ones, but the problem was that they were framed incorrectly in a constitutional way – almost as if to suggest that they were somehow more fundamental than they really were. In all too rapid a succession of events, observations about the rule of law soon descended into allegations of 'breaking the law' which is an entirely different thing!

It is, I believe, perfectly possible to avoid that sort of wrangling by being much clearer about what the rule of law means and how it interacts with politics. Political positions are not the preoccupation of the rule of law, nor should they be. Anyone who attempts to characterise them as such is, in my view, overreaching. This is an example of what Professor Tasioulas calls 'conceptual overreach'. According to him, this occurs when 'a particular concept undergoes a process of expansion or inflation in which it absorbs ideas and demands that are foreign to it'. The ultimate consequence of it is that 'a single concept … is taken to offer a comprehensive political ideology'. Tasioulas points out that this runs the risk of diluting those concepts and also that it makes public debate more difficult 'because it makes it difficult to find any point of common ground or shared understanding with [those we disagree with]'.[22]

In the context of statutory interpretation, there is another danger to guard against. If the courts end up reading too much into the rule of law, we could get into a situation where they do not give effect to Parliament's intention because they applied the presumption when it should not have been applied. When adopting a strained interpretation on the grounds that not to do so would lead to an outcome that is contrary to legal policy, the courts are on much stronger grounds when assessing the requirements of the rule of law, where it is uncontroversial that one possible outcome in a case would be an unfair one.

---

[21] AV Dicey, *An Introduction to the Study of the Law of the Constitution*, 10th edn (first edition published in 1885, ECS Wade ed, London, Macmillan, 1959) 205.
[22] J Tasioulas, 'The Inflation of Concepts' (*Aeon*, 29 January 2021) https://aeon.co/essays/conceptual-overreach-threatens-the-quality-of-public-reason.

Take, for example, *R v Registrar General* – where a convicted murderer applied to get the name of his birth mother under the Adoption and Children Act 2002.[23] Now, the terms of that statute were absolute. However, there was a real risk that he may cause serious harm or even worse to her if he got this information. The Court of Appeal held that, notwithstanding the absolute terms of the statute, the court should presume that Parliament did not intend for such a result as it would quite clearly be against public policy. In the absence of any evidence that Parliament had addressed its mind to this issue, the court interpreted the statute as not requiring disclosure. I think we can all recognise that disclosure would have been unjust. There is no need to appeal to contested premises for this. So, I believe the courts were on safe territory in using this as a trigger for saying 'we won't allow this outcome unless we can be sure Parliament really intended this'.

But the situation is otherwise when it comes to other decisions where the rule of law has been invoked. In the case of *Privacy International*,[24] there was a disagreement between the majority and the minority on whether it could be consistent with the rule of law to allow the Investigatory Powers Tribunal to make ordinary errors of law. In *Evans v Attorney General*, there was a disagreement between the majority and the minority on whether the rule of law was infringed by the ministerial veto provision under the Freedom of Information Act.[25] In both cases, this led the majority to require the clearest words (which were not present) to give the effect intended by the government. By contrast, the minority applied a more natural interpretation to those provisions.

With any principle, there are going to be borderline cases in terms of how it is applied. But these cases were not instances of everyone agreeing on the applicable concept, realising that its application was borderline and then coming out on different sides of the line. Rather, there was a substantive disagreement about what the relevant principles were. That disagreement was obscured by the use of the term 'rule of law'. In *Privacy International*, Lord Carnwath thought that it was important 'to ensure that the law applied by the specialist tribunal is not developed in isolation ([to coin a phrase] "a local law"), but conforms to the general law of the land'.[26] Lord Sumption did not share that view or apply that principle. Neither did Lord Wilson.

It is also noteworthy that in both *Privacy International* and *Evans* those who dissented thought that the meaning was perfectly clear but those in the majority did not. Why is this important? Because legislating is an act of communicating to the courts what the legislature intends. For such communication to be possible, it is necessary to speak the same language. Provided that there is a shared understanding of when certain interpretative presumptions apply, and what level of clarity is required to rebut that presumption, then there is no difficulty.

---

[23] *R v Registrar General, ex p Smith* [1991] 2 QB 393.
[24] *R (on the application of Privacy International) v Investigatory Powers Tribunal and others* [2019] UKSC 22.
[25] *R (Evans) v Attorney General (Campaign for Freedom of Information intervening)* [2015] UKSC 21.
[26] *R (on the application of Privacy International) v Investigatory Powers Tribunal* [2019] UKSC 22, [139].

For things like the presumption against retrospectivity, this is perfectly clear. But the more high-level the presumption is stated at, such as by appeal to protean concepts like the rule of law or fundamental common law rights, the more difficulty this causes. In such cases, there is a great degree of scope for reasonable disagreement over whether the rule of law has been infringed. After all, when enacting the provisions at issue in *Privacy International* and *Evans*, Parliament did not believe that it was infringing the rule of law (and, indeed, the judges in the minority in both cases agreed). It was also perfectly clear, as the minority recognised, what Parliament actually intended. Provided Parliament's assessment was not wholly unreasonable, it does not appear to me to be right to frustrate that intention by, in the absence of the clearest possible words, saying that actually this does breach the rule of law and so a presumption against the interpretation applies and it can only be rebutted by words that are even clearer to what Parliament has used.

There is here, I think, an interesting contrast with the Human Rights Act. It is true that in the vast majority of cases Parliament believes that the legislation it enacts is compatible with ECHR rights. Nonetheless, the courts can disagree and can read down the provision to ensure compatibility. But, importantly, they can do so because Parliament has given them that power – the power to determine whether the legislation is compatible with the Convention and the power to read it down. That is what makes this legitimate. However, section 1 of the 2005 Constitutional Reform Act cannot be said to enact something similar with regard to the rule of law.

The case law on all this is in a state of flux – you can see, for example, the careful judgments of Lord Reed and Lord Carnwath in *Elgizouli*,[27] and there is plenty of very good academic commentary on it.[28] Taking all of this together, this gives me a high degree of confidence that the courts will indeed end up in a benign and stable position.

I would like us to end up in a position where the courts only read down legislation in cases where there is a clear and unarguable breach of the core components of the rule of law. If we are to protect the rule of law from becoming a political football, then we must ensure that its focus continues to be laser sharp, rather than allowing it to become amplified as a weapon to fight battles of politics. It is a concept which is quite rightly above politics. It exists to protect the principles of justice, not to advance somebody's political agenda.

VII. Reform of the Reform Agenda

Today, the Lord Chancellor's duties are to properly balance our constitutional arrangements, and so to protect the judiciary. To maintain a clear delineation

---

[27] *Elgizouli v Secretary of State for the Home Department* [2020] UKSC 10.
[28] JNE Varuhas, 'The Principle of Legality' (2020) 79 *CLJ* 578.

about where the power lies, one must avoid drawing judges into the political realm and forcing them to adjudicate on moral or philosophical issues. The best solution is to avoid getting into this situation in the first place by Parliament taking the lead and ensuring that the discretionary field of judgement is appropriately construed.

I agree with Lord Sales that, when faced with an unclear statutory provision, the court should seek to construe it by 'looking to infer what the legislating Parliament would have decided had it addressed itself directly to the issue at hand'.[29] But in doing so, the courts should not be asked to replace Parliament's reasoning with their own. The responsibility to avoid dragging the courts into moral and political issues does not lie solely with the judges; Parliament and the executive also have a vital role in this regard. We must confront the fact that there have been instances where Parliament glossed over its own divisions by passing legislation that was vague and which had the effect (if not the intention) of exporting the determination of certain moral or political issues to judges. I want us to be clear about where the power lies and why; and to strike a balance in our constitutional arrangements – on which issues the courts should adjudicate, and in doing so how they should adjudicate them.

Some have suggested that the constitutional reform agenda of the Conservative government elected in 2019 is some sort of authoritarian executive power grab, but I think Colm O'Cinneide got it right when he said we are attempting to return to the political constitution model that was the orthodoxy for much of the twentieth century.[30] This is not to grab power for the executive, and I reject the notion that the government is something to be mistrusted fundamentally. I do, however, believe it will be possible to achieve a balance that reflects the realities of the modern justice system and the world in which we live today. The truth is that neither the executive nor the judges are, to borrow a regrettable and wholly wrong headline, 'Enemies of the People'. Far from it, we are both the servants of Parliament and the people. And in that common endeavour, the balance of our constitution will be maintained.

I want to restore what was at one time the very conventional thinking that parliament makes laws that give power to the executive and are checked by the judiciary. When given the opportunity to address our foremost thinkers on our constitution, I hope that it is possible to open up a debate about the rule of law and what sovereignty means today. My view is that we diminish the former by allowing it to be applied in that overtly political way, and we damage the latter by expecting the courts to adjudicate on the expressed will and intent of Parliament.

---

[29] Lord Sales, 'In Defence of Legislative Intention' (November 2019) 16, www.supremecourt.uk/docs/speech-191119.pdf.
[30] C O'Cinneide, 'The UK's Post-Brexit "Constitutional Unsettlement"' *Verfassungsblog*, 16 April 2021, available at https://verfassungsblog.de/the-uks-post-brexit-constitutional-unsettlement/.

PART II

Westminster and Whitehall

6

The Fixed-term Parliaments Act 2011: Out, Out Brief Candle

ROBERT CRAIG

I. Introduction

This chapter comes not to praise the Fixed-term Parliaments Act 2011 (FTPA), but to bury it. The theme of this edited collection is scepticism about the myriad constitutional reforms since 1997. The FTPA must be a leading contender for the most damaging constitutional change of this period, although the competition is fierce. Its demise is likely to be welcomed by those who value the traditional constitution. It must be recalled that its unpopularity in Westminster was such that *both* major parties committed to its repeal in their manifestos at the 2019 general election.[1] The Act repealing the FTPA – the Dissolution and Calling of Parliament Act 2022 (DACPA) – received Royal Assent in March 2022. It restores the previous tried and tested approach.

Unmoored, unpopular and unlamented, the indefatigable defenders of the FTPA will no doubt agitate for a similar Act in the decades to come. The experience gained from the problems caused by the first attempt, however, are not likely to be forgotten in a hurry. With luck, the abject failure of the experimental attempt to fix the term of parliaments in the 2010s will have permanently jinxed the idea – in a similar way to the seemingly long-term damage inflicted by the 2011 Alternative Vote referendum to the cause of electoral reform. The FTPA has strutted and fretted its hour upon the stage, and it is to be hoped that it is heard no more.

The detailed terms of the FTPA were the result of slightly grubby negotiations behind closed doors and the machinations by various parties as to its terms would not have looked out of place in the 'smoke-filled rooms' made infamous in the 1970s.[2] Before the FTPA, the Prime Minister had the power to precipitate a general election by a process called dissolving Parliament. The legal power to

---

[1] See https://labour.org.uk/wp-content/uploads/2019/11/Real-Change-Labour-Manifesto-2019.pdf, 82; www.conservatives.com/our-plan/conservative-party-manifesto-2019, 48.

[2] D Laws, *22 Days in May* (London, Biteback, 2010) 183–84.

do this was technically vested in the Crown as one of the remaining 'prerogative powers'. These are a set of residual, but sometimes very important legal powers, duties and rights historically possessed by the monarch but now exercised on the advice of ministers. It is entirely appropriate that these historical legal powers are nowadays exercised on the advice of the democratically elected executive branch. Dissolution of Parliament was, and now will be again, a paradigm example of such a prerogative power.

In the modern era, the prerogative power to dissolve Parliament was always exercised on the advice of the Prime Minister.[3] The revival of the prerogative power of dissolution by DACPA does, however, mean that there has been a renewal of speculation about the exercise of the power in some unusual hypothetical circumstances.[4] In particular, there remains the slightly thorny question of whether the monarch could possibly decline to dissolve Parliament. This chapter addresses this issue, but also considers the wider constitutional implications of the restoration of the previous system by DACPA.[5]

This chapter focuses on issues raised by the repeal of the FTPA by DACPA and the revival of the prerogative power to call an election within the maximum five-year term. The first section addresses the doctrine of confidence. It is suggested that this doctrine's central importance needs to be clearly explained and articulated in order to illustrate the deleterious effects of the FTPA on the constitutional balance of the UK.

The second section considers the way in which the FTPA affected that constitutional balance. Repeal of the FTPA means the restoration of the constitutional balance that had been distorted by it. Prior to the FTPA, both of the key forces within Parliament had the power to bring about a general election: on the one hand, the government could ask for a dissolution; on the other hand, MPs could pass a vote of no confidence in the government, thus precipitating a dissolution of Parliament outside some fairly unusual factual scenarios. This constitutional balance was undermined by the FTPA, which removed the power of the government to threaten a general election without Commons approval, and is considered in section III. The restoration of that balance is to be welcomed.

The fourth section deals with some of the implications of returning to the status quo ante. The final section deals with an unusual aspect of DACPA, which is a clause, known as an 'ouster clause', that attempts to stop the courts ever considering an application for judicial review in respect of a decision to dissolve Parliament.

---

[3] There is some dispute over whether a dissolution is requested or advised, the distinction being that the former is said to be something that can be refused, whereas the latter is not. The question of any alleged residual discretion possessed by the monarch is discussed further below. Reform of the prerogative of dissolution was in both the Labour (s 9:3) and Liberal Democrat (p 88) manifestos in 2010.

[4] See discussion in Joint Committee on the Fixed-Term Parliaments Act, *Report of Session 2019–21* (2019–21, HL 253, HC 1046) [124]–[145], https://committees.parliament.uk/publications/5190/documents/52402/default/, addressed further below.

[5] Dissolution and Calling of Parliament Act 2022, s 3. Final debate in the House of Lords on 22 March 2022: https://parliamentlive.tv/Event/Index/889d1c3f-6f0b-41ac-8324-ad755dc30433.

This follows what was for many observers the surprising decision of the Supreme Court to interfere in the prorogation of Parliament in 2019 in the *Miller II* case.[6] The chapter addresses whether the attempt to exclude the courts from this area through such an ouster clause would be effective and considers some recent commentary suggesting that such a clause would be ineffective.

II. Constitutional Balance

A. The Doctrine of Confidence

The British constitution is known for prizing flexibility and pragmatism over ideological purity. The FTPA had a major impact on the delicate pre-existing constitutional balance that existed prior to its passage. In particular, it prevented the executive from being able to call a general election. This detrimentally affected the dynamic balance within Parliament between the government and MPs which the restoration of the previous system will restore. The largest benefit of reviving the dissolution prerogative via DACPA is the resurrection of real reciprocity within Parliament, which was damaged by the FTPA. This interdependence had developed over time into a sophisticated symbiotic relationship, with the ultimate sanction of calling a general election being available to *both* the government and MPs. This potential for mutually assured destruction was fundamental to the balance between the two key democratic forces within Parliament. The FTPA detrimentally altered that delicate balance, thankfully only temporarily.

The British system has grown organically, lacking the kind of top-down 'rational' structure exhibited by, say, the French system, which is famous for reflecting a 'pure' separation of powers.[7] Many of the resulting processes and systems are haphazard and piecemeal, a function of legacy rather than theory. Nevertheless, it is fair to say that as the system has adapted to changing circumstances, the tensions and pressures in the system have evolved to reflect developments over time in highly flexible and responsive ways. This organic system of accountability is sometimes known as the partial separation of powers.[8] One of the most ancient of the malleable concepts that is illustrative of this chameleonic process is the doctrine of confidence.

The doctrine of confidence has undergone radical change over the centuries. It originated in the notion that the king can do no wrong, which itself was, and to some extent still is, seen as a function of prerogative power.[9] In its most basic

---

[6] *R (Miller) v Prime Minister; Cherry v Advocate General for Scotland* [2020] AC 373; [2019] UKSC 41; 3 WLR 589; [2019] 4 All ER 299 (*Miller II*).

[7] C Munro, *Studies in Constitutional Law*, 2nd edn (Oxford, Butterworths, 1999) 302.

[8] ibid.

[9] AV Dicey, *An Introduction to the Study of the Law of the Constitution*, 8th edn (London, Macmillan, 1927) 246; *Council for the Civil Service Unions v Minister for the Civil Service* [1985] AC 374, 409.

form, the concept simply reflected the fact that the monarch could not be criticised directly. This was partly due to respect for the office, with its alleged divine mandate, and partly through the practical politics of the potentially dangerous consequences of criticising the monarch. This reality is what led to the novel doctrine that the king could only ever be in error through poor or faulty *advice*. This meant that blame was attributed to the king's advisers, who would thereby come under political pressure. The king could blame the advisers and sack (or even execute) them precisely because they had lost his confidence due to their faulty advice. It can be seen, therefore, that the archetype of the doctrine of confidence goes back centuries. It long predates democracy in this country.

The original conception of the doctrine of confidence broke down in the seventeenth century. Famously, Earl Strafford bitterly remarked on the wisdom of putting your trust in princes as he was forced, fatally, to take the blame as a proxy for the early mistakes and failures of Charles I's rule.[10] This only postponed the inevitable and ultimate confrontation between the Crown and Parliament that culminated in the Civil War and eventually the final defeat and execution of the king. The Glorious Revolution saw the resulting *transfer* of supreme legal and constitutional power from the monarch to the King-in-Parliament – or, as it is now more accurately known, the Crown-in-Parliament.[11] This entrenched the checks and balances approach that marks the British constitution because it moved the centralised decision-making power from the Crown to the Crown-in-Parliament. In the latter, the decisions of the government are subjected to considerable scrutiny and debate. A direct result of that change was the fact that both the executive and the legislature were then drawn from inside a parliament that is a conglomerate of both elements. The two limbs were, and remain, fused – the very opposite of the notion of a pure separation of powers.[12]

Although absolutely not designed to achieve this goal, this fusion permanently achieved the constitutional *balance* that is the key theme of this section. No longer were advisers to the monarch determined by the king on a whim. On the contrary, it slowly became clear that in a constitutional monarchy, the confidence that ministers needed to maintain was no longer that of the monarch, but of Parliament.[13] Thus, the ancient doctrine of confidence gradually moved its centre of gravity with the times and thus converted Parliament to the great debating chamber of the nation, where to this day government ministers must justify their policies and be held to account. This constitutional requirement is known as the responsible government view and flows directly from the confidence doctrine. As is well known, the government must nowadays maintain the confidence of the House of

---

[10] A Cromartie, *The Constitutionalist Revolution* (Cambridge, Cambridge University Press, 2006) 257–59.

[11] *R (Jackson) v Attorney General* [2005] UKHL 56, [2006] 1 AC 262, [2005] 3 WLR 733, [2005] 4 All ER 1253, [9] (Lord Bingham).

[12] Munro (n 7) 322–28.

[13] Munro (n 7) 303–04.

Commons and is held responsible to it for its decisions.[14] This simply means that until and unless the Commons brings down a government through a vote of no confidence, the government can be presumed to have the right to continue governing in accordance with its policy platform and its electoral mandate.

B. The Effect of Democracy on the Confidence Doctrine

The democratisation of the system has further altered the doctrine of confidence. Historically, it could fairly be said that the processes of constitutional accountability in effect were contained within Parliament and the groupings were more fluid. If a government fell, then an alternative grouping of MPs could form a slate and put itself forward as being best placed to command the confidence of Parliament. As Bagehot pointed out, the Cabinet was originally just one committee of Parliament.[15] Parliament could vote to dissolve that committee and appoint another in its place. In this original sense, the confidence doctrine was confined within Parliament. This has now changed. In a modern democratic assembly, MPs directly represent their constituents. The representative function of MPs is not new, but has gained increased force as direct democratic electoral accountability has bedded in. The overwhelming importance of that democratic mandate has affected the doctrine of confidence in important ways.

The doctrine of confidence within the Commons slowly developed as the requirement to maintain the confidence of the *representatives* of each constituency. Crucially, however, the doctrine of confidence now operates at two different levels. If the government loses the confidence of the representatives of the people, it has (except whilst the FTPA was in force) the option of seeking the confidence of the people directly unless an alternative government could be formed.

> [T]he reason why the House can in accordance with the constitution be deprived of power and of existence is that an occasion has arisen on which there is fair reason to suppose that the opinion of the House is not the opinion of the electors.[16]

The mechanism by which this was achieved requires some unpacking. When the Crown dominated the country, with Parliament as a subordinate adjunct, there could be long periods where Parliament would not sit. The sitting of Parliament was naturally controlled by the divinely mandated monarch, who could use his or her prerogative powers to call Parliament to sit, to prorogue (suspend) Parliament and ultimately to dissolve it at his or her pleasure.

After the Civil War and Glorious Revolution, executive power was effectively transferred over time inside Parliament and conferred on the Cabinet.[17] It became

---

[14] Dicey (n 9) 210.

[15] W Bagehot, *The English Constitution* (first published 1867, edited with an Introduction and Notes by Miles Taylor) (Oxford, Oxford University Press, 2001) 11.

[16] Dicey (n 9) 288.

[17] Dicey (n 9) 305.

clear that this body had then acquired, at least de facto, the prerogative powers once exercised by the monarch. This included wielding the powers to prorogue and dissolve Parliament, as well as other important legal powers such as royal assent, the final stage by which Bills passed by the two Houses become Acts of Parliament. Most importantly, perhaps, ministers inherited the power to propose legislation and, therefore, to govern the country as a matter of law. In essence, governance passed from the unelected monarch to the elected government. The power to dissolve Parliament and call a general election, in particular, created a constitutional balance in Parliament whose importance is difficult to understate.

Once it became clear that the government had the power to advise the monarch to call an election, it can be seen that both branches possessed a 'nuclear option' to which they could resort at any time to put the future governance and direction of the country to the people. The government could dissolve Parliament and precipitate an election. MPs had an equal and opposite power to pass a vote of no confidence in the government which would either see an alternative government installed, spelling the end of the original government, or a general election being called.[18] Dicey puts it well.

> the right of dissolution ... enables the ... Ministry to appeal from the legislature to the nation ... The right of dissolution is the right of appeal to the people, and thus underlies all those constitutional conventions which ... are intended to produce harmony between the legal and the political sovereign power.[19]

The FTPA rolled back the democratisation of Parliament by constraining the power of the executive to make a direct appeal to the electorate. In a sense, the FTPA therefore made Parliament less democratic by diminishing the executive's right of appeal to, and direct accountability to, the electorate.[20]

C. Bifurcated Votes at General Elections

The mechanism of choosing both government and MPs also had an important effect. Historically, MPs were chosen locally, albeit sometimes on an opaque basis, to represent their area and seek the redress of grievances from the Crown. This function remains an important aspect of an MP's role in the modern system. Some take the view that the purpose and mandate conferred by a general election relates solely to the election of MPs – this view holds that *only* MPs, *qua* MPs, secure a

---

[18] It should be noted that s 22(6) of the Parties, Elections and Referendums Act 2000 means that candidates standing for a 'qualified registered party' must be given a certificate to that effect by the 'registered nominating officer of the party'. This gives the leadership of the party the power to deselect MPs at a general election. It might be thought that this changes the balance of power significantly. I am grateful to David Howarth for this point.

[19] ibid 291.

[20] I am grateful to Richard Johnson for this point about the impact of the FTPA on democratic accountability.

democratic mandate.[21] This is known as the representative government view or, sometimes, the Westminster view. On this conception, the government itself has no *direct* electoral mandate.

In the UK, the constitution always reflects practical reality. The constitution is 'no more and no less than what happens'.[22] Over time, it has become clear that a general election does not just elect local MPs. On the contrary, it is now plain that in reality the *executive* is also chosen at a general election. Major parties stand on their policy platform, in part expressed in their manifesto, and put forward a slate of potential ministers to give effect to their policy choices and direction. Our vote at a general election is therefore *bifurcated*. We vote for both executive *and* legislature.

It is, of course, the case that in some constituencies, one or both of the major parties are not represented or have no chance of winning that seat. The claim that the voters in that constituency are choosing the government as well as the local MP has less force in such circumstances. This does not undermine the central claim that a general election now supplies not only local representatives to be the MP for particular constituencies but also confers a direct electoral mandate on the winning executive slate to implement their electoral programme, policies and political philosophy. It is for this reason that governments are frequently described as 'going to the country', when they seek to gain or refresh their 'mandate'.[23] The first-past-the-post system effectively operates at both the micro- and macro-levels. The party that wins the most seats is likely to form the government. This mandate is weaker, but still real, even if no overall majority in seats is achieved.

Those who believe that governments secure a democratic mandate from a general election in addition to the mandate conferred on local MPs defend what might be called the 'responsible government' view, sometimes known as the Whitehall view.[24] The responsible government conception recognises that the executive's responsibility to govern the country is not a subordinate and ancillary aspect of the legislative function within Parliament. Rather, it is suggested that the executive gains its own direct democratic mandate at general elections and is in fact an equal democratic partner of MPs within Parliament, albeit always responsible and accountable to MPs. This reinforces the constitutional balance discussed above. In a fused constitutional system, based on checks and balances, it can now safely be observed that *both* executive and legislature have a direct electoral mandate within Parliament.[25]

---

[21] M Elliott and R Thomas, *Public Law* (Oxford, Oxford University Press, 2020) 125; A Tomkins, *Public Law* (Oxford, Oxford University Press, 2003) 132.

[22] JAG Griffiths, 'The Political Constitution' (1979) 42 *MLR* 1, 19.

[23] O Wright, 'Winter general election: Chill wind blew for the Tories in 1923', *The Times*, 30 October 2019, available at www.thetimes.co.uk/article/winter-general-election-chill-wind-blew-for-the-tories-in-1923-7fpf3ntb2.

[24] AH Birch, *Representative and Responsible Government* (London, Unwin University Books, 1964) 115.

[25] ibid 116–17. Both extremes of the two main schools of thought (Whitehall and Westminster) have difficulties explaining some aspects of the system. The extreme Westminster view has trouble explaining why Bills implementing government manifesto promises are treated with caution in the House of Lords and why a by-election must be called if a candidate with a formal party affiliation dies during

Within Parliament, both executive and legislature are therefore fully aware that *both* limbs have a direct electoral mandate, although their views on policy may sometimes diverge. Normally, these divergent interests coalesce because the government generally has a majority in the Commons, so they are usually able to pursue their legislative agenda to implement their policies and political philosophy.[26] Sometimes, however, this norm does not hold, either because a government has no majority or because a particular issue is such that the majority is lost. In those circumstances, the responsible and representative conceptions of government can come into direct conflict where the executive and backbench MPs have diametrically opposed views as to the appropriate direction for the country.

It is the constitutional balance argument that underpins the justification for the government to have the power to dissolve Parliament. Both the government and MPs have a direct democratic mandate due to the bifurcated nature of the vote in the modern system. It is the fact that both limbs have a democratic mandate that demonstrates and explains the value to the system of having a balance within Parliament. It follows, therefore, that it makes complete sense for both limbs to have the ability to bring about a general election to test their respective mandates.

III. The Effect of the FTPA

The authors of the FTPA gave insufficient weight to these cross-currents and competing conceptions within the modern constitutional framework, and in particular the responsible government view. Instead, the Act privileged the representative government view by handing the power to dissolve Parliament solely to MPs – the Act gave little weight to the responsible government view. The primary effect of the FTPA was to remove from the Prime Minister and the government the power to call a general election. Under the FTPA, the standard term was to be five years between elections.[27] Before an early election could be called, a vote in the House of Commons was necessary with a two-thirds majority in favour of an early election.[28] Alternatively, a statutory vote of no confidence in the government would result in a general election if no alternative government was formed within 14 days and a positive motion of confidence passed in it.[29] In addition, s 2(7) FTPA

---

a general election campaign but not if they are independent. The extreme Whitehall view has trouble explaining why MPs can switch parties and why a new mid-term Prime Minister has no duty to call an immediate general election or continue the policies of their predecessor. The better view, of course, is that both extremes are wrong, and the government and MPs *each* secure a democratic mandate at a general election. This might be labelled the 'moderate Whitehall' view.

[26] See further the evidence of Vernon Bogdanor to the Joint Committee: https://committees. parliament.uk/writtenevidence/18881/html/; there are 'two fundamental principles, the principle of parliamentary government and the principle of democratic government ... Normally ... the two principles coincide'.

[27] FTPA, s 1.

[28] FTPA, s 2.

[29] ibid.

stated that the date of a future general election was to be determined on the advice of the Prime Minister. This author has considered in depth elsewhere some of the potential problems with the FTPA, but these issues are not really relevant to a more general analysis of the constitutional problems with the underlying rationale for the FTPA in the first place, which is the focus of this chapter.[30]

Section 7(4)(a) FTPA required that a review be undertaken of its operation 'no later than 30 November 2020'. This led to a Joint Committee Report on the FTPA that was published on 18 March 2021. It sets out a number of 'principled' arguments for the FTPA.[31] They rest mainly on the claim that there exists a so-called 'incumbency advantage' as well as permitting better planning for the civil service, potential candidates and others. The report cites Petra Schleiter and Valerie Belu in support of the claim that an incumbency advantage exists.[32]

A. The Alleged 'Incumbency Advantage'

Schleiter and Belu have argued that not having fixed-term Parliaments in the UK confers an incumbency advantage on the government because the ability to select the date of the election improves their electoral chances.[33] They claim that analysing actual general election results since 1945 demonstrates a 3.5 per cent advantage in vote share and 11.3 per cent advantage in seat share to the incumbent government. This research has been quoted in Parliament.[34] They argue that this is a 'substantively large difference' between the actual outcomes and the alternative predicted outcomes had the term of Parliament been fixed.[35] The claims made by the authors raise a number of issues that might be thought to undermine the salience of their points.

The first point to make is that Schleiter and Belu openly concede that the data is by no means unequivocal, and any difference could be explained by 'signalling effects', or a 'selection effect', whereby 'only successful governments make use of the opportunity to call a premature poll'.[36] These are stark admissions. The authors very fairly summarise the contradictory points made against their view in the literature:

---

[30] R Craig, 'Restoring Confidence: Replacing the Fixed-term Parliaments Act 2011' (2018) 81 *MLR* 480.

[31] Joint Committee Report (n 4) [17].

[32] ibid [22].

[33] P Schleiter and V Belu, 'Electoral Incumbency Advantages and the Introduction of Fixed Parliamentary Terms in the United Kingdom' (2018) 20 *British Journal of Politics and International Relations* 303. See also the Joint Committee Report (n 4) [19]–[25].

[34] eg HL Deb 30 November 2021, vol 816, col 1286 (Lord Newby): 'Research in the UK by Schleicher [sic] and Belu shows that, where elections have been called opportunistically before the statutory end point of a Parliament, it has given the incumbents an average increase in vote share of 3.5% over what might otherwise have been expected, which has translated into an 11% seat advantage. In circumstances where no party has a majority in the Commons – a highly likely scenario for the UK in the future – it gives the largest party a massive advantage'.

[35] Schleiter and Belu (n 33) 314.

[36] ibid 304.

'The literature on opportunistic election calling – including the signalling effects of this strategy and the competence of governments that select it – lends support to both sides in this policy debate.'[37] The existing literature therefore gives rise to contradictory views about the conditions under which opportunistic elections are triggered and the electoral consequences of this strategy.[38]

In one sense, it is tempting simply to cite those important admissions and leave the matter there, precisely because no real further argument is needed to take the view that little weight need be given to the claims made in the paper. It is difficult to see how it could ever be appropriate to cite the claimed figures as allegedly probative evidence without very detailed caveats. Notwithstanding this overarching and admitted problem, there are other issues with that paper.

One problem with the methodology of Schleiter and Belu is that they exclude two elections on the perhaps somewhat questionable grounds that those elections were allegedly forced upon those governments rather than being freely chosen.[39] Given the paucity of examples since 1945, this kind of cherry-picking is puzzling. They further claim that a case study – Wilson's early election in 1974 – aids their argument. They suggest that the early election was beneficial to him because without it his government's 'fate would likely have been sealed by parliamentary defeat and given its dwindling public support, the electoral consequences of a later election appeared deeply unfavourable'.[40] Unfortunately, this is pure speculation and assumes what it purports to prove.

The authors also place considerable and surprising reliance on public opinion polls taken in the period shortly after early general elections. They suggest that these polls show that governments would not have 'performed equally well' if they had not been able to schedule an election in 'favourable circumstances'.[41] This takes no account of the significant alteration in the political reality in the period straight after an election for a re-elected government. Schleiter and Belu's overt reliance on such shaky data is therefore troubling.[42] It is disappointing to see, in the Joint Committee report for example, such reliance placed on a paper whose underlying data is contradictory, partial and to some extent appears to rely on arguably discredited opinion poll data as substantiating counter factual and hypothetical claims.

B. The FTPA During Brexit

For our purposes, the most important aspect of the FTPA was the removal of the ultimate sanction of calling a general election from the Prime Minister. This was

---

[37] ibid.
[38] ibid 306.
[39] ibid 308.
[40] ibid 318.
[41] ibid 316.
[42] This author is not a professional psephologist or political scientist and is grateful to Richard Johnson, the editor of this collection, who has cast an expert eye over the claims made in this section.

flatly contradictory to the responsible government view because it undercut the constitutional balance generated by both the government *and* MPs previously having the power to call an election. By handing the power solely to MPs, the FTPA privileged the representative government view. It is, of course, difficult to engage in meaningful counterfactual narratives, but it is at least worth considering the tortuous, bitter and extended machinations over the Brexit process in the 2017–19 Parliament. Meg Russell has argued that the FTPA 'did not cause the Brexit impasse', quoting an unnamed source to the effect that 'the Conservative Party would not have let [Theresa May] go into another general election'.[43] This is, of course, mere speculation.

Readers will have their own views, but it is worth addressing the fact that the Brexit deal that was negotiated by the Prime Minister, and which was the central plank of government policy, was voted down by Parliament no less than three times. The first vote, on 15 January 2019, was lost by an enormous margin: 432–202.[44] It is at a minimum plausible that one or more of those votes might have had a different outcome if there was a meaningful threat that defeat for the government would precipitate an immediate general election. Indeed, Russell is forced to concede this possibility in her note.[45]

The bottom line is that since the government could no longer threaten its backbenchers with a general election directly, voting against the government came at a commensurately reduced potential political cost. Neither this possibility nor the counter-claim that it made no difference can be treated as anything more than conjecture in the end. It seems, at least to this author, to be quite the fluke that these machinations happened in a Parliament where the evident refusal to endorse the most important policy objective of the government led not to a general election, but to political paralysis. It is worth noting that John Stuart Mill not only predicted this potential outcome if the executive could not dissolve Parliament, but also was highly critical of the potential for deadlock.

> Other reasons make it desirable that some power in the state (which can only be the executive) should have the liberty of at any time, and at discretion, calling a new Parliament. When there is a real doubt which of two contending parties has the strongest following, it is important that there should exist a constitutional means of immediately testing the point and setting it at rest. No other political topic has a chance of being properly attended to while this is undecided.[46]

Henry Hill has described the assumption of control of the business of the House of Commons by Oliver Letwin MP and others in February 2019 as a

---

[43] M Russell, 'The Fixed-term Parliaments Act did not cause the Brexit impasse', *The Constitution Unit*, 6 September 2021, available at https://constitution-unit.com/2021/09/06/the-fixed-term-parliaments-act-did-not-cause-the-brexit-impasse/.

[44] The second vote, on 12 March 2019, was lost 391–242. The third vote, on 29 March 2019, was lost 322–277.

[45] ibid: 'As Bogdanor suggests, there would have been two possible outcomes. First, as happened with John Major, theoretically the Brexit rebels might have backed down.'

[46] JS Mill, *Representative Government* (first published 1861, Kitchener, Batoche Books, 2001) 160–61.

'wildcat executive' leading to a 'constitutional cordyceps'.[47] Letwin claimed that the Commons must 'take on the government of our country' and 'be, so to speak, a Cabinet'.[48] Memorable language for a memorable time. Readers who subscribe to the responsible government conception may perhaps be permitted a wry smile at claims that the privileging of the representative government conception inherent in the FTPA played no part in framing such contemporaneous attitudes and debate that resulted in the extraordinary scenes in Parliament during that period.

The FTPA arguably helped to create the circumstances where a wildcat executive could be formed, overtly catapulting backbench MPs into the awkward position, lamented by Letwin, of making real executive decisions that actually affected people's lives. As John Stuart Mill sagely pointed out, 'there is a radical distinction between controlling the business of government and actually doing it'.[49] The normal role of backbench MPs is to hold the executive to account, not make executive decisions themselves. Worse still, the usual mechanisms of accountability and responsibility became inapplicable precisely because those who drove through the legislation refused, despite their clear numerical majority, to topple the government, install themselves as a new executive and, crucially, be held accountable for their conduct at the despatch and ballot boxes.

It is not outlandish to suggest that the apparent temporary suspension of the responsible government conception by the FTPA would appear to be rather more than just a coincidence. This is not to deny that the obvious fact that the then government was also at fault in numerous ways. The central point, however, is that it is at best a surprising coincidence that the *unprecedented* aspects of the situation happened to be at a time when the government could no longer threaten an immediate general election.

IV. The Implications of Returning to the pre-FTPA Rules – Some Lessons

Now that DACPA has passed, some long-standing debates over the role of the monarch in the exercise of the dissolution prerogative may be revived. I have canvassed these elsewhere in more depth, but suffice to say that it is arguable that the effect of the recent ructions may have some important consequences on the norms that guide the behaviour of the relevant political actors.[50]

---

[47] H Hill, 'Letwin's wildcat executive would reduce ministers to marionettes', *Conservative Home*, 16 February 2019, available at www.conservativehome.com/thetorydiary/2019/02/letwins-wildcat-executive-would-reduce-ministers-to-marionettes.html; https://capx.co/the-case-for-withholding-royal-assent/.

[48] 'Letwin – The Commons must "take on the Government of our country" and "be a Cabinet"', *Conservative Home*, 14 February 2019, available at www.conservativehome.com/video/2019/02/watch-letwin-the-commons-must-take-on-the-government-of-our-country-and-be-a-cabinet.html, 4.05m and 4.54m.

[49] Mill (n 46) 58.

[50] R Craig (n 30).

The constitutional fireworks of the last few years will be considered for a long time to come. What is sometimes missed, however, is the dog that did not bark. A century earlier, no less fiery constitutional disputes took place over the role of the House of Lords in passing legislation and exercising its then veto. Ingeniously, the then Prime Minister sought to break the deadlock by appealing to the monarch to create sufficient peers under the royal prerogative to pass the contested Budget Bill, inspired by a previous crisis in 1832. A little-known aspect of the 1911 story is that the monarch was reluctant to accede to the request and it was not until there had been a further general election, fought squarely on the issue of constitutional reform, that the monarch was persuaded to agree.[51]

The saga a century ago has at least two relevant lessons for today. First, it proves that there can be a general election purely on one issue. This was also confirmed by the more recent 2019 election, which was in effect fought on the slogan of 'Get Brexit Done'. It is suggested that this rather bolsters the claim made earlier in this chapter that preventing the Prime Minister from threatening a general election on her central policy, no less than three times, is evidence that the FTPA was a significant constitutional disaster precisely because the Prime Minister could not take the issue to the country.

The second important lesson that might be drawn from a century ago relates to the monarch. It is suggested that the logical consequence of the steady removal of residual monarchical power over time makes it unthinkable for the monarch to play any similar role, or indeed *any* role, in the UK today as a modern, mature democracy. This author takes the view that is already unthinkable, but since the Joint Committee report appears to support the idea, the author's claim must necessarily also be treated as a normative one.[52] No sensible person could defend the idea of hereditary power in principle. The author also, therefore, disagrees with the government, who published a set of guidelines in which they claimed that the monarch would regain some residual theoretical role if the Bill was passed.[53] That is why the language of 'request' rather than 'advice' is used.

Traditionally, alleged residual discretion of the monarch was covered by what are known as the Lascelles principles.[54] These envisaged three circumstances where the monarch could refuse a dissolution.

1.   The existing Parliament was still 'vital, viable, and capable of doing its job'.
2.   A general election would be 'detrimental to the national economy'.
3.   The monarch could 'rely on finding another Prime Minister who could govern for a reasonable period with a working majority in the House of Commons'.

---

[51] *Jackson* (n 11) [151]; I Loveland, *Constitutional Law, Administrative Law and Human Rights* (Oxford, Oxford University Press, 2009) 163–64.

[52] Joint Committee Report (n 4) [124]–[145]. See also C Gardner, *What a Fix-up!* (2015); Gardner's evidence to the Constitution Committee of the House of Lords (https://committees.parliament.uk/writtenevidence/463/pdf/) as part of their report 'A Question of Confidence', https://committees.parliament.uk/work/14/fixedterm-parliaments-act-2011/publications/.

[53] https://assets.publishing.service.gov.uk/government/uploads/system/uploads/attachment_data/file/940028/Dissolution-Principles.pdf.

[54] https://publications.parliament.uk/pa/ld5802/ldselect/ldconst/100/10005.htm.

The second criterion is generally accepted to be no longer relevant. The two other limbs relate to whether the existing Parliament could continue and secondly whether an alternative Prime Minister could be found. If the recent Brexit period had any silver lining, it is suggested that one of the most striking aspects was the absolutely universal agreement that the monarch should under no circumstances be drawn into the political fray, as a former Cabinet Secretary has suggested in a related context.[55]

A. Potential Scenarios

In her evidence to the Joint Committee, which the report quoted seemingly with approval, Anne Twomey postulated a number of potential scenarios where she thinks that the monarch could potentially refuse a dissolution.[56] The main example she gives is where a government, immediately after an election, seeks to dissolve Parliament and have a fresh election despite the existence of a potentially viable alternative government. This fails to account for the overwhelming pressure that such a Prime Minister would face, not least from within Cabinet and their party, not to precipitate the almost inevitable demolition that would be inflicted on a party that forced another election without good reason. Furthermore, if there *were* remotely plausible reasons to call an immediate further election, it is not at all obvious that the monarch could properly refuse. The mooted residual discretion to refuse seems, therefore, to be redundant in all but the most fanciful circumstances. Setting a rule allegedly to cover such extreme circumstances seems to be either pointless or potentially damaging.

The Joint Committee expressly suggested that the government should use 'request' instead of 'advice' in seeking an election to make clear that a residual discretion remains for the monarch to refuse to dissolve Parliament in such circumstances.[57] They appeared to be persuaded that the possibility of intervention by the monarch, however remote, has some positive value. Whilst superficially attractive, this mooted power to refuse a dissolution fails to learn the lessons of the Brexit period. It was then discovered that norms formed with the best of intentions arguably caused an enormous crisis in unusual circumstances. The requirement for a two-thirds majority for an early election did not result in increased stability, as

---

[55] During the turbulent post-election period in 2010, the Cabinet Secretary, Gus O'Donnell, gave his view that the monarch must not be involved under any circumstances in appointing the Prime Minister: 'I believe it is the responsibility of the Prime Minister to ensure that the monarch remains above politics and when the Prime Minister resigns it is very apparent who the Queen should be calling to produce the next stable government … It is the Prime Minister's responsibility not to resign until that situation is clarified.' The same approach must logically extend to dissolutions. See www.theguardian.com/politics/2010/feb/24/whitehall-gus-odonnell-hung-parliament-purdah. If a Prime Minister dies suddenly, the Cabinet should appoint an interim leader if there is no Deputy Prime Minister.

[56] Considered with approval in Joint Committee Report (n 4) [132]–[138]. Her evidence on this point is at https://committees.parliament.uk/oralevidence/1549/pdf/, Q183.

[57] Joint Committee Report (n 4) [142].

many might have thought.[58] Instead, the inability of the Prime Minister to threaten to call an election and directly seek the confidence of the electorate led to total political paralysis.[59]

Those who defend a residual monarchical discretion to refuse a new general election are perhaps also guilty of underestimating the potential constitutional and political carnage that could ensue. Imagine a Prime Minister who is refused an election. They could nominally continue in office but publicly state that until the monarch granted an election, they could not put forward any policies or proposals. What if the Prime Minister then publicly promulgated some superficially plausible reasons for a fresh election (which are bound to exist, however flimsy)? What if the criticism and pressure thus placed on the monarch, who by definition would be acting without advice from the government, led to calls for abdication?

These nightmare scenarios are not just plausible in the event of a mooted refusal, they are even *likely*. The chances of the optimal outcome occurring, that the government meekly accepts the refusal and just disregards the overwhelming political pressures that no doubt led to the unusual decision to seek another election, seems to be somewhat overstated as an expected outcome. Rather than involving a hereditary monarch, Gus O'Donnell's argument that the politicians must sort it out seems manifestly sensible.[60] If that leads to two elections in quick succession, so be it. Those who are tempted to postulate ever more extreme hypothetical scenarios culminating in a putative intervention by the monarch fail to account for the potentially catastrophic unintended consequences of such an intervention for the constitutional system currently in place.[61]

Another scenario mooted by Twomey is where a junior coalition partner breaks off, mid-Parliament, and supports the opposition, where such a realignment could potentially create an alternative viable government. Twomey suggested this possibility in her oral evidence to the Joint Committee.[62] Again, if and to the extent there is perceived to be any sharp practice by the incumbent in calling an election in such circumstances, that is something that will be held fully and immediately to account, politically, by the electorate. The machinations and political factors that would swirl around in public discourse would fully ventilate the reasonableness of holding an election in such circumstances and the electorate would give their verdict.

---

[58] FTPA, s 2(10(b)).

[59] An illuminating analysis of the precedents and history can be found in a House of Commons Library paper, R Kelly, 'Confidence Motions', No 02873 (14 March 2019).

[60] See n 55.

[61] The claim that some potential extreme scenarios could be so bad that intervention by the monarch could be the *lesser* of two bad options is a popular view. This author simply disagrees with that view. In a democracy, democratic politicians and processes are the only legitimate methods of solving any such crisis. The exercise of hereditary power is flatly inconsistent with the direction of travel of decades, nay centuries, of democratic development. Furthermore, the postulation of extreme hypothetical examples is itself unhelpful. See the text to n 87.

[62] https://committees.parliament.uk/oralevidence/1549/html/, Q183.

The one scenario that must be avoided at all costs is the monarch intervening directly, because such actions could then be politically criticised without the protective shield of the government. The doctrine of confidence was established centuries ago to protect the monarch from criticism. The moment the monarch deviates from governmental policy, he or she would be left naked in the political fray. This would be flatly contradictory to one of the oldest principles of the constitution, which is that the monarch never acts independently of the government. For this reason alone, it is completely unacceptable.[63]

Exposing the monarch to the inevitable direct political criticism that would ensue is far *more* unacceptable, it is suggested, than the potential negative effects of a second election in quick succession or other mooted scenarios where the Joint Committee, and others, believe the monarch should have the right to intervene personally in the political domain. The voting public will no doubt make their own views clear as to the acceptability or otherwise of an election that is perceived as having happened after sharp practice. That is a matter for them. What is not feasible, it is suggested, is to identify circumstances where the monarch could properly refuse a dissolution requested by the government in the modern constitution.

An interesting example occurred recently when Boris Johnson faced a wave of resignations from his government that culminated in his resignation. Having so comprehensively lost the confidence of his party, and therefore of Parliament as a whole, his resignation was the inexorable result. He could not properly have sought to advise the monarch to dissolve Parliament and, unsurprisingly, he did not act in a way that would have put the monarch in an awkward position. In any event, it is technically the cabinet, representing the government as a whole, that advises the monarch, not the Prime Minister. This demonstrates that the pressure on a Prime Minister not to act in a way that could draw the monarch into the political realm is always overwhelming, and indeed at no point did Johnson seek an audience with the monarch. The system worked perfectly, even when the holder of the office of Prime Minister was one of the most stubborn ever to take on the role.

The Joint Committee appear to view the role of the monarch as purely being a deterrent, it being of paramount importance that the monarch be kept out of the political fray.[64] It is suggested that a far greater deterrent to any perceived sharp practice in calling an election, for example immediately after a previous election, would be the likely reaction of the general public in the voting booth. A purported residual monarchical backstop, acting by definition without ministerial advice, is a recipe for disaster – or pointless if it is always granted. It is also somewhat surprising to have to argue, in all seriousness, that an unelected hereditary monarch

---

[63] It might be thought that examples from similar Westminster-style systems could be useful. I addressed some of these examples in my *MLR* article (n 30). The core difference, however, is that a Governor-General (or equivalent) can, in extremis, resign and be replaced. The monarch cannot. The imperative to keep the monarch out of the political arena is commensurately greater as a result.
[64] Joint Committee Report (n 4) [144].

should not wield any actual personal political power in a twenty-first-century democracy, however remote the possibility.

It is perhaps also worth noting that there is deep-rooted scepticism about whether the monarch in reality has any residual discretion to refuse to permit a general election. Walter Bagehot puts the point well: 'Theoretically, indeed, the power to dissolve parliament is entrusted to the sovereign only; and there are vestiges of doubt whether in *all* cases is sovereign is bound to dissolve parliament when the cabinet ask him to do so.'[65]

It would seem, therefore, that even Bagehot, 150 years ago, believed that the sovereign was bound to accede to a general election request in all cases subject to some extreme exceptions, which he clearly thought were minimal and scarcely relevant. He does, however, leave the door slightly ajar, which may explain the basis upon which the Lascelles principles were later developed. If a mooted residual power to refuse was vestigial 150 years ago, when modern democratic accountability was considerably less established, it must now be reduced to vanishing point. This is without even dwelling on the normative argument against the possession of even the most limited real political power by an unelected, unaccountable hereditary individual, however outstanding the recent incumbent was.

The author therefore respectfully differs from the views of the Joint Committee and others on the appropriate role of the monarch in this area. Retaining even a vestigial substantive political role also offends against Bagehot's powerful insight that the constitution has both 'dignified' and 'efficient' elements. The role of the monarch falls quintessentially under the dignified aspect.[66] It is nowadays difficult to identify any element of the monarch's role that is part of the 'efficient' aspect.[67] The restoration of the prerogative of dissolution is not justification for reviving any purported residual personal discretion of the monarch. The serious and weighty constraints on the Prime Minister in calling an election are, and should remain, political, not legal.

B. Potential Statutory Power to Dissolve Parliament Following a Majority Vote in the Commons

The Joint Committee said that their preferred solution, absent the manifesto commitments by both major parties, would have been that a simple Commons majority would have been necessary for a general election.[68] In this they were

---

[65] Bagehot (n 15) 13–14.

[66] ibid 7.

[67] This issue is outside the scope of this chapter, but the appointment of the Prime Minister is now governed by strict convention that requires the person best placed to command a majority in the House of Commons be called. The only other potential tricky area is the weekly meeting with the Prime Minister, which should probably cease, but in any event is entirely in private and in confidence.

[68] Joint Committee Report (n 4) [80]–[82].

joined by Robert Hazell, Meg Russell and Andrew Blick, amongst others.[69] Others urged caution, including Margaret Beckett, who said that such a vote could cause 'complications' and expressed her view that the decision should be left 'in the hands of the prime minister of the day'.[70]

I have elsewhere argued for the repeal of the FTPA.[71] In that article, I suggested that the problem of the alleged residual monarchical discretion marginally tipped the scales in favour of conferring a statutory discretion on the Prime Minister to call a general election subject to a bare majority approval vote via a motion in the House of Commons. This would be approved by the monarch as a formality, but without any discretion to refuse.[72] I proposed that the House of Commons should approve the decision.

The idea of asking the House of Commons to approve any dissolution by simple majority was the only amendment that was successfully passed by the House of Lords to DACPA when it was a Bill.[73] The suggested amendment was swiftly rejected by the House of Commons when the Bill was returned, and the House of Lords did not put up any further resistance to returning the power, in effect, to the Prime Minister.[74]

The events in Parliament during the Brexit process have caused me to rethink my previous view. Earlier in this chapter, I argued that the well-intentioned attempt in the FTPA to seek the approval of the Commons for dissolution backfired spectacularly. My view now is that securing the approval of the Commons would be either pointless or damaging, despite the best intentions. In almost all cases, the vote will be a formality, either because the government has a majority or the main opposition votes in favour of the election, as one would expect. In almost all cases, the vote would therefore be pointless. This was seen in April 2017, when Theresa May secured a huge vote (522–13) in favour of an election.[75]

On the other hand, as Brexit proved, there may be circumstances where such a vote cannot be secured. Discussion of this possibility risks the error of dabbling in extreme hypotheticals, which is rarely useful or enlightening in a flexible constitution such as the UK. On the other hand, it is hard to simply ignore such recent history, even bearing in mind the impossibility of predicting future events and outcomes with any certainty.

---

[69] A Blick, https://committees.parliament.uk/writtenevidence/22206/html/, [29]; R Hazell and M Russell, https://committees.parliament.uk/writtenevidence/22206/html/, [28].

[70] Oral evidence of Margaret Beckett, https://committees.parliament.uk/oralevidence/1640/html/, Q326.

[71] R Craig (n 30).

[72] ibid 506.

[73] HL Deb 9 February 2022, vol 818, col 1584ff.

[74] HC Deb 14 March 2022, vol 710, col 643; HL Deb 22 March 2022, vol 820, col 856.

[75] N Walker, 'Brexit Timeline: Events Leading to the UK's Exit from the European Union' Briefing Paper 7960 (House of Commons Library, 6 January 2021) https://commonslibrary.parliament.uk/research-briefings/cbp-7960/.

In 2019, Parliament initially refused to grant an election to Boris Johnson, ostensibly because the election date would be too uncertain with Brexit day looming.[76] This was despite the fact that a Bill mandating that the government seek and agree an extension of the deadline to 31 January 2020 had already passed through the Commons.[77] Thus the government faced the possibility of repeated extensions in a Parliament that refused to agree a deal, was unable to agree an alternative path forward and refused to topple the government and install an alternative. This appeared to be genuine political paralysis. It was only resolved by the passage of the Early Parliamentary General Election Act 2019, itself only made possible by the Liberal Democrats breaking ranks.[78]

Were the Commons to refuse to permit a general election in a similar way in future, such a scenario could be highly damaging precisely because political paralysis would quite possibly again ensue, not least because it is hard to imagine such a scenario outside a hung Parliament. This could again potentially open the door to the type of deeply unfortunate and inappropriate scenes we saw with Letwin during Brexit, where the most basic principle of confidence is seriously breached by a quasi-executive that refuses to be held to account at the despatch and ballot boxes. Experience has now shown, it is suggested, that such a statutory power with Commons approval is either a pointless charade or potentially very destructive indeed. As new evidence has emerged, I have changed my mind – and I am now persuaded that Parliament was right to have restored the status quo ante.

The revival of the previous system is therefore to be welcomed. DACPA has restored the balance in the constitution and rightly recognises the importance of the responsible government view in a constitution that appeared to be leaning too far towards the representative government view. It means that both parts of the fused system of executive and legislature within Parliament have a 'big red button', so to speak, as part of the necessary, positive creative tension between the two elements of the system.

V. The Ouster Clause

The controversial *Miller II* case caused considerable consternation in Westminster circles.[79] The Supreme Court famously overturned a unanimous and powerful Divisional Court and struck down the prorogation of Parliament by the

---

[76] It was suggested that the Prime Minister could set the election date to be after Brexit under s 2(7) of the FTPA ('the polling day for the election is to be the day appointed by Her Majesty by proclamation on the recommendation of the Prime Minister'). www.bbc.co.uk/news/uk-politics-49584907. The vote was on 4 September 2019. See further the exceptionally useful paper by Walker (ibid).

[77] European Union (Withdrawal) (No 2) Act 2019.

[78] M Savage and T Helm, 'Lib Dems offer Johnson route to December election', *The Guardian*, 26 November 2019, available at www.theguardian.com/politics/2019/oct/26/boris-johnson-no-brexit-until-january-block-christmas-general-election.

[79] *Miller II* (n 6 above).

government during the Brexit process.[80] This is not the place to criticise the reasoning in that decision. Its relevance to this chapter is the backlash evidenced in DACPA as a result of the astonishment generated in the political realm by the completely unexpected judicial intervention in the political domain in *Miller II*. Indeed, the notes to DACPA specifically make clear that the ouster clause in the Bill was inserted directly as a result of the *Miller II* decision.[81] The ouster clause in DACPA is therefore an important aspect of the wider backlash against not just the FTPA, but the wider constitutional changes that have occurred in recent years. The necessity for the ouster clause received heavyweight support in evidence given to the Joint Committee from, inter alia, Sir Stephen Laws and Richard Ekins.[82] Ekins, in particular, says that the ouster clause 'or something like it is indispensable if Parliament is to restore the law as it stood before the FTPA'.[83]

The reason why Parliament inserted the ouster clause (considered below) following *Miller II* relates to the close conceptual connection between prorogation and dissolution. Indeed, dissolution is almost always preceded by prorogation.[84] Prorogation suspends Parliament. Dissolution brings Parliament to an end. The two prerogative powers are umbilically linked. It can therefore be no surprise that the drafter has specifically taken steps to try to prevent the courts interfering in a decision to dissolve Parliament after the Supreme Court's decision to cross the Rubicon by interfering in the decision to prorogue Parliament.[85]

It is important to make clear that, at one level, the insertion of the ouster clause might be thought to bolster the claim of those who insist that the prerogative of dissolution cannot be revived, and the new power must be statutory. This is because ouster clauses normally relate to *statutory* provisions. However, there is no particular reason to suggest that Parliament cannot, if it so chooses, oust the jurisdiction of the ordinary courts over not just statutory legal powers but also prerogative legal powers. This might be thought to be particularly true when the prerogative of dissolution was long thought to be not justiciable by the courts in the first place anyway.[86]

---

[80] *R (Miller) v Prime Minister* [2019] EWHC 2381 (QB), [2019] ACD 136.

[81] https://assets.publishing.service.gov.uk/government/uploads/system/uploads/attachment_data/file/940027/Draft-Fixed-term-Parliaments-Act-Repeal-Bill.pdf. 'Clause 3 further provides that the courts cannot consider the limits or extent of those powers. This is to address the distinction drawn by the Supreme Court in [*Miller II*] as regards the court's role in reviewing the scope of a prerogative power, as opposed to its exercise. It seeks to clarify that neither is justiciable in the context of decisions relating to dissolution'.

[82] See, eg Richard Ekins's written evidence to the Joint Committee, submitted on 11 January 2021: https://committees.parliament.uk/writtenevidence/20951/pdf/, [22]–[32]; see also Sir Stephen Laws's oral evidence on 10 December 2020: https://committees.parliament.uk/oralevidence/1386/pdf/, Q21 and Q22.

[83] ibid [31].

[84] Chitty J, *A Treatise on the Law of the Prerogatives of the Crown: And the Relative Duties and Rights of the Subject* (London, Butterworth, 1820) 73 fn (i).

[85] The threshold of 'high policy' exercises of prerogative power, which the courts used to treat as non-justiciable, was laid down in *R v Secretary of State for Foreign and Commonwealth Affairs, Ex parte Everett* [1989] QB 811, 817. The Supreme Court claimed not to be reviewing the decision itself, but rather its 'limits', though the distinction they purport to draw is hard to follow.

[86] *Council for the Civil Service Unions v Minister for the Civil Service (GCHQ)* [1985] AC 374.

A. The Paradox of Ouster Clauses

Ouster clauses are exceptionally controversial amongst the legal community. This is because they prevent the courts ensuring that particular legal powers conferred on various bodies by Parliament are exercised in accordance with the meaning and intention of Parliament – admittedly as interpreted by the courts. The paradox of the treatment of ouster clauses by the courts is that in their relentless attempts to limit the *effect* of ouster clauses, the courts have strayed closer and closer to disregarding the intention of Parliament in *imposing* an ouster clause. This is done, slightly ironically, in the name of protecting the alleged intention of Parliament in conferring the power whose exercise is contested in the particular case. This has led to some heroic interpretation of what at first sight appears to be fairly clear and unequivocal language in statutes. Consider, for example, the language of a famous example considered in a case called *Anisminic*: 'The determination by the commission of any application made to them under this Act shall not be called in question in any court of law.'[87]

To the lay reader, this might appear to be comprehensive and clear as day. The courts, however, got round it and held that a determination by the Foreign Compensation Commission to award compensation using public funds in a particular case could indeed be questioned, and overturned, by the courts, as they duly did in that case. This was achieved, in effect, by the transparent mechanism of holding that a determination that was legally flawed was not a true determination and therefore the ouster clause did not apply. The Commission's decision was described as only a 'purported determination'.[88] The courts went further, in fact, and held that such determinations took the Commission wholly outside their jurisdiction, as if they had decided to randomly award public funds to their friends and family.

The latter point may seem strange, but it illustrates an important but slightly puzzling argument frequently trotted out by commentators which is to postulate some extreme hypothetical example and then insist that this establishes that the courts must reserve the power to prevent such examples from happening. Once the principle is conceded, then it is but a short step to treating the ouster clause as nugatory. None of this is to suggest that academics and others are wrong to consider these kinds of examples (indeed, it is their job to do so). It is the *response* to these arguments that is crucial. If the principle is conceded, the argument is lost. The better view, it is suggested, was evidenced in a paragraph from the Divisional Court judgment in the *Miller II* case, which, in this author's opinion, cannot be too regularly recited.

> We do not believe that it is helpful to consider the arguments by reference to extreme hypothetical examples, not least because it is impossible to predict how the flexible constitutional arrangements of the United Kingdom, and Parliament itself, would react in such circumstances.[89]

---

[87] *Anisminic v Foreign Compensation Commission* [1969] 2 AC 147, 169.
[88] ibid 199.
[89] *Miller (HC)* (n 80) [66].

This admirable sentiment is the right way to frame these kinds of disputes. This is particularly the case for the revival of the dissolution prerogative. It is plain and obvious that the purpose of the ouster clause in DACPA is to prevent the courts ever considering the exercise of the prerogative of dissolution once it is revived. It is worth setting it out in full.

3. Non-justiciability of revived prerogative powers

A court or tribunal may not question –

(a)   the exercise or purported exercise of the powers referred to in section 2,[90]
(b)   any decision or purported decision relating to those powers, or
(c)   the limits or extent of those powers.

The clear desire of Parliament to lay down a red line for the courts in regard to the dissolution prerogative would not be a novelty, given the almost universal agreement historically that the dissolution prerogative was not justiciable by the courts under any circumstances. Rather, Parliament would be making crystal clear to the courts and the public that it expressly agrees with the prior consensus that accountability for dissolution decisions rests solely in the political domain, and the courts should not intervene. It could also be pointed out that if the drafters had *not* inserted such a clause, there might have been some who would argue that the failure to do so constituted a concession that it was justiciable. Heads the courts win, tails Parliament loses. In relation to *Miller II*, it is worth pointing out that the wording of section 3C above overtly references the reasoning of the Supreme Court where it held that the prorogation was voided because it was exercised in a way that breached the limit of that power.[91]

B.   Critiques of the DACPA Ouster Clause

A number of leading public law academics disagree with the claims in this section that the above ouster clause is a clear and binding parliamentary directive that the courts should never interfere in any decision to dissolve Parliament using the prerogative. This chapter will consider the views of Mark Elliott in a blog post, Alison Young, also in a blog post, and Gavin Phillipson, in his evidence to the Joint Committee considering the FTPA. They each make arguments that they suggest could be used by a court that wished to circumvent the ouster clause above, notwithstanding the apparent clarity of Parliament's intention.

In a post on the widely respected and heavyweight UK Constitutional Law Association blog, of which she is an editor, Young draws a direct analogy with the *Miller II* case in her analysis of the ouster clause.[92] She argues that a court

---

[90] DACPA, s 2 revives the prerogative power of dissolution, which was put into abeyance by the FTPA.

[91] *Miller II* (n 6) [48]–[51].

[92] https://ukconstitutionallaw.org/2020/12/04/alison-l-young-the-draft-fixed-term-parliaments-act-2011-repeal-bill-turning-back-the-clock/.

could well be justified in reviewing a dissolution because otherwise any residual supervision would be left to the monarch. She asks, clearly rhetorically, 'Is it really preferable to rely on the Monarch as opposed to the courts to check such potential abuses of the constitution?', and her post as a whole makes clear that she thinks that the judiciary indeed should circumvent the ouster clause in principle. She seeks to bolster her argument through the use of two hypothetical examples where she claims intervention by the courts would be justified.

> What if the Prime Minister deported all elected MPs, and then said Parliament was dissolved? What if he dissolved Parliament because his family had been kidnapped and there was a realistic threat that their lives would be in danger if he did not dissolve Parliament? Would these be controls over the existence of the power of dissolution, or its limits, or its exercise?

Mark Elliott takes a similar robust view on whether the courts could overturn the ouster clause.[93] He considers the example of the government seeking to 'deport all immigrants' by invoking the prerogative power of dissolution of Parliament. Although he admits that 'it would be a bold court that adopted such an approach', he argues that a determined court would be justified, in his view, in circumventing the ouster clause – or even 'decline' to give effect to the provisions of the statute.

Elliott and Young's extreme hypothetical examples are concerning. For them, the courts in these hypothetical scenarios would be justified in circumventing and therefore disregarding the ouster clause in DACPA. The beauty of their examples is in their stark illustration of what we might call 'the ouster clause three card trick'. Step one is to postulate a scenario, however ridiculous, where legal intervention is said to be conceivable. Step two is where the interlocutor may inadvisably be drawn into conceding that judicial intervention might be warranted, but only in such extreme circumstances. Step three is the *coup de grace*, where critics can then claim that the ouster clause cannot possibly be intended to be applied in *all* situations. It follows that the clear wording of the statute can be disregarded as functionally meaningless. The courts should therefore construe the clause in any way they please, as with other such clauses, to ensure that the courts retain a general supervisory jurisdiction over the underlying legal power.

In his evidence, Phillipson engages in a more subtle and therefore more difficult example of this kind of reading down of ouster clauses. His example is clever. He postulates the extreme hypothetical example of a rogue Westminster government purporting to 'dissolve' one of the devolved institutions, such as the Scottish Parliament, and bring about an election.[94] The example is, of course, complete nonsense because the Scottish Parliament is a wholly statutory body and there is no connection between prerogative and that body in any way. The cleverness of his idea rests in its marriage of an action that is obviously and clearly wholly outside

---

[93] https://publiclawforeveryone.com/2020/12/02/repealing-the-fixed-term-parliaments-act/.

[94] Dissolution must be distinguished from abolition. Phillipson is postulating prerogative being used to call an election.

any possible conception of a lawful exercise of the dissolution prerogative coupled with the seemingly plausible claim that judicial intervention would be appropriate in such circumstances. Phillipson expressly deploys the argument that since, in his view, the clause cannot mean what it purports to mean on its face, then effectively the courts are theoretically free to do whatever damage they deem necessary to the ordinary and natural meaning of the clause in order to preserve judicial supervisory power.

> The point here is not to try and argue that such powers might actually be used for terrible or ridiculous ends. Rather it is to show that since a literal reading would be a nonsense … it could not be adopted by the courts. And once a literal reading becomes impossible then the courts must find a non-literal one … Hence passing statutes whose literal meaning is an absurdity hands the courts the tools to unpick Parliament's intent. The very extremity of the wording of the clause invites its judicial undoing.[95]

It is important to note that Phillipson, unlike Young, is not expressly calling for the courts to eviscerate the clause in some situations. Rather, he is claiming that the lengths the drafter has gone to somehow *weakens* its effect. This is a Catch-22 situation. If Parliament is insufficiently clear, then the courts could find, and have always historically found, a loophole. Conversely, if Parliament is explicit and detailed, then the courts could treat the clause as an 'absurdity'. There appears to be no escape for parliamentary drafters from this Kafkaesque linguistic trap.

Nowhere do Young, Elliott or Phillipson consider the potentially catastrophic implications of the courts taking the logical next step of intervening, presumably during an actual general election, to stop the public voting on a new government and parliament. This could only occur if the courts were to treat the clause as nugatory and is the logical endpoint of their arguments – although, to be fair, they do not argue for this expressly. For them, the principle of judicial supervision is so inviolable that any potential negative constitutional consequences are worthwhile. Indeed, Phillipson even suggests that *Parliament* should capitulate by dropping the clause, and if it failed to do so, Parliament would be behaving in an 'irresponsible' way.[96] Tom Hickman makes a similar claim, suggesting that 'when making constitutional laws, Parliament must therefore assume that some gross abuse could occur'.[97]

It is suggested that the appropriate response to these critics is similar. Their *premise* must be denied. Rather than accepting that in some extreme circumstances judicial intervention would be justified, the better view is to deny that such

---

[95] https://committees.parliament.uk/writtenevidence/22214/pdf/, [24].

[96] ibid [27].

[97] Tom Hickman's evidence to the Joint Committee, https://committees.parliament.uk/writtenevidence/21616/default/, [14]. Hickman also claims at [13] that 'Those who make constitutional laws are playing the long game. Such laws must regulate the exercise of power far into the future and provide protections for exceptional circumstances that cannot be foreseen', but at [15], 'One does not have to subscribe to all of Burke's views to see the good sense in his strictures against tinkering with the constitution by legislating in the abstract without it being needed to remedy some demonstrable problem'. These two claims might be thought to be in some tension.

scenarios are appropriately treated as *legal* questions at all.[98] On the contrary, it is better to insist that Parliament has made crystal clear that the constitutional framework within which all such questions fall to be decided is the *political* sphere. Let the politicians sort it out. For the government to try something as extreme as trying to deploy prerogative against a devolved body would cause an explosive political and constitutional crisis that could only (and should only) be solved in the political domain. Just as with the coronavirus legislation and local council rate capping, the courts would doubtless, and rightly, refuse to be drawn into the fray.[99] It is therefore not useful for clarity or understanding to postulate such 'extreme hypothetical examples'. Any suggestion that the courts would be forced to intervene in some imaginary extreme situation can (and should) simply be rejected, citing the Divisional Court in *Miller II*.[100]

One of the beauties of the dissolution prerogative is that its exercise is subjected to the most immediate and powerful political accountability through the ballot box. Judicial intervention has no place here under any circumstances. This political framing would also be consistent with the claim made earlier that any exercise of the dissolution prerogative should be held to account by the electorate, and an unelected hereditary monarch no longer has any substantive political role to play. In this respect, dissolution can be materially distinguished from prorogation, which is why the insistence of some that the courts might be justified in eviscerating the ouster clause in some situations is so surprising – and misguided.

VI. Conclusion

This chapter has sought to argue that the repeal of the FTPA is a welcome restoration of constitutional balance because both the executive and MPs will in future be able to precipitate a general election. This restores the original, deeper meaning to the doctrine of confidence, one of the oldest and most well-established core aspects of the political constitution of the UK. The doctrine of confidence operates at two levels, so that the government must demonstrate it has the confidence of the elected representatives of the people or the people themselves voting directly. The prerogative system permits both branches to precipitate a general election. MPs can bring a vote of no confidence that will almost invariably result in an election. The Prime Minister can seek the confidence of the electorate directly through the restored prerogative of dissolution.

---

[98] I am grateful to Gavin Phillipson for pointing out in conversation that the question of whether the ouster clause is valid in itself is necessarily a legal question that a court could determine, even if its determination was to refuse to intervene in any way due to the clear terms of the provision.

[99] *R (Dolan) v Secretary of State for Health and Social Care* [2020] EWCA Civ 1605; *Nottinghamshire County Council v Secretary of State for the Environment* [1986] 2 AC 240.

[100] *Miller (HC)* (n 80) [66].

As argued above, votes at general elections are bifurcated. We vote not just for our local MP, but also for the executive and the platform on which they stand, as well as the slate of ministers put forward by the relevant party to act as the government. In fact, the power of the executive acting on its own democratic mandate to bring about a dissolution of Parliament and precipitate a general election promotes and increases democratic accountability. When both halves of the two parts of our fused system within Parliament have the power to bring Parliament to an early end, genuine mutual respect and accountability is woven into the system. The FTPA unbalanced that historical stasis because it made the executive's power to go the country conditional on Commons approval, when the Commons already had a mechanism to bring about an election if it wished. The repeal of the FTPA is therefore a significant improvement in democratic accountability and a positive development generally.

Finally, it has been suggested that the ouster clause drafted in response to the alarming decision in *Miller II* is comprehensive, clear and unassailable. Suggestions that it could be or should be circumvented by semantic dissimulation should be resisted as Parliament has made crystal clear that it wishes exercises of dissolution prerogative be held to account in the political realm – as it always has been historically.

The FTPA was a misguided and half-hearted reform which has no place outside of a fully codified revolutionary novel constitutional settlement. Its demise is strongly to be welcomed. The saga illustrates some of the dangers of tinkering for short-term goals with a constitution whose flexibility is a feature, not a bug – and ill-suited to the grubby compromises that led to it being passed in the first place. The candle of reasons for its passage burnt out long ago, and if there is one silver lining from the cloud of this temporary real-world experiment, it is that the chances of any future such fixed-term legislation being successfully proposed and passed must be slim to negligible, at least in this author's lifetime.

7

Reform of the House of Commons: A Sceptical View on Progress

TONY McNULTY

I. Introduction

In a parliamentary democracy, the key legislative body should be at the centre of both the governmental architecture and the constitutional settlement on which the country relies. Consequently, the first point of reference of any constitutional reform should be an assessment of how it impacts on the Commons. Although much has been made of the supposed 'democratic' features of parliamentary reform since 1997, there has been little attempt to link them to the key legislative chamber. Norton notes that 'Parliament has to adapt to constitutional change … [and] that it has an important role in monitoring such change', but this implies a rather passive role for Parliament.[1] The foundation of constitutional change would be stronger if its political impact on the House of Commons, and indeed on Parliament itself, was considered before 'reform' decisions were taken. It will be argued that changes to the broader constitution have implications for the role of the Commons and the role of the MPs within it – and there are dangers in treating this as an afterthought.

Over the years in the UK, the driver of parliamentary reform has often been partisan, political or expedient considerations. Reforms have been introduced without analysis of their impact on the Commons or MPs. They have offered solutions to problems with little regard for either the parliamentary system as a whole or its constituent parts and scant understanding of the consequences.

---

[1] P Norton, 'Reforming Parliament in the United Kingdom: The Report of the Commission to Strengthen Parliament' (2000) 6 *Journal of Legislative Studies* 1, 11. A good example of the post hoc issues raised by constitutional reform is the issue of English Votes for English Laws (EVEL) in the wake of devolution to the nations of the UK. These issues are explored in great detail by Daniel Gover and Michael Kenny in articles such as D Gover and M Kenny, 'Answering the West Lothian Question? A Critical Assessment of "English Votes for English Laws" in the UK Parliament' (2018) 71 *Parliamentary Affairs* 760, 782.

Norton suggests that there are essentially three preconditions to reform:

One is a window of opportunity ... the second is a reform agenda. MPs may favour change but they need a coherent set of proposals to unite behind. Third, there has to be leadership: this may come from the back-benches but may also come from the Leader of the House ... or from a combination of both.[2]

He is right to maintain that all three elements were evident in 1979, when the reform of Departmental Select Committees was introduced. The 'window of opportunity' was immediately after the general election, the reform agenda was clear – the creation of the committees to provide greater scrutiny, and the leadership of Norman St John-Stevas, as Leader of the House, was apparent. The confluence of these three elements created a broad consensus around the desirability for action and agreement that the impact on the Commons would be a positive one. Even the government – through St John-Stevas – saw how this reform would enhance the Commons' scrutiny role.

Institutionalist scholars have developed the notion of a 'critical juncture'[3] to explain how such change sometimes works and sometimes fails. Capoccia and Keleman describe a 'critical juncture' as the moment when 'structural (economic, cultural, ideological, organisational) influences on political action are significantly relaxed for a relatively short period'[4] and times when political actors can [sometimes must] 'overcome the usual bias towards inertia caused by lock-in and feedback effects'.[5]

This relates as much to the internal machinations of politics – how the Commons functions and what its roles are – as it does to any other organisation. Institutional change is characterised by 'long periods of path dependence punctuated by critical junctures, the origin of which lay in the institution itself'.[6] Consterdine and Hampshire argue that such critical junctures are useful for 'examining ... case studies where a period of policy inertia is punctuated by a period of transformation which ... leaves an enduring legacy'.[7]

There are parallels here to Norton's 'window of opportunity'. It is clear that the 1979 reforms took place in such a critical juncture. The proposals had their origins firmly within the Commons and its functions and roles. The same cannot be said of the later reforms considered in this chapter. Indeed, it will be argued that these reforms were ultimately flawed as they were not based on a serious analysis of the

---

[2] Norton, 'Reforming Parliament in the United Kingdom' (n 1) 13.

[3] The phase was first coined by SM Lipset and S Rokkan, *Party Systems and Voter Alignment: A Cross National Perspective* (New York, The Free Press, 1967).

[4] G Capoccia and RD Keleman, 'The Study of Critical Junctures: Theory, Narrative and Counterfactuals in Historical Institutionalism' (2007) 59 *World Politics* 341, 369

[5] E Consterdine and J Hampshire, 'Immigration Policy under New Labour: Exploring a Critical Juncture' (2014) 9 *British Politics* 275, 281–82.

[6] V Lowndes and M Roberts, *Why Institutions Matter: The New Institutionalism in Political Science* (Basingstoke, Palgrave Macmillan, 2013) 199

[7] Consterdine and Hampshire, 'Immigration Policy Under New Labour' (n 5) 282.

functions and roles of the Commons. This is particularly the case in the context of the effective delivery of government business and the efficient dispatch of scrutiny.

This chapter examines three specific periods of reform: the New Labour government of 1997–2010; the responses to the financial and expenses crises of 2008–10; and the Conservative–Liberal Democrat coalition government of 2010–15. It also discusses the reform of the Lords and suggests that it is not possible to seriously assess the nature of such reform without a commensurate and comprehensive review of the role and functions of the Commons. Further, it argues that such a reform would be flawed as it would represent a challenge to the primacy of the Commons – the central tenet of the constitution.

The targets of the early reforms, implemented by the Labour government from 1997 onwards, such as the sitting hours, the location of adjournment debates and the topicality of questions, were more to do with process than detail. Whilst there was some discussion on matters on substance such as pre- and post-legislative scrutiny, many of the actual reforms implemented merely tidied up discrepancies that existed, such as working hours. Yet again, though, reformers labelled such reforms as significant, radical and transformative – which they were not.

In the wake of the expenses crisis, Brown established a Select Committee in 2009 on the Reform of the House of Commons (the Wright Committee, so named after its chair, Tony Wright[8]) to look at how things could improve. In the Prime Minister's words, Wright was asked to 'advise on necessary reforms, including making Select Committee processes more democratic, scheduling more and better time for non-Government business in the House, and enabling the public to initiate directly some issues for debate'.[9]

The internal reforms to the Commons procedures based on the 2010 Wright Committee's report were not developed in the context of their impact on the functioning of the House. The three key reforms – the election of Select Committee chairs, the establishment of a Backbench Committee and the creation of a Business Committee – were all existing proposals and not rooted in a deep analysis.

The coalition government of 2010–15 tackled constitutional change with all the piety and sanctimony of a 'religious cult',[10] and with similar conviction and certainty. The then Deputy Prime Minister, Nick Clegg was charged with pushing the constitutional reform agenda. He offered a number of instant solutions to perceived problems and they were advanced because they were simply existing pet projects. The key reforms were the introduction of fixed terms for Parliament, electoral reform, a reduction in the number of MPs, the equalisation of the size of constituencies and reform of the Lords. All reforms were offered as a remedy to the failings of the political system, with no attempt to analyse how they would impinge on the role of the Commons or the role of MPs, nor indeed how the reforms would

---

[8] Tony Wright, MP for Cannock and Burntwood 1992–97 and for Cannock Chase 1997–10.
[9] HC Deb 10 June 2009, vol 493, col 797.
[10] P Riddell, 'In Defence of Politicians: In Spite of Themselves' (2010) 63 *Parliamentary Affairs*, 545.

improve the system at all.[11] They were also presented as somehow separate from the internal machinations and processes of the Commons and, at best, tangential to its role when, in fact, each of these issues could prove to be of fundamental importance.

There had been no serious analysis of how significant reforms, such as establishing fixed terms for the Commons or the introduction of electoral reform and changes to the House of Lords, would impact on either the existing constitutional settlement or the ability of the Commons to conduct its roles and functions efficiently. Reform of the Lords is discussed separately later in this chapter as the relationship between the two houses is of paramount importance to the constitutional settlement and should only be broached when there is clarity over the roles and functions of the Commons.

Critical junctures can lay the ground for change, and the change can be both profound and transformative, but this does not invariably follow. As Russell indicates, change can happen 'when key circumstances come together to make it possible'.[12] It will be argued that this was the case in 1979 but was not the case in these more recent reform periods, when protagonists for reform exploited the political system's dysfunctionality. The reform packages that followed were not rooted in an analysis of what was wrong with the system. As a consequence, the depth of the change was not rooted in the nature of the Commons and therefore there was no critical juncture. As a result, the change was neither profound nor transformative, and as a consequence would not prove to be durable or address the key needed for transformative reform.

II. What is the Commons for? Government and Scrutiny

Parliament is the supreme legislative body of the UK. Within that, the Commons is a legislative factory that, as well as being the national forum for political debate, both sustains the government in power and is the centre of parliamentary scrutiny of the government. The balance between these functions is important. However, primacy needs to be given to the facilitation of the government's ability to govern and the government needs to control business in the Commons to govern effectively. This tension between governance and scrutiny is not a new or modern dilemma.

---

[11] N Clegg, 'Bar the Gates: No Summer Holiday before the Overhaul' *The Guardian* (27 May 2009); see also the full text of Clegg's reform speech (*BBC News*, 19 May 2010) http://news.bbc.co.uk/1/hi/8691753.stm

[12] M Russell, 'Never Allow a Crisis to Go to Waste: The Wright Committee Reforms to Strengthen the House of Commons' (2011) 64 *Parliamentary Affairs* 612, 615.

In a discussion on the relevance of Parliament in the 1830s, Young described how the 'procedural history of Parliament is a struggle between an old principle (freedom of debate) and a new one (to make a programme and get through it)'.[13] If the latter point represents the Commons sustaining a government, the former relates to its scrutiny of the government.

These two functions – sustaining and scrutinising government, together with its role as the cockpit of national debate – remain central to what the Commons does. At the core of the UK system is the notion that governments are chosen by commanding a majority in the House of Commons and only function by prolonging this majority. Flinders contends that this is problematic as 'parliament has two inherently contradictory roles – first, to sustain the executive, which it would appear to do well, and second, to hold the executive to account between elections, which it does rather less well'.[14] A serious review of the functions and roles of the Commons as the prerequisite for durable reform would help address this apparently problematic dichotomy, but unfocused and untargeted reform is unlikely to do so.

Some commentators argue that the Commons is weak and in decline. King and Crewe contend that as 'a legislative assembly the parliament of the UK is, much of the time, either peripheral or totally irrelevant. It might as well not exist.'[15] Interestingly, though, they base this on a detailed analysis of a series of government blunders, many of which had no significant legislative or other input from the Commons. In fact, as Russell and Cowley make clear, many of the solutions to these government blunders had their origins in the very Commons they dismiss as weak and ineffectual.[16]

Flinders and Kelso strongly challenge this view on the decline of the Commons. They argue that 'the dominant public, media and academic perception of an eviscerated and sidelined parliament provides a misleading caricature of a more complex institution'.[17] The Commons is neither eviscerated or sidelined, yet 'the constant promotion and reinforcement of this caricature by scholars arguably perpetuates and fuels public disengagement and disillusionment with politics'.[18] Such a view also undermines the Commons' key role as the representative voice of the nation.

Riddell contends that the notion that Parliament 'has never been weaker, and that backbenchers are just lobby fodder, subservient to an all-powerful

---

[13] GM Young, *Portrait of an Age* (first published 1936, London, Phoenix Press, 2003) 29. Note the publication date.

[14] M Flinders, 'Shifting the Balance? Parliament, the Executive, and the British Constitution' (2002) 50 *Political Studies* 23.

[15] A King and I Crewe, *The Blunders of Our Governments* (London, Oneworld, 2013) 361.

[16] M Russell and P Cowley, 'The Policy Power of the Westminster Parliament: The "Parliamentary State" and the Empirical Evidence' (2016) 29 *Governance* 121, 135.

[17] M Flinders and A Kelso, 'Mind the Gap: Political Analysis, Public Expectations and the Parliamentary Decline Thesis' (2011) 13 *British Journal of Politics and International Relations*, 249, 249.

[18] ibid 250.

government', is a 'gross-simplification'.[19] He argues that those who have maintained that Parliament has been weak and getting weaker over time are wrong now and were wrong in the past. As with other commentators, he agrees with the need for reform, but not on the lines of 'big bangers' who want big bang constitutional reform and who 'condemn the whole system as rotten and corrupt'.[20]

Whether in the Commons or in terms of the broader constitutional issues, the message in the period from 2010 onwards was clear – a vote against reform was a vote for the 'broken system'.[21] This was not a sound basis for the development of a detailed discourse on the nature of the reform needed.

III. The New Labour Government: Tinkering Reforms and Low-Hanging Fruit

None of the suggested internal reforms to the Commons implemented by the New Labour government was radical or new. They had been floating around for some time as part of a wider tapestry of fashionable reforms that protagonists wanted to see implemented. The reforms were solutions looking for problems without any attempt at a fundamental review of the role of MPs or the role of the Commons itself.

The targets of early reform, such as the sitting hours, the location of adjournment debates and the topicality of questions, did little to impinge on the relationship between the executive and the Commons. The impact of each of these reforms may have been considered, but they were not analysed in any comprehensive way. Every time that reform has been suggested over the last 30 years, it has been couched in terms of existential threat. Rather than presenting a clear rationale for reform, it is proffered as essential for the continued existence of the Commons as an institution, with opponents painted as Luddites or dinosaurs. It should have been incumbent on those proposing reform – large or small – to justify it in terms of how the Commons does its job and the twin roles of delivery of government business and the efficient dispatch of scrutiny. Without doubt, a House of Commons that does not sit through the night on a regular basis should be much more efficient and effective. However, little thought was given to how this change might impact on the parliamentary year, the constituency business and duties of MPs or the scrutiny function of the House.[22]

As Russell and Cowley have shown, Parliament has significant influence, at all stages of the policy process.[23] This conclusion is based on a substantive empirical

---

[19] Riddell (n 10) 549.

[20] ibid 549–50.

[21] Russell, 'Never Allow a Crisis to Go to Waste' (n 12) 630.

[22] See, eg R Cook, 'Modernisation of the House of Commons: A Reform Programme for Consultation' Memorandum submitted by the Leader of the House of Commons (December 2001) https://publications. parliament.uk/pa/cm200102/cmselect/cmmodern/440/44003.htm

[23] Russell and Cowley (n 16) 132.

study of divisions in the Lords as well as the Commons, on Standing/Public Bill Committee proceedings and on an extensive analysis of Select Committees. They also point to other potential mechanisms of influence, including parliamentary questions (of all departments, not just PMQs), Private Members' Bills and non-legislative debates. Other opportunities for scrutiny could be added to this list, such as ministerial statements, urgent questions, Ten Minute Rule Bills, opposition day debates and written questions. This challenges Wright's notion that 'there is a fundamental fact in Britain that the executive is particularly strong and Parliament commensurately weak'.[24] Very often the areas in which the Commons works and works well – these potential mechanisms of influence – are ignored so as to advance the cause of individual, small-scale reforms.

Some of these mechanisms are more effective than others, but collectively they challenge the 'frequent caricature of Westminster that parliament is weak, government always gets its way, and backbenchers mostly do what they're told'. Russell is clear that this is 'a myth, and politicians who fall for it tend to wind up in trouble'.[25] Opportunities for scrutiny are varied and, of course, could be better used, but the issues with the current system of control and scrutiny do not stem from these mechanisms. Improving them is not helped by reformers again offering solutions without any significant analysis. One such case is the use of evidentiary sessions at what are now called Public Bill Committees, previously Standing Committees.

The ability of Standing Committees to take evidence before starting to scrutinise Bills was introduced as a result of the recommendations of the Modernisation Committee in 2006.[26] Whilst Cowley was right to contend that this had 'the potential to improve the quality of the parliamentary scrutiny of bills',[27] there was no guarantee that this would prove to be the case. This reform suggested that the absence of information was part of the failing of the Standing/Public Bill Committee system. Anyone who had ever served on such a committee will know that this was far from the case – the avalanche of information from all quarters verges on the oppressive.

Thompson has suggested that it has helped the process. However, there is little evidence to confirm that the scrutiny of Bills has improved because of these evidence-taking sessions. Some suggest that it is the same people giving the same evidence to a range of parliamentary fora. Indeed, a Labour MP described the evidence sessions for the Counter-Terrorism Bill 2007–08 as being like 'Groundhog Day' as the Bill 'heard from the same people who gave evidence to the

[24] T Wright, 'Prospects for Parliamentary Reform' (2004) 57 *Parliamentary Affairs* 867, 867.

[25] M Russell, 'Boris Johnson and Parliament: Misunderstandings and Structural Weaknesses' (*Constitution Unit Blog*, 5 February 2021) https://constitution-unit.com/2021/02/05/boris-johnson-and-parliament-misunderstandings-and-structural-weaknesses/.

[26] Modernisation Committee, *The Legislative Process: First Report of Session 2005–2006* (2006, HC 1097).

[27] P Cowley, 'Parliament' in A Seldon (ed), *Blair's Britain 1997–2007* (Cambridge, Cambridge University Press, 2007).

Home Affairs Committee' and, of the 15 witnesses giving evidence, six had already given evidence to the Home Affairs Select Committee.[28] My own experience is that the evidence sessions were limited in their impact. Relationships that began as naturally antagonistic remained so and no one, particularly government ministers, took notice of the evidence unless it supported their already held views.

The difficulty in part here is that this particular reform looked at simply one element of the legislative process when many of the problems with the process lie elsewhere. More difficult reforms, such as pre- and post-legislative scrutiny, were sidelined for the easier reforms – the low-hanging fruit.

IV. Response to Crisis: Never Let a Crisis Go to Waste – A Question of Numbers

The period of 2008–10 in UK politics was marked by the failures of the banking system and the MPs' expenses crisis. There was major criticism of the parliamentary system for its failure to prevent either of these crises. Some politicians looked to reform as part of the solution, including the then Prime Minister, Gordon Brown. There were constant attacks on the political system as a 'broken system' ripe for reform. But the reforms proposed were not new ideas, nor were they rooted in any analysis of the crises. As Russell argues, many of the reforms sought had 'little to do with the problems at hand, but reform advocates seemed to share the sentiment … that one should never let a crisis to go to waste'.[29] The crises could certainly have offered the 'window of opportunity' suggested by Norton's preconditions for reform, but there was no agenda for reform rooted in an analysis of the problems, nor was there any clear leadership.

Conservative leader David Cameron and others in the Opposition made much of the absence of reform in the past being part of the problem, without any detailed explanation of what exactly was wrong. Liberal Democrat leader Nick Clegg suggested that 'for decades reformers have been thwarted by Westminster inertia … [and that] … the MPs expenses scandal has … made change possible'.[30] In other words, there was a 'window of opportunity', but no substantive analysis of the problems or of how the system should best respond to them. Had they pursued this approach, they might have created Norton's two other preconditions: a shared agenda for reform and the leadership to see it to fruition. They could have investigated how the Commons could be best organised to facilitate both 'the effective delivery of government business and the efficient dispatch of scrutiny', but instead there was too general a focus on the 'broken system' and preordained,

---

[28] L Thompson 'Evidence Taking under the Microscope: How Has Oral Evidence Affected the Scrutiny of Legislation in House of Commons Committees?' (2014) 9 *British Politics*, 385, 387, 389.

[29] Russell, 'Never Allow a Crisis to Go to Waste' (n 12) 629.

[30] Clegg, 'Bar the Gates' (n 11). See also D Cameron, 'A New Politics: We Need a Massive, Radical Redistribution of Power' *The Guardian* (25 May 2009).

'oven ready' solutions to it. Ironically, the 'alibi' of a broken system provided cover for tinkering with reform rather than pursuing any reform of a substantive and transformative nature. Again, reformers chose petty reforms and dressed them as transformative – which they were not. There was no review of the functions of the Commons, nor of its key role – the legislative process. There was no discussion on pre- or post-legislative scrutiny, no review of the role of secondary legislation, no analysis of the role of the backbencher nor of the role of Select Committees. The extent of the reformers' radical response to crises was to attack the role and number of special advisers.

The focus on special advisers – 'spads' – illustrates this point. Brown suggested that one such problem with the broken system was the preponderance of special advisers. These 'people who live in the dark' were picked out as indicative of the broader malaise in the system.[31] Brown emphasised that his government only had 73/74 'spads' compared to a peak of 84 under Blair – although this reached 82 before the end of the government in 2010.[32] When Cameron entered No 10, he made a great play of cutting the numbers from 82 to 61. None of this was based on any analysis, let alone evidence about the role of 'spads' and how they relate to the work of ministers, government or relations with MPs. The wrong issue was used as a pretext for reform to give the impression of action.

From 2010, the two parties in the coalition continued the practice of introducing reform without any depth of evidence or analysis. The Coalition Agreement included an ill-thought-out commitment to 'put a limit on the number of special advisers'.[33] It was useful for populist rhetoric, but not necessarily for good government. Having 50 rather than 60 or 70 special advisers did not mean that a government would be any better or worse, but it projected an image of reducing political bureaucracy and addressing the broken system.

Having a particular number and type of special advisers might mean a greater degree of competence and cohesion in policy-making, but there is no 'right' number. There is a case for there being as many 'spads' as necessary to support efficient government, for example in developing policy, and, in a complex world, they could help rather than hinder the craft of governance. This might even explain the increase in the numbers under the coalition. By 2012, the number of 'spads' was back to the Blair heights of 84 and by 2019 there were over 117.[34] Interestingly, too, when Clegg became Deputy Prime Minister, he needed 14 special advisers to assist him in the role. The issue for 'reformers' was never really about the numbers of

---

[31] See S Whale, 'Living in the Dark: The Truth about Special Advisers' *Politics Home* (2 June 2020) www.politicshome.com/thehouse/article/living-in-the-dark-the-truth-about-special-advisers; L Sidnick, 'First, Fewer Special Advisers. Now, a Record Number. But Where's Much of the Growth? Step Forward, Nick Clegg' *Conservative Home* (12 June 2013) www.conservativehome.com/thetorydiary/2013/06/the-number-of-special-advisers-keeps-growing-but-they-keep-going.html; Institute of Government, 'Special Advisers' (9 December 2021) www.instituteforgovernment.org.uk/printpdf/9504.

[32] Sidnick (n 31).

[33] HM Government, *The Coalition: Our Programme for Government* (London, The Cabinet Office, 2010).

[34] Institute of Government (n 31).

'spads' impinging on the democratic process but rather using the issue politically to give the appearance of action and reform.

This is a charge that can be levelled at aspects of reform to procedures inside the Commons as well in the broader constitutional context. The chapter will return to these broader constitutional issues, but will first look at internal reform within the Commons.

V. The Wright Stuff? Reform for Reform's Sake

As indicated earlier, the Wright Committee produced some reforms, quick fixes that were based on the broader notion that the system was broken and needed fixing. What it did not do was focus on fundamental questions about the role and functions of MPs or the Commons. As Natascha Engel MP, a member of the Committee, queried 'why did we [the Committee] not start with the questions, "What do we think Parliament is for?" and, therefore, "What is the role of Members of Parliament?" Those questions were not asked at any point during the Committee's deliberations'.[35] Answers to these questions are central to a clear understanding of the role of an MP and what the functions of the House of Commons should be, as discussed above. They were not considered because the reformers had their ready-made solutions to hand.

By resisting a fundamental review of the Commons, reformers succumbed to the temptation of incrementalism or the 'tinkering' that Engel suggested.[36] Worse than this, suggesting that the three key reforms offered by the Wright Committee were the transformative reforms that the system needed meant that there was little scope or room for real substantive reform.

The media chose to see the reforms as transformative in the context of the 'broken system'. On the election of the membership and chairs of Select Committees, Coates saw it as a victory for backbenchers as 'MPs voted to wrest control of Commons business from the whips yesterday in the most significant change to the way that the House operates in 30 years'.[37] This implies that the most serious problem with Select Committees since their creation in 1979 had been how the members were appointed and the selection of chairs, implying that all the committee chairs were under the control of the whips. This was not the case.

There have been some excellent reports by the Select Committees since the implementation of the Wright reforms and certainly some outstanding chairs, but this would have been true before the reforms too. Indeed, the history of the Select Committees since their introduction in 1979 is one of clear success – both in terms of reports and chairs – given their limited resources. Equally, as with

---

[35] HC Deb 22 February 2010, vol 506, col 73.
[36] HC Deb 22 February 2010, vol 506, col 74.
[37] S Coates, 'New Reforms to Take Control of Commons Business from Whips' *The Times* (5 March 2010).

other reforms, it is difficult to treat any revitalisation of the Select Committees in the 2017–19 Parliament as normal, given the absence of a parliamentary majority, notwithstanding the confidence and supply agreement with the Democratic Unionist Party. Nor is it clear that such a reform would 'strengthen the chamber against the executive', as Russell contends.[38] There are many examples of chairs being selected despite the wishes of the whips, not because of them. Nicholas Winterton, Tory MP for Macclesfield, was Chair of the Health Select Committee from 1990 to 1992 and a constant thorn in his own government's side on health issues. Similarly, whist Donald Anderson MP and Gwyneth Dunwoody MP were exemplary Chairs of the Foreign Affairs and Transport Select Committees respectively, they did not simply carry out the government's bidding; far from it. Both successfully resisted a government push to deprive them on their respective chairs in 2001. The issue here is essentially the narrative of the reform, not its substance. Indeed, by common consent, the Select Committees had been a real success despite various constraints, yet reforms were hailed as transformative rather than administrative in nature.

It is not clear how this reform strengthened the Commons against the executive or improved the scrutiny function. Although Le Roux has stated that 'there is no doubt that the authority and legitimacy of Select Committees have grown in consequence',[39] little evidence was offered to sustain this view. Some evidence to the contrary was provided by Bates et al in a submission to a Liaison Committee Inquiry on Select Committees.[40] They concluded that there was no improvement in members' engagement as measured by attendance and turnover. They also made clear that 'there is little evidence that chair elections have in themselves improved committee independence and effectiveness' and that even 'if there has been an improvement in the performance of select committees, the new system of electing chairs does not seem to be the direct cause'.[41]

It is also difficult to unpick the impact on the Select Committees of Jeremy Corbyn as Leader of the Labour Party during the 2015–19 period. It appears that many senior Labour MPs, such as Yvette Cooper and Rachel Reeves, opted to serve as Select Committee chairs instead of serving on the front bench of a leader they clearly disagreed with. Yet it is also important to understand the cyclical nature of politics. Many of these individuals had been in ministerial positions for the

---

[38] Russell, 'Never Allow a Crisis to Go to Waste' (n 12).

[39] N La Roux, 'The Wright Reforms Changed Parliament, but There Remains Scope for Further Reform' (*Democratic Audit UK blog*, 25 February 2014) www.democraticaudit.com/2014/02/25/committees-scotland-and-the-right-of-recall-the-potential-for-parliamentary-reform/

[40] S Bates and M Goodwin, 'Submission from Dr Stephen Bates, Senior Lecturer in Political Science, University of Birmingham & Dr Mark Goodwin, Lecturer in Politics, Coventry University to the Liaison Committee Inquiry into the Effectiveness and Influence of the Select Committee System' SCS0014/15 (2019) http://data.parliament.uk/WrittenEvidence/CommitteeEvidence.svc/EvidenceDocument/Liaison/The%20effectiveness%20and%20influence%20of%20the%20committee%20system/Written/97227.html.

[41] ibid para 4.4, 3.

duration of the New Labour government, served on the front bench under Ed Miliband in the 2010–15 period and stood down from the front bench exhausted and in need of a degree of respite. There is little evidence that a new career path in Select Committees had been established at all. Many of them rapidly rejoined the front bench when Keir Starmer took over the leadership.

While, of course, Select Committees sometimes do very effective work, reformers again rather overegged this. Bates et al rightly suggest that they 'are only moderately successful in getting parliament to engage with their work, although they are (probably) getting better'.[42] They conclude that 'this ought to lead to some reflection as to why this is and whether or not there is a need to re-focus the work of departmental select committees'. It could have been transformative if the Wright Committee had focused on what the committees do and how change might strengthen the work of scrutinising the executive. This would have required a deeper review of the role and purpose of both the House of Commons and the MPs who sit within it rather than focusing simply on the method of electing the members and the chairs. As Engel suggests, for all the positive reviews this reform has received, it has proved to be more 'tinkering' than transformative.

The Wright Committee also recommended the creation of a Backbench Business Committee and this was created in 2010. The notion of a backbench committee charged with scheduling some of the business of the House was rooted in a Constitution Unit report of 2007.[43] The advent of such a committee was greeted as having the potential to be transformative, but again has not fulfilled this promise. The Wright Report suggested that 'A new committee made up of backbenchers (the "Backbench Business Committee") should be established to determine the timetable of House Business'. House business was defined as all 'non-government business' except opposition days, which were to remain the purview of the opposition parties. The Wright Committee broadly agreed that there should be an elected Backbench Business Committee responsible for scheduling 'backbench business'. The first problem with this approach is the lack of a clear definition of what is 'backbench business'. The Constitution Unit report divided business in the House into five broad categories – government business, members' business, opposition business, committee business and parliamentary questions.[44] Arguably, each of these requires some degree of government input, so it is not clear what is meant by backbench business.

Most of these five categories would not, in the end, be included as 'backbench business', and rightly so. Indeed, under the new standing order of the House, the

---

[42] S Bates, M Goodwin, S McKay and WL Ting, 'Debating the Effectiveness of House of Commons Departmental Select Committees in Informing the House' (*PSA Parliaments Blog*, 17 July 2019) https://psaparliaments.org/2019/07/17/select-committees-commons-chamber/.
[43] M Russell and A Paun, 'International Lessons for Enhancing the Autonomy of the House of Commons' (Constitution Unit UCL, 2007) www.ucl.ac.uk/constitution-unit/sites/constitution_unit/files/142_1.pdf.
[44] ibid 16.

nature of backbench business is arrived at by exclusion.[45] It is defined as 'all business which is not Government business, opposition business, motions for adjournment of the House, private business, amendments to SO 14 or business set down at the direction of the Speaker.'[46] This includes parliamentary questions – written and oral. Under Standing Order 14.4, the Committee is permitted to schedule business on 35 days each session, 27 in the Commons chamber and the rest in Westminster Hall. It is difficult to see how these changes could be described as transformative.

Whilst the Backbench Business Committee has been responsible for a wide range of debates, its motions are not binding on the government. Consequently, although it is reasonable to say that it has had a positive effect on MPs' morale,[47] it remains to be seen whether or not it is 'the most important reform that has happened since the Select Committee system was introduced in 1979 … [and] it has been remarkably effective.'[48] Its impact on House activity is relatively minor, and on government business even less. Certainly, the notion that it improves the 'ability of Parliament to hold the Government, the Executive, to account' has yet to be proven.[49]

Nonetheless, some debates might not have taken place had the government still determined the subjects for discussion. These include those on the contaminated blood scandal, prisoner voting rights and Hillsborough. Yet, as Evans suggest, this 'permanent backbench revolution' had 'party managers and the usual channels … [only] … mildly unsettled but certainly not shaken'. He is right to conclude that whilst the existence of the Committee has 'made the … Commons a more lively place on some Thursday afternoons', he is equally correct to suggest that 'it has done no very obvious harm'.[50] Again, hardly a transformative revolution.

Wintour reported that a 'long campaign to wrest control of the parliamentary agenda from government triumphed today when MPs voted overwhelmingly to establish an elected backbench committee to take responsibility for tracts of Commons business'. He went on to declare that 'the reforms, passed in the dying days of a discredited parliament, represent the most radical erosion of the authority of party whips for many years'.[51] As with other reforms, its proponents sold the change as transformative when, to date at least, it is no such thing. It is more of an expansion of the opportunity for debates by backbenchers – some of which

---

[45] L Maer, 'The Backbench Business Committee House of Commons Library Research Briefing, London' (2010) https://researchbriefings.files.parliament.uk/documents/SN05654/SN05654.pdf.

[46] R Kelly, 'The Backbench Business Committee' House of Commons Library Briefing Paper No 7225 (2020) 8.

[47] La Roux (n 40).

[48] Procedure Committee, 'Review of the Backbench Business Committee – Corrected Evidence' (23 May 2012) Q.17 and response, www.publications.parliament.uk/pa/cm201213/cmselect/cmproced/c168-i/c16801.htm.

[49] ibid Q.19 and response.

[50] P Evans, 'The Backbench Business Committee: An Unfinished Revolution?' (*Constitution Unit blog*, 22 January 2021) at https://constitution-unit.com/2021/01/22/the-backbench-business-committee-an-unfinished-revolution/

[51] P Wintour, 'Backbench Reformers Win Big Role in Controlling Commons Business' *The Guardian* (4 March 2010).

can challenge government. But the motions that emerge from these debates are not binding on the government. The Committee itself has stated that if they were, then 'The result would be that backbench debates would be heavily whipped and each motion defeated'.[52] Furthermore, 'it would mean that the freedom currently enjoyed by backbenchers to explore issues and speak relatively freely (much more so than ever before) would be sacrificed'.[53] For others, this means that the Committee is 'always the supplicant and the government business managers the holders of the key to the treasure trove of time'.[54]

VI. Standing Order 14 – A Matter of Time

The 'treasure trove of time' is at the heart of the government's control of its business and its ability to govern. Such control is rightly conceived through scrutiny and process, but the government must be able to govern. Many reformers appear to think that this is a secondary consideration, but it is not. Much of the Commons business is, in some form or other, government business, or at least has a substantive government input. In order to govern, time is essential in a fully functioning Parliament. Governments are obsessed by parliamentary time, not out of control freakery but because access to time dictates how the government is able to legislate. This should be looked at as part of any major review of the government and the Commons and how they work together.

At any given time, up to 10 Bills or sometimes more are at various stages of progress in both the Lords and Commons, and many key decisions and functions rely on each Bill becoming an Act in a specified time at a specified date. The result is a complicated four- or five-dimensional matrix – carefully calibrated to deliver. This is why government needs to control time in the Commons. This also needs to be seen in the context of approximately 20–40 Bills progressing each year. Clearly, how governments legislate should be a key feature of any detailed assessment of the role and functions of the Commons.

Central to the control of time by government is the rather infamous Standing Order 14.[55] The opening line of the standing order states that 'save as provided in this order, government business shall have precedence at every sitting'.[56] As Cowie and Samra make clear:

> there are, however, three important exceptions to this general rule included in the standing orders. On 20 days per session, opposition business is given priority.

---

[52] Backbench Business Committee, *Work of the Committee in the 2010–2015 Parliament* (2014–15, HC 1106) 3, paras 18–27 and 81. See also Kelly, 'The Backbench Business Committee' (n 47) 11.

[53] Backbench Business Committee (n 53) 3, paras 18–27 and 81.

[54] Evans (n 51).

[55] For text of SO14, see 'Standing Orders of the House of Commons – Public Business 2018' https://publications.parliament.uk/pa/cm201719/cmstords/1020/body.html.

[56] G Cowie and S Samra, 'Taking Control of the Order Paper' (2019) https://commonslibrary.parliament.uk/taking-control-of-the-order-paper/.

On 27 days per session, priority is given in the Commons chamber to backbench business. On 13 Fridays per session, precedence is given to the consideration of Private Members' Bills, with priority being given to those on the ballot.[57]

The Wright Committee reported quite fairly that 'the default position is therefore that time "belongs" to the government, subject to a number of exceptions and practices which allow others to influence and even determine the agenda'. This is an accurate assessment, and the report continues by saying that 'put crudely, and subject to maintaining a majority, the government enjoys not merely precedence but exclusive domination of much of the House's agenda and can stop others seeking similar control'.[58] The key phrase here is 'subject to maintaining a majority'.[59]

Once the government secures a majority in a general election or through deals, formal and informal, with other parties, then its business should prevail – fulfilling the role of the Commons to provide and sustain a government. The Wright Committee saw this as problematic; others see this as central to the prevailing constitutional settlement.

The implication that Parliament, not the government, should control the agenda fails to realise the importance of time in the Commons and how essential it is for a government to govern. The Commons is a place of statecraft and governance – not simply a debating chamber, although this role is very important. The effective delivery of government business and the efficient dispatch of scrutiny are paramount roles for the Commons. A failure to understand the importance of the control of the agenda also shows an inability to understand how Parliament really functions – especially in the context of this scrutiny of the executive. It also shows how tinkering with the system can cause undesirable consequences and lead to ungovernability. Importantly, it misses the key systemic constitutional point – governments are formed by those who command majorities in the Commons. Whilst it is reasonable to debate how best to secure time both for the government programme and to manage and protect the remaining non- Standing Order 14 time for the parliamentary scrutiny function, these are not the same issues as completely scrapping government control of the order paper.

The government cannot cede control of the agenda without losing its ability to govern, but it should be ready to ensure that those areas of business that facilitate scrutiny are preserved and protected. Judge is right to suggest there is already a presumption that there is 'a dual willingness – a willingness of government to be scrutinised and a willingness of Parliament to scrutinise, alongside a singular capacity: the ability of Parliament to scrutinise'.[60] This is the price for government dominance of business and control of parliamentary time.

---

[57] ibid 1.

[58] House of Commons Reform Committee, 'Rebuilding the House First Report of Session 2008–09', https://publications.parliament.uk/pa/cm200809/cmselect/cmrefhoc/1117/1117.pdf.

[59] ibid 40.

[60] D Judge, 'Walking the Dark Side: Evading Parliamentary Scrutiny' (2021) 92 *The Political Quarterly* 283, 283.

Judge is also right to suggest that there is a 'dark side' to scrutiny connected to what White contends is an 'excessive fear of governments of "failure and public criticism" and "blame and scapegoating" which result in "defensive reactions" by the executive'.[61] The argument here is not that there is no problem with the scrutiny function of government by the Commons; it could always be better. The issue is that the tinkering by the Wright Report and others has done nothing to improve the scrutiny function and is potentially an impediment to serious and radical reform.

In commenting on the control of the Commons agenda, Russell and Gover note that:

> most recently, the government's handling of the COVID-19 crisis – both in terms of the Commons' own procedure, and the extent to which MPs have a say over policy – has raised significant concerns, including among government backbenchers and key Select Committees.[62]

They therefore argue for the implementation of the 'last' Wright Report recommendation, on giving control of the Commons agenda to the Commons – with or without a House Business Committee. Whilst there have certainly been concerns about how the government managed the COVID crisis and the role played by both the government and scrutiny, Russell and Gover are less convincing on how control of the agenda would have changed this. They report that such an arrangement would have 'significant benefits', although they are not explained at any point. They suggest that any problems would be dealt with by 'safeguards' that 'could be built in to avoid time wasting and mischievous amendments'.[63] Again, though, these safeguards are not articulated further.

The absence of a detailed analysis of the role and functions of the Commons prior to any reform undermines both the efficacy and legitimacy of the reforms. The need and nature of these reforms and how they may improve matters are unlikely to be well thought out, given the lack of analysis. The same is true of constitutional reform at the national level.

It is normally incumbent on reformers to show the legitimacy and need for any proposed reform – but this has not been readily forthcoming in terms of constitutional reform. Rather, as Riddell contends, some reformers:

> spit out Westminster as a term of insult. They mistrust elected politicians and parties as inherently self-serving and obstacles to the expression of the Peoples' will. There is something of the piety, self-satisfaction, and all-or-nothing certainty of a religious cult about them.[64]

---

[61] H White, *Parliamentary Scrutiny of Government* (London, Institute of Government, 2015).

[62] M Russell and D Gover, *Taking Back Control: Why the House of Commons Should Govern Its Own Time* (London, The Constitution Unit, 2021) 6, www.ucl.ac.uk/constitution-unit/sites/constitution-unit/files/190_taking_back_control_-_why_the_house_of_commons_should_govern_its_own_time_final_report_110121.pdf.

[63] ibid 23.

[64] Riddell (n 10) 549.

VII. '1832' and All that – Constitutional Expediencies, the FTPA and Electoral Reform

The constitutional reforms proposed by the coalition government of 2010–15 were offered as a remedy to the failings of the political system, with no attempt to analyse how they would impinge on the role of the Commons or the role of MPs, or indeed how the reforms would improve the system at all.[65] They were also presented as somehow separate from the internal machinations and processes of the Commons and, at best, tangential to its role when, in fact, each of these issues could prove to be of fundamental importance.

The constitutional reform proposals were outlined in detail by Clegg and were portentously described by him as 'the biggest shake up of our democracy since 1832'.[66] This was a huge claim to transformative reform without any of the substance that sat beneath the Great Reform Act. None of the elements of reform proposed was a new idea, but all were offered in the simplistic spirit that 'reform is good, status quo bad' and without any real evidence for each particular change.

One of the reforms was the introduction of the Fixed-term Parliament Act 2011 (FTPA). The genesis of the Bill was rooted in a long-desired reform, which can be traced back to the 1930s, to remove the power of the PM to call general elections.[67] When he introduced the legislation, Clegg told MPs that 'This bill has a single, clear purpose ... for the first time in our history the timing of general elections will not be a plaything of governments'.[68] Whatever the merits of this argument, there were more strongly partisan and political reasons behind the legislation. It was not just a 'constitutional innovation'. It was, according to a senior Liberal Democrats advisor, a device 'designed to create a commitment between the two political parties' and to ensure that they 'would stick it out for the full five years, to make it just a little bit more difficult for the main party to do the dirty on the smaller party'.[69]

Thus, although dressed up as a significant constitutional reform brought in for virtuous reasons, the FTPA was a political device to prevent the Tories from going for an early dissolution when the polls favoured them. It was also clear from the problematic progress of the Bill through the Houses of Parliament that little thought had been given to how this piece of legislation changed the relationship between the Commons and the executive in general and, more specifically, in terms of confidence and no-confidence motions and their consequences. As a result, the proposals had to change 'essentially as a result of those responsible for the

---

[65] Clegg, 'Bar the Gates' (n 11).
[66] Clegg reform speech (n 11).
[67] A Blick, 'Constitutional Implications of the Fixed-Term Parliaments Act 2011' (2016) 69 *Parliamentary Affairs* 19, 19.
[68] J Fenwick, 'Is Axing Fixed-Term Parliaments a Good Idea?' (*BBC News*, 7 March 2021) at www.bbc.co.uk/news/uk-politics-56297664.
[69] ibid 3.

coalition Government not appreciating the nature and significance of the convention governing confidence votes'.[70] The FTPA was presented as needing no debate because the argument in favour was so compelling. The counter argument went beyond simply a defence of the status quo. Bogdanor presents this clearly as 'the traditional arrangement allowed for a responsiveness that is crucial to the democratic system, and that would be lacking under fixed-terms'. This view emphasised the appropriateness of early polls in such circumstances as an unworkable parliamentary balance, a mid-term change of premier, the need for a new mandate for a particular policy or changes in the party configuration of the government.[71]

Fixed terms have an impact on how the Commons conducts it work and this should have been a central consideration, but political interest seemed to be more important than impact or efficacy. At the very least, a range of legitimate options and concerns should have been recognised and discussed. Both the Conservative and Labour parties went into the 2019 election committed to repealing the FTPA – and this finally happened on 24 March 2022 with the Dissolution and Calling of Parliament Act 2022.

There was little parliamentary discussion on other elements of supposed constitutional reform, including proportional representation, a reduction in the number of MPs and the equalisation of the size of constituencies. A referendum on electoral reform – specifically the Alternative Vote (AV) – was simply the price exacted by the Liberal Democrats for joining the coalition. No rationale was provided for the plans to cut the number of MPs except that it was based on Cameron's panicked notion that the number of MPs was part of the problem inherent in the 'broken system'. This mirrored the numbers game on special advisers, rather than the promise of substantive reform.

Although there is a long-established practice of periodically reviewing first local government boundaries and then parliamentary boundaries, the 2013 review instigated by the Conservative–Liberal Democrat coalition government was different.[72] The review was charged with trying to equalise the size of parliamentary constituencies, echoing the People's Charter of 1838.[73] The problem here was not the periodic review of the boundaries, but rather carrying this out within the context of ensuring 50 fewer MPs. However dressed up, the rationale was simply a numbers game that had serious consequences for communities in terms of representation.[74] Even in this key area of reform, the motivation was narrow. There is no evidence of any serious analysis of the impact of any of these three items on the

---

[70] P Norton, 'The Fixed-term Parliaments Act and Votes of Confidence' (2016) 69 *Parliamentary Affairs*, 3, 13.

[71] V Bogdanor, *The Coalition and the Constitution* (Oxford, Hart Publishing, 2011) 20.

[72] See, eg I White and N Johnston, 'Constituency Boundaries: the Sixth General Review in England' House of Commons Library Standard Note SN/PC/06229.

[73] The equalisation of the size of constituencies was one of the Chartists' six demands.

[74] In the end, the 2013 Boundary Commission Report that redrew the boundaries for a 600-seat Parliament was abandoned because of disagreements between the coalition partners.

role and functions of MPs or the Commons in general. Furthermore, they lacked Norton's three preconditions for real reform.

The basis on which reform in 2010/11 was proposed was that the political system was broken and the perception of radical reform was all important. Although both of the coalition parties included a reduction in the number of MPs in their manifestos, there had been no obvious analysis on how this might impact on the relationship between the legislature and the executive. For example, should the number of ministers be reduced on a pro rata basis, would fewer MPs require larger resources to service larger constituencies or what would the impact be on the role of MPs in general? The absence of any significant research points to a rather crude equation that the fewer MPs the better – hardly a substantive basis on which to build the elements of the legislature.

Miles deals with the key issues around electoral reform elsewhere in this volume, including the merits of the first-past-the-post electoral system, accountability and electoral reform.[75] Across all three elements of coalition government reform, it is clear that their impact on the nature and role of the Commons was again not considered at all. Such consideration would have shown clearly that they would impact directly on the role of MPs, the work of the Commons and the relationship between the executive and the legislature. The only significant analysis that took place at all was on the detail of the processes involved.

VIII. Waiting for Godot: House of Lords Reform and the Primacy of the Commons

The reform of the House of Lords, as proposed by the coalition government, is another key area where an understanding of the roles and functions of the Commons and how they relate to a second chamber should have been essential. Yet the relationship between the two houses and how a reformed Lords would sit alongside the Commons was barely discussed. Most of the substantive debates around Lords reform related to composition, size and democracy – whether it should be elected, appointed or a mixture of the two.[76] Its functions and roles were seldom discussed. This is yet another case of a preoccupation with form over function, yet it is again offered in absolutist terms – how on earth could anyone possibly disagree with reform?

Opening the debate on a previous reform proposal back in 2003, Robin Cook, the then Leader of the House, drew the analogy of House of Lords reform becoming the parliamentary equivalent of 'Waiting for Godot', as it 'never arrives and some have become rather doubtful whether it even exists, but we sit around talking

---

[75] J Miles, 'Accountability and Electoral Reform', ch 9 in this volume.
[76] Royal Commission on Reform of the House of Lords, *A House for the Future* (Cm 4534, 2000).

about it year after year'.[77] Nevertheless, the Commons proceeded to vote down every option for reform that was presented in 2003.[78] Some suggested that this was a failure by the Commons and showed how it was already 'broken' as early as 2003. Although subsequent votes in 2007 showed Commons majorities for either 80 per cent or 100 per cent elected, the debate was again largely about composition, size and election rather than about the relationship of the second chamber to the Commons, its roles and its functions.

This was all the more apparent in the 2011 proposals for reform from the coalition government. The draft Bill introduced by Clegg explicitly referred to the existing functions of the Lords and stated that the 'Government believes that these functions should remain unchanged when the House of Lords is reformed and that it should continue this valuable work'.[79] In the course of the debate on the draft Bill, much of the criticism revolved around its limited nature and government proposals to limit the time for debate. Critics suggested that the government's proposals would create a 'a sham democratic chamber which will consist overwhelmingly of members who would rather be in this chamber [the Commons]', or that the proposal 'will damage the fabric of our government', that it was 'back of a fag-packet legislation' or that it did 'not adequately address fears about the primacy of the Commons'.[80]

Clegg was largely dismissive of these criticisms and those who resisted reform. He argued in very general terms that there were 'three reasons to vote in favour of the bill and its orderly passage. Because we believe in democracy; for the sake of better laws and because reform cannot be ducked.' The countervailing arguments around democracy and the primacy of the first chamber were dismissed. How exactly better laws would result from the reforms without any investigation or analysis of how laws are made by the first chamber, least still how they are revised by the second chamber, were ignored. The rhetoric of his third point essentially meant that 'we should reform because we should reform' – tautology to support legislation.

In debate, Clegg did not recognise any argument to counter the reforms and accused opponents of simply fearing change. Yet the concerns raised about the relationship of a reformed House of Lords to the Commons were legitimate and should have been explored. As Norton suggests:

> there was the objection of principle that an elected House would challenge the core accountability at the heart of the political system. Supporters of an elected second chamber rest on the basic premise that the existing appointed House is undemocratic. The case is stated as if self-evidently true.[81]

---

[77] HC Deb 4 February 2003, vol 399, col 152.

[78] HC Deb 4 February 2003, vol 399, col 243.

[79] House of Lords Reform Bill Volume 548: debated on Monday 9 July 2012.

[80] 'Nick Clegg Says Lords a Flawed Institution' (*BBC News*, 10 July 2012) www.bbc.co.uk/news/uk-politics-18759639

[81] P Norton, 'The House of Lords: A Sceptical View of "Big Bang" Reform', ch 8 in this volume.

In any substantive review, the discussion would start with an appraisal of the functions and roles of the principal chamber and a discussion on whether or not these functions and roles should remain the same or be reformed in any way. A key part of this discussion would be whether there needed to be a second chamber at all. If it was agreed that a second chamber was required, then, and only then, should there be a discussion on the nature, roles and form of the second chamber.

Notwithstanding the rhetoric of Clegg and others, it is strange to propose determining the second chamber's size and how it was to be elected or appointed before any consideration of its purpose, form and nature. The absence of this kind of analysis is what led to the bizarre proposal that an elected second chamber should have exactly the same functions as the previous House of Lords.[82] The notion that an elected second chamber would not challenge the primacy of the Commons was either naive or deliberately obtuse. Substantive reform was thwarted by those with easy answers who feared detailed analysis rather than those who feared change.

IX. Conclusion

As the Commons is at the centre of both the governmental architecture and the constitutional settlement, constitutional reform and how the Commons conducts its business are hugely important. Reform of the Commons is not a minor matter of lesser importance than the wider constitutional issues, but is central to them. If this is ignored, then any wider constitutional reform will be flawed.

The absence of a full understanding of what a reformed Commons should be doing both to facilitate the implementation of the legislative programme and to hold the executive to account means that the target of reforms over the last 20 years has largely been low-hanging fruit. Reforms sold as major innovations are often nothing of the sort, but as they do little harm to the executive, they are indulged, though some have had unintended consequences and have been repealed. A fundamental reform of the Commons in the interest of both MPs' work and better government, particularly in terms of legislation and scrutiny, is long overdue. This would allow government to work better on behalf of UK citizens. Reforms such as backbench debates, tinkering with the hours and consigning much backbench work to Westminster Hall do little to improve the efficacy of the Commons in terms of either scrutiny or good government. Like many of the recommendations of the Wright Report, they start from a fundamentally flawed premise on control of the order paper.

There are strong arguments for further reform of the Commons, but this needs to be substantive reform – to facilitate both the effective delivery of government business and the efficient dispatch of scrutiny. At various times, there has been cursory discussion on and some rudimentary plans for pre- and post-legislative

---

[82] Ibid.

scrutiny, but never in a significant and substantive fashion, and much more is required.[83] Russell argues that the way in which the Johnson administration has treated Parliament throughout the COVID pandemic[84] shows very clearly why further, but substantive, reform is needed – not least of the scrutiny function. Other areas, such as the reliance on secondary legislation as suggested by Jones[85] and Private Members' Bills as suggested by Brazier and Fox, need urgent review too.[86] But it is time to look at these processes more deeply in the context of better government and through a deeper review of the functions and accountabilities of the Commons and MPs.

Changes should not be considered in isolation or through the prism of 'oven ready' reforms posing as radicalism. The more recent contribution to proposed reform suggests that all that is needed in addition to proportional representation is 'an elected senate of the nations and regions to replace the Lords and maximum devolution of power out of Westminster'.[87] Yet again, this represents the triumph of form over function, shape over substance. There is no suggestion as to how these reforms would relate to the roles and functions of the Commons – the fulcrum of the UK's constitutional settlement.[88]

Unless politicians choose to centre the Commons at the heart of the constitutional settlement, and re-evaluate and reassess its roles and functions, then it will be impossible to properly reform the key constitutional areas, such as devolution, the voting system, the role of the judiciary and a reformed Lords – or, indeed, the internal workings of the Commons itself. A revitalised democracy requires nothing less than an energised Commons confident in its relationship with the government because it has finally been taken seriously enough to have its entire constitutional raison d'être, roles and accountabilities reviewed and confirmed. Once the roles and accountabilities of the Commons are properly determined in this fashion, both Norton's 'window of opportunity' and a clear agenda and leadership for reform can be generated.[89] This is the basis for genuine and lasting reform.

---

[83] See, eg R Kelly, 'Pre-legislative Scrutiny under the Coalition Government: 2010–2015' House of Commons Library Briefing Paper Number 05859 (2015) https://commonslibrary.parliament.uk/research-briefings/sn05859/; R Kelly and M Everett, 'Post-Legislative Scrutiny' House of Commons Library Research Briefing SN/PC/05232 (2013) https://researchbriefings.parliament.uk/ResearchBriefing/Summary/SN05232.

[84] See Norton, 'The House of Lords' (n 82), particularly on the Johnson government. See also M Russell, 'Boris Johnson and Parliament: an Unhappy Tale in 13 Acts' (The Constitution Unit, 2020) https://constitution-unit.com/2020/09/01/boris-johnson-and-parliament-an-unhappy-tale-in-13-acts/; M Russell, 'Boris Johnson and Parliament: Misunderstandings and Structural Weaknesses' (n 25).

[85] J Jones, 'Reliance on Secondary Legislation Has Resulted in Significant Problems' (The Constitution Unit, 2021) https://constitution-unit.com/2021/10/13/reliance-on-secondary-legislation-has-resulted-in-significant-problems-it-is-time-to-rethink-how-such-laws-are-created/.

[86] A Brazier and R Fox, *Enhancing the Role of Backbench MPs: Proposals for Reform of Private Members Bills'* (London, The Hansard Society, 2011).

[87] A Burnham, 'Why It's Time for Labour to Back Proportional Representation' *The Guardian* (25 June 2022).

[88] ibid.

[89] Norton, 'Reforming Parliament in the United Kingdom' (n 1) 11.

8

The House of Lords: A Sceptical View of 'Big Bang' Reform

PHILIP NORTON, LORD NORTON OF LOUTH

I. Introduction

Reform and demands for change of the UK's second chamber, the House of Lords, are nothing new. The House has been subject to criticism and reform for several centuries.[1] It was briefly abolished in the seventeenth century[2] and faced Liberal demands to 'mend or end' in the nineteenth.[3] It was subject to major change in the twentieth century, in the first half of the century to its powers (Parliament Acts 1911 and 1949)[4] and in the second half to its composition (Life Peerages Act 1958, Peerages Act 1963, House of Lords Act 1999).[5] There are critics who have regularly called for its abolition.

That it has been the target of demands for reform is not that surprising. Second chambers generally, as Meg Russell has shown, are the subject of criticism.[6] In the UK context, it derives especially from the fact that it is not elected – and for most of its history with members there by reason of inheriting their seats – and by the political composition of its membership. From the time of Pitt the Younger as Prime Minister at the start of the nineteenth century through to 1999, there was a Conservative predominance in the House.

Most of the changes of the twentieth century were first-order changes, stipulating the powers and composition of the House, and introduced by the government.

---

[1] See WS McKechnie, *The Reform of the House of Lords* (Glasgow, James MacLehose & Sons, 1909); C Jones and D Lewis Jones (eds), *Peers and Power: The House of Lords, 1603–1911* (London, Hambledon Press, 1986); P Raina, *House of Lords Reform: A History*, vol 1 (Bern, Peter Lang, 2011).

[2] FC Firth, *The House of Lords during the Civil War* (London, Longmans, Green, & Co, 1910).

[3] P Norton, *Reform of the House of Lords* (Manchester, Manchester University Press, 2017) 19–22.

[4] C Ballinger, *The House of Lords, 1911–2011* (Oxford, Hart Publishing, 2012); C Ballinger 'The Parliament Act 1949' in D Feldman (ed), *Law in Politics, Politics in Law* (Oxford, Hart Publishing, 2013) 171–86; P Norton, 'Parliament Act 1911 in its Historical Context' in Feldman (ibid) 155–69.

[5] Norton, *Reform of the House of Lords* (n 3) 23–27.

[6] M Russell, *Reforming the House of Lords: Lessons from Overseas* (Oxford, Oxford University Press, 2000).

The Acts of 1958, enabling life peers to be created, and 1999, removing most hereditary peers from membership, changed the very nature of the House, from one based on inheriting one's seat to one based on being appointed for one's own lifetime, and – given that those appointed were chosen usually to make some commitment to the House – facilitating a more active and assertive House. Prior to 1958, the House was becoming moribund, with short sittings and low attendance rates.[7] Since the passage of the Life Peerages Act, the House has essentially reinvented itself as an active and effective body of scrutiny, especially detailed legislative scrutiny.[8] Like the House of Commons, it is one of the most active legislative chambers in the world, and in terms of legislative scrutiny makes more of a difference to the detail of Bills than the Commons.

Its composition has facilitated its revitalisation. In terms of political composition, no one party has an overall majority. Government thus has to engage and take the House seriously in order to gets its measures through. At the individual level, the House is one of experience and expertise, members appointed usually because of the positions they hold or have held, or because they are the leading specialists in their field. Ministers have to be well briefed to respond to informed scrutiny, not least from members that other peers take seriously and whose arguments they may prefer over those advanced by the government. As a result, the culture of the House is very different to that of the House of Commons. The Commons is characterised by a culture of assertion, the Lords by a culture of justification.[9] The composition also facilitates another distinctive feature. As the Chief Rabbi Lord Sacks observed in evidence to the Joint Committee on the Draft House of Lords Reform Bill in 2012, the House also serves as an arena for a discourse of civil society.[10]

The House of Lords is thus qualitatively different to the elected House. The fact that the House of Lords is not elected ensures it defers to the elected chamber, seeking to complement, rather than challenge, the work of the Commons through fulfilling functions that MPs may not have the time or the political will to undertake. The House of Lords undertakes the tasks of not only detailed scrutiny of the provisions of Bills brought forward by the government, but also of delegated legislation, both in terms of order-making powers included in Bills and of the orders promulgated under the powers contained in Acts. The Commons lacks the political will and consequently the means to examine what may appear dry and specialised provisions, scrutiny of which entails no notable public and political profile. Peers lack the motivation to prioritise 'look at me' activities that necessarily and understandably predominate among members of the elected chamber.

---

[7] PA Bromhead, *The House of Lords and Contemporary Politics* (London, Routledge, 1958) 31; Norton, *Reform of the House of Lords* (n 3) 23–24.

[8] See P Norton, 'Legislative Scrutiny in the House of Lords' in A Horne and A Le Sueur (eds), *Parliament: Legislation and Accountability* (Oxford, Hart Publishing, 2016) 117–36.

[9] ibid 219.

[10] Joint Committee on the Draft House of Lords Reform Bill, *Draft House of Lords Reform Bill Report, vol III* (2012–13, HL 284–III, HC 1313–III) 175–78.

The House of Lords Act 1999 was advanced by the Labour government as the first stage of a process of reform 'to make the House of Lords more democratic and representative'.[11] It committed to appointing a joint committee of the two Houses to undertake review of possible future changes, but in the event established a Royal Commission to make recommendations. The Commission, chaired by Tory peer Lord Wakeham, a former Leader of both Houses, recommended that a minority of members be elected.[12] Attempts to achieve a political consensus on a part-elected chamber floundered. A joint committee was established to consider reform, but came to no conclusion, rather identifying options. These were put to each House in 2003: peers voted for an all-appointed House and against all the others; MPs voted down every option – all-appointed, part-elected, elected and an amendment proposing abolition. When invited in 2007 again to vote on the options, peers repeated their votes of 2003, but MPs voted for an 80 per cent elected House and a wholly elected House. The lobby for a wholly elected House was swelled by MPs opposed to election, but who believed a 100 per cent elected House would be unacceptable to the government. In the light of the vote, the government accepted the case for a largely elected House, publishing a White Paper, *The Governance of Britain*, stating its position. However, given that there were more pressing priorities, no measure was enacted during the period of the Labour government. Proposals for a draft Bill, announced early in 2010, were overtaken by a general election.

The commitment to achieve first-order change through the creation of a largely or wholly elected second chamber was taken up by the Conservative–Liberal Democrat coalition government of 2010–15. At the same time, there were attempts to achieve second-order changes, essentially incremental reforms internal to the House of Lords, including allowing peers to retire from membership. These were promoted by Private Members in the two Houses. The other notable difference is that the first-order change failed to be achieved, whereas second-order changes have made it to the statute book.

Here, I address the reasons for the failure of the first-order reform and for the success of incremental change.

II. The 'Big Bang' Failure

The Liberal Democrat Party has for some years embraced a liberal approach to constitutional change, seeking to fragment power as a means of limiting state authority and protecting the individual.[13] The reforms that form part of the agenda

[11] Labour Party Manifesto 1997.
[12] Royal Commission on Reform of the House of Lords, *A House for the Future* (Cm 4534, 2000).
[13] See P Norton, 'The Changing Constitution' in B Jones, P Norton and I Hertner (eds), *Politics UK*, 10th edn (London, Routledge, 2021) 319.

include a system of proportional representation for parliamentary elections and an elected second chamber.

The indeterminate result of the 2010 general election provided the opportunity for the party to be a partner in government. In negotiations with the Conservatives, the Liberal Democrats were perceived to have got the better of the deal in respect of constitutional issues.[14] Conservative leader David Cameron was formally in favour of an elected upper chamber – the party's manifesto promised 'to build a consensus for a mainly-elected second chamber' – but had made clear that he regarded it as a 'third term' issue, in other words a proposal that was not a priority and may never see the light of day. The manifesto was worded knowing that a consensus was unlikely to be achieved. Had the Conservative Party won an overall majority, Lords reform would not have appeared in the government's programme. However, now he was seeking Liberal Democrat support to form a government, Cameron had no principled objection to embracing a proposal for an elected chamber. The Coalition Agreement included a commitment 'to establish a committee to bring forward proposals for a wholly or mainly elected upper chamber on the basis of proportional representation. The committee will come forward with a draft motion by December 2010.'[15]

In the event, the government published a draft House of Lords Reform Bill in 2011 providing for a House of just over 300 members, with 240 elected and 60 appointed, 12 bishops and up to eight ministerial members. The elected members were to be returned under the single transferable vote (STV) method of election, with the election taking place at the same time as elections to the House of Commons. Each member was to be returned for a non-renewable term of three Parliaments, expected to be 15 years.

The draft Bill was sent to a joint committee of the two Houses for pre-legislative scrutiny. After something approaching 90 hours spent considering the measure, the committee endorsed most of the Bill's provisions, albeit frequently by majority vote, but recommended a House of 450 rather than 300 and noted that the two Houses would need to agree rules governing the relationship between them.[16] It also recommended that the proposed reform be subject to a referendum, a proposal that was rejected by the government. Almost half the members of the committee (12 out of 26) produced their own 'alternative report', arguing that the issue of Lords reform should not be treated as a discrete issue, given that it had consequences for the nation's constitution, and recommended appointing a constitutional convention to look more broadly at constitutional change.[17]

---

[14] R Fox, 'Five Days in May: A New Political Order Emerges' in A Geddes and J Tonge (eds), *Britain Votes 2010* (Oxford, Oxford University Press, 2010) 34.

[15] HM Government, *The Coalition: Our Programme for Government* (London, The Cabinet Office, 2010) 27.

[16] Joint Committee on the Draft House of Lords Reform Bill (2012) *Draft House of Lords Reform Bill Report, vol I* (2010–12, HL 284–I, HC 1313–I).

[17] 'Alternative Report, House of Lords Reform: An Alternative Way Forward' A Report by Members of the Joint Committee of Both Houses of Parliament on the Government's Draft House of Lords Reform Bill (London, 2012).

The government then introduced its House of Lords Reform Bill.[18] It followed the draft Bill, other than in one major respect: it stipulated that the elected members would be returned under a regional list system, rather than under STV. The Second Reading of the Bill in the Commons was scheduled for two days (9 and 10 July 2012). It faced substantial opposition from a large number of Conservative MPs as well as from several senior Labour MPs. The opposition on the Conservative benches was both broad – drawing members from different parts of the party, including some, such as Sir Nicholas Soames, who previously had been serial loyalists – and deep, with a dedicated group, led by Tory MP Jesse Norman, coming together to mobilise opposition to the Bill. They formed themselves into a body, self-styled 'the Sensibles', and undertook a dedicated whipping operation of their own. Drawing on the guidance of two supporters who were former whips, they arranged canvasses of backbenchers, meeting regularly to discuss tactics and assess support. Their operation essentially outmatched that of the government whips.

The effectiveness of the activity of 'the Sensibles' was borne out in the debate of the Second Reading. Tory opponents of the Bill were notable both for their presence in the debate and for dominating the contributions. Of 35 Tory backbenchers to speak over the two days, 29 opposed the Bill. Although most Labour MPs who spoke supported the Bill, 12 spoke against it, including former Cabinet ministers David Blunkett, Dame Margaret Beckett, Frank Dobson and Hazel Blears. Of Labour MPs to support the Second Reading, several emphasised the case for a referendum. Deputy Prime Minister Nick Clegg in opening the debate and junior minister Mark Harper in closing it faced a barrage of interruptions. When the Bill came to a vote, the government, with opposition support, won easily, by 462 votes to 124. The 'No' lobby included 91 Conservatives. A further 19 abstained. It was the largest rebellion by government MPs on the Second Reading of a Bill in post-war history. The opposition had made clear it would oppose the programme motion for the Bill, arguing that more time was needed for detailed scrutiny. It was clear that the combined votes of opposition MPs and Conservative opponents would lead to the motion being rejected. As a result, the government decided not to move it. This opened the door for unrestricted debate in committee, similar to that on the Parliament (No 2) Bill in the 1968–69 session.[19] Given that it would be taken in committee of the whole House, it would block out or delay other business the government wanted to transact. Senior Tory MP Oliver Letwin was asked by David Cameron to sound out Conservative rebels to see if there was scope for compromise. When the feedback was that they were adamant in their opposition, ministers took the decision not to proceed with the Bill. The announcement that it was being abandoned was made in August, and on 3 September Nick Clegg confirmed in the Commons that it had been withdrawn. Its withdrawal elicited no notable public reaction. Major House of Lords reform was viewed as off the agenda for the foreseeable future.

---

[18] See P Raina, *House of Lords Reform: A History, vol 4: 1971–2014: The Exclusion of Hereditary Peers, Book 2: 2002–2014* (Bern, Peter Lang, 2015) 440–556.

[19] J Morgan, *The House of Lords and the Labour Government 1964–1970* (Oxford, Clarendon Press, 1975) 208–22.

III. Why Reform Failed

What accounts for the failure of the government's Bill? Three reasons can be identified.

First, there was the Bill itself. It was deemed to go too far by opponents of an elected House. That was to be expected. They had principled objections. However, for supporters of an elected House, it did not go far enough. Even though the opposition supported the Bill, it adopted a critical stance, Sadiq Khan, from the opposition front bench, claiming that the government had 'cherry-picked from the Joint Committee's report, while blindly ignoring its other key recommendations and concerns'.[20] He regretted that the Bill did not embrace a wholly elected House and identified what was missing from the Bill, including provisions to deal with disputes between the two Houses.

Other MPs picked up on what they saw as basic failings of the Bill. The Coalition Agreement stated that 'It is likely that this will advocate single long terms of office. It is also likely that there will be a grandfathering system for current Peers'.[21] The Bill followed this commitment by providing for a fixed non-renewal term. For critics, this meant that members could not be held to account at the next election. During the Second Reading debate, Conservative MP Richard Shepherd challenged Nick Clegg, who had asserted the principle that those who make the law should be elected by those who bear it, arguing 'the older and greater principle is that those who make the laws should be accountable to those who bear the laws, and there is no accountability in the process that he is introducing'.[22] The Deputy Prime Minister responded simply that there was 'neither accountability nor legitimacy in the status quo', the first part of which did not deny the truth of Shepherd's assertion and the second part of which was not only irrelevant to the point, but also contestable. Even MPs sympathetic to an elected House pursued the issue, exemplified by the intervention of Labour MP Toby Perkins:

> Will the Deputy Prime Minister tell us what it was in his recent experiences that has suggested that the kind of democracy we need is one where politicians can say what the hell they like, stay for 15 years and never have to face the voters again?[23]

And as another Labour MP, Karl Turner, put it: 'This could be said to be just a bung for party loyalty: 15 years' salary without really having to do much more than that.'[24]

The Bill also barred those who had served in the new House from standing in an election to the House of Commons within four years and one month of ceasing to be members of the upper house. The Explanatory Notes to the Bill were explicit

---

[20] HC Deb 9 July 2012, vol 548, col 40.
[21] HM Government, *The Coalition: Our Programme for Government* (n 15) 27.
[22] HC Deb 9 July 2012, vol 548, cols 25–26.
[23] ibid col 29.
[24] HC Deb 10 July 2012, vol 548, col 214.

in stating the reason: 'This is to limit the extent to which membership of the House of Lords can be a "stepping stone" to election to the House of Commons.'[25] It was a point pursued by former Foreign Secretary Sir Malcom Rifkind, the first back-bench speaker on the Bill: 'Essentially, it will be a sham democratic Chamber, consisting overwhelmingly of Members who would rather be in this Chamber and who will be elected under a party list system that is an insult to the electorate.'[26] Election was thus seen as a route for ambitious politicians who had not achieved a parliamentary candidature rather than serving in the upper house being seen as an end in itself, although that is how Nick Clegg sought to justify the position: 'They will not be allowed to leave the Lords and immediately seek election to the Commons, so they will be encouraged to see their time in the House of Lords as their one real chance to make their mark.'[27]

There was also to be a lengthy transition period, with members elected in tranches, one-third at a time. Assuming each Parliament lasted five years under the provisions of the 2011 Fixed-term Parliaments Act, it was thus possible that it would take 15 years before the reform was completed.

For supporters of an elected second chamber, the Bill thus fell short of what they wanted. Some of the flaws identified by Sadiq Khan were also core to the objections of opponents of an elected House, not least in failing to relate form to function.

Critics also drew attention to the implications of 80 per cent of the members being elected. For advocates of a wholly elected chamber it fell short, whereas for opponents of election it went too far and opened the prospect of a two-tier chamber, the appointed members lacking the electoral legitimacy of the rest. In the event of the appointed members being the swing voters in a division, there was the potential of the media attacking the outcome as illegitimate.

Opponents were also able to pick up on the method of election, as is apparent from Sir Malcolm Rifkind's comments. He was followed by another former Foreign Secretary, Labour's Margaret Beckett, who developed the objection:

> The Deputy Prime Minister has waxed lyrical about the fact that Members of the existing upper Chamber are there by reason of patronage, but that is also what a party list system is – everyone in this House knows that that is the reality – so he proposes replacing one patronage system with another.[28]

The party list system provided a stronger target for opponents than STV, though there was an underlying objection to any electoral system that challenged the position of MPs and also because within both main parties there was a wariness or fundamental objection to a system of proportional representation. Such a system, argued Labour's Baroness Taylor of Bolton, a former Leader of the

[25] House of Lords Reform Bill, Explanatory Notes, 23.
[26] HC Deb 9 July 2012, vol 548, col 50.
[27] ibid col 35.
[28] HC Deb 9 July 2012, vol 548, col 54.

House of Commons, in debate on the Joint Committee's report, 'will always lead to post-election deals that no one has voted for' and raise the prospect of Senators claiming '"My mandate is bigger than your mandate. My mandate is stronger than your mandate. I was elected on PR". Why on earth would we give way in those situations?'[29]

Allied to the limitations of the Bill's provisions was a failure of leadership on the part of the government. Nick Clegg was committed to the measure, and pressed David Cameron to deliver on the agreement, but he was not decisive in pressing the case. Although he held monthly cross-party meetings, one senior Conservative recalled that he appeared not really interested. 'The meetings dragged on and on but he hadn't read the papers, or mastered the details or the implications.'[30] Cameron, for his part, although he wanted the Bill passed, showed no notable enthusiasm for it. In response to questions in the House, his answers were described by one lead-ing Liberal Democrat as 'distinctly lukewarm'.[31] He was reported to be 'nodding and winking to backbench opponents in private, saying "I know none of us want this"'.[32] Ministers were notably restrained in pressing backbenchers to support it. Foreign Secretary William Hague, given the task of mobilising support for the Bill, was reported as approaching rebels and saying he needed to speak to them about Lords reform. 'He pauses and then adds: "There we are. I've spoken to you about Lords reform"'.[33]

The lack of enthusiasm for the Bill extended to the opposition benches. Though Labour was in favour of the principle of Lords reform, there were tactical consid-erations in the leadership's approach to the Bill. Defeating the programme motion would not only embarrass the government, but the loss of the Bill may lead to the Liberal Democrats joining them to scupper boundary changes, a move favoured over Lords reform given its implications for the party.[34] As we have seen, the party was also divided on the Bill, some leading members being notably opposed to the Bill, others – while voting for it – being at best lukewarm.

The contents of the Bill and lack of leadership militated against overcoming the enthusiasm and organisation of those opposed to the Bill. Opponents drew on principled objections to pursue their case.

Second, picking up on Sadiq Khan's critique, the proposal failed to comprehend that input and output legitimacy are not discrete phenomena. One cannot sepa-rate who forms the body from the capacity of the body to fulfil its functions. The government's position was that the two could be so separated. The 2011 White Paper adumbrated the functions carried out by the House of Lords and declared: 'The Government believes that these functions should remain unchanged when

---

[29] HL Deb 1 May 2012, vol 543, col 2085.
[30] A Seldon and P Snowden, *Cameron at 10: The Verdict* (London, William Collins, 2016) 232.
[31] D Laws, *Coalition* (London, Biteback, 2016) 151.
[32] Seldon and Snowdon (n 30) 235.
[33] ibid 235; also confirmed to the author by one of those approached.
[34] C Bowers, *Nick Clegg: The Biography* (London, Biteback, 2012) 308.

the House of Lords is reformed and that it should continue this valuable work.'[35] This assertion was repeated by Nick Clegg when appearing before the House of Lords Constitution Committee.[36] The problem with this contention was that it assumed that elected members could continue to fulfil tasks previously accomplished by a House characterised by the experience and expertise of its members. It was unclear from the government's proposals why those who were leading figures in their field would devote time to seeking election for a term of up to 15 years and how the culture of the existing House would be maintained. Elections would presumably be contested and thus encourage partisanship. Candidates standing under party labels would squeeze out the potential for independents to be elected in any numbers, if at all. Experience and expertise in the House of Lords is not confined to the cross-benches. It is not clear what value would be added by elected members – who, as the Explanatory Notes to the Bill recognised, would likely be MPs manqué – and how they would be distinguishable in form and goals from members of the House of Commons.

Lord Young of Cookham, who, as Sir George Young, served in various ministerial positions in the House of Commons and later, when in the Lords, as a government whip (in effect, a departmental spokesperson), told an audience of students that when he was a minister in the Commons appearing at the despatch box he often knew more about the subject than those questioning him, whereas in the House of Lords it was the other way round.[37] Removing the potential for members with extensive experience and expertise to question ministers threatens the capacity of the upper house to scrutinise the actions and policy of the government in a way that complements the work of the Commons. The threat, in the eyes of the opponents of an elected House, is one of duplicating what MPs do rather than complementing it.

Third, and fundamentally, there was the objection of principle that an elected House would challenge the core accountability at the heart of the political system. Supporters of an elected second chamber rest on the basic premise that the existing appointed House is undemocratic. The case is stated as if self-evidently true. Opponents counter that there is a democratic case for not having a second elected chamber.

MPs, during debate on the Bill, variously stressed the importance of maintaining the primacy of the Commons. This may appear a self-serving point, but it embodied a key principle. Taken in terms of its roots (*demos kratia*), democracy is about how people choose to govern themselves. Absent a system of direct democracy, citizens choose who will govern. Election is both a means of selection

[35] HM Government, *House of Lords Reform Draft Bill* (Cm 8077, 2011) 10.

[36] Constitution Committee, House of Lords, Meeting with Nick Clegg MP, Deputy Prime Minister, unrevised transcript of evidence (1 February 2012) 27.

[37] Young of Cookham, 'Government and Parliament', talk to University of Hull students (30 November 2021).

and a way of calling those elected to account the next time they seek election. In a parliamentary system of government, those who are to form the executive are chosen through elections to the legislature. The government of the UK is determined through elections to the House of Commons. There is one body – the party (or parties) in government – responsible for public policy and answerable for that policy at the next election. Through the doctrine of collective ministerial responsibility, the government stands as a single entity before both the House of Commons and the electorate.[38] The House of Lords fulfils tasks that complement the work of the House of Commons, but does not act in such a way as to challenge the accountability at the heart of the political system.

Opponents of an elected second chamber believe that election would challenge the accountability of the government. There would be nothing to stop an elected second chamber demanding more powers than the existing House, the rationale for the Parliament Acts having disappeared. Even if not acquiring additional powers, it could deploy the powers still residing in the second chamber, which at present the House refrains from exercising, such as rejecting a Bill promised in a party's manifesto (and indeed any measure in the government's programme). An elected House could amend a Bill and engage in 'ping pong' with the Commons, ensuring the Bill's demise through the use of double insistence. The key point here is that there would be no one body standing before the electorate to be held to account for the outcomes of public policy. Negotiations between the two Houses could be opaque and produce outcomes not promised to electors and with those electors not being able to determine who was responsible.

Having an appointed second chamber that does not challenge the capacity of the House of Commons ultimately to get its way ensures that the government, commanding a majority in the Commons, remains responsible, and answerable, to electors for public policy. As such, there is a democratic argument for an appointed second chamber, a point put succinctly in evidence to the Joint Committee on the Draft Bill by a specialist in democratic theory, Professor Colin Tyler.[39] Voters would be able to elect the individual members who would form the chamber, but would lack the capacity to hold to account any one body for what they did collectively. The change would be value detracting in that the existing House is, and accepts that it is, accountable to and through the elected House of Commons, whereas with an elected House of Lords there would be no such accountability.

Under the existing system, electors know what they are voting and how their votes translate into the formation of a government. Under the government's plans, it would not be clear what electors would actually be voting for in elections to the upper house – they would not be affecting the formation of the government nor returning members who would have an incentive to pursue the grievances

---

[38] P Norton, *Governing Britain* (Manchester, Manchester University Press, 2020) 6, 165.
[39] C Tyler, *Evidence, Joint Committee on the Draft House of Lords Reform Bill: Report, Vol. III* (2012–13, HL 284–III, HC 1313–III) 200.

and concerns of constituents. The value added by the House of Lords in fulfilling functions complementary to the Commons would be lost and not replaced by any obvious or significant value to electors.

The demise of the House of Lords Reform Bill enraged Nick Clegg and his party – voting against boundary changes in retribution – but appears to have no wider repercussions within the main parties and made no obvious dent on the national consciousness.[40] As even Nick Clegg acknowledged, it was 'a subject of spectacular indifference to the vast majority of the British people'.[41] For the government, the issue was off the agenda and its successors took the stance that the commitment remained to a fundamental reform of the upper house rather than piecemeal changes. No action was therefore envisaged. In the event, pressure to achieve change was to come from outside the government.

IV. Incremental Change

Where the government failed, Private Members succeeded. In the House of Lords, opposition to the House of Lords Reform Bill came not primarily from those who took a High Tory approach to constitutional change, believing that everything as it stood should be preserved, but from peers who took a Burkean approach.[42] For them, the goal of reform was to strengthen the existing House in fulfilling its functions.

At the start of this century, a group of parliamentarians, led by an MP (Sir Patrick, later Lord, Cormack) and a peer (this writer), formed the Campaign for an Effective Second Chamber (CESC). Drawing support from members from different parties and of none (it included cross-benchers), it opposed an elected chamber, but campaigned for changes designed to strengthen the Lords in fulfilling its functions. It mobilised peers in opposing the elected options put forward in the votes in 2003 and 2007, but was active in proposing a programme of reforms to the existing House. These were drawn together in a House of Lords Reform Bill, drafted by this writer and introduced on behalf of CESC by a senior Liberal Democrat peer, Lord Steel of Aikwood (the Steel Bill). The proposals comprised putting the House of Lords Appointments Commission (set up to nominate cross-bench peers and to vet other nominees) on a statutory basis, closing the by-election provision for hereditary peers (under which when one of the existing hereditary peers retained under the 1999 Act died, they were replaced by another), removing peers from membership who failed to attend the House or committed a serious criminal offence, and enabling peers to retire.

---

[40] See Laws (n 31) 151–53; Seldon and Snowdon (n 30) 236–39.
[41] Bowers (n 34) 306.
[42] Norton, 'The Changing Constitution' (n 13) 356.

The Bill was first introduced and debated in March 2007 (HL Bill 52 of 2006–07), but, because of time constraints in the Lords, did not complete the committee stage. Lord Steel introduced the Bill on three further occasions.[43] On the fourth occasion, in 2010, the Bill – retitled the House of Lords (Amendment) Bill – completed all stages in the Lords, but made no progress in the Commons. However, at the start of the 2013–14 session, Conservative MP Dan Byles was successful in the ballot for Private Members' Bills and, as a supporter of CESC, opted to introduce a House of Lords Reform Bill to deliver on some of the Campaign's aims. It focused on provisions that were not generally contentious. Those likely to elicit opposition, such as removing the hereditary peers' by-elections (opposed by some hereditary peers), were omitted. The Bill enabled peers to retire, removed those who failed to attend for a session, and removed peers convicted of an offence and sentenced to 12 months' imprisonment or more. Byles was energetic in lobbying government and sceptical backbenchers to support the Bill. It was given a Second Reading on 18 October 2013, the Minister for the Cabinet Office, Greg Clark, announcing that it 'contains modest proposals that the Government are prepared to support'.[44] It made it through the remaining stages in the Commons and was then taken through the Lords by Lord Steel.

The following session, another supporter of CESC, former Lord Speaker Baroness Hayman, introduced a Private Members' Bill – the House of Lords (Expulsion and Suspension) Bill – extending what were limited powers of the House to suspend a member and introducing a power, previously not available to the House, to expel a member. The House had in 2009 resuscitated a power of suspension, last used in the seventeenth century, but it only extended to being able to suspend a member until the end of a Parliament. Under the Bill, the suspension could extend beyond the end of the Parliament. Acquiring the power to expel a member brought the Lords into line with the position in the House of Commons, where the power to expel had been variously used over the centuries, although the last occasion was in 1954.

The Bill was not notably contentious and no party opposed it. Similar provisions had been contained in the Labour government's 2010 Constitutional Reform and Governance Bill, but had been lost in the 'wash up' after a general election was announced, as well as in the Conservative–Liberal Democrat coalition government's 2012 House of Lords Reform Bill. It went through the Lords without opposition. What amendments were agreed were moved by Lady Hayman. In the Commons, a small number of Conservative MPs, led by Christopher Chope, sought to amend it – the debate took place around the power to expel – but were unsuccessful. The Bill received royal assent in March 2015 and took effect three months later.

---

[43] See S Rushbrook, 'Lord Steel of Aikwood's Private Member's Bills on House of Lords Reform', House of Lords Library Note LLN 2012/017 (London, House of Lords, 2012).

[44] HC Deb 18 October 2013, vol 568, col 1011.

Both measures were modest, but not ineffective. Over 100 peers had, by the end of 2021, retired from the House and a further eight had been removed for failing to attend for the whole of a session The House in November 2020 utilised the provisions of the 2015 Act and voted to agree a report from the Conduct Committee recommending the expulsion of a peer, Lord Ahmed, following allegations he had sexually exploited a vulnerable woman. He resigned from the House shortly before the report was debated.

Peers, not least those gathered in the Campaign for an Effective Second Chamber, continued to press for further reforms, including ending the by-election option for hereditary peers and putting the House of Lords Appointments Commission on a statutory basis, both pursued through Private Members' Bills. In the 2021–22 session, Labour peer Lord Grocott was successful – not for the first time – in achieving a Second Reading of a Bill to deliver the former. A Conservative peer (this writer) introduced a Bill to achieve the latter. Neither was going to make it to the statute book, the former because of determined opposition from a small number of (mostly hereditary) peers, the latter because it was not successful in the ballot for debate, but both served to signal support for further change. In exchanges with Cabinet Office Minister Lord True, this writer raised the prospect of the combination of the measures constituting stage 2 of Lords' reform.[45] The CESC has also continued to press for measures to reduce the size of the House. The House does not have the space or resources to accommodate all peers if they attend and is vulnerable to criticism if they do, for reasons of cost, and also if they do not, membership being deemed to incur a commitment to contribute to the work of the House. The numbers make it look a bloated chamber, with the media drawing attention to the fact that it is the second largest legislative chamber after the Chinese National People's Congress. The CESC initiated a debate in December 2016 in which the House agreed without a vote that 'this House believes that its size should be reduced, and methods should be explored by which this could be achieved'.[46] Consequent to the debate, the Lord Speaker, Lord Fowler, established a committee under former Treasury official Lord Burns to address the size, which made various recommendations to slim the membership with a view to achieving a membership no bigger than that of the House of Commons. The issue has remained a live one, with peers pressing for a reduction in numbers and self-restraint on the part of Prime Ministers in appointing new peers. Theresa May indicated such a willingness, but her successor in No 10 did not.

V. Explaining Success – And Failure

Why has such second-order change made it to the statute book, whereas first-order change has not, not least given that the government has continued to embrace the

---

[45] HL Deb 10 November 2021, vol 815, col 1704.
[46] HL Deb 6 December 2016, vol 777, cols 500–92.

latter? The explanation is relatively straightforward in that the incremental changes have been treated as necessary and sufficient by those opposed to an elected House and as necessary, but not sufficient by those who support an elected second chamber. Supporters of an elected second chamber have not had any powerful reason to oppose incremental reform. To argue that piecemeal change would hamper achieving fundamental reform would be to concede that such change would enhance the legitimacy of the unelected House. Given that first-order change has been ruled out by the government for the foreseeable future, piecemeal reform constitutes the only viable way forward in terms of achieving any change to the second chamber. Taking the reforms through Parliament in the form of Private Members' Bills has not encroached on government time, or indeed much on Private Members' time (the Second Reading of the House of Lords (Expulsion and Suspension) Bill was taken formally in the House of Commons), and by constituting second-order change it has not achieved much political prominence. With a few exceptions, MPs have not taken a notable interest – the changes are essentially internal to the Lords and do not impact upon the work and primacy of the Commons – and the measures have not engaged media interest.

Contrast this with the first-order changes, which not only impact on the role and primacy of the Commons, but also generate controversy as to the most appropriate form that the second chamber should take (if, indeed, there should be a second chamber). What unites supporters of first-order reform is that the existing House of Lords is not acceptable and something else should be put in its place. They are therefore agreed on what they are against (the House of Lords in its present form). However, there is no agreement as to what they are for. Theresa May was derided during her premiership for repeating the mantra 'Brexit means Brexit', but faced MPs who took different views as to what form Brexit should take. There were several options. One can see the equivalent with first-order reform of the House of Lords: 'Lords reform means Lords reform'. As we have seen, the Joint Committee that reported at the end of 2002 identified seven options. The House of Commons voted against every one. The results tended to bear out the observation of the late Lord Denham, who once observed that if you put four people in a room and ask for their opinions on reform of the upper house, you get five different responses.[47]

Bills designed to implement a 'Big Bang' approach, cresting an elected second chamber, will face the same obstacles as the 2012 Bill. Schemes of reform entail detailed provisions. Proponents may agree on the ends, but not the means. Opponents will seize on the means as well as the ends and be united in principled opposition. The objections of principle will be constant. Engendering and maintaining enthusiasm to get a big Bill through both Houses is likely, as in 1968–69 and 2012, to be a major challenge. Enthusiasm may wane in the face of concerted attacks, presupposing government enthusiasm for the measure in the first place.

---

[47] P Norton, *The Constitution in Flux* (Oxford, Martin Robertson, 1982) 130.

David Cameron's less than energetic support for the 2012 Bill was not dissimilar to that of Harold Wilson's for the Parliament (No 2) Bill: 'In moving the second reading, I made no effort to suggest that there was any enthusiasm about the Bill, one way or the other.'[48] House of Lords reform does not rank highly in the priorities of the government or its supporters. However much some MPs may concede the case for an elected second chamber, protecting the primacy of their own chamber will prove a powerful counterweight.

VI. Conclusion

Opposition to an elected second chamber may be portrayed as self-serving, both on the part of peers wishing to retain their membership and by MPs who may have eyes on themselves ending up in the Lords. However, there is a powerful and principled case to be made for their stance. The House of Lords is not so much a challenge to a democratic system of government as a facilitator of it. Without its legislative work, the statute book would be in a far worse state than it is. It adds value at relatively little cost to the public purse. Critics note the cost of running the institution without ever seeking to monetise the value of changes it achieves to legislation. How does one price a major change to a Bill that has the effect of protecting citizens' rights or reducing a burden on businesses and other organisations? The House complements the work of the elected House – it neither challenges nor duplicates – and leaves intact the direct line of accountability between electors and the government derived from elections to the House of Commons. It thus serves, in the words of Colin Tyler, 'to maintain the democratic character of the whole.'[49]

There is thus a case for reform, but reform to strengthen the House of Lords in fulfilling its functions, not to destroy it. There is a persuasive case for having a second chamber.[50] Having an appointed chamber characterised by experience and expertise can, and in the UK does, add value to the political process. The case for it should not go by default.

---

[48] H Wilson, *The Labour Government 1964–1970* (London, Weidenfeld & Nicolson/Michael Joseph, 1971) 608.
[49] Tyler (n 39) 38.
[50] P Norton, 'Adding Value? The Role of Second Chambers' (2007) 15 *Asia Pacific Law Review* 3.

9

Accountability and Electoral Reform

JASPER MILES

I. Introduction

The debate over electoral reform prompts a variety of responses. Some see it as the panacea to the nation's ills, believing it will transform politics, government policy, economic performance and the management of the economy. In sum, it will create a more cohesive and successful polity. On the other hand, defenders of the plurality system argue that the present system continues to deliver a strong, stable and single-party government. As such, it avoids the mush of coalition government created by proportional representation and the breaking of promises in post-election bargaining. Consequently, under the plurality system, a clear line can be drawn between the elector casting their vote and the creation of the government. Others dismiss electoral reform as a niche, liberal, middle-class issue, the preserve of academics in their ivory towers, *Guardian* readers and the North London dinner table set – 'a middle class game, like Scrabble' and of interest 'only to obsessives and those with an interest in the esoteric'[1] – a distraction from the real concerns of working people. The final, and perhaps largest, group do not think about electoral reform in any way, shape or form. The opinion polling evidence from Britain suggests that when people are asked their priorities, electoral reform does not register.

However, its lack of resonance with the public should not diminish its importance. Bogdanor notes that 'the differences between the various systems can be of crucial importance in relation to the health of the democratic polity'.[2] Moreover, as Gallagher and Mitchell write, 'Electoral systems matter. They are a crucial link in the chain connecting the preferences of citizens to the policy choices made by governments.' They matter in other ways too, including the shape of the party systems, the nature of government, the kind of choices facing voters at elections,

---

[1] R Blackburn, *The Electoral System in Britain* (London, MacMillan, 1995); V Bogdanor, *The New British Constitution* (Oxford, Hart Publishing, 2009) 303.
[2] Bogdanor (n 1) 303.

the ability of voters to hold their representative(s) to account, the behaviour of parliamentarians, the representativeness of institutions, the cohesion within political parties, the quality of government and the quality of life of the citizens ruled by that government.[3] On that basis, electoral reform is an important topic, and it should prompt greater interest.

To explore electoral reform and accountability, this chapter will begin by outlining the different ways we can measure and think about the appropriateness of an electoral system.

Next, the chapter will reveal how the debate over electoral ties into competing visions of democracy, namely pluralism and democratic elitism. Generally, and as explored below, we could place the pro-electoral reform lobby into the pluralist camp as they prioritise greater consensus in decision-making. On the flip side, we can broadly place supporters of the present system into the democratic elitist camp, favouring a narrower and more elitist conception of politics and democracy. Here, democracy resembles a competition between two teams, with the victor enjoying the spoils and the electorate acknowledging that it is the government that is to do the governing. Rooting the debate over accountability and electoral reform in the democratic theory allows the reader to consider the arguments and implications of reform beyond the strengths and weaknesses of particular systems. Accordingly, this section touches on the nature of democracy and what these theories can tell us about accountability.

The third section outlines the British experience of electoral reform, considering some of the implications and issues raised by the range of systems now used across the UK. Interestingly, the matter is likely to return to the political fore, fuelled by the British Labour Party's prolonged period in opposition. Much like the 1980s and 1990s, thoughts within the Labour Party will turn to coalition government, proportional representation and electoral pacts as a method of returning to power, correcting the supposed inability to win under the first-past-the-post electoral system (FPTP). Also, in an age of widespread disillusionment with mainstream politics and, by historical standards, low voter turnout, some see changing the electoral system as a method of reversing this trend. While there are other examples, such as New Zealand or Italy, the British experience offers an excellent case study, with electoral reform enacted at the periphery but FPTP maintained at the centre. Far from this being a form of cultural myopia on behalf of the author, the debate in Britain stretches back centuries and cuts across party and ideological lines, thus offering the interested observer the opportunity to engage with material of significant breadth and depth.

The final section assesses three core arguments in favour of retaining FPTP for Westminster elections: local representation; the mandate and the manifesto; and single-party government. It will conclude that while the present system is imperfect, it should not be lightly dismissed, as it scores highly when measured

---

[3] M Gallagher and P Mitchell, *The Politics of Electoral Systems* (Oxford, Oxford University Press, 2005) 3, 4.

against accountability. First, let us turn our attention to how we can 'measure' electoral systems.

II. Measuring Electoral Systems

There are various ways to measure an electoral system's suitability. Renwick identified six measures: (i) rewarding popularity, ensuring that popular support translates into political influence; (ii) fair representation in Parliament and government, with votes fairly translating into positions of power; (iii) effective and accountable government, with the emphasis shifting towards choosing a government and allowing structures to operate effectively and accountably; (iv) voter choice and turnout, although, as Renwick notes, choice can be interpreted in different ways, for instance, the choice of government, the range of options available to us, the degree to which we can express our preferences or the frequency with which we can make our voices heard through the ballot box; (v) the constituency link, which even most electoral reformers are keen to retain, allowing voters to choose the individuals who represent them, not just the parties; and (vi) keeping MPs in check and avoiding or eliminating misbehaviour, which Nyblade and Reed distinguish as looting or cheating.[4]

Commonly, 'fairness' is seen as the litmus test of an electoral system. Essentially, the argument goes that FPTP is 'unfair' due to its disproportionality, how it encourages a two-party system at the expense of small parties and the limits this place on voter choice. On the other hand, proportional or hybrid systems are 'fair/fairer' as there is a stronger correlation between votes cast and seats won, leading to a more representative assembly. Moreover, electoral reformers argue that 'all votes count' under alternative systems, whereas under FPTP there are wasted votes, safe seats and electoral deserts in which some parties have little to no chance of gaining representation. This is 'unfair' to both voters and political parties: the former as they are discouraged from participating in the democratic process, considering it to be hopeless, the latter as they focus their time, energy and resources on winnable 'marginal' constituencies, the seats that supposedly decide the outcome of a general election.

Yet, as Plant noted, the claim to fairness does not stand on its own but according to the criteria by which one is judging fairness: 'Electoral mechanisms cannot be assessed in a wholly neutral way, as it were giving them points against a set of neutral criteria.'[5] Furthermore, a procedural notion of fairness may not result in a fairer and more equal society. This should be of particular concern to social

---

[4] A Renwick, *A Citizen's Guide to Electoral Reform* (London, Biteback, 2011) 12–23; B Nyblade and S Reed, 'Who Cheats? Who Loots? Political Competition and Corruption in Japan' (2008) 52 *American Journal of Political Science* 926.

[5] See *Report of the Working Party on Electoral Systems (The Plant Report)* (London, Guardian Studies, 1991) 25; R Plant, 'Criteria for Electoral Systems: The Labour Party and Electoral Reform' (1991) 44 *Parliamentary Affairs* 552.

democratic parties. Conceivably, a procedurally 'fair' electoral system may strengthen the forces of the status quo through the centrism of coalition government, in which the politicians change but government policy stays the same. In turn, the central government's power may be constrained to the benefit of various ruling elites, thus acting as a brake on a radical government. Peter Hain, who would go on to serve as a minister in the New Labour Cabinet, wrote that 'a judgement on the desirability of PR [proportional representation] over first-past-the-post is more finely balanced than most PR advocates concede, and is ultimately a political question about democratic priorities rather than a moral question about fairness'.[6]

Another way of thinking about electoral systems and electoral reform is to consider the function of an institution and the according suitability of an electoral system. Here, Plant distinguished a legislative assembly and a deliberative one, the former more concerned with legislation, the latter more concerned with dialogue. Of course, a legislative assembly also must deliberate, and a deliberative assembly may also have to legislate, but the distinction helps to frame our thinking about the purpose of institutions. This was evident in New Labour's constitutional reform agenda, as they understood that different kinds of institutions can use different electoral systems. For example, many accused New Labour of self-interest when introducing the Regional Party List system for elections to the European Parliament but maintained FPTP for Westminster. They argued that Blair's power depended on his majority at Westminster, not at Brussels; therefore, it mattered little how many Labour MEPs were elected. Yet, it is not simply a matter of self-interest. The European Parliament is a very different institution from the House of Commons; therefore, a different criterion underpinned the decision to adopt the Regional Party List and keep FPTP.

New Labour's approach to devolution reflected this principle. At its core was the view that Holyrood, the Senedd and Stormont should foster a different type and approach to politics than that found at Westminster, as these bodies did not have to sustain the executive of the UK. Admittedly, Northern Ireland is different to Scotland and Wales as the political system is built upon consociationalism, but different assumptions supported the adoption of the particular electoral system. Whereas Westminster was to maintain single-party government through the continued use of FPTP, a more consensual and pluralistic style was to be encouraged – at least in theory, though not necessarily in practice – one party dominating. As such, it was permissible to adopt the Additional Member System (AMS) for the devolved bodies in Scotland, Wales and the London Assembly, the Single Transferable Vote (STV) in Northern Ireland and for Scottish local government elections, and the Supplementary Vote (SV) for mayoral elections in English cities, boroughs and city regions, as well as for the election of politics and crimes commissioners in England and Wales. Also,

---

[6] P Hain, *Proportional Misrepresentation: The Case against PR in Britain* (Hampshire, Wildwood House, 1986) 48.

Great Britain moved from FPTP to a Regional Party List system for the European Parliament, while Northern Ireland used STV. However, the Regional List system has been eliminated following the UK's departure from the European Union.

Lastly, we can consider the issue of electoral reform as a division between *process* and *outcomes*. Here, we can see reformers centring their attention on *process*. For instance, they may stress the advantages of electoral systems which give the elector greater choice through preferential voting or allowing electors to vote for different parties at constituency and regional level. Furthermore, coalition formation will involve consensus, compromise and dialogue, supposedly representing a more comprehensive range of views and ideas, which is seen as beneficial. Supporters of FPTP emphasise *outcomes*, arguing that single-party government is better placed to deliver on what it has promised. Traditionally, this argument was often utilised by those within the Labour Party, believing that the advancement of policies which would help bring about a more equitably society was more important than the electoral mechanisms which sent them to Parliament. Recently, Johnson argued that the Labour Party should avoid fetishising process and would do well to remember that *outcomes* matter.[7] As with Plant's distinction between legislative and deliberative assemblies, it would be an error to think that reformers have little to say about outcomes and supporters of the plurality system care little for process. After all, reformers claim that effective policies emerge through broader participation and supporters of FPTP highlight, for example, the processes within political parties. However, it is possible to discern a different emphasis.

We can draw four conclusions from the discussion above. Firstly, claims to 'fairness' do not stand on their own and electoral reform is not simply an argument about moving from an unfair to a fair system. Much will depend on how individuals prioritise the different measures as identified by Renwick. Secondly, institutions' purpose and role are important criteria when considering electoral systems. If we accept that elections to the House of Commons entail creating a very different type of body to that found at the devolved level, then FPTP can be justified contrary to the reformers' claims. Thirdly, distinguishing between process and outcomes does help clarify what is seen as important in the democratic process, whether that is the reaching of decisions or 'getting on with the job' of implementing policy. Lastly, electoral reformers in Britain have had some notable successes, primarily linked to New Labour's constitutional reform agenda. While important political considerations and motivations influenced Labour's embrace of constitutional reform, there are links between those advocating constitutional reform and the pluralist and decentralist tradition. Indeed, it is worthwhile to consider how electoral reform and accountability relate to both the pluralist and democratic elitist traditions. Doing so will help clarify the different understandings of accountability. We begin with pluralism.

---

[7] See R Johnson, 'Proportional Representation Would Spell Disaster for Labour. Party Members Should Reject It' *The Guardian* (27 September 2021).

III. Pluralism and Electoral Reform

At its core, pluralism is concerned with the dispersal of power and the decentralisa-tion of decision-making. An overbearing or powerful central government should be limited and replaced by an environment that encourages greater participation. Pluralism encompasses a view of society that prioritises voluntary organisation and civic society. It has a rich heritage, encompassing thinkers and practition-ers from across the political spectrum, often relating back to Edmund Burke and the 'little platoons'. According to its proponents, this approach has a dual benefit. Firstly, it fosters consent – severely lacking with decisions taken at the centre – and secondly, individuals are better placed to understand the problems affecting them rather than distant politicians and bureaucrats. Pluralism was *rediscovered* in Britain towards the end of the twentieth century by thinkers such as Paul Hirst, David Marquand and Will Hutton, who criticised what they saw as the 'top-down' view of politics which came at the expense of civil society. Recently, it found expression in David Cameron's Big Society and Maurice Glasman's Blue Labour.

Pluralism also offers a view of politics and political institutions, stressing the need for cooperation, dialogue, openness and negotiation, and is, therefore, seen as being at odds with the narrow and elitist style of the Westminster model of poli-tics. Democracy is deemed to be more than periodical elections in which voters can pass judgement on the government. David Beetham wrote that

> democracy is not an all-or-nothing affair, which a society either has or does not have, but a matter of the degree to which the people control the decision-making process, and the extent of equality in the exercise of that control.[8]

Much of the academic literature prior to New Labour's constitutional reforms argued that there was a lack of accountability within the British system of govern-ance. For instance, Oliver wrote: 'the institutions of the state are in many respects insufficiently accountable – politically, publicly, legally and administratively – both for their modus operandi (the ground rules of the system of government) and for the substance of what they do'.[9] Hirst and Barnett wrote, 'The principal problem in Britain's institutions is the strong tendency to exclusive party government and its control of a highly centralised state with few checks on the executive'. They continued:

> Exclusive government, concentrated in the hands of the Prime Minister and the Cabinet, narrowly confined in Whitehall and Westminster, has prevented the development of a collaborative political culture that makes possible the cooperation of the major social interests one with another and with the state ... The UK needs fundamental reforms

---

[8] D Beetham, 'Democratic Criteria for a Democratic Audit', paper presented to the Democratic Audit of the United Kingdom, the Human Rights Centre, University of Essex (1988), quoted in M Evans, *Charter 88: A Successful Challenge to the British Political Tradition?* (Aldershot, Dartmouth, 1995) 40.

[9] D Oliver, *Government in the United Kingdom* (Milton Keynes, Open University Press, 1991) 202.

in its central governmental institutions in order to ensure accountability, stability and efficiency in policy.[10]

Proponents argue that only a move away from FPTP will bring about a consensual style of politics. Moreover, FPTP is considered a significant obstacle to creating a pluralistic democracy. Marquand considered that the plurality system had created a political duopoly, with the two major parties 'running the club', 'viewing the public outside the walls as the raw material for top-down social engineering rather than as active citizens making their own history from the bottom up'.[11] He continued, believing PR to be a fundamental reform required to reform Britain's 'elective dictatorship', 'a precondition of the wider and deeper changes that are needed to create a truly civic culture in this country'.[12] Lord Hailsham's 'elective dictatorship' thesis compiled a range of pre-existing concerns but unified them around calls for a written constitution that would limit Parliament both by law and by a system of checks and balances.[13] Indeed, this argument persists and is often the starting point for those critical generally of the Westminster model, and specifically of FPTP.

FPTP encourages a tendency to hoard power at the centre, as it fosters single-party governments and a 'winner-takes-all' mentality. Supposedly, governments govern in the interests of those they represent, excluding all those who fall outside of the winning party's electoral base, as are the parties that lost. PR, it is claimed, would correct this stifling approach to politics and force political parties to reach common ground through mutual learning. Consequently, the narrow sectional interest of single-party government will be replaced by consensus politics, offering a more accurate depiction of the electorate's centrist preferences, embodied in coalition government. After all, a coalition government will be in tune with the concerns of a greater number of voters, thus corresponding more closely to the policy views of a majority of electors than under FPTP. For Lord Blake, electoral reform provided additional benefits:

> The avoidance of flagrant minority rule is, we believe, more important than any disadvantages which coalition may have … It is said that this choice will be made, not by the electors, but by politicians in backstage bargains and wheeler-dealing in 'smoke-filled' rooms. We are not much impressed by this argument … It may be better to have visible coalition between parties than to have invisible ones between sections of one party … Nor is it obvious that decision to join or not to join a major partner in a coalition must

---

[10] P Hirst and A Barnett, 'Introduction' in A Barnett, C Ellis and P Hirst (eds), *Debating the Constitution: New Perspectives on Constitutional Reform* (Cambridge, Polity Press, 1993) 5–6.

[11] D Marquand, 'Closing the Westminster Club' in G Smyth, *Refreshing the Parts* (London, Lawrence & Wishart, 1992) 3.

[12] ibid 3.

[13] Lord Hailsham, *The Dilemma of Democracy: Diagnosis and Prescription* (London, Collins, 1978) referenced in M Foley, *The Politics of the British Constitution* (Manchester, Manchester University Press, 1999) 123–24.

be taken in 'smoke-filled rooms'. A party could convene a conference after an election or it could announce its stance in advance.[14]

Pluralists claim it is wrong to dismiss coalition government as weak and unstable. After all, coalition government is the norm across much of Europe, some of which are long-lasting and produce effective policies. Also, it is a method to promote compromise and collaborative culture with legitimacy emanating from inter-party and interest bargaining, rather than manifestos. Tony Wright, the former Labour MP and academic, wrote that an election had traditionally been seen to offer a 'democratic' solution to the problem of accountability – 'he who says election says accountability'. Wright continued, saying that the doctrine of electoral account-ability 'is really an argument for a particular kind of democracy. The kind, in fact, represented by Britain's elective dictatorship'.[15] The concentration of power at the centre is compounded by the inability of the winning party to achieve over 50 per cent of the national vote. This pours doubt on the legitimacy of the mandate and the support for the governing party's policy programme. For Birch, election results of this kind mandated compromise or coalition, not radical or ideological policies.[16] Consequently, the pluralist perspective stresses that FPTP offers only a weak link between voters and the government, a limited view of accountability and a narrow view of democracy.

IV. Democratic Elitism and First-Past-the-Post

Democratic elitism recasts democracy. As Bachrach writes, it emphasises the competitiveness of political elites, their accountability to the electorate at periodi-cal elections and the open, multiple points of access to elite power for those who bother to organise to voice their grievances and demands. The electorate still has a role, albeit a limited and largely passive one according to the pluralists, as there is the freedom to vote, pressurise the elites and rise to an elite position.[17] This theory is associated with the writings of Joseph Schumpeter and Karl Popper – 'the two modern political thinkers who have made the most trenchant observa-tions on the nature of democratic choice' and 'common sense theorists'.[18] This approach can also be found in the writings of Giovanni Sartori, Max Weber and Eric Schattschneider. For Schumpeter, 'we now take the view that the role of the people is to produce a government, or else an intermediary body which in turn

---

[14] Quoted in Blackburn (n 1) 409–10.

[15] T Wright, *Citizens and Subjects: An Essay on British Politics* (London, Routledge, 1994) 101–02.

[16] AH Birch, 'The Theory of Representation and Practice' in S Finer (ed), *Adversary Politics and Electoral Reform* (London, Wigram, 1975) 62–63.

[17] P Bachrach, *The Theory of Democratic Elitism* (London, University of London Press, 1969) 8.

[18] M Pinto-Duschinsky, 'Send the Rascals Packing: Defects of Proportional Representation and the Virtues of the Westminster Model' (1999) 36 *Representation* 118, 126.

will produce a national executive or government'.[19] Popper considered an election to be a 'Day of Judgement' on the government, focusing on the ability of the electorate to remove a government.[20] Sartori noted how the competitive theory of democracy entailed the rule of anticipated responses. Moreover, the power of deciding between the competitors is in the hands of the demos. The unorganised majority becomes the arbiter in the contest among the organised minorities of the politically active, and the competition between them is democracy.[21]

Recently, Michael Pinto-Duschinsky, John Pepall and James Forder have articulated the democratic-elitist position, all strongly influenced by the work of Schumpeter and Popper. Pinto-Duschinsky wrote that elections and representation are not ends in themselves. 'The key condition of people power is that the voters should have a direct effect on the selection and – even more important – on the expulsion of Prime Ministers and cabinets.' He continued: 'What is at stake is not mathematical "fairness" but democracy itself. Where the people are unable to control the arrogance of power, there is no democracy.'[22] Moreover, the standard test for democracy is not the degree of correspondence of views between the public and political leaders – for this happens in totalitarian regimes where the leadership pursues popular policies – but that governments should, through the electoral process, be ruled by the voters.[23] For Pepall, voting is a procedure for letting the people decide, and if there is no unanimity, then any decision must involve one choice winning and one or more losing. 'The PR goal that "everyone wins and all get prizes" means that the voters do not decide. That is a real waste of voting.'[24] Forder considered:

> We cannot separately assess each and every policy of the government but we can decide whether the leaders we have should continue or whether they should go. When we decide that they should go, democracy furnishes the tools with which we can make it happen. Perhaps even more importantly, the threat of rejection keeps the government working to avoid the outcome … The power of the people to dismiss the government is the greatest gift of democracy and should be treasured.[25]

The participatory democracy envisaged by the pluralists is unattainable. In Britain, as in many other Western democracies, only a minority of citizens engage in *everyday* politics, taking the time to organise and mobilise. Generally, those who do mobilise are wealthy, formally educated, well informed and well connected, tending not to be socially typical. Consequently, most citizens only formally participate

---

[19] J Schumpeter, *Capitalism, Socialism and Democracy* (London, George Allen & Unwin, 1976) 295.

[20] K Popper, 'Popper on Democracy' *The Economist* (23 April 1988) 28.

[21] G Sartori, 'Anti-Elitism Revisited' (1978) 13 *Government and Opposition* 58, 71.

[22] Pinto-Duschinsky, 'Send the Rascals Packing' (n 18) 118, 126.

[23] M Pinto-Duschinsky, 'A Reply to the Critics' (1999) 36 *Representation* 153.

[24] J Pepall, 'First-Past-the-Post: Empowers Voter, Accountable Government' in L Miljan (ed), *Counting Votes: Essays on Electoral Reform* (Vancouver, Fraser Institute, 2016) 9.

[25] J Forder, *The Case against Voting Reform: Why the AV System Would Damage Britain* (Oxford, OneWorld Publications, 2011) 26.

in the democratic process at election time, the prime example being a general election. Norris considered that on that basis, only elections 'let the majority of British citizens become involved in public life on a regular basis, and only elections connect the policy preferences of voters to parties which remain accountable for the actions in government'. However, the issue raised is how effectively elections function as a link between citizens and leaders.[26] To consider this question, we can reflect on the British experience of electoral reform, particularly the implications and issues raised since New Labour's constitutional reform experiment.

V. The British Experience

The debate concerning reforming the electoral system in Britain stretches back to the nineteenth century, cutting across party lines and fluctuating party attitudes. For instance, the Liberal Party stuck by FPTP until the 1920s, when the Labour Party challenged its position as one of the two main parties and it went into retreat. Initially, many in the Labour Party favoured reform. However, the influence of Ramsay MacDonald and the electoral successes enjoyed in the 1920s convinced the Labour Party that all that was required to implement reform was a parliamentary majority. This was fulfilled in 1945. Yet, the matter returned to the fore in the 1980s as Labour struggled against Thatcherism's electoral and political dominance. The Conservative Party have long favoured FPTP, but exhibited some interest in the 1970s, concerned about the introduction of socialism on a minority of the vote. While much of the debate in the twentieth century centred on Westminster, it spilt over into wider discussion on territorial questions and membership of supranational bodies. For instance, the debates in the 1970s over devolution and elections to the European Parliament considered the appropriateness of different electoral systems.

By the late 1980s, electoral reform had taken on renewed importance. The Labour Party was holding an internal party enquiry led by Raymond Plant, considering the merits of systems as part of Labour's wider constitutional reform agenda. In Scotland, there was the Scottish Constitutional Convention, consisting of political parties, trades unions, churches and civil society, leading to a blueprint for Scottish Devolution. The Labour Party understood that it would have to concede electoral reform to other parties if its constitutional reform agenda was to progress. At Westminster, the leadership of both Labour and the Liberal Democrats had engaged in 'the project', an elite-level attempt to unite the progressive forces in Britain. 'The project' centred on constitutional reform, including reform of the Westminster electoral system, leading to the Independent Commission on the Voting System, led by Roy Jenkins. Its recommendation of AV Plus (the Alternative

---

[26] P Norris, *Electoral Change Since 1945* (Oxford, Blackwell, 1997) 235.

Vote in the constituencies combined with regional top-up areas) was kicked into the long grass.

However, as mentioned, this did not mark the end of the matter, as by the early twenty-first century, the UK was using no fewer than six electoral systems: FPTP; the block vote (otherwise known as the multiple nontransferable vote and used in some local council elections in England and Wales, most notably in London Boroughs); the supplementary vote; the single transferable vote; the regional list system; and the additional member system. Therefore, depending on where voters in the UK reside, they encounter various electoral systems to elect representatives at different levels of governance. For example, before Britain departed from the European Union, a voter in Scotland faced the prospect of four different electoral systems: putting an x next to one party in the European elections; putting an x next to one party and an x next to one individual candidate on the ballot for the Scottish Parliament; ranking candidates in order of preference for Scottish council elections; and putting an x next to one candidate for Westminster elections.

To reflect on some of the issues raised by these systems, we can build upon the discussion and ideas found in the UK government's 2008 *Review of Voting Systems*.[27] The report highlighted that any move to PR for Westminster would increase the number of small parties represented, a greater likelihood of coalition governments and multi-member constituencies. In addition, it would not guarantee higher turnout or better social representation, and it could produce unintended consequences, especially around the relationship between constituency and list members, and effective ballot design. Moreover, the report found that there is limited public knowledge of, and interest in, electoral reform. Interestingly, public support for PR has not increased, despite the plethora of systems now used, and there is concern about the influence of small parties and coalitions on government decision-making.

According to the proponents of electoral reform, alternative electoral systems would promote trust in politics and boost participation as the result would be considered 'fair'. Consequently, whether the electorate understand the mechanics of how their representatives came to be there is deemed less important. Anecdotally, an elector in London in 2004, having just engaged with three different electoral systems, was quoted as saying 'What the hell's going on in there?'[28] A similar picture emerges from other parts of the country. During the 2004 European elections, an exit poll in Greater Manchester found that 'nobody' understood how votes under Party List were counted. Two examples from 2007 are noteworthy. Firstly, the North Wales newspaper *Daily Post* found that 'hardly anyone' was aware of the way in which the regional seats were allocated for the

---

[27] Lord Chancellor and Secretary of State for Justice, *The Governance of Britain Review of Voting Systems: The Experience of New Voting Systems in the United Kingdom since 1997* (Cm 7304, 2008).

[28] *Evening Standard* (4 June 2004), quoted in R Kelly, 'It's Only Made Things Worse: A Critique of Electoral Reform in Britain' (2008) 79 *The Political Quarterly* 263.

Welsh Assembly.[29] Secondly, a total of 146,097 ballots were 'spoilt', largely because voters misunderstood various requirements of simultaneously voting for the Scottish Parliament and Scottish councils. To make matters worse, local and national results may have been different had voters understood the mechanics and expectations. In 2009, a survey conducted by BBC Radio Manchester found that less than five per cent of voters understood how winners and losers were calculated under the D'Hondt formula.[30] One writer concluded that 'the more PR is used, the more baffled voters seem to become', perhaps leaving them feeling more estranged from politics than in the FPTP-only days.[31] Defenders of FPTP are on firm ground when they claim one of the strengths of the system is its simplicity and that in a democracy, voters must understand how their representatives come to be elected.

Elsewhere, the evidence that alternative electoral systems promote higher voter turnout and a more engaged citizenry is patchy. Here, a critical caveat is based on a distinction between 'first order' and 'second order' elections. 'First order' elections relate to elections for national parliaments, whereas 'second order' concerns sub-national elections. One of the expectations of 'second order' elections is that turnout will be lower than for 'first order' elections; therefore, the extent to which the electoral system will promote turnout is debatable. It is also noteworthy that turnout across much of the West has declined recently. That said, the evidence from the devolved assemblies does not easily align with the vigour with which reformers claim that PR will enthuse the electorate. Turnout for Stormont elections dropped by almost 15 per cent between 1998 and 2016, but both the 2017 and 2022 elections saw the turnout return to the low-to-mid 60s. A similar picture emerges from Scotland, where turnout fell by 9 per cent from 1999 to 2011 but improved in both 2016 and 2021. Turnout in Wales remains low, hovering in the mid-40s.[32] Some might view rising turnout in Scotland and Northern Ireland as systematic of the electorate becoming accustomed to PR. However, it is perhaps better explained by other variables, particularly the prominence of the territorial question in Scottish and Northern Irish politics. Consequently, it is difficult to argue that introducing PR schemes alone has reinvigorated electoral turnout.

Alternative electoral systems such as AMS, Regional Party List and STV raise interesting questions regarding the relationship between the elector and the representative. The voter–representative link is diluted through bigger and sometimes very diverse geographical constituencies, reducing the identification between the elector and the representative. As such, does the elector blame or praise one or all

---

[29] *Daily Post* (5 May 2007), quoted in Kelly, 'It's Only Made Things Worse' (n 28) 261.

[30] Quoted in R Kelly, 'The Worst of All Worlds? Electoral Reform and Britain's 2009 European Elections' (2009) 82 *The Political Quarterly* 103.

[31] Kelly, 'It's Only Made Things Worse' (n 28) 263.

[32] See K Bunker, 'What Turnout Can We Expect in Northern Ireland, Scotland and Wales?' (Democratic Audit UK, 2016) www.democraticaudit.com/2016/05/02/what-turnout-can-we-expect-in-northern-ireland-scotland-and-wales/; E Uberoi, Turnout at Elections' House of Commons Library No 8060 (2021).

of the representatives? Is a representative responsible for a particular part of the region or all of it? In 2004, Arlene McCarthy, then a Labour MEP, admitted that the move to multi-member constituencies had seen 'the lines of communication' between her and her constituents become 'blurred'. Furthermore, sometimes she had to refer her constituents to other MEPs who understood a particular town better.[33] Elsewhere, there is evidence from Scottish local council elections that voters are influenced by the candidates' place on the ballot paper. Candidates with surnames near the start of the alphabet from the same party are at an advantage over candidates of the same party with surnames at the end of the alphabet.[34]

In addition, such systems bring into focus the relationship between the representatives elected by different mechanics for the same institution. For example, AMS in Scotland and Wales entails representing voters by constituency and regional members. There has been friction between constituency and list members in the Scottish Parliament and Welsh Assembly over the imbalance in constituency work and dual candidacy. Constituency members have complained about being 'shadowed' by regional members, as the latter seek recognition and opportunities to enhance their reputation. Lundberg comments that this competition could be good for constituents as it removes the safety of constituency incumbents and improves responsiveness.[35] However, what type of role regional members should play, especially within constituencies, remains. Moreover, the role of regional members touches on accountability. After all, are they accountable to constituents or to the party organisation?

Certainly, electoral reform has contributed to changes in the party systems found across the UK. Indeed, the UK now has several party systems linked to more complex voting behaviour which has seen independents and minor parties performing better in these elections than in Westminster elections.[36] As a result, coalition is commonplace in the devolved bodies in Scotland, Wales and Northern Ireland, the latter in-built through consociationalism. Also, it is evident in Scottish local government through the introduction of STV. Consequently, there is no shortage of evidence of parties with different interests and ideas working together. However, critics point to the disproportionate influence of minor parties in shaping the executive and policy. In 2009, the Liberal Democrats played a key role in Scotland and Wales, despite coming fourth in both elections on less than 14 per cent of the vote. In Scotland, they refused to continue to support Labour, opening the door to the SNP to form a government. In Wales, they refused to form a 'rainbow coalition', allowing Labour to stay in power. More recently, following

---

[33] *North West Tonight* BBC TV report (27 May 2004), quoted in Kelly, 'It's Only Made Things Worse' (n 28) 264.

[34] See J Mitchell and A Henderson, 'Elections and Electoral Systems' in M Keating (ed), *The Oxford Handbook of Scottish Politics* (Oxford, Oxford University Press, 2020) 216.

[35] TC Lundberg, 'Competition between Members of the Scottish Parliament and the Welsh Assembly: Problem or Virtue?' (2006) 77 *The Political Quarterly* 107.

[36] M Garnett, P Dorey and P Lynch, *Exploring British Politics* (London, Routledge, 2020) 557.

the 2021 Scottish Parliament elections, the Scottish Greens, who finished fourth on eight per cent of the regional vote and with eight MSPs, ended up in government following a power-sharing agreement with the SNP. While PR schemes have resulted in greater proportionality in the legislature, the executive can witness small parties wielding disproportionate influence.

Moreover, despite the incessant calls for proportional representation from *The Guardian* and *The Independent*, its popularity in academic and intellectual circles, and the widespread use of alternative electoral systems across the UK, support for reforming the Westminster electoral systems remains marginal. The scale of defeat for reformers during the 2011 Alternative Vote Referendum was revealing. Firstly, it provided a snapshot of the support for the present system. Secondly, it showed the limits of the electoral reform lobby to unite a broad electoral coalition. Thirdly, there was a relative lack of interest in voting reform, especially when compared to greater levels of engagement and participation in the Scottish Independence Referendum, 2014 and the Referendum on Continuing British Membership of the European Union, 2016. Of course, this has not deterred the electoral reform lobby. Yet, when asked about their priorities, people raise health, education, the economy and immigration – not the D'Hondt formula or the Droop quota.

As an aside, the British experience of electoral reform should serve as a warning to the Labour Party about the dangers of electoral reform and proportional representation. Scotland offers an example of how an alternative electoral system provided a foothold for an opposition party to eat into the Labour vote. Nor has it led to the creation of innovative policies that have resolved the deep-seated economic and social problems found across the UK. If the British left embraces electoral reform for Westminster, hoping it will lead to a fundamental shift in economic relations or the transformation of society, then the evidence thus far from across the UK and further afield suggests they will be disappointed. As such, electoral reform sceptics are right to reject the more far-fetched claims about the transformative impact of proportional representation. As Peter Hain pointed out,

> one of the least convincing characteristics of the PR case is the fervour with which it is pressed as almost a panacea for all Britain's ills … PR is often peddled in an entirely escapist manner, as an illusory way out of the economic and political crisis which has steadily been closing in on Britain.[37]

VI. In Praise of FPTP

Some have argued that FPTP 'has lost the battle of ideas',[38] perhaps reflecting the electoral reformers mistaken belief that they are the superior custodians of

[37] Hain (n 6) 43.
[38] A Blais and M Søberg Shugart, 'Conclusion' in A Blais (ed), *To Keep or to Change First Past the Post? The Politics of Electoral Reform* (Oxford, Oxford University Press, 2008) 206.

democratic traditions. It would be more accurate to state that supporters of the plurality system make an essential and well-reasoned contribution to the debate over electoral reform. There are, of course, a range of arguments in favour of FPTP. However, this section will centre on three: local representation through the constituency link; the theory of the mandate and the manifesto, a cornerstone of the British political tradition; and the superiority of single-party government over coalition government. The three arguments explored below have a close relationship to accountability. We begin with local representation.

Under FPTP, there is a clear link between the MP, the constituency and their constituents. The single-member constituency provides for an obvious and *direct relationship* between the MP and his or her constituents, offering clear lines of local accountability. Moreover, as Caroline Flint makes clear in her chapter, an MP strongly identifies with their constituents. Regardless of whether the constituent has voted for the MP, the MP seeks to gain their vote at future elections by addressing their concerns. It is not, as the reformers would have us believe, a case of the MP only working in the interests of those who voted for them. Systems that consist of large, multi-member constituencies based upon many electors or hybrid systems that deliver two types of MP could undermine links between local communities and their elected representatives. In turn, this would weaken the principle of democratic accountability. In addition, the simplicity and straightforwardness of FPTP should not be dismissed. The winner is the candidate who has received the largest number of votes. There is a clear and unambiguous winner, namely the person most people positively want. Under a preferential system, it is possible that a candidate with the most first preferences could lose out to a candidate as a result of second, third or fourth preferences. Notably, under the plurality system, the voter can see what happened to their vote both locally and nationally.

As we have seen, critics of the theory of the *mandate and the manifesto* claim that very few people read the manifesto, governments are unable to deliver on all their promises as they are blown off course or lack the political will and very few people participate in the writing of the manifesto. Nevertheless, the theory of the mandate and the manifesto is an integral part of the British political tradition, providing a clear line between an elector casting their vote and the actions of government. It acts as a contract between the electorate and the government. Should a government be unable to fulfil its manifesto, it has to explain why, and if a government's failings are so significant, then the electorate can insert a new government with different priorities. Indeed, ensuring that the electorate can choose between rival political programmes is a critical element of democracy.

In addition to the formal manifesto, there is the implied manifesto. The government cannot do all it promises and cannot promise all that it does. With FPTP, the electorate understands that when unexpected events happen, such as economic recession, a Labour government will boost public spending and a Conservative government will cut taxes. Under PR, there is a greater chance that a government's policy agenda is set after the election, and both the formal and implied manifestos are bartered away during the negotiations or obscured once in office.

In such situations, power is transferred from the electorate to politicians, which will damage trust in politics. Consequently, far from invigorating British politics, it is possible that the introduction of PR for Westminster elections would breed further public disillusionment with party politics. For instance, it could see debate moved even further from the public to the private arena, with policy decisions made in secret deals and governments changing hands without prior consultation with voters.

The claim of the superiority of single-party government relates to the theory of the mandate and the manifesto. This links back to the earlier discussion on process and outcomes as single-party government is justified because it is better placed to 'get things done'. For supporters of FPTP, there is nothing inherently superior about coalition government. Pepall scorned electoral reformers for idealising coalition as 'benign compromise' as it was unclear where responsibility lay and it allowed parties to 'offer programs for a niche with no way of knowing, or assuring voters, that they can be effective'.[39] Indeed, while small parties and independents claim that they have greater independence, once in the House of Commons they find their independence compromised, as it is here that majorities must be formed. In addition, PR systems offer great opportunities for minority parties to be given power disproportionate to their support. Pinto-Duschinsky raised the question of whether PR systems assure that each party's proportion of governmental office (as distinct from the proportion of legislative seats) will be proportional to its share of the vote.[40] For instance, a 'hinge party' may emerge, achieving a small proportion of the vote, but pivotal in deciding which major parties form the government. Moreover, it may extract sectional policy concessions that have little support in the country. In that situation, the proportionality of votes would not match proportionality of power, thus undermining the case for PR.

VII. Conclusion

Despite the far-reaching constitutional changes enacted by New Labour, supplemented by further reforms by subsequent governments, concerns about accountability in British politics persist. Many of these relate to the electoral system and other themes explored elsewhere in this volume. As for the electoral system, the continued use of FPTP encourages a range of complaints. Broadly, the argument goes that the present system is unfair, fostering remote decision-making taken by a small group at the centre, thus limiting involvement in the political process. One critical way of giving people greater power is reforming the Westminster electoral system. Importantly, reformers claim that a move away from FPTP will transform politics. Allegedly, it will offer greater accountability to

---

[39] Pepall (n 24) 17.
[40] Pinto-Duschinsky, 'Send the Rascals Packing' (n 18) 119.

the electorate, with the oft-mentioned claims that it will boost voter turnout as 'all votes count under proportional representation', that it is an accurate representation of interests and that the government will have to be open to a greater range of ideas and voices, resulting in better policy which aligns with the electorate's preferences. Outside of Parliament, introducing PR will encourage voters to become active citizens rather than disengaged bystanders.

The extent to which the evidence supports these claims is, as we have seen, contested. FPTP is imperfect, but adopting alternative electoral systems across the UK has proved that to be the case for every other electoral system. One of the great strengths of FPTP is accountability. Given that FPTP generally fosters single-party government, it is clear who to praise or blame. Should the government fail to fulfil its promises or is incompetent or corrupt, it is clear where responsibility lies: the single party in office. Moreover, the electorate can 'kick the rascals out' and insert a new government. Under PR and the increased likelihood of coalition, the government may be produced after the election based upon elite bargaining rather than the electorate's preferences, producing a policy programme that shares little resemblance to the policies placed before the electorate during the election. In addition, we should remember that one of the critical roles of the House of Commons is to sustain the government of the UK. This entails a different criterion to that of other institutions, and a system that fosters strong, stable and effective government that can deliver on the promises made to the electorate during the election should be prioritised.

Supporters of FPTP in Britain must continue to make a case for retaining the system, and tackle the pro-reform lobby head-on. Fundamentally, FPTP offers clear accountability about where responsibility lies and gives the people of this country the most important ability, the power to remove their government.

10

Delegated Legislation in an Unprincipled Constitution

I. Introduction

This edited volume invites its contributors to provide sceptical perspectives on aspects of the British constitution. For such a project, the role and legitimacy of delegated legislation is an ideal subject. Over the last 30 or so years, the British constitution has been in an almost permanent state of development and flux. Yet, curiously, ever increasing recourse to delegated legislation in a constitutionally unprincipled manner has featured in the activity of all governments, regardless of their political hue. This practice undoubtedly reflects pressures on parliamentary time, and the sheer complexities of governing a modern state. Nevertheless, academic commentary has railed against this activity since Lord Hewart's *The New Despotism*, published in 1929. In this text, the author lambasted the broad delegation of rule-making powers to ministers, characterising such practices as a form of 'administrative lawlessness'.[1]

Regrettably, the aphorism *plus ça change, plus c'est la même chose* (the more things change, the more they stay the same) is entirely apposite.[2] So much so that Gabriele Ganz's concluding remarks in her pioneering study of delegated legislation published in 1997 still ring true. She explained that delegated legislation is

> a necessary evil. The classic reasons for its use, i.e. lack of parliamentary time, its technicality, flexibility, and detail, are as valid today as they ever were. The danger in recent developments is that the exceptional types of delegated legislation, which amount to government using non-legal means, may become the norm.[3]

* Thanks to Leah Trueblood, Alison L Young, Jonathan Greenacre and the editors for helpful comments. All errors and omissions remain mine alone.
[1] Lord Hewart of Bury, *The New Despotism* (London, Ernest Benn, 1929) ch 4.
[2] So apposite, in fact, that it forms the title of a report into the phenomena from 2020. See A Sinclair and J Tomlinson, 'Plus ça Change, Plus c'est la Même Chose: Brexit and the Flaws of the Delegated Legislation System' (London, Public Law Project, 2020).
[3] G Ganz, 'Delegated Legislation: A Necessary Evil or a Constitutional Outrage?' in P Leyland and T Woods (eds), *Administrative Law Facing the Future: Old Constraints and New Horizons* (Oxford, Oxford University Press, 1997) 80–81.

It might be reasonable to question the need to re-tread this well-worn path in 2022, then. After all, legislation (in all its forms) is often dismissed by academic common lawyers as 'block-heads' law', as on its face it offers considerably less intellectual stimulation than the reasoning of judgments.[4] Recent and ongoing trends in the use of delegated legislation suggests a ring of truth to former Labour MP Austin Mitchell's quip that the British constitution 'is whatever government can get away with'.[5] Although scholars tend to represent the constitution as underpinned by foundational constitutional principles such as parliamentary sovereignty, the rule of law and the separation of powers (among others), the use of delegated legislation serves as a sharp reminder that these principles are aspirations as opposed to entrenchments. The British constitution affords a government with a majority in the House of Commons ample opportunities to follow the path of least resistance in policy-making. Delegated legislation is one such path.

However, in the last 12–18 months, several parliamentary committees have once again sounded the constitutional alarm in relation to the proliferation and content of delegated legislation. The frequent and unprincipled resort to delegated legislation has been labelled 'democracy denied'[6] and 'government by diktat',[7] whilst another committee centred on threats to the rule of law posed using delegated legislation in the context of the pandemic.[8] Clearly, the twin challenges of Brexit and COVID-19 are not free-standing problems. In parliamentary terms, they are merely symptoms of a pre-existing condition.

Through examining the nature of delegated legislation, the methods by which it is scrutinised and the forms which it takes, this chapter echoes the need for a 'culture change' in the constitution in which the relationship between primary and secondary legislation is rebalanced in favour of the former, so as to give the fullest possible effect to 'the principles of parliamentary democracy, namely parliamentary sovereignty, the rule of law and the accountability of government to Parliament'.[9] If anything, delegated legislation demonstrates that our constitutional culture is continually 'up for grabs'. In recent years, the intensification of a constitutional culture which prioritises the dominance of Whitehall over Westminster[10] starkly illustrates that the 'good chaps' theory of the constitution, which recognises

---

[4] N Duxbury, *Elements of Legislation* (Cambridge, Cambridge University Press, 2012) 57.

[5] A Mitchell, 'The Mandate Man' *Prospect Magazine* (20 November 1997).

[6] Delegated Powers and Regulatory Reform Committee, *Democracy Denied? The Urgent Need to Rebalance Power between Parliament and the Executive* (2021–22, HL 106).

[7] Secondary Legislation Scrutiny Committee, *Government by Diktat: A Call to Return Power to Parliament* (2021–22, HL 105).

[8] Joint Committee on Statutory Instruments, *Rule of Law Themes from COVID-19 Regulations* (2021–22, HL 57, HC 600).

[9] *Government by Diktat* (n 7) [29].

[10] D Howarth, 'Westminster versus Whitehall: What the Brexit Debate Revealed about an Unresolved Conflict at the Heart of the British Constitution' in O Doyle, A McHarg and J Murkens (eds), *The Brexit Challenge for Ireland and the United Kingdom: Constitutions Under Pressure* (Cambridge, Cambridge University Press, 2021).

that the UK's uncodified constitution relies to an unprecedented degree on the 'self-restraint of those who carry it out',[11] is not a self-sustaining ecosystem.

II. What is Delegated Legislation?

Delegated legislation is sometimes alternately described as 'secondary' or 'subordinate' legislation, or collectively as 'statutory instruments'. As a matter of purely technical definition, 'delegated' legislation is any legislation which owes its authority to a parent statute.[12] However, this technical or 'source-based' definition alone is unpersuasive. After all, all Acts of the devolved legislatures owe their authority to parent Acts of Parliament. However, McHarg astutely noted in 2006 that Acts of devolved legislatures have 'more in common with primary than with delegated legislation'[13] because Westminster had 'delegated' authority to a representative democratic institution, as opposed to the executive alone.[14] In *AXA General Insurance v Lord Advocate*,[15] decided in 2011, the Supreme Court endorsed this argument. The true hallmark of delegated legislation, then, is not merely that it derives its validity from a 'parent' Act, but primarily that it is generated by the executive alone, with only a remote connection to wider democratic and parliamentary processes.

It is this remote relationship with legitimising institutions[16] and processes that explains why delegated legislation is generally tolerated by constitutional commentators, as opposed to celebrated. The lack of institutional legitimacy when compared with Acts of Parliament (primary legislation) means that delegated legislation can be invalidated by the courts using common law powers and through the process in section 6 of the Human Rights Act 1998. The Supreme Court noted that 'Although [delegated legislation] can be said to have been approved by Parliament, draft statutory instruments … are not subject to the same legislative scrutiny as bills; and, unlike bills, they cannot be amended by Parliament'.[17] This reduced engagement with, and validation from, the parliamentary process brings delegated legislation within the full jurisdiction of the courts. Unlike Acts of Parliament, delegated legislation is not imbued with the force of Parliament's sovereignty.

---

[11] A Blick and P Hennessy, 'Good Chaps No More? Safeguarding the Constitution in Stressful Times' (London, The Constitution Society, 2019) 5.

[12] UK Parliament, 'What Is Secondary Legislation?' www.parliament.uk/about/how/laws/secondary-legislation/.

[13] A McHarg, 'What Is Delegated Legislation?' [2006] *PL* 539, 561.

[14] ibid 561.

[15] *AXA General Insurance Ltd and Others v Lord Advocate and Others* [2011] UKSC 46, [2012] 1 AC 868.

[16] For a taxonomy of legislative legitimacy, see M Russell, 'Rethinking Bicameral Strength: A Three Dimensional Approach' (2013) 19 *Journal of Legislative Studies* 370.

[17] Sinclair and Tomlinson (n 2) [22].

However, there is no doubt that as 'a matter of principle, the use of subordinate or delegated legislation is clearly possible and legitimate within our constitution'.[18] Loveland goes further, asserting that it would not be 'possible to govern ... solely through primary legislation'.[19] As a form of governance, delegated legislation is not merely necessary, it is ubiquitous. In 1993, the Delegated Powers Scrutiny Committee explained that the 'ever-increasing mass of detail in statutory instruments could not be scrutinised by Parliament if it formed part of primary legislation'.[20] Reducing the workload and 'enabl[ing] government to act expeditiously'[21] are the essential justifications for proliferating delegated legislation. *Erskine May*, the authoritative manual of parliamentary practice, notes that the benefits of delegated legislation are its 'speed, flexibility and adaptability'.[22] Delegated legislation, therefore, is a constitutional essential. In recent years, however, we have seen its use generate concerns that constitutional principles are being eroded.

III. Creating and Scrutinising Delegated Legislation

Delegated legislation is a ubiquitous and necessary part of all mass liberal democracies. However, its ubiquity and how it is created challenges well-worn constitutional assumptions regarding the primacy of parliamentary and representative democracy in the British constitution. This is in large part due to the 'rules of the game' for creating delegated legislation not being the subject of any binding prior legal commitments. There is no equivalent in the British constitution of the USA's Administrative Procedure Act of 1946, which requires that draft delegated legislation is the subject of notice and public comment procedures designed to 'bring regularity and predictability to agency decisionmaking'.[23]

Every student of constitutional law or politics learns by rote that in the British constitution, Parliament is sovereign. The foundational articulation of this principle is that Parliament has 'the right to make any law whatever; and further, that no person or body is recognised by the law of England as having a right to override or set aside the legislation of Parliament'.[24] This statement of the orthodox position of Parliament in the constitution is, in essence, a statement of unqualified supremacy.

---

[18] J Jones, 'The Rule of Law and Subordinate Legislation' www.statutelawsociety.co.uk.

[19] I Loveland, *Constitutional Law, Administrative Law, and Human Rights: A Critical Introduction*, 9th edn (Oxford, Oxford University Press, 2021) 120.

[20] *Democracy Denied?* (n 6) [23].

[21] R Fox and J Blackwell, 'Fox and Blackwell: Parliament and Delegated Legislation' (London, Hansard Society, 2014) 32.

[22] D Natzler and M Hutton (eds), *Erskine May's Treatise on the Law, Privileges, Proceedings and Usage of Parliament*, 25th edn (London, 2019) [31.1], erskinemay.parliament.uk/.

[23] C Copeland, 'The Federal Rulemaking Requirement' RL32240 (Washington DC, Congressional Research Service, 2013) 5.

[24] AV Dicey, *An Introduction to the Study of the Law of the Constitution*, 2nd edn (London, Macmillan, 1886) 36.

Recently, the Supreme Court has sought to venerate and explain the good reasons for parliamentary supremacy in the constitution. The widely publicised cases brought by Gina Miller provide the foremost examples. In *Miller v Secretary of State for Exiting the European Union*,[25] the majority, led by Lord Neuberger, emphasised that the effect of giving notification to withdraw from the European Union under Article 50 of the Treaty on European Union 'will constitute [a] significant ... constitutional change' which could not lawfully be achieved by the executive alone.[26] The principle of parliamentary sovereignty meant that beginning the process of Brexit negotiations required 'the authority of primary legislation' to authorise a paradigm shift in the UK constitution.[27]

Further flesh was put on the bones of parliamentary sovereignty by a unanimous eleven justice panel in *Miller; Cherry v Prime Minister*.[28] The Supreme Court held that proroguing Parliament for five weeks was unlawful. The prorogation would have prevented scrutiny of the withdrawal agreement from the European Union. Using the Royal Prerogative in this way went beyond the scope of the government's lawful powers and offended the constitutional principle of parliamentary sovereignty. Part of what made this breach of the principle of sovereignty so constitutionally offensive was that parliamentary sovereignty was the catalyst which gave effect to the principle of parliamentary accountability. The core legal wrong in the prorogation can be summed up in the following statement: 'the longer that Parliament stands prorogued, the greater the risk that responsible government may be replaced by unaccountable government: the antithesis of the democratic model'.[29]

But the constitution as described by the apex courts and viewed from the ivory towers of academe reads like mythology when we consider the role of delegated legislation. Both the volume of delegated legislation created and the minimalistic role of parliamentarians in scrutiny and amendment undermine parliamentary sovereignty, political accountability and democracy. The forward march of delegated legislation can be rendered compatible with foundational constitutional principles if we are willing to adopt impoverished and diluted versions of those principles. Tucker suggests that if we envision parliamentary sovereignty as merely 'a doctrine about supremacy, or who has the last word', then 'delegated legislation does not impinge on Parliament's authority'.[30] Unsurprisingly, such a narrow definition has proven unsatisfactory to most (the Supreme Court and this author included). The prevailing mood at the time of writing is summed up by a

---

[25] *R (on the Application of Miller and Another) v Secretary of State for Exiting the European Union* [2017] UKSC 5, [2018] AC 61.

[26] ibid [81].

[27] ibid [101].

[28] *R (on the Application of Miller; Cherry) v Prime Minister* [2019] UKSC 41, [2020] AC 373.

[29] ibid [48].

[30] A Tucker, 'Parliamentary Scrutiny of Delegated Legislation' in A Horne and G Drewry (eds), *Parliament and the Law* (Oxford, Hart Publishing, 2018) 359.

committee of the House of Lords, whose report declared that the ongoing 'abuse of delegated powers is in effect an abuse of Parliament and an abuse of democracy'.[31]

In numerical terms, the use of delegated legislation far outweighs Acts of Parliament. Delegated legislation 'is not merely a common practice ... it is the standard form of law-making'.[32] Watson observes that legislation using Acts of Parliament, which receive full legislative scrutiny,[33] has been declining steadily over the last 40 years. In the 2010–20 decade, there were around 52 Acts per year, marking a slight increase in the previous decade. By contrast, the number of statutory instruments has risen exponentially since the 1990s, and approximately 3000 per year were created during the 2010–19 period.[34] In fact, the Cabinet Office's 'Guide to Making Legislation' contains a presumption in favour of rule-making by statutory instrument. This is because legislative slots are competitive. Government departments must 'bid' for a slot for their Bill on the legislative programme.[35] Central government departments are asked to appraise whether 'the ends they wish to achieve could be reached by purely administrative means [or] secondary legislation ... before embarking on primary legislation'.[36] A Select Committee described the 'Guide to Making Legislation' as a 'functional document' lacking any sense of 'the fundamental principles underlying why Parliament ... scrutinise[s] delegated powers so closely'.[37]

Compared with primary legislation, which can be scrutinised and amended by both Houses of Parliament, delegated legislation suffers from a severe democratic deficit. There is a patchwork of methods for scrutinising delegated legislation which have developed piecemeal over time. In their 2014 study, Fox and Blackwell explain that 'the majority of [Statutory Instruments] are not subject to any form of parliamentary scrutiny at all'.[38] Delegated legislation which receives no parliamentary scrutiny is simply 'made' (as opposed to 'laid') by the relevant government department and then signed off or 'made' by a minister.[39] An alternative to this is to simply lay the legislation before Parliament. This laying before Parliament of delegated legislation does not afford parliamentarians any opportunity for scrutiny either.

For delegated legislation that is subject to parliamentary scrutiny, there are three main procedures: the affirmative resolution procedure; the negative resolution procedure; and enhanced scrutiny procedures. The negative resolution

---

[31] *Democracy Denied?* (n 6) 5.

[32] Tucker (n 30) 350.

[33] Cabinet Office, 'Legislative Process: Taking a Bill through Parliament (Guidance)' (20 February 2013) www.gov.uk/guidance/legislative-process-taking-a-Bill-through-parliament/.

[34] C Watson, 'Acts and Statutory Instruments: The Volume of UK Legislation 1850–2019' Commons Library Briefing Paper 7438 (2019) 8.

[35] Cabinet Office, 'Guide to Making Legislation' (London, Stationery Office, 2017) [3.1].

[36] ibid [5.3].

[37] *Democracy Denied?* (n 6) [125].

[38] Fox and Blackwell (n 21) 5.

[39] ibid 5.

procedure allows legislation to be laid before Parliament. It is considered law on the day in which a minister signs it into force unless there is a motion in the Commons or Lords to reject it within 40 days. Affirmative resolution, by contrast, requires the active approval of both Houses of Parliament. Neither of these procedures permit the amendment of delegated legislation, only its wholesale rejection. Wholesale rejection is extremely rare. In 2016, it was reported that only 17 statutory instruments had been rejected in the last 65 years. During that period, almost 170,000 such instruments were made.[40]

Enhanced scrutiny procedures are only available if Parliament chooses to include them in the parent Act. This is the only process which allows parliamentarians to amend delegated legislation. Despite calls to create such a model, there is no standard template for enhanced scrutiny procedures.[41] In general terms, however, enhanced scrutiny involves a two-stage process. First, a proposal for a draft order is laid before Parliament. The draft order itself is then laid and subject to a specified time period for scrutiny. After the period expires, a revised or amended draft order may be laid before Parliament. The Northern Ireland Act 1998 and the Human Rights Act 1998 provide for enhanced scrutiny procedures. Section 85 of the Northern Ireland Act enables His Majesty to make provision about certain of the 'reserved matters' in Schedule 3 to the Act and section 10 of the Human Rights Act 1998 enables a minister or His Majesty to amend a provision of legislation to remove incompatibility with a European Convention on Human Rights right or a UK obligation under the Convention. The European Union (Withdrawal) Act 2018, Schedule 8, section 14 provides an enhanced scrutiny procedure for instruments which 'amend or revoke subordinate legislation under section 2(2) of the European Communities Act 1972 (including subordinate legislation implementing EU directives)'.[42] It is clear, then, that Parliament has chosen to adopt enhanced procedures in these Acts because their subject matter significantly impacts upon the constitution and legal system.

Several problems emerge clearly from this patchwork. The most serious issue is that there is no mechanism or principle for determining what process should be used. Neither the subject matter of the legislation nor the breadth of the powers is determinative. In 2021, the Delegated Powers and Regulatory Reform Committee decried a culture in Whitehall 'which appears to encourage a tendency to see the delegation of legislative powers as a matter of political expediency'.[43] The Hansard Society derided the approach to allocating forms of scrutiny to delegated legislation as 'neither rigorous nor rational'.[44]

---

[40] House of Lords Constitution Committee, *Delegated Legislation and Parliament: A response to the Strathclyde Review* (2015–16, HL 116) [40].

[41] Delegated Powers and Regulatory Reform Committee, *Strengthened Statutory Procedures for the Scrutiny of Delegated Powers: Third Special Report* (2010–12, HL 19) [2].

[42] European Union (Withdrawal) Act 2018, sch 8, s 14.

[43] *Democracy Denied?* (n 6) 4.

[44] Fox and Blackwell (n 21) 171.

Although parliamentary sovereignty is repeatedly reaffirmed as the 'bedrock'[45] of the constitution, Parliament rarely exercises its right to reject delegated legislation. On the one occasion in recent memory when it did so, the government sought to undermine that exercise of power, even by suggesting it was unconstitutional. In October 2015, the House of Lords rejected the Tax Credits (Income Thresholds and Determination of Rates) (Amendment) Regulations 2015. Baroness Manzoor tabled this amendment because the regulations, if passed, would make draconian cuts in the budget for welfare, amounting to £12 billion.

Far from accepting the autonomy of the Lords, let alone the wider sovereignty of Parliament, the immediate response of the government was to suggest that peers in the Lords were in breach of a constitutional convention (a politically enforceable rule of the constitution considered binding on the actors to whom it applies in the context of their official role).[46] According to a statement issued by John Penrose MP, the House of Lords had breached the 'long-standing convention' that they do 'not seek to challenge the primacy of the elected House on spending and taxation'. The House of Lords also 'does not reject statutory instruments, save in exceptional circumstances'.[47]

The government commissioned an independent review into the actions of the House of Lords (the Strathclyde Review). The Review returned three recommendations regarding the Lords' relationship with delegated legislation. The first, and furthest-reaching, recommendation was that the House of Lords should play no further role in the scrutiny of delegated legislation. The second, somewhat more moderate, recommendation was that the House retain its power in relation to delegated legislation, but should nonetheless pass a resolution to define 'in a more precise way, the restrictions on how its powers to deny approval or to annul should be exercised'. The final recommendation was that a new statutory procedure should be created which would allow any defeats imposed on delegated legislation by the Lords to be overruled by the House of Commons.[48]

The Review was not well received by Select Committees.[49] By way of response, the Commons Public Administration and Constitutional Affairs Committee (PACAC) noted that, contrary to the government's assertion, there was 'no consensus as to whether there is a convention regulating the House of Lords' ability to exercise its formal powers to block secondary legislation'.[50] There was some suggestion that 'a convention had developed whereby the House of Lords did not

---

[45] *Jackson v Attorney General* [2005] UKHL 56, [2006] 1 AC 262, [9] (Lord Bingham).

[46] A McHarg, 'Reforming the United Kingdom Constitution: Law, Convention, Soft Law' (2008) 71 *MLR* 853, 860.

[47] HM Government, *Strathclyde Review: Secondary Legislation and the primacy of the House of Commons* (Cm 9177, 2015) 18.

[48] ibid 18.

[49] *Democracy Denied?* (n 6) [49] summarises the conclusions of all the reporting Select Committees.

[50] Public Administration and Constitutional Affairs Committee, *The Strathclyde Review: Statutory Instruments and the Power of the House of Lords* (2015–16, HC 752) [24].

defeat Statutory Instruments' save in exceptional circumstances. However, PACAC concluded that 'there is not universal agreement on what precise form this convention might take and this therefore indicates that no clear convention exists'.[51] PACAC conceded that the Lords' vote to reject the tax credits regulations 'may have been political drama and an embarrassment for the Government, but they did not constitute a constitutional crisis'. It stated pithily that the House of Lords 'was behaving well within the powers available to it on statutory instruments'.[52] It would be highly unusual, not to mention wholly unwise, to allow a convention to crystallise which seeks to limit parliamentarians from holding the executive's powers of legislation to account. This is especially true in view of the unprincipled and limited scrutiny procedures to which delegated legislation is subject.

IV. The Subject Matter of Delegated Legislation

Compromises to parliamentary sovereignty and representative democracy inherent in the scrutiny of delegated legislation would be tolerable if its subject matter were purely technical or trivial. There is an instinctive pull towards the argument that the absence of meaningful opportunities for parliamentary scrutiny should mean that such legislation should be restricted to the 'technical refinement of previously agreed policy'.[53] Acts of Parliament, by contrast, seem to be the most legitimate way of ensuring scrutiny of substantive policy-making. However, Jones notes that there is no 'pre-existing constitutional dividing line between "acceptable" uses of secondary legislation – say, to make "minor, technical or ancillary" provisions – and "unacceptable" ones – say, to make "substantive policy changes"'.[54] In short, the constitutional rules pertaining to the content of delegated legislation are either absent, or unprincipled.

King observes an 'unmistakable trend towards the expanded use of delegated powers to deal with questions of sometimes quite substantial policy'.[55] This trend has been undoubtedly 'accentuated by Brexit and the pandemic', resulting in a change in 'the balance of power between Parliament and government'.[56] However, the absence of any concrete principle against executive legislation on matters of substance has not prevented concerns being raised. The phenomenon discussed in the remainder of this chapter represents a worrying 'general strategic shift'[57] away from the principles of parliamentary democracy and the rule of law.

---

[51] ibid [24].
[52] ibid [28].
[53] *Government by Diktat* (n 7) [17].
[54] Jones (n 18).
[55] J King, 'The Province of Delegated Legislation' in E Fisher, J King and A Young (eds), *The Foundations and Future of Public Law: Essays in Honour of Paul Craig* (Oxford, Oxford University Press, 2020) 154.
[56] *Government by Diktat* (n 7) [15].
[57] ibid [24].

One long-standing issue with delegated legislation is the use of Henry VIII powers. These powers are found in Acts of Parliament, but they confer a discretion on a minister to amend primary legislation unilaterally, using delegated legislation. The name itself calls to mind 'the King's "impersonation of executive autocracy".[58] The term itself comes from the Statute of Proclamations in 1539, which gave Henry VIII, as the sitting monarch, the power to amend parliamentary legislation by proclamation.[59]

Henry VIII clauses are constitutionally problematic because they 'entrust the executive, or potentially some other body, with the power to overturn prior Acts of Parliament'.[60] Generally speaking, such clauses exist to permit the alteration of pre-existing legislation. But Barber and Young, writing in 2003, note that the most remarkable species of Henry VIII powers 'create a power to change Acts of Parliament passed after the empowering Act'.[61] Clauses of this nature are present in the Parliament Acts 1911 and 1949, the Devolution Acts and the Human Rights Act 1998. Ironically, all of these Acts are generally deemed by courts[62] and scholars[63] to fall within the definition of 'constitutional statutes', a designation that denotes a category of statutes which are, by virtue of their important subject matter, only subject to repeal by the most explicit statutory language.

In more recent years, Henry VIII powers have been fiercely criticised by a senior member of the judiciary as resulting from 'bad precedents, invaluable to someone seeking arbitrary powers, like Henry VIII, and bad on that ground alone'.[64] The process of legislating for withdrawal from the European Union has led to the enactment of legislation replete with such clauses.[65]

Henry VIII clauses are frequently created by a species of Act of Parliament known as 'skeleton legislation'. This term describes an Act which sets out the 'general shape and structure of the intended law, but leave[s] all the detail to be provided in secondary legislation'.[66] The name 'skeleton legislation' comes from a critique of the practice advanced in a report by the Scrutiny of Delegated Powers Committee. It proclaimed that Bills which left large swathes of substantive policy-making to the executive amounted to 'little more than a licence to legislate and so give flesh to the "skeleton" embodied in the bill'.[67]

---

[58] *Report of the Committee on Ministers' Powers ('Donoughmore Report')* (Cmd 4060, 1932) in N Barber and A Young, 'The Rise of Prospective Henry VIII Clauses and Their Implications for Sovereignty' [2003] PL 112, 113.

[59] Delegated Powers and Regulatory Reform Committee, *Third Report* (2017–19, HL 22) [93].

[60] Barber and Young (n 58) 113–14.

[61] ibid 112.

[62] *Thoburn v Sunderland City Council* [2002] EWHC 195 (Admin), [2003] QB 151.

[63] F Ahmed and A Perry, 'Constitutional Statutes' (2017) 13 *OJLS* 461; T Khaitan, '"Constitution" as a Statutory Term' (2013) 129 *LQR* 589.

[64] Lord Judge, 'Ceding Power to the Executive; the Resurrection of Henry VIII' (Public Lecture, King's College London, 12 April 2016) www.regulation.org.uk/library/2016_Henry_VIII_powers-Lord_Judge.pdf./.

[65] Sinclair and Tomlinson (n 2) 4.

[66] Fox and Blackwell (n 21) 19.

[67] *Democracy Denied?* (n 6) [59], citing Scrutiny of Delegated Powers Committee, *1st Report* (1992–93, HL 57) [15].

The Welfare Reform Act 2012 is a central example of skeleton legislation. It was intended to reform social security law, which is highly complex in and of itself. However, the Bill was 174 pages in length and made provision for a mind-boggling 374 delegated powers.[68] By way of justification for this approach, Chris Grayling MP, the minister sponsoring the Bill, employed the following metaphor. He explained that the Bill would 'create a bookcase on which we can lodge the books of the detail of the future benefits system. [The] Bill and the debate are about build-ing that bookcase … the debate is not about the detailed content of every single book.'[69] Regardless of how apt the metaphor might have been (this author reserves judgement), one parliamentarian was less than impressed in the Bill's committee stage, remarking that the House could not scrutinise the Bill because 'Ministers have not yet decided what the legislation is'.[70]

Specific numbers on the use of skeleton Bills are not available, but the Delegated Powers and Regulatory Reform Committee expressed its concern that in recent years their use has 'grown markedly'.[71] Examples of the subject matter of skeleton Bills include Brexit legislation, the Childcare Bill and the Civil Liability Bill. The same Committee took the view that the practice 'signifies an exceptional shift in power from Parliament to the executive'. The central wrong in this shift, according to the Committee, is that 'the real operation of the legislation [is] to be decided by ministers'. In constitutional terms, then, this practice 'will rarely be justifiable'.[72]

Nevertheless, there is an element of truth in Jones's supposition that 'excep-tional situations – like the huge constitutional and legal shift of Brexit, or a national emergency like covid – may call for exceptional responses'.[73] Most, if not all, constitutional orders either feature explicit constitutional provisions dealing with emergencies or have similar provisions in ordinary legislation. For example, the UK has the Civil Contingencies Act 2004, which includes an 'event or situation which threatens serious damage to human welfare in a place in the United Kingdom' within its definition of an emergency.[74] The definition of 'serious damage' includes the loss of human life.[75] However, the processes in the 2004 Act were disregarded in favour of the 'much weaker' scrutiny processes of the Coronavirus Act 2020 in a move that has been characterised as a 'neglect of constitutionalism'.[76]

Critics of the use of delegation in response to Brexit and the pandemic have been acutely aware of the challenges posed to the government by these succes-sive crises.[77] Yet, there remains pervasive support for the idea that the practices

[68] Fox and Blackwell (n 21) 133.
[69] ibid 134, citing HC Deb 29 March 2011, vol 526, col 171.
[70] ibid 135, citing S Timms (Lab) citing HC Deb 29 March 2011, vol 526, col 169.
[71] *Democracy Denied?* (n 6) [63].
[72] ibid [66].
[73] Jones (n 18).
[74] Civil Contingencies Act 2004, s 1(1)(a).
[75] ibid s 1(2)(a).
[76] A Blick and C Walker, 'Why Did the Government Not Use the Civil Contingencies Act?' *The Law Society Gazette* (2 April 2020) www.lawgazette.co.uk/legal-updates/why-did-government-not-use-the-civil-contingencies-act/5103742.article.
[77] See, eg *Rule of Law Themes from COVID-19 Regulations* (n 8) [4]; *Democracy Denied?* (n 6).

surrounding delegated legislation during Brexit and the pandemic pose risks to Parliament's position at the apex of the constitution and respect for the rule of law.

The rule of law is a deeply contested constellation of ideals.[78] To that end, its role in the British constitution is dynamic, not static. It occupies no fixed position. Definitions range from the barest procedural criteria to the inclusion of fundamental human rights and substantive moral values. However, most definitions, ranging from thin to thick conceptions (sometimes described as 'formal' or 'substantive' models), agree that legal rules which comply with the rule of law promulgate laws which vindicate the values of 'generality; publicity; prospectivity; intelligibility; consistency; practicability; [and] stability'.[79] In layman's terms, legal rules must apply to everyone as opposed to specific individuals, be well publicised and easy to understand, and apply only to future conduct. They cannot sanction someone for a wrong that was legal yesterday. Additionally, legal rules must treat similar cases in a consistent manner, and must be practical, somewhat predictable and stable, as opposed to fleeting.

Beatson demonstrates that rule-of-law values are in general decline in Britain. Large bodies of legislation remain inaccessible to the ordinary public,[80] and the criminal law (which requires rules to be particularly clear) suffers from increasing complexity.[81] On top of these concerns, we can see that delegated legislation has been used during Brexit and the COVID-19 pandemic in several ways which are frankly inimical to even the most basic definitions of the rule of law. Justifications of 'emergency' or 'necessity' can only offer so much in the way of mitigation when we step back and view the practices surrounding delegated legislation as part of the routine compromise of foundational constitutional principles.

There are four practices in the promulgation of delegated legislation which raise real rule-of-law concerns: circumventing scrutiny procedures; the sub-delegation of legislative power (known as 'tertiary legislation'); blurring the boundary between law and guidance; and the creation of new criminal offences.

Procedures for scrutinising delegated legislation may be scant, but the exigencies of Brexit and COVID-19 saw even these meagre safeguards being pushed aside. In its report on the challenges posed to the rule of law by the pandemic, the Joint Committee on Statutory Instruments observed that 'of the 461 coronavirus instruments laid before Parliament by 5 July 2021, more than one in nine were made to come into force before being laid'.[82] In relation to Brexit, Sinclair

---

[78] J Waldron, 'Is the Rule of Law an Essentially Contested Concept (in Florida)?' (2002) 21 *Law and Philosophy* 137; J Raz, *The Authority of Law: Essays on Law and Morality* (Oxford, Oxford University Press, 1979) ch 11; L Fuller, *The Mortality of Law* (New Haven, Yale University Press, 1954); T Bingham, *The Rule of Law* (London, Penguin, 2010).

[79] J Waldron, 'The Rule of Law', *The Stanford Encyclopedia of Philosophy* (2016) [5.1].c.

[80] J Beatson, *Key Ideas in Law: The Rule of Law and the Separation of Powers* (Oxford, Hart Publishing, 2021) 33.

[81] ibid 36.

[82] *Rule of Law Themes from COVID-19 Regulations* (n 8) [68].

and Tomlinson have highlighted the poor explanations given to parliamentarians regarding the purpose of various statutory instruments. Deficiencies in the explanatory memoranda which accompany statutory instruments are described as 'pervasive'. The authors note that the nadir of this situation came in relation to the explanatory note to the Law Enforcement and Security (Amendment) (EU Exit) Regulations 2019.[83] This 75-page document was described by the Secondary Legislation Scrutiny Committee as 'impenetrable'. Its report asked the Home Office to relay the instrument with an improved memorandum.[84] Both of these practices undercut minimal rule-of-law requirements, namely, that laws promulgated should be clear, intelligible and prospective in their application.

The next practice which engages rule-of-law concerns is known as legislative sub-delegation, also called the creation of 'tertiary' legislation. In this situation, an Act of Parliament confers 'a legislative power [to the executive] which may, in turn, include provision for further delegation of legislative power'.[85] This 'tertiary' legislation carries the same force as any other form of delegated legislation. However, the nature of the body to which legislative powers are sub-delegated means that these powers cannot be scrutinised by Parliament. Examples of this sub-delegation include leaving powers conferred upon the minister to local actors (such as local authorities and prison governors) to vary pandemic safety rules at short notice in specific local areas.[86] This practice was described by the Delegated Powers and Regulatory Reform Committee as a 'potentially more egregious'[87] erosion of democratic accountability than ordinary delegation. It also has a less immediate, albeit no less severe, rule-of-law cost. The threat to the rule of law is manifested in the government's attempt to construe the powers in statutory instruments very broadly. On this basis, the Committee claimed sub-delegation was lawful. When interpreting statutes, however, the courts apply a general presumption against the sub-delegation of legislative power.[88] The arguments about modern statutory construction permitting such sub-delegation were considered by a parliamentary committee tasked with investigating the rule-of-law implications of the pandemic. They described the government's position on tertiary legislation as unable to 'survive the 2016 decision of the Supreme Court in *Public Law Project*',[89] which endorsed general presumptions against the sub-delegation of broad statutory powers. This common law presumption is underpinned by broader theoretical presumptions within the rule of law, namely, that the law should be clear, stable and predictable.

---

[83] SI 742/2019.
[84] Sinclair and Tomlinson (n 2) 25.
[85] *Democracy Denied?* (n 6) [107].
[86] *Rule of Law Themes from COVID-19 Regulations* (n 8) [14]–[28].
[87] *Democracy Denied?* (n 6) [111].
[88] D Greenberg, *Craies on Legislation*, 12th edn (London, Sweet & Maxwell, 2020) paras 3.5.1–3.5.4 and 19.1.22.6.
[89] *Rule of Law Themes from COVID-19 Regulations* (n 8) [17].

During the pandemic, the boundary between law and guidance was also frequently blurred. The amount of non-legally binding guidance proliferated significantly under the Coronavirus Act 2020. The guidance expressed commands which exceeded the legal powers conferred by the Act. Obligations such as staying two metres apart from anyone outside was a rule which appeared in guidance as opposed to law. However, it was presented to the public at large as law, despite having no legal force of its own. Ewing comments that guidance which stated that 'every citizen is instructed to comply with these new measures' was 'oblivious to [the] basic constitutional formality' that restrictions on general liberties could not be imposed by non-legal means.[90]

Parliamentarians also expressed concerns about the 'disturbing new trends'. including 'disguised law' and over-reliance upon guidance as a means of rule-making. The phenomenon of 'disguised law' refers to an increase in recourse to 'instruments which are legislative in effect but often not subject to parliamentary oversight'.[91] Examples of this included 'mandatory guidance', 'Requirements "to have regard to" guidance' and 'powers to make a "determination", to make "directions", to determine "arrangements", and to issue a "code of practice", a "protocol" or a "public notice"'.[92]

Enshrining legal rules in mandatory guidance has the effect of what the Leader of the House of Commons described as 'circumvent[ing] the usual way of regulating a matter'.[93] The Justice Committee of the House of Commons expressed rule-of-law concerns regarding the impact of this practice during the pandemic. The Committee emphasised that

> [i]n a free society that respects the rule of law, only legislation can criminalise conduct, and it should be open to a person to decide whether to follow government guidance. The Government has a responsibility to ensure that the public and the police have a clear understanding of the distinction between guidance and the law.[94]

Undoubtedly the most egregious wrong – when viewed through the lens of constitutional principle – was the use of delegated legislation to create new criminal offences. This practice is not new, however. A Law Commission consultation from 2010[95] expressed concerns about the increased resort to criminal sanctions in the regulatory context, including under the Consumer Protection Act 1987.[96] The Consultation Report expressed 'concerns about the use of delegated powers to create criminal offences, especially when these offences can be met with a sentence

[90] K Ewing, 'Covid-19: Government by Decree' (2020) 31 *King's Law Journal* 1, 18.
[91] *Democracy Denied?* (n 6) [89].
[92] ibid [90].
[93] ibid [94].
[94] House of Commons Justice Committee, *COVID-19 and the Criminal Law* (2021–22, HC 71) [44]
[95] Law Commission, 'Criminal Liability in Regulatory Contexts: A Consultation Paper, No 195 (London, The Law Commission, 2010)
[96] ibid [3.83] onwards.

of imprisonment'.[97] The Law Commission took the 'provisional view' that criminal offences should only be created using primary legislation.[98]

During the pandemic, this advice went unheeded. The Joint Committee on Statutory Instruments pointed out that offences created using delegated legislation in response to the pandemic were both unclear and irrational. The difficulties ranged from the relatively benign – failure to adequately define a 'suitable place' in a regulation concerning accommodation[99] – to the ridiculous. The Health Protection (Coronavirus, Local COVID-19 Alert Level) (Medium, High and Very High) (England) (Amendment) (No 3) Regulations 2020, enacted by the Department of Health and Social Care, made it a criminal offence to remain open for the purposes of selling alcohol at certain times. However, in a parliamentary evidence session, a representative of the Department admitted to the ridiculous implications of this prohibition. It would have been 'entirely lawful' for an off-licence to remain open and to allow customers to enter and select their preferred alcohol without making a purchase. Immediately upon leaving the shop, they could 'telephone to the counter … and place an order, and … re-enter the shop and buy the alcohol'.[100] One cannot help but speculate that a drafting error which produced such absurd results may well have been intercepted and corrected by the parliamentary process if it had appeared in primary legislation.

V. Cementing Principles in an Unprincipled Landscape

The above analysis of delegated legislation aims to stir the consciences of those committed to representative democracy and the rule of law. It is a source of personal frustration and disappointment that this chapter (and many others) continues to repeat the same grievances over the course of a generation. Perhaps this is because public law scholars tend to suffer from both naivety and utopianism. Much of what is discussed in this chapter may be undesirable when measured against abstract principles, but it is perfectly constitutionally permissible. Perhaps Griffith was right when he lamented that: 'Societies are by nature authoritarian. Governments even more so.'[101] In this volume, Professor Harlow's illuminating chapter points out that Griffith never defined the political constitution in his Chorley lecture, and he recognised the need for 'a strong executive government capable of pushing through a reformist agenda'.[102] But, as Harlow remarks, he was 'no authoritarian'[103]

---

[97] ibid [3.112].
[98] ibid [3.145].
[99] *Rule of Law Themes from COVID-19 Regulations* (n 8) [30], citing The Health Protection (Coronavirus, Restrictions) (Steps) (England) Regulations 2021, SI 364/2021.
[100] *Rule of Law Themes from COVID-19 Regulations* (n 8) [34].
[101] JAG Griffith, 'The Political Constitution' (1979) 42 *MLR* 1, 3.
[102] C Harlow, 'Judicial Encroachment on the Political Constitution?' ch 2 in this volume.
[103] ibid.

either. He strongly recognised the role of the political institutions of the constitution in securing accountability for executive action.

Delegated legislation and the damaging practices which surround it cast our well-worn and lazy assumptions about principles in the British constitution into sharp relief. The enduring legacy of Griffith's essay is the sentiment that the (somewhat skeletal) architecture of the British constitution means 'that we get no more or no less than the constitution we as a polity deserve'.[104] Principles in the British constitution are not conveniently built into a pre-existing, entrenched framework. Their continued presence requires consistent effort on the part of the government, parliamentarians and the electorate. Like the crumbling edifice of a historic building, constitutional principles must be consistently and assiduously maintained.

In this regard, the efforts by various Select Committees suggesting that resort to delegated legislation should be the subject of last resort and eschew policy choices are to be welcomed. A 'culture change' in the practices surrounding the making and scrutiny of delegated legislation which places the principle of parliamentary democracy at its centre is undoubtedly required.[105] This should include, among other measures, an amendment to the 'Guide to Making Legislation' to include a 'statement of principles of parliamentary democracy, with a requirement that it should underpin to the fullest extent possible decisions about proposed delegations of legislative power'.[106] But the flexibility of our constitutional settlement means that any such commitment requires political will. There is no doubt that if we want a principled constitution, then we must all commit, in short, to being 'good chaps'.[107]

Brexit and the pandemic left a severe (potentially indelible) dent in the constitutional landscape. Ewing observed that the pandemic saw parliamentary accountability recede in favour of 'briefings by ministers (flanked by government experts) in an empty room with journalists, not MPs, on the receiving end remotely to ask questions. Broadcast live to the nation, the spectacle reinforces the marginalisation of Parliament'.[108] This constitutional shift has not gone unobserved. In February 2022, the Institute for Government launched a review of the British constitution, because the time had come to 'consider whether reforms are necessary to make the UK's constitutional order more coherent, effective and legitimate'.[109]

---

[104] H Hooper and V Fikfak, *Parliament's Secret War* (Oxford, Hart Publishing, 2018) 237.
[105] *Democracy Denied?* (n 6) [164] 'Box 2'.
[106] ibid [165] 'Box 3'.
[107] Blick and Hennessy (n 11).
[108] Ewing (n 90) 24.
[109] M Thimont Jack, J Sargeant and J Pannell, 'A Framework for Reviewing the UK Constitution' (London, Institute for Government, 2022) 11.

VI. Conclusion

There is no doubt that executive power has increased, and we now stand at a cross-roads between two potential models of the British constitution. Howarth, a former parliamentarian, dubs these competing models (first proposed by AH Birch)[110] the 'Westminster' and 'Whitehall' models.[111] The Whitehall model views the executive as the dominant constitutional entity. According to Howarth, on this view, the party which wins a general election 'is not merely entitled to implement its manifesto (to exercise its "mandate") but obligated to do so'.[112] Therefore, the Whitehall model sees 'parliamentary activity that tends to obstruct the implementation of the winning party's manifesto … as anti-democratic'.[113] The Westminster view, by contrast, celebrates Parliament as the central constitutional actor. It is no mere ideal.[114] On this model, Britain is viewed as 'a representative democracy in which members of parliament exercise their own judgment, in the tradition of Edmund Burke, and do not automatically follow the views of their party'.[115] In this regard, what happens in Parliament matters: it has real consequences, including ministerial resignation when the confidence of the Commons is lost.

Obviously, the prevalence of each model shifts according to time and circumstance. Ideally, neither should dominate entirely and for all time coming. Whilst hierarchies in constitutions and legal systems are inevitable to some degree, constitutionalism inherently requires and promotes tension between institutions and the continued justification of the exercise of public power.

The role of delegated legislation in the last 30 or so years is a poignant illustration that constitutional principles are contingent and even potentially illusory. The dicta from the Supreme Court in the *Miller* cases illustrate how starkly understandings of the constitution can vary between its key actors at any point in time. The Supreme Court adopted a view which was 'very much Westminsterist' in marked contrast to 'the determinedly Whitehallist' views of the government and other political actors.[116] The efforts of various Select Committees which have highlighted the desire to return Parliament to the centre of the legislative process come at an important time in history. After all, its function in this author's view is to 'protect us from authoritarianism, from despotism, from an over mighty monarch, but also from an over mighty executive'.[117]

---

[110] A Birch, *Representative and Responsible Government: An Essay on the British Constitution* (London, Allen & Unwin, 1964).
[111] Howarth (n 10) 217.
[112] ibid 218.
[113] ibid.
[114] ibid.
[115] ibid 218–19.
[116] ibid 238.
[117] Lord Judge (n 64).

11

A Defence of the Dual Legal–
Political Nature of the Attorney
General for England and Wales

CONOR CASEY[1]

'The role of Attorney General, which combines legal and ministerial functions, needs to change'.

The Prime Minister, the Rt Hon Gordon Brown MP, 3 July 2007.

I. Introduction

In February 2022, the House of Lords Constitution Committee opened an inquiry into the role of the Law Officers.[2] The Committee outlined several questions that would frame its investigation, including whether it is 'appropriate or helpful for the Law Officers, as Government legal advisers, to be politicians serving in Government?'.[3] This inquiry represents the most thorough examination of the office of Attorney General since the period between 2007 and 2009, during then Prime Minister Gordon Brown's campaign for constitutional reform.[4] Part of the Labour government's proposals involved holding a consultation on the role of the Attorney General, which was kickstarted by the publication of a document setting out several options for changing the role and functions of the office.[5]

---

[1] The author would like to thank Richard Ekins, Richard Johnson, Conor McCormick and Yuan Yi Zhu for helpful comments and discussions.
[2] See https://committees.parliament.uk/work/6540/role-of-the-lord-chancellor-and-the-law-officers/.
[3] 'Constitution Committee calls for evidence on the role of the Lord Chancellor and the Law Officers', available at https://committees.parliament.uk/work/6540/role-of-the-lord-chancellor-and-the-law-officers/news/161171/constitution-committee-calls-for-evidence-on-the-role-of-the-lord-chancellor-and-the-law-officers/.
[4] Government of the United Kingdom, *The Governance of Britain* (Cm 7170, July 2007).
[5] Government of the United Kingdom, *The Governance of Britain: A Consultation on the Role of the Attorney General* (Cm 7192, 2007) 2.

Impetus for the consultation stemmed from debate over whether there was unacceptable tension between the 'various functions of the Attorney General – being a minister and a member of the government and being an independent guardian of the public interest and performing superintendence functions', and 'between being a party politician and a member of the Government, and the giving of independent and impartial legal advice'.[6] The consultation document provided that the government's view was that the 'test for any proposal for change should be whether it enhances the effective administration of justice, the maintenance of the rule of law and the protection of the public interest, and enhances public confidence in the office'.[7] It was clear that some in government were open to reform, with the then Prime Minister, Gordon Brown, announcing to the House of Commons that the Attorney General 'needs to change'.[8]

Around the same time, the House of Commons Constitutional Affairs Committee[9] and House of Lords Select Committee on the Constitution[10] both issued reports on potential reform, with the former advocating significant change. The Commons Committee recommended reform along the lines that responsibility for providing legal advice to the government and superintending the prosecution services should be vested in a statutorily independent career lawyer and not a politician or member of the government.[11] In the end, however, the government and Parliament did not proceed with significant reform. While some recommendations made by the House of Commons Committee were received positively by the Labour government (even if not acted upon), its most consequential proposals were rejected.[12] Although the government initially appeared enthusiastic about the prospect of reform, it ultimately quickly rowed back from the idea, eventually agreeing with the majority of submissions to their consultation that the current set up had – upon reflection – very strong merits after all.[13]

The recommendations of the current House of Lords Constitution Committee – whose members include a former Supreme Court president, an ex-Lord Chancellor and ex-Solicitor General – will no doubt spark renewed debate on the Attorney General and their proper role in the constitutional order. This chapter aims to contribute to this ongoing reflection by arguing that the Labour government had

---

[6] ibid.

[7] ibid.

[8] HC Deb 3 July 2007, vol 462, col 817.

[9] House of Commons Constitutional Affairs Committee, 'Constitutional Role of the Attorney General' (5th Report of Session 2006–07, 17 July 2007).

[10] House of Lords Select Committee on the Constitution, 'Reform of the Office of Attorney General' (7th Report of Session 2007–08, 18 April 2008).

[11] House of Commons Constitutional Affairs Committee (n 8) para 18.

[12] See Government of the United Kingdom, *The Government's Response to the Constitutional Affairs Select Committee Report on the Constitutional Role of the Attorney General* (Cm 7355, 2008).

[13] Government of the United Kingdom, *The Governance of Britain: Constitutional Renewal* (Cm 7342–I, 2008) para 51.

acted prudently by rejecting significant constitutional reform, and that current political actors should follow suit.

As such, I offer a defence of the Attorney General and the institutional status quo of the Office. I suggest that the current configuration of the Attorney General, as an officer with dual legal–political dimensions, is reasonable and defensible. I also argue that the costs of moving to an alternative model of Attorney General could be steep and not worth incurring. However, my defence is slightly qualified in that I suggest several moderate reforms would be prudent to ensure proper balance is maintained between the political and legal dimensions of the office, so that the former does not compromise the latter. I proceed in four parts.

Section II offers an overview of the Attorney General's Office and its diverse set of functions and responsibilities. This section provides an account of the dual legal–political nature of the office. Section III outlines the strongest critiques of the office and why calls for reform arise intermittently. Section IV offers a defence of the office and argues successive Attorneys General have, for the most part, maintained appropriate balance when simultaneously carrying out their role as legal advisor and guardian of the public interest and rule of law on the one hand, and their position as a highly political animal and member of government on the other. Section V outlines a slight qualification to my defence, which is that several reforms would be prudent responses to some legitimate concerns raised in section IV and would help solidify appropriate balance between the dual dimensions of the Attorney General's Office. A brief conclusion follows.

II. Role and Functions of Attorney General

Parliament and the judiciary are the most visible actors helping ensure the executive and its officials adhere to the rule of law. The former does so by subjecting ministers to parliamentary scrutiny for their actions and censure where appropriate, the latter through the mechanism of judicial review. However, *within* the executive it is government lawyers who are at the frontline of ensuring the rule of law is respected. Government lawyers ensure that concern for law and legality remain 'ever-present considerations' for politicians and officials by being on hand to provide legal advice in respect of policy concerns or legislative proposals.[14]

The organisation of government lawyers in England and Wales is somewhat complex but, for simplicity's sake, can be pictured as having a pyramid-like structure. At the base of the pyramid are career civil service lawyers who provide day-to-day legal advice to ministers and officials on countless legal questions. The Government Legal Department (GLD) – which has a staff complement of

---

[14] B Yong, *Government Lawyers and the Provision of Legal Advice within Whitehall* (London, The Constitution Unit, 2013) 94.

around 2000[15] and is headed by the Treasury Solicitor[16] – provides this function for most government departments and ministers. A minority of departments, like the Foreign Office and Cabinet Office, rely on their in-house departmental legal advisors. These lawyers play a critical role in ensuring that the routine work of dozens of departments – from administrative decisions to the formulation of legislation, both primary and secondary – remains compliant with statute, human rights law and constitutional conventions.[17]

Atop this base, at the apex of the government lawyer pyramid, stand the Law Officers.[18] This group includes the Attorney General for England and Wales,[19] the Solicitor General for England and Wales[20] and the Advocate General for Scotland (who advises the UK government on Scots law). The Attorney General of England and Wales is a constitutional office ancient in origin, with roots traceable to the thirteenth century.[21] Initially the Attorney General was the King's lawyer, an eminent counsel expected to fiercely represent the sovereign's interests, defend their prerogatives in legal proceedings and provide advice where requested. Over time, as the effective exercise of executive authority shifted to the government, the Attorney General stopped acting as a personal lawyer to the sovereign and became a salaried minister of the Crown whose work focused exclusively on government business in the courts and Parliament.[22]

Today, the main function of the Attorney General and other Law Officers remains to serve as legal advisors to the Crown via her Prime Minister and government.[23] The Law Officers are, by convention, members of government but not members of the Cabinet.[24] Traditionally, Attorneys General attended Cabinet meetings on request as the need for advice arose.[25] However, recent Attorneys

---

[15] www.gov.uk/government/publications/workforce-management-information-for-gld-ago-and-hmcpsi-201819.

[16] BK Winterobe, 'Legal Advice and Representation for Parliament' in D Oliver and G Drewry (eds), *The Law and Parliament* (London, Butterworths, 1998) 95.

[17] Yong (n 13) 15–17.

[18] For more fulsome overviews of the Law Officers place in the constitutional order, see J Edwards, *The Law Officers of the Crown: A Study of the Offices of Attorney-General and Solicitor-General of England with an Account of the Office of the Director of Public Prosecutions of England* (London, Sweet & Maxwell, 1964); C McCormick, *The Constitutional Legitimacy of the Law Officers in the United Kingdom* (Oxford, Hart Publishing, 2022).

[19] The Attorney General of England and Wales also holds the Office of Advocate General for Northern Ireland and advises the UK government on Northern Irish law.

[20] Pursuant to the Law Officers Act 1997, any function of the Attorney General may be exercised by the Solicitor General, and anything done by or in relation to the Solicitor General in the exercise of those functions is treated as if it were done by the Attorney General.

[21] See WS Holdsworth, 'Early History of the Attorney and Solicitor General' (1918–19) 13 *Illinois Law Review* 602.

[22] *The Governance of Britain: A Consultation* (n 4) 4–5.

[23] The Attorney General is also, by convention, expected to be available to provide legal advice to Parliament in several limited instances, including the conduct of House proceedings, disciplining of members and the effect of proposed legislation.

[24] The Attorney General has not been a member of Cabinet since 1928.

[25] E Jones, 'The Office of Attorney-General' (1969) 27 *CLJ* 43, 47.

General have reported that there is now an 'expectation' that the Attorney General will regularly attend Cabinet meetings.[26] The Law Officers handle only a very small fraction of legal questions concerning the government, namely the most difficult, pressing and politically important.[27] Successive versions of the Cabinet Office's Ministerial Code have referred to the importance of the Law Officers' advice, and specified they must be consulted where: the legal consequences of action by the government have important policy repercussions; if a department legal advisor is unsure of the legality or constitutionality of legislation; if the vires of subordinate legislation is in dispute; or where two or more departmental legal advisors are in disagreement.[28] A request for legal advice may also be made directly to the Attorney General at Cabinet level, particularly if it involves an issue on which the Prime Minister has taken a policy lead. The Law Officers' decision is, by convention, accepted as binding, making it the last word on internal legal questions for the government.[29]

The Attorney General also has several important functions in the legislative process. Departmental Bills submitted to the Parliamentary Business and Legislation Cabinet Committee must be accompanied by a legal memorandum drafted by GLD advisors or other in-house advisors. This memorandum includes 'full and frank assessment of legal risk' arising from the issues engaged by the Bill,[30] including, inter alia, analysis of its compatibility with the Human Rights Act 1998 (HRA). This memorandum is shared with the Law Officers, who also consider its HRA compatibility and satisfy themselves with the memorandum's cogency. The Attorney General also scrutinises Bills for consistency with rule-of-law values by examining them for (i) potentially oppressive retrospective effect and (ii) likelihood of early commencement before the typical two-month period post-royal assent elapses.[31] In such circumstances, the Law Officers' consent must be given for Bills to proceed to Parliament.

The Attorney General has accrued a diverse range of common law and statutory responsibilities under the broad heading of defending the public interest. Examples include power to prosecute for contempt of court or repeat initiation of vexatious litigation, to refer 'unduly lenient' sentences or points of law to the Court of Appeal, to appoint amicus curiae in certain important proceedings where an important point of law is at stake, to make or consent to an application for a

---

[26] C McCormick and G Cowie, 'The Law Officers: A Constitutional and Functional Overview' House of Commons Library Briefing Paper No 08919 (May 2020) 49.

[27] SSC Silkin, 'The Function and Position of the Attorney-General in the United Kingdom' (1978) 12 *Bracton Law Journal* 29, 34.

[28] See *Ministerial Code: A Code of Conduct and Guidance on Procedures for Ministers* (London, Cabinet Office, 2001) para 22; *Ministerial Code: A Code of Ethics and Procedural Guidance for Ministers* (London, Cabinet Office, 2005) paras 6.22–6.44; *Ministerial Code* (London, Cabinet Office, 2018) paras 2.10–2.13.

[29] McCormick, *The Constitutional Legitimacy* (n 17) 52.

[30] Guide to Making Legislation' (Cabinet Office 2022) 11.11.

[31] ibid 3.10.

new inquest, and to intervene as a party in litigation concerning charity law.[32] More recently, Attorneys General have been given an important responsibility in respect of devolution, and been vested with statutory authority to refer questions to the Supreme Court about whether the three devolved assemblies have exceeded their respective legislative competences.[33] In discharging all these responsibilities, the Attorney General is – per the widely accepted and embedded Shawcross principles – expected to exercise their judgement independently of direction from other members of the government.[34] Named after former Attorney General Sir Hartley Shawcross QC, the basic thrust of the principle is that while Attorneys General may consult with their colleagues when discharging their public interest functions, ultimate decision-making responsibility rests with the Attorney General alone, who is not to be put under pressure by any colleagues.[35]

Finally, and significantly, the Attorney General has a heavily political dimension to their work. The Attorney General is a government minister and typically a senior politician of the governing party drawn from the Commons as an elected MP or from the Lords as an appointed peer. They are subject to dismissal by the Prime Minister, subject to collective responsibility and take the whip in Parliament. The Attorney General superintends the Crown Prosecution Service and Serious Fraud Office, and has an important role in helping set their priorities and broad policy objectives, and ensuring the offices are adequately resourced. The Attorney General also has reserved a right to make representations to the Director of Public Prosecutions (DPP) in a small subset of national security cases, for which they must inform Parliament after doing so. But day-to-day operations and individual prosecutorial decisions are left to statutorily independent civil servants and the DPP. The superintendence functions of the Attorney General are now subject to detailed framework agreements, which make the Attorney General's ability to influence the DPP's prosecutorial decisions vanishingly small.[36] The division of responsibility between the Attorney General and the directors of the prosecution agencies is, suggests McCormick, 'clearer than it has ever been before … it could scarcely be much clearer to my mind'.[37]

Attorneys General will also tend to share the basic normative goals and political philosophy of their party and ministerial colleagues. Thus, as with any minister, part of their general workload will be to help advance the policy goals of the

---

[32] McCormick, *The Constitutional Legitimacy* (n 17) 62–70.

[33] C McCorkindale and A McHarg, 'Continuity and Confusion: Legislating for Brexit in Scotland and Wales (Part II)' (*UK Constitutional Law Blog*, 7 March 2018) https://ukconstitutionallaw.org/2018/03/07/christopher-mccorkindale-and-aileen-mcharg-continuity-and-confusion-legislating-for-brexit-in-scotland-and-wales-part-ii/.

[34] McCormick, *The Constitutional Legitimacy* (n 17) 66–67.

[35] ibid.

[36] Attorney General's Office, *Framework Agreement between the Law Officers and the Director of Public Prosecutions* (18 December 2020); Attorney General's Office, *Framework Agreement between the Law Officers and the Director of the Serious Fraud Office* (21 January 2019).

[37] Written evidence of Conor McCormick to House of Lords Constitution Committee, RLC0005 (14 March 2022) 14.

government, which may well touch upon sensitive legal issues like human rights law, criminal justice, judicial review and the government's conception of the correct balance of the British constitution. It is a constitutional truism that Attorneys General must avoid political partisanship in their public interest determinations, and (of course) the kind of political activity that would bring the judiciary or rule of law into contempt. But Attorneys General have never been considered apolitical in the richer sense of that word, so that they must avoid good-faith political activity taken to advance the policy objectives and legislative agenda of the government.[38] In recent years, Attorneys General have, for example, been at the forefront of executive engagement with the jurisprudence of the senior judiciary treating the HRA and core constitutional principles. Several recent Attorneys General have engaged in these political debates by offering respectful, but often very firm, public remarks voicing disagreement with the superior courts and defending the legitimacy of the government inviting Parliament to correct what it views as erroneous and constitutionally heterodox judgments.[39]

According to Appleby, simultaneously discharging this diverse range of functions requires the Law Officers to vigilantly maintain a

> delicate balance between the necessary loyalty they must exhibit as executive ministers and the independence from political interests that is fundamental to the provision of accurate and robust legal advice and for making decisions about where the public interest lies.[40]

Whether they have, or even can, strike this balance is at the heart of debates over reform.

III. Controversy and Arguments for Reform

At the heart of intermittent academic and political calls to reform the Law Officers is the belief that the incumbent dual legal–political model of government chief

---

[38] See C Casey and J Larkin, 'Crossing the Line: The Attorney General and the Law/Politics Divide' (Policy Exchange Judicial Power Project, January 2022).

[39] See R Wright and J Croft, 'UK Attorney-General Backs Calls to Curb Judges' Powers' *Financial Times* (12 February 2020). The *Financial Times* article is a report based on Geoffrey Cox QC MP's extended interview with the Institute for Government think-tank. The headline represents quite an unfair and lopsided summary of what was an extensive and nuanced hour-long conversation. However, the then Attorney General did make the comments cited in the article about the appropriate balance of power between the courts and Parliament and also mentioned there were legitimate concerns that decisions were increasingly being taken by the former that ought to be reserved to the latter. For the full interview, see www.youtube.com/watch?v=N5TzdjkGu2k. See also J Wright, 'The Attorney General on Who Should Decide What the Public Interest Is' (8 February 2016) www.gov.uk/government/speeches/the-attorney-general-on-who-should-decide-what-the-public-interest-is; D Grieve, 'European Convention on Human Rights: Current Challenges' (24 October 2011) www.gov.uk/government/speeches/european-convention-on-human-rights-current-challenges.

[40] G Appleby, 'The Evolution of a Public Sentinel: Australia's Solicitor General' (2012) 63 *Northern Ireland Legal Quarterly* 397, 398.

legal advisor is imprudent and should be reformed in favour of an apolitical model. Behind this conviction is an implicit scepticism that striking a sound balance between the different dimensions of the Attorney General's current role is possible or realistic.

The Labour government's 2007 consultation document on reform, for instance, outlined that the current multifaceted nature of the Attorney General's role had given rise to a debate about whether there is unacceptable tension between the Attorney General's political status as a government minister and their functions as the government's chief legal adviser. More specifically, a core concern noted by the consultation was that

> some believe that the Attorney General cannot truly be (or be seen to be) independent from the Government (or party), with the result that the Attorney General's advice lacks at least the appearance of complete impartiality, or even that the Attorney may come under pressure to slant the advice in a particular way to support the Government or political party in Government.[41]

A similar concern, phrased in a similar way, was also raised in respect of the Attorney General's public interest functions.

One thing to notice about these kinds of critiques is that they equivocate between two very distinct risks associated with the Attorney General's political dimension. One is that there is a risk the Attorney General will substantively allow partisan considerations to colour, or 'slant', their legal advice.[42] The other is that there is a risk the public may *perceive* advice to be politicised, which will undermine faith in the Office and in the government's dedication to the rule of law,[43] perhaps even breeding cynicism towards the notion of the rule of law itself.

There is a stronger evidential basis for the latter concern than the former. To be sure, in the last several decades there have been some allegations of improper political influence being brought to bear on the Attorney General while discharging their independent functions. However, this has mainly occurred in the realm of prosecutorial decision-making,[44] final say over which is now near exclusively in the hands of the independent Director of Public Prosecution, save for a subset of exceptional cases implicating national security or which justify a *nolle prosequi*.[45]

When it comes to the provision of legal advice, however, there are only rare occasions when concerns about actual politicisation have been explicitly raised. The most prominent and well-trodden controversy is the long-running debate

---

[41] *The Governance of Britain: A Consultation* (n 4) 12.

[42] N Walker, 'The Antinomies of the Law Officers' in M Sunkin and S Payne (eds), *The Nature of the Crown* (Oxford, Oxford University Press, 1999) 161.

[43] House of Lords Constitution Committee, 'Reform of the Office of Attorney General: Appendix 3 Written Evidence by Professor Sir Jeffrey Jowell QC' (7th Report of Session 2007–08) 29.

[44] McCormick, 'Written Evidence' (n 36) 12–13. Discussed at more length in s IV.

[45] A Horne, 'The Law Officers: Standard Note' House of Commons Library SN/PC/04485 (August 2014) 8.

over whether political pressure was brought to bear on then Attorney General Lord Goldsmith when he gave legal advice in the run up to the Iraq war. This (hotly contested) outlier aside, no commentator of whom I am aware maintains that successive Attorneys General have allowed partisan bias to substantively affect their legal advice-giving work. For example, although the House of Commons Constitution Committee ultimately recommended reform of the office back in 2007, neither it nor the respondents who supplied evidence to the Committee suggested it was a live concern.[46]

The more well-grounded critique of the status quo concerns the risks of *perceived* politicisation. This is a concern advanced by several prominent commentators. Professor Sir Jeffrey Jowell KC, for example, argued that 'where legal advice is proffered to the Government by a serving politician who is also a member of that government, that advice is vulnerable to being construed as influenced by partisan political considerations'.[47] This concern has a point. If one were to ask a reasonably informed observer – the proverbial person on the street – they would likely agree that it should be more difficult in principle for a politician-lawyer to give objective detached legal advice to a party colleague – including their political boss – relative to an entirely apolitical official with civil service tenure protections.

But while such concerns are legitimate, they must be weighed with several other considerations before they should be used to undergird calls for wide-reaching form. For a start, if one thinks the office is largely functioning well and that there is no evidence of *actual* partisanship in its advice-giving work, then one may reasonably ask: is an ultimately mistaken *perception* about the Law Officers a strong enough foundation on which to justify significant change to a long-standing constitutional institution?

To be sure, for some critics of the status quo, the risk of perceived bias or politicisation – whether factually misplaced or not – is indeed sufficient to justify reform.[48] But absent tangible evidence of the damaging impact perceptions of political bias is actually having – such as demonstrating erosion of public or parliamentary faith in the government's commitment to the rule of law – a more measured approach would be to advocate less radical change to meet such concerns, such as a codified restatement of the Attorney General's role and responsibilities to accompany the Ministerial Code which stresses the importance of independence to their role. In other words, what should be advocated is the kind of targeted reform that would address the perceptions of the concerned citizen but without involving radical constitutional surgery.

---

[46] Government of the United Kingdom, 'The Government's Response to the Constitutional Affairs Select Committee Report on the Constitutional Role of the Attorney General' (April 2008) para 44; Ministry of Justice, 'The Governance of Britain – Constitutional Renewal' (March 2008) para 53.

[47] Jowell (n 42) 28. See also Walker (n 41) 149.

[48] Professor Jowell writes the 'tradition of actual independence is not the only point here. The appearance of lack of independence is what matters. Justice must not only be done, but also seen to be done.' Jowell (n 42) 29.

Proponents of reform might also suggest that arguments in favour of the status quo based on the proposition the Attorney General is democratically accountable to Parliament for their advice-giving role are naively overstated. They are ostensibly overstated because parliamentarians cannot truly assess, for example, whether there actually has been politicisation of legal advice because of the intense levels of confidentiality pervading the Law Officers' work. There is, once again, clearly truth to this concern, given the constitutional conventions against both revealing that advice was given by the Officers and disclosing the content of the advice itself. The latter convention is quite rigorously (though not absolutely) enforced, and this fact clearly militates against Parliament being able hold the Law Officers accountable for the impartiality and cogency of their legal advice.

But this concern can also be addressed without altering the fundamentals of the status quo. This concern can be addressed, for example, by consciously re-examining the parameters of the convention against the disclosure of the fact or content advice. The last two decades have demonstrated that the convention against disclosing that legal advice has in fact been taken is effectively moribund. It has also demonstrated that the convention against disclosure of the content of legal advice is simply not understood by anyone to be absolute, as advice *has* been disclosed in full or in precis form on several occasions. This includes advice concerning the legality of the Iraq war,[49] use of armed force against Islamic State forces,[50] drone strikes against British citizens fighting for Islamic State,[51] use of armed force against Syrian government forces,[52] the legal effects of the Northern Irish backstop contained in Prime Minister May's doomed Withdrawal Agreement[53] and the legality of the Internal Market Bill.[54] Indeed, it is worth noting that in its 2009 response to the House of Commons Justice Committee Report on potential reform of the Office, the then Labour government itself suggested that 'in exceptional cases' it would be 'prepared to waive legal professional privilege and disclose the

---

[49] J Chilcot, *The Iraq Inquiry: Volume 5*, https://webarchive.nationalarchives.gov.uk/ukgwa/20171123122743/www.iraqinquiry.org.uk/the-report/.

[50] Prime Minister's Office, 'Memorandum to the Foreign Affairs Select Committee Prime Minister's Response to the Foreign Affairs Select Committee's Second Report of Session 2015–16: The Extension of Offensive British Military Operations to Syria', www.parliament.uk/globalassets/documents/commons-committees/foreign-affairs/PM-Response-to-FAC-Report-Extension-of-Offensive-British-Military-Operations-to-Syria.pdf.

[51] UK Parliament Joint Committee on Human Rights, 'The Government's Policy on the Use of Drones for Targeted Killing' (2nd Report of Session 2015–16) https://publications.parliament.uk/pa/jt201516/jtselect/jtrights/574/574.pdf.

[52] Prime Minister's Office, 'Syria Action – UK Government Legal Position' (14 April 2018) www.gov.uk/government/publications/syria-action-uk-government-legal-position/syria-action-uk-government-legal-position.

[53] G Cox, 'Legal Effect of the Protocol on Ireland/Northern Ireland' (Attorney General's Office, 13 November 2018) https://assets.publishing.service.gov.uk/government/uploads/system/uploads/attachment_data/file/761852/05_December-_EU_Exit_Attorney_General_s_legal_advice_to_Cabinet_on_the_Withdrawal_Agreement_and_the_Protocol_on_Ireland-Northern_Ireland.pdf.

[54] See https://assets.publishing.service.gov.uk/government/uploads/system/uploads/attachment_data/file/916702/UKIM_Legal_Statement.pdf.

advice that it has received'.[55] Explicit recognition by the government that voluntary disclosure of legal advice – in full or in precis form – may be constitutionally proper, in limited and exceptional circumstances, to aid parliamentary debate and scrutiny when it concerns issues of national importance may take much of the sting from the critique that the Attorney General is not truly accountable to Parliament for their advice-giving function. I will discuss this possibility in more depth in section IV.

IV. Defence of the Status Quo

The history of the Law Officers demonstrates they can, for the most part, maintain careful balance when simultaneously carrying out their role as legal advisor and guardian of the public interest/rule of law on the one hand, and their position as a highly political animal and member of the government on the other. Law Officers have largely been able to do their advisory and public interest work in a way that can withstand political pressure because of a combination of several factors: namely, a combination of a supportive constitutional culture and tradition, a dedication by the Officers to constitutional norms of independence in functions concerning the public interest and rule of law, and adherence to legal professional ethics and expertise.[56]

Successive Attorneys General have strongly rejected the contention partisan politics clouds their provision of legal advice. Instead, they maintain that when responding to legal queries they try to offer impartial advice in the manner of a professional lawyer's advice to any client: to give an objective and reasonable analysis of the law as they see it using their legal expertise and judgement.[57] This task frequently involves seeking additional expert input, and in difficult cases it is not unusual for the Attorney General to get preliminary advice from the lawyers in the Attorney General's Office, from the GLD or 'from a silk, and in particular from First Treasury Counsel'[58] to aid their deliberations.[59] Some Attorneys General have

---

[55] Government of the United Kingdom, 'The Government's Response to the Justice Committee Report on the Draft Constitutional Renewal Bill (Provisions Relating to the Attorney General)' (July 2009) 9.

[56] C Casey and J Larkin QC, 'Crossing the Line' (n 37) 12.

[57] C Casey, 'The Law Officers: The Relationship between Executive Lawyers and Executive Power in Ireland and the United Kingdom' in O Doyle, A McHarg and J Murkens (eds), *The Brexit Challenge for Ireland and the United Kingdom: Constitutions under Pressure* (Cambridge, Cambridge University Press, 2021) 296; T Daintith and A Page, *The Executive in the Constitution: Structure, Autonomy and Internal Control* (Oxford, Oxford University Press, 1999) 297.

[58] The first treasury counsel is a barrister nominated by the government to provide legal advice and representation in the most sensitive and impactful public law matters. It is invariably a barrister of considerable esteem.

[59] Yong (n 13) paras 4.7 and 4.20.

sought legal advice from external academic experts.[60] Law Officers have expressed strong commitment to, in the words of former Advocate General Lord Keen KC, not sanctioning the legality of a course of action unless they can advise 'government that there is a respectable argument for the implementation of a policy and that it can, therefore, in theory fall within the bounds of the rule of law'.[61]

The fact that previous Attorneys General have felt confident in offering what they consider forthright, politically detached advice – even if it might have unwelcome consequences for the government – is testament that their ability to maintain a stance of detachment is not idle talk. This is especially so when combined with the absence of actual evidence of partisanship over the recent history of the office.[62] A recent concrete example of this can be seen with Attorney General Sir Geoffrey Cox KC MP's advice on the legal effects of the so-called Northern Irish 'backstop' element of the EU–UK Withdrawal Agreement; advice which undoubtedly proved a serious political thorn in he then-prime minister Theresa May's attempt to secure parliamentary approval for her deal.[63] The then Attorney General's advice on the backstop, and its international law implications, clearly proved a major obstacle to May's ability to gain support for the agreement. Parliamentarians from the opposition benches, the Prime Minister's confidence and supply partners and her own party all explicitly cited the legal risk identified in the advice as a reason to reject the agreement.[64] This episode is a vivid case study of the Attorney General's capacity to withstand political pressure to slant legal advice to make it more favourable to the executive, even in issues of high political salience.

It is fair to say, however, that while Attorneys General strive for political detachment when giving advice, they do not regard themselves as legal technocrats. They instead seek to combine their professional expertise as trained lawyers with a desire to assist their ministerial colleagues in a common goal of implementing the government's policy agenda.[65] In many respects, the political dimensions of the office are *complementary* to the Attorney General's role as legal advisor. The political aspect of the role provides the Attorney General with tacit and intimate knowledge of the policy goals and priorities of ministerial and party colleagues and the political pressures they are under. This makes them well placed to act as

[60] P Lewis and O Bowcott, 'Government's top Legal Advisers Divided over Move to Override Brexit Deal' *The Guardian* (10 September 2020) www.theguardian.com/politics/2020/sep/10/governments-top-legal-advisers-divided-over-move-to-override-brexit-deal.

[61] Oral evidence of The Rt Hon the Lord Keen of Elie QC, former Advocate-General for Scotland (2015–20) to the House of Lords Constitution Committee (27 April 2022) 2.

[62] Casey (n 56).

[63] G Cox, 'Legal Opinion on Joint Instrument and Unilateral Declaration concerning the Withdrawal Agreement' (Attorney General's Office, 12 March 2019).

[64] R Mason and R Syal, 'ERG Signals It Could Back May's Brexit Deal if Legal Advice Is Clearer' *The Guardian* (13 March 2019) www.theguardian.com/politics/2019/mar/13/erg-signals-itcould-back-may-brexit-deal-legal-advice-is-clearer.

[65] JLJ Edwards, *The Attorney-General, Politics and the Public Interest* (London, Sweet & Maxwell, 1984) 70; O Heald, 'The Role of the Law Officers' (speech by the Solicitor General to Kent Law School, 18 October 2012) www.gov.uk/government/speeches/the-role-of-the-law-officers.

a 'buffer between politicians and the lawyers', translating 'purist legal thinking into something that ministers could understand'.[66] It also aids the task of offering constructive advice which not only speaks to the constraints the Attorney General's colleagues are bound by, but also any possible lawful and proper alternatives those colleagues can avail themselves of so they might still advance their policy agenda for the common good.[67]

The argument that the political and ministerial dimensions of the Attorney General's work compliment their legal work has been endorsed (perhaps unsurprisingly) by several previous incumbents. Sir Geoffrey Cox MP KC, a recent former Attorney General, stated that one of the advantages of having a political element is that the Law Officer is better attuned to 'which issues his colleagues are struggling with, which issues have to be accentuated and emphasised to drive home the point, and which points are not necessarily so important'.[68] Jeremy Wright KC, another recent Attorney General, maintained that while the legal advice they gave was not coloured by party politics, it was also

> important that all lawyers have the ability to give advice to their clients in ways that their clients find most useful. And it seems to me that having somebody who also has a political background enables the Law Officers to do that.[69]

Yet another former Attorney General said his ability to give good legal advice was aided by his getting to know his colleagues' 'policies, their intentions, their methods, indeed their very temperaments and characters'.[70] This former Law Officer added that the better an Attorney General is able to understand the 'stresses and the strains' of the policy-making process, the better able they are to 'assist in ensuring that if there is a lawful and a proper way of achieving its objectives, that way will be found'.[71]

Several academic commentators have equally observed how the political status of the Attorney General helps lend their advice weight and status. Professors Daintith and Page write that, as politically responsible lawyers, the work of the Law Officers has a 'special quality and status' amongst both their ministerial peers and other civil servant government lawyers.[72] In a similar vein, in written evidence supplied to the House of Lords Constitution Committee in 2007, the late distinguished Professor Anthony Bradley QC doubted 'whether an "independent" lawyer outside the structure of central government and not holding ministerial

---

[66] Yong (n 13) para 4.8.
[67] ibid 61.
[68] Evidence of Sir Geoffrey Cox QC MP to House of Commons Justice Select Committee HC 1887, 23 January 2019.
[69] Evidence of Jeremy Wright QC MP to the House of Commons Justice Select Committee, 15 September 2015.
[70] Silkin (n 26) 37.
[71] ibid.
[72] Daintith and Page (n 56) 297.

office would command the authority that at present goes with the office of Attorney General'.[73]

Professor Yong's 2013 study of government lawyers commissioned by UCL's Constitution Unit demonstrated that this sentiment was shared by many senior career civil service lawyers then working in the GLD. All those interviewed suggested the dual legal–political dimensions of the Attorney General's role were complementary.[74] Yong documents that those interviewed:

> [S]aw no need for reform. The key benefit, they argued, in having the chief legal adviser as a minister, was that he – or she – had knowledge of the political pressures on ministers, which in turn aided the Attorney General in carrying out the act of 'translation'; but it also helped from the point of view of the Attorney General's colleagues – it gave his or her advice more weight.[75]

More recently, in oral evidence presented to the House of Lord's ongoing inquiry into the Law Officers, former Director of the Government Legal Department Sir Jonathan Jones KC conceded, when put to him by the House of Lords Constitution Committee, the point there was a hypothetical greater risk a more politically oriented Attorney General would be more 'willing … to give convenient advice'[76] than a statutorily protected civil servant lawyer. But Sir Jonathan proceeded to maintain that there were very significant countervailing advantages in the 'Government's senior legal adviser being a politician who is regarded as an equal … is trusted to be part of the inner circle, attends Cabinet … and is seen to be on the Government's side'.[77] These kinds of Attorneys General are, suggested Sir Jonathan, the 'best placed to give the best advice' to the government, advice informed by legal expertise and political acumen.[78]

Whatever the *perceptions* of the pernicious effects of the Attorney General's political dimension, there appears to be a consensus amongst all stripes of government lawyer that it has had a largely beneficial impact, by adding greater weight to the advice and making it more constructive and politically attuned. In his testimony to the House of Lord's Constitution Committee's inquiry, the former Advocate General Lord Keen of Elie KC gave an interesting insight into just how seriously the weight of the Attorney General's legal advice is held by the executive. He noted that he could not think of an instance during his five-year tenure when the government 'decided to proceed in the face of express advice that there was no respectable argument to support a particular policy proposal'.[79] In contrast,

---

[73] House of Lords Constitution Committee, 'Reform of the Office of Attorney General: Appendix 2 Written Evidence by Professor Anthony Bradley' (7th Report of Session 2007–08) 25.
[74] Yong (n 13) 4.9.
[75] ibid.
[76] Testimony of Sir Jonathan Jones QC to House of Lords Constitution Committee, 23 March 2022.
[77] ibid.
[78] ibid.
[79] ibid.

there appears to be broad consensus that the advice of a technocratic apolitical apex legal advisor may not command the same level of weight, or be as politically attuned, as that from a Law Officer with dual legal–political dimensions.

Another advantage advanced in favour of the status quo concerns democratic accountability. As noted above, the Law Officers do not handle the routine legal questions faced by the government. Instead, they handle the most controversial and politically salient legal questions. They also settle the most contested questions, for example where conflicting advice is given by government lawyers advising different departments. Is it not appropriate for these kinds of sensitive legal questions – which can have wider policy and political repercussions – to be determined by a legal figure who is ultimately democratically accountable to Parliament for their decision-making? As ministers, the Law Officers are ultimately accountable for their decisions and advice in a way that a career civil servant with statutory tenure protections cannot be. One former Attorney General stressed the fact that 'every decision which the Attorney-General takes, every piece of advice which he gives, every statement which he makes, is one for which in some form or other he may ultimately be held accountable in Parliament'.[80] An alternative apolitical model, whatever its merits, involves vesting enormous influence over the direction of sensitive policy decisions in an official who would by deliberate design be highly insulated from political accountability.

The constitutional culture surrounding and suffusing the Attorney General's Office is also conducive to maintaining a proper balance between its legal and political dimensions. Respecting the values of legality and the rule of law – central to the UK's constitutional culture – requires an Attorney General, *at a minimum*, to not allow partisan bias, party political concerns or pressure from colleagues to obscure good faith attempts to offer proper legal advice, to taint a conclusion that a particular decision is in the public interest or to cause them to sign-off on the legality of government policies under flimsy and strained legal justification.[81] What ensures these boundaries are respected? One mechanism helping promote respect for the Office's norms and boundaries is, as just noted, the fact that the Attorney General is subject to ministerial accountability to Parliament. If an Attorney General acts in a manner Parliament considers inappropriate,[82] they can inflict sanctions and hold them to account via censure. A recent prominent example was Parliament's decision in 2018 to hold the government in contempt for the Attorney General's refusal to disclose a copy of their advice to the House for scrutiny.[83]

---

[80] Silkin (n 26) 38.

[81] Casey and Larkin, 'Crossing the Line' (n 37) 12.

[82] To be clear, I am not commenting on whether the government or Sir Geoffrey Cox acted inappropriately in initially refusing to publicly disclose the advice. I am merely stating that Parliament clearly took the view that their refusal to disclose advice was unacceptable behaviour and after forming such a view was able to inflict a sanction it deemed necessary.

[83] UK Parliament, '"Contempt Motion" on Publishing of Legal Advice' (4 December 2018) www.parliament.uk/business/news/2018/december/contempt-motion-on-publishing-of-legal-advice/.

This formal accountability walks hand in hand with willingness by political actors to sanction perceived misuse of authority. An Attorney General who is perceived to have descended into partisan decision-making or to have succumbed to political pressure not only risks breaching the constitutional and professional norms that underpin the work of the Office (and, more broadly, those that underpin the legal profession generally), but the public and parliamentary confidence and credibility on which the office depends.[84] Where such norms are breached, serious political controversy and criticism tends to follow.

For example, the decision of former Attorney General Suella Braverman KC to publicly defend Mr Dominic Cummings, the Prime Minister's former special adviser, following allegations he breached COVID-19 lockdown guidelines was viewed by many as an ill-judged party political intervention into a matter that could have found itself under criminal investigation, and generated significant political scrutiny.[85] Several years prior, the allegation that former Attorney General Lord Goldsmith KC succumbed to political pressure to alter his initial advice over the legality of the UK's involvement in the Iraq war was a major focus of the long-running Chilcot Inquiry, and continues to generate deep controversy nearly two decades later for all the main actors involved.[86] Lord Goldsmith also faced controversy over whether he permitted political representations from the Prime Minister to influence how he superintended a Serious Fraud Office investigation into the arms company BAE Systems over allegedly corrupt payments made to Saudi Arabian officials.[87] The crux of the controversy was whether the Prime Minister's representation to the Attorney General – along the lines that a prosecution of BAE could harm the UK's national security interests – swayed the latter's advice to the Director of the Serious Fraud Office that a prosecution should not proceed.[88] The political blowback from this controversy was a major impetus in establishing the detailed framework agreements now governing how the Attorney General's Office superintends the prosecution services. These agreements make very clear and unambiguous the limited scope of the Attorney General's ability to issue a direction to halt a prosecution. The protocols also make clear that if the Directors seek public interest representations from the executive, such public interest consultation exercises are 'conducted with propriety; that consultees are informed that the decision is for the prosecutor alone; and that the wider Ministerial representations tending to any particular conclusion are probed appropriately'.[89] Perhaps even

---

[84] Casey (n 56).

[85] O Bocott, 'Attorney General Faces Calls to Resign after She Defends Dominic Cummings' *The Guardian* (25 May 2020) www.theguardian.com/politics/2020/may/25/attorney-general-faces-calls-to-resign-defends-dominic-cummings-suella-braverman.

[86] See R Verkaik, 'Goldsmith under Pressure from Legal Profession over Impartiality' *The Independent* (29 April 2005) www.independent.co.uk/news/uk/crime/goldsmith-under-pressure-from-legal-profession-over-impartiality-3903.html.

[87] S Fidler and C Adams, 'BAE Systems Faces Allegations of Secretly Paying Saudi Prince' *Financial Times* (7 June 2007) www.ft.com/content/e37553d2-147f-11dc-88cb-000b5df10621.

[88] McCormick, *The Constitutional Legitimacy* (n 17) 187–89.

[89] Casey and Larkin, 'Crossing the Line' (n 37).

more politically explosive in its day was the controversy that brought down the first Labour government of Ramsay MacDonald in 1924. A large factor in that government's collapse was the allegation that Attorney General Patrick Hastings KC had acceded to political pressure from Cabinet colleagues in discontinuing a prosecution which had been initiated against a communist newspaper editor for incitement to mutiny.[90] The decision caused a storm of political controversy and allegations of inappropriate political influence. All of which is to say that the seriousness of these previous controversies is a measure of how entrenched the constitutional norms and expectations surrounding Attorneys General are, and how those who might be seen as overstepping their boundaries may be held to account by parliamentary or public censure.

To recap the arguments made thus far, for proponents of the status quo there is no convincing evidence that contemporary Attorneys General have failed (save for a handful of allegedly documented instances discussed above) to successfully balance the political and legal elements of their role in a manner justifying broad reform. On the contrary, they consider there is good reason to think having a democratically accountable politician-lawyer at the heart of government decision-making has been beneficial to upholding the rule of law and the provision of independent, yet politically attuned and usefully constructive, legal advice.

The final argument I advance in defence of the status quo is that there would be potentially serious costs involved in replacing the UK's current model with an apolitical chief legal advisor drawn from the civil service or private practice. Models of apex legal advisors come in all shapes and sizes, and decisions about how to structure them involve difficult normative trade-offs:[91] between values and principles like legal expertise, concern for the rule of law, independence from partisanship, concern for the government's ability to vigorously implement policy for the common good and democratic accountability; and there is good reason to believe – based on comparative experience – an apolitical chief legal advisor would affect a worse balancing of these important considerations than the status quo. I illustrate this with some comparative constitutional examples I have treated elsewhere.[92] Some legal systems – like Ireland, Japan and Israel – do opt for non-elected career lawyers to serve as chief legal counsel to government, with very high levels of insulation from politics.[93]

---

[90] Jones (n 25) 50.

[91] C Casey and D Kenny, 'The Gatekeepers: Executive Lawyers and the Executive Power in Comparative Constitutional Law' (2022) *International Journal of Constitutional Law*.

[92] See C Casey and J Larkin, 'The Attorney General and Renewed Controversy over the Law/Politics Divide' (2022) 26 *Edinburgh Law Review* 228.

[93] M Asimow and Y Dotan, 'Hired Guns and Ministers of Justice: The Role of Government Attorneys in the United States and Israel' (2016) 49 *Israel Law Review* 3, 12; D Kenny and C Casey, 'Shadow Constitutional Review: The Dark Side of Pre-enactment Political Review in Ireland and Japan' (2020) 18 *International Journal of Constitutional Law* 51.

In Japan, the Cabinet Legislation Bureau (CLB)[94] is the key advisory organ to the government over legal and constitutional affairs. A highly autonomous[95] and technocratic[96] institution, it is staffed by career lawyers appointed on the basis of academic excellence and promoted on the basis of seniority. The Director of the CLB is formally nominated by the government, but by convention the latter will accede to the former's internal choice of successor, a fact which underscores its influence and autonomy. The CLB's influence on executive policy-making is very significant, and its advice is generally regarded as binding by the government.[97]

In Israel, the Attorney General is formally appointed by the government, but its choice is highly fettered. The Attorney General can only be chosen from an approved list drawn up by an independent panel. This panel consists of a former Supreme Court judge appointed by the Chief Justice, a former Attorney General appointed by the government and a representative appointed on behalf of the legal academy and bar association. It is also a requirement that a candidate be eligible for appointment to the Supreme Court. Upon appointment, the Attorney General serves a fixed term of six years and cannot be removed save in very limited circumstances.[98] The Attorney General is guardian of the public interest, in charge of state litigation, final decision-maker in respect of prosecutions and exclusive legal counsel to the government. The Attorney General's advice on the legality of policy decisions or proposed Bills is *binding* on the government, and the latter cannot seek advice from any other lawyer without the former's prior consent.[99]

The Irish Constitution provides that the Attorney General is 'the adviser of the Government in matters of law and legal opinion'. The Attorney General is assisted in their work by an office of several hundred civil service lawyers, and Attorneys General have been known to also draw on the expertise of barristers in private practice when the need arises. The Attorney General is appointed at the discretion of the Taoiseach and serves at their pleasure. They must also vacate their position should the Taoiseach resign. Aside from stipulating they are not to be members of the government, the Constitution says nothing else in terms of eligibility criteria. But there is a strong constitutional convention that the appointee must be a barrister of some eminence; indeed, most who serve as Attorney General go on to join the superior courts and several have been appointed Chief Justice. A minority of Attorneys General have been parliamentarians, but in recent years most have had looser political affiliations with the political party in government.

---

[94] H Yamamoto, 'Interpretation of the Pacifist Article of the Constitution by the Bureau of Cabinet Legislation: A New Source of Constitutional Law?' (2017) 26 *Washington International Law Journal* 99, 109.

[95] NS Ghaleigh, 'Neither Legal nor Political? Bureaucratic Constitutionalism in Japanese Law' (2015) 26 *Kings Law Journal* 193, 205.

[96] M Seki, 'The Drafting Process for Cabinet Bills' (1986) 19 *Law Japan* 168, 183.

[97] Casey and Kenny (n 90).

[98] A Bakshi, 'Legal Advisers and the Government: Analysis and Recommendations' (2016) *Kohelet Policy Forum* 17.

[99] E Rubinstein, 'The Attorney General in Israel: A Delicate Balance of Powers and Responsibilities in a Jewish and Democratic State' (2005) 11 *Israel Affairs* 417, 422.

Although the Constitution says nothing on the issue, the Attorney General's legal advice is, by convention, accepted as binding on the executive, and advice that some measure will likely be found unlawful will signal the end of a policy. Despite high levels of confidentiality over the content of legal advice, there is evidence that Attorney General advice is quite conservative and risk avoidant in its tenor. For example, it frequently seems to prevent the government from pursuing policies that are, at the very least, arguably constitutional/lawful and which the government strongly wished to pursue.[100]

The model of apex government legal advisors in these systems is very apolitical and technocratic compared to the UK. The work of these lawyers – who are drawn from the civil service or private practice – also tends to have a larger degree of detachment from the policy-making and political concerns of the government.[101] This more apolitical and technocratic model has several undoubted qualities. For example, opting for an entirely technocratic and apolitical system can act as a powerful safeguard against more lurid abuses of executive authority. They also ensure, whether by rule or convention, that the chief legal advisor will always be someone with very considerable professional expertise and seniority. They may also decisively remove any *perception* that the provision of legal advice or public interest functions have been subject to inappropriate politicisation. But it is sometimes overlooked in debates over reform that such qualities must be balanced against potentially serious costs.

One such cost is that highly technocratic and apolitical legal advisors often tend towards conservatism and caution when giving legal advice. Apex government lawyers who lack political experience might opt for a risk-averse disposition they consider best respectful of the rule of law and constitution, approving only those policies they feel are consistent with the 'best view' of the law they think a court might reach.[102] They may also generally be less likely to approach legal analysis with the same inclination to constructively assist the government in implementing its policy mandate while staying within lawful bounds, at least when compared to a lawyer whose office has dual legal–political dimensions.[103] This kind of 'constitutionally conservative' approach to legal advice can therefore risk developing several pathologies. It might, for example, excessively legalise the

---

[100] Attorneys General's advice has been highlighted as a very considerable obstacle to addressing Ireland's ongoing housing crisis. Successive Attorneys General have been accused of offering overly conservative interpretations of the scope of private property rights that excessively hinder Parliament's ability to regulate them for the common good. See H Hogan and F Keyes, 'Housing Crisis and the Constitution' (2021) 65 *Irish Jurist* 87.

[101] See Yamamoto (n 93) 111.

[102] Jack Goldsmith contrasts two different approaches that executive lawyers might take to legal interpretation. One, which carries an 'obligation neutrally to interpret the law as seriously as a court', takes what he calls the 'best view'. This approach can be contrasted with the 'reasonable legal position' approach, which requires less – that a legal argument merely be respectably plausible and taken in good faith. J Goldsmith, 'Executive Branch Crisis Lawyering and the "Best View" of the Law' (2018) 31 *Georgetown Journal of Legal Ethics* 261, 263.

[103] Kenny and Casey (n 92).

policy-making process, hamstring the political branches from testing the boundaries of the law where it is uncertain and prevent or impede good-faith dialogue between the political branches and courts about such matters as the content of the law, the extent of constitutionally permissible change or how the law should be best interpreted.[104]

More generally, it cannot be overlooked that there are democratic costs that accompany embracing a highly technocratic and apolitical model of apex legal advisors, given that it will inevitably allow unelected lawyers to wield considerable influence and power over the policy-making process. In the countries I have mentioned, apex legal advisors wield what is tantamount to a veto over policy-making and the initiation of legislation. This type of model is prone to vesting 'considerable and controversial influence over the functions of the elected branches'[105] in legal officials who will be, by deliberate design, largely unaccountable for their decisions.[106]

None of the above warrants the conclusion that an apolitical and technocratic model of apex legal advisor lacks merit. Such systems can and do work perfectly well. But the legal rules and political norms that govern a government's appointment of its leading lawyers, and the appointee's self-understanding of their constitutional role, will have serious ramifications for constitutional politics. Some may welcome the kind of cautious, legalistic and risk-minimising approach a more apolitical and technocratic apex legal advisor may bring to the executive branch. They may regard an overabundance of caution as a valuable safeguard against abuses of state power. For others – and I include myself here – a very cautious and highly risk-averse approach to the provision of legal advice has the capacity to seriously hamstring the state's capacity to project public power to robustly respond to socio-economic challenges for the common good. Given the overall robust health of the Attorney General's office, such costs are simply not worth risking.

V. A Slight Qualification

The qualification for my defence is this: some critiques consistently raised by advocates for reform have a reasonable basis, including concerns about *perceived* politicisation of the advice-giving function and the fact that high levels of confidentiality surrounding the advice diminish the ability for Parliament to police whether this is in fact occurring and hold the Attorney General democratically accountable.[107]

---

[104] G Appleby and A Olijnyk, 'Executive Policy Development and Constitutional Norms: Practice and Perceptions' (2020) 18 *International Journal of Constitutional Law* 1136; C Casey and E Daly, 'Political Constitutionalism under a Culture of Legalism: Case Studies from Ireland' (2021) 17 *European Constitutional Law Review* 202, 221–24; Bakshi (n 97) 34.

[105] Casey and Kenny (n 90) 63.

[106] ibid.

[107] Written evidence of Conor McCormick (n 36) 3.

I have argued elsewhere that institutionalising a measure of transparency over legal advice can combat some of the potentially negative consequences of both technocratic and political models of executive lawyering. For example, in the former case, transparency would help deter an executive from citing overly cautious or risk-averse legal advice to defend political inaction on important issues. More relevant for the context of the UK's dual legal–political model, it could help deter an executive from attempting to leverage flimsy legal cover for their policies by putting pressure on their advisors or appointing partisan hacks. As Professor Goldsmith puts it, a measure of transparency facilitates scrutiny of the 'accuracy, persuasion, and consistency' of legal advice and critique of 'self-serving or mistaken or excessive interpretations'.[108]

This transparency could come in the form of a non-statutory government policy statement that it will consider limited disclosure in exceptional circumstances on a case-by-case basis. This, of course, need not involve exhaustive disclosure of all relevant preparatory material, nor issues engaging acutely sensitive national security questions or pending litigation. Rather, disclosure could be reserved for critically contentious issues of national importance, where the soundness of the legal advice in question is critically bound up with the overall legitimacy of the executive's action, and where it is most important to involve Parliament in debate, deliberation and scrutiny.

VI. Conclusion

The biggest challenge for any constitutional order with a chief legal advisor with dual political–legal dimensions is maintaining an apt balance between their attachment to a 'particular government and its political objectives' and their commitment to a 'broader set of values associated with the integrity of the legal and political order'.[109] Both facets are important features of the Attorney General's constitutional framework and, when rightly balanced, each is conducive to the political common good in their own way; whereas an imbalance in either dimension risks deleterious consequences. Attorneys General have, I suggest, largely managed to successfully tread this 'constitutional tightrope'.[110] This fact, more than any other reason, highlights the wisdom of the 2007–09 Labour government's ultimate decision to row back on pursuing the kind of significant reform it had initially proposed.

---

[108] J Goldsmith, 'The Irrelevance of Prerogative Power and the Evils of Secret Legal Interpretation' in C Fatovic and B Kleinman (eds), *Extralegal Power and Legitimacy: Perspectives on Prerogative* (Oxford, Oxford University Press, 2013) 228.

[109] Walker (n 41).

[110] Edwards, *The Law Officers of the Crown* (n 17) ix.

12

The Public Appointments System

JOHN BOWERS

Though the public appointments system has generally worked well in recent years, it is highly dependent on informal mechanisms, including the willingness of ministers to act with restraint and the preparedness of the Commissioner to speak out against breaches of the letter or the spirit of the code.[1]

Committee on Standards in Public Life, 'Standards Matter 2' (2020)

I. Introduction

Quis custodiet ipsos custodes, asked Juvenal in *Satire* 6: 'But who will keep guard on the guards?', and this is an important question to be asked about public appointments and one on which views legitimately differ. The Public Administration Select Committee concluded in 2014 that 'public appointments are not sufficiently transparent, representative, or accountable'.[2] Yet the Grimstone Report, set up by the Cameron government to review the public appointments system and render it less bureaucratic, concluded that the system of public appointments in the UK has been a 'major success', and in particular commended the 'pragmatic and sensible' recommendations originally made by Lord Nolan's Committee in 1995.

There are, however, serious concerns about the way in which the public appointments system is currently operating. These are somewhat different to the problems which were identified at the time of the Nolan Report, although some of them overlap. There have in particular been some high-profile cases which have occasioned real alarm about whether the whole system is now fit for purpose,

---

[1] Committee on Standards in Public Life (CSPL), 'Upholding Standards in Public Life', Final Report and Recommendations of the Standards Matter 2 Review (November 2021) 10 www.gov.uk/government/collections/standards-matter-2.

[2] Public Administration Select Committee, *Who's Accountable? Relationships between Government and Arm's-Length Bodies* (HC 110, 2014) 27.

although there is inevitably some controversy about what the purpose of the system actually is.

There is no real compulsion to obey the code on public appointments beyond the court of public opinion, and most such appointments are not sufficiently high profile actually to cause much public interest. This no doubt lies behind the comment made by Sir Peter Riddell, the former Commissioner for Public Appointments (CPA), that 'Ministers are in a strong, even dominant, position in public appointments but some are now seeking to tilt the process even further to their advantage'.[3]

II. Nolan

Since the mid-1990s, it has been Lord Nolan who has metaphorically kept guard on the guards in this arena, both during his distinguished life and, after he died, through his extraordinary legacy in his groundbreaking Report on Standards in Public Life. He was a member of the Appellate Committee of the House of Lords and the first chair of the Committee on Standards in Public Life, which produced the so-called 'Nolan Principles'. This august body was set up largely as a reaction to the cash-for-questions scandal which plagued the Major government, one of several 'sleazy' episodes at the time, including sex scandals. It was charged with considering the 'standards of conduct of all public office-holders'. In John Major's words, the Committee was to serve as 'an ethical workshop'. And it did, and acted as a research laboratory and policy generator too.

The Committee's creation was a major step forward in ethical standards in the public sector. It insisted on the principles of 'Integrity, Openness and Honesty', among others, and laid down the important and still used Seven Principles of Standards in Public Life. It begat an independent system for public appointments (the CPA, an office now held by William Shawcross) and it also led to the establishment of the Parliamentary Commissioner for Standards, amongst other important initiatives.

The system of public appointments was already a major concern into which it had to enquire. More specifically, at the time of the report there was, according to Lord Nolan, a 'widespread perception of bias in appointments', although the Nolan Committee acknowledged that 'much of the evidence was circumstantial or inconclusive' (as, indeed, much of it is now). This, of course, is partly because all of the processes are quite properly private and confidential, people prefer not to come forward to say that they have been turned down for a particular role and feedback from appointing panels may be sparse (and not necessarily wholly accurate).

---

[3] P Riddell, 'Pre-Valedictory Speech to the UCL Constitution Unit on Public Appointments' (The Commission for Public Appointments, 29 April 2021) https://publicappointmentscommissioner.independent.gov.uk/pre-valedictory-speech-to-the-ucl-constitution-unit-on-public-appointments/.

There was also concern at the time of the Nolan Committee that the appointments were going overwhelmingly to Conservative placemen, which is a complaint that resurfaced under the Johnson administration.[4]

There is a danger with informality, as there is with too much formality and bureaucracy. In evidence to the Public Administration and Constitutional Affairs Committee (PACAC), Sir David Normington, who was at the time of the Nolan Report a senior civil servant, told it that these concerns had merit:

> I was a civil servant in the 1990s, before 1995, when there was no regulation and I do remember it. It was a very informal time. People's names popped rather surprisingly out of hats. People got together and said, 'Do you know anybody who could have this role?' I don't exaggerate. Sometimes there were selection panels and sometimes there were not but it was a wholly informal system and – this is really important – [the people] who we saw appointed, some of them very good, were mainly white men of a certain age from a certain background.[5]

The likelihood then as now was to appoint 'people like us' to public roles. The Nolan Report also stressed something which maybe has been lost since, that 'an effective member of a NDPB [non-departmental public body] board must be committed to the goals of the organisation'.[6] The story since on diversity in public appointments is positive but not perfect.[7]

A central issue is what is the appropriate role of ministers in the process and what is most in keeping with a democratic mandate? Is the optimum that ministers should mould public appointees to their political viewpoint or should there be a wholly independent system which could resemble the Judicial Appointment Commission, which limits ministerial involvement? The former approach is represented by Normington himself, a consummate insider who said, as stated in PACAC Report 17:

> It is essential for the health of the democratic process and the effective conduct of Government that Ministers make the final decision on who is to sit on the boards of those bodies and it is inevitable and desirable that they should choose people who are willing to work within the policy framework of the Government of the day.[8]

The latter would be extremely expensive. Before addressing these questions, the present system for appointments should be considered.

---

[4] There were some cross-party appointments under Cameron, such as Alan Milburn being appointed as chair of the Social Mobility Commission in 2012 and Andrew Adonis being appointed head of the National Infrastructure Commission in 2015.

[5] Cited in PACAC report, 17.

[6] 'Nolan Report', 3.37.

[7] 'Public bodies should reflect the communities they serve. When appointments are made without any assessment of merit there is a tendency for like to appoint like, and for candidates from diverse backgrounds who do not see themselves as "fitting the mould" not to apply for roles': CSPL, 'Upholding Standards in Public Life' (n 1) 5.4.

[8] Review of the Office of the Commissioner for Public Appointments, Note by Sir David Normington, Public Appointments Commissioner and First Civil Service Commissioner, 8.

III. What are Public Appointments?

The contours of public appointments covered by the CPA are not clearly drawn and are regularly changing. There are hundreds of public bodies which have a role in the processes of national government, but are neither government departments nor part of government departments. They operate to a greater or lesser extent at an arm's length from ministers. NDPBs are of varying size and scope, and include bodies like art galleries, museums, inspectorates, regulators, NHS boards and advisory committees. They cover the whole gamut, from chairing a big, high-profile body like the BBC to governing institutions like the Bank of England and heading up small, technical advisory bodies for which competition may not be so fierce. As of 31 March 2020, which is the latest figure available, there were 4739 public appointees in the UK. Of these appointments, 52 per cent were made directly by ministers and 48 per cent were delegated by the Ministry of Justice, by the Department of Health and other ministries to, for example, NHS trusts.

Most of them are 'real' jobs that frequently come with heavy responsibilities and major decision-making potential. Many intersect directly with the political process, or at least with governmental priorities. Some may be valuable in providing experience that is of interest to the private sector, and even if not will certainly create good networks of contacts.

The public bodies which fall under the CPA are listed in an Order in Council, and this can be easily amended and expanded from time to time. It is revised every year or so to ensure full coverage of public appointments. This method of legislating means that the very office could be abolished without primary legislation being needed. This should be put on a full statutory footing.

The public appointments edifice must be sharply distinguished from the way in which appointments of senior civil servants are managed. These are separately overseen by a statutory Civil Service Commission, including the First Civil Service Commissioner.[9] Judicial appointments are regulated separately, by the Judicial Appointments Commission (who put forward only one name for appointment in each case). The cases of Dido Harding and Kate Bingham in relation to respectively NHS Test and Trace and vaccines also need to be distinguished as they were directing civil servants so there is a confluence; these controversial appointments will be considered later.

A. Office of the Commissioner for Public Appointments

The post of CPA was established in 1995 to give people more confidence in the system of public appointments, which is mainly run by ministers and civil servants.

---

[9] Sir David Normington held both posts at the same time.

The CPA thus has a bulging in tray, with a very large number of appointments to consider. In 2020/21, there were 693 such appointments within the CPA's remit (ie much lower than the 4739 figure cited above for all appointments). Of these, 67 proceeded without competition.

Broadly speaking, the Commissioner oversees the appointments which are made to over 300 public bodies by ministers in Whitehall and another 56 by the Welsh government.[10] The coverage of the CPA incorporates executive NDPBs; advisory NDPBs; certain health bodies but not NHS trusts; public corporations; public broadcasting authorities; certain utility regulators; non-ministerial departments; national park authorities; and conservation boards for Areas of Outstanding Natural Beauty.

There are some apparent anomalies of coverage, so that the office does not regulate the Governor and Deputy Governors of the Bank of England but does cover the Court of the Bank, ie the non-executives who form what elsewhere would be seen as a board of directors. That is because the Governor and Deputy Governors are executives.

With such a challenging brief, one would expect the Office of the Commissioner for Public Appointments (OCPA) to be well resourced. But this expectation is wrong. Instead, the Office is a shoestring operation and has only three members of staff – including the part-time Commissioner – and is based within the Civil Service Commission Secretariat. In many ways, the most direct power the CPA has is to draw attention to abuses of the system, which would normally be behind the veil of official secrecy. There is a serious embarrassment factor for ministers and civil servants from the OCPA intervening in the public arena. Sir Peter Riddell, a former *Times* journalist and Director of the Institute of Government, was more willing to be in the public arena than his predecessors and probably his successors.

OCPA also undertakes an annual audit of the handling of appointments by government departments to assess generally whether the Governance Code is being followed and to discuss best practice and the scope for improvements to be made. The Commissioner chooses which competitions he will examine in detail and may then see all the relevant papers about how the competition was handled.

B. The Normal Method of Appointment

The role of the CPA has shrunk over time. The system for making public appointments itself is now set out by the government in its Governance Code on Public Appointments, a document drawn up in 2016 by ministers (in consultation with the Commissioner). As the Commissioner's website explains, 'the Code is based on three core principles – merit, openness and fairness – and sets out the essential requirements for meeting those principles'.

---

[10] The Scottish and Northern Ireland executives have separate arrangements.

The process is run by the sponsoring government department, which establishes an advisory assessment panel for each appointment. Roles must be advertised on the government's public appointments website.

Ministers must be consulted about the quality of the field at the sift stage, which is when they have the maximum chance to mould the pack. A shortlist is selected for interview by the panel, which is usually chaired by a senior official.

Ministers make the final choice from the list of appointable candidates with whom they are presented by the interview panel. The ministers are entitled to meet with all the appointable individuals and can be informed at all stages of the process as to its progress. The interest taken by ministers inevitably varies between individual ministers and the weight, prominence and reach of the particular appointment. Under the Nolan Principles, a panel puts people 'above the line' or not, and the minister can only choose anyone above the line, save in the limited circumstances considered below. The Commissioner's role now is chiefly limited to the audit of departments' choices against the Governance Code and to investigate complaints.

The Committee on Standards in Public Life (CSPL) review in 2005 spoke of the 'difficult and perennial task of balancing ministerial responsibility, merit and independent oversight'. The Committee warned that 'it is unlikely that a system so dependent on personal responsibility [both of ministers to act with restraint and of the Commissioner to speak out] will be sustainable in the long term'. In 2005, the Parliamentary Public Administration Committee re-emphasised that ministers should be involved in appointments as they were 'the legitimate embodiment of ministerial responsibility'.[11] The CSPL has suggested that all discussions with ministers at shortlisting stage are properly recorded.

Ministers may in a particular appointment reject the whole candidate list and ask for a competition to be rerun, while the latest amendment to the Ministerial Code allows them to appoint someone whom an appointment panel has found to be unappointable – although this is not believed to have happened yet, and would no doubt cause outrage if it did. If appointing a candidate deemed 'unappointable', however, ministers 'must consult the Commissioner for Public Appointments in good time before a public announcement and will be required to justify their decision publicly'.[12] The CSPL believed that the nature of any such public justification 'should be in Parliament, at a meeting of the department's relevant Select Committee'.[13]

---

[11] CSPL, *Getting the Balance Right, Implementing Standards of Conduct in Public Life* (Cm 6407, 2005).

[12] Cabinet Office, Governance Code for Public Appointments (2016) clause 3.2, https://assets.publishing.service.gov.uk/government/uploads/system/uploads/attachment_data/file/578498/governance_code_on_public_appointments_16_12_2016.pdf.

[13] CSPL, 'Upholding Standards in Public Life' (n 1) 5.12.

There is also evidence that many roles are only being filled by interim appointments, who have to show blind loyalty in the hope of a longer-lasting role. This was a favourite tactic of Donald Trump as US President, although there it was to avoid the need for Senate confirmation, which in some cases would prove difficult.[14]

C. Senior Independent Panel Members

Panels for the core list of important high-profile bodies must include an independent member and a senior independent member, and this is another one of the Commissioner's key means of influence on the public appointments system. There are, of course, varying shades of what is known as 'independence'. Senior independent panel members (SIPMs) cannot be 'currently politically active', must be independent of the department and the body concerned, and must be familiar with senior recruitment and the public appointments principles, but beyond that there is no guidance. It is odd that there is currently no requirement that the SIPM should report back on the assessment.

There are some dilemmas attaching to the independent members; you want people who are independent, but if they know the area they are likely to know people in the frame, so to speak. This is particularly so in the cultural sector, where everyone seems to know everyone else. There is also the suspicion that ministers interfere with appropriate processes to promote candidates of their political persuasion and to deter those of the opposite politics. Riddell has complained of repeated 'attempts by ministers to appoint people with clear party affiliations', which he has had to rebuff.

There are some lessons here that might be learnt from the devolved administrations, which take a stronger line to provide independence. In Scotland, there is no ministerial involvement at all in the shortlisting stage. In Wales, ministers can sit on selection panels for appointments to upper tier bodies. When they do this under the Commissioner's Code for the National Assembly of Wales, they must invite two nominated members of the relevant assembly subject committee that shadows each ministerial portfolio to sit on the panel with them. It seems entirely right that SIPMs have a 'specific duty of reporting' on the conduct of their competitions, as many already do informally. Such a reform would provide an additional check against unfair panel assessments.[15]

---

[14] See S Skowronek, J Dearborn and D King, *Phantoms of a Beleaguered Republic* (Oxford, Oxford University Press, 2021).

[15] CSPL, 'Upholding Standards in Public Life' (n 1) 5.18, citing a suggestion made by Peter Riddell.

D. Compelling the Production of Documents

Although there are powers under the Order in Council to compel documents to be disclosed to the Commissioner either in response to a complaint from a candidate or as part of an investigation which he decides to undertake because the appointment is high profile or controversial, it is difficult for him to tell that all documents are in fact disclosed and there are no legal sanctions if they are not (such as a court would have). The details are in any event kept confidential because of the need not to reveal the identity of any candidates. The role and power of the Commissioner was diminished by the Grimstone Review, to which I now turn to critique.

IV. The Grimstone Review

Just at the time when there was again rising concern about the politicisation of public appointments, the Cameron government set up a review in 2015 to reduce the jurisdiction of the central regulator. This was the Grimstone Review. Gerry Grimstone was a former chairman of Barclays plc and has recently (in 2020) been made a Conservative peer.

The overall effect of his report was to increase ministerial power. The primary responsibility for ensuring that ministers comply with the rules was put onto permanent secretaries and away from the Commissioner himself.

There were 41 recommendations made altogether, the most important of which for present purposes were

1. the need for ethnic gender and social diversity;
2. providing chairs of boards to which a candidate is being appointed with a voice in the appointment; and, most importantly,
3. the Commissioner should not play a role in recruitment process itself but merely assure Parliament and the public that it is carried out in accordance with the Public Appointment Principles.

Sir David Normington said that the effect of these proposals would be to relegate the Commissioner to a 'sort of commentator and bystander'.[16]

The Parliamentary Public Administration Committee was not impressed by the results, concluding:

> In particular, the Grimstone proposals significantly weakened the role of the Commissioner for Public Appointments. The Commissioner's role was merely to expose and publicise flaws in the process for any particular appointments rather than to set the parameters of the Code which henceforth was set by Ministers so there was a sense of their marking their own homework.[17]

---

[16] Evidence to PACAC.
[17] Public Administration and Constitutional Affairs Committee, *Better Public Appointments? The Grimstone Review on Public Appointments* (HC 495, 2016).

The role of the Commissioner's office thus fundamentally changed. Before these changes, the Commissioner owned the Code of Practice and worked with a team of centrally appointed assessors who acted as independent members of panels. Post-Grimstone, the Commissioner now regulates public appointments against the government's own code. It is a passive role. As set out in the Governance Code, there are circumstances in which the Commissioner must be consulted in advance by ministers, but the Commissioner's role is merely to audit departments against the Code, report annually and thematically on compliance with the processes and the principles which are set out in the Code, and investigate complaints.

It is likely that a determined team of a Secretary of State and their special advisers who want to push through a political appointment will simply not worry about the very busy permanent secretary to the same degree as they would about an effective external regulator who can operate more in the public eye.

A. Critique of Grimstone

The Grimstone Report indeed did not garner many friends. Sir David Normington, who was the Commissioner for Public Appointments and Civil Service Commissioner at the time the Review appeared, outlined serious criticisms of the Grimstone Review and in particular about the reduced role of the Commissioner:

> Currently, the Commissioner provides public assurance that those who are appointed to public bodies are up to the job. It is not clear from the Grimstone report how much of this will continue. Indeed the report appears to remove most of the Commissioner's powers.

Professor Matthew Flinders and Dr Alexandra Meakin agreed: 'Some of Sir Gerry's recommendations risk undoing much of the work completed over the last twenty years to restore public trust in ministerial appointments ... giving the impression-correct or incorrect- that ministers are policing their own appointments.'[18]

Although a degree of political accountability is desirable, it is also necessary to preserve and police the independence of the system. The Public Administration and Constitutional Affairs Committee Report, *Better Public Appointments? The Grimstone Review on Public Appointments*,[19] concluded: 'Although the Government has adopted them [the Grimstone Recommendations], it should think again. The Commissioner's powers should be restored in order to safeguard public trust and confidence in the system.'

In unusually direct and trenchant comments, the Committee said:[20]

> We do not question the merits of holding a review of the public appointments process, but this review should have aimed to reinforce the changes made by Sir David

---

[18] Cited in ibid.
[19] ibid.
[20] ibid para 85.

Normington. Instead, the Grimstone review threatens to undermine the entire basis of independent appointments. Rather than build on Sir David's work, it effectively demolishes the safeguards built up by Lord Nolan … The Government must make significant changes to the proposals in order to robustly deliver a public appointments process in which the public can have confidence.

V. Abuses

These problems have been compounded by several recent abuses of the system in different forms which illustrate why the present system is not working when people do not act as 'good chaps' and why rules need to be tightened.

It is hard to put it better than Peter Riddell as the Commissioner for Public Appointments:

> [S]ome at the centre of government want not only to have the final say but to tilt the competition system in their favour to appoint their allies … I have on a number of occasions had to resist … attempts by ministers to appoint people with clear party affiliations.[21]

Various abuses of the system may be distinguished. They are: packing; leaking; changing sponsors; and appointment with no competition. The controversy over the Ofcom chairmanship spans two of these areas, which I shall look at first, before considering the specific cases of Dido Harding and Kate Bingham.

A. Leaking

Briefing the media in relation to forthcoming appointments before the appointment process is complete is an abuse because it can make it appear to those outside the gilded circle of preferred candidates that the result of a competition is already a foregone conclusion (and thus put off other candidates from applying or pursuing the application). This habit has gained greater traction recently, and has received the critical attention of the Public Appointments Commissioner. In his report for 2019/20, Peter Riddell, the outgoing Commissioner, noted that telling the press that 'someone is a favoured candidate for a post – or has been effectively lined-up – is damaging, not only by appearing to pre-judge the outcome of an open competition but also by discouraging other strong and credible candidates from applying'.

This happened most recently and blatantly in two important appointments to media bodies, the second of which was especially fraught. The first was the case

---

[21] OCPA Report in November 2020, https://assets.publishing.service.gov.uk/government/uploads/system/uploads/attachment_data/file/932513/Peter_Riddell_to_Lord_Evans.docx.pdf.

of Richard Sharp, who was widely touted in the media as the next chairman of the BBC well before his actual appointment, so that no other serious candidates put their head above the parapet. He was a Conservative Party donor, a partner in Goldman Sachs and the brother of Dame Victoria Sharp, a senior judge. It is interesting to look back to less partisan days on public appointments when Harold Wilson appointed Lord Hill, who had been a former Conservative Postmaster General, to that position and Tony Blair nominated a known Tory for that key role. It was reported that only 10 applied for the BBC chair because Sharpe's imminent appointment had been so widely trailed.

The second was the controversial on–off process for Paul Dacre as the favoured candidate of No 10. He was the former editor of the *Daily Mail* and the combative chief spokesman of the Tory Right for many years, who was frequently trailed as chair of Ofcom. This also had a chilling effect on other appointees applying. Ofcom is especially sensitive because it regulates media companies and operators, including the BBC, of which the Conservative government and Party have been very critical. Oliver Dowden, then the relevant Secretary of State, somewhat disingenuously said on the *Today* programme on Radio 4 on 15 November 2021 that the reason Dacre was not appointed and the process had to be rerun was because there were so few applicants. This was disingenuous because the government, by its incessant leaking that he was the preferred applicant, had discouraged applicants.

Peter Riddell, in his final report, drew public critical attention to the leaking of preferred candidates in this way:

> For instance, it is quite reasonable for ministers to suggest names and also to reject the advice of an advisory assessment panel and to order the re-running of a competition. But what is against the spirit of the Code is to seek to influence the work of an assessment panel by leaking the names of preferred candidates beforehand which can be, and has been, a deterrent and discouragement to other potential applicants from putting their names forward.

B. Changing Sponsors and Job Requirements

Usually, it is clear which department will take responsibility for a particular appointment, but some have vague lines of responsibility. This appears to be what happened in the case of Paul Dacre, who was initially turned down as an appointable candidate for the role of chairman of Ofcom when the panel was (as it should have been) under the tutelage of the Department of Digital, Culture, Media and Sport, but a second panel was to be held under the control of No 10 before Dacre eventually withdrew.

The subtle changing of the job requirements in the second round for the Ofcom post are also of interest and show how the department can mould the job to the person. These would have been likely to favour Dacre if he had stayed in the race. The successful candidate originally had to demonstrate they could work 'collegiately' with other board members and have a 'positive relationship' with the

Ofcom chief executive. These were not likely to be seen as virtues obviously to be found in the combative Paul Dacre. It was, however, watered down by No 10 to working 'effectively' with board members and creating a 'productive relationship' with the chief executive.

There were also subtle features of the board for the appointment. A lobbyist with close connections with the Conservative Party was to be on the board for the selection of the chairman of Ofcom: Michael Prescott, a former political editor of the *Sunday Times* and now a lobbyist with Hanover Communications. He was to sit with Sue Gray, the former Director of Ethics and Integrity at the Cabinet Office.

Then, in December 2021, there was an unexpected turn of events and an attack on the system. Dacre was appointed to be Editor-in-Chief of the *Daily Mail* (he had stepped down as their long-term editor three years before in favour of Geordie Greig, who was then defenestrated) and he withdrew his name from consideration. He did not, however, depart the field quietly, but rather with a flourish. He described his trauma in a letter to *The Times* that is as good an example of the Tory critique of public appointments as one could find. He said his experience of 'an infelicitous dalliance with the Blob' had not been good, and he went much further and claimed that senior Whitehall figures were determined to exclude anyone with convictions on the right of centre from public appointments. The Blob was the term famously used by Michael Gove to describe the liberals in the education establishment who opposed his reforms in education policy when he was the Secretary of State of Education.

Dacre said:

> To anyone from the private sector, who, God forbid, has convictions, and is thinking of applying for a public appointment, I say the following: The civil service will control (and leak) everything.
>
> The process could take a year in which your life will be put on hold; and if you are possessed of an independent mind and are unassociated with the liberal/left, you will have more chance of winning the lottery than getting the job.[22]

Although stated in characteristically trenchant language, this does contain a kernel of truth which should not be overlooked.

C. Panel Packing

The appointment of the new chair of the Office for Students in 2020 appears to be a blatant case of panel packing. A Conservative-dominated panel appointed a former Conservative MP, James Wharton, without experience in the education sphere (he had been a solicitor and then a lobbyist), to this sensitive role, which is

---

[22] 'Former Daily Mail editor Paul Dacre pulls out of race to be chairman of Ofcom while launching blistering attack on left-wing civil servants and public sector 'blob', *Daily Mail*, 19 November 2021, available at www.dailymail.co.uk/news/article-10222441/Former-Daily-Mail-editor-Paul-Dacre-blasts-liberal-civil-servants-quits-Ofcom-chairman-race.html.

at the heart of the 'culture wars' because universities are increasingly under attack for being too woke and restrictive of free speech.

At the time, the Commissioner raised concerns about a packed selection panel, but to no avail – which shows the limits of his power. The panel consisted of the former Tory councillor Baroness Wyld, former Tory candidate Patricia Hodgson, Eric Ollerenshaw (a Conservative MP between 2010 and 2015) and Nick Timothy, former chief of staff to Theresa May (full disclosure: a friend of mine), along with a representative from the Department for Education. Riddell has been rightly strident in his public statements about this particular process, but he can huff and puff as much as he likes; he has no power to restrain the appointment going ahead.

D. Appointments without Competition

Appointments made without competition can be a big problem too, although there are some limited circumstances where they may be legitimate. Paragraph 3.3 of the Governance Code is quite circumscribed in stating:

> In exceptional cases, ministers may decide to appoint a candidate without a competition. They must make this decision public alongside their reasons for doing so. They must consult the Commissioner for Public Appointments in good time before the appointment is publicly announced.

The Grimstone Report noted that there will be 'exceptional occasions when ministers may decide that a full appointments process is not appropriate or necessary'. In those instances, however, Grimstone recommended that 'there should always be an independent scrutiny before the appointment is announced, perhaps by the lead non-executive board member of the relevant department, to ensure that the process has been conducted with integrity'.[23]

Pages 28–31 of the CPA 2019–20 Annual Report state that the most common reasons behind appointments without competition and extensions of tenure were, according to the OCPA:

- To allow time for a competition, for example, to cover the time ahead of a new appointee taking up their post, where a competition has failed to recruit or to delay the start of a competition for necessary reasons (eg the Welsh government's suspension of competitions).

- To provide stability and experience to the board, for example, to protect quoracy, during a period of significant change to its powers or strategic direction, to support other new leaders (such as a new Chief Executive) or when it is subject to an independent review.

---

[23] Public Administration and Constitutional Affairs Committee (n 17) 10.

- To allow for a board to be merged, established or closed down where a fresh competition would be redundant.
- To allow for a specialist project to be completed, or to retain skills where an individual is required to see it through to the end, for example, to help steer a board through the pandemic.

Election campaigns lead by convention to the freezing or suspension of appointment competitions. The same happened initially during the first coronavirus pandemic lockdown in March 2020, but Whitehall adapted quickly and the normal competitions resumed. However, for a variety of reasons, there has been a backlog of some big competitions straying beyond the departure date of the outgoing chair (for example, Ofcom and the Charity Commission), and the Commissioner agreed to the appointments of interim chairs in each case. The former Cabinet Secretary Lord Sedwill told PACAC that 'unregulated appointments were a temporary response to the pandemic and not a precedent for future appointments'.[24]

VI. Dido Harding and Kate Bingham

The appointments without competition of Dido Harding and Kate Bingham to important NHS bodies during the COVID-19 pandemic raise various issues of abuse of the system and merit separate consideration because of the centrally important and unusual nature of their roles. They happened close together, and in the case of the former led to legal action by the First Division Association. Harding became the head of NHS Test and Trace and Bingham head of the vaccine programme, and both happen to be the wives of Tory MPs – the former the wife of John Penrose, who, ironically enough, serves as the Anti-Corruption Tsar. Bingham had relevant experience in biotech venture capital and, as things stand, appears in retrospect to have been an inspired choice because of the great success of the vaccine rollout programme – but it is still a case study in how public appointments should not work. In Bingham's case, however, this could be considered a case of the end justifying the means.

The consecutive positions of Dido Harding are the more complex to disentangle. She had been chief executive of the mobile phone company TalkTalk, which was involved in a serious data breach. Pre-pandemic, she was appointed as chair of NHS Improvement, a quango, through the normal process for public appointments. She was then brought in to run Test and Trace. She was also subsequently appointed to head up the National Institute of Public Health without open competition.

---

[24] Lord Sedwill, 'The Work of the Cabinet Office', oral evidence given to the House of Commons Public Administration and Constitutional Affairs Committee (17 November 2020) response to Q517, https://committees.parliament.uk/oralevidence/1208/pdf/.

These 'taskforces' – unlike government departments on the one hand or quangos/NDPBs on the other – have no legal standing. But what both did was spend huge amounts of money and direct a massive amount of civil service effort for months. This is extraordinary in terms of constitutional propriety. In the case of Dido Harding, civil servants were reporting directly to her instead of to the permanent secretary at the Department of Health, and she was deciding how large sums of money were to be spent. Bingham was doing the same. These were not regular quango appointments; they were actually bringing people into the heart of the executive branch, bypassing the civil service and its normal procedures for spending money.

Whilst the third Harding appointment is just a straightforward decision to ignore the Nolan Principles, the second appointment – and that of Bingham – is far more significant as, for a substantial period, two outsiders were brought directly into the heart of the government and allowed to direct massive expenditure of money and direct huge amounts of government effort in ways that not only bypassed Nolan (1995) but also the Northcote–Trevelyan civil service reforms (1854) and the public accountability reforms of the first Gladstone administration.

In *Spike*, Jeremy Farrer and Anjana Ahuja say that it was a grave error to appoint Harding.[25] Although Hancock praised her 'significant experience in healthcare and fantastic leadership', Farrar could not see what skills she brought to the role.

VII. Charity Commission Chairmanship

One of the areas where culture wars (ie using aspects of culture to provide dividing lines between the parties) may be seen being played out is the chair of the Charity Commission. In advance of the competition, Oliver Dowden, then the Secretary of State for Digital, Culture Media and Sport, said the new chair of the Charity Commission would 'reset the balance' after he said some charities had been 'hijacked by a vocal minority seeking to burnish their woke credentials'. After a long process which was heavily influenced by the government leaking of the sort of person they required, Martin Thomas was appointed. One noticeable thing about him was that he had been a friend of Boris Johnson at Oxford. He was chair at two charities, Downside Up and the Forward Arts Foundation, and before that the chair at Women for Women International UK.

Before he took up the post, however, he resigned because he had been found out sending a photo of himself at Victoria's Secret to an employee of the charity he ran. He said that this was because the company were thinking of investing in a charity in which he was involved (although he was not found guilty of misconduct on this head). What had not been picked up by the civil servants involved

---

[25] J Farrer and A Ahuja, *Spike: The Virus vs The People – the Inside Story* (London, Profile Books, 2021) 145.

in the process was that whilst he was chair of the latter charity he was the subject of three formal complaints, one of which was the subject of a serious incident report to the Charity Commission. It appears surprising that inquiries were not made of the Charity Commission as to whether his record was known to them. This was described as 'shambolic, incompetent and shocking' by Julian Knight MP, the chair of the Culture, Media and Sport Select Committee. After many months and another selection process, Orlando Fraser KC, another friend of Johnson, was appointed.

VIII. Tsars

What should also not be permitted is the sort of flanking movement created by setting up wholly new institutions and then not submitting them to the public appointment processes at all. There has, however, been a proliferation of rather vague tsar positions[26] which are not subject to the Order in Council listing public appointments or, indeed, any regulation at all or due process for appointment because they are not listed in it. The creation is purely by the executive action of a minister or the Prime Minister. This has occurred ad hoc and is classic territory where 'chumocracy' rules (or, rather, a spectacular lack thereof) apply. Some of the roles fizzle away after a little while, such as the Shale (Fracking) Tsar, but some have real influence and staying power, such as the Tsar for Problem Families. Tsars can be called to appear before Select Committees, but are not bound to face other parliamentary or even media questioning, notwithstanding the influence that they may wield. The obvious point is that if you can set up a new body or tsardom and appoint whomever you like to run it, you can effectively bypass other institutions and the inconvenience of the public appointments criteria at all. Prime Minister Johnson relied on his favoured informal approach of appointing 'tsars' to lead core parts of the pandemic response, including vaccines, test and trace, personal protective equipment (PPE) and – recently – education catch-up. A friend of the Prime Minister and Carrie Johnson, Nimco Ali, was appointed in October 2020 as an adviser on tackling violence against women and girls without any clear appointment process.

---

[26] Ruth Levitt calculated as long ago as in 2013 that more than 300 tsars have been appointed since 1997, more than 100 of them appointed by coalition ministers alone. Gordon Brown holds the ministerial record, with 46 appointments in all, 23 as chancellor and 23 as Prime Minister; David Cameron made 21, Michael Gove has made 11. Levitt's research suggests that tsars come principally from business (40% of the total) and the public service (37%); several are serving or former politicians (18%) and the rest include academics and researchers, lawyers and media people. Some are specialists, others are generalists or advocates with known views. Overall, they are strikingly undiverse: predominantly male (85%), white (98%), over 50 years old on appointment (83%) – and, indeed, 38% were titled.

There are no rules, procedures or codes to govern the appointment, role or indeed payment of these tsars. The CPA should set out what he sees as a transient appointment for which full procedure is not needed.

The first Greensill Report by Nigel Boardman showed up the problems caused by ministers making ad hoc appointments to ill-defined roles, in that Lex Greensill had successive ill-defined roles in the heart of the government. Boardman drew attention to the ever-expanding number of tsars and trade envoys with often unclear responsibilities and opaque appointment procedures. The process for direct ministerial appointments is, Boardman says, 'opaque and poorly understood'. He recommends a new Code of Practice 'which makes clear the expectations on both departments and appointees' in these areas. Crucially, it reaffirms that express ministerial approval should be required for such posts.

IX. Non-executive Directors

Another yawning gap in this coverage are the many non-executive directors (NEDs) of government departments which also do not fit within the public appointments regulated regime. They may, however, have considerable influence over government policy,[27] although this is not so in all cases (it is often a question of the personalities involved, both of the ministers and the NEDs) and some have made no impact at all.[28] The 2010 Ministerial Code emphasised that NEDs should largely be drawn from the 'commercial private sector'.[29] They do, however, have access to very sensitive information and formal roles in departments (eg chairing audit committees, input to performance reviews of permanent secretaries and other officials, and some specific responsibilities in managing public money), as well as much scope for informal influence. This may be helpful in private sector arenas.

Michael Gove paved the way in appointing personal allies as NEDs during the Cameron government. Liz Truss put on the board at the Department of International Trade two former Tory MPs, Douglas Carswell and Stephen O'Brien, and a former vice-chair of the Conservative Party, alongside a public relations man and former Labour special adviser.

The idea of including them in the public appointments structure was in fact debated in 2016 by the Public Administration Committee, but the conclusion then was that their role depended so much on the secretary of state and what he or she

---

[27] eg Henry Dimbleby on food.

[28] According to the UCL Constitutional Unit, the average term for NEDs is 42 months; 2–35 days' work pa; salary £15,000, rising to £20,000 for lead NEDs.

[29] Institute for Government, 'Government Departments' Boards and Non-executive Directors (2021) www.instituteforgovernment.org.uk/explainers/government-departments-boards-and-non-executive-directors#:~:text=How%20are%20non%2Dexecutive%20directors,appointed%20by%20the%20prime%20minister.

wanted them to do that it would be very hard to classify them with other public appointments. However, the announcements of some non-executive members of departmental boards say that the appointment has followed an open competition when there is in fact no check or scrutiny – in other cases, they are announced as the result of direct ministerial appointment. What is needed at the very least is greater transparency about how they are appointed, why and what they will be doing. Grimstone recommended that NEDs should come within the remit of OCPA, and this is surely correct. The CSPL was recently categorical that 'The appointments process for Non-Executive Directors of government departments should be regulated under the Governance Code for Public Appointments'.[30]

The conclusion of the government was that their role depended so much on the secretary of state, and what he or she wanted them to do, that it would be very hard to classify them with other public appointments. Also, there has been a mass appointment of Tory MPs as unpaid trade envoys (a role which started under Theresa May's government) and other such jobs, so the 'payroll' vote of those signed up to support the government no matter what gets bigger, even though they are not paid.

X. Encouraging Applications

One aspect of the Grimstone Review that has been positive is the encouragement of applications. According to Sir Gerry, relying on 'people sufficiently knowledgeable or motivated enough to read the Cabinet Office newsletter or look at the Cabinet Office website is clearly in itself not sufficient'. He therefore suggested that 'much more active processes are needed to reach out to people and to publicise vacancies across, for example, private sector corporate talent programmes, talent management programmes, relevant specialist networks and associated social media'.[31]

XI. Back to Politicisation

Increasing politicisation is, however, a major part of the problem. Ministers' desire to have tighter control is the driving force behind a series of changes of rules and approach which can be dated back to the Grimstone Review in 2016 but accelerated under Johnson. It is possible to make the case that the appointments process has been undermined by political meddling. The practice of picking political allies can be traced back decades, which in particular ensured that the chairs of most NHS trusts were Labour-leaning, and James Callaghan appointed his son-in-law

---

[30] CSPL, 'Upholding Standards in Public Life' (n 1) Recommendation 25.
[31] Grimstone Report, 24.

Peter Jay as Ambassador to Washington without his having any diplomatic experience. There was what were dubbed in the tabloid media as the Quango Queens under Labour, such as Lin Homer and Suzi Leather, who acquired a series of appointments. What we are seeing now, however, is unprecedented: so many posts being ideologically driven and large swathes of people who are not ideological feeling there is no point applying.

The strong counter narrative from the Right, however, is that Britain is still, so many years after his retirement as Prime Minister, run by a Blairite elite and that this needs to be broken down. This was voiced eloquently by Paul Dacre in stepping back from his application for the role as chair of Ofcom, for which he was generally touted and apparently encouraged by Downing Street to apply.

The Conservative Home website has a feature entitled 'Calling Conservatives: New public appointments announced', which encourages its readers to apply for vacant posts because of the theory that so many are in the hands of 'liberal metropolitans'. The Taxpayers' Alliance reported in 2018–19 that of 1844 appointments where the political allegiance was declared, 47.4 per cent were Labour-supporting, while 31.6 per cent were Tory-supporting. This is, however, a contested area, given that the 2019–20 Annual Report by the Public Appointments Commissioner cites the figures of 38.3 per cent and 36.8 per cent respectively (although this the percentage of those who declare their political allegiance which is only 10% of the total).

What is clear is that it is at the present time virtually impossible for Labour supporters to be appointed to major boards (or even selection boards), including in the cultural sector, where one would have thought politics should have minimal influence. One columnist of my acquaintance was not called back as a member of an independent scrutiny board because they used to write for *The Guardian* and that in itself was anathema to ministers (as they were informed by civil servants involved). The civil servants wanted the person back, but they had no choice.

One of the least publicly discussed issues is the frequent strains and misunderstandings between the chairs of public bodies and ministers/departments over appointments to those bodies. The former can feel that their interests are neglected and brushed aside by ministerial diktat. This argues for reaffirming, and in some cases strengthening, the independent element in the appointments process, particularly for those bodies which scrutinise the actions and conduct of ministers and the executive.

XII. Parliament's Role

Parliament's role in public appointments is somewhat vague. It is confined to pre-appointment hearings for preferred candidates to chair a list of more than 50 public bodies as set out in Cabinet Office guidance. Parliament cannot, however, veto these appointments. There have, though, been cases where a candidate has withdrawn when it has become clear a Select Committee would recommend against their appointment – but in other cases, ministers have proceeded to appoint notwithstanding an adverse view from the relevant Select Committee. Recent examples include the appointment of Amanda Spielman to head Ofsted and that of Baroness Stowell (a Conservative peer) to chair the Charity Commission, although she only served one term.

John Wadham, formerly General Counsel of the Equality and Human Rights Commission, has argued that all appointments that have 'a role in holding the Government to account, protecting the rights of the citizen or promoting equality or human rights' should face parliamentary scrutiny. The government did not agree to this when it was proposed in 2012, but it is a good idea. This has been taken up by the CSPL in their Standards Matter 2 paper.

XIII. Diversity

Nolan made the obvious point that whilst individual posts should always be made on merit, the overall field of selection should represent an appropriate mix of relevant skills and backgrounds. More still needs to be done to address the lack of diversity amongst public appointments so that the boards of public bodies are more reflective of the communities which they serve. Of the appointments discussed by the Commissioner for Public Appointments in his report, the worrying figures are that only 11.2 per cent come from ethnic minority backgrounds and only 41.5 per cent go to those who are 54 and under. Now 50 per cent are women and this has happened without special measures being taken beyond encouragement. The hopes raised by the 2018 report of Lord Holmes of Richmond into opening up public appointments to people with disabilities largely remain unfulfilled. Too many such appointments are filled by the recently retired.

XIV. Conclusion

If the erosion of the Nolan Principles continues, the landscape could be completely different by 2024. We should return to the Nolan Principles. Alex Thomas, of the Institute for Government, sums up the situation in a measured, judicious response:

> In the end, making the right public appointments is about getting the best people in to do the job. The tried-and-tested way to do that is with an open competition, and ministers shouldn't undermine those competitions by stacking panels or cherry-picking candidates. There will be times when someone is needed more quickly and the process is set aside – then it is really important that public appointees have a clear remit, are properly held to account and only serve a time-limited term.[32]

---

[32] www.prospectmagazine.co.uk/politics/public-appointments-ministers-government-cronyism.

At present, there is no real compulsion to obey the code on public appointments beyond the court of public opinion, and most of the public are disinterested. The role of CPA should be put on a statutory basis. In particular, ministers should not have the exclusive say in the appointment of political and ethical regulators, and there should be an independent majority on interview panels and/or Commons committees should be more involved.

13

Standards and the British Constitution

GILLIAN PEELE[1]

I. Introduction

This chapter examines the role of standards in the contemporary debates about the UK's constitutional arrangements. A good deal of attention has necessarily been devoted to the high-profile changes to in the UK's constitutional framework over the last quarter century. Many of these changes, such as devolution and the passage of the 1998 Human Rights Act, occurred as a result of the 1997–2007 Blair governments' constitutional reform programme. The 2016 referendum and the UK's subsequent exit from the European Union have subsequently produced an additional dimension of constitutional turbulence.[2] This chapter argues that, important though those high profile changes are, it is equally essential to examine the more diffuse area of standards or integrity issues. By 'standards or integrity issues', I mean the wide range of questions which relate to ethical conduct in public life and the methods by which we try to guarantee high standards of probity in the public sector.

Although this element of the constitutional fabric might have been assessed favourably until relatively recently, the period after 2019 witnessed a growing concern with integrity issues. Much of this concern was generated by a series of scandals which occurred in the government elected in 2019 and culminated in the forced resignation of the Prime Minister, Boris Johnson. Not only had Johnson's personal conduct in government been heavily criticised, but he was held responsible for failing to provide the ethical leadership required for the government as a whole. Integrity issues and the maintenance of high standards in public life became key issues in the debate about the choice of a successor to Johnson and the style of government which that successor should adopt. Reasserting the importance of integrity in the political system thus seems at least initially to have become

---

[1] The opinions expressed in this represent the personal views of the author and cannot in any way be attributed to the Committee on Standards in Public Life.

[2] For reflections on the impact of Brexit on the constitution, see V Bogdanor, *Beyond Brexit: Towards a British Constitution* (London, IB Tauris, 2020).

a political priority for politicians and the public alike. Yet, while a commitment to high ethical standards in government is a necessary precondition to restoring public trust, the process is likely to be a challenging one. For, as this chapter will show, the construction and maintenance of an integrity system is a complex and demanding task, and is thus always likely to be in danger of being sidelined in favour of other priorities.

II. The UK's Integrity System

Any democracy's integrity system will have three elements: a set of laws, rules and principles specifying the ethical values to which those in public life should adhere; machinery for enforcing those law, rules and principles; and some arrangements for maintaining relevant ethical values at the forefront of the consciousness of those in public life. Different systems will display differing degrees of coherence and consistency, and will vary in the use of formal or legal mechanisms as opposed to conventions or informal understandings. The UK's integrity framework is very much a patchwork. The Committee on Standards in Public Life (CSPL), which since 1994 has been responsible for keeping integrity arrangements under review, described it more favourably as a 'tapestry'. Both descriptions reflect the country's traditional emphasis on a wide range of constitutional conventions, informal understandings and parliamentary mechanisms of political accountability. They also reflect the extent to which the system, if it can properly be called a 'system', has developed incrementally, and been refined and adjusted as circumstances have altered.

Although political corruption was widespread in the eighteenth and nineteenth centuries, key reforms were generally assumed to have eliminated much of this 'taint' from public life.[3] The UK's modern integrity institutions therefore developed against the background of a somewhat complacent narrative that corruption, abuse and misconduct were relatively absent from British public life. Of course, scandals have never been absent from British politics, but when one such as the Poulson affair of the early 1970s did occur, it was often treated as an unfortunate deviation from the normal standards of political propriety, a one-off incident to be investigated but not having implications for the wider structures of government.[4] The cash for questions scandal of the early 1990s dented this complacency and triggered an overhaul of Britain's ethics machinery. That scandal

---

[3] For an excellent overview of the pre-modern history of corruption in the pre-modern era, see M Knights, *Trust and Distrust: Corruption in Office in Britain and Its Empire 1600–1850* (Oxford, Oxford University Press, 2021).

[4] On the Poulson affair, see R Fitzwalter and D Taylor, *Web of Corruption: The Story of JGL Poulson and T Dan Smith* (London, Granada, 1981).

exposed the willingness of some MPs to engage in paid advocacy and to use their parliamentary position for financial reward.[5] In its wake, the CSPL was created.

The CSPL is a small, independent, arm's-length body, sponsored by the Cabinet Office and reporting to the Prime Minister. Although it is only an advisory body, it was intended to be permanent, and has been the driving force in the development of the UK's standards machinery. Its membership is small, comprising now a chairman, who serves for one term of five years, and four independent members, who are recruited by open competition and also serve for one term of five years. In addition, there are three representatives of the parliamentary political parties. The CSPL is served by a small secretariat of civil servants. There have been changes to the CSPL's remit. Following controversy over a donation to Labour from Bernie Ecclestone, the 1997–2001 Blair government added party funding to the CSPL's responsibilities and asked it to conduct an inquiry. That inquiry was the basis for the 2000 Political Parties, Elections and Referendums Act, which altered the framework of party funding regulation and established a new body, the Electoral Commission, to administer electoral finance. After devolution, the CSPL's remit was changed further to exclude Scotland, Wales and Northern Ireland from its jurisdiction as the new devolved authorities were expected to set up their own standards machinery.

The CSPL is not itself a regulator, but since its inception it has undertaken a wide-ranging programme of analysis and appraisal of many of key institutions and regulatory bodies in the British system of government. Through the identification of the overarching principles which ought to govern public life, the CSPL has set integrity standards for the whole public sector and developed a model which has influenced standards in the private sector also. The seven principles of public life – the 'Nolan Principles' of selflessness, integrity, objectivity, accountability, openness, honesty and leadership – have been unchanged since they were first enumerated, although the CSPL has sometimes amended the descriptors of the principles to take account of changes in the social context. Thus, the descriptor of the leadership principle was amended to incorporate the need for holders of public office to treat others with respect following rising concern about bullying and harassment. The CSPL largely decides its own agenda, although sometimes it may be asked by the government to report on a specific problem, as occurred with its inquiry into intimidation of parliamentary candidates.[6] The CSPL has encouraged the formulation and refinement of codes of conduct to apply these principles to specific sectors of government. It has also examined the machinery through which conduct is regulated and standards enforced across the many diverse areas of the public sector. And it has focused attention on the importance of creating and maintaining a culture which promotes ethical conduct within different organisational settings.

---

[5] On the cash for questions scandal, see D Leigh and E Vulliamy, *Sleaze: The Corruption of Parliament* (London, 4th Estate, 1997).

[6] Committee on Standards in Public Life, 'Intimidation in Public Life' (December 2017).

The CSPL has probed many of the key governmental institutions and political problems. Thus, it has scrutinised, inter alia, the machinery for regulating the conduct of MPs and of peers, the ethical rules of local authorities, the rules governing the raising of money by political parties, the regulation of electoral administration, lobbying and the revolving door between the public and private sectors.[7] In addition to these familiar topics – which trouble all democracies – the CSPL has tackled issues of fairly recent origin. Thus, it has addressed the intimidation of parliamentary and local government candidates, which became increasingly threatening after the 2016 referendum on Brexit and the 2017 general election. It has also tackled issues created by technological change in the public sector, such as the safeguards needed for the use of artificial intelligence in decision-making and the delivery of services.[8] It has further been an active voice on standards issues in public debate. Thus, for example, in its Annual Report for 2021–22, the CSPL again expressed its opposition to the government decision to proceed with provisions in the Elections Act 2022 which in its view threatened the independence of the Electoral Commission by giving the government the power to set the strategic direction of the Commission through a strategy and policy statement.[9] Looking back over nearly 30 years of initiatives, it is clear that the impact of the CSPL on the handling of integrity issues in British public life has been profound. It has given the UK what it certainly did not have before – the elements of an integrity system and a body which could focus attention on standards issues whenever they arose. Its methodology of taking evidence from a wide cross-section of individuals and organisations within the field under review as well as from academics and other outside experts has given its recommendations authority and influence, even if governments have not always accepted them.

Despite the achievements of the CSPL in building the country's ethics machinery, by 2020 there was a sense that the approach to ethical regulation pioneered by the CSPL was losing some of its leverage. The chair of the CSPL, Lord Evans of Weardale, asked in a 2020 lecture whether we were living in a post-Nolan age in the sense that the Nolan Principles no longer seemed to guide all aspects of public life.[10] Lord Evans cited a number of episodes which suggested that the government was falling below the standards of probity which ought to have been shown by its members. These episodes included the initial approval given by a Cabinet minister, Robert Jenrick, to Richard Desmond's application for planning permission for the Westferry Printworks. Desmond was a Conservative Party donor and the application had already been turned down by a planning inspector.[11]

---

[7] A full list of publications of the Committee on Standards in Public Life can be found at www.gov.uk/government/organisations/the-committee-on-standards-in-public-life.

[8] Committee on Standards in Public Life, 'Artificial Intelligence and Public Standards: Report' (February 2020).

[9] Committee on Standards in Public Life, 'Annual Report 2021–2022' (8 July 2022).

[10] Lord Evans of Weardale, 'Are We in a Post-Nolan Age?' Hugh Kay Lecture to the Institute of Business Ethics (12 November 2020).

[11] J Gardiner, 'Government U-Turns to Refuse Westferry Printworks Scheme' *Housing Today* (18 November 2021).

(The minister's decision was later overturned.) There were also allegations that the Home Secretary, Priti Patel, had bullied civil servants, allegations which were investigated by the Independent Adviser on Ministerial Interests, who resigned after the Prime Minister refused to accept the findings. There were also, as Lord Evans noted, worrying pressures on other rules designed to protect against corruption and misconduct – for example, on the independent elements of the public appointments system and on the rules governing procurement.

Since that 2020 lecture, there have been further scandals which have pushed integrity issues centre stage, exposed weaknesses in different parts of the integrity system and generated intense public mistrust of the government's honesty and integrity among voters.[12] The Greensill affair revealed that it was possible for a recruit to the government from the private sector to use his position for private gain. It also exposed the extent to which former ministers (in this case a former Prime Minister) could continue to use their governmental contacts for lobbying purposes after leaving office. Lobbying was also at issue when, following a *Guardian* investigation and a damning inquiry by the Standards Commissioner in 2021, a Conservative MP, Owen Paterson, was found to have engaged in extensive lobbying for financial gain.[13] The episode was escalated when there was a brazen but short-lived attempt to save Paterson by using the governmental majority to reform the system for adjudicating allegations of misconduct in the Commons. The government had, however, to withdraw its attempt to recast the system and Paterson resigned his seat, which the Conservative Party subsequently lost in the resultant by-election.

Two subsequent episodes inflicted further damage on the public's perception of standards in government. The first was the discovery that a series of social gatherings had occurred inside Downing Street at a time when lockdown rules were in force. An investigation by the Metropolitan Police resulted in a number of fixed penalty notices being issued to senior members of the government, including the Prime Minister. A specially commissioned report from Sue Gray, the former Cabinet head of Propriety and Ethics, was damning in its condemnation of the events. The whole affair caused extensive public anger and created the impression of a government which was not obeying the rules it was imposing on the country at large.

The 'Partygate' saga had not been entirely concluded when another controversy exploded. This episode concerned a government deputy whip, Conservative MP Christopher Pincher, who was accused of groping two men while drunk at the Carlton Club in July 2022. The scandal was followed by allegations about previous misconduct by Pincher and that this was known to senior officials, including the Prime Minster, when Pincher was appointed to government. The attempt by

---

[12] See, eg the Survation survey 'Polling the Nolan Principles: The Public's Take on Ethical Standards in Public Life' based on fieldwork conducted 11–15 November 2021.

[13] On the Committee report, see F Lawrence, D Pegg and R Evans, 'Lobbying for "Naked" Bacon: How the Owen Paterson Scandal Began' *The Guardian* (5 November 2021).

Boris Johnson to deny that he knew of Pincher's history was refuted by the former permanent secretary at the Foreign and Commonwealth Office, Lord (Simon) McDonald, thereby exposing the Prime Minister as having inadvertently or deliberately been untruthful about his awareness of the allegations about Pincher. This particular case proved a breaking point for many in the Conservative Party and the government, and forced Boris Johnson to announce his resignation as Prime Minister in July 2022.

These episodes underline the importance of leadership and culture in establishing ethical standards in government. Boris Johnson had by July 2022 lost credibility as someone who could provide the ethical leadership for the government and convince the public of its integrity. The tsunami of standards issues which hit the Johnson government after 2019 also called into question the robustness of the existing approach to standards regulation. Of course, much of the UK's constitutional system depends upon respect for conventions and a degree of self-restraint on the part of government. Yet that self-restrain may not always be forthcoming and, as Simon Case noted in evidence to the House of Commons Public Administration and Constitutional Affairs Committee (PACAC), this was a government which believed it had a mandate to take controversial initiatives and to test boundaries.[14] The purely advisory nature of the CSPL has always meant that if the Prime Minister wishes to ignore the recommendations it is offered, they can do so. Indeed, the CSPL, in its 2021–22 Report, noted with regret the increase in the time taken by the government to respond to CSPL Reports and the fact that some reports had received no response at all.[15]

Not surprisingly, some radical suggestions for reform of the standards system have surfaced. The Labour Party has committed itself to setting up an Ethics and Integrity Commission, which would restructure and merge some existing standards bodies. Although the details of how it would work are as yet unclear, it seems likely that it would be given an oversight role in relation to the implementation of the Ministerial Code and strong enforcement powers over the ability of ministers and civil servants to move between the public and private sectors.[16] The Institute for Government has also suggested reforms which attempt to streamline and strengthen some of the regulatory bodies responsible for standards.[17] So too has the Constitution Unit.[18] Both of these bodies to a large extent support and reinforce the CSPL major review of 2021,

---

[14] Public Administration and Constitutional Affairs Committee, *Propriety of Governance in Light of Greensill* (28 June 2022, HC 212) oral evidence from Simon Case, Cabinet Secretary and Darren Tierney.

[15] Committee on Standards in Public Life, 'Annual Report 2021–2022' (n 8).

[16] See P Walker, 'Labour Proposes Watchdog for Ministers' Ethics to Stop Revolving Door' *The Guardian* (28 November 2021).

[17] See T Durrant and C Hadden, 'Reinforcing Ethical Standards in Government' (Institute of Government, March 2022).

[18] R Hazell, M Boo and Z Pullar, 'Parliament's Watchdogs: Independence and Accountability in Five Constitutional Watchdogs' (London, Constitution Unit, July 2022).

which published a range of recommendations for improving the machinery of standards regulation.[19] This Report was the CSPL's first comprehensive review of the whole terrain of standards regulation. Although the Report ranges widely, at the heart of its analysis are areas where serious concerns about ethical conduct had surfaced in recent years. These areas primarily involve relationships and behaviour at the centre of government: the role of the Ministerial Code as a mechanism for regulating ministerial behaviour; the effectiveness of the Business Appointment Rules as a mechanism for regulating the revolving door between the public and private sectors; the role of the Commissioner for Public Appointments in ensuring that appointments are properly made on the basis of merit, not patronage; and maintenance of transparency around lobbying. Before examining these recommendations in more detail, I want to explore some features of the context of standards regulation in more detail. These features of the context are important both because they shape the debate and shed light on why it has taken the course it has in recent years.

III. The Changing Context of Standards Regulation

The overview of the standards landscape in the two-volume report by the CSPL of June and November 2021 provides an up-to-date and comprehensive survey of the field following a detailed mapping exercise of the various bodies responsible for maintaining standards.[20] I want to highlight three aspects of the contemporary context of standards regulation that have changed since the 1990s and identify new tensions that have emerged in relation to maintaining ethical values in public life. Some of these tensions reflect an altered political climate; others reflect features of the political system which are always going to prove challenging.

The three aspects that I am highlighting are: the role of public opinion; the conflict between claims of legitimacy based on the ballot box and legitimacy claims derived from broader understandings of constitutional practice; and the tensions generated by adversarial politics.

A. Public Opinion

Questions of improper conduct in public life tend to gain attention when scandals hit the headlines; and the technicalities of standards issues may sink beneath the radar of public consciousness once the immediate cause of concern has been addressed. But that does not mean that they will not leave an impression.

---

[19] Committee on Standards in Public Life, 'Standards Matter 2: Committee Findings' (June 2021); Committee on Standards in Public Life, 'Upholding Standards in Public Life' (November 2021).
[20] See R Dobson Phillips, 'British Standards Landscape: A Mapping Exercise' (report commissioned by the Committee on Standards in Public Life).

The media has played an important part in exposing some of the key scandals of the last 30 years. Thus, *The Guardian* was a crucial player in the cash for questions saga, while the *Daily Telegraph* ran a systemic investigation into the abuse of the expenses system by MPs. *The Guardian* was also instrumental in producing the material which led to Owen Paterson's censure by the House of Commons Standards Committee. Of course, the news media have their own agendas and priorities. Moreover, the reportage often needs to focus on individual wrongdoing to gain audience attention (or what Howard Tumber calls 'flawed people') rather than on either the institutional or structural conditions which enabled the misconduct to occur.[21] There may not be any sustained follow-up of such reforms as do occur afterwards, although some dedicated advocacy groups such as Transparency International and the Good Law Project do help to keep integrity issues under review.[22] It is also important to note that changing trends in where the public obtains its information are important: social media are now a significant source of knowledge and opinion about integrity issues.

Episodes of impropriety and misconduct make headlines and inevitably risk reputational damage trust both to particular individuals and political parties, but also to other institutions, especially Parliament and the government. The contemporary debate about standards takes place against the background of a more widespread concern about trust, not just in the UK, but across the democratic world. Whether or not there is a 'crisis' of trust is unclear; but what we can see in the UK is a low level of trust in politicians and government.[23] What we can also see is that the public values integrity and honesty very highly as components of the democratic system. A study by the Constitution Unit showed 75 per cent of respondents agreed that a healthy democracy requires that 'politicians always act within the rules', while only six per cent supported 'getting things done even if that requires politicians to break the rules'.[24] So ethical values matter to the public and are indeed central to what they think defines a democracy. And when it comes to the Nolan Principles specifically, a Survation poll found that 59 per cent did not believe the government was upholding the Nolan Principles of integrity and 62 per cent did not think it was upholding the principle of honesty.[25] Such a finding is not just uncomfortable for the current government; it is a problem for future governments of whatever political persuasion since it is likely to be challenging to reverse this judgement.

---

[21] H Tumber, 'Media Scandals: Sound and Fury but in the End Little Changes' *The Conversation* (17 November 2021).

[22] On Transparency International, see www.transparency.org.uk/. On the Good Law project, see https://goodlawproject.org/.

[23] For a recent excellent discussion of the trust issue, see Ipsos/Mori, *Trust: The Truth* (London, Ipsos/Mori, 2022).

[24] A Renwick, B Lauderdale, M Russell and J Cleaver, 'What Kind of Democracy Do People Want?' (London, Constitution Unit, January 2022).

[25] See Survation panel survey on the Seven Principles of Public Life, www.survation.com/polling-the-nolan-the-publics-take-on-ethical-standards-in-public-life.

Ultimately, though, it is necessary to be very cautious about the relationship between public opinion and standards. Not only is public attention likely to wane, but even if it has a clear view of what standards are important, it does not always have a clear idea about how to achieve adherence to these standards and values. It is also likely that concern for standards will diminish in the face of conflicting public priorities.

B. Conflicting Legitimacies

Since its establishment, the CSPL has been viewed as both a shield and an irritant. It could be seen as a shield when it allowed a Prime Minister confronting an ethical dilemma or scandal to export it to an authoritative body. The CSPL does not investigate individual cases, but it can examine the extent to which the regulatory arrangements of an institution need overhauling to prevent such abuses in future. Yet it could also be seen as an irritant because reform might challenge long-established ways of doing things and will sometimes conflict with principles which have become baked into the mindset and practices of politicians. A good example of such a long-established principle is the notion of exclusive cognisance – the idea that the House of Commons has exclusive jurisdiction over its own proceedings and disciplinary arrangements. The highly significant changes which the CSPL promoted in relation to standards in the House of Commons, including the creation and frequent review of a Code of Conduct and a Commissioner for Parliamentary Standards, were a break with past practice and not universally welcomed by MPs.

Since those early reforms there have been other, more radical steps. The introduction of lay members to the Committee on Standards in 2013 (and the enhancement of their number to parity with MPs in 2016) was a major step in taking disciplinary arrangements out of the exclusive control of MPs. (Lay members were given full voting rights on the Committee in 2019.) There was also the creation of a separate new body – the Independent Parliamentary Standards Authority (IPSA) – to handle the administration of MPs' pay and allowances after the 2009 expenses scandal. Yet, while these reforms gradually gained acceptance, there remained an undercurrent of parliamentary resentment about the erosion of MPs' autonomy and an opposition to the work of the new regulators. Given the historical importance attached to the right of Parliament to control its own proceedings, some of this concern was understandable, even if overshadowed in the public mind by the evident possibility of abuse of their privileges by some MPs. Some of the resentment of regulatory provisions came out in the Owen Paterson case as criticism of Kathryn Stone, the Parliamentary Commissioner for Standards, as a section of Conservative MPs sought to defend Paterson from censure.

The criticism of Kathryn Stone in the Paterson case had echoes of the earlier situation when Elizabeth Filkin (who served as Commissioner for Parliamentary Standards between 1999 and 2001) found her role and office under attack.

She had been criticised by MPs and had encountered obstruction especially when ministers' behaviour was under scrutiny. This sniping and obstruction, as well as a reduction in the resources available to her office, led to her decision not to apply for a renewal of her initial two-year term of office.

There was also intense opposition to the new regime for handling pay and allowances set up in the wake of the parliamentary expenses scandal. The 2009 Parliamentary Standards Act took the determination and administration of pay and allowances out of the House of Commons' hands and transferred it to an external body. This body (IPSA) encountered extensive criticism from MPs as it attempted to establish the new system. Some of that criticism reflected administrative problems at the beginning of IPSA's life; but some of the sniping at IPSA, as at the Parliamentary Commissioner for Standards, reflected resentment at the shift from arrangements where MPs' claims were largely self-policed, lightly overseen by the Fees Office, to one that appeared bureaucratic, remote and inefficient. The obituaries of the first chief executive of IPSA, Andrew McDonald, recorded the 'unrelenting hostility' to the new body from some parliamentarians.[26] Of course, IPSA's role was always likely to be sensitive, given the way in which it impinged on MPs' working lives. The hostility also reflected the assumption that the fact of election protected MPs from regulation of their conduct by officials and gave them a degree of autonomy which would not be normal in any other profession.

The assumption that those who have been elected should enjoy a degree of freedom from regulatory control is an argument which has frequently resurfaced in debates about standards. In the controversies about second jobs for MPs, some MPs argued that it was up to constituents alone to decide whether they wished to elect an MP who had additional outside earnings. Thus, Sir Geoffrey Cox, who retained a very successful and remunerative legal practice alongside his parliamentary duties, argued on his website that it was up to the electors of his constituency of Torridge and West Devon whether or not they voted for someone 'who was a senior and distinguished professional in his field and still practiced that profession'.[27]

At a more general level, there is likely to be tension between the priorities of an elected government and the priorities of appointed regulatory and advisory bodies. This tension is likely to be especially acute when there is a change of government or when the political weather changes substantially. From the Thatcher period onwards, there was a marked change in political values and a deliberate celebration of an entrepreneurial style of government and market principles. This shift saw a questioning of the traditional culture of the civil service and a desire to

---

[26] See 'Andrew McDonald Obituary' *The Times* (10 November 2021); E Owen, 'Andrew McDonald Obituary' *The Guardian* (5 November 2021).

[27] See 'Statement from Sir Geoffrey Cox, 10 November 2021' www.geoffreycox.co.uk/news/statement-sir-geoffrey-cox.

make government more responsive to ministers and to absorb more of the values of the private sector. In the quest for modernisation of government, the public service ethos was implicitly undervalued and marginalised. The general dynamic was not reversed in the Blair/Brown years, which brought a new concern for the effective delivery of policy. The period since 2010 has seen a series of crises – the global financial crash, Brexit and the COVID pandemic – all of which have further reshaped attitudes to the public sector. The language of getting the government's goals done, of bypassing orthodox procedures to achieve desired outcomes and of the importance of flexible and speedy decision-making have all tended to make concern for procedural safeguards seem somewhat academic.

The government formed by Boris Johnson in 2019 was distinctive both for its radical objectives and for its espousal of a populist and anti-bureaucratic style. It was also distinctive for the extent to which Johnson personally claimed to have a mandate as a result of the 2019 electoral victory. Although Johnson's political authority had been severely weakened and he was forced to resign in 2022, during his time in office he seemed to believe that he had an unusually free rein in relation to constraints on governmental decision-making and on standards of conduct. As has been noted, a series of episodes occurred in which Johnson appeared to have been at the very least careless about the importance of providing ethical leadership and setting the moral tone for the administration. Johnson's approach to government was partly idiosyncratic. It was, however, supported in part by elements of the Conservative Party and press, which viewed efforts to impose procedural limits on elected politicians by advisory and regulatory bodies or by bureaucrats as undemocratic. Thus, some argued that the controversy surrounding 'Partygate' was trivial by comparison with the real issues that ought to dominate the political agenda. Others argued that in such matters as public appointments the government ought to have a free hand despite the procedures designed to ensure that such appointments are transparent and incorporate an independent element and concern for merit and competence. For example, Allister Heath, the editor of the *Sunday Telegraph*, made frequent attacks on the 'Blob' and argued that it had no right to see itself as a constitutional restraint on the executive. The elected government, he argued, should 'control all parts of the state (other than the judiciary) and have the right to appoint and control all quangos and agencies, as is the case in many countries'.[28] This quasi-populist elevation of an elected government over constitutional conventions and those who are in appointed positions has become a familiar argument in recent political discourse. Former Prime Minister Sir John Major, in his evidence to PACAC on the Greensill affair, attacked its implications, noting that while the ballot box gave a government power, it did not give it a licence to do anything it wanted.[29]

---

[28] A Heath, 'The Blob Is Taking Back Control and Destroying Boris Johnson's Premiership' *Sunday Telegraph* (24 November 2021).

[29] Public Administration and Constitutional Affairs Committee, *Propriety of Governance in Light of Greensill* (n 13) oral evidence from Sir John Major.

C. Weaponising the Standards Debate

It is perhaps inevitable that in an adversarial party system the issue of standards will be weaponised. Scandals affecting today's government will be seized upon by opposition parties, who will try to attach the label of sleaze or corruption to those in power. For its part, the government is likely to move onto the defensive in such circumstances, however weak its case. This dynamic limits the extent to which it is possible to move the arguments and analysis beyond the short-term zero-sum games of daily politics, much less develop any consensual basis for reform. It also impedes progress by highlighting the self-interest of the actors involved and by sharpening the polarisation of debate.

Two points should, however, be made about the current way in which standards issues and party competition intersect. The first is that, although party concerns have obviously shaped the prominence given to these issues on the political agenda, these debates have had the effect of keeping standards concerns before a wider public.

The second point to note is that, although party cohesion is generally very strong in Parliament, the recent handling of standards issues has revealed internal divisions inside the Conservative Party and a willingness to challenge the leadership on them, as the government's U-turn on the Paterson affair revealed. The inquiries of PACAC under Conservative William Wragg's chairmanship have probed a number of standards issues in a way which has often been critical of the government. And the anger over the Pincher affair which led to Johnson's decision to step down from the leadership of the Conservative Party and ultimately the premiership followed a torrent of resignations from Conservatives angered by the Prime Minister's conduct. The resignation showed that the political checks on a Prime Minister who has lost party and public confidence can still be very effective and that indeed they may operate more speedily than formal inquiries such as the Privileges Committee investigating whether Johnson had misled Parliament over 'Partygate'.

D. The Erosion of a Shared Culture

The turbulence in recent British political life has unsurprisingly seen a good deal of uncertainty about whether there remains any set of shared values or acknowledged rules of conduct among political elites. Peter Hennessy and Andrew Blick have pointed to the erosion of the 'good chaps' theory of government and argued that there is no longer a set of shared values and understandings which can be relied on to socialise politicians and civil servants into behaving with integrity in office public office or to guide them when ethical dilemmas arise. As Hennessy and Blick put it, the good chaps theory embodied the idea that the public could trust politicians to regulate themselves and that those who rose to high office would know and have internalised the unwritten rules of government, the rules which politicians and other office holders would want to adhere to even if doing so might frustrate their policy objectives, party political goals or personal ambitions. Indeed, the experience of the Johnson resignation could be interpreted in very different ways in relation to the continuing unwritten rules of government. It could be seen to show that inbuilt understandings and rules of conduct still operated and would operate to curb a politician who defied them. But the very fact that Johnson was himself so unwilling to accept that he had been in any sense blameworthy and the talk from some of his supporters of a comeback suggest that questions of ethical principle and personal integrity had been sidelined in these debates.

If the assumption that politicians have lost what they used to have – a kind of inbuilt moral compass – is true, that erosion makes reliance on self-regulation and informal and unwritten rules problematic. Such considerations suggest the need for stronger and more explicit rules governing behaviour in public life, as well as stronger safeguards for those who wish to raise objections to a policy on ethical grounds. There must thus be a renewed effort to keep integrity issues at the forefront of decision-makers' consciousness, whether through recruitment processes, training and induction processes or through dedicated opportunities to discuss ethical dilemmas and challenge conduct. Yet such emphasis on ethical awareness and challenge inevitably creates a possible tension between ministerial responsibility for policy decisions and objections from those constitutionally bound to carry out ministerial decisions.

IV. A Standards Overhaul? The 2021 Report

The 2021 Report 'Upholding Standards in Public Life' was thus delivered against a growing awareness of weaknesses in the standards system and the background of mounting concerns about the handling of integrity issues in the Johnson government.[30] The review itself explored the whole landscape of standards regulation and identified areas where it had become manifestly apparent that reforms were needed to strengthen the effectiveness of the institutional arrangements by giving them more enforcement powers and more independence.

A. The Ministerial Code and the Independent Adviser on Ministerial Interests

Ensuring high standards of conduct within the executive is inevitably a sensitive but essential issue for any government. Those who hold public office and serve in government, whether as ministers or civil servants, are expected to operate within the law, to adhere to the Nolan Principles and not to exploit their

---

[30] Committee on Standards in Public Life, 'Upholding Standards in Public Life' (n 18).

position for private gain. The rules governing ministerial conduct are set out in the Ministerial Code, a document which was originally called 'Questions of Procedure for Ministers'. It originated in the Second World War, but was made public in 1992. Although the Code remains the personal responsibility of the Prime Minister who issues it, the very act of making it public had an impact on its status, giving a benchmark for judging ministerial conduct and allowing debate about its application.

While it contains a variety of rules and procedural requirements relating to the work of government, Tony Blair's renaming of it in 1997 as the 'Ministerial Code' highlighted its role as a document prescribing ministerial standards in office. As a result, the status, interpretation and enforcement of the Code have become increasingly contentious. The Prime Minister's responsibility for the conduct of a government means that in the last resort it must be for the Prime Minister to decide whether any improper behaviour by a minister constitutes a breach of the Code and warrants dismissal. Here, of course, political judgment is inevitably crucial because a Prime Minister has to balance the need to maintain high standards of propriety in an administration with an assessment of the need of the political value of an individual minister.

Deciding whether an individual minister has breached the Code also involves a difficult process of fact-finding. Before the creation of the new post of Independent Adviser on Ministerial Interests in 2006, investigations into possible breaches of the Ministerial Code usually would be conducted by a senior civil servant, such the Cabinet Secretary. This process was problematic because the Cabinet Secretary might be thought to lack impartiality and might be reluctant to question the word of a minister – or, indeed, the Prime Minister – for fear of harming their relationship.

The post of Independent Adviser on Ministerial Interests was created to circumvent this problem. The job has two aspects. The first aspect is to scrutinise the interests of ministers to ensure that no conflict arises between their personal affairs and their public responsibilities. The second aspect of the job, which became highly controversial during Johnson's premiership, is to investigate alleged breaches of the ministerial code by ministers and to make recommendations to the Prime Minister. At the time of writing (mid-2022), it is for the Prime Minister alone to refer an alleged breach of the Code to the Independent Adviser. The Independent Adviser may not initiate an inquiry. Indeed, the Prime Minister may choose in some instances of alleged breach to continue with the older model of investigation by referring an investigation to someone other than the Independent Adviser, for example to the Cabinet Secretary or, as in the 'Partygate' investigation, to another individual such as Sue Gray, currently (mid-2022) the second Permanent Secretary at the Cabinet Office and formerly a Director General of the Cabinet's Propriety and Ethics division. It is also possible for the Independent Adviser to suggest an inquiry to the Prime Minister, but it can only be pursued with the Prime Minister's consent.

Despite a lack of clarity about powers, the role worked reasonably well under Blair, Brown, Cameron and May. However, under Boris Johnson an allegation that Priti Patel, as Home Secretary, had breached the Ministerial Code by bullying her civil servants exposed the need to strengthen the authority of the Independent Adviser in cases where his findings were opposed by the Prime Minister. In the Patel case, the Independent Adviser, then Sir Alex Allan, found evidence of bullying and reported that a breach of the Code had occurred. However, the Prime Minister refused to accept the findings and Patel continued in post without sanction. This outcome not only cast doubt on the effectiveness of the Independent Adviser's role, but also undermined faith in the efficacy of the Ministerial Code, not least among civil servants. Sir Alex Allan then resigned as Independent Adviser, to be replaced some months later by Lord Geidt. He, in turn, resigned in mid-2022 after a series of standards issue arose involving not just individual ministers, but the Prime Minister himself.

The double resignation of two successive Independent Advisers focused much attention on the office and prompted a range of suggestions for its reform. The CSPL 2021 Report (which was published before Lord Geidt's resignation) had recommended putting the office on a statutory basis; and it also recommended that the Independent Adviser should have the power to initiate investigations, a proposal which is echoed in Labour's proposals for reform.

The CSPL also recommended that there should be speedy publication of any report of an inquiry. Although the CSPL recommended that the Prime Minister should necessarily remain the final judge of what sanction to apply to a minister found to have breached the Code of Conduct, it proposed introducing a graduated range of sanctions so that a breach would not necessarily result in resignation.

The government's response to these resignations was largely negative and, although it accepted the idea of graduated sanctions, by rejecting the other recommendations for strengthening the Independent Adviser's role it ignored the extent to which these proposals were a package. With the resignation of Lord Geidt, other proposals surfaced. Although the CSPL called for a swift refilling of the role, the government itself raised the question of whether there should be not one Independent Adviser but a panel. Sir John Major, giving evidence before PACAC, advocated a reform of the system which would support the independence of the Independent Adviser with a small committee of three Privy Councillors.

B. The Business Appointment Rules: ACOBA and the Revolving Door

A series of contraventions of the rules governing the take-up of jobs after leaving public office had long shown the weaknesses of the system for managing movement between the public and the private sector.[31] Although all govern-ments want to encourage constructive movement between the two sectors, such transfers present a range of ethical risks in democratic systems. Specialist knowledge obtained in government may be used improperly in the private sector, former contacts may be exploited for lobbying purposes and anticipation of securing a job in the private sector may influence behaviour in the public sector. The system for preventing such abuses (the Business Appointment Rules, administered by the Advisory Committee on Business Appointments, ACOBA) has been increasingly judged as inadequate for the task. The Committee itself is a mixture of people drawn from the private and public sectors, and its status has no statutory foundation. It has its origins in the Advisory Committee on Civil Service Appointments, which was set up in 1975 but then applied only to civil servants. The name was changed to the Advisory Committee on Business Appointments in 1995 and for the first time its remit was extended to minis-ters. At the same time, its work was made more transparent. The major problem with the Committee's role, however, was that it remained an advisory commit-tee. Its findings were not directly applicable to individuals, but were advisory opinions delivered to departments; and there was no way of enforcing its recommendations.

Although it was generally argued to have a strong level of compliance, it was the cases of non-compliance which gained headlines. When the CSPL looked at the issue in its landscape review, it recommended major reforms. The 2021 CSPL Report urged putting the Advisory Committee on Business Appointments on a statutory basis and making it a regulatory body. It also recommended strength-ening its powers of enforcement, by incorporating compliance with the Business Appointment Rules into contracts. New sanctions were proposed which might include the recoupment of pension and severance pay in cases of serious breach. There was also a suggestion that non-compliance with the Rules might be taken into account when an individual was being considered for an honour of any sort. One other major problem with the operation of the Business Appointment Rules is that the system does not cover the whole range of civil servants but only the most senior ones (permanent secretaries and director general grades). Civil servants below those very senior grades have their applications for approval of transfer to the private sector handled by departments which appear to show a good deal of inconsistency in the restrictions they apply.

Although at the time of writing no concrete proposals from the CSPL have found acceptance from the government, it is clear that there is a good deal of support for reform, not least because Lord Pickles, the current chairman of ACOBA, is in favour of major change.

---

[31] For a discussion, see D Hine and G Peele, *The Regulation of Standards in British Public Life: Doing the Right Thing?* (Manchester, Manchester University Press, 2016) ch 9.

C. Lobbying

Despite efforts to enhance transparency around lobbying, there has long been dissatisfaction with the timeliness and comprehensibility of the information about lobbying. Sometimes the data released obscures as much as it reveals. The CSPL Report recommended that the Cabinet Office should become responsible for managing a centrally collated database and that it should impose minimum standards for describing the nature and purpose of all official meetings with outside interests.

D. Public Appointments

The Office of the Commissioner for Public Appointment was set up in 1995 as a result of the CSPL's first report. The purpose was to ensure that the process of making appointments to a range of public appointments (including arm's-length bodies and a variety of other advisory committees and quangos) balanced the responsibility of ministers for those decisions with the need to ensure that the process itself was transparent. It also had to ensure that it could produce a diversity of candidates with the competence and skills to do the job. It should be noted that there is, and always has been, an inherent tension between these two principles, a point which has been made very cogently by Sir Peter Riddell, who was Commissioner for Public Appointment between 2016 and 2021. It is not that these appointments are intended to be apolitical; rather, it is that from 1995 onwards there was an attempt to build safeguards into the system. The role of the Commissioner for Public Appointment was designed to ensure that the process worked openly and effectively to assess the various candidates, even though ultimately the final decision would be for the relevant government minister. Riddell has described this as a system of 'constrained patronage'. However, since 2016 many of the mechanisms of constraint have weakened and the balance between patronage and merit, which was always delicate, has shifted towards the government. Part of this shift was the product of the Grimstone Review of 2016, which greatly enhanced the role of ministers and reduced the Commissioner's role in the appointment process.[32] But part of it reflects the alleged use of tactics which constitute a threat to the spirit of the Nolan Principles, including stacking appointment panels, floating the names of preferred candidates in advance in a way which would necessarily deter competitors and, in some cases, making appointments without any formal competitive process. In addition, a range of new, unregulated appointments, such as tsars and non-executive directors, within the government's

---

[32] G Grimstone, 'Better Public Appointments: A Review of the Public Appointments Process' (London, Cabinet Office, March 2016).

gift have appeared. Public appointments are the subject of the chapter by John Bowers (chapter twelve) and will therefore not be dealt with in detail here except to outline the recommendations of the CSPL Report designed to meet the perceived threat to the integrity of the system as a result of government manipulation.

The CPLS Report recommended that the Code on Public Appointments should be amended so that a minister could not normally appoint someone deemed by a selection panel not to be of sufficient calibre to merit appointment. If a minster wished to persist and make such an appointment, the minister would be required to explain the decision and to appear before the relevant Select Committee to justify the appointment.

V. Conclusions

It is evident that the CSPL has hitherto been instrumental in building up the infra-structure of the standards machinery in the UK. In doing so, it has worked with the grain of British constitutional practice, recognising the need to complement, rather than compete with, parliamentary accountability and acknowledging the extent to which so much of its work depends upon conventional understandings and self-restraint. It has also benefited from the willingness of successive govern-ments to respond to its suggestions for reforms, and to accept them wherever possible. The integrity system which has emerged may not be the tidiest or most logical, but it continues for the most part to work, not least because it is able to devise pragmatic solutions which can command the support of those who have to implement them. However, the period since 2019 has seen a shift in the political environment and much greater pressure on the capacity of the existing arrange-ments to deter malfeasance and protect standards. Doubts about the continuing fitness for purpose of the existing standards regime has led to increasing demands (including from the CSPL itself) for reforms to strengthen the standards machin-ery by placing many of the regulatory bodies on a statutory basis, specifying more clearly their mode of operation and giving them effective enforcement powers.

The 2021 Report did not make any recommendations about the status of the CSPL itself. As noted earlier, it could be abolished by simple government decision. (There was a danger that this might have happened at the time of the triennial review of 2013, but in fact the CSPL survived, albeit with reduced resources.) Other bodies have, however, suggested strengthening the independence of the CSPL either by putting it on a statutory basis or by Order in Council.[33] It is not, of course, entirely clear how far putting a body on a statutory basis is a guarantee of protection against abolition, although it does give it additional independence and may enhance its status. A government determined to eliminate a standards body

---

[33] See, eg Hazell et al (n 17).

may always do so regardless of that body's statutory basis. Thus, the Standards Board for England, although a statutory body, was abolished by the Localism Act of 2011, which swept away the whole standards regime for local government in England and arguably left it with a number of deficiencies which have not as yet been remedied.[34]

Placing a regulatory body on a statutory basis also widens the possibility that its decisions may be subject to judicial review. However, the balance of opinion is firmly in favour putting some standards bodies on a statutory basis to signal their independence. Implementing any recommendations of the CSPL of course depends on the government accepting them and acting on them. Recently, the response of the government to CSPL reports has, as noted, tended to be slow and negative, even when there has been a demonstrated degree of support from stakeholders in the area under review (as with local government) or where, as with the 2021 Report 'Upholding Standards in Public Life', there has been a large degree of consensus behind the proposals.

The approach pioneered by the CSPL now stands at something of a crossroads. It is possible that much, if not all, of its 2021 Report will be accepted by a new Conservative leader anxious to reset the government's image on standards and to draw a line under the Johnson administration's record on integrity issues. Alternatively, it is possible that the recommendations may be sidelined because of the press of other business or because their impact is viewed as placing undesirable checks on governmental processes. If that should happen, the likelihood is that more radical solutions will gain traction, even though some of them would present greater difficulties of integration into existing constitutional assumptions. What is clear, however, is that standards issues are an area of constitutional significance, vital to the life and functioning of our democracy. Even if its views are not always coherent or consistent, the public cares about these issues and does not regard them as subordinate to the delivery of substantive economic and social policy objectives. All governments and all politicians are likely from time to time to encounter ethical dilemmas and perhaps to fall short of the demanding standards embodied in the Nolan Principles. The important point is that they should recognise this and move swiftly to remedy any such failures, and to reassert the centrality of high standards throughout public life. This involves not just keeping a watchful eye on standards issues in public life, but attempting to educate the public on their significance for democratic politics. The flexible and pragmatic character of the UK's standards regime still has the potential to meet the challenges of a changing environment, although its credibility now requires the reforms needed to strengthen its independence and enforcement powers discussed in this chapter. It remains to be seen how far and how quickly the government will move to repair this element of the UK's constitutional life.

---

[34] For a recent discussion, see Committee on Standards in Public Life, 'Ethical Standards in Public Life: Report' (January 2019).

PART III

Beyond Westminster and Whitehall

14

Devolving and Not Forgetting

SIR VERNON BOGDANOR

I. Introduction

Devolution is the transfer of powers from Parliament and government to directly elected sub-national bodies over such public services as education, health and transport, while reserving matters such as foreign affairs, defence and macro-economic policy, essential to the integrity of the UK, to Westminster.

With devolution, by contrast with federalism, Westminster retains full power to legislate for a devolved body. Section 28 of the Scotland Act of 1998 providing for a Scottish Parliament declares that it 'may make laws, to be known as Acts of the Scottish Parliament'. It is immediately followed by section 29 declaring that this 'does not affect the power of the Parliament of the United Kingdom to make laws for Scotland'. It is for the courts and, in the last resort, the Supreme Court to determine whether legislation of the devolved bodies lies within their competence.

Devolution was first proposed for Ireland by Gladstone in 1886, when it was called Home Rule. There were to be four Irish Home Rule Bills, none of which were successful. The first, in 1886, was defeated in the House of Commons, the second, in 1893, was defeated in the House of Lords. The third reached the statute book in 1914, but was suspended owing to the outbreak of war. A fourth Bill also reached the statute book, in 1920. This provided for not one but two Home Rule Parliaments, one for the six counties of Ulster, the other for the remaining 26 counties in Ireland. But the 26 counties rejected it, Irish nationalists demanding full independence. This was achieved in 1921, following a guerrilla war. Ironically, Home Rule was to operate only in the six counties of Northern Ireland, which had not wanted it. The six counties preferred to remain under rule from Westminster but accepted devolution as, in the words of the first Prime Minister of Northern Ireland, Sir James Craig, a 'final settlement and supreme sacrifice in the interests of peace although not asked for by her representatives'.[1] The Northern Ireland

---

[1] 'Correspondence between Her Majesty's Government and the Prime Minister of Northern Ireland', letter from Sir James Craig to Lloyd George, 11 November 1921, 5.

Parliament was, for most of its existence, from 1921 to 1972, elected by the first-past-the-post electoral system, and it was alleged that there was widespread discrimination by the Unionist, primarily Protestant, majority, especially in housing, against the Nationalist, primarily Catholic, minority, particularly in that part of the province west of the River Bann. Catholic resentment led in the late 1960s to a civil rights movement and IRA terrorism. In consequence, the Northern Ireland Parliament was prorogued, in effect abolished, in 1972. It was in part to avoid such majority domination, and in part to contain the SNP in Scotland, that the devolved bodies created at the end of the twentieth century were all to be elected by proportional representation.

This historical excursus is of importance in understanding the motives for devolution in 1997. Faced with nationalist pressures in Scotland, the Blair government was determined to avoid what it saw as the mistakes of previous UK governments towards Ireland since it seemed that the refusal of Home Rule had fuelled separatism. Devolution, it was hoped, would prevent Scotland following the same course. In 1995, Labour's Shadow Secretary of State, George Robertson, predicted that it would 'kill nationalism stone dead'.[2] The 1997 Labour Party manifesto declared that with devolution, 'The Union will be strengthened and the threat of separatism removed'. Critics of devolution, however, feared that it would put Scotland on the slippery slope to independence, while the SNP supported it precisely because it believed that it would prove a path to separation.

A further motive for devolution was to fill what has been called a 'legitimacy deficit' in Scottish and Welsh politics.[3] Until 1970, the Secretary of State for Scotland had always belonged to a party which had a majority in Scotland as well as at Westminster. But, since 1970, the Conservatives have been in a minority in Scotland, which meant that under Conservative rule, Scotland was governed by legislation opposed by those representing the majority. The legitimacy deficit was highlighted in 1989 by the introduction of the unpopular community charge, the so-called poll tax, in Scotland before its introduction in England and Wales. Scotland was in the anomalous condition of having a separate judicial system, a separate executive in the form of the Scottish Office headed by a Secretary of State, but no separate legislature to hold that executive to account. Devolution, therefore, was enacted for Scotland in 1998, following a referendum which showed a three to one majority in favour of it.

In Wales, nationalism has always been weaker than in Scotland. That is primarily because, whereas in Scotland nationalism is an integrative factor – almost all Scots, whether they support the SNP or not, take pride in their nationality – in Wales nationalism is divisive. It has been based primarily upon language. But only around 20 per cent of the Welsh population speaks the Welsh language. Support

---

[2] Quoted, eg in G Baldini, 'Devolution and Scottish Politics Ten Years On' (2013) 48 *Government and Opposition* 127, 128.

[3] A Paun and S Macrory (eds), *Has Devolution Worked: The First 20 Years* (London, Institute of Government 1998).

for the Welsh nationalist party, Plaid Cymru, has always been strongest in the Welsh-speaking areas of North West Wales. Elsewhere there have been fears that separatism or even autonomy would disadvantage English speakers.

But Wales, like Scotland, suffered from a legitimacy deficit, the Conservatives not having won a majority of the vote there since 1859. A separate Welsh executive was set up in 1964, but since then whenever there has been a Conservative government at Westminster, the Secretary of State has represented only a minority in Wales. The Blair government took the view that it could hardly refuse devolution to Wales once it had been offered to Scotland. In Wales, the referendum was held one week after the referendum in Scotland, and the outcome was a wafer-thin majority for devolution by 50.3 per cent to 49.7 per cent. Since the referendum, however, Welsh identity appears to have been strengthened. The Senedd has no doubt played a large part in strengthening identity and is now firmly established as part of the Welsh political landscape. Its powers, originally confined to secondary legislation, were extended into primary legislation following a referendum in 2011, and in 2017 the settlement was transformed from a conferred powers model into a reserved powers model, as with Scotland. The reserved powers model is generally believed to be more favourable to the devolved body than the conferred powers model.

Northern Ireland has been called by one authority 'the embarrassing relative kept in the UK's constitutional attic'.[4] Unlike Scotland and Wales, it is not a nation, but a province contested by two nations, the British and the Irish. The primary motivation for devolution in Northern Ireland was quite different from the motivation in Scotland and Wales. It was designed primarily to ensure a role in government for the minority nationalist community, and it was just one part of a wider settlement embodied in the Belfast or Good Friday Agreement of 1998. By contrast with Scotland and Wales, devolution in Northern Ireland required power-sharing between representatives of the two communities. The largest party – currently Sinn Fein – is required to enter into coalition with the second largest party – currently the Democratic Unionist Party – and important or controversial legislation requires the consent of representatives of both communities. It is as if at Westminster, whatever the result of the election, the Prime Minister were to be required to enter into coalition with the Leader of the Opposition.

In 1999, Ron Davies, a former Secretary of State for Wales and seen by some as an architect of devolution in Wales, declared that it was 'a process not an event'.[5] The powers of the devolved bodies have expanded considerably since 1998, and Scotland and Wales now enjoy the power in effect to vary Scottish and Welsh income tax rates. Indeed, they enjoy more fiscal powers than provinces in many federal states, including Switzerland, often thought of as the most decentralised

---

[4] J Mitchell, 'Has Devolution Strengthened the UK Constitution' in Paun and Macrory (n 3) 148.
[5] Quoted in *Irish Times* (20 February 1999).

country in the world. But, of course, the more powers that are devolved, the smaller the role of Scottish and Welsh MPs at Westminster, something that would please the separatists.

England, the largest part of the UK, has no devolved body, and is, according to one writer, 'the last stateless nation in the United Kingdom'.[6] This means that the Westminster Parliament is also in effect a Parliament for England, and the government of the UK is also in effect the government of England. Ministers for matters devolved to the non-English parts of the UK, such as education and health, are in effect ministers for education and health in England only. So, when Boris Johnson announced policies to combat COVID, he was announcing policies to combat COVID *in England*. Other parts of the UK had the freedom to propose quite different policies (and did).

Some have proposed the establishment of an English Parliament to secure symmetry. Critics have, however, retorted that this would unbalance the country and that in no system in the world does one of the devolved bodies represent 85 per cent of the population. An English Parliament, moreover, would mean that Westminster would become little more than a debating chamber on macro-economic policy, defence and foreign policy.

Others have proposed, alternatively, devolution to English regions, combined perhaps with a reformed second chamber comprising representatives of Britain's nations and regions. But no one has proposed *legislative* devolution to the English regions, which would mean different laws in Newcastle from those in Bristol. What is proposed is devolution of executive powers, currently held by ministers, to regions.

Critics retort that regions in England are artificial and ghostly constructs. Those living in Bath or Canterbury do not believe that they inhabit a 'region'. In a referendum in 2004 in the North East, thought to be the region most sympathetic to devolution, it was rejected by a four to one majority.

For the foreseeable future, therefore, it appears that devolution will remain asymmetrical. The English have never insisted on the integration of the non-English parts of the kingdom, but they have always rejected federalism – though perfectly prepared to advocate it for ex-colonies!

Survey evidence, however, has shown that devolution to the non-English parts of the kingdom has strengthened the sense of Englishness. Many in England, so it is alleged, feel excluded because of the lack of effective representation. It has been alleged that English nationalism was a contributory factor in the Brexit verdict of 2016. Therefore, so it is argued, there is a need for devolution in England, even if not legislative devolution, so as to combat the resentment felt at the greater influence exerted by the non-English parts of the UK following the creation of the devolved bodies.

---

[6] R Weight, *Patriots: National Identities in Britain, 1940–2000* (London, Macmillan 2002) 726.

Devolution in England has taken the form of combined local authorities with directly elected metro mayors, of which there are currently 10, under the 2014 Cities and Local Government Devolution Act. But a 2022 White Paper[7] proposes that devolution be extended to any area in England that seeks it. Combined authorities will not be necessary. Instead, devolution is to be based on the top tier of local government, ie county or unitary authorities. Nor will a directly elected mayor be necessary, although local authorities which choose a mayoral regime will enjoy greater powers than those which do not.

Currently, 40 per cent of the inhabitants of England live under mayoral regimes. The metro mayors enjoy powers previously held by ministers, and the legislation has led to the emergence of strong, visible local leaders such as Andy Burnham in Greater Manchester and Andy Street in the West Midlands. In Greater Manchester there is an experiment in integrating health and social care which, if successful, may be adopted in other areas. Devolution in England was emphasised by Boris Johnson as part of his levelling up agenda; and since devolution to the combined authorities and mayors is non-legislative, it does not raise the awkward questions of sovereignty that are raised by devolution to the non-English parts of the UK.

The introduction of metro mayors could alter the constitutional balance between central and local government. One of the reasons why local government has traditionally been little valued in Britain and was unable to resist centralisation is that there has been a sharp separation between local and national political roles, with the local role being seen as distinctly subordinate. The metro mayors may well alter that perception.

Before establishment of the London mayoralty in 2000, only three politicians had been able to build national careers upon their record in local government – Joseph Chamberlain, Radical mayor of Birmingham between 1873 and 1876; Herbert Morrison, first Labour leader of the London County Council between 1934 and 1940; and Ken Livingstone, Labour leader of the Greater London Council from 1981 until its abolition in 1986. But these were very much exceptions to the general rule that central and local politics remained in separate spheres, with local government being strictly subordinate. Indeed, when Herbert Morrison stood for the Labour leadership in 1935, his critics argued that he was a local rather than a national political figure, and that is one of the reasons why he was defeated by Clement Attlee. Morrison's leadership role in local government was seen as a handicap, not an advantage.

The sharp separation between central and local politics in Britain contrasts sharply with politics on the Continent and in the USA, where success at local or provincial level allows politicians to gain executive experience and provides a springboard for national political leadership. In the USA, presidents such as

---

[7] Department for Levelling Up, Housing and Communities, *Levelling Up the United Kingdom* (White Paper, CP 604, 2022) para 3.5.1.

Franklin Roosevelt, Jimmy Carter, Bill Clinton and George W Bush were state governors before reaching the White House. In Germany, every Chancellor between Kurt Kiesinger in 1966 and Olaf Scholz in 2021, except for Helmut Schmidt and Angela Merkel, had been the leader of a provincial government. In France, Jacques Chirac was mayor of Paris before reaching the Élysée, while Nicolas Sarkozy had been President of the General Council of Hauts de Seine in Paris before becoming President of France. In Britain, by contrast, of recent Prime Ministers before Boris Johnson, only John Major and Theresa May had executive experience, as chair respectively of a local housing committee and a local education authority, although Andy Burnham, mayor of Greater Manchester, is currently seen as a possible future candidate for the Labour leadership.

The metro mayors, therefore, could transform the relationship between central and local government by showing that a major contribution to British politics can be made from a local base, so providing an alternative route for political leaders and making territorial leadership a springboard for political power at national level.

II. Devolution and Legitimacy

Devolution had a further rationale in addition to containing nationalism and filling the legitimacy deficit. It was to bring government closer to the people and stimulate healthy competition between sub-national units. Each unit would, so it was argued, seek to perform better than the others and claim that it was achieving wonders even with limited resources. Devolution, then, would enable local patriotism to be used as a lever to improve public services. A nationally organised public service, by contrast, institutionalises grumbling, since, if ever such a service, for example the NHS, claims to be doing well, the government has an excuse for diverting resources elsewhere. An organisation which can never be seen to be successful but must always be in the position of pointing out its deficiencies so that it is awarded extra funds is hardly likely to stimulate pride in performance. So running public services locally, it is argued, is better for the morale of those working in them than running them from the centre.

Devolution might also, so it was suggested, encourage innovation. For innovations to be successful, there needs to be honest feedback on progress. Centralised decision-making and the uniform application of best practice are less likely to achieve this than experimentation by sub-national bodies, which can identify failure before it is replicated on a national scale. Devolution, therefore, is a form of pluralism which, as well as providing for necessary checks on government, could also lead to more effective government. If knowledge derives, as Karl Popper believed, from a process of trial and error, then devolution would help ensure that such a process actually takes place. By contrast, centralised government prevents crucial lessons from being learnt. It has been suggested, for example, that the movement towards comprehensive education in the 1960s was not 'inherently foolish', but that what was wrong

> was the scale of the experiment and the absence of honest feedback on progress. – The widening gap between the self-congratulation of the educational establishment and the everyday experience of parents propelled educational reform to the top of Britain's political agenda – the common-sense belief that central co-ordination and direction are bound to improve performance remains ingrained despite the contrary evidence derived from the failure of planning in both government and business organizations around the globe. In an uncertain, changing world, most decisions are wrong, and success comes not from the inspired visions of exceptional leaders, or prescience achieved through sophisticated analysis, but through small-scale experimentation that rapidly imitates success and acknowledges failure.

So, for public services, devolution offers an excellent institutional framework within which such 'small-scale experimentation' can take place.[8] Further, it has been suggested that many

> central government changes of a substantive or innovative kind, such as the introduction of new standards or methods of service provision, are – most frequently generalisations of existing local government practice or responses to demands produced by local authorities' practical experience, rather than ideas originating with government departments.[9]

How well has devolution lived up to the hopes of its supporters? It has certainly led to some improvements in democratic representation and legitimacy. Survey evidence indicates that the Scottish Parliament and the Welsh Senedd attract more trust than either Westminster or local government, showing that trust is not merely a matter of proximity, but is dependent on whether the institutions of government reflect a genuine sense of identity.[10] There has been greater percentage representation of women in the Scottish Parliament than at Westminster. The 2014 Scottish Cabinet contained equal numbers of men and women, while in 2015 three of the four leaders of the major parties – Nicola Sturgeon, Kezia Dugdale and Ruth Davidson – were female and the last two were members of the LGBT community. And devolution has ended the legitimacy deficit. It has therefore improved the quality of democracy in Scotland and Wales.

The evidence for improvements in public policy is far more limited. There have been a few significant changes. Scotland and Wales have lowered the voting age for elections other than Westminster elections from 18 to 16. Scotland has introduced the single transferable vote system of voting for local elections, while, under the Local Government and Elections (Wales) Act of 2021, Welsh local authorities can, if they wish, also adopt that system.

---

[8] J Kay, 'The Centralised Road to Mediocrity', *Financial Times* (27 February 2006).

[9] P Dunleavy, *Urban Political Analysis: The Politics of Collective Consumption* (London, Macmillan, 1980) 105.

[10] B Page, 'Has Devolution Enhanced Public Trust in the Political System?' in Paun and Macrory (n 3) 109–21.

Scotland has introduced free residential care and a ban on smoking in public places, and has abolished university tuition fees for Scottish students in Scottish universities. All three devolved bodies have abolished prescription charges. And there have been a small number of innovations which have been taken up in the rest of the UK, such as from Wales a charge on plastic bags and an opt-out system for organ donation.

Scotland and Wales decided not to adopt the New Labour reforms of the Blair government in the public services providing for private involvement in health-care and education. They remain strongholds of Old Labour. There is evidence that, in consequence, standards in education and health have not improved to the same extent as in England. This has, ironically, left a policy space in Scotland for the Conservatives, who have proposed New Labour policies. This may help account for the recent improved electoral performance of the Conservatives in Scotland.

But, of course, the main purpose of devolution was to kill nationalism stone dead. In Scotland, it has certainly not done so. Since 2007, the SNP has been the largest party in the Scottish Parliament, and, despite proportional representation, was able to win an overall majority in the 2011 Holyrood election. In consequence, Prime Minister David Cameron felt impelled to offer an independence referendum. This was duly held in 2014, and independence was defeated by 55 per cent to 45 per cent. But Brexit, which Scotland voted against, has led to pressure for a second referendum, which UK governments have so far been able to resist. But the question of a further referendum may arise again should the next general election result in a hung Parliament in which the Labour Party is dependent on the SNP for a majority at Westminster.

It is, of course, impossible to know what would have happened in Scotland had devolution been rejected. Arguably it has provided a forum for the SNP, which would have been weaker without the chance of exercising power in Edinburgh. But it is equally arguable that Scots, faced with a stark choice between the unitary state and independence, with no middle way, would have opted for independence. So, on the fundamental issue of whether devolution has succeeded in containing separatism in Scotland or whether it has encouraged it, the jury remains out.

On 17 November 2020, Prime Minister Boris Johnson was accused of having told a virtual meeting of Conservative MPs that devolution had been a 'disaster', and that it had been 'Blair's biggest mistake', remarks which he has denied. But, whether he made these remarks or not, there is hardly any support in Scotland or Wales for the devolution legislation to be repealed. From that point of view, it must be counted a success.

In Northern Ireland, the main purpose of devolution was, as we have seen, to bring the two communities together. That has not been achieved. But at least there has been a considerable decline in violence. During the period of the Troubles, between 1968 and the Belfast or Good Friday Agreement of 1998, there were around 3500 deaths. Since the Agreement and the establishment of devolution, the figure has been around 160. So, if Northern Ireland is not yet 'post-sectarian', it is 'largely post-conflict'.[11] But there has been little improvement in trust towards Northern Ireland's separate institutions, partly, no doubt, because of the long suspensions of the Assembly following inter-communal disputes. Indeed, since 1998, the Assembly has been suspended for a total of over seven years. In consequence, devolution in Northern Ireland 'has been neither a process nor an event – here devolution had been a vehicle and not a destination, but the vehicle has broken down again'.[12] Nevertheless, survey evidence indicates that devolution is still the most preferred constitutional option for Northern Ireland as compared to alternatives such as direct rule, integration or reunification.

III. Devolution and Brexit

Until Brexit, there was comparatively little conflict between UK governments and the devolved bodies. But Brexit has reignited conflict, primarily in Scotland and Northern Ireland, both of which voted against it. Scottish and Irish nationalists argue that they have been extruded from the EU against their wishes. The SNP favours an independent Scotland in the EU. But Brexit makes the cause of Scottish independence more difficult to argue for, not easier. For, with the rest of the UK outside the customs union and internal market of the European Union, Scotland would find herself excluded from the UK's internal market and she would be confronted by a hard border with England, by far her largest market.

Irish nationalists claim that Brexit makes it more difficult to achieve their aspirations within Northern Ireland and so strengthens the case for reunification with an Ireland, which of course remains in the EU. Northern Ireland is in a different position from Scotland in this regard. Indeed, it is unique in the UK, as it is the only part of it that could rejoin the European Union without needing to renegotiate entry. For, after reunification, Northern Ireland would be in the position of becoming part of an existing Member State of the European Union, as with East Germany after the fall of Communism when it joined with West Germany as part of the European Union. After the Brexit referendum, one commentator suggested that the prospect of a united Ireland was not only credible but inevitable[13] – a gross overstatement, of course, for by no means all of the 56 per cent who voted Remain were also supporters of Irish unity. It is in particular highly unlikely that the 34 per cent of self-designated Unionists who voted Remain were also voting to join with Ireland.

---

[11] C Gormley-Heenan, 'Has Devolution Brought Peace, Stability and Good Governance to Northern Ireland?' in Paun and Macrory (n 3) 55.

[12] ibid 56.

[13] S Fenton, 'For the First Time in My Life, the Prospect of a United Ireland is Not Only Credible but Inevitable' *The Independent* (27 March 2017).

In Scotland and Wales, Brexit has led to a constitutional dispute concerning powers repatriated from the European Union. Repatriated powers include areas such as agriculture, fisheries and environmental protection. These powers had been transferred to Scotland and Wales in the devolution legislation, but devolution in these areas was largely illusory since policy was made primarily by the European Union, which ensured the preservation of an internal market in Britain. While Britain remained a member of the European Union, her own internal market was upheld by the EU's internal market rules. In the words of the European Union Select Committee of the House of Lords, the European Union was, 'in effect, part of the glue holding the United Kingdom together since 1997'.[14] But that glue is now becoming unstuck. The government therefore has to face the problem of how the UK's internal market can be ensured after Brexit when neither Westminster nor the devolved bodies are collectively bound by EU law. If all EU functions in the devolved areas were transferred to the devolved bodies, that, in the government's view, would threaten the internal market of the UK. It would, for example, make little sense to have four entirely different systems of agricultural protection in the four parts of the UK. To preserve the internal market in goods and services within the UK, there must be common minimum trading standards as well as limits on the degree of variation of state aid, business support, environmental requirements and agricultural subsidies. Further, any country involved in trade negotiations will wish to be assured that it can gain trade access to the whole of the UK, not just England; and agriculture is bound to play an important part in such negotiations.

The government accordingly began to negotiate on common frameworks with the devolved bodies. However, it came to the conclusion that in a small number of areas – 18 out of 154, most of which were the responsibility of the Department of the Environment, Food and Rural Affairs – legislation was needed even if the devolved bodies did not agree to it. An Internal Market Bill was therefore introduced and duly passed by Parliament in 2020. In consequence of this legislation, not all of the powers being repatriated from the EU within the devolved areas will be repatriated to the devolved bodies. The Scottish and Welsh devolved bodies did not consent to the Bill and argued that it breached the Sewel Convention that Westminster would not normally legislate on matters affecting the devolved bodies without their consent. The European Union Withdrawal Act had also been passed without the consent of the devolved bodies in Scotland and Wales. The Scottish and Welsh governments regarded the Internal Market Act as an assault on devolution. But it could be argued that, had Britain never joined the EU, Parliament would have reserved the powers which, under the Act, it retains, so that not every function relating to, for example, agriculture and fisheries or state aid would have been devolved. Even so, the Internal Market Act could have implications for future policies within devolved areas. If, for example, the Scottish Parliament were to

---

[14] European Union Select Committee of the House of Lords, *Brexit: Devolution* (2017–18, HL 9) 12.

decide to reduce the sugar content in food and drink, such a policy could not apply to food and drink imported from the rest of the UK, so limiting the value of the Scottish legislation. The minimum pricing of alcohol, a policy of the Scottish Parliament, will, however, be unaffected since the Act does not apply to legislation already in existence.

The devolved bodies have not ruled out legal action, but in the first *Miller* case in 2017, the Supreme Court had unanimously ruled that the Sewel Convention was not justiciable, even though it had been put into statute in section 2 of the Scotland Act 2016 and section 2 of the Wales Act of 2017.[15] In 2018, the Supreme Court ruled that, under the European Union Withdrawal Act, Westminster could amend the terms of the Scotland Act of 1998 without the consent of the Scottish Parliament and that the Scottish Parliament lacked the power to incorporate directly applicable devolved EU law into domestic Scots law and the power to ensure that Scotland's laws kept pace with developments in EU law where this conflicted with Westminster legislation.[16] In April 2021, the Welsh government was refused leave for a judicial review of the Internal Market Act on the grounds that the claim was premature in the absence of specific circumstances. But the Welsh government has been given leave to appeal against this decision.

The Senedd has taken a less confrontational view than the Scottish Parliament. By contrast with Holyrood, Cardiff Bay is dominated by the Labour Party, a strongly Unionist party. The Welsh government has sought to protect Welsh interests by transforming the devolution settlement into a quasi-federal relationship. It wants the Joint Ministerial Committee, established at the time of devolution, to coordinate relationships between the devolved bodies and the UK government, to be transformed into an annual Heads of Government Summit and then into a Council of Ministers. This Council should, so it believes, require the UK government to secure the agreement of at least one devolved body before legislation affecting the devolved bodies is passed. This would mean that the devolved bodies acting together could veto the UK government and so the Welsh government's proposal would not be compatible with the sovereignty of Parliament. And, just as in Belgium the Walloon sub-national government was able to hold up the EU's trade agreement with Canada, it could prevent the UK government from signing a trade agreement with another country because the three devolved bodies, representing 16 per cent of the population of the UK, were opposed to it.

In Northern Ireland, the Northern Ireland Protocol, part of the EU Withdrawal Agreement, has imposed great strains on the devolution settlement. The Protocol provides that Northern Ireland, unlike the rest of the UK, remains in the EU's internal market; and although, like the rest of the UK, Northern Ireland has left the

---

[15] *R(Miller) v Secretary of State for Exiting the European Union* [2017] UKSC 5, paras 146, 148–49, 150, 151.

[16] *The UK Withdrawal from the European Union (Legal Continuity) (Scotland) Bill – a Reference by the Attorney General and the Advocate General for Scotland* [2018] UKSC 64.

EU's customs union, it is nevertheless required to conform to EU customs rules. That means there must be a customs border for goods moving between Great Britain and Northern Ireland, and it imposes new restrictions on the Northern Ireland Assembly. The Northern Ireland Assembly is required to continue to apply EU regulations, and to incorporate into its laws future EU regulations, which will not apply to the rest of the UK; while if and when the rest of the UK decides to diverge from EU rules, Northern Ireland will be left behind. Nationalists claimed that the Protocol was essential to protect the Belfast or Good Friday Agreement by preserving a soft border between Northern Ireland and the Republic. But Unionists argue that it contradicts the Agreement since it alters the constitutional position of Northern Ireland without the consent of the majority. At the time of writing, Unionist are threatening that if the Protocol is not radically revised, they will cease to participate in the Northern Ireland Executive, so causing yet another suspension of the Assembly.

IV. Devolving and (Not) Forgetting

The implementation of devolution has revealed two interrelated flaws in the original settlement. The first is that it has encouraged Westminster to forget about Scotland, Wales and Northern Ireland.

The policy of 'devolve and forget' had disastrous consequences in Northern Ireland after the 1920s. For, although Westminster retained its supremacy, by convention it did not legislate in devolved areas, and in 1923 the Speaker ruled that parliamentary questions could not be asked over matters transferred to Northern Ireland, since no government minister was responsible for them. This stultified discussion of alleged injustices in the province. In 1965, when a backbencher sought to raise the issue of the property vote in local government elections in Northern Ireland, which allegedly discriminated against Catholics, the Deputy Speaker ruled him out of order. In July 1964, the Home Secretary, Henry Brooke, ruled that alleged religious discrimination in Northern Ireland could not be debated at Westminster. In 1965, the Deputy Speaker ruled that 'discrimination in housing in Northern Ireland is not a matter for the United Kingdom Government; it is a matter for the Northern Ireland Government'.[17] One MP declared that, in consequence, it proved impossible to penetrate 'the blank wall of incomprehension and ignorance about Ulster'.[18] MPs were more aware of conditions in Brussels or Berlin than conditions in Belfast. During the years of devolved government, Westminster devoted on average two hours a year to Northern Ireland, and not until 1969 did Westminster legislate on transferred matters, against the wishes

---

[17] HC Deb 26 October 1965, vol 718, cols 45–46.
[18] P Rose, *Backbencher's Dilemma* (London, Frederick Muller, 1981) 179.

of the Northern Ireland government.[19] In 1968, Catholic grievances erupted into a civil rights movement, elements of which turned to violence, so inaugurating the troubles.

There is, of course, no similar danger of discrimination or terrorism in the case of Scotland or Wales. Nevertheless, what happens there must remain of concern to the whole of the UK. For devolution, as well as meeting the desire for self-government in the non-English parts of the UK, is intended also to sustain the integrity of the UK. Even in federal states such as the USA, the federal government cannot abdicate from responsibility for what happens in the states. Modern federalism is generally, to adopt the terminology of William Riker, centripetal rather than centrifugal, so federal governments are held responsible for national standards.[20] In the USA, the federal government has a number of strategies to influence the states, in particular its superior fiscal capacity. It has, for example, made funding for highways in the states conditional on adopting a 21-year-old drinking age.[21]

Similar issues arise in the British context. It has been alleged, for example, that skills are weaker in Scotland than in England. In 2019, according to the Programme for International Student Assessment, Scottish pupils scored the lowest levels in maths and science since they had first taken part in the survey nearly 20 years ago. Scottish pupils were trailing their peers in England in reading, maths and science. Further, to pay for free university tuition, the SNP government has cut around 120,000 places in further education. If that has resulted in a skills shortage in Scotland, that is a matter of concern to the whole of the UK, not just Scotland. Inadequate skills are a problem for the UK as a whole. Sections 50 and 51 of the Internal Market Act confirm that the UK government can spend directly in devolved areas to promote economic development, to provide infrastructure and to support education and training. The Act, therefore, is an important stage in showing that devolution is of significance for the UK as a whole and that the policy of devolving and forgetting in Northern Ireland will not be repeated in Scotland.

The second flaw with devolution is that it has been ad hoc and unplanned, a response to political pressures rather than based on principle. That flaw is exemplified in some of the hopes being placed in the Johnson government's levelling up agenda, a central part of its programme.

In his first major speech as Prime Minister at Manchester on 15 July 2019, Boris Johnson explicitly linked devolution with the levelling up agenda. He declared that the Brexit vote was not just against Brussels, but against 'all concentrations of power in remote centres', and that there was a demand for greater self-government

---

[19] C Coulter, 'Direct Rule and the Ulster Middle Classes' in R English and GS Walker, *Unionism in Modern Ireland* (London, Macmillan, 1996) 169–70.

[20] W Riker, *Federalism: Origins, Operation, Significance* (Boston, MA, Little Brown & Co, 1964).

[21] I owe this point to Richard Johnson.

in towns and cities. 'I do not believe,' he declared, 'that when the people of the United Kingdom voted to take back control, they did so in order for that control to be hoarded in Westminster.' Andy Burnham, mayor of Greater Manchester, echoed the Prime Minister when he told the *Financial Times* on 5 May 2021 that 'If the government is going to level up, you can't do it from an office in Whitehall'. Many would agree that levelling up requires much more devolution and decentralisation.

But there is a fundamental tension between devolution and the principle of territorial equity, which entails fairness between those living in different parts of the country so that benefits and burdens depend upon need and ability to pay rather than upon where one lives. That principle lay at the basis of the welfare state as implemented by the Attlee government after 1945. Aneurin Bevan, when he established the National Health Service, pointedly declined to devolve powers to Scotland or Wales, even though he himself was Welsh and represented a Welsh constituency. Health needs depended not upon where one lived, but upon the nature and degree of one's illness. Central control has not, of course, succeeded in achieving equality between regions, and there remain, for example, widely different standards of healthcare in different parts of the country. But whether devolution helps to remove or perpetuate these inequalities depends upon the political clout and leverage of local leaders. It is only accidental if their leverage equates with the degree of deprivation in their region. This means that only central government can determine what is the right balance between different parts of the country. But genuine devolution means, as has been seen in Scotland and Wales, at the very least a considerable diminution in Westminster's responsibility for transferred public services. It means that, when problems arise, voters must cease to complain to 'the government' and ask 'the government' to put it right. In the past, it was not just wicked politicians who encouraged centralisation, but we, the people, who insisted on blaming the central government for matters that were not within their remit.

The traditional argument of the Right against devolution, used in the past by many Conservatives, was that devolution, by undermining the sovereignty of Parliament, would threaten the unity of the kingdom. The traditional argument of the Left, used by Bevan, was that devolution would deprive Westminster not so much of sovereignty as of power, the power to correct territorial disparities.

Of course, few object to a devolved body supplementing basic provision with, for example, free long-term residential care for the elderly in Scotland or freedom from prescription charges in the devolved areas. But what are the limits to devolution in national services such as health and education? How much freedom should a devolved body enjoy to depart from national policies in transferred matters? Health is one of the devolved functions. Should that mean that a devolved body, if it so wished, should be able to charge for a visit to a doctor? On 25 November 2015, Lord Porter, the Conservative chairman of the Local Government Association, warned that devolution of healthcare could mean an end to national standards, in which case 'it won't be a national service. It will be a range of local services.'[22]

The principle of territorial equity, therefore, is bound to constrain the extent of devolution. But, if we are to preserve that principle, we need a clear statement of what functions are so fundamental to the welfare state, so much a part of the social union, that they are unsuitable for devolution. For unionism has a social and an economic dimension, as well as a constitutional one. If devolution is to be compatible with fairness to all of the citizens of the UK, we must be clear about those basic social and economic rights which all citizens of the UK, wherever they live, are entitled to enjoy. Ideally, a basic statement of those rights should be embodied in a constitution defining those powers that need to remain at the centre as embodying the fundamental social and economic as well as the constitutional and political rights of the citizen. But, short of that, a charter should be enacted laying down the basic principles which should govern the territorial division of powers between central government and the devolved bodies. Until now, devolution has consisted primarily of responding to pressures from the devolved bodies for further powers. It has been ad hoc and unplanned. But if the UK is to survive, devolution has to be understood in terms of the needs of the country as a whole, not just its component parts.

In May 2015, a report from the Bingham Centre titled 'A Constitutional Crossroads' advocated in its foreword 'a written constitution' that 'would most directly provide the advantage of clear ground-rules to serve as a framework for our territorial arrangements and to secure their permanence.'[23] But a constitution, a very distant project, should be preceded by a 'Charter of Union which would lay down the underlying principles of the UK's territorial constitution and of devolution within it'. The Charter would help to provide guidelines, a roadmap to the workings of government and the territorial distribution of power appropriate to a multinational state. Ideally, it would be drawn up with the consent of the devolved legislatures and so establish a principled framework for the UK as a whole.

If we are to make a success of devolution, then we need to lay down clear constitutional principles. And above all, we need to emphasise not only what divides those living in the UK, but also what unites us, what we have in common – our shared destiny.

---

[22] *Financial Times* (25 November 2015).

[23] *A Constitutional Crossroads: Ways Forward for the United Kingdom: Report of an Independent Commission*, Bingham Centre for the Rule of Law, May 2015, available at www.biicl.org/documents/595_a_constitutional_crossroads.pdf.

15

Scottish Secession and the Political Constitution of the UK

PETER REID AND ASANGA WELIKALA

I. Introduction

The comparative student of secession looking at the debate over Scotland's secession from the UK is often left fascinated, if not perplexed, by the uniqueness of it all. The debate is conducted with a civility and democratic maturity that contrasts strikingly with the violence and conflict that characterises secession debates elsewhere, including elsewhere within the UK. The territorial break-up of the state is contemplated in an entirely phlegmatic way. But most of all, the comparativist is struck by how unusual it is, not merely that the host state ungrudgingly grants the legal right to secede by a secession-seeking sub-state territory, but also to do so multiple times whenever the latter wishes to assert the right, and for the right to be exercised with no procedural constraint other than a democratic majority in the seceding unit. A second dimension to this UK response has been to grant devolved institutions to Scotland, and to increase these institutions' power when demands for independence are strong enough. It is this second dimension that we address in this chapter. Our purpose is, first, to identify the strengths and weaknesses of this distinctive UK approach to secession claims; and second, to suggest ways, based on the development of a new 'Union statecraft', by which the gaps and weaknesses within the organic ontology of British constitutionalism might be addressed.

II. Secession Diplomacy: Taking the Heat from the Fire

Since the 1960s, the UK government has developed a unique approach to Scottish secession. A kind of 'secession diplomacy' has evolved, whereby constitutional concessions have been made to the Scottish electorate whenever the appetite for secession politics has been strong enough. The policy has been to give away what is necessary to assuage nationalist sentiment in the country, while still giving away the least amount of power possible. These changes were not guided by a coherent vision and underlying principles for how devolution should contribute to UK constitutionalism. Of this, we explore two institutional responses: first, the now-defunct attempt to include a territorial Parliament within the House of Commons with English Votes for English Laws (EVEL); and second, the unsuccessful attempts to turn the House of Lords into a territorial second chamber. Both of these were unsuccessful responses to the institutional drift caused by devolution. They were bound to peter out, or create more problems than they solved, because the UK government lacks a clear and workable vision for the relationship of the devolved administrations with the centre. We explore EVEL and House of Lords reform through 'gradual institutional change' and 'intercurrence'. Secession diplomacy may be a democratic and workable approach to territorial tensions; however, it must be accompanied by vision and underpinning principles for UK constitutionalism. In order to respond to the institutional drift that has already taken place, the UK needs both institutional and political reform. The institutional response must be sensitive to the traditional institutional logics in Westminster and Whitehall. The political response should be a new kind of Union statecraft that builds more comprehensive political relations and conventions around the devolution leaders and those in the UK government.

Reflecting on 20 years of devolution, Hassan identifies three distinct 'time frames' on the road to devolved power in Scotland:

> [A] more-than-a-century-long campaign for Scottish home rule which dated back to Gladstonian home rule and Keir Hardie's Independent Labour Party in the 1880s; the more recent post-war attempt to progress constitutional change and self-government which accelerated after the SNP began to become a serious electoral force from the late 1960s onwards; and finally, the shorter period which encapsulated Labour's preparation for office pre-1997, followed by the relatively smooth last phase of 1997–99 legislating and preparing for a Scottish Parliament.[1]

In this chapter, we address the two most recent periods, from the 1960s onwards, as well as some more recent changes to the Scotland Act. Throughout this time frame, there has developed a consistent character to constitutional change in Scotland. The UK government has exercised a unique brand of secession diplomacy, whereby constitutional concessions have been made to the Scottish electorate whenever the appetite for secession politics has been strong enough. This strategy emerged from the Labour Party as a way to deal with the SNP as an electoral threat. However, after the SNP formed a government in Holyrood, it has become a UK government approach to secession. We call this strategy 'secession diplomacy'. We examine the 1979 devolution referendum, the passage of the Scotland Act 1998, and the Scotland Acts of 2012 and 2016.

---

[1] G Hassan, 'Back to the Future: Exploring Twenty Years of Scotland's Journey, Stories and Politics' in G Hassan (ed), *The Story of the Scottish Parliament: The First Two Decades Explained* (Edinburgh, Edinburgh University Press, 2019) 1.

A. The 1979 Referendum

Discussions of Scottish devolution were triggered by Winnie Ewing's victory in the Hamilton by-election in 1967.[2] McGarvey and Cairney note that:

> The SNP's breakthrough in 1967 marked it as a serious electoral force in Scottish politics and the party made further gains at the 1970 and both 1974 UK general elections. The two major UK parties were responding to the perceived demand for constitutional change.[3]

This led to the Royal Commission on the Constitution in 1969 (the Kilbrandon Commission), which was given a wide remit to appraise and make recommendations on UK governance in relation to sub-state trends. The Kilbrandon Report was published in 1973, and crucially set out the case for a Scottish assembly with legislative powers. The majority report recommended legislative powers broadly aligned to the powers of the Scotland Office, while the minority report further recommended the power to raise taxes through a sales tax or surcharge on income tax. During the second 1974 General Election, the Labour Party campaigned in Scotland on a manifesto promise (separate to the English manifesto) to deliver a 'Legislative Assembly for Scotland with substantial powers over crucial areas of decision-making'. However, the eventual White Paper was perceived by some within the Party to fall short of this commitment, and a breakaway group, the Scottish Labour Party, was formed. Nonetheless, after the failure of the Scotland and Wales Bill, the Scotland Bill was given royal assent on 31 July 1978, and the referendum took place on 1 March 1979. After a backbench amendment introduced by George Cunningham, 40 per cent of the electorate (ie all those on the voter register, including those who did not/could not vote) had to vote in favour of an assembly before one could be established. This was an additional barrier to the usual simple majority of voters, which was also required. In the end, 52 per cent of voters favoured an assembly; however, this represented only 32.9 per cent of the electorate, thus resulting in a 'No' victory.[4]

Throughout this process, we see the beginnings of secession diplomacy. The idea of Home Rule re-emerged because of the SNP's electoral success. The Labour Party won an election with promises for significant reform, only to put forward the weakest possible option when elected. However, we should not overstate this as a deeply engrained UK government strategy; rather, it was a calculated response by Labour to the electoral threat of the SNP. After the October 1974 elections, Labour held the smallest majority on record (three seats) and the SNP had only grown as an electoral threat. While the majority of SNP wins in the 1974 elections were at

---

[2] C O'Neill and C Himsworth, *Scotland's Constitution: Law and Practice* (London, Bloomsbury Professional, 2015) 3.17.

[3] P Cairney and N McGarvey, *Scottish Politics*, 2nd edn (London, Bloomsbury, 2013) 24–25.

[4] For a fuller description of the Bill's passage and the referendum, see O Gay, 'Scotland and Devolution' House of Commons Research Paper 97/92 (House of Commons Library, 1997) 18–23.

the expense of Conservative incumbents, Labour saw that the electoral balance was about to tip against them. McLean and McMillan write that:

> Astute politicians knew that, while the electoral system had protected Labour by giving the SNP only 10 per cent of the Scottish seats for its 22 per cent of the vote, it would swing round viciously if the SNP vote share were to rise by another 10 percentage points or so. On a vote share of somewhere between 30 and 35 per cent, the SNP would flip from victim of the electoral system to its beneficiary. With an evenly distributed 35 per cent of the vote, it could win more than half of the seats in Scotland – Labour had just won 40 out of 71 seats (ie 56 per cent) in Scotland on 37 per cent of the vote.[5]

Tam Dalyell's verdict was therefore that the devolution process was 'primarily an exercise in party politics' and 'the legislation was hastily cobbled together to meet the electoral threat posed by the Scottish National Party'.[6] Indeed, establishing the Kilbrandon Commission was itself a response to electoral pressure.[7] Sillars describes October 1973 as a 'double whammy', as the Kilbrandon Commission reported in favour of devolution and Labour lost the Govan by-election (thought to be one of their most secure seats).[8] While McLean and McMillan see a mixture of electoral calculation and concern for the Union in this process,[9] the electoral imperative was probably the strongest factor. Even with the discovery of North Sea oil, the SNP was still a long way from convincing a majority of Scots that independence was in their best interests. This was perhaps reflected in the Conservatives' rejection of devolution. The Labour leadership also wanted to minimise the damage that devolution could do to the Party's unity. Devolution had ideologically divided the membership – both in whether it was an effective response to the SNP and whether it fitted with the Party's identity.[10] Therefore, the electoral imperatives of Labour's slim majority, its dependence on Scottish seats and the SNP's growing electoral success were the motivations behind the 1979 referendum. The Labour government's response was derailed by its own MPs; however, it also set in motion the beginnings of secession diplomacy. The leadership's strategy was to grant small constitutional concessions in order to draw the heat from the SNP.

For a more detailed analysis of the Act, see 24–30; see also V Bogdanor, *Devolution* (Oxford, Oxford University Press, 1979).

[5] I Mclean and A McMillan, *State of the Union: Unionism and the Alternatives in the United Kingdom since 1707* (Oxford, Oxford University Press, 2005) 162.

[6] T Dalyell, *Devolution: The End of Britain?* (London, Jonathan Cape, 1977) 43.

[7] Jack Geekie and Roger Levy, 'Devolution and the Tartanisation of the Labour Party' (1989) 42 Parliamentary Affairs 399, 399–400.

[8] J Sillars, *A Difference of Opinion: My Political Journey* (Edinburgh, Birlinn, 2021) 95.

[9] Mclean and McMillan (n 5) 162.

[10] D Torrance, *Standing Up for Scotland: Nationalist Unionism and Scottish Party Politics, 1884–2014* (Edinburgh, Edinburgh University Press, 2020) 133–34; G Brown, 'The Labour Party and Political Change in Scotland, 1918–1929: The Politics of Five Elections' (PhD thesis, University of Edinburgh, 1982) 527.

B. Scotland Act 1998

While a sincerely pro-devolution movement influenced the shape of the Scotland Act 1998, in holding a referendum on devolution, the Blair government was motivated by the electoral threat of the SNP and the Union's stability. The Thatcher governments of 1979–90 and the growing political divide between Scotland and England revitalised nationalist politics in Scotland. It gave new impetus to Unionist, pro-devolution figures. The Campaign for a Scottish Assembly (later dubbed Campaign for a Scottish Parliament) was launched in 1980. This movement produced a document called 'A Claim of Right for Scotland', which was signed at the 1989 Scottish Constitutional Convention. Labour, the Liberal Democrats and civil society participated, whereas the Conservatives did not, and the SNP withdrew after the first day. Therefore, although the SNP was later able to succeed electorally under devolution, many party activists did not originally see it as valuable. In 1990, the Convention published its first report. A commission was established in 1993 to flesh out what it wanted some of the Parliament's details to be, particularly its procedures. The Scottish Constitutional Convention published its ultimate report in 1995, 'Scotland's Parliament, Scotland's Right'. Many of these recommendations were incorporated into the Labour government's 1997 White Paper, *Scotland's Parliament*. In the September 1997 referendum, 74 per cent of voters favoured a Scottish Parliament and the Scotland Act 1998 was passed.[11]

While civil society obviously shaped the contours of the 1998 Act, particularly in delivering a Parliament designed to promote 'new politics', the best explanation for the Act's passage is still the Blair government's attempts to neutralise the SNP as an electoral threat. The Union's stability was also an important factor. Despite the Labour government's massive electoral success, it was clear that the SNP were still competitors in Scotland. This was likely seen as a threat to both the territorial state and the Labour Party. Linked to this, the Labour Party's reputation was also at stake, particularly as John Smith had committed the Party to devolution as leader and Labour had been such an important force in shaping the Convention. There had been fears that another Conservative government would do irreversible damage to Scots' perception of the Union and the SNP had polled strongly in 1992. Torrance notes that the government's 'broader strategic aim, naturally, was keeping the SNP under control'.[12] Devolution was believed to be the institutional response that would 'kill nationalism stone dead'.[13] Therefore, while other devolution events have responded to strictly immediate pressure, the introduction of a Scottish Parliament was part of a pre-emptive strategy. There was no immediate electoral pressure from the SNP. The 1998 Act was

---

[11] A Brown, 'Designing the Scottish Parliament' (2000) 53 *Parliamentary Affairs* 542, 547.

[12] Torrance (n 10) 143.

[13] S MacNab, 'Scottish Parliament at 20: Why Devolution Failed to "Kill Nationalism Stone Dead"' *The Scotsman* (8 May 2019) www.scotsman.com/news/scottish-news/scottish-parliament-20-why-devolution-failed-kill-nationalism-stone-dead-1418095.

partly caused and shaped by a faction of Scottish Labour members that genuinely believed in the benefits of devolution. However, the interests of both the Labour Party and the Union, using devolution to assuage nationalist sentiment, was also part of the process. This was the midway point between using devolution to protect the Labour Party's electoral interests and entrenching secession diplomacy as a UK government approach to the independence movement. The Conservatives, opponents of devolution in 1979, now softened their approach. While Conservatives were far from wholehearted supporters of the Scotland Bill, the Party accepted the necessity of its passage and engaged constructively in its debate and amendment.[14] The immediate threat to Labour was not as severe as previous years; however, the 1980s had seen growing resentment and alienation of Scots against the government in London. The SNP was seen as more of a threat to the Union's long-term survival than it had been previously.

C. Scotland Acts 2012 and 2016

Since 1998, the Labour Party's strategy of using constitutional concessions to assuage nationalist sentiment has become part of the UK government's approach. Electoral politics are no longer a factor in this approach; instead, it has been used to avoid the break-up of the Union. The interests at play have therefore moved from the electoral to the existential. The Scotland Acts 2012 and 2016 were direct results of this secession diplomacy. Both Acts increased the power of the Scottish Parliament, and both transfers of power were the smallest increments possible given the circumstances. The SNP's 'victory' in 2007, where they leapt from 27 seats to 47 and ousted the Labour–Liberal Democrat coalition, was met with panic by Scottish Unionist parties. After the SNP government published its 'National Conversation' report, an opposition motion was passed to establish a commission

> [t]o review the provisions of the Scotland Act 1998 in the light of experience and to recommend any changes to the present constitutional arrangements that would enable the Scottish Parliament to serve the people of Scotland better, that would improve the financial accountability of the Scottish Parliament and that would continue to secure the position of Scotland within the United Kingdom.[15]

The motion was opposed by the SNP as overly restrictive in its exclusion of independence, however welcome as part of a broader constitutional discussion.[16]

---

[14] BK Winetrobe, 'Enacting Scotland's "Written Constitution": The Scotland Act 1998' (2011) 30 *Parliamentary History* 85, 88; O Gay, 'The Scotland Bill: Devolution and Scotland's Parliament' Research Paper 98/1 (House of Commons Library, 1998) 8.

[15] See Des Browne's Written Statement to the Commons: HC Deb 25 March 2008, vol 474, cols 7–8WS.

[16] For a discussion of context, terms of reference and the SNP's position, see H Holden, 'The Commission on Scottish Devolution – the Calman Commission' Standard Note SN/PC/04744 (House of Commons Library, 2010) 6–10.

The commission's recommendations were introduced by the Scotland Act 2012 after the SNP won an overall majority in the 2011 elections. In hindsight, particularly in comparison to the Scotland Act 2016, the new powers were only modest. The SNP's 2011 victory was particularly worrying for Unionists because the devolved electoral system was designed to avoid such an outcome.[17]

The 2016 Act was similarly a response to nationalist sentiment, this time in the form of the 2014 independence referendum. In 2012, and throughout 2013, support for the Union maintained a strong lead over independence. When the referendum was granted, therefore, the UK government (along with almost everyone else) thought there was almost no chance of a 'Yes' victory. However, no one foresaw how quickly 'Yes' would inflate in the polls during the campaign process.[18] As a response to this, particularly when some polls showed overall support for independence, David Cameron, Ed Miliband and Nick Clegg made a statement promising changes to devolution. This statement, known as 'The Vow', promised more powers and putting the Scottish Parliament on a permanent footing.[19] After the 'No' victory, the Smith Commission was established, leading to the Scotland Act 2016. While there has been concern over the true scope of the 2016 powers and whether the Act 'promise[s] more than it actually delivers', the breadth of new powers is nonetheless substantial and the 2016 Act is widely seen to deliver on the promises made in 2014.[20]

We accept that there were also other factors at play in the devolution process. Even when the Union was most popular amongst Scots, they identified along 'Unionist nationalist' lines, viewing the Union as a necessary machine for advancement while maintaining the Scottish identity.[21] This was contributed to by the establishment and subsequent development of the Scotland Office in 1885, which further institutionalised Scotland as a distinct territory with distinct interests and governance.[22] Constitutional space created by central UK actors' laissez-faire approach to many Scottish issues also gave local authorities some level of practical autonomy.[23] Scottish devolution is also part of a wider global phenomenon

---

[17] R Johns, J Mitchell and CJ Carman, 'Constitution or Competence? The SNP's Re-election in 2011' (2013) 61 *Political Studies* 158, 158–78.

[18] See the opinion poll analysis in R McInnes, S Ayres and O Hawkins, 'Scottish Independence Referendum 2014: Analysis of Results' Research Paper 14/50 (House of Commons Library, 2014) 16–22.

[19] M Foote, 'Inside the Vow: How Historic Daily Record Front Page Which Changed the Course of Britain's Constitutional Settlement Was Born' *Daily Record* (17 September 2015) www.dailyrecord. co.uk/news/politics/inside-vow-how-historic-daily-6464878.

[20] A McHarg, 'A Powerhouse Parliament: An Enduring Settlement: The Scotland Act 2016 Special Section: The Scotland Act 2016' (2016) 20 *Edinburgh Law Review* 360, 361. For a discussion of the various powers, see this special section of the *Edinburgh Law Review* more generally.

[21] Cairney and McGarvey (n 3) 21; A Brown, *Politics and Society in Scotland*, 2nd edn (London, Macmillan, 1998) 11.

[22] J Mitchell, *Governing Scotland: The Invention of Administrative Devolution* (London, Macmillan, 2003).

[23] J Bulpitt, *Territory and Power in the United Kingdom: An Interpretation* (Manchester, Manchester University Press, 1983) 29–30.

of sub-state nationalism that has become more nuanced in recent years, with an increasing number of sub-state actors looking for more autonomy and formalised institutions, although not full secession.[24] However, as we have demonstrated, the key causal factors were electoral pressures and then secession diplomacy as a response to the SNP's popularity.

Thus, the UK government has developed a uniquely responsive and pragmatic approach to Scottish secession – 'secession diplomacy'. The government has always favoured the retention of power at the centre. However, when the appetite for independence in Scotland has been strong enough, devolution has been used to cool the nationalist movement. This is clearly seen in 2012 and 2016. The most important moment, in 1998, is slightly more complicated. While there was always a latent threat from the SNP, Labour did not face immediate pressure. However, growing support for devolution within the Labour Party and the belief that it would be a decisive victory over the SNP led to the Scottish Parliament. While there was no immediate pressure, therefore, the move was part of a pre-emptive strategy. Secession diplomacy grew out of Labour strategies in the second half of the twentieth century. In the 1970s, devolution was more of a Labour strategy against the SNP than it was a UK strategy against Scottish secession. The Scotland Act 1998, on the other hand, was perhaps a response both to the weakened Union and the SNP's dormant threat to Labour seats. This is reflected in Conservatives' reluctant support. However, in 2012 and 2016 we see secession diplomacy being deployed by all Unionist parties and a Conservative-led government.

III. The Missing Piece: Vision

Although the UK government has taken a non-authoritarian, democratic and pragmatic approach to secession, its secession diplomacy has also created issues in UK constitutionalism. The root cause of these issues is a lack of guiding principles behind the founding and strengthening of devolved institutions. Just as decisions were often made in the moment and as a response to Scottish political pressure, so too they were not accompanied by any sustained vision for stable constitutional relations.

The UK devolution process therefore has been characterised by ad hoc development. By this, we mean piecemeal and in response to immediate pressures *plus* lacking in a consistent framework of underlying principles for devolution. The lack of guiding principles is evidenced by a deficit of institutional developments in London to properly accommodate the newly devolved nations. The Scotland and Wales Acts (particularly) were not accompanied by significant

---

[24] S Tierney, 'Reframing Sovereignty? Sub-state National Societies and Contemporary Challenges to the Nation-State' (2005) 54 *International and Comparative Law Quarterly* 161; M Keating, 'Sovereignty and Plurinational Democracy: Problems in Political Science' in N Walker (ed), *Sovereignty in Transition* (London, Bloomsbury, 2006) 203.

formal change of the way in which Westminster conducts its business. The original extent of institutional change was the Sewel Convention, where Westminster will not normally legislate on devolved matters or alter the devolution agreements without consent from the affected devolved assembly. This convention arose prior to the passing of the Scotland Act.[25] It is not a justiciable rule and it came under pressure during the Brexit process.[26] However, it is normally characterised by well-developed procedures, even if the agreements are often conducted by the respective governments rather than the parliaments.[27] Nonetheless, the House of Lords Constitution Committee warned that there are existential questions raised by devolution which require a more comprehensive framework:

> There is no evidence of strategic thinking in the past about the development of devolution. There has been no guiding strategy or framework of principles to ensure that devolution develops in a coherent or consistent manner and in ways which do not harm the Union.[28]

This report was particularly concerned that developments were made in 'silos', that is, bilateral talks between the UK government and an individual devolved government. There was no overarching plan for devolution, and developments were reactions to political changes within the devolved nations. It was emphasised that devolution in one nation could have an impact on the overall UK structure.[29] The report examines the 'devolution deals' being struck across England, which were welcomed in principle but also characterised as ad hoc.[30] Surveys have shown that a significant minority of English believe that they are not given a fair share of public spending and there is a common theme that English do not perceive the 1998 deals as good for them.[31] Tierney warns that the UK may be engaging in 'decentralisation without direction'.[32] This is reflected in the informal interactions between the Scottish and UK governments. In a report on the devolution process, the Bingham Centre observes: 'That Whitehall has changed so little as a result of devolution gives the unfortunate impression that the centre has not fully caught up with the magnitude of the changes to the state that devolution has triggered.'[33]

---

[25] HL Deb 21 July 1998, vol 592, col 791.

[26] *R (on the application of Miller and another) (Respondents) v Secretary of State for Exiting the European Union (Appellant)* [2017] UKSC 5.

[27] P Bowers, 'The Sewel Convention' Standard Note SN/PC/2084 (House of Commons Library, 2005).

[28] House of Lords, Select Committee on the Constitution, 'The Union and Devolution' (10th Report of Session 2015–16) 30 https://publications.parliament.uk/pa/ld201516/ldselect/ldconst/149/149.pdf.

[29] ibid 89–101.

[30] ibid 390–406.

[31] C Jeffery et al, 'Taking England Seriously: The New English Politics The Future of England Survey 2014' (Edinburgh, Centre on Constitutional Change, 2014) 11–14.

[32] S Tierney, 'Drifting Towards Federalism? Appraising the Constitution in Light of the Scotland Act 2016 and Wales Act 2017' in R Schütze and S Tierney (eds), *The United Kingdom and the Federal Idea* (Oxford, Hart Publishing, 2018) 102.

[33] 'A Constitutional Crossroads: Ways Forward for the United Kingdom' (London, Bingham Centre for the Rule of Law, 2015) 9.

The House of Lords Constitution Committee made similar observations in a 2015 report on intergovernmental relations in the UK. The report observed that intergovernmental relations tend to be informal and bilateral, and the key formal forum – the Joint Ministerial Committee – is not well regarded by devolved governments.[34] Intergovernmental relations have been described as 'weakly instituted'[35] and 'inadequate.'[36] Although the effects of devolution on the UK constitution are beginning to be explored and addressed, devolved governments have limited political capital to help establish a more coherent system. Contrasting UK intergovernmental relations with those in Canada, Anderson and Gallagher argue that: 'IGR are not just a recent novelty, they are mostly an irrelevance, with little or no sense that they affect the political fortunes of the government, whose MPs are overwhelmingly English.'[37]

Therefore, although devolution has clearly raised questions on the character and constitution of the UK, there are also political barriers to a more coherent structure. Westminster and Whitehall are only beginning to acknowledge that devolution will inevitably have a fundamental impact on their own work, if not status. This is a consequence of the UK government's ad hoc approach to devolution.

This is not an argument against secession diplomacy, which by definition requires pragmatic responses to pressure; however, it is a call for clearer guiding principles in future reform. Secession diplomacy needs to be guided by vision and firm principles if it is to be sustainable. Cracks appearing in devolved relations with the centre suggest a lack of vision for devolution's future. It is the combination of secession diplomacy with a lack of vision that makes the reforms ad hoc. It is still possible to grant further devolved powers in a responsive manner while also conforming to a plan which sets out a positive vision for relations between devolved administrations and Whitehall. These relations should not be left to develop in a wholly unguided fashion.

---

[34] House of Lords Select Committee on the Constitution, 'Inter-Governmental Relations in the United Kingdom' (11th Report of Session 2014–15).

[35] W Swenden and N McEwen, 'UK Devolution in the Shadow of Hierarchy? Intergovernmental Relations and Party Politics' (2014) 12 *Comparative European Politics* 488, 488. See also House of Lords Select Committee on the Constitution, 'Respect and Co-operation: Building a Stronger Union for the 21stCentury'(10thReportofSession2021–22)ch5,https://committees.parliament.uk/publications/8562/documents/86664/default/; Lord Dunlop, 'Review of UK Government Union Capability' (2019) https://assets.publishing.service.gov.uk/government/uploads/system/uploads/attachment_data/file/972987/Lord_Dunlop_s_review_into_UK_Government_Union_Capability.pdf.

[36] Welsh Government, *Brexit and Devolution: Securing Wales' Future* (White Paper, 2017) 17.

[37] G Anderson and J Gallagher, 'Intergovernmental Relations in Canada and the United Kingdom' in M Keating and G Laforest (eds), *Constitutional Politics and the Territorial Question in Canada and the United Kingdom: Federalism and Devolution Compared* (Cham, Springer International Publishing, 2018) 40.

IV. Intercurrence and Gradual Institutional Change

This section discusses 'intercurrence' and 'gradual institutional change', which are the theories by which we explore the unintended effects of devolution on UK constitutionalism and politics. Historical institutionalists are increasingly interested in processes of gradual change, whereby institutions change profoundly over long periods of time rather than being formed, abolished and altered during critical junctures. Because of the mechanisms of change identified by this work, it is closely associated with the theory of intercurrence – whereby institutions containing conflicting logics may coexist and interact with each other.

A. Intercurrence

Intercurrence was first identified as a distinct approach to historical institutional studies by Orren and Skowronek in 1994, writing in the context of American Political Development.[38] In their main work on the subject, *The Search for American Political Development*, the authors defined intercurrence with reference to two other approaches, institutions *in* time and politics *over* time. Intercurrence combines features of these two approaches and also adds some new perspectives. As with approaches that evaluate institutions in time, the authors accept institutions' use by politicians to bring order to politics and their capacity to entrench processes. Also, the authors draw on approaches which describe the path-dependent nature of politics over time.[39] However, those who deploy an intercurrence analysis are particularly concerned with the 'partial and uneven' nature of change. Politics and institutions are left partially reformed, with embodiments of conflicting eras existing simultaneously – long after the reasons and proponents of their creation. Orren and Skowroneck therefore promulgated an approach which addressed the relationship between multiple institutions over time. Institutions (particularly political ones) may coexist and influence each other even though their underlying purposes, temporalities and logics are distinct. Intercurrence therefore refers to a particular approach to historical institutionalism, one that views institutions as a matrix – each affecting the other – in the fullness of time. It addresses politics in an environment where there are 'rules evolved in separate centuries, purposes pursued within different professional traditions, experience drawn from separate policy legacies, coexisting laws with separate lineages'.[40]

---

[38] K Orren and S Skowronek, 'Institutions and Intercurrence: Theory Building in the Fullness of Time' (1996) 38 *Nomos* 111, 111; K Orren and S Skowronek, *The Search for American Political Development* (Cambridge, Cambridge University Press, 2004).
[39] Orren and Skowronek, *The Search for American Political Development* (n 38) 108.
[40] ibid 112.

B. Modes of Gradual Change

Historical institutionalists have begun to develop a typology of gradual institutional change. As mentioned in this section's introduction, intercurrence and theories of gradual institutional development are not dependent upon each other, even though they are frequently linked in the literature. Works by authors such as Thelen, Streeck and Mahoney have pushed writers to theorise the various modes by which change, particularly gradual change, takes place.[41] Thanks particularly to Streeck and Thelen's seminal piece, there is now a sophisticated toolbox for the various modes of exogenous and endogenous institutional change.[42] This work identifies five mechanisms of institutional change: displacement, layering, drift, conversion and exhaustion. For this chapter, we are particularly interested in layering and drift. Layering is the process whereby new features are added to institutions in such a way that alters their 'status and structure'.[43] This is typified by the proliferation of private pension schemes in the USA after they were added as optional supplements to the public pension. The private system was deliberately expanded to undermine support for the public pension.[44] The institutional landscape can therefore be transformed simply by adding new features to existing institutions rather than tearing institutions down and building new ones afresh. Drift describes an unresponsiveness to exogenous change by those tasked with maintaining institutions. In this way, the essential features of the institution may be unaltered on paper, though their status and function becomes depleted in reality. The authors associate this with deliberate neglect and deterioration, and therefore describe it as a destructive force.[45] Theorists emphasise the deliberate nature of drift, whereby policymakers deliberately fail to adopt, or block, changes that may mitigate the drift process.[46] In this chapter, we rely on a much looser definition of drift, which simply acknowledges the tendency for exogenous changes,

---

[41] K Thelen, 'How Institutions Evolve: Insights Form Comparative Historical Analysis' in J Mahoney and D Rueschemeyer (eds), *Comparative Historical Analysis in the Social Sciences* (Cambridge, Cambridge University Press, 2003); W Streeck and K Thelen, 'Introduction: Institutional Change in Advanced Political Economies' in W Streeck and K Thelen (eds), *Beyond Continuity: Institutional Change in Advanced Political Economies* (Oxford, Oxford University Press, 2005); J Mahoney and K Thelen, 'A Theory of Gradual Institutional Change' in J Mahoney and K Thelen (eds), *Explaining Institutional Change: Ambiguity, Agency, and Power* (Cambridge, Cambridge University Press, 2009); JS Hacker, 'Policy Drift: The Hidden Politics of US Welfare State Retrenchment' in Streeck and Thelen, *Beyond Continuity* (ibid); JS Hacker and P Pierson, *Winner-Take-All Politics: How Washington Made the Rich Richer-and Turned Its Back on the Middle Class* (London, Simon & Schuster. 2010).

[42] Streeck and Thelen (n 41); K Thelen and J Conran, 'Institutional Change' in O Fioretos, TG Falleti and A Sheingate (eds), *The Oxford Handbook of Historical Institutionalism* (Oxford, Oxford University Press, 2016) 60–65.

[43] Streeck and Thelen (n 41) 31.

[44] Hacker (n 41).

[45] Streeck and Thelen (n 41) 24–29.

[46] JS Hacker, P Pierson and K Thelen, 'Drift and Conversion: Hidden Faces of Institutional Change' in J Mahoney and K Thelen (eds), *Advances in Comparative-Historical Analysis* (Cambridge, Cambridge University Press, 2015) 184.

including changes in other parts of the institutional landscape, to have knock-on effects on individual institutions. In this chapter, drift is when institutions' internal structures are unchanged, but their status and functions are altered by gradual exogenous change. We do not include deliberate neglect as a necessary component.

V. The Failed Layering of Institutions

A lack of vision with regard to devolution has led to failed layering processes in both the Commons and the Lords. These processes were intended to accommodate the changes introduced by devolution. In the Commons, EVEL was an ill-designed attempt to address the West Lothian Question (WLQ)[47] by incorporating a territorial assembly with limited power into a sovereign Parliament. On the other hand, House of Lords reform has failed primarily because further legitimacy for the Lords could threaten the Commons' absolute primacy. Both of these attempts were triggered by institutional drift in Westminster and Whitehall. Devolution has unexpectedly undermined the democratic primacy of the centre in both Scotland and England. In Scotland, the devolved government has become the de facto Scottish mouthpiece on all UK politics, not just those acts within devolved competence. In England, there is frustration with the apparent lack of an English counterweight to Scottish devolution. This reflects one of the limitations with conceiving devolution along traditional federal lines, which would imply some kind of balance. The UK constitution should instead be conceived as devolution within a unitary state. The constitutional settlement has evolved after concerted effort by Scotland against the centre rather than a deliberate design based on territorial parity (in terms of wealth and population) and plurality (distinct territorial units that nonetheless have an overarching commitment to the state). In this way, Scotland is a constant exception to the dominant vision, which is monist. On the other hand, devolution in England is growing – but even this is taking a different character to that in Scotland.[48]

A. EVEL

EVEL was an attempt to fix democratic disparities created by the 1998 agreements. Ad hoc devolution led to inconsistencies in the UK constitution which created tensions between the nations. One of these inconsistencies is the English

---

[47] The WLQ was raised by Tam Dalyell, the MP for West Lothian, in 1977. Dalyell questioned why Scots (and Welsh and Northern Irish) MPs could influence the outcome of laws which only affect England, while the English had no such say (under normal circumstances) over the laws within devolved competence which affected only devolved nations. HC Deb, 14 November 1977, vol 939, cols 122–23.

[48] 'Respect and Co-operation: Building a Stronger Union for the 21st Century' (n 35) 93.

Question, of which the WLQ is a component. The English Question refers to a mix of policy considerations raised by devolution: 'How, within the Union, should England be governed? Is there a way to allow England a separate voice within the UK without undermining the Union? Should power be devolved or decentralised, and if so how?'[49]

Perhaps the most renowned component of this discussion is the WLQ. EVEL tried to address this by giving MPs representing English constituencies a veto over legislation that only affected England and was also within a devolved legislature's competence. This was known as the 'double veto', whereby English MPs would have to veto a provision twice (the first veto triggered procedures for the Commons to reconsider the provision) before it was scrapped. It is important to note that this was only a veto; a majority of votes, including those from Scottish MPs, was still required before a Bill could be passed. Because the Scottish Parliament has more competencies than the Welsh Assembly, this veto occasionally included the votes of Welsh MPs, too. These changes were achieved through changes to the Commons' Standing Orders.[50]

However, an unusual unity of opposition MPs from all parties and government backbenches saw them as further ad hoc reform. EVEL was variously described as an 'abuse of process', 'constitutionally outrageous',[51] an example of how the Commons 'stagger and stumble with ad hoc steps'[52] and 'back of a fag packet'.[53] EVEL also went against the findings of the McKay Commission, which had looked into the English Question and advised against a Commons veto.

We consider EVEL to be an example of ad hoc reform because it meets our two-part test. Firstly, it was piecemeal. Although addressing the WLQ had been a Conservative manifesto promise since 2001,[54] this was nonetheless an individual, limited-focus reform designed to remedy a gap in the original devolution deal. Secondly, it also lacked consistent principles for an underlying vision of devolution. EVEL was part of a General Election campaign that depicted Ed Miliband as (literally) in the pocket of Scotland's former First Minister, it failed to draw cross-party or cross-nation support and it actively went against its own commission's findings.[55] While we do not present a comprehensive framework of

---

[49] 'The Union and Devolution' (n 28) 89. For a fuller discussion of the WLQ and its repercussions, see V Bogdanor, 'The West Lothian Question' (2010) 63 *Parliamentary Affairs* 156.

[50] D Gover and M Kenny, 'Finding the Good in EVEL: An Evaluation of "English Votes for English Laws" in the House of Commons' (Edinburgh, Centre on Constitutional Change, 2016) 14–17.

[51] HC Deb 6 July 2015, vol 598, col 56.

[52] HC Deb 2 July 2015, vol 597, cols 1655–56.

[53] HC Deb 7 July 2015, vol 598, col 222. However, it should be noted that the changes were subject to review after one year and thoroughly debated in the Commons. The Lords also held a debate on the changes.

[54] D Gover and M Kenny, 'Deliver Us from EVEL? Is the Government Right to Abolish "English Votes for English Laws"?' (*The Constitution Unit Blog*, 27 June 2021) https://constitution-unit.com/2021/06/27/deliver-us-from-evel-is-the-government-right-to-abolish-english-votes-for-english-laws/.

[55] F Perraudin and R Mason, 'Tory Election Campaign Poster Depicts Ed Miliband in Pocket of SNP' *The Guardian* (9 March 2015) www.theguardian.com/politics/2015/mar/09/tory-election-poster-ed-miliband-pocket-snp-alex-salmond.

devolution principles in this chapter, such a campaign is intuitively contrary to any positive vision for the territorial state.

EVEL tried to address the WLQ, the product of ad hoc reform, with further ad hoc reform. In doing so, it created further inconsistencies in the UK's territorial constitution. EVEL addressed the best-known component of the WLQ described above. However, the WLQ also has a second component, as asked by Dalyell:

> Under the new Bill, shall I still be able to vote on many matters in relation to West Bromwich but not West Lothian, as I was under the last Bill, and will my right hon. Friend be able to vote on many matters in relation to Carlisle but not Cardiff?[56]

Therefore, Dalyell also saw another side to devolution, which went beyond the reaction of English voters to the Scottish Parliament. Devolution also altered the position of devolved nation MPs and split devolved nation representatives into two independent groups. For example, there are Scottish MPs and MSPs; and Scottish MPs vote on devolution matters with no more frequency than English MPs. Scottish MPs can vote on England-only issues; however, they (as individuals) are not represented in Holyrood. Because it was part of an approach to constitutionalism that lacks underpinning principles, EVEL built on this inconsistency. In doing so, it created two new inconsistencies. Firstly, it affected the voting power of devolved nations' MPs even though those MPs have no voting rights in their devolved parliaments. EVEL therefore required the Speaker (who decided when EVEL applied) to adjudicate between nations' rights rather than simply MPs. For example, when deciding whether English, Welsh and Northern Ireland MPs exercise a veto over a provision, the Speaker reviewed the Scotland Act to determine whether similar provisions could be passed by the Scottish Parliament. Although it is Scottish MPs who were affected, therefore, the test was based on powers of the Scottish Parliament. This can only be explained as adjudication on the rights of the Scottish nation, taken as a whole and represented jointly by MPs and MSPs, rather than simply Scottish MPs.

The second inconsistency was the lack of a veto for devolved nations. Because the English nation was represented by a body of MPs within a sovereign Parliament, and because devolved nation MPs were completely excluded from voting in the relevant Grand Committee, English MPs exercised a complete veto power.[57] This contrasted with the Sewel Convention, whereby Westminster will not normally legislate on devolved matters without the consent of the devolved legislature, but retains the discretionary power to do so.[58] Both of these inconsistencies could have

---

[56] HC Deb 3 November 1977, vol 938, col 30.

[57] This raised questions about the justiciability of EVEL procedures and whether UK courts would involve themselves in the application of devolution laws, despite Westminster's *exclusive cognisance*. See comments from Lord Hope of Craighead and Lord Lisvane, HL Deb 21 October 2015, vol 765, col 762 and HL Deb 16 July 2015, vol 764, col 759. See also V Bogdanor, *The Crisis of the Constitution: The General Election and the Future of the United Kingdom* (London, The Constitution Society, 2015) 23–24.

[58] For the non-justiciability of the Sewel Convention, see *R (on the application of Miller and another) v Secretary of State for Exiting the European Union* [2017] UKSC 5 [147]–[151]. In particular, the words 'not normally' and 'recognises' were taken to limit this to convention. This created an even more complex

feasibly exacerbated territorial tensions if (i) the Supreme Court held an Act of the Scottish Parliament to be ultra vires even though similar powers were exercised under EVEL and protected by *exclusive cognisance* or (ii) Westminster decided to break the Sewel Convention, particularly if Scottish MPs were also blocked from voting on similar legislation in England. The first scenario would draw attention to the Commons' power to unilaterally misapply devolution legislation for itself; the second scenario would bring attention to English MPs' numeracy in the Commons and devolved legislatures' legal subordinacy. There was an added threat of Scottish MPs holding the balance of power and opposing parties forming the majority for UK-wide and EVEL legislation. Therefore, by building more inconsistencies into a sensitive aspect of the UK's constitution, EVEL could have created further tensions if it had been maintained.

B. House of Lords

Particularly since devolution, House of Lords reform has been mooted as a way to accommodate regionalism at the centre with a chamber of nations and regions. Meg Russell gives a thorough account of why such reform has never come to fruition.[59] Russell identifies five barriers to a territorial House of Lords. One barrier is the 'worldwide phenomenon that achieving second chamber reform is almost always very difficult'. This is a product of first chambers' vested interest against second chamber reform as well as other factors. Four other, more UK-specific, factors are the tendency for incremental change rather than constitutional moments; the lack of concurrent responsibilities with devolved administrations; devolved administrations' irresoluteness towards Lords reform; and commentators' engrossment with whether the Lords should be directly elected at all, rather than whether there should be a link with devolution. The first 'worldwide' factor is perhaps most acute in the UK context because of Parliament's unique history. In addition to the usual vested interests against second chamber reform, Westminster has built an identity around the unitary state and the constitutional moment of the Parliament Act 1911.

The Parliament Act 1911 unequivocally established the Commons' primacy over the Lords. Unsurprisingly, parliamentary conventions on the raising of tax began their formation in its earliest days, particularly when the Lords and Commons were first separated. Each House would agree how much it would tax

---

situation than the previous anomaly. English MPs exercised a complete veto, whereas the devolved nations did not. Nonetheless, if Westminster were to legislate contrary to the Sewel Convention, then it would do so with the consent of a majority of MPs, including those from devolved nations. However, devolved nation MPs are vastly outnumbered by English MPs and they may have voted against the legislation. Furthermore, those devolved nation MPs are not taken to exclusively represent their nation when EVEL procedures are applied.

[59] M Russell, 'Attempts to Change the British House of Lords into a Second Chamber of the Nations and Regions: Explaining a History of Failed Reforms' (2018) 10 *Perspectives on Federalism* 268.

itself and, as the House which raised the most tax, the granting of finance to the Sovereign eventually became the prerogative of the Commons, while the Lords consented and advised. This was recognised by Henry IV in an ordinance from 1407, and by the end of the seventeenth century the most important modern principles of public finance had been established.[60]

However, the constitution found itself under pressure at the turn of the twentieth century. The Liberals had won a large Commons majority in 1906; however, their numbers were small in the Lords. Henry Campbell-Bannerman had plans for radical change and his government quickly found itself on a collision course with the Lords. It was not until 1911 that the Asquith government – after another general election and a constitutional conference – passed the Parliament Act, having struck a deal with Irish Nationalist MPs and threatened the Lords with a swamping of new peers.[61] Ballinger notes that this Act gives a statutory footing to the Commons' rights over financial legislation. From this point, the Lords could only delay Money Bills for a maximum of one month.[62] The Lords had the right to delay most non-Money Bills for around two years. Later, under the Parliament Act 1949, this time frame was reduced to one year. The Acts themselves have rarely been relied upon, and it is perhaps the experience of the Liberals' triumph itself that has had the most enduring effect.

Lower house dominance in the UK is a product of the usual vested interests against upper house reform, but is also entrenched by the romance of its own origins. Westminster's institutional identity, the product of a rich history, makes second chamber reform especially difficult. Parliament is instilled with logics that are hostile to a territorial second chamber. These are not simply window dressings that contextualise other interests against reform, but inhibiting factors in themselves.

C. Layering and Institutional Priorities

By appreciating the intercurrence of UK institutions after devolution, we can observe the defects that ad hoc reform has created for the UK's constitution and the challenges in remedying these defects. This holds lessons for any states that may adopt a secession diplomacy strategy. Devolution has caused institutional drift in Westminster and Whitehall. The UK constitution is increasingly a landscape of different institutions and the centre has been unable to adapt to the waves caused by devolved counterparts. The democratic legitimacy of the centre is under

---

[60] A Rogers, 'Henry IV, the Commons and Taxation' (1969) 31 *Mediaeval Studies* 44, 44; D Morris, '"A Tax By Any Other Name": Some Thoughts on Money Bills and Other Taxing Measures: Part I' (2001) 22 *Statute Law Review* 181, 181–84.

[61] C Ballinger, 'Hedging and Ditching: The Parliament Act 1911' (2011) 30 *Parliamentary History* 19.

[62] ibid 19; R Kelly and L Maer, 'The Parliament Acts' Briefing Paper 00675 (House of Commons Library, 2016).

scrutiny and the institutional makeup of Westminster and Whitehall is insufficient to deliver a stable equilibrium. The UK government has attempted to respond by layering the Houses of Parliament with new features. However, these features have come into conflict with the underlying logics of both Houses and the processes have proved unsuccessful. Secession diplomacy must include measures to balance the logics of the pre-existing state with demands for regionalisation.

The establishment of the Scottish Parliament and government caused drift in Westminster and Whitehall. This 'centre' of the UK's constitution was deliberately left unaltered and only a minimum amount of procedural change (the Sewel Convention and a weak Joint Ministerial Committee) was introduced to accommodate devolution. Although Westminster and Whitehall did not adopt new rules or form of statecraft to accommodate devolution, the devolved institutions nevertheless caused drift in their status. In Scotland, this was partly intentional. For example, when the Salmond government changed the 'Scottish Executive' into the 'Scottish Government', it was sending a signal that the devolved institutions would be more autonomous. They were then used in a more assertive way against the centre than they had been before. Salmond used his position as First Minister to bring new scrutiny to the centre during the referendum debate. This was most vivid when he repeatedly challenged Prime Minister Cameron to a televised debate, which Cameron refused. Cameron's position was widely seen as untenable and the relationship between First Minister and Prime Minister was given new attention.[63]

The Scottish Parliament's debating chamber has also become a new forum for publicising Unionist and nationalist arguments. This has had a knock-on effect for the rest of Scottish politics.[64] However, the Sturgeon government has used the Scottish administration's powers most assertively to change the dynamics of British constitutionalism. A string of ultra vires Bills have brought the Scottish government into courtroom battles with the UK government. While these were not necessarily intentionally ultra vires, the Sturgeon government seems more willing to test the boundaries of vires than previous Scottish governments.[65] The risk of judicial clashes is anyway inherent in devolution, even with significant political safeguards.[66] The drift in the status of the UK's centre was most apparent during

---

[63] S Carrell, 'Alex Salmond Challenges Cameron to St Andrew's Day TV Duel' *The Guardian* (15 September 2013) www.theguardian.com/politics/scottish-independence-blog/2013/sep/15/salmond-cameron-debate-challenge.

[64] S Daisley, 'To Save the Union, Ignore Gordon Brown' *The Spectator* (12 January 2022) www.spectator.co.uk/article/to-save-the-union-ignore-gordon-brown.

[65] *The Christian Institute et al (Appellants) v The Lord Advocate (Respondent) (Scotland)* [2016] UKSC 51; *The UK Withdrawal from the European Union (Legal Continuity) (Scotland) Bill – A Reference by the Attorney General and the Advocate General for Scotland* [2018] UKSC 64; *Reference by the Attorney General and the Advocate General for Scotland – United Nations Convention on the Rights of the Child (Incorporation) (Scotland) Bill and Reference by the Attorney General and the Advocate General for Scotland – European Charter of Local Self Government (Incorporation) (Scotland) Bill* [2021] UKSC 42.

[66] C McCorkindale and JL Hiebert, 'Vetting Bills in the Scottish Parliament for Legislative Competence' (2017) 21 *Edinburgh Law Review* 319.

the Brexit process. The Scottish Parliament, working in tandem with the Welsh Assembly, brought in its own legislation to alter the return of EU powers as far as they applied to Scotland. This Bill was itself challenged in court and ultimately found ultra vires.[67] The Scottish government consistently complained that the UK government was refusing to cooperate with it during the Brexit process, while the UK government accused the First Minister of 'undermining' negotiations.[68]

Nicola Sturgeon, in particular, has used her political clout as First Minister to carve out roles not originally envisaged for that office. This has included a role in international events such as COP26 and voicing concerns over the UK's refugee policy.[69] Most recently, to the chagrin of Conservative MSPs, the SNP has also used First Minister's Questions as a platform to call for the Prime Minister's resignation.[70] The intended divide of devolved institutions being simply for devolved affairs and the centre being for UK policy has not sustained itself. Devolved institutions have used their democratic legitimacy as a basis to challenge the UK government on reserved matters.

There has also been a change in Westminster's institutional status amongst the English. As described above, EVEL was an attempt to answer the English Question. English politicians, and to a certain extent the public, have become frustrated with devolved nations' status within the institutional framework and there have been some calls for more of an 'English voice'.[71]

While secession diplomacy deliberately tried to avoid asking difficult questions about the nature of the UK constitution as far as possible, the effect was simply to delay these questions rather than avoid them completely. As pragmatic and responsive as the UK government approach has been, it was perhaps only a matter of time before it ran into obstacles. In both aspects of institutional drift – Scotland and England – the change has been in the centre's status as democratic representatives. Devolution has created a democratic forum of Scottish voices which can better formulate and support a uniquely Scottish position against UK policies. Although the Scottish Parliament and government may be restrained in their powers, the politicians who form them have a high status in Scottish political culture and are

---

[67] UK Withdrawal from the European Union (Legal Continuity) (Scotland) Bill. The majority of the Bill's provisions were within competence at the time of passage.

[68] M Wade and G Keate, 'Sturgeon Accused of Subverting Brexit Talks' *The Times* (25 August 2016) www.thetimes.co.uk/article/sturgeon-accused-of-subverting-brexit-talks-rl0jt398v.

[69] G Campbell, 'How Nicola Sturgeon Has Carved out a Role at COP26' (*BBC News*, 8 November 2021) www.bbc.com/news/uk-scotland-scotland-politics-59206425; R Mason, 'Nicola Sturgeon Calls on UK Government to Step up Help for Afghan Refugees' *The National* (18 August 2021) www.thenational.scot/news/19521564.afghanistan-nicola-sturgeon-calls-uk-government-step-help-refugees/.

[70] J Bradley, 'Nicola Sturgeon Calls for Boris Johnson's Resignation as She Says the "Corrupt Incumbent of Number 10" Has to Go' *The Scotsman* (9 December 2021) www.scotsman.com/news/politics/fmqs-nicola-sturgeon-calls-for-boris-johnsons-resignation-as-she-says-the-corrupt-incumbent-of-number-10-has-to-go-3488893.

[71] Jeffery et al (n 31); D Gover and M Kenny, 'Answering the West Lothian Question? A Critical Assessment of 'English Votes for English Laws' in the UK Parliament' (2018) 71 *Parliamentary Affairs* 760.

increasingly concerned with politics outside their institution's vires. It is not clear that the 1998 reforms and those that followed definitely made independence more likely, though they have certainly institutionalised the Scottish national voice as a distinct part of all UK politics. The locus of Scottish politics, in both devolved and retained competences, has shifted from Westminster to Holyrood.

The 1998 Act was deliberately designed to minimise institutional contact between the centre and the devolved administrations. Indeed, the court proceedings over vires are perhaps the most prominent form of deliberately designed contact within the Scotland Act. However, the democratic and nationalist character of devolution has given the institutions relevance outside their prescribed powers. The First Minister, and the Scottish Parliament and the Scottish Government, have become vanguards of the Scottish political voice in all areas of UK politics. In England, as a repercussion of this, the centre has been characterised as inadequate to represent the English public fully and balance the power of the devolved nations. Therefore, as effective as secession diplomacy has been in minimising support for independence (at least in the short term), it has also created a new institutional dynamic that will not leave the centre unchanged.

Secession diplomacy should not be engaged in without a vision to balance the logics of the pre-existing state with the new regional arrangements. EVEL and House of Lords reform are examples of layering that failed because they came into conflict with deeply entrenched institutional logics. EVEL effectively tried to establish a limited power, regional Parliament within a sovereign, unitary Parliament. These conflicting logics proved untenable. The regional/unitary divide was politicised by MPs during EVEL's passage reference, with some parliamentarians complaining that 'two classes' of MPs were being created.[72] Also, as described above, the job of the Speaker was to adjudicate between the nations rather than assemblies, and the role of devolved nation MPs was incoherent. These disparities reflected conflicting logics between the traditional status of the Commons and the new role of English MPs under EVEL. Eventually, EVEL was scrapped because it was too complicated and did not sit comfortably with the principles of Westminster.[73]

Both reasons were related to the conflicting logics of EVEL and the Commons. The procedures were necessarily complex because they tried to accommodate regionalism within a unitary chamber. They also built upon devolution legislation normally handled by courts and gave the adjudication role to the Speaker instead. While there is certainly an adjudication in Money Bills, too, devolved competence is far more complex. Similarly, although it may be a hyperbole to say that two classes of MPs were created, EVEL did redefine the role of different MPs to an extent not previously seen.[74]

---

[72] ibid 772.

[73] 'Commons Scraps English Votes for English Laws' (*BBC News*, 13 July 2021) www.bbc.com/news/uk-politics-57828406; Gover and Kenny, 'Deliver Us from EVEL?' (n 54).

[74] For limited precedent, see Gover and Kenny, 'Answering the West Lothian Question?' (n 71) 772–73.

On the other hand, the key hindrance in reforming the Lords was the possible change in its relationship with the Commons. Since 1911, the supremacy of the Commons has been a permanent feature of the UK's constitution. The Commons is effectively a sovereign chamber. New democratic legitimacy for the Lords would allow the House to challenge its subordination. Even indirect elections could be a paradigm shift in the Houses of Parliament. This has been too big a pill to swallow for successive governments. The difficulties in creating indirect elections in England is also a reflection of the unitary state. Therefore, both attempts at reform failed because the newly introduced logics fundamentally conflicted with the established institution. This emphasises the need for states to have visions and underpinning values for their constitutional character if they are to engage in secession diplomacy. Ad hoc reform has created the need for reform of Westminster; however, this institution is diametrically opposed to such reform. Without proper vision for the UK's constitution, we have created institutions that are extremely difficult to balance with each other. To have balance, we need a new vision for devolution, which would probably require new features in Westminster. However, this could cause an overhaul in the Parliament's foundations. Given this situation, future attempts at reform must address this underlying conflict and (somehow) find a solution. The problem is therefore set; however, the solution is unclear.

VI. New Union Statecraft

The nature of institutional drift in Westminster and Whitehall demonstrates the need for a new 'Union statecraft'. Working with a coherent vision for devolution, this should be the political arm existing in tandem with structural reforms. Commentators on intergovernmental relations have tended to focus on incoherent institutional design. It is argued that the lack of proper procedures and bodies for cooperation has contributed to poor relations. While we agree with this, our discussion of drift in Westminster and Whitehall suggests that Unionist parties (at least) must develop a new political consensus in managing devolution. We call this 'Union statecraft'. Apart from the Scottish government's vires court battles, devolution procedures have not (purely in themselves) triggered any direct conflict with Westminster and Whitehall. This is perhaps to be expected, because devolution was deliberately designed without concurrent responsibilities. Also, since 2007, the SNP have focused on showing governing competence rather than simply trying to pitch battles with Westminster.[75] Instead, drift has been a product of political change that is intrinsic to any kind of devolution. The Scottish

---

[75] M Harvey and P Lynch, 'Inside the National Conversation: The SNP Government and the Politics of Independence 2007–2010' (2012) 80 *Scottish Affairs* 91.

Parliament and the Scottish Government have largely usurped Westminster and Whitehall as the Scottish forums for debate and the national voice. This political status is totally removed from devolved administrations' legal competence. It comes from the nature of elected assemblies and state leaders that feel as though they are 'closer to home' than UK-wide counterparts. While institutional redesign may be part of the answer, therefore, the 'problem' is essentially political. Part of the answer must also be political. For Westminster and Whitehall to adapt to this change, officeholders must find a new way of dealing with each other that will be as much a political craft as it is a structural design. Drawing on a coherent vision for devolution, a new approach to devolved politics must be developed that can incorporate the Scottish administration's unforeseen political status.

A key feature of the new Union statecraft should be political acceptance of (and adaptation to) the institutional drift caused by devolution. For this 'statecraft', we do not envisage the purely party-political, pragmatic strategy offered by Bulpitt, based on governing competence as a key to winning elections.[76] Nor do we envisage a very thick account such as that offered by Will in *Statecraft as Soulcraft*.[77] Instead, we envisage Union statecraft as a political approach adopted by Unionist politicians at both the UK and Scotland levels to emphasise and develop the values of the Union while still accepting their status as competitive political actors. Unlike conventions such as the Sewel Convention, which create only a thin consent-based link with the centre, this is a fully fledged cooperative approach. As mentioned, therefore, the full content of statecraft must come after the Union's underpinning values and principles have been agreed upon. Much of this work is already underway, particularly in the Lords' Select Committee on the Constitution's 2016 report, which identified six 'principles underlying the Union and devolution'.[78] It must be motivated by mutual benefit rather than coercion. For example, in contrast with many federal infrastructures where the centre has coercive fiscal leavers, Barnett depoliticises allocation. This reflects the original strategy behind devolution, which was to separate Scottish competences rather than link devolved apparatus to the centre.

There is, nonetheless, a preliminary component of Union statecraft that may be recommended based on this chapter's findings. Recognising Holyrood as the new, premier locus of Scottish politics, and accepting that this is unchangeable and tied to its status as the democratic forum closest to a people with a strong sub-state national identity, Unionist parties should approach and utilise Holyrood as a more expansive player. The approach to Holyrood should include its de facto political status rather than being strictly limited to its legal powers. It should also demonstrate the value of deeper cooperation with the centre rather than compartmentalising UK policy separately from devolved competences. There is

---

[76] J Bulpitt, 'The Discipline of the New Democracy: Mrs Thatcher's Domestic Statecraft' (1986) 34 *Political Studies* 19.

[77] GF Will, *Statecraft as Soulcraft: What Government Does* (New York, Touchstone, 1984).

[78] 'The Union and Devolution' (n 28).

a perception that, at devolved level, Unionist parties have preferred to fly under the radar in designing policy. Flagship policies such as the smoking ban tended to mirror movements south of the border rather than representing a truly distinct path for Scotland. Also, both Scottish Labour and Scottish Conservatives are restricted in their actions because of tight loyalties to their counterparts in the rest of the UK. Richard Leonard was seen as Corbyn's man in Holyrood[79] and Scottish Conservatives have been hesitant to criticise damaging actions by the party in Westminster (however, Douglas Ross's recent intervention in 'Partygate' and other comments represent an important break with this trend).[80]

As a forum for the distinct Scottish political voice, Holyrood favours those who are willing to criticise actions in Westminster that go against Scots' interests and 'stand up' for the Scots as a political group. Union statecraft must leave space for this kind of exchange if it is to be electorally attractive and Unionist parties should not be afraid to capitalise on these kinds of opportunity. Criticising the UK government, or a UK-wide party, should not be equated with anti-Unionism. The flip side is that Unionist parties are in a stronger position than independence parties to coordinate initiatives with Westminster and Whitehall. By adopting an approach which accepts the political potency of devolution and the way in which policy plans can cut across devolved and retained competencies, parties can use Union statecraft to reinforce the benefits of the Union. In exercising autonomy from their counterparts in the rest of the UK, Scottish Unionists can engage meaningfully in political bargaining and cooperation with the UK government. By publicly finding and implementing mutually beneficial agreements, Unionists will reinforce the advantages of working together.

This represents a break from the original vision of devolved administrations as restricted to their own territories and vires. It also raises serious questions about the institutional changes required to make such a statecraft viable – the role of Scottish MPs in this framework is a particularly important issue. Nonetheless, the best response to the changed nature of Scottish politics is a new focus on cooperation rather than compartmentalisation. This may tie into the recent Lords Constitution Committee report on the territorial state, which argues for a more cooperative approach to strengthening the Union which recognises its pluralism.[81] Devolution and Holyrood *are* Scottish politics, and it is difficult to show the value

---

[79] S Carrell, 'Richard Leonard Wins Scottish Labour Leadership in Decisive Victory' *The Guardian* (18 November 2017) www.theguardian.com/politics/2017/nov/18/richard-leonard-voted-scottish-labour-leader.

[80] 'New Scottish Tory Leader Douglas Ross Promises to "Stand up" to Boris Johnson as Meeting with Ruth Davidson Revealed' *Politics Home* (6 August 2020) www.politicshome.com/news/article/new-scottish-tory-leader-douglas-ross-promises-to-stand-up-to-boris-johnson-as-meeting-with-ruth-davidson-revealed; H Stewart et al, 'Scottish Tory Leader and Senior Backbencher Call for Johnson to Resign' *The Guardian* (12 January 2022) www.theguardian.com/politics/2022/jan/12/scottish-tory-leader-calls-for-boris-johnson-to-resign; L Webster, 'Scottish Tories Let Boris Johnson Off "Scot-Free" in Commons Sleaze Vote' *The National* (1 December 2021) www.thenational.scot/news/19754472.scottish-tories-let-boris-johnson-off-scot-free-westminster-sleaze-vote/.

[81] 'Respect and Co-operation: Building a Stronger Union for the 21st Century' (n 35) 26.

of UK institutions to this politics without direct cooperation. One precursor to this must be more political autonomy for Scottish Unionist parties.

VII. Conclusion

In this chapter, we have applied some new concepts, and adapted an old one, to help explain both the genius and failures of secession politics in the UK. Firstly, there is the idea of secession diplomacy. This has been a responsive and pragmatic approach to repeated calls for Scottish independence. Where other countries have suppressed secession movements, the UK government has been willing to grant concessions wherever demands have been strong enough. These concessions were intended to cool demands for independence. Secondly, there is our conception of ad hoc constitutional change. Secession diplomacy is necessarily piecemeal; however, it does not have to be totally unguided by long-term vision and principle. Finally, there is Union statecraft. This is an approach to UK politics that fully accounts for the political status of devolved administrations and their leaders. It is a consistent way of working these relations based on a long-term vision for devolution. We have shown the basic parameters of these concepts and how they relate to each other, but much work remains to be done to fully flesh out their content and implications.

Devolution is structurally different to federalism, and it has also developed out of a political context that is distinct from many federal systems. Therefore, to address devolution and make it productive, we need to respond with a different political craft to what one would normally find in a federal system. Naturally, it must also move beyond the current Indi/Unionist rigidity. Union statecraft should recognise the limited coercive leavers at the centre's disposal, as well as the changed nature of Scottish politics, and develop through cooperation.

The UK's underdeveloped approach to devolution is reflected in failed reform in the Commons and Lords. Westminster's status has been altered by the diffusion of democratic legitimacy at the sub-state level. Although the Scottish Parliament may be limited in its powers, politicians are individuals with beliefs and interests that go beyond their institutions' law-making competence. Devolution politicians and officeholders have used their platform to alter the political landscape in the UK. Some have therefore tried to reform Westminster to better meet the imperatives of devolution. However, the logics of a devolved assembly, or a national assembly within a devolved state, are different to those deeply entrenched in Westminster. Constitutional layering has found its limits in Lords reform and EVEL. Proposals were found to be too conflicting with the Parliament to work. To make things more difficult, EVEL also continued a pattern of ad hoc reform that lacks vision for the UK's constitutional future.

If both devolution and the Union are to be sustained – in other words, recognising that secession diplomacy has run out of road – the UK requires both political and institutional reform which must be informed by vision, principle and statecraft.

16

Northern Ireland's Constitutional Position in the UK

KATE HOEY, BARONESS HOEY

I. Introduction

In the months before the 2016 referendum on the UK's membership in the European Union, I travelled around the country recommending a Leave vote. I spoke at numerous rallies, where ordinary men and women told me that their concerns about EU membership had been ignored for many years. They understood that the referendum was their opportunity to reassert control over the future direction of their country. From their passion and the turnout at these events, I was not at all surprised when the country voted to leave, but many in the UK and EU establishment were shocked. They just could not understand the anger people felt about the EU in many parts of country.

Over the past few months, I have witnessed something similar taking place in Northern Ireland. There is genuine anger, especially in the Unionist community, about the constitutional status of Northern Ireland within the UK. Far too many in the UK political establishment, as well as in academia and the media, do not fully appreciate this discontent. They fail to take seriously the strength or legitimacy of British identity among many people in Northern Ireland. They therefore cannot see that many people in Northern Ireland feel that their Britishness is being dismantled brick by brick.

At the core of this anxiety is a very serious concern about how the Brexit process is being implemented in Northern Ireland. When the UK voted to leave the EU, most people quite rightly assumed that *all* of the UK would leave the EU on the same terms. Yet, in the years that followed the vote, many pro-Remain politicians tried to block Brexit altogether, and they thought Northern Ireland would be their vehicle to do so. Politicians who had shown no concern for Northern Ireland before the Brexit vote started waxing lyrical about the importance of the Belfast (Good Friday) Agreement and the supposed need for 'no border' on the island of Ireland. These discussions were often very misinformed, bearing little resemblance to the actual terms of the Belfast Agreement.

Statements by Irish and EU politicians were often treated as purely factual, while Unionist voices, if they were heard at all, were taken with a heavy dose of scepticism.

Those of us who believe in a UK independent of the European Union *and* in the territorial integrity of the UK were placed in an almost impossible situation. The Chequers Plan, announced by Theresa May in 2018, seemingly had the advantage of treating the whole of the UK on (mostly) equal terms, but it had the serious disadvantage of not properly implementing the result to leave the European Union. Conversely, the Northern Ireland Protocol, negotiated by Boris Johnson's government in October 2019, had the advantage of extracting Great Britain fully from the European Union, but it contained the serious disadvantage of leaving Northern Ireland under many aspects of the EU legal regime. As a result of the Protocol, which received legislative assent in the Withdrawal Act after the December 2019 general election, not only does Northern Ireland need to follow laws that the rest of the UK does not, but this arrangement means that internal UK trade (Britain to Northern Ireland) is now treated as if it were foreign trade, subject to customs bureaucracy.

For Unionists, this is an unacceptable state of affairs. Crucially, it was never given consent by the Unionist community in Northern Ireland. In this chapter, I will argue that the Northern Ireland Protocol is a violation of two key constitutional principles. The first is the idea that Northern Ireland is an equal part of the UK and therefore its residents should be treated as equals to those in any other parts of the UK. The second is the principle of consent that has been at the heart of the post-Troubles political system in Northern Ireland. Any change to the constitutional status of Northern Ireland within the UK cannot be made unilaterally by Westminster. The people of Northern Ireland must agree to it. Community consent was at the core of the Belfast Agreement, yet it has been blithely ignored by those who now profess to care so much about it.

II. The Political Significance of Unionism

In order to understand how we have arrived at this unfortunate position, it is first important to explain the significance of Unionist identity in Northern Ireland. Too often, Unionism is treated by the media as some kind of backward, inward-looking and sectarian position. There could be nothing further from the truth. Unionism is a broad church in terms of left and right. There are Catholics who are pro-Union, as well as members of non-Christian faiths and those of no faith. What unites Unionists is the fact that their British identity is significant to them, that they regard the UK as the relevant political unit for that identity and that they see Northern Ireland as an integral part of the UK.

For many decades, Northern Ireland Unionism has been treated with disdain by successive UK governments. From the 1880s until the 1910s, three major attempts were made to introduce Home Rule (devolution) in Ireland, which would have had the effect of ensuring that most of the laws governing all of the island, including Unionists in Ulster, were made in Dublin. In 1914, the Third Home Rule Act passed, but its provisions were suspended pending the end of the First World War. The war changed things in really important ways. Above all, British politicians in Westminster became more alert to the Unionist cause thanks to the sacrifice of many Northern Irish soldiers on behalf of the UK in the war. In just two days (1–2 July 1916), over 5500 members of the 36th (Ulster) Division perished at the Battle of the Somme. As Paul Bew writes, this sacrifice gave Unionists 'new credibility within British political life'.[1] A consensus grew in London that the terms of the 1914 Act were no longer tenable. Unionists in the North could not have rule from Dublin imposed on them without their consent.

Consequently, when Home Rule was revisited after the war, partition was the new suggestion. The island would be divided into two: a six-county Northern Ireland would have its own governing institutions based in Belfast and the 26-county Southern Ireland would have its own separate institutions based in Dublin. Ulster Unionists never claimed to be a separate nation, and so partition and Home Rule were not really the demands of the community. They saw their nationality as British. They accepted the Government of Ireland Act 1920 as a pragmatic compromise – not because they were particularly fond of partition, but because it recognised Unionists' democratic demands to stay in the UK.

By this point, in the middle of the Anglo-Irish War, things were too late for the South. A truce was declared in July 1921 and the Anglo-Irish Treaty was signed on 6 December 1921. One year later, the Irish Free State was declared, and the devolved government of Northern Ireland exempted itself from this new state, choosing to remain within the UK. This marked the birth of Northern Ireland as a political unit within the UK.

The international border between Northern Ireland and the Irish Free State was agreed by the governments of the UK, the Free State and Northern Ireland in December 1925. Although the Free State government initially accepted the partition of the island, many in the nationalist cause still insisted that the Irish nation was unitary and must cover the whole of the island of Ireland. The 1937 Constitution of Ireland asserted a territorial claim to the North. Article 2 proclaimed, 'The national territory consists of the whole island of Ireland, its islands, and the territorial seas'. This was an illegal statement, in contravention of an internationally agreed treaty. Yet, it remained in the Irish constitution for over six decades.

The campaign to tear Northern Ireland from the UK and annex part of a constitutional monarchy to a neighbouring republic has been going on since the island of Ireland was partitioned. Right throughout my early childhood in the 1950s, there was sporadic armed insurgency. Attempts were made to use political reforms to quell violence. The Sunningdale Agreement of 1973, the Anglo-Irish

---

[1] P Bew, *Ireland and the Politics of Enmity* (Oxford, Oxford University Press, 2007) 382.

Agreement of 1985 and the Belfast (Good Friday) Agreement of 1998 all sought to establish a principle of cross-community governance.

III. The Belfast (Good Friday) Agreement: Separating Myth from Reality

The most significant of these efforts was the Belfast (Good Friday) Agreement, signed by Tony Blair and Bertie Ahern on 10 April 1998. It is in fact two agreements: a short UK/ROI treaty and a more detailed multiparty agreement. The following month, as a Labour MP, I travelled to Northern Ireland to campaign with pro-Union politicians, including the UUP leader David Trimble, for a 'Yes' vote in the referendum on the Agreement. As someone born and brought up in Northern Ireland, and with many deep and continuing connections, I perhaps had more credibility with the Unionist community in Northern Ireland than any other Labour MP. Therefore, my presence in the campaign was useful for Tony Blair, who wanted a big 'Yes' vote.

I had many misgivings about the Belfast Agreement. There were parts of it which were very unpalatable to Unionists. These included the release of terrorists from prison, the inclusion of former terrorists in the Northern Ireland legislature and Executive, the requirement that the Executive always be composed of a coalition between unionists and nationalists, and North/South political structures.

I nonetheless campaigned in its favour because I wanted (and still want) to see peace and stability in my home country. Many in the pro-Union community, including me, were prepared to accept this bitter pill because we thought the Belfast Agreement would achieve two things. First, it would very clearly cement the place of Northern Ireland within the UK. It established, once and for all, that Northern Ireland could not be removed from the UK without the express consent of its people. Likewise, it required the Republic of Ireland to abandon its unilateral claim over the whole of the island of Ireland. Second, we so wanted peace after all the years of bloodshed and strife. We were convinced that the Belfast Agreement was the tool to deliver this.

It seems we were deceived. The events of the last few years show that the principle of consent was merely symbolic. The Belfast Agreement does not protect Northern Ireland's equal place in the Union at all. You can change everything about Northern Ireland's sovereignty without the consent of the people of Northern Ireland except for technical secession from the UK. The Court of Appeal in *In Re Jim Allister* in March 2022 made it clear that Northern Ireland could be placed in an entirely different legal regime, subject to the powers of a foreign entity (in this case the EU), and the people of Northern Ireland could have no say over any of this. This is a very disturbing development. It means that one day Northern Ireland could theoretically be placed under the legal jurisdiction of Dublin, without any approval from the Northern Ireland people, so long as it remains technically part of the UK, if only in name. If I knew then what I know now, I would not have recommended a 'Yes' vote on the Belfast Agreement, and I think this is true for many Unionists who supported the treaty in 1998.

One of the biggest misunderstandings about the Belfast Agreement is the idea that it guaranteed an open border between Northern Ireland and the Republic of Ireland. It did not, and there is virtually no discussion of the border in the agreement. The word 'border' does not appear at all. There *is* a border between the North and South. Northern Ireland and the Republic of Ireland have completely different tax regimes, social services, currency, political systems, units of measurement, and much else. Even when the Maastricht Treaty removed customs controls on both sides of the border, VAT rates were different, leading to cross-border shopping and, in some cases, smuggling. That border is a real one, which has been recognised by the UK, the Republic and internationally on multiple occasions over the last century. When Ireland joined the euro in 1999, it hardened the border further, but no one seemed to complain about that at the time.

However, there has always been a Common Travel Area between the UK and the Republic of Ireland, which has nothing specifically to do with Northern Ireland separate from the rest of the UK. It has existed since 1923 and has survived all of the turmoil of the past century, resulting in 1.6 million Irish citizens moving to Britain, double the numbers who went to the USA in the same period.[2] This arrangement predates the EU, and it has never been under threat. The EU has shown that it is willing to be pragmatic about the integrity of its 'four freedoms' (free movement of goods, services, labour and capital) when it benefits from flexibility, whereas at other times it is utterly inflexible when it is in its interests not to make exceptions. The EU Withdrawal Treaty made a carve-out, allowing for the UK and the Irish Republic to 'make arrangements between themselves relating to the movement of persons between their territories'. Why could such pragmatism not be used when it came to trade?

Another key misunderstanding about the Belfast Agreement is the idea that it requires the UK government to be neutral on the question of Northern Ireland's future. This, in fact, goes a little further back to the Downing Street Declaration made by John Major in 1993. Major's joint statement with Albert Reynolds (Irish Taoiseach) was seen as a precursor to the IRA ceasefire, which made the Belfast Agreement possible. Major declared that the UK government has 'no selfish strategic or economic interest in Northern Ireland'. This phrase has often been misinterpreted. The Declaration does not say that the UK government has no interest *at all* in Northern Ireland, simply that its interests are not *selfish*. It is not selfish to protect the right of self-determination of people in Northern Ireland, including those who feel British or would prefer to remain part of the UK than be submerged in a culture which they do not feel is their own.

The practice of the Irish government here is instructive. The Irish government is not a neutral actor, nor does it really pretend to be on this issue. Although, as part

---

[2] D Ferriter, 'How the Irish Became Britain's Oldest, Loneliest Ethnic Group', *Irish Times*, 17 May 2022.

of the Belfast Agreement, the Irish government changed the language of its 1937 Constitution's territorial claim over the North, it has not abandoned the aspiration of a united Ireland as a matter of policy. The new language in the Constitution is softer, but still makes an aspirational claim for a united Ireland as 'the firm will of the Irish nation … to unite all the people who share the territory of the island of Ireland'. The Constitution does qualify that 'a united Ireland shall be brought about only by peaceful means with the consent of a majority of the people, democratically expressed, in both jurisdictions in the island'.

The amended Irish Constitution thus still asserts a desire for a united Ireland, albeit requiring consent to be achieved. The UK government, equally, should also feel free to express its preference for a UK, with Northern Ireland being an equal member. This position is simply a mirror of the Irish government's position and is in no way a violation of the principles of the Belfast Agreement. Yet, in practice, the UK government presents itself as a 'mediator rather than sovereign power'.[3] Unionists feel betrayed by their own UK government, while the Irish government constantly backs up nationalists.

IV.   Devolution: Has it Delivered?

One of the main things the Belfast Agreement *did* do was re-establish devolved government in Northern Ireland. As has been mentioned, the Government of Ireland Act 1920 made provisions for Home Rule in Northern Ireland. The state opening of the Northern Ireland Parliament took place in June 1921. Just over 50 years later, in 1972, direct rule was imposed in Northern Ireland, bringing devolved government to an end. The new Northern Ireland Assembly met in 1998 under new terms. Unlike before, when the principle of majority rule applied, the Executive requires cross-community power-sharing. All Executives must contain both nationalist and Unionist members.

The record of devolution has not lived up to the aspirations of those who supported the creation of the Northern Ireland Assembly. There has repeatedly been a failure to reach consensus between nationalist and Unionist parties, leading to a regular collapse in the Executive. On a political level, devolution seems to have done little to subside the orientation of politics around constitutional questions at the cost of real political debates over the substance of policy. There is even a term for this – 'Ulsterisation' – which is sadly now being used to describe Scottish politics, too. For example, while Northern Ireland has long had a different set of parties from the rest of the UK, devolution entrenched rather than weakened this divide. I have always argued that UK parties should compete in all of the UK. There is no reason, for example, why the Labour Party should not stand candidates in Northern Ireland. In 1998, I was part of a small group of Labour MPs who wrote to the Prime

---

[3] WB Smith, 'The British State and Ulster Unionism' in JW Foster and WB Smith (eds), *The Idea of Union: Great Britain and Northern Ireland* (Vancouver, Belcouver Press, 2021) 187–88.

Minister Tony Blair arguing that the ban 'institutionalises sectarian patterns, stunts political growth, increases tensions and fears, and makes it difficult to develop trust and popular political empowerment'.[4] Our concerns were sadly ignored.

As I write in the summer of 2022, the threat to Northern Ireland's place in the Union of Great Britain and Northern Ireland is perceived to be even more threatened. For the first time since devolved government institutions were created, there will be a Sinn Fein First Minister (should the Executive ever be reformed). Despite not winning a single extra MLA and despite the First and Deputy First Ministers being on an equal standing, the media commentators have decided the writing is on the wall for Unionism. Of course, that is entirely false. What happened was that there are three main Unionist parties in Northern Ireland and despite a united call for Unionists to transfer their vote right down the list, this did not happen, so the Democratic Unionist Party lost 2 seats (one DUP (Alex Easton) had become independent before the election and held his seat).

The Belfast Agreement stated that the largest bloc of MLAs would nominate the First Minister, but the St Andrew's Agreement a few years later agreed to change this to the party with the largest number of seats nominating. It was ironic that the DUP, who had supported the change, became the victim of their own negotiations.

V. Brexit and the Northern Ireland Protocol

I strongly believe that leaving the EU was the right thing to do for the UK, and this includes for Northern Ireland, too. British politicians in Westminster have done Northern Ireland a grave disservice by keeping it under EU laws while the rest of the UK is exempt. Under the Protocol, Northern Ireland remains in large part under control of the EU. About 70 per cent of Northern Ireland's economic activity – agriculture, manufacturing and environment – are subject to all present and future EU laws, while the rest of the UK is not. Northern Ireland remains subject to the European Court of Justice as its highest court, whereas the rest of the UK does not. Trade barriers have been erected between Northern Ireland and the rest of the UK, a position that would be unthinkable anywhere else in the country. Can you imagine customs checks between the East and West Midlands?

This problem stems from critical errors made by the UK government in the Brexit negotiation process. Pro-Remain politicians, who wanted to scupper Brexit, saw their opportunity with Northern Ireland.[5] They believed they could force the whole of the UK to stay in the EU single market and/or Customs Union. They argued that it was absolutely essential that there should be no trade barrier

---

[4] 'You Can Join Labour in Dublin but Not Derry' *Daily Telegraph* (5 June 1998).
[5] M Barnier, *My Secret Brexit Diary* (Cambridge, Polity, 2021), 90.

between Northern Ireland and the Republic of Ireland. The UK government made clear very early on that it had no intention to reimpose customs controls on the island. Earlier in the process, the Irish Taoiseach Enda Kenny seemed sympathetic to the idea that the UK and the ROI could resolve this problem bilaterally. Arguably, bilateralism was required by the Belfast Agreement, which provided for a British–Irish intergovernmental conference to ensure 'bilateral co-operation on all matters of mutual interest within the competence of both Governments'.

This changed, however, when Kenny was replaced by Leo Varadkar in June 2017, shortly after Theresa May lost her parliamentary majority in the 2017 election. Varadkar sided with the EU and abandoned the principle of bilateralism, stating that the Republic of Ireland would not negotiate separately from the European Union. This placed the Irish border at the heart of the Brexit negotiations, rather than a *sui generis* issue which could be addressed by the governments separately, as so many other issues, not least the Belfast Agreement itself, had been done without EU interference.

Nonetheless, Theresa May foolishly declared that there would be no hard border between Northern Ireland and the Republic in the Joint UK/EU report on 8 December 2017. This was reckless and a complete failure of UK statecraft. Really, what this pledge came down to was a fear of physical infrastructure on the border. The reason for this was some nationalist politicians had raised the possibility of terrorist violence at the border.[6] This was cynical and not a legitimate way of carrying out political debate. Theresa May's Chief of Staff Gavin Barwell reveals in his diaries the panic at No 10 when unnamed Northern Ireland politicians told them that the peace process would collapse if Northern Ireland detached itself from the EU single market.[7] Furthermore, no one was talking about the kind of infrastructure generally associated with a 'hard' border, like walls or customs buildings. May ruled out very modest, non-intrusive technological infrastructure.

By making this commitment, the UK government gave the EU enormous bargaining power. It meant that either the rest of the UK would need to fall under the EU's legal orbit, too (basically nullifying the Brexit vote), or Northern Ireland would have to be treated as akin to an EU territory for the purposes of the UK government. May chose the former; Boris Johnson chose the latter.[8] Neither is acceptable.

By keeping the pledge of 'no checks' between North and South while also committing to taking Britain fully out of the EU, Boris Johnson divided our own country internally. The Northern Ireland Protocol leaves one part of the UK under

---

[6] 'Varadkar Warns EU a Hard Border Risks Return to Violence of the Past in Ireland', *Belfast Telegraph* (19 October 2018).

[7] G Barwell, *Chief of Staff: An Insider's Account of Downing Street's Most Turbulent Years* (London, Atlantic Books, 2021), 160.

[8] It should be noted that May's deal included the worst of both worlds. While she would have kept the whole of the UK in the EU customs union, she would have also kept Northern Ireland (only) in the single market.

a different set of laws than the rest of the UK. This represents an unacceptable change in the status of Northern Ireland, different from the rest of the country, without the consent of the Northern Irish people or the devolved institutions.

Would any other country in the world have offered to divide its sovereign territory and leave part of its country under the jurisdiction of a foreign court? I can hardly imagine the USA allowing Alaska to operate under Canadian law, with the Canadian Supreme Court as the highest court in Alaska, merely to enable easy trade between Alaska and Canada, especially if that would mean border checks between goods coming into Alaska from California. It would be an absurd situation and, rightly, viewed as such by the rest of the world. Only recently, German Chancellor Olaf Scholz argued in favour of the territorial integrity of Russia when it comes to trade between the exclave Kaliningrad and the rest of Russia.[9] Yet, when it comes to Northern Ireland within the UK, a different standard seems to apply.

Ill-informed or actually quite hostile politicians in the EU and USA talk about the Protocol as if it is somehow necessary for the endurance of the Belfast Agreement. Nothing could be further from the truth. David Trimble, who won the Nobel Peace Prize for his role in the creation of the agreement, rejects the Protocol entirely. He has written in no uncertain terms: 'Make no mistake about it; the Protocol does not safeguard the Belfast (Good Friday) Agreement. It demolishes its central premise ... that democratic consent is needed to make any change to the status of Northern Ireland.'[10]

In the discussions about the Protocol, it is sometimes implied that the economy of Northern Ireland has more in common with the economy of the Republic of Ireland than with the rest of the UK. This is not the case. It is a significant exaggeration.

Pro-EU politicians will often talk about the 'all-Ireland' economy as if it is more significant than the UK economy of which Northern Ireland is a part. In fact, a very small proportion of goods and services from Northern Ireland enter the Republic (about six per cent of its output). Lord Trimble was absolutely right when he said, 'the EU has nothing to fear from the miniscule level of trade that crosses into its territory from Northern Ireland'.[11]

The Republic of Ireland is 'the world's largest tax haven'.[12] The reporting of multinational firms' huge profits in the Republic of Ireland distorts comparative figures of the North and South's GDP and GDP per capita. While, on paper, these are much higher in the South, in reality these are profits that are hardly taxed and not generated by economic activity in Ireland itself. A better gauge of prosperity for ordinary people is 'actual individual consumption', which is based on

---

[9] H von der Burchard, 'Germany's Scholz urges free transit for Russian goods to Kaliningrad', *Politico*, 30 June 2022, available at www.politico.eu/article/olaf-scholz-urges-free-transit-for-russian-goods-to-kaliningrad/.

[10] D Trimble, 'Ditch the Protocol' in Foster and Smith (n 2).

[11] ibid 342.

[12] G Gudgin, 'The Island Economies' in Foster and Smith (n 2).

consumer spending and government spending on services such as education and health. By this metric, Northern Ireland is a bit better off than the Republic.[13]

In addition, the UK state is much more generous in Northern Ireland than Dublin likely would be. Government spending per head in Northern Ireland (on PPP[14] prices) is 18 per cent higher than in the Republic. There are many economic advantages which Northern Ireland enjoys being in the UK. One of them is that NI public workers will often receive UK-wide rates of pay, even though prices in Northern Ireland tend to be lower than in Great Britain. Equally, if Northern Ireland joined the Republic, it would be rejoining the EU, where Ireland is now a net contributor rather than beneficiary of European Union spending.

In June 2021, I joined with other pro-Union politicians (Jim Allister MLA,[15] Ben Habib, Arlene Foster MLA, Steve Aiken MLA, Lord Trimble) to challenge the Protocol on the grounds that it was incompatible with Article 6 of the Act of Union 1800 and with section 1 of the Northern Ireland Act 1998.

The Act of Union 1800 makes it quite clear that Northern Ireland must be treated as any other part of the UK. Northern Ireland's place in the Union should not be regarded as more contingent or less secure than any other part. People from Northern Ireland should not be treated by the UK government differently than residents of any other part of the United Kingdom. Article 6 of the Act of Union 1800 spells out that residents of Great Britain and (Northern) Ireland shall 'be entitled to the same privileges, and be on the same footing'. The Act singles out 'trade and navigation in all ports and places in the United Kingdom' and that 'subjects of Ireland shall have same the privileges, and be on the same footing as his Majesty's subjects of Great Britain'. The Northern Ireland Protocol clearly violates the terms of the Act of Union.

Our initial complaint was refused judicial review in the Royal Courts of Justice in Belfast. Mr Justice Colston declared that 'much constitutional water has passed under the bridge' and that the legislation implementing the Protocol had, in effect, repealed these provisions of the Act of Union. This is an astonishing conclusion.

In March 2022, the High Court in Belfast dismissed our appeal of this decision. The court did say

> there was a valid argument that the EUWA 2018 as amended conflicts with the same footing provision in Article VI of the 1800 Act because the citizens of NI remain subject to some EU regulation and rules as part of the withdrawal framework which does not apply to other citizens of the UK.[16]

The court held that the Withdrawal Agreement legislation can subjugate earlier legislation where it conflicts, including the Act of Union. As a matter of urgency,

---

[13] ibid.

[14] Purchasing Power Parity.

[15] Member of the Legislative Assembly.

[16] *Court Dismisses Appeal Against EU Exit Protocol*, Judicial Communications Office, 14 March 2022, available at https://www.judiciaryni.uk/sites/judiciary/files/decisions/Summary%20of%20judgment%20-%20In%20re%20Jim%20Allister%20and%20others%20%28EU%20Exit%29%20-%20CA%20-%201403222.pdf.

the UK government must restore this vital provision of the Act of Union. Until there is a border poll which votes to leave the UK, Northern Ireland is entitled to remain a full and integral part of the Union.

VI. Conclusion

At the time of writing (summer 2022), the legislation designed to give the UK government the power to abrogate any part of the Protocol is going through Parliament. There will be attempts to sabotage it by many of the same MPs who tried to stop Brexit. However, whatever the outcome in Parliament, the campaign to ditch the Protocol has brought to the forefront just how little understanding citizens of the rest of the UK have for Northern Ireland. Over many years, governments, whatever their political persuasion, have sidelined Northern Ireland, ignoring what was happening there until forced to deal with the IRA upping their terrorist campaign, first in Northern Ireland and then on mainland Britain. Sadly, it is a widely held view that everything Tony Blair did to bring about the Belfast Agreement was first and foremost to stop bombs going off in London.

By refusing to nominate a First or Deputy First Minister, the DUP has finally drawn serious attention to the fact that the Protocol is jeopardising the hard-won peace brought about by the Belfast Agreement. The increased vote for the Traditional Unionist Voice (TUV) party led by Jim Allister QC has undoubtedly pushed the DUP into this more militant policy. The Executive is thus frozen and its life time-limited. The issue now is the very future of the Agreement, something which the Irish government for several years claimed it was trying to protect. Neither the Republic nor the European Union should be happy that we are in extremely dangerous territory as a result of the mistakes made in the earlier negotiations. London certainly is not. Sadly, Irish government ministers always speak out on the side of the nationalists and then criticise the UK government for not being even-handed in their approach.[17]

No one should underestimate the threat to the entire UK of any border poll in Northern Ireland. Once granted and when lost (as polls consistently predict) under the Agreement, there would have to be a poll every seven years. This instability would also add fuel to the Scottish independent campaign.

If the Government really wants to defend the Union, then seeing Northern Ireland as 'a place apart' can no longer be tolerated. Ministers in the Northern Ireland Office need to be out and about meeting local communities and listening. Conor Burns, the former Minister of State who is a Unionist and a Catholic, spent more time in the Province than any other minister except under direct rule. Secretaries of state who fly in and out on the same day are doing a huge disservice to the Union. All legislation going through Parliament should include Northern

---

[17] J McCormack, 'Brexit: UK government not "even handed" in protocol row, says tánaiste', *BBC News*, 30 June 2022, available at www.bbc.co.uk/news/uk-northern-ireland-62002402.

Ireland when the Executive is not sitting. The Higher Education Freedom of Speech Bill is a current example of when this needs to happen. More and more people living in Northern Ireland are questioning the cost, the efficiency and the need for a devolved Assembly. Planning for a longer-term governance of Northern Ireland needs to happen now. Mandatory coalition when one of the parties in that coalition wants to destroy the country they are meant to be governing is not sustainable.

Professor John Wilson Foster wrote:

> Unionism is not just a 'tradition' to be accommodated in a united separate Ireland like some quaint folk custom. It is a cultural reality which cannot breathe the air of Irish Republican separatism than which it is bigger and to which it is diametrically opposed.[18]

My Britishness, just like for the majority of citizens living in Northern Ireland, is not up for negotiation and never will be. That is what all UK governments need to understand.

---

[18] JW Foster, 'Why I Am a Unionist' in Foster and Smith (n 2) 86.

17

The European Union and
the British Constitution

JOANNA GEORGE AND GISELA STUART,
BARONESS STUART OF EDGBASTON[1]

> Just at this moment Alice felt a very curious sensation, which puzzled her a good deal
> until she made out what it was: she was beginning to grow larger again, and she thought
> at first she would get up and leave the court; but on second thoughts she decided to
> remain where she was as long as there was room for her.
>
> Lewis Carroll, *Alice's Adventures in Wonderland*[2]

I. Introduction

Alice's awareness of growing larger and then considering leaving the court in
Wonderland is in some ways similar to the UK's membership of the EU. The
difference, of course, is that the UK chose to leave via a referendum instead of
remaining in the UK-shaped space that it had uniquely cultivated for itself over
47 years. Like Alice's 'burning curiosity'[3] to follow the White Rabbit into an
unknown Wonderland, the UK's relationship with the EU had initially been driven
by economic 'curiosity'. But by 2016 this economic curiosity, which was the basis
for the Remain campaign, had waned, just as the EU's political and constitutional
ambitions had expanded into an unrecognisable institution from the one the UK
had joined. The EU's institutional architecture, as implemented by the EU Treaties
of the 1990s and 2000s, no longer worked to serve the UK's political interests.

The UK's impact on EU constitutional developments was ultimately mixed
and inconsistent. Yet its historical position within the EU is predicted to significantly influence Member States when they proceed with future EU constitutional

---

[1] We are grateful to Ollie Randall and the editors for comments on an earlier draft; the usual
disclaimer applies.
[2] L Carroll, *Alice's Adventures in Wonderland* (1865).
[3] ibid.

developments. In contrast, the impact of the EU on UK constitutional developments was notable as it generated a hierarchy of laws that had not previously existed, and which has since become deeply embedded in the UK's legal and devolution framework.

Writing in 2013, Qvortrup stated that 'The British Constitution has been subject to more or less constant change from 1997 onwards, but the reforms have not "dominated the nation's life".[4] In 2016, the Brexit vote completely changed this. This chapter examines how changes to EU constitutional structures had an impact on UK governance and the UK's relationship with the EU. We seek to highlight the lessons that can be learnt from UK–EU dynamics since the 1990s and analyse how its successes and failures can help navigate the post-Brexit relationship.

II. The UK's Role in Changes to EU Governance in the 1990s and 2000s

A. Sowing the Seeds of Brexit: The Maastricht Treaty

In order to offer an analysis of constitutional reform since 1997 and to provide a richer picture of the post-Brexit relationship between the UK and EU, it is necessary to consider *why* and *how* this distinct constitutional and political relationship first emerged.

The origin of the UK's relationship with the EU stems from the UK's late entry into the then European Communities, the original members of which had formed close ties for two decades before the UK joined in 1973. This made it more challenging for the UK to develop naturally close ties with other Member States, in comparison to original Member States such as France and Germany, whose relationship was 'heavily institutionalised'[5] from the outset. But also, unlike her European counterparts, the UK's status as an undefeated and uninvaded country from World War II made a relationship with Europe important, but not existential to the UK's future. Similarly, the UK's constitutional evolution, political system, religious history and geography had always differentiated her from her neighbours. These factors shaped an attitude of ambivalence towards UK political integration in an increasingly institutionalised Europe.

The issue of how much the UK would integrate itself into European affairs first came to a head in 1992 with the signing of the Maastricht Treaty, which lay the political, legal and historical foundations of what we now know as the European Union. This marked the beginning of 'a new stage in the process of creating an

---

[4] M Qvortrup, *The British Constitution: Continuity and Change: A Festschrift for Vernon Bogdanor* (Oxford, Hart Publishing, 2013) 2.

[5] J Smith, *The United Kingdom's Journeys into and out of the European Union* (London, Routledge, 2017) 16.

ever closer union among the peoples of Europe'.[6] Yet Britain originally joined the European project for largely economic reasons.[7] This wording was one of the tension points in the negotiation of the treaty. An earlier draft prepared by Ruud Lubbers proposed a 'federal' Europe,[8] which was rejected by the UK delegation and replaced with 'ever closer union' – a phrase that has been core to the EU's aims since the Treaty establishing the European Community in 1957 and which Cameron later sought to exempt the UK from in 2015 with the hope that the UK would remain in the EU.[9] Whilst the changing of words initially worked to appease the UK, the unintended consequence was a relationship with the EU that was not consistently comfortable on either side for over 20 years.

Maastricht was both a victory and a failure for Britain's place in the EU. Firstly, the negotiation of the Treaty, led by the Major government, demonstrated a way forward of accommodating the UK in an EU of increasing and variable geography. By actively voicing what the UK was willing and not willing to accept as a Member State, the Major government was able to remove the protocol on the Social Chapter from the body of the Treaty and obtain opt-outs from the monetary union and the Schengen borderless area. This, in turn, led the way for other Member States, such as Denmark, who also sought opt-outs.

But a consequence of Major's role in negotiating the Treaty intensified the idea of a Europe that no longer had a common destination. Major's need to appease Conservative politics also reduced the UK's ability to shape developments[10] within the EU, an action that was later repeated by Cameron.

Academics, commentators and politicians have since observed that Maastricht tried to do too many things. Issues that arose were attempted to be resolved by later EU Treaties. Whilst the UK's 'hostile stance'[11] at Maastricht did restrict the political ambitions for a federal Europe, problems at EU level, such as the analysis paralysis problem faced by Member States over what powers and authority would be dispersed to the EU, meant that EU governance would remain unsettled. That is, of course, until Member States provide the EU 'with the tools for effective action'[12] on key issues such as EU fiscal policy.

Maastricht showed that it was possible for the UK to be a Member State and voice its own needs and preferences by speaking of 'red lines' to accommodate

---

[6] Treaty on European Union, 7 February 1992, Art A.

[7] G Stuart, 'The Strange Thing Is Not That Britain Is Leaving the EU – It's That We Ever Joined' *The Guardian* (31 January 2020) www.theguardian.com/commentisfree/2020/jan/31/britain-eu-economic-political-maastricht.

[8] S de Mars, *EU Law in the UK* (Oxford, Oxford University Press, 2020) 17.

[9] V Milner, '"Ever Closer Union" in the EU Treaties and Court of Justice Case Law' Briefing Paper No 07230 (House of Commons Library, 16 November 2015).

[10] A Menon and JP Salter, 'Britain's Influence in the EU' (2016) 236(1) *National Institute Economic Review*.

[11] A Menon and V Wright, 'The Paradoxes of "Failure": British EU Policy Making in Comparative Perspective' (1998) 13(4) *Public Policy and Administration* 46.

[12] A Menon, 'Unhappy Anniversary: Maastricht 25 Years On' (London, UK in a Changing Europe, 7 February 2017) https://ukandeu.ac.uk/unhappy-anniversary-maastricht-25-years-on/.

domestic politics. Yet this came at a cost to the consensus-orientated relationship that is required to maintain long-term connection and understanding within the EU, regardless of where it is seeks to go.

B. New Labour and the Amsterdam and Nice Treaties

By the 1990s and 2000s, the EU had become a 'very different animal and a product of other historical forces'.[13] This was due to the growing political and social identity the EU was seeking to inhabit at the expense of national governments. Maastricht had awakened European citizens to this in countries such as France, which narrowly approved of it in a referendum (51 per cent), whilst Denmark rejected it outright in a first referendum (50.7 per cent) before accepting it in a subsequent one. Whilst the concept of a 'democratic deficit' was first used in the late 1970s, it was Maastricht that truly paved the way.

This is because Maastricht provided the European Parliament with greater legislative powers and the ability to branch out into more policy areas, but critically failed to clearly outline when Member States could make law or when the EU could.[14] For the UK, this was 'deemed very problematic',[15] especially as there was limited scope within the Major government and the British media to nurture a positive perception of the tangible benefits of EU membership under the EU's new functions.

Unlike Major, Blair was a more passionate and politically unrestrained supporter of the EU, with a party that was mostly united on a manifesto promise to 'give Britain the leadership in Europe which Britain and Europe need'. Powerful European leaders, such as Helmut Kohl, had already developed a good relationship with Blair prior to his election to office and this worked to the UK's advantage when signing the Treaty of Amsterdam little more than a month after taking office. Amsterdam emphasised the shift 'to the EU's political responsibilities at home and on the wider international stage';[16] an ambition that was in sync with New Labour's geopolitical ambitions. This active interest in European affairs alongside practical action to shape and integrate UK involvement within the EU made Blair an effective and exemplary leader of UK–EU relations during his first five years as Prime Minister.

This can be illustrated by several initiatives. Firstly, regular 'Mini-Corp' meetings enabled junior ministers to discuss what was happening in Brussels in their respective areas. This encouraged greater understanding of what was happening

---

[13] C Bickerton, *The European Union: A Citizen's Guide* (London, Pelican Books, 2016) 48.
[14] de Mars (n 7) 17.
[15] ibid.
[16] European Commission, 'Treaty of Amsterdam: What Has Changed in Europe' (June 1999) 5, http://aei.pitt.edu/15098/1/MOVE-TREATYOFAMSTERDAM-1999.pdf.

on specific policy issues and how they related to each other. Secondly, the development of bilateral relations with European sister parties enhanced awareness of what they were thinking, which in turn created successful working relationships across the EU. This was crucial for initiating, instead of reacting to, events which later proved damaging under the Cameron government, whose disengagement with EU-oriented processes, combined with his 'uncollegiate'[17] strategy to appeal directly to Member States for help, proved fatal by the time he tried to renegotiate the UK's EU membership. Thirdly, junior ministers were encouraged to learn foreign languages to develop stronger cultural connections with their European counterparts, with some pursuing lessons at the old Foreign Office Language School located in Admiralty Arch. In addition, from 2002, MPs were permitted to claim expenses for up to three return visits a year to national parliaments of Council of Europe Member States, EU institutions and agencies.

Not only did this deepen ministers' connections to and understanding of European cultures, but it made Britain 'sound and think' like an engaged Member State concerned with wider EU interests beyond those of the UK's. At domestic level, close relations were cultivated with Labour MEPs, who would attend Parliamentary Labour Party meetings and provide updates from the European Parliament. These approaches were integral to Blair's strategy for Britain to lead within Europe.

Timing was also a significant factor in Blair's initial EU success. The UK held the Presidency of the Council of the EU during the first half of 1998, which gave Blair the authority to push for enlargement towards the East. The Treaty of Nice, agreed in 2000, set out to accomplish this. So, in this respect, Blair succeeded in shaping and solving an issue that was of paramount concern to the direction of the EU's future.

But the unintended consequence of being *too* eager to shape the future of the EU meant that the UK was effectively a guinea pig for an immigration policy that caused significant and long-term divisions within the UK.[18] Arguably, the immigration policy was one of the most visible EU policies that UK citizens and residents *felt* and *saw* the impact of when Blair decided to immediately allow the 10 new Member States to benefit from free movement of people in the UK in advance of their 2004 joining date. Inadvertently, reducing immigration from EU Member States subsequently became a key issue for Brexit voters.

Schmidt observed in 2006 that the 'democratic deficit' is at the national, not European, level because 'national leaders and publics have yet to come to terms

---

[17] M Bevington, 'Brexit: David Cameron Did Even More Damage Than You Think' (London, UK in a Changing Europe, 13 August 2018) https://ukandeu.ac.uk/brexit-david-cameron-did-even-more-damage-than-you-think/.

[18] See Lord Ashcroft Polls, 'How the United Kingdom Voted on Thursday ... and Why' (24 June 2016). In this poll, a third of Leave voters said that their main reason for voting for Brexit was to control immigration.

with the institutional impact of the EU on the traditional workings of the national politics'.[19] Blair's decision in the case of EU enlargement illustrates this. What this shows is that careful attention is consistently required to strike the right balance between national concerns and EU ambitions. Without this, one is likely to fall short.

C. The Convention on the Future of the European Union

Critics have argued that aspects of the British constitution which have been subject to piecemeal and reactive constitutional reform since 1997 have failed to solve the problems they set out to achieve. This criticism intrinsically applies to the EU. Following the signing of the Nice Treaty, which aimed to make EU institutions more efficient and legitimate,[20] it soon became clear that the 'arcane business'[21] of EU constitutional treaty changes was no longer workable. In response, the Laeken Declaration was drafted in December 2001, and this established the Convention on the Future of Europe. The Convention put forward questions on acute issues such as resolving the EU's democratic deficit, bringing the EU closer to its citizens and integration of the Treaties into a Constitutional Treaty.[22]

Intriguingly, prior to the establishment of the Convention, Blair had advocated for an intergovernmental and political 'Statement of Principles' – a stark change to the pattern of another legal treaty.[23] This, he advocated, would be a more pragmatic way of shaping a 'responsive'[24] EU to accommodate 25 Member States[25] without turning it into a 'superstate'.[26]

Blair failed to gain support for a Statement of Principles within the European Parliament. But the Convention was a formative moment in the UK's approach to the EU and an opportunity for Blair to shape a constitution for Europe[27] beyond a post-World War II reaction. A strength of the Convention was that it actively included national parliamentarians[28] and government representatives. This

---

[19] VA Schmidt, *Democracy in Europe: The EU and National Polities* (Oxford, Oxford University Press, 2006) abstract.

[20] European Parliament, 'The Treaty of Nice and the Convention on the Future of Europe', www.europarl.europa.eu/factsheets/en/sheet/4/the-treaty-of-nice-and-the-convention-on-the-future-of-europe.

[21] J Rankin, 'Lack of Citizens at EU's Citizens' Debate Raises Eyebrows', *The Guardian* (18 June 2021) www.theguardian.com/world/2021/jun/18/eu-citizens-debate-future-europe-talks.

[22] 'The Laeken Declaration and the Convention on the Future of Europe', Research Paper No 02/14 (House of Commons Library, 8 March 2002) 13, https://researchbriefings.files.parliament.uk/documents/RP02-14/RP02-14.pdf.

[23] Tony Blair, speech to the Polish Stock Exchange, Warsaw, 6 October 2000.

[24] ibid.

[25] A Seldon and D Kavanagh, *The Blair Effect 2001–5* (Cambridge, Cambridge University Press, 2010) 374.

[26] ibid.

[27] G Stuart, 'The Convention on the Future of the European Union' (London, UK in a Changing Europe, 2 November 2020) https://ukandeu.ac.uk/brexit-witness-archive/gisela-stuart/.

[28] Gisela Stuart was a UK Parliamentary Representative to the Convention.

provided an open channel for them to voice their opinions in the treaty negotiation process; a perspective that up until that point had not been considered. For the UK, this enabled Parliament to be more involved in European affairs,[29] and this worked well for the UK as its national representatives were made accountable for decisions made at the Convention.[30] However, this process was not repeated, to the detriment of UK–EU understanding.

This understanding had concurrently begun to weaken between Blair and EU leaders as the 9/11 attacks in the USA plunged the West into a geopolitical crisis. This proved a distraction for Blair, whose attention had swung towards supporting the USA in the lead up to the Iraq war in March 2003 – suggesting that Blair was, at heart, an Atlanticist more than a European. Simultaneously, this period was critical for UK–EU relations in the finalising of the draft Constitutional Treaty in July 2003. By diverting his focus, Blair failed to entrench the UK's potential within the EU. After 2003, that opportunity had passed. Despite saying in 2000 that he wanted Britain to 'be the bridge between the EU and the US',[31] Britain unintentionally ended up becoming a wall. By not consistently prioritising EU relations, Blair had, like his predecessors, become a defiant obstacle to collective EU interests.

It was well accepted within the EU that its citizens did not have the same popular interest in European institutions as national ones, but attempting to reduce the 'democratic deficit' through national referendums proved to be too risky in the Netherlands and France, both of which rejected the draft Constitutional Treaty in 2005. This spooked Blair, who had initially promised to hold a referendum in light of the quadruple success of the devolution referendums, but, like six other Member States, he dropped such plans. This reactive hesitation to call a referendum would later become the go-to response for British Prime Ministers for a further eight years.

Had the EU Parliament opted for Blair's proposed Statement of Principles instead of a draft Constitutional Treaty, would this have put the EU on a different trajectory and made the UK a more willing Member State? Possibly. Fundamentally, the UK's influence within the EU after 2003 never recovered as a result of Iraq, which internally permeated UK–EU relations. Simultaneously, Blair's creative method of contributing towards the EU's 'common destiny' narrative had begun to weaken with the introduction of the euro in 1999, highlighting the growing divide between euro and non-euro countries such as the UK. Moreover, the beginning of the UK's political conflict over a referendum on Europe, combined with decreasing trust in UK politicians to deliver on one, became one of the most significant consequences of the EU's most famous and failed constitutional ambition that would pervade the UK throughout the 2010s.

[29] Stuart, 'The Convention' (n 26).
[30] G Stuart, *The Making of Europe's Constitution* (London, The Fabian Society, 2003) 18, https://fabians.org.uk/publication/the-making-of-europes-constitution/.
[31] Blair speech (n 22).

III. Political Dynamics Leading Up to the 2016 EU Referendum

A. The Legacy of the Lisbon Treaty

Despite the failed Constitutional Treaty, EU momentum for another treaty to replace it was back on the agenda again in 2007. Angela Merkel advanced the Berlin Declaration, which facilitated this process and set 2009 as a deadline for the new treaty. Months previously, José Manuel Barroso had announced that an 'institutional settlement' was a priority to make the EU more effective, coherent, transparent and democratic,[32] particularly in the face of globalisation. But the consequence of this urgent need to finish unsettled business following Nice, instead of having a longer period for reflection, exacerbated the 'EU problem' for subsequent UK governments.

Yet there were some successes for the UK from the Lisbon Treaty. Blair's push for a long-term President of the European Council, in contrast to six-month rotations, was implemented, highlighting his success at shaping the EU's institutional architecture. Lisbon also clarified the exclusive, shared and supporting competences of the EU for the first time, providing a clear remit for the UK and other Member States. Of later importance, it offered Article 50, a formal procedure to withdraw from the EU.

What differentiated this treaty from the previous ones was that it was seen as a conclusive document for subsequent years, with no other immediate treaty reform proposed. The contents within Lisbon are identical in substance to those found in the failed Constitutional Treaty. Yet differing interpretations of the constitutional status of Lisbon, with the word 'Constitution' itself having 'been consciously excised',[33] ignited controversy within UK politics.

From a UK political perspective, the House of Commons European Scrutiny Committee stated that Lisbon is 'substantially equivalent to the Constitutional Treaty'.[34] Through a legal lens, the High Court rejected the idea that the Constitutional Treaty was the same as Lisbon in the 2008 *Wheeler* case.[35] Yet from an EU political perspective, Giuliano Amato[36] said in the months leading up to the signing of Lisbon that EU leaders 'decided that the document should

---

[32] ibid.

[33] P Craig, *The Lisbon Treaty, Revised Edition: Law, Politics, and Treaty Reform* (Oxford, Oxford University Press, 2013) 25.

[34] House of Commons European Scrutiny Committee, *European Union Intergovernmental Conference* (2006–07, HC 1014) para 45.

[35] *R (on the application of Stuart Wheeler) v Office of the Prime Minister & Anor* [2008] EWHC 1409 (Admin), paras 26 and 32.

[36] The former Prime Minister of Italy (1992–93 and 2000–01). He was also the Vice-Chair of the Convention and head of the Amato Group, which was set up to consider what action should be taken following the rejection of the Constitutional Treaty.

be unreadable. If it is unreadable, it is not constitutional, that was the sort of perception,[37] so that national leaders could pass it off as a 'typical Brussels treaty'[38] and not an accessible constitutional document. Valéry Giscard d'Estaing[39] has also said similar, acknowledging that it was 'unpenetrable for the public'[40] to understand the difference between Lisbon and the Constitutional Treaty.

This meant that significant developments took place, arguably, without voters really being aware of them. The EU 'democratic deficit' issue, which had been a core challenge for the Convention to resolve, was not being treated with the same importance in the drafting of Lisbon. The consequence of this was a growing sense of resentment and distrust about the EU among UK citizens, with research commissioned by the European Commission in this period highlighting that only a quarter of Brits trusted the EU[41] – a fact not aided by Gordon Brown's deflection of holding a long-discussed referendum on EU Treaty changes. It was becoming increasingly clear that Euroscepticism, both inside and outside of Parliament, was becoming a serious issue, albeit one gestating in the background.

A weakness of the Brown government was that it missed the opportunity of creating a Cabinet Office position for the Europe Minister outside of the Foreign Office to address this. Caroline Flint, Minister of State for Europe during this time, observed that the Foreign Office 'wasn't really about talking to the public in the UK, to explain our role and relationship with the EU'[42] – a missed opportunity to provide a government source of information to counterbalance hostility in the British press towards the EU. Alongside this, the move to elect MEPs in England, Wales and Scotland[43] via a closed party list system in 1999 reduced the connection with voters and their sense of place. As a result, the misunderstanding about Europe became not only a trust issue with the country, but also an institutional one within the UK and European Parliaments.

B. Cameron and UK–EU Understanding

As with the party under Major, the 2010 intake of Conservative MPs were highly concerned with Europe. One commentator observed at the time that the new

---

[37] L Kirk, 'Treaty Made Unreadable to Avoid Referendums, Says Amato' *EUobserver* (16 July 2007).

[38] ibid.

[39] Valéry Giscard d'Estaing, the former President of France (1974–81), was also the Chair of the Convention.

[40] V Giscard d'Estaing, 'Giscard d'Estaing: The EU Treaty Is the Same as the Constitution' *The Independent* (30 October 2007) www.independent.co.uk/voices/commentators/val-eacute-ry-giscard-d-estaing-the-eu-treaty-is-the-same-as-the-constitution-398286.html.

[41] F Nelson, 'Europe Returns to the Commons – and, This Time, Nobody Is Safe' *The Spectator* (19 January 2008) www.spectator.co.uk/article/europe-returns-to-the-commons-and-this-time-nobody-is-safe.

[42] C Flint, 'The EU and British Politics, 2010–2015' (London, UK in a Changing Europe, 29 January 2021) https://ukandeu.ac.uk/brexit-witness-archive/caroline-flint/.

[43] In contrast, Northern Ireland used the Single Transferable Vote system.

intake was 'far and away the most Eurosceptic'[44] in the party's history, with many of them reflecting the views of their constituency associations. On top of this, the 2010 general election saw more MPs standing down than at any election since 1945. This led to a new generation of MPs unable to 'speak' Europe and with no means of learning it either[45] as the initiatives established under the Blair government fell by the wayside. Additionally, as part of modernisation reforms in the House of Commons,[46] key issues such as European debates on annual fisheries and agriculture were allocated to the new Backbench Business Committee. Before this, these debates were scheduled as Government Business in the House of Commons. A consequence of this modernisation was that it reduced debate and priority on these issues.

Such EU paralysis amongst UK politicians contributed towards the Conservatives' 'stop talking about it' strategy when faced with challenging questions about the EU during the 2010s. Whilst it can be argued that in the early 2000s few MPs could competently deal with EU issues,[47] Cameron's 'inconsistent and ambiguous'[48] EU policy may in part be due to his neglect of learning how the EU connected with the UK's political system – an error he could have rectified at any moment.

At EU level, Cameron's actions were shortsighted and politically damaging even before he became Prime Minister, with his decision to withdraw Conservative MEPs from the centre-right and highly influential European People's Party group in the European Parliament. Alienation from pro-European Conservative MEPs ensued – people whom he would later turn to for support when campaigning to remain in the EU. The move also restricted immediate access to informal meetings, such as the one held shortly before the EU euro crisis summit in December 2011, with prominent European leaders including Angela Merkel and Jean-Claude Juncker. This proved highly isolating for Britain.

It is plausible to conceive that had Cameron resisted demands from Eurosceptic Conservative MPs to switch groups in the European Parliament, he would have been able to exert greater levels of 'soft' power to build much-needed allies and supporters at EU level from the very beginning of his premiership. His strategy can be contrasted with that of the Blair government, which used 'soft' power to significantly influence constitutional developments from the outset.

More often than not, the Conservatives appeared to forget that the UK's relationship with the EU was – and still is – a two-way relationship and not one

---

[44] E Stourton, 'Euroscepticism among Conservative MPs' (*BBC News*, 17 October 2011) www.bbc.co.uk/news/uk-politics-15291712.

[45] Stuart, 'The Convention' (n 26).

[46] See House of Commons Reform Committee, *Rebuilding the House* (2008–09, HC 1117).

[47] Stuart, *The Making of Europe's Constitution* (n 29) 11.

[48] M Brusenbauch Meislova, 'All Things to All People? Discursive Patterns on UK–EU Relationship in David Cameron's Speeches' (2018) 14 *British Politics* 224.

centrally occupied by 'the UK's own narrow interests'.[49] As a result, the Coalition Agreement, which promised that the UK would play 'a strong and positive role with our partners',[50] turned out to be anything but.

C. The Referendum

Having promised a 'cast iron guarantee' to hold a referendum on Lisbon, Cameron later dropped this, citing that it was no longer an option because of the Czech Republic's decision to ratify it. Unusually, the idea of holding an EU referendum subsisted, despite it being a topic that 'no one really wanted to raise'.[51] The 2010 Conservative manifesto condemned Labour's decision not to hold a referendum, describing it as a 'shameful episode' which 'can never happen again'.[52] To 'restore democratic control',[53] the Conservatives promised a 'referendum lock', which would require the UK government to hold a referendum before any further treaty changes which would transfer competences or powers from the UK to the EU. On coming into office, the Cameron–Clegg coalition government implemented the 'referendum lock' via the European Union Act 2011. Coined by Gordon as an 'unprecedented constitutional experiment',[54] the Act came under criticism for its drafting and the 'manner and form' in which the sovereignty of Parliament is exercised.[55] For Cameron, the Act proved to be politically self-destructive. For the UK, it added an additional layer of tension to the relationship it had with the EU.

Cameron narrowly avoided triggering the referendum lock at the 2011 EU summit by vetoing the Fiscal Compact Treaty (which aimed to tackle the eurozone debt crisis), thus removing the UK as a contracting party. Whilst the 2011 Act acted as a political point of defence on EU matters in the UK, its creation arguably led to Cameron becoming more cautious in giving any meaningful concessions to the EU in negotiations over reform. To do so would have risked provoking a referendum in the UK. It is, of course, impossible to decipher if he would have taken the same approach had the 2011 Act not existed. But its absence may have made him more willing to engage on a more consensual and committed basis towards EU matters. Instead, the 2011 Act served to remind Cameron that his

---

[49] House of Lords European Union Committee, *The Post-Crisis EU Financial Regulatory Framework: Do the Pieces Fit?* (2014–15, HL 103) para 39.

[50] HM Government, 'The Coalition: Our Programme for Government' (Cabinet Office, May 2010) 19, https://assets.publishing.service.gov.uk/government/uploads/system/uploads/attachment_data/file/78977/coalition_programme_for_government.pdf.

[51] J Smith, *The Coalition Effect 2010–2015* (Cambridge, Cambridge University Press, 2015) 381.

[52] Conservative Party Manifesto 2010, 113.

[53] ibid.

[54] M Gordon, 'Mike Gordon: European Union Act 2011' (UK Constitutional Law Association, 12 January 2012) https://ukconstitutionallaw.org/2012/01/12/mike-gordon-the-european-union-act-2011/.

[55] P Eleftheriadis, 'A New Referendum is a Constitutional Requirement' (University of Oxford, 4 July 2016) www.law.ox.ac.uk/business-law-blog/blog/2016/07/new-referendum-constitutional-requirement.

loyalty and priorities lay with managing the Conservatives, especially in advance of the 2015 general election, when he sought a single-party government. This fact was bolstered by the increasing popularity of UKIP in the 2012 local elections and a Conservative MP defection to UKIP in 2014. Significantly, UKIP also gained the highest number of seats amongst British MEPs in the 2014 European Parliament election.

Cameron took the position that a renegotiation followed by a referendum would be the 'correct way forward'[56] following his 2013 Bloomberg speech. But he failed to formulate substantive asks that addressed the main concerns of Leave voters. This was to keep Angela Merkel on side – despite her appreciation of Cameron's domestic political difficulties – before and during the renegotiations so that she would offer an agreement for the UK to stay in the EU. When Cameron planned on asking for an emergency brake on immigration in a 2014 speech,[57] he watered this down to appease Merkel and other EU leaders.[58] His reluctance to 'put Merkel to the test'[59] underlined the UK's weak influence within the EU.

This stems from several incidents in the lead up to the renegotiation, including Cameron's defiance by opting the UK out of the EU's emergency proposal to relocate 120,000 refugees in 2015.[60] The timing of the renegotiation itself – which happened during a time of multiple crises within the EU, such as Schengen and the euro – further undermined Britain's bargaining ability for concessions as these issues did not impact the UK. As noted by Thompson, 'British preferences appeared irrelevant to the EU's future',[61] with the Remain campaign's argument about achieving reform from within the EU sounding unpersuasive. Against the backdrop of the eurozone crisis, the Remain campaign's economic argument appeared weak against Vote Leave's focus on immigration and UK sovereignty.

Could Cameron have prolonged the UK's 'status quo' relationship with the EU? There was certainly potential for him to explicitly advocate change in the EU's institutional architecture during the renegotiation which recognised that there are two separate groups of Member States – 'a core and a periphery'.[62] The eurozone Member States would require deeper political and economic integration whilst the rest would need a looser framework. Had Cameron offered a clear and alternative vision of the future of Europe during a period of reduced crisis within the EU, he could have potentially formed better UK–EU relations whilst also appeasing Eurosceptics within his own party. Instead, he had, according to Ivan Rogers, no

---

[56] Smith, *The Coalition Effect* (n 50) 392.

[57] David Cameron, speech at JCB Staffordshire, 28 November 2014.

[58] H Thompson, 'Inevitability and Contingency: The Political Economy of Brexit' (2017) 19 *British Journal of Politics and International Relations* 434.

[59] ibid.

[60] European Commission, 'Refugee Crisis – Q&A on Emergency Relocation' (22 September 2015) https://ec.europa.eu/commission/presscorner/detail/en/MEMO_15_5698.

[61] Thompson (n 57).

[62] Stuart, 'The Strange Thing' (n 6).

'effective operation on the European question',[63] with very few people within the Conservatives actually 'deeply informed and focussed enough' to have conversations about it in the lead up to the referendum.

IV. The Post-Brexit Relationship with the EU and UK Governance

A. UK Governance Post-Brexit

Changes to the system of UK governance arising from devolution reforms introduced since 1997, in combination with the tectonic shift of Brexit, has driven the devolution settlement to a constitutional crossroads and our modern interpretation of devolution. Where policy areas with devolved competence corresponded with EU competence, the obligation to legislate within the constitutional structure of EU law reduced divergence in the policies pursued by the UK and devolved governments. The response to devolution post-Brexit by the May and Johnson governments had mixed success.

When initially drafted, the EU (Withdrawal) Act proposed to give the UK Parliament sole authority over retained EU laws in policy areas that were devolved. However, following concerns by the Scottish and Welsh governments that this was a 'power grab' by Westminster, the legislation as enacted returned devolved competencies back to the devolved institutions. The Act provided the UK government with the powers to temporarily 'freeze' devolved competence in any policy areas under section 12. Yet these powers, which expired on 31 January 2022, were never exercised, and have since been repealed. Further, the UK and devolved governments have cooperated on developing UK Common Frameworks which ensure that a common approach is collectively taken where powers have returned from the EU which intersect with policy areas that concern devolved competence. At present, such a consensus-oriented approach has worked well and is a positive step towards strengthening the Union through shared understanding and interest. The UK government must, however, be consistently committed to respecting the views and interests of the devolved governments if this is to continue.

One area for improvement remains intergovernmental relations. Tension has increased in parallel with the centralising of the UK's Union and the constraining of devolved power. This can be evidenced in the Internal Market Act 2020. In response to the Internal Market Bill, the Scottish and Welsh Parliaments refused 'legislative consent', which would usually be required under the Sewel Convention, whilst the Northern Ireland Assembly did not hold a formal legislative consent

---

[63] I Rogers, 'Cameron and the European Union, 2012–2015' (London, UK in a Changing Europe, 27 November 2020) https://ukandeu.ac.uk/brexit-witness-archive/ivan-rogers/.

vote. This has since led the Scottish government to declare that the Internal Market Act is an 'assault on devolution',[64] whilst in 2022 the Welsh government pursued legal action against the UK government, claiming that the Act 'severely curtails' the powers of the Senedd. This 'hyper-unionism',[65] which can be observed through Johnson's designation of himself as the 'Minister for the Union' in 2019, has encouraged the growth of a more 'muscular strain of unionist sentiment'.[66] Despite this, the recent review of intergovernmental relations has outlined new structures which have the potential to help navigate sensitive post-Brexit issues, such as allocating money from the UK Shared Prosperity Fund.

Arguably, 'without a compelling story about the UK's place in an uncertain world, nations may develop divergent visions of their geopolitical futures'.[67] This has led to the four parts of the UK seeking different outcomes for their own individual relationships with the EU, with pro-EU Irish and Scottish nationalists seeking re-entry as a Member State of the EU. Meanwhile, England and Wales, which voted to leave the EU, wish to remain outside.

Scottish independence, which has remained at the forefront of constitutional and political discussion despite the 'No' vote in the 2014 independence referendum, has been reignited by the Brexit process. But Scotland already has one of the most powerful devolved governments in the world.[68] Through interdependence mechanisms, such as section 104 orders,[69] the UK government routinely gives effect to Scottish legislative choices.[70] This means that the relationship between England and Scotland is already legally framed on shared power. So, too, is the relationship between England and Wales through section 150 orders.[71]

If an independent Scotland wished to regain EU membership, it would require a willingness to accept obligations as part of its Union relationship. This would mean leaving the UK Union to join another one. Arguably, this would lead Scotland to become independent in name, but not in a political or constitutional nature. Northern Ireland's distinctive land border has added tension to the Brexit process. Without such a border, the EU could have had wider scope to provide a variety of deals.

The 'glue'[72] of the EU which had held the UK together since 1997, both culturally and constitutionally speaking, must be substituted with a sturdier substance that can withstand the test of time. Serious reflection is needed about what shape

---

[64] Scottish Government, 'UK Internal Market Bill: Scottish Government Consent Impossible' (8 September 2020) www.gov.scot/news/uk-internal-market-Bill/.

[65] M Kenny and J Sheldon, 'When Planets Collide: The British Conservative Party and the Discordant Goals of Delivering Brexit and Preserving the Domestic Union, 2016–2019' (2021) 69 *Political Studies Association* 965.

[66] ibid.

[67] J Simons, 'The British Constitution after Brexit' (Cambridge, Bennett Institute for Public Policy, March 2020) www.bennettinstitute.cam.ac.uk/publications/british-constitution-after-brexit/.

[68] A Tomkins, 'Don't Believe All the Bluster: Devolution Means Cooperation' *The Herald* (1 December 2021).

[69] See Scotland Act 1998.

[70] ibid.

[71] See Government of Wales Act 2006.

[72] European Union Committee, *Brexit: Devolution* (2017–18, HL 9) 12.

devolution should take post-Brexit and the nature of the Union relationship in the UK's dealings with the EU. A purposeful alternative to the status quo Union may be one that is federal in nature, as suggested in a new Act of Union Bill,[73] which advocates that the Union is a voluntary association of four component parts and 'should determine its own affairs to the extent that it considers it should'.[74]

In the absence of the EU's stabilising impact on devolution, a new Act of Union has the potential to substitute and enhance it. To do so would require the UK's 'raw and unresolved'[75] existential question about the role and relevance of parliamentary sovereignty to be confronted. If parliamentary sovereignty has 'prevented us [from] fully coming to terms with the constitutional implications of devolution',[76] then it is imperative to interrogate its place in a post-Brexit devolved UK. This, in turn, would perhaps encourage England, the largest and the least politically and culturally nurtured nation within the Union, to come into full fruition, with a clearer sense of identity and belonging within the Union.

Like the relationship between the UK government and the EU, the relationship between the UK and its devolved governments would collectively benefit from a more meaningful instead of a tense and transactional relationship. A UK government which places less emphasis on short-term party political interests would help. So too would serious consideration of all policy areas which have a Unionist element, such as the proposed Bill of Rights Bill as drafted in June 2022 which could weaken and undermine the Union. It is consistent curiosity into how all of the UK's component parts work individually and together that will make the Union a collective and long-term success. Without it, the future of the Union post-Brexit is highly contested.

B. UK versus EU Understanding of Brexit

Although 'Leave' was one of two options in the 2016 EU referendum, the Cameron government prepared no contingency plans for Brexit. Because of this, the May government formulated the UK's Brexit policy in a Brexit White Paper[77] based on its own analysis, whilst also incorporating some of the promises of the 'Vote Leave' campaign on issues such as controlled immigration and continued collaboration with European partners on major science research. Yet differing interpretations of the referendum result by the UK government and the EU meant that the Brexit negotiation process was tense and challenging from the outset.

---

[73] Both authors have contributed to the Act of Union Bill as Steering Committee members of the Constitution Reform Group.

[74] Constitution Reform Group, 'Explanatory Notes to the Act of Union Bill', 2018.

[75] M Russell, 'Brexit and Parliament: The Anatomy of a Perfect Storm' (2021) 74 Parliamentary Affairs 443. P Craig, *The Lisbon Treaty, Revised Edition: Law, Politics, and Treaty Reform* (Oxford, Oxford University Press, 2013) 25.

[76] V Bogdanor, *Beyond Brexit: Towards a British Constitution* (London, IB Tauris, 2019) 277.

[77] UK Government, Department for Exiting the European Union, *The United Kingdom's Exit from, and New Partnership with, the European Union* (Cm 9417, 2017).

The Withdrawal Agreement, which was negotiated between the May government and the EU over an 18-month period, was rejected three times by the House of Commons. This led to the European Council, at the request of the May government, extending Article 50 three times. Unable to pass a meaningful vote in the House of Commons, which was required by section 13 of the European Union (Withdrawal) Act 2018, the Johnson government bypassed the meaningful vote with the European Union (Withdrawal Agreement) Act 2020. Inevitably, such a delay meant that the proposed date on which the UK was supposed to leave the EU – 29 March 2019 – was postponed until 31 January 2020.

Alongside the Withdrawal Agreement, the Political Declaration on the Framework for Future EU–UK Relations establishes the direction and tone of future negotiations. Whilst not legally binding, it asserts that the relationship 'will be rooted in the values and interests that the Union and the United Kingdom share' which 'arise from their geography, history and ideals anchored in their common European heritage'.[78] In practice, this has so far not been clearly adhered to. Looking to the past for direction for the future relationship, whilst positive in intent, is arguably a weaker starting point in this instance as the relationship has endured deliberate separation. A more ambitious and forward-thinking relationship should be formed based on shared objectives and action-orientated goals on issues such as climate change and the migrant crisis. Focus would be sharper and motivation to succeed together more intentional.

A weakness in the EU's approach to understanding Brexit is that it has 'obsessively focused on Brexiteer misrepresentations of Europe',[79] with less consideration of other Brexit viewpoints. Even as late as 2018, EU officials such as Michel Barnier were encouraged to believe that the UK would change its mind about Brexit.[80] Meanwhile, the UK government's approach has led to accusations that it has acted in such a way that it is an untrustworthy partner. Consequently, relations have become strained.

From a UK perspective, a key question to be seriously contemplated is what right does the UK have to expect to be treated as a significant neighbour by the EU? This is particularly dependent on the conduct and good faith of the UK government, which initially sought to violate international law in a 'specific and limited way' in the Internal Market Act 2020. Arguably, such action undermines the UK's commitment to a rules-based order as well as its credibility as a trusted treaty partner. Yet, as a former Member State and close geographical neighbour, the UK has a strong case for and expectation of how it should be treated in both the short and long term.

---

[78] European Commission, Revised Political Declaration, 17 October 2019.

[79] E Drea, 'Europe Has Learned Nothing from Brexit' (*Politico*, 24 November 2021) www.politico.eu/article/europe-brexit-lessons-single-market-economy/.

[80] M Barnier and R Mackay, *My Secret Brexit Diary: A Glorious Illusion* (Cambridge, Polity, 2021) 164, Wednesday 18 July 2018: Tony Blair.

From an EU viewpoint, what are the risks of not treating the UK as a significant neighbour? How would this restrict the EU's long-term development and relationships with Member States that have Eurosceptic governments? Without intentional reflection on these concerns, the post-Brexit relationship between the UK and EU will be paralysed by hesitation and ambiguity.

C. Future UK–EU Dynamics

What shape will the UK's relationship with the EU take as a former Member State and now 'third country'? The question has been a fundamental one for both the UK and EU since the 2016 EU referendum. Yet, for the EU, Brexit and the political symbolism of a Member State and its citizens intentionally expressing a vote to leave the project has threatened to undermine the project's perceived function and importance to current EU citizens. The referendum was an exercise in democratic decision-making about the EU at UK national level, a method that the EU has historically been cautious of as a result of the rejection of previous treaties by other Member States. Because of this, there has been a 'determined effort'[81] to limit the direct participation of national citizens in the project of EU integration, with the only link being initiatives overseen and monitored by national governments and EU officials.

This can be reflected in the recent Conference on the Future of Europe, as hosted by the European Commission, the EU Council and the European Parliament, which aimed to provide a direct space for EU citizens to have their say. In contrast to the Convention on the Future of Europe, the Conference attempted to be EU citizen driven through a primarily multilingual digital platform. Yet very few EU citizens were involved in the process (652,532[82]), and it is disputed how many were aware of its actual existence.

One key objective of the Conference is to give young Europeans 'a central role in shaping the future of the European project'.[83] For young Europeans and Brits, a strong relationship between the UK and EU is in their best interests, particularly for those seeking study and work opportunities. Recent statistics show that whilst there has been a drop in students coming to the UK from major EU countries since 2011/2012, applicants from Italy and Spain have increased by almost half.[84] This is partially linked to high levels of youth unemployment in these countries in comparison to the UK.

---

[81] C Bickerton, 'The Future of the EU: A Retrospective' (Real Instituto Elcano, 9 December 2021) www.realinstitutoelcano.org/wps/portal/rielcano_en/contenido?WCM_GLOBAL_CONTEXT=/elcano/elcano_in/zonas_in/ari105-2021-bickerton-the-future-of-the-eu-a-retrospective.

[82] Conference on the Future of Europe, 'Report on the Final Outcome' (May 2022) 13.

[83] Joint Declaration on the Conference on the Future of Europe Engaging with Citizens for Democracy – Building a More Resilient Europe [2021] OJ C91I/1.

[84] S Hubble and P Bolton, *International and EU Students in Higher Education in the UK FAQs*, Briefing Paper CBP 7976 (House of Commons Library, 15 February 2021).

Similarly, research shows that young people in the UK want close ties with their European counterparts. Among those aged under 45, 63 per cent would vote to join the EU whilst 69 per cent of those who did not vote in 2016 (many of whom were too young to do so) would also vote to join if given the opportunity to do so in 2021.[85] Failing to recognise the opportunities the UK offers young Europeans and vice versa is detrimental to the future relationship, and also ignores the international context and culture for cooperation that appeals to younger age groups.

Twenty years ago, the issue of the EU's 'democratic deficit' was a cause of political and constitutional concern and curiosity. Today, the momentum and urgency for constitutional reform within the EU as witnessed in the early 2000s no longer exists. Whether the findings and recommendations of the conference's work will result in EU Treaty changes is unclear; however, at the time of writing, the European Parliament has passed a resolution to progress with preparing treaty proposals. In any event, a relationship where the only way a country can relate to the EU is by being receptive to the prospect of membership is *not* a meaningful neighbourhood relationship.[86] The Russian invasion of Ukraine in February 2022 and Ukraine's immediate application to join the EU (followed by Georgia and Moldova in the days following) is likely to confront this issue as EU Member States remain divided over speeding up EU candidacy status and enlarging the EU in response to war.

Despite the UK's fractious relationship with the EU, especially in relation to the operation of the Northern Ireland Protocol, the united response on supporting Ukraine – which was one of the opening items on the agenda for the first meeting of the EU–UK Parliamentary Partnership Assembly – could prove a breakthrough in UK–EU relations. The UK has been able to position itself as a core EU ally by leading on European diplomatic efforts to support Ukraine and through its membership of NATO, a re-emerging power with geopolitical support and capabilities that include but also expand beyond the European continent.

V. Conclusion

Prior to the 1997 referendum on devolving power from Westminster to Wales, the then Secretary of State for Wales, Ron Davies, memorably referred to devolution

---

[85] J Curtice, 'Voters Still Divided over Brexit – but Back UK Government in Battles with Brussels' (London, UK in a Changing Europe, 7 December 2021) https://ukandeu.ac.uk/voters-still-divided-over-brexit-but-back-uk-government-in-battles-with-brussels/.

[86] G Stuart, 'British Politics, 2010–2015' (London, UK in a Changing Europe, 2 November 2020) https://ukandeu.ac.uk/brexit-witness-archive/gisela-stuart/. In this respect, the creation of the new European Political Community in October 2022 is an initiative that should be welcomed. The UK would benefit from being actively involved from the outset, unlike its membership of the EU. This is especially pertinent in light of Russia's invasion of Ukraine in February 2022 and Ukraine's immediate application to join the EU followed by Georgia and Moldova in the days following. With EU Member States divided over speeding up EU candidacy status and enlarging the EU in response to war, a new European Political Community could prove valuable and act as a meaningful way to address these concerns.

as 'a process, not an event'. We suggest that this applies equally to Brexit, which is a long-term constitutional and political task in progress. As exemplified by the first Blair government, mutual recognition and support can go a long way in sustaining and enhancing relationships with strategic allies. Yet the historical and cultural differences between the UK and the European continent proved too challenging for both to overcome and persist with within the supranational shape of the EU.

A workable and successful two-way relationship between the UK and the EU will require constant vigilance, maintenance and patience, just as it did when the UK was a Member State. The meaning and intention of Brexit will undoubtedly evolve over time with the changing guard of political actors, parties and negotiators who will take responsibility for Brexit negotiations. Responsibility for the initial constitutional framework and direction of Brexit rests with the current political actors. It is their duty to make a success of it for future generations.

18

Against (Many Kinds of) Representation

RICHARD TUCK

There are two ways in which I can be represented in a political process. One is through what political scientists call a 'principal–agent' relationship: I choose someone to act on my behalf at a meeting I cannot myself attend. In the case of a legislative assembly, all the inhabitants of a territory cannot be present, so they choose a relatively small group of legislators, but (with various qualifications) the legislators are the agents of the electors. This is an old and familiar kind of representation, and even in the ancient world of citizen assemblies it played some part, though on nothing like the scale and importance which it assumed in the post-classical states of Western Europe.

The agent may be under strict instructions, or he may have a degree of discretion. Both kinds of agents have in the past been sent to legislative assemblies, though the practice of local mandation has fallen into disuse in most Western democracies. It was in fact quite common in England at least until the Reform Act of 1832 for the public meetings which elected MPs subsequently to vote on instructions to be given them about how they were to vote in the Commons, and on the Continent mandation was widely used in the form of instructions given to the delegates to the various national estates, such as the famous *cahiers* presented by the delegates to the French Estates-General in 1789.

To modern eyes, however, the well-known refusal by Edmund Burke to accept the instructions which the electors of Bristol had customarily given their MPs often looks like a kind of holy writ. The other MP elected at the same time (in the old two-member format of English parliamentary elections) had agreed to be mandated, but Burke told his electors (conveniently, after the vote had been counted):

> My worthy Colleague says, his Will ought to be subservient to yours. If that be all, the thing is innocent. If Government were a matter of Will upon any side, yours, without question, ought to be superior. But Government and Legislation are matters of reason and judgement, and not of inclination; and, what sort of reason is that, in which the determination precedes the discussion; in which one sett of men deliberate, and another decide; and where those who form the conclusion are perhaps three hundred miles distant from those who hear the arguments?

In fact, the instructions in a city like Bristol had usually dealt either with the particular economic interests of its merchants, who had a perfectly good knowledge of the issues involved, or with big national questions which had already been widely debated, so that the force of this argument was rather blunted. And they scarcely apply in a modern society, where the quality of debate outside the assembly is usually incomparably superior to that inside, where whipping, procedural constraints and all the rest of a parliamentary apparatus take us far away from a Burkean ideal.

The principal reason for Burke's refusal to accept mandation – and the reason which modern politicians who cite Burke are also (if they are honest) motivated by – was in fact what he said a couple of paragraphs later:

> Parliament is not a Congress of Ambassadors from different and hostile interests; which interests each must maintain, as an Agent and Advocate, against other Agents and Advocates; but Parliament is a deliberative Assembly of one Nation, with one Interest, that of the whole; where, not local Purposes, not local Prejudices ought to guide, but the general Good, resulting from the general Reason of the whole. You chuse a Member indeed; but when you have chosen him, he is not Member of Bristol, but he is a Member of Parliament. If the local Constituent should have an Interest, or should form an hasty Opinion, evidently opposite to the real good of the rest of the Community, the Member for that place ought to be as far, as any other, from any endeavour to give it Effect.

But this was a very far-reaching claim, since it amounted to a declaration that an elected member is under no obligation to respect the views of the people who chose him. Modern parliamentary practice is actually quite different, despite the lip-service paid to Burke, both because Members of Parliament are mostly elected because they belong to a political party and are committed to the policies of that party, and because it is taken for granted that on local issues such as (say) a new airport, a responsible MP *should* represent the local interest against the national one. Though MPs (in particular) are unsurprisingly fond of citing the Address to the Electors of Bristol, the reality of modern democratic politics is much closer to the pre-Burkean practice of the city.

It was for this reason that the language of mandation reappeared after the decline of local instructions, in the shape of the 'national mandate' claimed by victorious parties for implementing the terms of their manifestos. The idea that a party's manifesto is a special document whose provisions have been approved by the electorate has played a powerful role in modern British politics; in particular, the constitutional position of the House of Lords now rests on a convention agreed at the time of the Attlee government that the Lords would not use their delaying power against measures which had been specified in the governing party's manifesto. Though it has been argued that manifestos have now ceased to have any special significance, and it is obviously the case that not many voters read them, it is revealing that very few politicians are prepared to say to their electorates that they should disregard them: there is a general understanding that there has to be *some* respect for the positions which were formally put before the electors in a general election. In the parliamentary debates over the Brexit agreement, for example, it was taken for granted by most participants that the parties' manifestos had to be respected, even though their interpretation could be stretched well beyond what common sense would allow.

So a full-blooded Burkean position is no more persuasive now than it was in 1774 (Burke, it should be remembered, recognised that he could not get re-elected at Bristol, and opted instead for a pocket borough in Yorkshire, where his few constituents were willing to let him use his own judgement in Parliament as long as he stayed loyal to the borough's owner, Lord Rockingham). Local mandation has gone, but a sense that a member *is* mandated, though now predominantly at a national level, has not disappeared. The idea that a Parliament is a deliberative assembly in which the members are able to follow the arguments and make their own minds up about the matters under consideration is patently now a fantasy, and indeed always was one. Nor, on a strict view of democracy, *should* it be such an assembly, for if it were to be, the voters would have very little part to play in the politics of their nation.

The second way I can be represented, other than through the principal–agent relationship, is by a process that 'mirrors' me. An accurate picture represents its subject, but is not the subject's *agent*. Again, the idea that an assembly should mirror the population is an old one, though there is always implicit in this idea a theory about what kinds of attributes are relevant to political decisions. There can only be mirroring of a few specific traits, normally such things as gender, class and race; these are the selected traits because in our societies they are thought to have some kind of association with political loyalties. One could imagine other societies in which height, for example, was a relevant trait (indeed, there are societies which have come quite close to this, such as Rwanda and the Punjab under Sikh rule), but that would not be something which in our society we want mirrored.

A distinction has to be made here. One reason for demanding a mirror assembly is that if these traits are not represented, their absence may be evidence that the process whereby principals choose agents is flawed: black citizens, for example, might be unable to find agents they trust to act on their behalf. In principle, however, if the citizens could properly authorise their delegates (through a system of mandation, say), mirroring would not be necessary: the need for it arises only because the delegates are rather loosely tied to their principals, and cannot be trusted to use their discretion on behalf of their electors.

But another reason is the belief that an assembly ought to be representative of the country as a whole because the members of the assembly would then make the kinds of decisions which the citizens would have made, had they been able to gather in one place. This is not the same as the belief that an assembly which does not mirror the population is evidence of a flaw in the electoral system, since on this view it would not really matter if the members had not been chosen by the citizens *at all*, as long as they were appropriately representative of the population.

This idea resembles the use which governments and political parties make of opinion polling. A well-designed opinion poll builds into its samples appropriate weighting for the salient groups, and polls have (despite their occasional eye-catching failures) remarkable success in predicting what an electorate will do. The sample of the population questioned by the pollsters accurately represents the population as a whole, and can be used as representative when decisions are made, without being *chosen* by the citizens or acting as their agents.

Although a pure instance of this kind of representation has rarely been used as a basis for political institutions, and the demand for it has often been confounded with what we might term the evidential type of representation, its underlying logic does not require any active participation by the general public. Indeed, a short story by Isaac Asimov, published in 1955, depicted an America in which Asimov's famous supercomputer 'Multivac' picked one completely representative citizen to be that year's Voter![1] And in our own time, this logic has begun to work its way out, bolstered (I think) by the sophistication of modern sampling techniques. It is worth remembering that almost all our classic political theories, and the institutions constructed upon them, predate practices such as opinion polling. Many of the primitive arguments for representative assemblies would in fact have been pointless had such practices been available: after all, a poll can apparently give a much better sense of what the public wants than the cumbersome and flawed process of electing delegates. (I say 'apparently' for reasons I will return to presently.) Influenced by these thoughts, political theorists – and, indeed, activists – have become increasingly drawn to institutions such as citizen juries empanelled to decide policy, and even methods of sortition to choose delegates to a legislature. These theorists argue that elections in practice are corrupted by all sorts of forces, and that a lottery would be free of corruption; it would also be more democratic, in the sense of more *egalitarian*, since it would offer every citizen an equal chance of taking part in acts of legislation.

Most schemes of proportional representation (PR), although they do not (mostly) attempt to mirror the distribution of traits such as wealth or race, are still varieties of mirror representation.[2] The traits with which they are concerned are people's political opinions, possibly (though not necessarily) expressed through adherence to particular political parties. The assumption behind this is that there is a certain distribution of opinions throughout the population, and that this distribution ought to be properly represented in a legislature. As Thomas Hare said in the first systematic treatise on proportional representation, 'the object be

---

[1] I Asimov, 'Franchise', originally published in *If: Worlds of Science Fiction* (August 1955), reprinted in *Earth is Room Enough* (Doubleday, 1957). It is said that Asimov was inspired by CBS News's use of the Remington Rand UNIVAC I computer on election night 1952 correctly to predict a landslide for Eisenhower after only three million votes had been counted – the first instance of what has become a familiar feature of US elections, to the degree that most people treat the 'calling' of the result early in the evening by the networks as the actual outcome of the election.

[2] Some 19th-century universal suffrage schemes did in fact build in distinctions of wealth (eg the Prussian franchise), but this was not an attempt to mirror the society; rather, it was the opposite – to give disproportionate weight to the wealthy.

to gather the sense of the nation', and, given this assumption, he quite reasonably concluded about the English electoral system in 1857 that 'a contrivance more inefficient for the purpose can hardly be conceived'.[3] All schemes of PR since then share Hare's governing assumption that there is objectively 'the sense of the nation' on any subject, and the job of a political process is to represent that sense as accurately as possible.

Hare himself accepted that once the representatives met in Parliament

> it is … by the majority of the representative body that the decision must be pronounced. It is that majority which speaks for the whole, and is irresistible. It may be likened to an engine of enormous power which crushes all opposing forces.

But

> it is not necessary to the efficiency of the engine that the same overpowering force should have been employed in the process of its construction. It is when the engine is formed that we require its power to be exercised; – whilst the engine is being made, – it is the engine we want, and not the power.[4]

In other words, the assembly should be representative of the wider population, but the legislators themselves would have to form coalitions of various kinds in order to make a final decision about a policy; *decisions* were to be left to the representatives.

This remains a feature of most schemes of PR, and illustrates the fact that integral to them is the idea that legislators should to a significant extent be free to use their own judgement rather than dutifully follow the instructions of their constituents. A thorough-going PR system cannot straightforwardly coexist with mandation, since a mandate is likely to pre-empt the kind of discussions over (say) forming a government subsequent to the election which PR is supposed to facilitate. It was partly for this very reason that local mandation was employed in pre-Reform Act England, since the old English constitution had a kind of PR built into it, in the shape of two-member constituencies. Local mandation ensured that the two members would both vote in the same way on the issues which were important to their constituents, and thereby made the primitive PR method more like the modern first-past-the post English system.

Two-member constituencies did not in fact vanish from England until 1950, when the remaining two-member boroughs (and the University seats) were abolished. But they had been under constant attack since the beginning of the modern movement for parliamentary reform; every scheme for universal suffrage and what was termed 'equal representation' (that is, constituencies of equal size), from the Duke of Richmond's proposals in the 1780s through Bentham's *Plan of Parliamentary Reform* and the People's Charter of 1838, took it for granted

---

[3] T Hare, *The Machinery of Representation* (London, W Maxwell, 1867) 13.
[4] T Hare, *The Election of Representatives, Parliamentary and Municipal. A Treatise* (London, Longman, Green, Longman, Roberts & Green, 1865).

that (in Bentham's words) 'In and for each election district, one Member and no more shall be elected'.[5] And the Third Reform Act of 1884, which effected the greatest extension of the franchise, was also the Act which effectively abolished two-member constituencies, leaving (for the whole UK) only 27. This is a remarkable fact: the cause of universal suffrage in England was always linked to the *abolition* of an existing PR system. Periodic attempts were made to salvage multi-member constituencies, but the thrust of parliamentary reform throughout the nineteenth century was always towards their abolition.

Many countries on the Continent, however, saw a new turn to PR in the late nineteenth and early twentieth centuries, and this was perfectly well understood by contemporaries to be a conservative response to the growth of new mass political movements in the age of universal (or near-universal) manhood suffrage. The Royal Commission Appointed to Enquire into Electoral Systems, which reported to Parliament in 1910, in fact observed about the vogue for schemes for PR in the preceding 20 years that the major extension of the franchise in the Third Reform Act 'had aroused those apprehensions of the tyranny of the majority which at all times have accompanied large increases of the electorate, and in some countries have actually led to the adoption of proportional methods'.[6] This view has been endorsed by a number of contemporary scholars, who have concluded that PR in

---

[5] Richmond's Bill proposed 'That every commoner of this realm, excepting infants, persons of insane mind, and criminals incapacitated by law, hath a natural, unalienable, and equal right, to vote in the election of his representative in parliament. That the election of members to serve in the House of Commons ought to be annual. That the manner of electing the Commons in parliament, and all matters and things respecting the same, be new-modelled according to the present state of the kingdom, and the ancient unalienable rights of the people. That the number of members in the House of Commons being 558, the total number of electors should be divided by that, to give the average number of those, having a right to elect one member.' Charles Grey, the future author of the Reform Act, proposed in 1797 that 'the country should be divided into districts, and no person permitted to vote for more than one member'; Bentham, as we have seen, said the same, and *The People's Charter* of 1838 used an almost identical form of words in Article V of its section on Electoral Districts: 'That each electoral district return one representative to sit in the Commons' House of Parliament, and no more' (*The People's Charter: Being the Outline of an Act to Provide for the Just Representation of the People of Great Britain in the Commons' House of Parliament* (London, Working Men's Association, 1838) 14). The USA is an interesting case. The US Constitution does not prescribe any system of congressional districts, and many states in the first 50 years of the Republic elected all their Representatives on a state-wide basis; and, of course, the Senate has two-member constituencies. However, an Act was passed in the 1842 Congress stipulating single-member congressional districts (though it was to some extent ignored, particularly in the South): A Hacker, *Congressional Districting: The Issue of Equal Representation* (Washington, DC, Brookings Institution, 1964). Hacker argued that the single-member districts were an attempt to get more proportionality in the representation, since it was possible under the state-wide system for a single party to sweep the board. But comparison with England would also suggest that radical democrats in general were committed to single-member representation. Certainly, in the debates in 1842 over the abolition of what was called 'general-ticket voting', Northern radicals joined with the conservative Whigs in pushing for the measure against the wishes of the Southern Democrats.

[6] Royal Commission on Systems of Election, *Report of the Royal Commission Appointed to Enquire into Electoral Systems, with Appendices* (London, Eyre and Spottiswoode, 1910) 2.

Europe was largely a device for weakening left-wing political movements, since (at least on the Continent) the Right before the First World War was split between Catholic and non-Catholic parties, whereas the Left tended to be more unified.[7]

Fear of the power which is in the hands of a majority of the electorate has continued to be a major motive behind proposals for PR, though, as Hare understood, no one has seriously suggested constraining the power of a majority of *legislators* (except through schemes for constitutional constraints of various kinds, which could equally well be applied to the mass electorate itself). It is usually presumed by advocates of PR that legislators will be immune to the dangers of majoritarianism, despite the fact that if their numbers were genuinely to correspond to the distribution of opinion in the wider society, the principle of majoritarianism in the assembly ought to lead to the same outcomes as would have been the case had the electorate spoken directly, for instance in a referendum. But in fact, what is implicit in schemes for PR is, as I said earlier, an unspoken version of the old assumption that legislators are not really mirror representatives of the electorate, nor should they be, since they will bring capacities to the legislative process which do not correspond to those which are widespread in the population.[8]

---

[7] See in particular C Boix, 'Setting the Rules of the Game: The Choice of Electoral Systems in Advanced Democracies' (1999) 93 *American Political Science Review* 609. Boix's view was criticised by T Cusack, T Iversen and D Soskice, 'Economic Interests and the Origins of Electoral Systems' (2007) 101 *American Political Science Review* 373, who argued instead that the critical factor in the adoption of PR was an economic structure which privileged industrial cooperation over industrial conflict. They accepted that in general PR schemes in the early 20th century were sponsored by right or centre-right parties, but they pointed out that they tended in practice to benefit centre-left policies. Boix defended his position in C Boix, 'Electoral Markets, Party Strategies, and Proportional Representation' (2010) 104 *American Political Science Review* 404. It is clear that radical socialist parties tended to oppose PR and campaign for straightforward universal suffrage. To some extent, the dispute between Boix and Cusack et al is really a dispute about what counts as 'left', and, more particularly, what politicians of the period thought was 'left', and what the political systems of Western Europe would have looked like without PR. It is noteworthy that the countries with the longest or proudest history of electoral participation have tended to stick with first past the post (this being true even of France, though the Fourth Republic used PR during the 22 years of its existence). In Belgium, the first country to introduce a national PR system (the 'd'Hondt system' now used in Scotland), in 1899, it was forced through by the Catholic Party government against the votes of the Belgian Socialists. It was also, it should be said, a strange version of PR, since it maintained the plural vote system, weighting votes towards the wealthier classes, which had been introduced in 1893 as a condition of allowing universal suffrage, and which was not abolished until 1919. Interestingly, and something which is usually overlooked, a demand for a better kind of representation than conventional elections provided was part of the programme of the Italian Fascists. 'The electioneering mentality of democracy has disappeared and the idea of political representation has been enlarged to include every means whereby popular sentiments and aspirations are revealed, with the result that old parties have been eliminated and all political forces have been concentrated in Fascism. It was hence necessary that a new organ should arise alongside the government, and that one of its functions should be to constitute the national representative body. It is thus that the Grand Council of Fascism designates the representatives of the nation': *Il Resto di Carlino* (4 December 1932) (at the time a Fascist newspaper), quoted in G Salvemini, 'Totalitarian "Elections" in Italy Today' (1937) 4 *Social Research* 108, 113.

[8] I should add at this point that these considerations might not apply to, say, a single transferable vote system used to elect a single executive officer, as in the case of the recent New York mayoral election. Such a figure does not himself go forward to negotiate the formation of an executive, unlike the

The current keenness for systems of mirror representation and PR is, however, particularly curious, given that during the second half of the twentieth century it became clear that it is not possible to have any system which actually delivers an accurate representation of a society's wishes, and that the very notion of 'the wishes of a society' may be an illusory one. This was the great discovery of the theorists who worked on what were called 'social welfare functions' in the area of collective choice, though their discovery failed to make much impact on the enthusiasts for schemes of representation. This was partly because of the highly technical character of the literature and partly because their work did not employ the language of representation, and its relevance to the question of representation could easily be missed.[9] But I think that to a great extent the fact that it has been ignored is testimony to it being the case that people do not *actually* believe that electoral democracy is a method of mirror representation. What they do believe it to be is something I shall turn to presently.

The collective choice literature was concerned with systems of representation in the following sense. The idea was that there could be a 'function', to use the mathematical term, whose inputs were individuals' choices or preferences and whose output was a collective choice which corresponded in some fashion to the individual preferences. The scope of the functions was very wide; they included systems of voting, but also such things as market mechanisms which took individual consumers' choices as the inputs and produced out of them a collective allocation of goods.[10] At first glance, this might not seem to be a theory of representation, but in fact it is, since the essence of a representative system, in the sense of one that 'mirrors' the citizens, is that their existing preferences, beliefs, values, traits or whatever other term we choose to use are taken as given, and put into

member of an assembly elected through PR. The system, however, still renders the actual process of choosing a tentative one: I am not really making a *decision* when I and people who think like me vote for a particular candidate, as we may have all sorts of different second preferences which we might hope to play a role in the final outcome. It is not really feasible for voters to behave strategically. This is regarded by some people as a desirable feature, but the heart of my argument in this chapter is that it is *not* desirable: strategic voting is an essential part of real democratic assemblies which are tasked with making a determinate decision. Far preferable as a democratic exercise, I think, is the French Fifth Republic system of two rounds, which in the end presents the electorate with a clear choice, and where strategic voting is possible and, indeed, widely practised. One could also say that the first round in a French Presidential election is rather like open primaries in the USA, in which people can vote on the candidates they want to go forward to what everyone understands will be a two-person race, even though (unlike France) legally it can be a multi-person election. Straw votes in committees play a similar role.

⁹ Amartya Sen is an exception. See, eg his throwaway remark in A Sen, *Collective Choice and Social Welfare*, (San Francisco, Holden-Day, 1970) 65, 'One might not wish to raise a revolution every time one's preferences fail to get complete representation in collective choice, but then there are circumstances in which one would like to do precisely that and would try to change the mechanism of collective choice'. There are a number of similar remarks throughout the book.

¹⁰ L von Mises, *Human Action: A Treatise on Economics* (New Haven, CT, Yale University Press, 1949). See also Sonenscher's discussion of Sieyès's radical reformulation of the division of labour as a representative system: M Sonenscher, *Before the Deluge: Public Debt, Inequality, and the Intellectual Origins of the French Revolution* (Princeton, NJ, Princeton University Press, 2007) 12.

some social mechanism which generates a result which in some rather loose sense 'corresponds' to them. Mirror representation always presupposes that there is a separate object to *be* mirrored.

This was also the central assumption of the 'social welfare function' literature; as Kenneth Arrow, the greatest of the theorists in this field, said in his classic work, 'we will … assume in the present study that individual values are taken as data and are not capable of being altered by the nature of the decision process itself'.[11] If the individuals were allowed to behave strategically, in the sense that each one wanted to produce a certain kind of collective outcome and would behave accordingly, up to and including falsifying their expressed preferences in order to bring about the desired collective result, then social welfare function theory could not deal with this situation. A social welfare function could even treat people in principle as entirely passive, as long as there was some way of determining what their wishes were. Imagine, for example, a machine which could read people's minds without their being aware that this was being done. The data from the machine could be put into a social welfare function and an outcome generated by whatever the function was, and that would be a perfectly good instance of the process; but it would obviously be very different from voting as we normally understand it.

This was a more general idea of representation than had been the case when people thought about how a representative assembly could be constructed, since it was also concerned with the question of how the result of a vote *as such*, in an assembly or outside it, could be properly representative of the wishes of the voters. Would majoritarianism or some elaborate system of PR – a market or some other, as yet untried system – allow the result to be taken as a representation of the votes? But the literature of function theory tended for natural reasons to concentrate on familiar systems of voting.

Formal reasoning of the kind employed by the function theorists quite quickly revealed, however, that hopes for an effective system of representation of this kind were illusory. This was shown particularly by Arrow's famous 'Impossibility Theorem', which established that any system might (among other counter-intuitive results) hand the power of decision ultimately to a 'dictator'; or the result might be internally contradictory – in particular, it might exhibit the kind of 'cycling' which Condorcet in the 1780s diagnosed as a deformity in majority voting, whereby there could be a majority for A over B, B over C and C over A. Internal contradiction of this kind was a failure of representation, since it implied either that there was no stable object to be represented[12] or that there was a stable object, but the method of representation was faulty. Arrow was expressly critical of the hope that systems of PR could solve the problem of representation, pointing out that his 'Theorem' was entirely general and encompassed all possible methods of social choice.[13]

---

[11] KJ Arrow, *Social Choices and Individual Values* (New York, Wiley, 1951) 7.
[12] One might perhaps say that it was like cubism versus realism.
[13] Arrow (n 11) 59.

The obvious conclusion to draw from this literature was that *representative* democracy was fatally flawed in principle, but that other kinds of mass democracy might still be possible, and this indeed was the conclusion which Arrow himself came to, though with some reluctance.[14] But his conclusion was largely disregarded; more characteristic was the use made of Arrow by the influential political scientist William H Riker, who argued that it was now clear that what he called 'populist' democracy was logically impossible, and that the only version of democracy which was feasible was a 'liberal' form.[15] By 'populism', Riker understood a political theory which believed in a general will 'which is the objectively correct common interest of the incorporated citizens', and that the way to discover it

> is to compute it by consulting the citizens. The computation will be accurate if each citizen, when giving an opinion or vote, considers and chooses only the common interest, not a personal or private interest. Thus, by summing the common interest regarding wills (votes) of real persons, one can arrive at the will of the great artificial person, the Sovereign.[16]

This was a picture of 'populism' based on what was becoming at the time (1982) the standard way of reading Rousseau.[17] Again, though Riker did not use the language of representation, his concept of populism was really a theory of representation in the broad sense: there is an objectively specifiable 'general will' or 'common interest' which is conceptually distinct from the result of a majority vote, but which can be represented by the result if certain other conditions are met – like Hare's 'sense of the nation'. Riker simply assumed, in a very revealing way, that the only theory of mass democracy was 'populist' in his sense, and that democracy could therefore only be understood in its 'liberal' meaning, as a somewhat etiolated system of public control over state officials. Like most advocates of 'liberal' democracy, however, Riker could not provide many arguments for the desirability of specifically *electoral* control over officials rather than other possible forms, and it might currently be argued (for example) that, given his assumptions, citizen juries are a better means of control, if control is what we are concerned with. The prevalence of notions of liberal democracy may indeed be one of the reasons why citizen juries and sortition are enjoying a vogue, since the absence of mass participation in such systems is in accord with its absence in most ideas of liberal democracy.

But there is another way of looking at democratic politics, which was arguably the way in which its great theorists in the late eighteenth and early nineteenth centuries looked at it, but which has largely been forgotten today. This is the idea

---

[14] ibid 7.

[15] WH Riker, *Liberalism against Populism: A Confrontation between the Theory of Democracy and the Theory of Social Choice* (Long Grove, IL, Waveland Press, 1988); see also A Weale, 'Taking Back Control as Democratic Theory' (2022) 13(52) *Global Policy* 89.

[16] Riker (n 15) 11.

[17] I suspect he got it from BM Barry, *Political Argument* (London, Routledge & Kegan Paul, 1965), which is included in his bibliography.

that democracy is a site of what we might call *active* citizenship, and that people *create* their opinion in the act of deciding. As I observed above, representation can in principle be an entirely *passive* process; the vote is treated as a means of acquiring information about people's preferences over political outcomes, but the only activity required of the citizens (if that) is conveying the information to a body or mechanism which will process it and produce the appropriate result. And as I said, if there were a way of gathering the information without asking the citizens to do anything, that would function just as well as the basis for the final decision.

No one has ever seriously supposed that a body of legislators would behave in this way. The point of the assembly is not only to deliberate – and modern assemblies do not actually deliberate in any very impressive way – but to *decide*, and the decision involves all kinds of political action on the part of the legislators, including elaborate strategies to secure the outcome they want, such as falsifying their real preferences. This is what Hare recognised: that the legislators cannot *themselves* be represented. Legislative assemblies, for example, have for many centuries devised procedures to avoid the kinds of contradictions which Arrow's Impossibility Theorem outlined, since they have recognised that their purpose is to come to a common decision about what a law or other kind of policy proposal should be. Ancient Rome, which was a sophisticated voting democracy with getting on for one million citizens at the time of Caesar, devised a system of choosing 10 tribunes each year without Condorcet cycling, by using serial voting among the 35 'tribes', which functioned in effect as virtual constituencies. Each candidate was withdrawn from the vote as soon as he commanded a majority of the tribes, and in that way his ranking in the preferences of the later tribes was never known.[18] This was quite compatible with Arrow's Impossibility Theorem, since one of the conditions for the theorem is that there should be full information about the preferences of the voters, and under the Roman system the full preferences of almost half the voters might never be known. More commonly, assemblies have avoided voting on more than two options, and have used simple majorities (or in some circumstances supermajorities) to choose between them.

But the central idea of the early democrats (among whom I include Rousseau, Bentham, Marx and some of the American Founding Fathers) was that even in a modern state all the citizens can think of themselves as, and indeed actually *be*, the legislators, and can behave in exactly the same way as they would in a legislative assembly. The most obvious way in which they can do that is by voting on a plebiscite, and that became a not uncommon means of deciding on fundamental constitutional issues from the 1780s onwards, and was theorised by the more Rousseauian figures in the French National Assembly in the early 1790s.[19] Rousseau himself, rather oddly, did not consider a plebiscite as a mechanism in a

---

[18] The order in which the tribes voted was determined by a lottery, in order to avoid giving a permanent advantage to the tribes which voted first.

[19] See R Tuck, *The Sleeping Sovereign: The Invention of Modern Democracy* (Cambridge, Cambridge University Press, 2015).

large modern state, such as Poland, but he did favour systems of mandation, and they too were adopted by radical democrats, particularly the socialists, though, as I said earlier, mandation has mostly disappeared from modern politics.[20]

The French Revolutionary defenders of the plebiscite understood that the final popular vote would have to be a 'Yes' or 'No' vote on the proposed measure. This necessarily involved simplifying or ignoring the preferences of many voters, but they believed that this was not an argument against the system (though that charge was levelled against them by some of their opponents), since the object of the exercise was to allow all the citizens to take part in an act of legislation, under the same constraints which the members of a legislative assembly were under. The same, interestingly, was said by the members of the Royal Commission Appointed to Enquire into Electoral Systems in defence of the existing parliamentary system:

> On the question whether the representation of all parties in proportion to their voting strength is in itself desirable, we may point out that it is not a fair argument against the present system that it fails to produce such a result, because it does not profess to do so. A general election is in fact considered by a large portion of the electorate of this country as practically a referendum on the question which of two Governments shall be returned to power. The view may be right or wrong, but it has to be taken account of in any discussion which turns on the composition of the House of Commons.[21]

I think the members of the Commission were correct, and that this was a profound observation about British politics. The general public still sees an election as a kind of referendum, and appeals by smaller parties to – in effect – leave the business of deciding who the government should be to the elected representatives have always fallen on deaf ears. The decisive vote in the 2011 referendum (appropriately enough) against an Alternative Vote system for parliamentary elections was testimony to this intuitive sense on the part of the electorate. But if this view is correct, it is necessary that the electorate is presented with a simple choice, just as the MPs at Westminster would be in the end, were a proportional representative system be employed. The great parties which can potentially form a government have a responsibility to keep themselves as coherent alternatives, if the citizens are to be legislators. Again, the electorate seem to have an intuitive sense of this, as the dismal fate of breakaway parties demonstrates; people do not *want* their views to be represented if that means not having a say in legislation.

From this perspective, there is a critical difference between an opinion poll and a vote, since the latter is decisive in a way the former is not. When we know that we are *actually* making a decision, we have a different view about what we are doing from when we merely give an opinion to an interviewer – even if we have been asked to imagine taking part in an election. A real election is different from an imaginary one. The undeniable fact that opinion polls are surprisingly accurate is only relevant if one takes for granted that *representation* and not *participation* is

---

[20] Marx, for example, was an enthusiast for the *mandat impératif* used in the Paris Commune.
[21] Royal Commission on Systems of Election (n 6) 34.

the touchstone of democracy – again, ask yourself whether the USA of Asimov's short story could really have been understood as a democracy. The fact that I will probably vote along the lines of what I told someone is useful for politicians (and, I would say, for my fellow citizens, since it helps them to think about what parties are most likely to achieve power, and this may – rightly – influence how they vote), but it is not a substitute for the actual act of voting.[22]

One of the reasons why this view of voting fell into decline in the later twentieth century was the increasing prevalence of a conviction that in a large group of people, the act of voting could have little or no effect on the outcome.[23] If this was right, an entire body of citizens could not possibly function like a legislature. In an assembly, even one as large as the British House of Commons, an individual member has a reasonable chance of being what political scientists call 'pivotal', that is, they could cast the decisive vote – as we witnessed at various dramatic moments during the Brexit debates. But it is extraordinarily unlikely that an individual member of the public could be pivotal in a referendum vote.

If my vote cannot *achieve* an outcome, the point of my voting has to be something else. The favourite choice of political scientists has been that it is 'expressive', ie that my vote is a means of registering or affirming my loyalties. There are, however, many problems with this. One is that a *secret* affirmation is a rather curious phenomenon; after all, we normally think that an expression of something has to be *public*. In the days before the secret ballot, it might have been easier to think of voting as expressive, though in fact it was always assumed then that it had some kind of instrumental force, but it is hard to think of it in this way now. Another is that the point of a public expression (taking part in a demonstration, for example) is most obviously to bring about some result, and to get other people to do something. But if there is no instrumental purpose in an individual's voting, there can be little more instrumental purpose in their demonstrating. It is true that it might get more people to vote, and that one's activity might therefore be thought to have more impact than one would have had merely by going to the polls oneself. But the extra numbers must still be trivial, and one's own participation in the demonstration should have (on the pivotal voter view) as little effect on the outcome of the demonstration as one's participation in the poll should have on the result of the election.

The expressive view ends up as treating politics purely as a theatre of self-expression rather than a zone of responsible action – and that indeed seems to be the view which has become deeply embedded in our culture. It also has an affinity with the idea of mirror representation, since both ideas preclude strategic behaviour on the part of the voter: the voters simply manifest their sincere commitments, and the representative mechanism picks the commitments up and consolidates them in some fashion.

---

[22] See my remarks about the so-called 'bandwagon effect' in R Tuck, *Free Riding* (Cambridge, MA, Harvard University Press, 2008) 60.

[23] For the history of this, see ibid.

But in fact, we can think of voting as an act with an instrumental purpose, even in a very large group. To be pivotal is to be *necessary* to the result – without my vote the result would have been different. But that is not the only kind of instrumental action. My vote might not be necessary, but it might be *sufficient*. To see the difference, imagine a serial vote, rather like the Roman system I mentioned above, in which we vote one after the other. Once a candidate receives a majority of the votes, he is declared elected and withdrawn from the list. Suppose my vote is the one which tips the balance and secures his election. There is no reason to think it was *necessary*, and indeed the chances are very small that it would have been: there may be plenty of his supporters ready to step up and vote for him if I had not turned up. But my vote undeniably secured his election: given the other votes, it was sufficient.

You might say that serial voting of this kind is very rare, and irrelevant to modern electoral practices. But it is in effect embedded in *any* election. A count in an English general election is a vivid example of this. The ballot papers pile up on long tables as they are counted, and at some point it is clear that there are enough ballots for Candidate A to be returned as the MP; this is the point at which the journalists spot the gloomy faces among the members of the losing party, and quickly relay their prediction of the result to the TV operations room. Suppose my ballot is in one of these piles: is it not reasonable to say that I have secured the election of my candidate? And the chances of my ballot being in what we might call an 'effective set' of ballots is quite high: even if 90 per cent of the electorate vote for A, the chance of my vote for A being in the effective set is 5:9, well worth a trip to the polling station.

The difference between this view of voting and the pivotal view actually rests on quite a profound difference in how we think about our own actions. If I want an outcome but do not in general care about how it is achieved, I will only vote when my vote is necessary, just as I will only pay for something in a shop if I can only get it by handing over money. But I might care about whether *I* have brought about the outcome, and want to be (or have a good chance of being) causally responsible for it. The most obvious example of this is altruistic behaviour: it seems strange, and rather abhorrent, to say that I really care about (for example) fighting famine, but would on balance prefer someone else to do it; but this is the equivalent of saying that unless my vote is pivotal, I would rather not bother to go to the polls. The same, I would say, is true about democratic citizenship: if I care about democracy, and in particular if I feel that *I* must have played some part in legislating, that I have not merely been the passive recipient of other people's political decisions, then I will want to be one of the people who has brought about what I wish for.

In any particular instance, of course, I may fail to be one of a winning (or 'effective') set of votes. This has often been thought, again, to be an argument against placing too much weight on majority voting, since it seems to some people to be a means of exercising tyranny against the minority. Actually, the track record of genuine majority voting (that is, where there is true universal suffrage) is not very bad; most eye-catching examples of modern tyranny involve either denying the vote to large numbers of people, as in the American South before 1965 and Northern Ireland before 1968, or manipulating a legislative assembly by excluding or corrupting some of the members, as in the Enabling Act, which granted dictatorial powers to Hitler. The Nazis in fact lost the few plebiscites they contested in the years before Hitler finally led them to power. This track record is not accidental: given genuinely free and full elections, minorities can usually engineer coalitions with some of the majority to tempt them away from the rest.[24] If there is one all-important issue which radically divides a population, that may not be possible; but then we are likely to be in a world where no normal political process will have any effect, and civil war may be the only outcome. It is curious that these rather obvious facts are so often ignored – testimony, I think, to the strong desire of many political scientists and historians to believe that mass democracy is more dangerous than its 'liberal' counterpart, as their precursors have done ever since the French Revolution.

Moreover, even if I lose a vote, I have played a part in the legislative process. Once more, we should think of citizens as if they were members of a legislative assembly. When a member of an assembly is outvoted, we do not think that they have ceased to be responsible for the outcome (unless, like Sinn Fein MPs at Westminster since 1918, they refuse to take their seats). Once the vote has been taken, they line up as legislators with the majority, and would (if this were required) sign their names to it as members of the assembly which voted on the law; it is ultimately an act of the *entire* assembly. But if this is true of the assembly, it should also be true of the whole electorate. At some point, like the Sinn Feiners, I might feel so comprehensive an alienation from my fellow citizens that I will play no part in their affairs: but again, we are likely in that case to be in a situation where no ordinary processes can keep the political community intact.

If we revert to a picture of democracy of this kind and repudiate the more thorough-going ideas of representation, what follows from the point of view of modern politics, especially in the UK? The first thing is that referendums, at least on constitutional matters, are going to be an accepted feature of British politics. Until Britain entered the EEC, as I have argued elsewhere,[25] there was

---

[24] A tragic example of this is the way African Americans under Reconstruction were able to form coalitions with poor whites in order to topple the Southern oligarchs; this, after all, was why the old rulers of the South were determined to deprive the new black citizens of the vote. Although we often suppose that the expansion of the franchise has been a one-way process, as it has mostly been in the UK (though see below), this is far from true generally. Thus, France saw the introduction of universal manhood suffrage in 1793, its withdrawal in 1795, its reinstatement in 1799, its effective abolition in 1815, its reappearance in 1848, its modification in 1849 and its final enactment in 1852. And that is to leave to one side the representation of women in France, many of whom could vote before 1789, but all of whom lost the vote in 1793 and did not recover it until 1945. In England, too, some women could vote before 1832, when all women lost the vote and did not regain it until (for some women) 1918 and (for all women) 1928. Quite a lot of working-class men also lost the vote in 1832 (the residents of boroughs which had had in effect manhood suffrage, such as Westminster), and not all of them regained it until 1918.

[25] R Tuck, *The Left Case for Brexit* (Cambridge, Polity, 2020).

no urgent need for special procedures to decide on constitutional questions, since the ordinary processes of parliamentary elections could do the job. But membership of the EEC locked us into a constitutional system which could not be amended by Parliament but only repudiated in its entirety, and the Wilson government recognised that under these circumstances the only way of securing democratic authority for such a far-reaching constitutional innovation was a referendum.

Since then, it has come to be taken for granted that major constitutional questions have to be decided by referendums: the very fact that opponents of Brexit in Parliament after 23 June 2016 wanted to engineer a second national vote rather than exercise their legal right to ignore what was technically a consultative referendum is testimony to the fact that there is no going back to our old way of doing things. Parliament in 1973 in effect forfeited the right to decide our constitutional arrangements, and the farcical nature of its proceedings under the May government merely confirmed that it had lost its old authority. Conceivably, in a generation or so outside the EU it could recover it, but that is now extremely doubtful, and the new role of referendums should instead be accepted.

Second, schemes for PR for major legislative assembles should be resisted. The question to be put about any proposed system of representation in a modern democracy must be, how far does it resemble a referendum? Representation, on this view, is a *pis aller* – a necessary one, perhaps, but inferior to a direct vote of the democratic electorate. So, just as in a referendum, or the vote on a Bill in Parliament, the final choice between representatives should effectively be a binary one, to avoid the problems which Condorcet and Arrow diagnosed. I say 'effectively', since one does not need to move to the French system, as long as (as in the USA) everyone understands that in the end it is a choice between two alternatives. But if smaller parties in the UK were seriously to challenge the role of the two major parties, the correct response (I believe) is not to allow them more weight through a PR system, but to think about ways in which the British people can continue to believe (as the Royal Commission in 1910 said) that they are taking part in a referendum on their government. Unfortunately, the current Labour Party threatens to put its weight behind the campaign for PR. This would merely be the latest step in its long march away from the genuinely democratic principles of the early socialists, but it may now be too late to avert this, given how deep the cultural shift away from its old principles has gone.

Third, the vogue for sortition and citizen juries should also be resisted (and it is no accident that the same people are often enthusiasts both for citizen juries and for PR). To put the case against them bluntly: what do I do while waiting for the tiny number of my fellow citizens, who have been chosen without election to represent me, to report on their decision? Have I played any role in their activity, other than to lobby or petition, rather as people could do in the monarchies of Ancien Regime Europe? These systems are the apogee of representation, and Asimov's fantasy of 1955 is simply their *reductio ad absurdum*: a state in which they had real power would be far less democratic, from the point of view of an 'active' democrat, than even one with our existing creaky and fallible structures. At least those structures, as they took their final shape in the twentieth century, had been created by people who took the idea of active democracy for granted, and who successfully resisted the various apparently enlightened schemes to undermine them. In a world which is turning against democracy while pretending that it wants to extend it, the best thing we can do now is in fact to preserve their achievement.

INDEX

Ingram Content Group UK Ltd.
Milton Keynes UK
UKHW022304290623
424318UK00004B/94